BIRTHRIGHT IN LAND

by William Ogilvie

and the STATE of SCOTLAND TODAY

*

Produced and written

by

Shirley-Anne Hardy

*

Birthright in Land, by William Ogilvie – and the State of Scotland Today

Produced and written
by
Shirley-Anne Hardy

*

Main texts by:

William Ogivie – end of 18th Century

D.C. MacDonald – end of 19th Century

Shirley-Anne Hardy – end of 20th Century and Eve of the New Millenium

*

Published by:
The Peregrine Press,
The Rocks, Pitlochry, Perthshire,
Scotland PH16 5QZ

Cover Design by Alan Torrance

ISBN 0 9535426 0 2

1. Economics. 2. Social and Political Studies.
3. The Environment.

Typesetting by Danscot Print Ltd., and Perth Secretarial Services.
(Some final pages typeset direct by S-A.H. See Ch. "The Making of This Book".)
Printed by: Danscot Print Ltd., 8 Kinnoull Street, Perth PH1 5EN.
It is intended that this book will be printed on re-cycled paper.

DEDICATION

This book is Dedicated to those who, through challenging times, managed still to keep alive the understanding of Justice and Liberty; to the many others who suffered and endured for it, unable to speak or act; and to others yet who both acted and spoke, and who paid a great price for it.

*

The first copy of this book will be presented to the National Library of Scotland, in Commemoration of the Life of William Wallace.

*

...Never yet
Share of Truth was vainly set
In the world's wide fallow:
After hands shall sow the seed,
After hands, from hill and mead,
Reap the harvests yellow.

(Whittier.)

WILLIAM OGILVIE
(1736 - 1819)

"This photogravure is from a miniature by Archibald Birnie, Artist, Aberdeen, dated 1819. It was kindly lent by Mrs. Davidson, of Gordon Terrace, Inverness, Professor Ogilvie's nearest relative now living, and one of the very few surviving descendants of seven nephews and six nieces, who survived him as next-of-kin, in 1819.

"The portrait is an undoubted likeness. When shown recently to Mrs. Gibb, of Old Aberdeen, she recognised it at a first glance. 'That's Professor Ogilvie', she said, 'Eh! but it's like him' – and critically examining it in detail, she continued – 'his hair', 'his eye', 'his nose', and 'his ear' – 'all is like him, except this' – pointing to his neckcloth. Then she explained, with a smile, that 'he was generally not so braw about the neck'. 'You see', she added, 'he was a great scholar, and was aye studying and writing, and was somewhat careless about his dress'.

"On being asked if she thought the portrait was taken after death, she replied: 'I don't know, but anyhow, *this is the image of the living man'.* Mrs. Gibb was born in Old Aberdeen, within a bow shot of King's College, in the year 1803. She is a most intelligent person, and her faculties are still wonderfully bright. She is the only person now alive that knows anything of any consequence about Professor Ogilvie, from personal knowledge."

Taken from D.C. MacDonald's
Biographical Notes.
See further note on the picture
at the end of "The Seven Wise Masters".

LIST OF CONTENTS

*

*

PART I: WILLIAM OGILVIE and THE STATE OF SCOTLAND TODAY

Note on Order of Part I. Since this book has been produced for Scotland today, I have had no hesitation in placing first the chapter which speaks for this very day of her history.

The further chapters are placed according to the same idea: that is, with the more topical to the fore, (but – according to the unusual journey of this book – in one sense "The Seven Wise Masters" comes first of all! ... as is explained above, in "Texts – D.C. MacDonald's Biographical Notes", which will be found on p. xxx). The reader, however, is free to take the chapters in exactly the order he chooses, for they are not so much chapters, as different sections of Part I.

The placing of Wallace last here is for another reason – for last is also a powerful place. It is that we may carry his spirit forward with us into the rest of the book.

*

PART II: SIGNPOSTS

*

*

A TRIBUTE

AT THE BEGINNING

*

A TRIBUTE AT THE BEGINNING

Having now reached a certain stage on life's journey, I should like to extend my acknowledgements, here at the start, to include earlier scenes.

And so:-

To my Father,
Harold Ernest Sanderson

- who departed the German prison camp,
carrying the commandant's sword! *

*

To my Mother,
Elsie Sanderson (née Stein)

- who to the end of her long life averred
that she once saw fairies dancing in the garden...

*

To my Aunts,
Chrissie, Nettie, Annie and Jessie Stein

- deeply woven into our childhood years,
who played something of the role
of "fairy godmothers" in our lives.

*

To my Sisters:

Diana Bremner, who has enriched my life
especially in our adult years; and to my almost-twin
- rock of my childhood, Marigold! **

*

And very specially to my dear Tom,

who remains ever close, and who, in making so much of this
life's journey with me, contributed so much to making me what I am.

*

Also to all the
four-footed Companions of my life,

and no less my Companions of the wild, including
the feathered ones, from whom I have learnt
many and wonderful things.

*

* My father, serving with the Royal Scots in World War I, was badly gassed, and taken prisoner by the Germans. When his temper was roused, his nature could be very stubborn, and on one occasion a fiery altercation took place between him and the German camp commandant. He was courtmartialled, and the defence lawyer and his friends feared that the outcome of the trial would be that he would be shot. Fortunately, the armistice was signed in the nick of time. The camp commandant was only too thankful to dispatch him along with the first contingent of soldiers from the camp - and Harold, with a final, superb stroke of boldness, walked out of the camp carrying the commandant's sword! (It remains in the keeping of the family to this day.)

*

** Marigold's surname can be discovered
in Part III!

*

I have just, at the last moment, come on this clearer picture of our Aunts to add - (its duplicate, which I have for long had framed, is very faded). In their very much older years. Chrissie, my mother, Jessie and Annie. Chrissie, the eldest, was as gifted as the others, but helped to run the home; Jessie was a nurse; Annie - a horticulturist, trained at Swanley. Nettie - not in this picture - was a doctor, painter and linguist.

*

ACKNOWLEDGEMENTS:

*

*

ACKNOWLEDGEMENTS

*

It is with especial gladness that I write this section, for many are those to whom I would express my thanks for help during the prolonged period of the production of this book.

THE COVER DESIGN

I feel that I must place very first of all my thanks to Alan Torrance for his wonderful cover designs, and in particular for the great trouble that I know he went to, amidst much other pressing work, to make these the radiant creations that they are.

The cover which he has produced makes me want to be my own distributor - to go round the bookshops and enjoy seeing all the response to it!

THE INITIATION OF THE JOURNEY

Turning to the contents of the book, I must place first here my special indebtedness to both Robbie Kemp and Peter Gould, whose successive visits during the winter of 1995-96 in unexpected ways helped to set this journey on foot; and to Robbie Kemp, in addition, for some words of his that became at once woven into one of my 1996 texts.

A SPECIAL INDEBTEDNESS

Next I must place a very special indebtedness to my friends, Sarah Farrand and Valerie Gould, who at critical moments in the early stages of this journey helped to illumine and strengthen the inner pathway.

A SPECIAL CONTRIBUTION

Thirdly here, my special acknowledgements must go to Denise Black and Alan Torrance, for our many inspiring conversations throughout these three years of the book's coming into being - conversations which contributed so much to the ideas woven into its pages, quite apart from their special contributions within its pages too.

MY READERS

Fourthly, I owe a debt beyond any computation of mine to those who gave so generously of their time to act as Readers, for the duration of a journey whose length extended far beyond what I had ever envisaged in its early days. I must mention here too, at the start, those briefer conversations with others of my readers, which proved no less to be of providential inspiration and timing.

As I discovered gradually both how wide and how deep the work on this book was taking me, I felt very much the need of those to whom I could look, who would be scrutinizing the text alongside me. As a starting-point, and holding the possibility of a wide-ish readership in mind, I wrote out a small list of "priorities" that my readers should check for...of which I will divulge no more than that the first placed on the list was - "nothing boring"! And this, I trust, at least has been achieved! But the remit went far beyond that, and was one that placed a very considerable demand upon those acting as readers.

From the beginning I made the rule that I would regard "no news as good news" - i.e., only to come back to me if anything seemed in any way amiss. This way of working proved 100% successful. My readers were spared the labour of replying to each assignment, whilst I in turn was able to give myself to the work in hand, with that total concentration which was essential to its accomplishment. Hence I was able to enjoy, for the latter part of the journey of this book, a state of peace which was a novel and extremely refreshing experience; whilst the knowledge that my readers were participating so fully in every step of the way, was of more help and support throughout this time than any words of mine could possibly express.

Whilst any shortcomings in the book must be acknowledged as mine alone, I should like to say that, during this time I leaned heavily upon the following - some of whom I turned to for particular parts of the text, but most of whom shared with me the full length of the journey:-

Bill Barber, John and Maggie Fraser, Valerie and Peter Gould,
Robbie Kemp, Trevor Parkin, and Denise Black and Alan Torrance.

To all of these, I owe a great and lasting debt; and whatever good fruitage this book may bring will be in considerable part due to their care of the work through all of this time.

THE PRINTERS AND TYPESETTERS

I have been led to write of the contribution of the two good typesetters of the book, Christine Bain and Valerie Davis, under the heading below, "Presentation of the Book".

Here, then, I would like to express my warm and heartfelt thanks to Mrs Jean Black, who, at the helm of Danscot Print Ltd. in Perth, has given me such great support in the matter of the book's production.

Jean has arrived here - in a snowstorm! - to collect and deliver work when the days got urgent, has been of unfailing help at every turn, and is finally meeting me off the train after Easter herself, to see that the book goes at once to the printers. (And this, only because I refused to consider her driving all the way out here to collect it, which she pressed me to allow.)

The final part of the book's journey proved a challenging time in many ways, through all of which Jean Black was of steadfast support. For when the writing of the main text was ended, and the stage arrived of putting the book together, I found myself faced with a task that was far beyond what I had <u>ever</u> envisaged! The first sight of the package of its papers finally put together - (without even Part III which was still to be worked on) - made me wonder just how wide a spine it was going to need! Then - simply trying to cope with all the variety of the papers involved, especially when I started on Part III, made me long for a six-yard trestle table on which to be able to set out everything visibly before me, in its proper sequence. But there was no space for that dream! - hence things had to remain in bundles... I found it so difficult to envisage the thing <u>whole</u>, lying in that hidden-up state, that I finally came to the idea of running through it a succession of title-pages, and putting these on a tag. Now at last I had in my hand a whole that I could <u>see</u>! - (and I expect readers will find them helpful too).

In addition to this daunting situation, the work of checking all the texts, and that involved in setting out Part III: these both took about three times as long as envisaged when at first embarked upon! (It is just as well I had no idea ahead of what the last lap of the journey would be like! - for while engaged on the writing I was totally concentrated upon it.)

Hence, twice in this last stage of the book I reached despair about the completion date ahead. But at each crisis Jean came immediately and swiftly to my aid, managed to re-organize the printing dates at once, and in general proved a tower of support - even more, of <u>kindness</u>. Therefore I could not express in words all that her help through this time has meant to me either. But I can say this. Before I knew only the 'downstairs' at Danscot - (and no more friendly or efficient place could be). Now I know the 'upstairs' too, and it has made that separate doorway a very special one for me now! Just as also the presiding presence of Jean Alston, at Perth Secretarial Services where some of the typesetting was also done - along with <u>all</u> those that work there - has always made the Perth Secretarial Services' doorway a special one in my life too; not forgetting either Jackie Rothwell, in the earliest days of my visits there, a long time ago.

PRESENTATION OF THE BOOK. (MAIN.)

The vital matter that I have kept before me, regarding the presentation of the book, is the production of a text that is easy on the eye, and therefore pleasant to read. That this has, I believe, been achieved, is due to the quite excellent work of its two typesetters, Valerie Davis of Danscot Print, (who did the main work), and Christine Bain of Perth Secretarial Services.

To Valerie I owe much, in particular, for the thought she gave to the setting out of William Ogilvie's "Essay", with both the (almost running) commentary accompanying it, and the footnotes at the start. Although the result appears simple, it was in fact a complex piece of setting-out which I was thankful to hand over to Valerie, who was at once ready with far better suggestions about it than mine, and I feel she has accomplished it excellently.

From Christine Bain have come some 'special touches' to the book in the parts she dealt with so competently too; and in addition I owe to her the inspiration of starting the book off in A4 size - (considering the length it has grown to, what a mercy!) - when I had been thinking of something a bit smaller. But then, no doubt Christine has some special intuition regarding work from me! - for I have known her now for over twenty years. (Indeed, it was Christine who first typeset "The Land Question" for me in 1981, and it has stayed in print in that format ever since.) I was grateful also to Christine for managing so swiftly (and soing so nicely) the belated additional string of title-pages for me (while Valerie was still engaged on the last of the texts).

My grateful thanks must also go to Jean's daughter, Hilary Black, who helped out at Danscot with my work during the university vacation-times. As already explained, I did not, at the start, have any idea of the length to which the book would grow, so that keeping up with the typesetting of all the material became quite a challenge, since both my typesetters were working part-time. Towards the end a lot of extra time had, in fact, to be given to the work, which was unstintingly given, and earns my wholehearted gratitude.

For pages that are pleasant and easy to read, my lasting thanks therefore go to those who set them out so well.

OTHER SPECIAL ACKNOWLEDGEMENTS

I would like here to make a special acknowledgement to the following by name, who - not necessarily all by direct means at all, but in the diverse ways of life - have strewed encouragement along my path, so helping to inspirit this work.

And I should like to say at the start that they are accompanied by others too, in my thoughts, unnamed - but whom equally I hold dear:-

Julia Bastian; Christine Blair - (and "Ellerys", of unfading memory, provider of much good sustenance over this time); Leyna Brinkmeyer; Mary Burns; Brenda Clark; Karen Curran: for the inspiration of her "St Brendan" - and for his sense of humour! Gordon Duncan; Don Bongers; Godfrey Dunkeley;

Alan Ferguson and Georgie, of Jesse Cottage - (from whom sprang so much for this book, as related within); Phil Ferguson; Derek Flyn; Rosalia Gentles; Kenneth Gibb; Paul Gill; Ron Greer; Sandy Greig; Fred Harrison - for his kind encouragement of my work over many years, (and for the heading, now added, to my letter to the Cairngorms Campaign, reprinted here); Alanna Hartzok; Mary-Rose Kaczorowski, ("Redwood Mary"); Nairn Kennedy - who kept the outdoor work going single-handedly all of this time - and trod as lightly in the role of 'major domo'...and eventually of 'nanny' too, the day I returned from a certain unexpected adventure in Edinburgh unable to tie my shoe-laces! Elspeth King - for the inspiration of the exhibition on Wallace she organized at the Stirling-Smith Museum and Art Gallery, in Stirling, in 1997, information gained from which I have gratefully made use of in this book; Diana Forrest; Paul and Adelaide Joseph;

Alex Jamieson; Calder and Joyce Jamieson; Ole Lefmann; Sandy Lindsay - whom I first met when he was a councillor, during my anti-fluoridation trip through the highlands in 1969, (and 'needed no telling' on that score!) - and his wife, Morag; Elizabeth McDonagh; Margaret Macrae - for the three 'smiles' on my desk! Dick Noyes; Alwyne and Christine Pilsworth; Muriel Proctor; the late Harry Rae; Tom Risk; Sylvia Robertson - for her encouragement shown in waiting for the book she originally ordered in 1996! Kevin Murphy; Tanya Roskoshnaya;

Joyce Sanderson; Stewart Sanderson; Ian Sillars - for his many informative dispatches of material over the years; John Smith; Barbara Sobrielo; Jocka Wakefield de Vos; Joanna Welsh; Marie Weyda-Wernick - for first telling me that the film "Braveheart" was showing in Perth, and urging me to go; Karl Williams; Ivan Willis; Robin Yellowlees.

Further:-

The National Library of Scotland - for their great help given at a certain stage in the writing of this book, (as recounted within).

Perth & Kinross Central Library, (the A.K. Bell Library in Perth) - for countless responses of much help from their Reference Department during this time.

Thins Bookshop in Perth - for their many helpful dispatches of books likewise.

Also: to all who have kept me supplied, by various dispatches, in every way, throughout this time, including my friends of so many years at the Highland Health Store in Perth; Woods of Perth, who have unfailingly sent by return the packages of "flimsy" required for my typewriter; and Royal Mail Pitlochry, whose Posties have sometimes walked up through snow to ensure I got my mail.

The Courier - of whose informative news reports I have made much use in this book, (where I have referred to it at first as "The Dundee Courier", for the interest of overseas readers, later merging simply into "The Courier"); and particularly for its lively correspondence columns, where you can soon see the issues that the people of Scotland are getting their teeth into!

ACKNOWLEDGEMENT TO H.M.S.O. - AND THE "UNKNOWN CONTRIBUTOR"!

This is an opportunity to express my appreciation, also, to whoever it was that contributed a certain entry in the little book, "25 Walks in Highland Perthshire", by Roger Smith, published by Her Majesty's Stationery Office in 1994.

It was only in 1998 that, greeting some walkers on the Craigower track as I turned in at my garden gate, and being tentatively greeted by name in return... some interesting information came to light! For on asking how these visitors to the area had come to know my name, they showed me a little entry in this HMSO book, which refers to "Rock Cottage" that walkers pass by, and that there lives "Mrs Shirley-Anne Hardy...noted for her radical views on land use and ownership".

Well! Four years late I would like to thank the contributor of that little entry, whoever it was - (Roger Smith acknowledges a number of sources of his information at the start of the book) - for the fun I have had with it since! Not least among various nephews and nieces...who had told me before now, with much interest, that the cottage was mentioned in some (other) Perthshire guide-book - but, in the way of one's family, I do not think had ever taken my work particularly seriously!

With HMSO more recently privatised, this particular book of the series is now o(ut) o(f) p(rint) - (but fame through HMSO? - I should have been writing "oops"!) - and difficult to find (for it is an excellent guide). What was my delight then, a few days ago, on going into the porch, to discover a little package lying there - a copy of "25 Walks in Highland Perthshire", so kindly tracked down and delivered to me by Betty and Allen Bradshaw, of Glasgow...my "visitors", whom I had met on the Craigower path almost exactly a year ago!

And so I take this opportunity to thank them, here, too - hoping my little message of thanks will also reach the "unknown contributor"!

*

ACKNOWLEDGEMENTS - "PERMISSIONS"

The content of this book has been greatly enhanced by the contributions of a great many other writers; and for these I should like to express my gratitude along with my more formal acknowledgements.

Some of the articles included here are ones long treasured by me. "Twenty Minutes of Reality" and "Imprisoned Ideas", for instance, came into my life nigh on half-a-century ago - I no more remember from what source... Together, these contributions add much variety as well as interest to the book; while the ones on Georgist land reform will enable readers to see just how universal has been the knowledge of this elementary law of natural justice - the history of whose hide-up is almost as interesting as the law itself!

The gathering of the "permissions" relating to these other contributions to the book has not, however, been exactly the easiest of tasks! It drew me to conclude that, in our age of technology, we have cluttered ourselves up with machinery and lost the better help of human hands - and heads. Antonia Swinson's words about IT (Information Technology), which you will find in Part III, are indeed illuminating!

While some responses were quick and efficient - and others, upon a prompting, could not have been more helpful - with yet others, as weeks passed into months of silence, (and in some cases with rather last-minute material I wished to add), I was finally driven to resolving an impossible situation by sending some batches of letters by special Recorded Delivery, saying - that I knew everyone's desk was very crowded today, that I did not wish to burden them with writing on what might well be to them a trivial matter amongst other work, and so - that I would take it, unless hearing from them to the contrary by a certain (stated) date ahead, that they would be happy for me to go forward as proposed.

Upon this basis, then, I would like to make the following acknowledgements, with a grateful sense of the riches that they represent. (I should add that they are in no particular order at all, but simply as they emerged from my two bulging files - most likely with the first last and the last first; for with time pressing, I had to do a preparatory listing of them from an 'airline' seat on a train journey, where there was only room to turn the pages over one by one.)

My gratitude, then, goes to the following:-

The publication "Land and Liberty", of the Henry George Foundation, and similarly "Progress", of Tax Reform Australia, for their permission to quote freely, with attribution, from the pages of both these valued organs of the Georgist movement.

Stephanie Sorrell, editor of the "Science of Thought Review", for her permission to quote freely, with attribution, from articles that have appeared in its pages; and also for her own poem, which I have been particularly grateful to include here.

Jill Edelstein, for her exceptional picture of Primo Levi.

Alick Bartholomew, of Gateway Books, for permission to reproduce my favourite picture of Viktor Schauberger.

Nick McGowan-Lowe, for the picture of Adam McIntosh in his tree-house, which adds so much to the article.

Harold Lane, for the six line-drawings so kindly done for me, and which make so special a contribution to the book.

The following, as listed:-

1) Cynicus Art Publ. Co., and the Third Eye Centre, Glasgow, for the postcard "The Land for the People".

2) Jim Crumley, and The Courier, for Jim's article "A Simple Equation".

3) Adam McIntosh, and The Scotsman, for "How I branched out into a leafy des. res."

4) The Land for the People, and The Big Issue in Scotland, for the article on the "Pure Genius" land occupation.

5) Nicholson, and The Melbourne AGE, (also to Tax Reform Australia) for the cartoon, "The Undertakers".

6) The C.W. Daniel Co. Ltd., for the extracts from "The Restoration of the Peasantries", by Dr G.T. Wrench.

7) The Agent for Allen Ginsberg, in New York, and also The Atlantic Monthly, (USA), for the poem "Morning in Spring", by Allen Ginsberg.

8) The Atlantic Monthly, and the Macalester Park Publ. Co., for the article "Twenty Minutes of Reality", by Margaret Prescott Montague.

9) Donald Clayton, for his poem on Gigha (Scottish island).

10) The Scotsman, and A.R. Edge and W. Watson Davidson, for the poem "The Tangle o' the Isles". (Note: I have been unable to contact Mr Edge and Mr Watson Davidson, but The Scotsman kindly wrote me that, after thirty years, there could surely be no objection - and I feel that overseas readers will greatly enjoy this unique piece of Scottish literature!)

11) The Family of the late Mr W.H. Marwick, for his article "The Common Market".

12) Art Rosenblum of Aquarian Alternatives, and Acres, (both USA), for the article on the work of Carl Weschke.

13) Briony Vanessa Lill, for her article "The Carp and the Butterfly".

14) The Tree Society Internat., for "The Purpose of Disease" by Albert Howard.

15) The Tree Soc. Int., or The Soil Assoc., for "The Earth's Healing Powers", by Prof. Lindsay Robb - (an article of many years ago, not recognised by either, but I think was undoubtedly a publication of one or the other).

16) Scotland on Sunday, and Antonia Swinson, for the extract from her article of 16 Aug 98.

17) EarthKind, and Ann Smith, for her article on CHOO.

18) Phil Rooksby, for the extracts from his book "My Kind of Self-Sufficiency", and for the picture of Midsummer Cottage.

19) The Economist, and David Manasian, for the extracts from his article "The Case for Reform".

20) The Price-Pottenger Fdn. (USA), for extracts from "Nutrition and Degenerative Disease", by Dr Weston Price.

21) Callum Coats, Olaf Alexandersson, and Alick Bartholomew of Gateway Books, for extracts from their books on the work of Viktor Schauberger: "Living Water" (by Olaf Alexandersson), and "Living Energies" and "The Water Wizard" (written and produced, respectively, by Callum Coats).

22) Fritjof Capra, and Harper Collins Publrs. Ltd., for the extract from "The Tao of Physics".

23) Cameron Thomson, of the SEER Centre Trust, for the extract from his article on Soil Remineralisation and Climate Shift.

24) **Lifeforce**, Health Action Network, for helpful information included in the book.

25) Joel Griffiths and Chris Bryson (USA), and the National Pure Water Assoc's publication "Watershed", for Joel and Chris's article "Fluoride, Teeth and the Atomic Bomb", with additions by the N.P.W.A.

26) Rider and Co., (Publishers), of Random House, UK Ltd, for the extract from Eugene O'Neill's "Long Day's Journey into Night", and from Lanza del Vasto's "Return to the Source".

27) The Hallberg Publ. Co., USA, for the extracts from A.J. Nock's "Our Enemy the State", (conveyed by The Nockian Society).

28) To the publication, Orion, (USA), for the article "These Green Things - Catherine Sneed and the San Francisco Garden Project".

29) The magazine "Grace", and Mrs E. Lewis, for the extract on Ragwort from her letter.

30) Fred Foldvary, (and "Land and Liberty"), for the article, "The Pied Piper".

31) The Talgarth Trust, for their leaflet on health, reproduced in Part III.

32) The Spectator, and W.J. Brown, for his article "Imprisoned Ideas".

33) Lindy Davis, and The Georgist Journal, for his article "By the Way".

34) The International Biogenic Society - (address given with article, in Pt.III) - for the extract from "The Essene Gospel", and the reproduction of their attractive opening lay-out for the text.

35) Giulio Einaudi, Publishers, of Turin, for the Italian text of Primo Levi's words; and to Stuart Woolf, and Little Brown & Co. (UK), for the translation of those words.

36) The Dr Edward Bach Centre, for the quotation from the writings of Dr Bach.

37) To the origins of the setting-out of Chief Seattle's statement, "This Earth Is Precious" - which came to me, without source, very many years ago, (and I feel sure is shared widely across the world by how, by others too, in this attractive form).

38) To the source of the article (or chapter in a book?), "Gosaba - A Modern Miracle", which so deserves resurrecting - and whose re-printing in this volume will, I hope, bring to light at last some information concerning its origins.

*

Finally: I have done my best to produce a wholly correct list. I sincerely hope there are no errors or omissions in it; but should there be, let me in advance record my sincere apologies.

FINER POINTS OF PRESENTATION OF THIS BOOK

*

There are a few things that remain, finally, to be said on the above, and so I must fit them in here.

As the reader will already know, (from my foregoing Acknowledgement to the Printers), the matter of this book's production has presented me with many challenges - not the least of which has been a sense of time pressing, all the way through. Two deadlines hoped for in its final stage have already been lost - I cannot lose the third! - and so here are a few points which I hope can forestall much that would otherwise seem only too well deserved criticism on the finer points of its presentation - (and even perhaps on some not-so-fine. For you reach a stage, with only three days to go and a lot of detailed work still to be done, when you feel you no longer see the wood for the trees!)

To make an attempt, however. Firstly: I have ended up having to do a lot of pages from my humble (now considerably "old-fashioned") typewriter, which does not justify at the right margins. There was simply no time left to send them for typesetting. However, I have tried to set them out neatly.

I did have a brief try, in 1997, at a more modern machine, when I thought I might do some of the typesetting myself. But the touch - ("You peck at it like a bird", as was explained by the kind proprietor of the shop, somewhat despairingly!) - was so different from that of an old "thumper", that I could not consider spending the time that would have been needed to master it. There are advantages in staying with an older machine, however. "We are seeing a lot of carpal tunnel syndrome now because everyone is using computers and are repeatedly injuring the median nerve in the wrist" - as I noted in an alternative health leaflet recently...(I have said enough about modern technology altogether in the book, I think!)

By contrast, the older machines are entirely friendly on the hands. I have beaten out type on mine for hour after hour, day after day - with never the smallest complaint, from either hands or machine. And here let me place a belated acknowledgement to my faithful Hermes 3000 which has been a friend indeed to me, throughout this entire project.

(...I have just realized that I said, on the opening "ISBN" page, that the explanation of my humbler typesetting would be explained in "The Making of This Book". But it comes in here instead, and I do not feel I can now alter that sacred "registered" ISBN page - such a milestone of achievement as it was!)

Almost on the eve of going to the printers - (I complete this over Easter weekend) - I can only now summarize rapidly just some of the points of presentation that I am aware leave much to be desired - while doubtless there are others more important I shall miss mentioning and only remember later. Here, however, is something of a jumble of those points on which I had collected some notes:-

1) Part III, in its setting-out, is much "a thing of seams and patches", which may well show through the printing - (no time to tidy). "A thing of themes and snatches" too, Gilbert and Sullivan!...But not perhaps quite aspiring to Jim Crumley's "darning"!

2) There is a disorder in the capital letters - used sometimes, and sometimes not, (esp. in II:2), for such words as "Water", "Earth", etc. No time to order now - or to explain!

3) "Birthright...and...Scotland Today" dances about at the foots of the pages, and the dots vary also. (The stick-on page numbers - my very last task - will no doubt dance at the tops, in some sections of the book, too, (as they are used to cover a scatter of pencilled numberings).

4) The namings of the chapters that run on the tops of the pages have had often to be minimal. I would much have liked to make these a more helpful part of the book.

5) Sections that should start uniformly on the right-hand page possibly sometimes start on the left.

6) "The Strathconon Chronicle" appears somewhere at the start of that section where it should have been the more formal "The Chronicle of Strathconon".

7) There are different type-settings - and different sizes of type withon the type-settings too. Part of the journey of the book which there is simply no time to explain!

8) I may have said in Part I somewhere that certain articles appear at the end of it. They are all finally grouped at the very end, in Part III.

9) There is an uncompleted footnote somewhere about boxed organic vegetables. Hopefully one of the organic organizations - (addresses given in text) - can help here. (But please send s.a.e., if enquiring of them.)

10) I have not perhaps replaced "landowner" with "landholder" as fully as I had intended.

11) If the sub-titles to the "Serendipities" remain slightly undersize compared with the text - they were not meant to be - (my cell-phone battery gave out at a crucial moment!) However, being in bold, I think they still sufficiently stand out.

12) Some of the dates of writing - (of which I have deliberately left a scattering in the book, as giving some account of the "travelling") - may appear to go backwards. This is because some belong to the original longhand script, while others relate to the date of its typing-out, to be handed to my readers. (...Yes - the book's first draft was written in an even more old-fashioned manner - simply a succession of A4 notebooks and a biro!...with a few coloured pens for clearer mapping in additions and alterations.) Perhaps I may be permitted to add here:

To allow a computer to come between you and the flow of ideas is, to this individual, uncontemplatable! And I believe this shows some sound intuition. The emissions from electronic-ware interfere with the bio-rhythms of life. If writing be a creative business - how, then, not affected in subtle and damaging ways?

There is also the matter of simplicity. Just so, my spinning-teacher - (so expert she spun flax - most challenging of all fibres - for King George V) - told me: the best of all - even better than the spinning-wheel - is the simple spindle. As she said - "just the spindle and you". Exactly so!

...I think a round dozen is enough for us all! But let me add a "baker's" one in the form of something a good deal more necessary.

A BIG THANK YOU to Trevor Parkin, who undertook a quite massive re-read through, almost at the last moment, of some of the longest texts for me, to re-check for errors. And thank you, too, for being so insistent on those sub-headings for Part II ch.2 - (which I had feared I simply didn't have time to do). Even I found it a relief to add them in the end!

I would much have liked to re-read the remaining (shorter) texts before printing, (for there may even be the odd one still unchecked). I shall try to fit this in. But if it cannot be done - my apologies, since this third printers' date is sacrosanct. ...For not only has the book's time come now - my time has come too! I can carry this 'child' no longer. Time for it to issue forth into the light of day!

S-A.H. - 3 Apr 99
* Easter *

3 MEMORANDUMS

*

(a) "Sexist" Vocabulary.

So far as this is concerned, I go for SIMPLICITY, (and I have in any case read that "he" may stand originally for a pronoun of common gender).

Therefore, so far as linguistics are concerned, in my vocabulary - man embraces woman!

(b) Identity of Author.

All the writing in this book, where not specifically appearing under the name of another, is by me, Shirley-Anne Hardy.

Use of Initials. Where it was especially necessary for my name to appear: since it is a long one, I have had recourse here and there, (especially in some of the title-sheets), to the use of my initials, instead of my name. Thus, wherever "S-A.H." appears in this book, it refers to myself, Shirley-Anne Hardy. (Sometimes it appears by the "travelling" dates too.)

(c) Price of Book.

My intention is to keep the price of the book as low as possible, providing that it covers all costs, since I would like this book to be available as widely as possible to readers.

I shall also be placing a number of copies of it in the public libraries.

*

ABOUT THE AUTHOR

*

Of Scottish parentage - (my mother was born in Falkirk, and my father in Peebles) - I was born in Africa, in the then British Protectorate of Nyasaland, now Malawi. For my father had been advised to go for health reasons to a warmer clime, after being badly gassed in World War I.

The circumstance which brought me early home to Scotland again has long seemed to me significant. As an infant in Africa, only a few months old, I contracted amoebic dysentery - an illness notoriously difficult then, (and, I believe, even now), for doctors to treat. My life being despaired of by the hospital in Durban where I was taken, my parents were advised by the kind doctors there that the only hope for me lay in getting me out of Africa, by smuggling me aboard a boat home. (Presumably the ship's captain would not have welcomed a dying infant aboard!) Once on the high seas, it seems my recovery was rapid and complete, and I never looked back. Thus my return to Scotland was an early one, and I grew up a strong and healthy child.

That I should have looked so simply to the forces of nature for that early healing, rather than to orthodox medicine, has often struck me since, in view of my unhesitating adoption of the pathway of natural healing, as soon as I stumbled upon its teachings in the early 1950s.

The second great directive to my life's pathway, I also came upon by chance. It was out of a waste-paper basket that I first made acquaintance with Henry George!

Having resolved to carry the Georgist message to today's young after completion of an honours degree in Russian in 1968 - (alas, before the era of exchange visits, so I never learned to speak the language) - I decided to enter the field of Liberal Studies lecturing. ...Orthodoxy, with velvet gloves, lost no time however in easing me out of that chosen pathway! - (and ensuring that <u>all</u> doors remained firmly closed upon any such further adventuring!) Forced to abandon that path, and following a long span of exile, I was then led to return to Scotland; a country which my husband (from Nottingham - and by then retired) came deeply to love.

...And so nigh twenty-five years have sped by here, much of it spent working on the land, and planting many trees.....here, where I find myself half-way between Edinburgh, the happy home of my earlier years, and Strathspey - that land of the Cairngorm mountains, where our Aunts had a house, and long and unforgettable childhood holidays were spent. And I have always been deeply aware that it was there, among the mountains of the Cairngorms, that my soul grew up...

*

AN ENCOUNTER

On the 10th January, 1997, I was travelling on the train to Edinburgh, spending the journey – (as I was well used to doing!) – writing, folding, clipping, sticking ... when towards the end a woman of senior years, sitting just across the aisle from me, remarked smilingly (something like): "You've been using your time well!"

I smiled in agreement, and we fell into conversation. She came from X ..., I from Pitlochry. She spoke of a friend in Pitlochry ... and this in turn led me to write down for her a helpful local address.

Taking the piece of paper in her hand, she looked at it for a moment – then said: "You're a very intelligent woman." (She had been scrutinising my handwriting)

Considering the other 'journey' I was on – (and indeed the very mission, which was taking me to Edinburgh) – I realised that such a golden opportunity should not be missed, and said quickly: "I would be humbly grateful for any tips you can give me".

Her response (immediately given), astonished me, especially in view of *that particular journey*: "Oh, you don't need tips. You should be giving others tips."

Then followed: "I think you take a great deal on too, and you're very efficient."

Finally, as we were about to leave the train: "I thought you were a nun in civvy clothes." (I had had a Bible open before me, during the first part of the journey. But hopefully it wasn't just that!)

I learned that reading handwriting was a natural gift for her. Yes, she had done a course too – but it really all came from within her, quite simply and naturally.

I was so overwhelmed at these messages – from so incredible a Providence, just at that time – that already, as we were about to disembark, I had given her a warm embrace. As we were parting on the platform, I turned and gave her another – and at that moment noticed that an earring had fallen at her feet. I thanked Providence again, since now I was able to restore it to her. (For she had not noticed her loss)

I was still so overwhelmed by this encounter, as I flew up Waverley steps, that after accomplishing the essential mission I could not think of following up my other plans. Instead – a quiet lunch at Henderson's,[1] where I might try to absorb this amazing event. ... And there I 'saw' the purple flying bluebirds!

Shirley-Anne Hardy
(As recorded in January, 1997)

---

[1] *A delicious wholefood and salad bar that I had long known. Edinburgh's 'Cranks'!*

"Someone a long time ago wrote that books too, like human beings, have their destiny: unpredictable, different from what is desired or expected." (Primo Levi.) *

*

Coming upon these words of Primo Levi's in the early weeks of 1997, I could not but be struck by them, on account of my involvement with another book at the time, whose journey was taking an unexpected course.

The words remind us, of course, of the frequent human folly of our "desires" and "expectations"! Sometimes it is good to withhold desire, and simply to travel. By such a journey, at any rate, a book has come into being (this book) which simply would not have come into existence otherwise.

There are several reasons why I owe to my readers some account of the journey of this book. To the fore in my thought are those many friends, meetings with whom have had to be delayed over months that extended into years, as all I could continue to reply to welcome invitations was that I was still "head hard down" and "living like a recluse"!

Then there is a certain annual event in Pitlochry which I attend, and particularly enjoy, where in early November 199<u>6</u> I had to explain that I was leaving early as I was helping to speed a book forward for the printers. Well! - when November 1997 came round, astonishingly I still had the same message for those present - and accompanied by the same early departure!

Imagine, then, my situation when November 199<u>8</u> arrived...and once more I stood up and gave forth **THE SAME MESSAGE!** By this time I felt some serious credibility was called for, and was thankful to be able to add to the message that Thins in Perth (well-known booksellers) had most kindly offered me an autograph-signing day. I was touched when one of those present then eagerly took out a pencil and asked the date the book would be available - and boldly answered (my cheerful hope at the time!) - "the end of January"...! Ever hopeful - and ever hoping - against an unvarying, almost mirage-like feature of this journey: that as I proceeded, it <u>**ever extended**</u>! - (and only the very last stages have seen its vanishing!)

But there are other reasons too for giving some account of the journey of this book. Why is there a chapter which carries the very words of the title of this book - as of its Part I - buried away towards the <u>end</u> of that Part I, and marked with a three-year-old date as well? And why - when the Othila Press published "William Ogilvie's Birthright in Land" in 1997 with an acknowledgement of my work in it - did no actual work of mine appear in the book? Is it possible that this individual really had nothing

---

* An Italian writer who survived Auschwitz to give us his remarkable books. (Mentioned in Part II ch.1.) The quotation above opens his Afterword to "The Truce": Qualcuno, molto tempo fa, ha scritto che anche i libri, come gli esseri, hanno un loro destino, imprevedibile, diverso da quello che per loro si desiderava e si attendeva."
(Translated by Stuart Woolf.)

herself to say about William Ogilvie? Those who know her would find this very unlikely! And so - let us start at the beginning.

We met here, one August day in 1994 - the 10th of August, to be precise - a few of us who had a shared interest in radical land reform. (This is sometimes - but incorrectly in the view of a growing number today - referred to as land value taxation; more correctly, land rent for revenue, or community ground rent.*) This movement - concerned with a natural and fundamental law of justice in economic relationships - was given great impetus by the work of the American, Henry George, towards the end of the last century - verily the inspiration of the movement today. Now the work of our own William Ogilvie of Aberdeen, in the late eighteenth century, upon this great matter had recently come to light through one of our number, in a copy of the book published a century later - a volume entitled "Birthright in Land", by D.C. MacDonald; and the decision was taken by us that afternoon to republish it.

The programme had a slow beginning, but in the autumn of 1995 work went forward on a flyer intended as a forerunner for our main work, to help awaken interest in it; and this was presented at a meeting in Glasgow at the end of December 1995.

Those last days of December 1995 produced a cold-snap of exceptional intensity. The rail-tracks froze, and I had to abandon my planned journey by train, so that I only arrived many hours late, by bus. Having missed the vital morning session, I returned home to a feeling of gradually deepening perplexity as to why it was that the little flyer - of mere A6 (6"x4") format - was now to go forward as our main production. The extremely limited extracts from Ogilvie it contained were hardly sufficient, I felt, to present a true idea of the worth of his work. Moreover, the date "1782" placed on the front cover by the title, seemed to me to give the production a positively archival look.

I should explain here that the whole point of the venture, to me, was to relate Ogilvie's writings to "the state of Scotland today" (as I put it). Treated merely as a historical piece of writing, it had no interest for me at all, since Ogilvie spoke as strongly for our times as he did for his. Most of my colleagues were quite happy about this, but there was also a strong vein of opposition to it among us.

I decided to consult a contact that I had on The Herald, (a major newspaper published in Glasgow), and he very helpfully summarized his view of an A6 for me as follows:-

1) That the A6 is used mainly for re-prints of classics (or extracts from them) if you want to remind yourself of them - maybe for getting up for exams, or for a read on a train;

2) That for new books they are "not a very good idea";

3) That they would be not much regarded for a review.

Well! - a production that was not really going to attract a review would hardly re-introduce Ogilvie to Scotland!... I also visited some bookshops in Perth to look at their A6 stands - and found it impossible to picture our very dull cover front amidst their bright arrays. Wondering if my view of the cover was an unbalanced one, I had already sought the view of one or two friends, as useful "outsiders"? (but understanding well enough the purpose of our work). But I found their reaction to the cover was the same as mine, and one even offered kindly to design something that might be more eye-catching for us.

---

* See Pt. III ch. 5: Letters to the Scottish Office.

I wrote of these findings to my fellows in the group, and my view that it would be an unworthy edition of Ogilvie, in a letter first of mid-January just to the chairman and secretary, but upon getting no reply - to all my colleagues on 26 Jan 96. On 23rd February I wrote a further letter to all, voicing my concerns over our proposals for MacDonald's "Biographical Notes" on Ogilvie, (which, with one or two other texts, were to be included in the book). To none of these letters did I receive any reply from any of my colleagues. However, being clear enough in my own mind as to what was needed, I had already set to work, and so - on the unforgettable Leap Year's Day of 1996 - sped to Edinburgh with six packages for central posting..... which would just allow 24 hours for perusal of their contents, ere our meeting planned for here on March 2nd.

The packages contained an extended version of my "Braveheart" article (which it had been proposed I provide as a "modern commentary" on the land question), and also an article I had quickly put together without which I felt the book would be quite incomplete - "William Ogilvie - and the State of Scotland Today". (These are the two "1996" chapters that appear in the present book.) Along with these I had included a "boxed" lay-out design of the various contents for a proper-sized book.

For some strange reason I attended that meeting here on 2 Mar 96 possessed of an adamantine resolve to bow out of the group there and then - to hand over my work and say that I felt my part in it was now completed. However, my colleagues, pleased with my work, unexpectedly proposed at the meeting that I should have charge of the contents of the book - a proposal which placed me in a quandary. To have refused their invitation would have been like delivering them the proverbial slap in the face. Following a silent inner struggle as the meeting proceeded - I knew that I could not do this. Hence, as I wrote them afterwards, (having explained what had been my intention): "You have after all persuaded me that that time is not quite yet!" (The contents of the book were of course the one thing I cared about. I would not have accepted a role of any other kind.)

So we worked on through 1996, gradually assembling the texts. Towards the end of that year, however, my colleagues and I fell out of step on a certain matter, and arrived at an impasse as to how to proceed forward together. At first I had thought that the best solution of this would be simply to allow our ways to divide, in which case I would have moved forward on my own. However, the general reluctance to abandon the joint project prompted me to offer to work on a third possible way forward which might yet keep us together.

At this point, providence intervened. I had been longing for a break - enjoy dancing (solo!) myself - and so had booked a seat for "Riverdance" in Edinburgh. However, somehow I managed instead to do a dance of my own on the pavement outside!...from which I came up with one hand dangling! Clearly, emergency aid was required - and the Playhouse Theatre were most helpful. I was soon in Edinburgh Royal Infirmary - but no sooner safely curtained off there than I was doubled up in stitches of laughter! So - she was longing for "a break" - and now she had got one! (However, the strange feeling, from the start, of some greater Providence behind the whole episode, was no doubt what really invoked those buoyant spirits.)

To the difficulties facing our group was now added a period of trying stagnation, (since trying to deal with paper on a typewriter with one arm in a sling is a very slow business). My colleagues then met together at Auchterarder on 1 Mar 97 and resolved that, should I remain unwilling to accept their proposal - although they very much hoped that I would do so - they would then go forward themselves with their own project - but omitting my two articles;

while adding that they fully understood I might wish to produce my own work likewise, and wished me well should I decide to do so.

Since this seemed indeed, now, the only practical solution to our situation, I accepted their decision on the matter, and informed them that I did in fact intend to go forward with a book on my own. This was followed up by further letters that March in which I detailed the matters where my copyright was involved, (these extanding beyond just my two articles). I received no reply to these letters regarding copyright, but being well used by now to my colleagues' policy of silence, I never doubted for an instant that that silence meant, in this case, an honourable acceptance of my communications on the matter of copyright.

A fresh approach was then made to me by my colleagues, in a letter of 6 Apr 97, proposing that it was time that the Scottish Ogilvie Society was dissolved, and that perhaps we might still go forward together if we found an outside publisher acceptable to all. By this time, however, I could both sense that there was a book inside me waiting to be born - and had in fact set certain matters on foot regarding it. I was therefore unable to retract from my new pathway and join with them again.

Eager as I was to move ahead, I found that internal Scottish Ogilvie Society affairs still, however, continued to bog my footsteps. (There was certainly an unresolved matter dating back to the end of Dec 96, but this I had firmly put aside by now to be dealt with only <u>after</u> the work on Ogilvie was done, since I felt that the needs of Scotland came decidedly first.) At the end of May 97 it seemed I was finally free, and on May 30th rang one of my former colleagues to ask if they had any further need of me, and also if any book of their own was going forward. He knew of none, and seemed thoroughly despondent about the whole matter, but I assured him that I was working on a book anyway; and ascended the hill that night rejoicing in freedom at last to get on with it.

But - "there was silence in heaven for the space of half an hour"! June was not more than half gone when there arrived a letter from the Othila Press in London (publishers especially of Georgist literature), stating that they had received the text of a book, "William Ogilvie's Birthright in Land", and seeing my name was included in it - and knowing there had been some difficulties up in Scotland - they wanted to make sure I was happy about it before going forward with its publishing. The matter was urgent.

This - complete "bolt from the blue" - was in fact welcome to me. It seemed perfectly right that my ex-colleagues should produce their own work - and I realized also that it was the best assurance of peace for me to pursue my own pathway. I made a quick telephone call and said, "Send it up - I'm sure I'll be able to send it back to you by return of post".

Alas for such sanguine hopes! Apart from my two articles, which had indeed been removed, there were other matters of copyright I had written about which left me with great concern. Work of my origination was, without ascription, now entangled in texts under others' copyright, as indeed one small item too of my actual writing. Moreover, my name, in an erroneous usage - <u>and my goodwill</u>! - were now woven into a book of whose existence I was not even aware.

I can never be grateful enough to the Othila Press, both for their alertness in telling me of the existence of this book, and for working on through the ensuing weeks on the trying details of the matter, (which should all, of course, have been sorted out long ere this). It now took a full month of my best time and energies, which I could ill afford now that I was embarked on my own real journey.

The movement in the south was understandably eager to have a text on Ogilvie for their own campaign work, at this special time in Scotland's history - and I knew it would be some time yet before my own book was out. The question of the copyrights was obviously a vital one, however, since I was concerned that I must have the freedom to make use of my own work. Eventually the errant copyrights were removed, and at the proposal of the Othila Press there was also placed at the start of the book a statement acknowledging my work on both the Ogilvie and the D.C. MacDonald texts.

Let us proceed swiftly now to the end of this journey. It was early June of 1997 - just after I had made that May telephone call - and I was free at last, (as I thought, though not quite, as it turned out), to continue my own journey. I pushed the chair back from my desk that summer evening. My energies had been so drained by the on-going internal entanglements with my former colleagues, that I was alarmed my very soul-forces now seemed to be withdrawing from my own work - the work I had so longed to do, and which was still a considerable task that lay ahead. I went out into the garden for the touch of the earth. As always, it was re-vitalising - invigorating. The answer came quickly. "Have fun!" it said - "Have fun! Because if you don't enjoy the work - nobody else will either!" Encouraged, I went to pick some herbs for the evening meal, and there came to me the word "Signposts" - with the idea that I could make the further part of the book - (the fuller look around at "the state of Scotland today" that I was eager to do) - a quite simple matter after all. Just a stringing together of some of the interesting press clippings I had gathered, with a few words of commentary to link them... And so - this is how Part II of this book came to be called "Signposts"!

...Six weeks later, emerging from the Othila Press episode, I had to face the fact that I could never now hope to get the book published for the 11th September 1997 - that 700th anniversary of Wallace's victory at Stirling Bridge, which I had so set my heart on marking the date of the book's appearing. I can only now smile, looking back at that early wish...in the light of Primo Levi's words placed at the start of this foreword!

...So autumn and winter of 1997 came and went - and of course the Stirling Bridge anniversary combining with Scotland's referendum entered into the book!...till by Easter 1998 chapter 1 of Part II was finally completed. During all of this time the most wonderful material was coming to me for the book, marking the stage of the journey where - "as it continued, so it extended"!

At midsummer of 1998 - and almost exactly a year after the copyright business - my work on Part II chapter 2,(following the absorbing study of the work of Viktor Schauberger recounted therein), was suddenly once more brought to an unexpected halt, with the necessity of embarking immediately upon an urgent environmental campaign. For it was impossible to stand by, even amidst such a task, and watch yet another bit of the Planet being gradually destroyed under one's nose by blundering practices. I did not manage to return to the work of the book until the 7th August 1998, and all-in-all I reckon it lost me roughly two months of work, with the on-going investment of some energies still required into the autumn - until in November I finally shelved it firmly until the book should be out. Alarming at the time as these successive delays were to me, for a book that was intended to be out many months ago, I realize now that the book knew its own journey far better than I did. For had it not been so, there are things now contained in the book that simply would not have been there - but that perhaps it was always meant to include.

There remains one final matter to touch on - I will do so as lightly as possible. It may be that there are some copies of an erroneous Law of

Rent sheet now abroad in Scotland. This would be unfortunate at a time when Scotland is just re-awakening to her "auld acquaintance" with, and lost knowledge of, so important a matter. This sheet was produced when the Scottish Ogilvie Society was in existence - but I must absolve myself from any responsibility for it. That sheet differs from the one presented in this book...(which is a copy of the one that appeared in my "The Land Question" in 1981 - see Pt.II ch.2 here - both acknowledged to the Henry George movement)...in that it contains a fundamental confusion of value with size. Ogilvie himself forcefully deals with this error that sometimes arises - with the distinction between the two, and the importance of it. *

The erroneous diagram - produced when the Scottish Ogilvie Society was in existence - was one that nearly slipped through to the printers unnoticed when that joint project was on foot, back in November 1996. That book being a joint production, our responsibility for it would be a shared one, and it was therefore important to me that we all see all of each others' texts ere they went to press, (just as all had seen mine). When I realized what was happening, I took the only course open to me, and at once withdrew my two articles from the project - thereby bringing the production to a halt on the very eve of its printing. (It was this which was the origin of the divide between us.**) When the Othila Press text arrived in the summer of 1997, I noted that the diagram was absent from the book, and it was only many months later that it came to my attention that an entry at the back of the book, concerning further reading matter, referred to it as available. I have to assume that it refers to the erroneous sheet, since I have never received any notice of its recall. (I could not have risked further delays to this book by taking the matter up in the interval, in view of past experience.)

When I think back now to the time spent with my former colleagues, I cannot help looking back at a passage early on in D.C. MacDonald's "Biographical Notes", where he quotes rather deliciously from a Mr P.J. Anderson (of the New Spalding Club, in his "Scottish Notes and Queries for June 1889... possibly not in my edition here - no time to check), about how the proceedings of the Senatus, during Ogilvie's membership of it, "bristle with (his) protests against, and reasons of dissent from, the decision of the majority" - ! I am sure my erstwhile colleagues believed they had an ugly duckling in their midst - they did not see that perhaps, as in the legend, she wasn't really a duckling at all! But how could they possibly know? - they were all drakes!

But how blest the whole journey has been! - and I cannot but feel that this goes for my former colleagues as well, and I wish them all blessing too. Certainly, without our divergence, this book would never have come into being, which I see so clearly now was waiting to be born.

It is nearing journey's end now. But ere closing there is a special

---

* "Almost all of Agrarian laws have proceeded on the plan of restricting that extent of landed property which an individual may acquire, and not the nature and the force of that right with which the landholder is invested. Thus endeavouring to establish an equality of fortune, they have been found impracticable..." See para. 6 of the edition here of Ogilvie's "Essay", and footnote added thereto.

** I did not in fact discover the alteration to the diagram until many weeks after, when I finally took it from the envelope in which it had subsequently been sent to me by another...by which time our own joint programme had fallen through.

part of the journey still to recount, for it concerns those Seven Wise Masters that have come to play such an unexpected role in this book!

In the spring of 1996 I had an extraordinary experience. It followed upon a lively Scottish Ogilvie Society meeting on the 25th May at another's house, after which a colleague had driven me home. I shall recount it as I wrote of it to another of my colleagues on the 24th September of that year:-

> "...It was when I was alone again that the strange thing happened. I suddenly became aware of the literal meaning of "walking on air". My feet just couldn't earth! Never have I had such an experience before in all my life - and now I knew, too, that the saying 'to walk on air' isn't just a made-up saying, but is born of the actual experience of people in extraordinary states. I could feel that something very powerful was at work - as though there were great jubilation going on in some higher sphere, and I was being drawn up into it.
>
> The experience lasted on into the evening, as I moved about on various small tasks, and walked in the garden. I suppose, when I looked at my feet, they appeared to be on the earth. So it was apparently I myself who had been drawn so far out of my physical, and into my etheric, form...which was dancing up - up.....that I experienced it in this way - that my feet just couldn't touch the ground! And all the while there was just this feeling that something very powerful was going on - something much bigger than seemed explained merely by the immediate circumstances.
>
> It was as soon as I awoke the next morning that this little verse pushed itself through to me - so clearly a part of that whole 'dance'!"

...And what was the little verse?

"We are the 'Septemviri' -
Of a slightly different brand,
For unlike those Seven Worthies
We won't write our names just in sand -
Like Ogilvie rather we'll go for
Staking man's birthright in land!"

This little verse was to have been included at the front of the Scottish Ogilvie Society publication, and this colleague had written me proposing a certain alteration to it. It was an alteration I could not allow, since it destroyed the rhythm of the dance! Thus - although I had not spoken of this experience to anyone - I was impelled to write of it to him, to explain...(when he at once kindly conceded the point, adding - "may you often walk on air!")

I had particularly never spoken of this experience to anyone, since I had not understood it myself. However, the meanings of things, not clear at the time, can sometimes become clearer in retrospect. And so I have decided to include this account of it here, especially as a tribute to Ogilvie, realizing, as I now do, that he was very much at the heart of it all. For it concerns a certain 'other chapter' in the journey of the book, a chapter of which perhaps only I among us at the time was aware... But it has also made me aware of how Ogilvie - who lived so austere, dedicated and lonely a life - had an enormous capacity for fun!

But I think this comes out well in any case, in a subtle way, in his very dealings with those Seven (not so!) Wise Ones - and it is perhaps no great wonder that they have come to play so special a role in this book!

This journey would not be complete without a pause to look back at the end, down the long vista - and in surveying it, to make this acknowledgement. I have spent an exceptional period, of nearly two years, much alone, in the company of many great souls. Of these, perhaps especially must be named - Ogilvie - Schauberger - and William Wallace. Their pictures about my room have accompanied this work, and brought their presence very close. I believe I shall always look back to this period of my life as to "a sacred time".

Finally: this book has been written for all who are looking for its message. But the primary inspiration and impetus for it have come from Scotland, my own country, and from the Scots - a people whose distinctiveness and worth have been for far too long dumbed down by the imposition of an alien culture, with its hierarchical structure rooted in a system of land tenure equally alien. The rest I have said in the opening chapter of this book, and in the further chapters right on to the last page. May it prove of interest, may it prove of impetus! - and may it be enjoyed!

S-A.H., 29 Mar 99.

*

(Primo Levi)

T E X T S

*

TEXTS

The texts used in this book for William Ogilvie's "Essay", as also for the "Biographical Notes" on Ogilvie by D.C. MacDonald - (with the various extracts also that I have taken from them) - and the "Preface" to Ogilvie's "Essay", also by D.C. MacDonald: all these are taken from the book entitled "Birthright in Land: An Essay on the Right of Property in Land, by William Ogilvie, with Biographical Notes by D.C. MacDonald", published in London by Kegan Paul, Trench, Trübner & Co. Ltd., in 1891; and re-printed in 1970 by Augustus M. Kelley, Publishers, of New York, in their "Reprints of Economics Classics" series.

*

Ogilvie's Essay

The passages from Ogilvie's "Essay" used in the edition in this book, are ones I originally selected for the Scottish Ogilvie Society's joint project, and grew out of the paragraphs selected for our early small flyer, (as related in "The Making of This Book"). Hence, although my book appears after the Othila Press publication, the edition of Ogilvie's "Essay" presented here was the more original.

To have gone back to the beginning again, and studied the whole of Ogilvie's "Essay" anew for this volume, in an attempt to achieve a greater variation from what has since appeared in the Othila Press publication, would have been timewise beyond me. I therefore chose to concentrate upon D.C. MacDonald's "Biographical Notes" instead.

However, on returning to Ogilvie's "Essay" again, to check it carefully for its order of passages, I found myself drawn to write a much fuller commentary upon it linking it with our time, than I had earlier achieved - (that is, in the 1996 chapter, which is also included in this book). In this sense, then, the Ogilvie "Essay" chapter in fact contains a good deal of new material.

D.C. MacDonald's Biographical Notes

My selections from the "Biographical Notes" - (which grew out of an excellent but much more restricted original Scottish Ogilvie Society selection, as already related) - having much the same history, I returned to the "Biographical Notes" in the summer of 1997, to discover what variations I might here too achieve. In fact, I found a number of passages which I now wished to include. In particular, I wanted to include those passages which linked Ogilvie's work with that of Dr G.T. Wrench of our own time, (whose work I have frequently referto in the contents of this book), in the efforts which <u>both</u> made on behalf of today's "Third World". For this Third World is simply the inevitable fruitage of false land tenure, introduced and imposed by Britain on every country that came under her dominion, there to wreak havoc likewise among their unfortunate peoples, creating the inevitable masses of the dispossessed and deprived now called the "Third World" for which Britain bears so heavy a responsibility today - (while the same "dispossessed and deprived" abundantly people her own terrain).

The chief fruitage of this further study of the "Biographical Notes" was perhaps, however, the decision to make a special extract of the section on Ogilvie's battle against the Seven Wise Masters - a section which drew me strongly for the special light it threw on Ogilvie himself. ...And this decision came to prove more fruitful than I had ever contemplated! For these Seven Wise Masters at once walked out of the "Biographical Notes" and entered into my own book! Thus, as I wrote my commentary on Ogilvie after the Seven Wise Masters section, so I found them - (as I seem to recall...two years later and no time to check back now!) - entering into my own commentary on Ogilvie's "Essay" too! Thus the reader may well wish to delve into the Seven Wise Masters section (or chapter - which stands usefully complete on its own), before reading Ogilvie's actual "Essay" with commentary.

D.C. MacDonald's Preface

MacDonald's "Preface" to Ogilvie's "Essay" is practically a 'prose poem' in itself - (a "pastoral prose poem" is how DCM refers to Ogilvie's "Essay" in the course of it). It requires, then, no special editing at all - (as we all in the Scottish Ogilvie Society felt) - beyomd simply the excision of the passages referring to the church and to women, as being now out of date.

However, in the end I decided that the passages on women by D.C. MacDonald were in fact of some interest to include here, as showing something of the subtle methods by which women were historically kept under - and also MacDonald's own decidedly advanced views on the position of women - not all of which we have perhaps quite caught up with yet. ...In addition, it includes that delightful summary of the matter from the pen of Rabbie Burns!

*

Scottish Ogilvie Society. Finally, let me add here an acknowledgement regarding the early work on the texts which was contributed by my former colleagues of the Scottish Ogilvie Society; as also for some helpful suggestions by them concerning my two 1996 chapters, (included in this volume).

*

VIKTOR SCHAUBERGER and DR WESTON PRICE

The books used here do not strictly, I realize, come under the heading of "texts", since my work was simply that of a discussion of their contents - albeit with numerous quotations - in presenting the work of these two great pioneers.

Nevertheless, the books on Viktor Schauberger, by Callum Coats and Olaf Alexandersson, (all published by Gateway Books), and Dr Weston Price's own book, "Nutrition and Degenerative Disease", (published by the Price-Pottenger Foundation in America), deserve, I feel, a special mention in this section, since the discussion of the work of both constitutes so large a part of Part II chapter 2, and since both contributed so much inspiration for the book as a whole.

I have been very glad, over the past two years, to be in touch with Alick Bartholomew of the publishers, Gateway Books, regarding the progress of the work I was engaged in. To have gone beyond this general contact, however - in the course of my work on either Viktor Schauberger or Dr Weston Price - in consulting with others at any stage about my own text, would - (as I well knew from the start) - have meant that this book would never come out at all! Alick Bartholomew of Gateway Books - whom, with his wife, Mairi,

I had the pleasure of meeting last summer - seems intuitively to have understood the situation from early on, and for this I am grateful indeed to him.

The responsibility for these sections of this book is therefore mine alone - but I greatly look forward to sharing the book, at last, with those of whose own inspiring books I have made so much use.

My trust is that, when this volume at last appears and I am able to make that contact with them, they will be able to feel that the use I have made of their work is not only sound, but in addition such as to spread a knowledge of these ideas, and to open up that practical pathway forward for them, which is so desperately needed in the world today.

*

Part I

*

William Ogilvie
and
the State of Scotland Today

*

"If you bring forth what is within you, what you bring forth will save you. If you do not bring forth what is within you, what you do not bring forth will destroy you.

(*Words of Jesus discovered from a Papyrus*)

"Who is he who has seen the danger and not given the warning?"

(*Source unknown*)

*

Produced by
Shirley-Anne Hardy
in the days immediately following

SCOTLAND'S REFERENDUM

11th SEPT. 1997

*

WILLIAM OGILVIE'S ESSAY ON PROPERTY IN LAND

*

1) A Few Words on Ogilvie's Essay, by S-A.H.

2) The Essay, with Ogilvie's own Preface, and Commentary by S-A.H.

3) A Few Words in Conclusion, by S-A.H.

*

A Few Words

on

William Ogilvie's Essay

As I write these words, Scotland has just taken a momentous first step towards the restitution of her full independence. And this marks Ogilvie's Essay as a work of extraordinary significance for us at this time.

Dealing, in his Essay, with the fundaments of injustice, which he saw to be rooted in false land tenure, Ogilvie knew that, if there is to be a restitution to the Scots of their *land,* then "the will of the collective body of the people" must be brought into operation to accomplish it.

Why is this?

Because more is caught in the term "land reform" (if it is to be *radical* land reform) than meets the eye – and certainly something more than merely the nation's "petty cash"! It was, of course, only radical land reform that interested Ogilvie – for his perceptions were radical. And is it not that *radical clear seeing* that we are so in need of today?

The most interesting comment I heard during the week that led up to the referendum – drifting through from a television programme in an adjoining room – came from an Asian-accented voice (hopefully of Scottish citizenship) : *the real meaning of freedom today is not political, but economic.*

He had a point! He had a mighty point!

Why so?

Because, (as the speaker himself seemed to convey, even in so few words), the whole of the political process, with all of its sickening corruptions, has grown up out of, and fattened itself upon, the apparently insoluble economic conundrum of the *continuing economic slavery of the vast majority, under whatever political flag.*

Whatever?

Aye!

Political . . . but what about *national?*

Look about you today!

. . . Clearly, then, this matter of the *economic structure under which we live* needs examining to its roots. And if we in Scotland would do this, we are fortunate. For we find that we have a child of our very own to address us – and who speaks his blazing message to us, across two hundred years, for this very time. For William Ogilvie shows us how the political will can be transformed into the truly national will, *by taking the economic question in its stride.*

How does Ogilvie speak his message to us?

Ogilvie detected – just as did our speaker on the programme – that it is *economic* power which is the real thing – (even apartheid was based on the land dispossession of the blacks). He shows us that the root of power in the political structure is always economic – and that it is *out of this economic root that political power springs.*

Therefore Ogilvie, in his Essay, addresses himself to the *root of the economic question.* And where does he find this root to lie? Where else could it possibly be found to lie, but in that word doubly emphasised by Mark Twain in trying to get the same message across: "*Get land,* young man, get LAND – THEY DON'T MAKE IT ANY MORE!"

Land – which is limited in supply, land – which no human hand made, land – which we all need for our very survival here – and which indeed was here, waiting for us when we arrived, like a mother with open and welcoming arms: how come we have allowed some to carry title-deeds to this Earth-Mother of ours, empowering them to hold others to ransom for a very living?

To ransom?

> "To whomsoever the soil at any time belongs, to him
> belong the fruits of it. White parasols, and elephants
> mad with pride are the flowers of a grant of land."
> (Translation of an Indian grant of land, found at Tanner.)

What exactly are "the fruits of it"?

Why! – exactly all that can be taken from the one who labours on that land, above what is yielded by land which is marginal – (i.e., that land for which no rent can be asked, as the labourer, if not actually starving, is already at the bottom end of society's scale).

THIS IS THE LAW OF RENT!

And this Law operates in the midst of industrial Britain just the same as in the midst of rural India! – In Britain, where great masses of people at the lower end of the social scale, though not outwardly starving, are indeed so drastically *starved of real nutrition* – and so, sickening in countless ways – that they are more and more collapsing upon our social services . . . which are less and less capable of acting as a safety net under the weight of a society . . . gradually collapsing under land rent robbery. (Examine for yourselves in Part III the unassailable, natural Law of Rent, with its correlative iron *Law of the Depression of Wages.*)

To return to those "white parasols, and elephants mad with pride".

Today's cadillacs and trips to the sun? How marvellously summed up are our more homely political prostitutions, just the same!

To Ogilvie, it was all an open book: the intricate, destructive interweavings of the Law of Rent through the whole social fabric – and the tragic stranglehold that such an economic power-base always exerts upon the political one.

It was therefore plain to him that the uprooting of such an economic order would require nothing less that one of those rarest of historical events – a time when the decisive power of the State (is) thrown for a . . . while . . . into the hands of the collective body of the people" (50th paragraph here)* He saw, moreover, that even given that rarest of moments in their history, the uprooting of such a powerful economic structure can still only be achieved – through insertion, in a new constitution, of the necessary bill of right – by a *people that knows what they are doing.*

Scotland is right now poised at just such an extraordinary moment in her history. But do the Scots yet really know *what it is that they must do if they would truly win their freedom?*

How remarkable a thing it is that just at the time, when profound change is a-foot in Scotland, we can summon from our past someone of Ogilvie's insights – insights both economic *and* political – to turn the searchlight of his gaze, for us, upon today's scene!

So now let us allow Ogilvie himself to show us – *what this decisive moment in our history is given us for.*

*

* See Ogilvie's Essay

OGILVIE'S ESSAY

Ogilvie's Own Introduction

The municipal laws of every country are not only observed as a rule of conduct, but by the bulk of the people they are regarded as the standard of right and of wrong, in all matters to which their regulations are extended.

In this prejudice, however natural to the crowd, and however salutary it may be deemed, men of enlarged and inquisitive minds are bound by no ties to acquiesce without enquiry.

Free inquiry, however it may give birth to vain theories and chimerical projects, has never in any department been productive of essential detriment to the true interests of mankind. What undesirable consequences have always arisen from the stagnation of inquiry, and from silent acquiescence, even in establishments that are beneficial, and in opinions that are true, the history of mankind bears witness in every age.

Property is one of the principal objects of municipal law, and that to which its regulations are applied with greatest efficacy and precision. With respect to property in moveables, great uniformity takes place in the laws of almost all nations; they differ only as being more or less extended to details, comprehending the diversity of commercial transactions; and this branch of jurisprudence may be said to have almost attained to its ultimate maturity and perfection.

But with respect to property in land, different principles have been adopted by different nations in different ages; and there is no reason why that system, which now prevails in Europe, and which is derived from an age not deserving to be extolled for legislative wisdom, or regard to the equal rights of men, should be supposed to excel any system that has taken place elsewhere, or to be in itself already advanced beyond the capacity of improvement or the need of reformation.

The leading principles of that system which (the author) now holds, respecting property in land, have been coeval in his mind with the free exercise of his thoughts in speculative inquiries; they have recurred often, they have been gradually unfolded, and for some years past he has been accustomed to review them frequently, almost in their present form, with still increasing approbation.

All that he would request in their favour (and the candid will readily grant this) is, that they may not be rejected on the first disgust, and that those who cannot adopt the opinions here advanced may at least bestow some pains in ascertaining their own.

It is to a free and speculative disquisition, concerning the foundation of this right of property in land, and concerning those modifications, by which it may be rendered in the highest degree beneficial to all ranks of men, that the author of these pages wishes to call the attention of the learned, the ingenious, and the friends of mankind.

OGILVIE'S ESSAY

(with sub-headings, commentary and footnotes by S-A. H.)

The Right to Land – and the specific meaning of this.

(Paras. 1-6 in this edition.)

All Right of property is founded either in occupancy or labour. The earth having been given to mankind in common occupancy, each individual seems to have by nature a right to possess an equal share. This right is little different from that which he has to the free use of the open air and running water[1]; though not so indispensably requisite at short intervals for his actual existence, it is not less essential to the welfare and right state of his life through all its progressive stages.

This right cannot be precluded by any possession of others and nor is it tacitly renounced by those who have had no opportunity of entering upon it. The opportunity of claiming this right ought to be reserved for every citizen. Rude societies have respected this right ; in the progress of arts it is overlooked, and by conquest generally subverted.

Speculative reasoners have confounded this equal right with that which is founded in labour, and ascertained by mutual law. The progress of cultivation gives an ascendant to the right of labour over that of general occupancy. But the public good requires that both should be respected and combined together, and although such combination is difficult, and has rarely been established for any length of time, it is the proper object of Agrarian laws, and effectual means of establishing it may be devised.

The collective body of the people, if at any time their power shall predominate, ought above all things to insist on a just regulation of property in land. It belongs to the community to establish rules by which this general right may become definite; but not to recognise such a right at all, not to have established any rules by which its claims may be ascertained and complied with, ought to be accounted essentially unjust[2]. Means may certainly be discovered by which this general right of the community in the property of the soil may be clearly and practically ascertained.

---

1. Tiberius Gracchus of ancient Rome, a Tribune of the People – (the *plebs*, for whom he stood, with his brother, in opposition to the *patricians*, or the rich and privileged) – in one of his speeches referred to land, air and water in just this way:-

   "Men of Rome, you are called the lords of the world, yet
   have no right to a square foot of its soil. The wild beasts have
   their dens, but the soldiers of Italy have only water and air."

   Ogilvie being the widely-read classical scholar that he was, we may find Tiberius Gracchus's thought woven into Ogilvie's here. However it was – we still haven't caught up with either of them!

---

2. Let us see that we linger no longer in that category of the "essentially unjust", where Ogilvie's statement so justly places us! Ogilvie has given us a prod. Do we need a *shove*? – !

The value of an estate consists of three parts – the original, the improved, and the improvable value.* The original and the improvable value of a great estate still belong to the community, the improved alone to the landholder. The original value is the proper subject of land-taxes; the improvable value may be separated from the improved, and ought to be still open to the claims of the community.**

---

* *Ogilvie saw the value of any piece of land as consisting of three parts:* the ***original*** *value – that which the land might have borne in its natural state; the* ***improved*** *value – that which it has received from the improvements or developments bestowed upon it by the occupier, (buildings, cultivation, etc.); and the* ***improvable*** *value – that further value which the land may still receive from any future improvements or developments, (including of course any planning permissions granted).*

However, more recent thought recognises that for the purposes of site valuation for public revenue, we need distinguish between only two values. Firstly, there is the value of the ***unimproved site****, (assessed, i.e., as though the improvements belonging to it did not exist, but taking into account all of the values bestowed upon it by the presence and activities of the surrounding community, including buildings, public works, roads, etc.) This value clearly belongs to the community.*

Secondly, there is the value of the ***improvements*** *bestowed upon it by the occupier; and these just as clearly belong to him.*

The essential point is that, in common with other radical land reformers, (those, i.e., advocating land rent for revenue), William Ogilvie recognised that it is the ***improved*** *value of the land* ***alone*** *– (that is, the value arising from the investment of his own labour in it) – that rightly belongs to the landholder.*

A special case exists regarding improvements that ***merge with the land****, such as manuring, draining, levelling, reclamation, etc. "Making allowance for improvements that merge in the land is a familiar feature in the legislation in several countries where land value taxation is in some measure already in operation. For example, in Denmark, provision for such allowance is made on proof of the expenditure incurred, setting however a time limit of thirty years during which the expenditure is considered to have been recouped. , Of similar effect are the provisions in United Kingdom law whereby occupiers of farmland are indemnified, on the transfer or sale of land, for the unexhausted value of the improvements they have made at their own expense during their tenure." (A.W. Madsen, in a footnote to ch. 18 of "Progress and Poverty" by Henry George, Hogarth Press, 1953.)*

Whether or not the U.K. law is still in operation, it was clearly of sound practice – and principle. Regarding the Danish law: where the main expenditure has been the labour of the occupier, it might be considered more just that, for the duration of his lifetime, the increased value should belong to him. **(Note:** *the* ***first two*** *paragraphs above draw upon a footnote of* ***joint*** *authorship, in an early unpublished Scottish Ogilvie Society edition of the Essay.* S-A.H.)

** *Ogilvie wrote for a largely agrarian society. But the laws regarding land tenure which he discusses apply equally, of course, to city land – where indeed the highest land values today arise.* **(Note:** *this footnote draws upon the same source as that above.* S-A.H.)

Almost all of Agrarian laws have proceeded on the plan of restricting that extent of landed property which an individual may acquire, and not the nature and the force of that right with which the landholder is invested. Thus endeavouring to establish an equality of fortune, they have been found impracticable, and, could they have been carried into execution, they must have proved detrimental to the progress of industry and of commerce.*

---

* *The "nature" of the landowner's right, under land monopoly, is the ability to extract from the labourer that rental payment which should go to the community – with the "force", accompanying that right, of keeping the labourer's wages at their lowest possible level. (See **Law of Rent and Wages** in Part III.*

*Exactly the same mistake is made by would-be land reformers today, as Ogilvie points out here – who miss the point that it is the land's **rental value**, and not its **physical extent**, that is the heart of the matter, and the issue at stake. (See discussion of this in Note 3).*

*This is a strong statement by Ogilvie, on this matter; and considering his extensive personal experience over many years, both as a hands-on land improver, and as a stalwart champion of the community's land values – (see his battle with the **Seven Wise Masters**) – we must concede that Ogilvie **knew what he was talking about**. Do not, then, let us make double fools of ourselves – by doing what is foolish, (i.e. attempting to combine **rental valuations** with **geographical measurements** – an absurdity!), **and** by doing it in the face of someone like Ogilvie: that is, someone of his immense stature in these matters, and born of our very own soil and culture too!*

(Note: My first five lines above were my original contribution for the Scottish Ogilvie Society project. S-A.H.)

Land Rental Value: the true Public Revenue. Industry should not be taxed. (Paras. 7-10.)

If the original value of the soil be the joint property of the community, no scheme of taxation can be so equitable as a land-tax,[3] by which alone the expenses of the state ought to be supported until the whole amount of that original value be exhausted; for the persons who have retained no portion of that public stock, but have suffered their shares[4] to be deposited in the hands of the landholders,[5] may be allowed to complain, if, before that fund is entirely applied to the public use, they are subjected to taxes, imposed on any other kind of property, or any articles of consumption.

---

3. It is important to note that – as pointed out in the third footnote – what is signified here is the levying of a tax upon the land's ***rental values*** – ***not*** a tax upon the *extent* of land-holding. A small holding may be creaming off far more value from the community than a large one, in any of the numerous aspects that come into play, be it in town or country, such as: soil fertility, direction of slope, accessibility, availability of public services, and prime or corner sites in city land.

This is an important point to grasp regarding radical land reform, and is made quite plain by Ogilvie himself, (most specifically in paragraph 5 here). Hence the beauty of radical land reform. It requires no bureaucratic play of dividing up land, limiting land, allocating land, or setting up those absurd "land banks" that we hear of from time to time – all of which "land business" will incontestably lay itself open to the widest uses of corruption. (And haven't we seen enough corruption, at national *and* at local level?)

If Scotland is to build herself anew from the soil . . . (that lies under her city land, no less) . . . she wants none of that. What she does want is the knowledge too long denied her – the knowledge, and understanding, of the land question already possessed by numerous of her forebears, and deliberately kept from her by established interests: forebears who gave themselves to study, observation, *and clear utterance* upon the principles, *and* practice, of this matter – and whose work we must bring again to the light.

Why was this knowledge of our history denied us, if not precisely because it is the key to the most thorough undoing of today's economic monopoly – (i.e., land-and-resources monopoly, *land* as an economic term embracing its resources) – and hence the key also to the dismantling of those inordinate, false accumulations of capital, those huge vested interests that rule us behind the scenes? Why else has it been so assiduously kept out of our schools and colleges, if not that it would unquestionably signal the demise of that Establishment which – alike under Tory and Labour – has bossed us according to our own ignorance for far too long?

Far from needing to import any foreign concepts of land tenure into Scotland, what we need to do is to re-discover, re-vitalise, RE-INSTITUTE – and then *export*, our own!

(See further, Law of Rent and Wages chart in Part III, and note upon it.)

---

4. Let us note Ogilvie's vocabulary here. We talk glibly enough of the market in stocks and shares. As Ogilvie points out: here is the original "stock" – and here are the original "shares". – And here is something we have originally overlooked! . . . There's a mighty lot for us to catch up with!

---

5. Note that "landholders" – or occasionally "proprietors of land" – are Ogilvie's preferred terms, not "landowners". We should emulate him in this – for psychologically it brings already a step into freedom. Let us consider the term "landowner". It is intimidating! For who can justifiably take away what another rightly *owns*? And doubtless the term "landowner" operates for just that purpose! It would be interesting to know whether it was a term Ogilvie deliberately eschewed, or whether it was simply not so current in his time. Either way provides interesting food for thought! Let us, then, decide to follow Ogilvie's example – (in the main, just as occasionally, for his purpose, he spoke of "proprietors", a term more akin to "owners"). The term "landholder" is also a far sounder ecological term for our time, since happily there is a growing awareness that it is nonsensical for us to speak of "owning" any part of Planet Earth!

How preposterous, then, is the system of that country which maintains a civil and military[6] establishment, by taxes of large amount, without the assistance of any land-tax at all! In that example may be perceived the true spirit of legislation, as exercised by landholders alone. Property in land is the fittest subject of taxation; and could it be made to support the whole expense of the public, great advantages would arise to all orders of men. What then, it may be said, would not in that case the proprietors of stock in trade, in manufacture and arts, escape taxation, that is, the proprietors of one-half the national income? They would indeed, be so exempted; and very justly, and very profitably for the State; for it accords with the best interests of the community, through successive generations, that active progressive industry should be exempted, if possible, from every public burden.[7]

All property ought to be the reward of industry; all industry ought to be secure of its full reward; the exorbitant right of the landholders subverts both these maxims of good policy. It is the indirect influence of this monopoly which makes a poors-rate necessary; requires unnatural severity in penal laws; and renders the improvement of machinery for facilitating labour unpopular, and perhaps pernicious. The oppressed state of the cultivators,[8] being universal, has been regarded by themselves and others as necessary and irremediable. A sound policy respecting property in land is perhaps the greatest improvement that can be made in human affairs. It might restore a sinking state.

Reformation in this important point is not to be despaired of; the establishment of property in land has changed, and may hereafter receive other innovations.

---

6. A reference by Ogilvie – slightly obliquely at that dangerous time – to the abolition of the military tenures, under which the armed forces had been paid for out of *rental revenues*. (See further in Part I, Patrick Edward Dove, and also the Biographical Notes.)

---

7. The true champion – of true business!

---

8. "The cultivators". Equally, the factory and office workers, etc., of today. As also, lamentably, the trades unionists – who are meant to be upholding all these workers' rights. As Ogilvie says, a little further on, "they feel indeed, and they complain, but . . ."
But . . . !

Present land tenure directly opposes the interests of the landholder to those of the community and is the FUNDAMENTAL EVIL IN OUR SOCIETY. (Paras. 11-12.)

Property in Land, as at present established in Europe, is a monopoly of the most pernicious kind. The interest of landholders is substituted for that of the community; it ought to be the same, but it is not. The landholders of a nation levy the most oppressive of all taxes; they receive the most unmerited of all pensions; if tithes are oppressive to industry, rents capable of being raised from time to time are much more so. The imperfection of this state arises from that right to the improvable value of the soil which landholders possess. The oppression proceeding from this right debases and corrupts. The rent which may be taken for land ought to be submitted to regulations not less than the interest of money.

That exclusive right to the improvable value of the soil which a few men, never in any country exceeding one hundredth part of the community, are permitted to engross is a most oppressive privilege, by the operation of which the happiness of mankind has been for ages more invaded and restrained, than by all the tyranny of kings, the imposture of priests, and the chicane of lawyers taken together, though these are supposed to be the greatest evils that afflict the societies of human kind.

Blame for the present wrong order does not rest with the proprietor of land – and those who suffer from the monopoly do not see it. (Para. 13.)

It were unjust to censure the proprietors of land, however, for retaining and exercising, as they do, a right whose foundations have not been inquired into, and whose extent no one has ever yet controverted. It is the situation in which they find themselves placed that prompts their conduct, nor can they readily conceive either the injustice or the detriment which the public suffers, by permitting such rights to be exercised. On the other hand, the farmers and cultivators have no clear perception of the injustice and oppression which they suffer. They feel indeed, and they complain, but do not understand, or dare not consider steadily, from what cause their grievances take their rise. The oppressive rights of the one order, and the patient submission of the other, have grown up together insensibly from remote ages, in which the present state of human affairs could not be foreseen.

Laws regulating land tenure are more vital for society than laws regulating the interest on money. (Paras. 14-16.)

Whatever good reasons may be given for restraining money-holders from taking too high interest, may with still greater force be applied to restraining proprietors of land from an abuse of their right. By exacting exorbitant rents, they exercise a most pernicious usury, and deprive industry that is actually exerted of its due reward. By granting only short leases, they stifle and prevent the exertion of that industry which is ready at all times to spring up, were the cultivation of the soil laid open upon equitable terms.

It is of more importance to the community, that regulations should be imposed on the proprietors of land, than on the proprietors of money; for land is the principal stock of every nation, the principal subject of industry,[9] and the use of which is most necessary for the happiness and due employment of every individual.[10]

Nor is it less practicable to adapt regulations to the use of land[11] than to the use of money, were the legislative body equally well inclined to impose salutary restrictions on both. The glaring abuses of the one might be as effectually prevented as those of the other; although the total exclusion of all manner of abuse from either, is not to be looked for.

---

9. There is no need to modify this statement for today. Since no industry can take place without land, for which rent must be paid, land still remains *the principal subject of industry* – regardless of the strenuousness of the attempts to obliterate this simple recognition from our minds!

---

10. Note that Ogilvie, just as other writers on this radical *land rent* reform, sees no possibility of *in*voluntary employment, in a society founded on land justice.

---

11. This reference to the *use of land* clearly refers to the opposing states under discussion in this respect: i.e., as to whether it is used for the extraction of rents from others, or whether for the direct application by the landholder, to it, of his own powers (physical, managerial – of whatever type these may be). Ogilvie makes no reference here to our present-day arena of squabbles over how land should best be *used* by those who "own" it

– and would never have entered into it. He saw too clearly that abuses of land *use* arise from the entire abusive system of land *tenure*: the false power gained by some – (as bestowed by false land tenure law) – over the rental value of land, whether this is enjoyed as rent, or capitalised into selling-value. He, of course, had his own fully bitter first-hand experience of this kind of abuse of land, in terms of its use, over the business of the sale of the potential botanic garden area belonging to King's College, (just for silver to line some people's pockets. See ch. "The Seven Wise Masters".) We need to cultivate Ogilvie's same clear vision – adopt radical land rent reform, and so cease from our countless misdirected disputes over false land use, with all the wastage of energies that such disputes involve – when we have made no attempt to understand the real nature of our land tenure laws and the fatal flaws they contain, and to *remake those laws in conformity with social – and planetary – justice.*

But that class of men in whom the strength of every government resides, and in whom resides also the right of making laws – (or the power of influencing and controlling those who possess the right of making them) – have generally been borrowers of money and proprietors of land.[12]

---

12. Those "in whom resides . . . the power of influencing and controlling" the law-makers, suggests vividly enough those who roam the world of the "Seven Wise Masters". (See ch. in Part I.) *Note:* I have simplified the wording here, which – (in those possibly more Latin-oriented days) – originally ran: ". . . in whom the strength of every government resides, and the right of making or the power of influencing and controlling those who possess the right of making laws, have generally been . . "

    With land to offer as collateral, how easy it is to borrow large sums of money . . . and so, by an astute use of such borrowings, to enrich oneself still further! (Such borrowings are not, however, open to the mere *bread-winners*, of course!)

Land monopoly militates against the improvement of agriculture. (Para. 17.)

The chief obstacle to rapid improvement of agriculture is plainly that monopoly of land which resides in the proprietors, and which the commercial system of the present age has taught them to exercise with artful strictness, almost everywhere. Hereafter, perhaps, some fortunate nation will give the example of setting agriculture free from its fetters. A new emulation will then arise among the nations hastening to acquire that higher vigour and prosperity, which the emancipation of the most useful of all arts cannot fail to produce.

The more concentrated use of land in industry, than in agriculture, brings a greater profit to the landholders – hence their chief interest in industry. (Paras. 18 -24.)

The monopoly of rude materials, indispensably requisite for carrying on any branch of industry, is far more pernicious than the monopoly of manufactured commodities ready for consumption. The monopoly possessed by landholders is of the first sort, and affects the prime material of the most essential industry.

The monopoly possessed by landholders enables them to deprive the peasants not only of the due reward of industry exercised on the soil, but also of that which they may have opportunity of exercising in any other way, and on any other subject; and hence arises the most obvious interest of the landholder, in promoting manufactures.

That nation is greatly deceived and misled which bestows any encouragement on manufactures for exportation, or for any purpose but the necessary internal supply, until the great manufactures of grain and pasturage are carried to their utmost extent. It can never be in the interest of the community to do so; it may be in that of the landholders, who desire indeed to be considered as the nation itself, or at least as being representatives of the nation, and having the same interest with the whole body of the people.

In fact, however, their interest is, in some most important respects, directly opposite to that of the great body of the community, over whom they exercise an ill-regulated jurisdiction, together with an oppressive monopoly in the commerce of land to be hired for cultivation.

The encouragements granted to commerce and manufacturers, and so universally extolled, seem merely schemes devised for employing the poor and finding subsistence for them, in that manner which may bring most immediate profit to the rich:[13] and these methods are, if not deliberately, at least without inquiry, preferred to others, which might bring greater advantage to the body of the people directly, and ultimately even to the rich themselves.

There are districts in which the landholder's rents have been doubled within fifty years, in consequence of a branch of manufacture being introduced and flourishing, without any improvement in the mode of agriculture, or any considerable increase of the produce of the soil. Here, therefore, the landlords are great gainers, but by what industry or attention have they earned their profits? How have they contributed to the progress of this manufacture, unless by forbearing to obstruct it? And yet from the necessity under which the manufacturing poor lived, of resorting to these landholders to purchase from them the use of houses and land, for the residence of their families, they have been enabled to tax their humble industry at a very high rate, and to rob them of perhaps more than one-half of its reward.[14]

---

13. These same "schemes and devices", which occupied the Tories throughout their eighteen years of ascendancy . . . now occupy "New Labour" no less. Ogilvie would have nothing to do with them, recognizing them as the direct offspring of land monopoly, to be *got rid of*, along with unemployment, and the *rotten land system lying at the root of both.*

---

14. Industrial workers – labour of every kind – and small (i.e. not land-investment-advantaged) businesses alike, groan under the heavy burden of taxation today. But *what* is it that in reality taxes industry at so high a rate, Ogilvie asks us to observe? His comments here fully accord with the views of other radical land reformers in indicating rent as sufficient in itself to bear the whole expenses of the State, with no taxation added thereto.

Had the manufacturers of such districts possessed what every citizen seems entitled to have, a secure home of their own,[15] had they enjoyed full property in their lands, would not then the reward of their industrious labour have remained entire in their own hands?

15. Note that Ogilvie sees land rent justice as bringing about a situation in which it is *normal* that every citizen should have "a secure home of their own" – (and "secure" does not, of course, mean weighted with a mortgage – whose chief component is in by far the most cases the monopolistic land values involved). "A secure home of their own"! Just think what this means in a land like Scotland, where most people live either as tenants of a private landholder, or as tenants of the State – and with the homes of most of the remainder mortgaged to the hilt.

The ill consequences for society of allowing the false capturing by the landholders of socially created land values. (Paras. 25-28.)

What is it that in England restrains the early marriages of the poor and industrious classes of men? Alas! not the Marriage Act but a system of institutions more difficult to be reformed; establishing in a few hands that monopoly of land by which the improvable as well as the improved value of the soil is engrossed. It is this which chiefly occasions the difficulty of their finding early and comfortable settlements in life, and so prevents the consent of parents from being given before the legal age. It is this difficulty which even after that age is passed still withholds the consent of parents, restrains the inclinations of the parties themselves, and keeps so great a number of the lower classes unmarried to their thirtieth or fortieth years, perhaps for their whole lives.[16]

Let it be considered what regulations a colony of men settling in a small island, just sufficient to furnish them subsistence, by the aid of high cultivation, would probably establish in order to render the independent subsistence of each individual secure, and to prevent any one, or a few, from engrossing the territory, or acquiring a greater share than might be consistent with the public good? Just such regulations respecting property in land, it would be in the interest of every state to establish at any period of its history.

What other reason can be given, than the influence of this monopoly, why in countries, for many ages not thinly inhabited, nor unacquainted with the arts of agriculture, so great a proportion of the soil should still remain barren, or at least far below that state of fertility, to which the judicious cultivation of independent occupiers could bring it?

---

16. While young people today have broken through the taboos of not living together before marriage, it is interesting to see our same underlying social and economic conditions, in this respect, described so exactly by Ogilvie two hundred years ago! "Plus ça change . . ." – but what really *can* change under land monopoly? . . . except for a progressive tightening of the screw . . .

While the cultivable lands remain locked up, as it were, under the present monopoly, any considerable increase of population, though it seems to add to the public strength, must have a pernicious influence on the relative interests of society, and the happiness of the greater number. By diminishing the wages of labour,[17] it favours the rich, fosters their luxury, their vanity, their arrogance; while on the other hand, it deprives the poor of some share of their just reward and necessary subsistence.

---

17. No more classic – or more piteous and terrible – exposition of this unvarying law of land monopoly, could be found than occurs "incidentally" in John Steinbeck's recounting of the wanderings of the desperate, dispossessed "Okies" – (people of Oklahoma) – in his book "Grapes of Wrath".

The present unjust fiscal policies – virtually created by the landholders – directly oppose the benefit of the community, and cause the debasement of advantaged and disadvantaged alike. (Paras. 29-33.)

When mention is made in political reasonings of the interest of any nation, and those circumstances, by which it is supposed to be injured or promoted, are canvassed, it is generally the interest of the landholders that is kept in view.[18]

Regarding the whole wealth of the community, as belonging of right to themselves, landholders stand foremost in opposing the imposition of exorbitant taxes by the State,[19] forgetting the exorbitancy of that taxation which they themselves impose on the cultivators of the soil, and which the sovereign may in justice, and in the way of retaliation ought to, regulate and restrain. They clamour aloud against pensions and sinecure places, bestowed by the sovereign, not adverting that their own large incomes are indeed pensions, and salaries of sinecure offices, which they derive from the partiality of municipal law in favour of that order of men by whom its regulations are virtually enacted.[20]

---

18. Note how this seems to reach an ultimate absurdity, when politicians – as for the past two decades – have continued to preach to us that "Scotland has never had it so good"! But – as we have said – what can change under land monopoly? Here is Robert Watson of Elgin – (a student of Ogilvie's?) – speaking at the end of the eighteenth century:-

   > "In James's reign, the people were borne down with poverty and oppression, whilst the courtiers were boasting of the flourishing state of the nation, and squandering thousands in luxury and debauch. During Mr. Pitt's administration, thousands are dying for want of the common necessaries of life; and yet his courtiers are extolling the goodness of the times, and adding insult to misfortune, by their extravagant profusion." – ! (Quoted from "The Thunderbolt of Reason", by Graham Bain. See ". . . and another Historic Statement", later in Part I.)

---

19. It may be observed how, in an age when *tax evasion* has reached a high art among the rich, landholders have no need to take this stand any longer. For the poor, on the other hand, who live from wages, tax evasion is a virtual impossibility.

---

20. Perhaps this may be considered one of Ogilvie's "gentle strokes"! (See D.C. MacDonald's *Biographical Notes*.)

The public good requires that every individual should be excited to employ his industry in increasing the public stock, or to exert his talents in the public service, by the certainty of a due reward. Whoever enjoys any revenue, not proportioned to such industry or exertion of his own, or of his ancestors, is a freebooter, who has found means to cheat or to rob the public, and more especially the indigent of that district in which he lives. But the hereditary revenue of a great landholder is wholly independent of his industry, and secure from every danger that does not threaten the whole State. It increases also without any effort of his, and in proportion to the industry of those who cultivate the soil.[21] In respect of their industry, therefore, it is a progressive tax of the most pernicious nature, and in respect of the landholder himself it is a premium given to idleness, an inducement to refrain from any active useful employment, and to withhold his talents, whatever they are, from the service of his country. If the circumstances in which he finds himself placed stimulate to any exertion at all, it is that insidious vigilance[22] by which he himself is debased, and his dependants at once corrupted and oppressed.

May not the landholder and his ancestors be described as a race of men whose business and whose industry have for successive generations consisted in buying up large tracts of land as cheap as they can, and letting them to others as dear as they can?[23]

---

21. . . . Or, today, who work in factories, offices, etc. – wherever, i.e., industry (in the basic meaning of that word) or *any* kind, utilises that first of all requirements for productive effort, which is LAND.

---

22. Vigilance for his own vested intereasts.

---

23. The first thing to be clear about here is that Ogilvie was speaking strictly , of course, about landholders *qua* landholders. There are many landholders – and Ogilvie was one himself for a time, (see interesting account of this in the Biographical Notes) – who do invest their labour in their holding, (whether in town or country); and that they deserve the full reward of that labour goes without saying.

Moreover, as to the "more" that may be taken from a landholding, under land monopoly, than a mere return to labour: the blame for this, as Ogilvie has already pointed out, cannot be laid at the door of the landholders. For so long as society allows an abusive system to operate, for so long will that society (*including its land*) be abused. And, at the deepest level, the landholders will suffer, as a result, along with everyone else. Indeed, there are undoubtedly those among their ranks who themselves recognise this – as well as any of us; and would be as thankful as any of us to see inaugurated radical change of a kind so just. A "coming together" is required to bring it about, of people from all walks of life.

It has been required of the magistrate that he should with the same assiduity apply rewards to virtue as punishment to vice. The part which he has to act in respect or these cases is very different. The natural sentiments of men are sufficient to repress smaller vices, and to encourage and reward great and striking virtues; but they are not vigorous enough to apply adequate punishment to great crimes,[24] nor steady and uniform enough to secure due reward and regular encouragement to the common and ordinary virtues of human life.

The falsity of wage restraints – and the equal futility of placing health and welfare in the inept hands of the State. (Paras. 34-37.)

Every man, and every order of men, have their peculiar commodity, which they bring to market for the service of the community, and for procuring the means of their own subsistence. It would be injustice and oppression, therefore, in any one order to impose restrictions on any other respecting the price they may demand for their peculiar commodity. This injustice, however, certain higher orders have attempted, though generally without success,[25] to put in practice, on various occasions, against their inferiors – against hired servants, day labourers, journeymen, artists of various kinds – by prescribing limits to the wages they are allowed to ask or to receive.

These lower classes of citizens have only the labour of their hand for their commodity, and if any is more than another entitled to the privileges of a free and equal market, it is surely that which may be accounted more immediately the gift of nature to each.

The community has a right, no doubt, to restrain individuals from doing ought that may be pernicious or offensive: what right it can have to compel them to exert their industry for the public service, at a regulated price, may admit of question, excepting only those cases in which the safety of the state is brought into immediate and evident danger.

---

24. A parallel and interesting comment on this, quoting Machiavelli, is found in the article "Our Daily Bread", by Dr. Viggo Starcke, Danish philosopher and historian – (published some years ago by *Land and Liberty*).

> "Some people . . . are so absorbed in details of small things that they do not see the great things at all. The shrewd Italian statesman Machiavelli understood that. He said: 'People are always provoked by small injustices,, but never by great injustices'."

---

25. What great "advance" in the "success" of this practice we have, seen since Ogilvie's time! Dear Trades Unionists – where have you hidden your wits?

The indirect and remote influences of this monopoly are productive of many unnatural situations and many pernicious effects, which the skill of legislature is frequently employed in vain to redress.[25] Were this monopoly anywhere removed, and the cultivation of the soil laid open upon reasonable terms, the lowest classes of men would not be destitute of wherewithal to maintain their decayed and infirm relations and neighbours. These charitable attentions, prompted by private affection, would be better discharged, than when they devolve on the public; and all that encouragement to idleness, that waste, and mismanagement, inseparable from poor rates, and other public institutions of this sort, would be spared.[27]

---

26. Exactly the point that Dr. Wrench makes – (see Goliaths Unmasked, Part III):- "The more evils it" (the errant principle) "causes, the more laws they have to pass". But these are incapable of reversing the "deeper causes" of the evil. As Dr. Wrench goes on to point out: "When social principles are not lacking in a State's organization,' little law is needed". Today we are presented not only with a plethora of laws – laws often incompetent, even ridiculous – but also, of course, with all those "directives" from Brussels. A Mad Hatter's Tea-Party of legislation is the only possible description of such a scene – and no wonder the Income Tax people have finally thrown up their hands saying "do-it-yoursel£!"

---

27. I reserve my chief comment on this aspect of today's scene to another section of the book – (easily recognizable!) And regarding the "certain matter" there discussed – how forcefully Ogilvy today would have said to us, "I TOLD YOU SO!"

    But we may pause for a moment on Ogilvie's words "and other public institutions of this sort" – which seem prophetic if we imagine the range of these that would have come under his scrutiny today. State involvements in such spheres as housing, health and education are due simply to the *impoverishment of the people*, who would otherwise have taken perfectly good care of what are, in reality, their own affairs – (unaccustomed as we are to viewing them as such, after so long a take-over).

In no sphere is *State intervention* more disastrous than in that of education – as we have seen from the very subject-matter of this book. But State involvement in health . . . stemming in huge part from its *prior* intervention in agriculture, involving the denaturing, chemicalization, and poisoning of the soil, hence of our food – and the cost of this adding untold millions to the N.H.S. bill, (all painlessly extracted from the *taxpayer*, of course!), from the resultant ill-health . . . and the untold sufferings placed upon countless families in turn . . . who innocently bear the end-fruitage of this damage to soil and creature alike in the food chain . . . all this adds a disaster of almost equal proportion; only that the perversion of education lies at the very foundation of all.

No doubt Ogilvie's vision included in its prophetic sweep, also, the thousands of dedicated individuals locked into such State systems, more and more only wishing to take early retirement as they watch these systems' increasing dilapidations under State "management" – evidence not only of the gargantuan waste of . . . that ever ill-fated system of taxation, but also of a truly horrendous waste of human talent and skills.

What is there left to say of State housing policy, directly responsible as it is for the breaking up of communities and positive encouragement of vandalism, through schemes displaying a profound incomprehension of human values? What indeed is there left to say of such policies, but to point to the huge task which courageous communities – of actual *people* – are now having to take upon themselves, in order – by various imaginative means – to reclaim such space for human families.

But again, it is not the actual people involved in this kind of "State enterprise" – *State folly* – who are to blame. It is the structures that we have, in our own folly, created, which are structures de-humanising in themselves. We need the new humanity of a society whose structures are all human-scale – and in which the role of the State is reduced to the role of government pure and simple. (See A.J. Nock, in "Our Enemy, the State" – Reading List; and Part II here.)

A fundamentally false economic structure burdens itself with false laws, false fears – and the encouragement of crime. (Paras. 38--41.)

Sumptuary laws (i.e. laws against luxury. S-A.H.) have been frequently turned into ridicule, and not unjustly, as pretending to maintain an impracticable simplicity, and an unnecessary austerity of manners, among the great body of citizens; but they deserve a very different estimation, if considered as means of directing the public industry to those exertions which may be productive of the most extensive utility, and most valuable enjoyments to the community at large.

Why should it be necessary to restrain the industry which ministers to luxury? Because the industry which is productive of essential plenty is restrained.

In a country where the opportunities of exercising a natural employment, and finding an easy subsistence, were thus laid open to all, the temptations to theft and other violations of property would be very much diminished;[28] nor could it be thought necessary to restrain such crimes by the unnatural severity of capital punishments.

In such a country no suspicion could arise, no surmise would be listened to, that the invention of machines for facilitating mechanical labour, could ever be pernicious to the common people, or adverse to the prosperity of the State.[29]

---

28. Let us pause on this simple, and so obvious, statement of Ogilvie's; pause until it really sinks into us how our prisons are bursting at the seams, while we foolishly wring our hands for money to build . . . yet more foolish cells of incarceration! Because we will not use our

plain common sense – our elementary powers of observation, reflection and deduction. Let us now put these into operation and realize our real tragedy – the real *crime that we have committed against ourselves*, and that we still have not caught up with. . . . Still have not caught up with William Ogilvie, of two hundred years ago!

---

29. How clearly Ogilvie sees that it is not machinery itself, but machinery *under monopoly capitalism* that is averse to the workers' interests – both in bringing about unemployment, and in becoming the master instead of the servant of work. There is a fine parallel with our technology today!

No attempt to address our social problems will bear any comparable fruit to that which sets itself to address them *at their root*. (Paras. 42-44.)

Perhaps no government can claim to itself the praise of having attended with the same impartial care, to the interests of the lower, as of the higher classes of men. Those who are employed in cultivating the soil are placed below the regard of men in higher stations of public dignity and trust; nor are their sufferings and wrongs obtruded on every eye, like the misery of the begging poor. They themselves are not much accustomed to reflection; they submit in most countries to their hard fate, as to the laws of nature, nor are they skilled, when severer oppression has at any time awaked them to a sense of the injustice they suffer, in making known their feelings and their complaints to others. But if the intelligent, and the friends of mankind, will take some pains to inquire into the nature and extent of that oppression, under which the industrious groan, and the force of that exorbitant monopoly, from whence their grievances proceed; and if such men will employ the talents which nature hath given them, in explaining these grievances, and the rigour of that monopoly, to the whole world, Europe, enlightened Europe, will not be able to endure it much longer;[30] and the subversion nay, even the abatement–of this monopoly, with the abuses flowing from it, may well deserve to be accounted the best and most valuable fruit of all her refinements and speculations.

---

30. Just think how Ogilvie would have challenged "Scotland, *enlightened* Scotland" – (*post-referendum*) – today! Is Scotland really going to "endure it much longer", when a second stride – into full Independence – will allow her at last to set her own house in order? . . . and show still *un*enlightened Europe the way! And what sort of a comparison would the much-vaunted Scottish Enlightenment of the 1700s – which Ogilvie cannot be presumed to have thought much of! – bear to *this*?

If it be indeed possible to accomplish any great improvement in the state of human affairs, and to unite the essential equality of a rude state, with the order, refinements, and accommodations of cultivated ages, such improvement is not so likely to be brought about by any means, as by a just and enlightened policy respecting property in land. It is a subject intimately connected with the proper occupation and the comfortable subsistence of men; that is, with their virtue and their happiness. It is of a real substantial nature, on which the regulations of law may be made to operate with efficacy, and even with precision.

So powerful and salutary might the good effects of such an enlightened policy prove, so beneficial such a restoration of the claims of nature and the general birth rights of mankind, that it might alone suffice to renovate the strength of nations, exhausted by civil war, or by great and unsuccessful enterprises; and even in the most flourishing states it might give rise to a new era of prosperity, surpassing all example, and all expectation that may reasonably be founded on any other means of improvement.

We need not despair of our task, since systems of land tenure have already evolved, and can further do so. (Paras. 45-49.)

If we consider how far the present state of property in land, even in the best governed nations, is removed from that more equitable and advantageous system, which tends to establish in every country the greatest number of independent freehold cultivators that the territory of the State can admit, we may almost be led to despair, that any great progress can be made towards so remote an improvement, however justly and however much it may be desired. On the other hand, the actual system of landed property in the west of Europe is greatly changed from what it has formerly been. It has varied its form with the prevailing character of successive ages; it has been accommodated to the rude simplicity of the more ancient times, to the feudal chivalry of the middle centuries, an to the increasing industry and cultivation of later more tranquil periods. It may now therefore be expected to receive a new modification, from the genius and maxims of a commercial age, to which it is too manifest that the latest establishment of landed property is by no means adapted, and that from this incongruity the most pernicious and most flagrant oppressions arise.

In the progress of the European system of landed property, three stages may be distinguished – the domestic, the feudal, and the commercial. In the first, the condition of the cultivator was secured from any great oppression, by the affectionate sympathy of the chief of his clan. In the second, it was still secured, and almost as effectually secured, by that need which his lord had of attachment, assistance, and support, in the frequent military enterprises and dangers in which he was engaged.

But in the commercial state there is no natural check which may establish the security of the cultivator; and his lord has hardly any obvious interest but to squeeze his industry as much as he can. It remains, therefore, for the legislatures of different countries to establish some control for protecting the essential interests of their common people. It is an object which deserves, and will reward, their care. In the dark and disorderly ages the oppression exercised over the cultivators could not be reduced to a system. Their landlords depended on their assistance and military services,[31] and would not, therefore, hazard the diminution of their attachment. If at any time the landlord endeavoured to exact more than they were inclined to give, means of concealment and evasion were not wanting, by which his rapacity might be effectually eluded. But in the present times there is no reciprocal dependence, and all means of concealment and evasion are rendered by the order of our laws uncertain, or, indeed, vain.

In those disorderly times, whatever oppression, or chance of oppression, the cultivators of the field were exposed to, they saw their landlord exposed to others, perhaps greater and more frequent; there was common to both an uncertainty in the possession of their just rights; and to compensate this, a chance of obtaining, by address, somewhat beyond these rights. In the present times, these common chances are removed by the protection of established government. The rights of the higher orders are rendered perfectly secure, while those of the cultivators are laid open to their oppressions.

That free discussion which every subject now receives gives reason to hope that truth and utility will always triumph, however slowly. In politics, in agriculture, in commerce, many errors have been rectified in theory, and even the practice in some, though not in an equal degree, reformed. And shall it be reckoned, then, that in this, the most important of all temporal concerns to the greatest number of mankind, the most pernicious errors will be suffered to remain still unrefuted, or if not unrefuted still unreformed? It is not permitted to the friends of mankind to despair[32] of ought which may tend to improve the general happiness of their species, any more than it is consistent with a magnanimous and genuine patriotism ever to despair of the safety of our country.

---

31. Another reference to the shameful abolition of the *military tenures*, which, so long as they stood, did at least ensure a roughly reciprocal relationship between landlord and tenant, by placing upon the receivers of rent a definite responsibility for the supplying of an armed force.

---

32. Let us pause for a moment on these words, to appreciate the strength, in Ogilvie, of this quality of faith. D.C. MacDonald's Biographical Notes bring home to us just how dark a time Ogilvie lived in. It is a sign of the peculiar strength of his character, amongst all its other virtues, that he *did not permit* himself to despair. In this aspect of his character, he followed truly in the footsteps of Wallace.

The *collective body of the people* must establish their own *Bill of Rights*. But first they must grasp the FUNDAMENTAL NATURE OF THEIR RIGHT TO PROPERTY IN LAND.

(Para. 50.)

Internal convulsions have arisen in many countries by which the decisive power of the State has been thrown, for a short while at least, into the hands of the collective body of the people. In these junctures they might have obtained a just re-establishment of their natural rights to independence of cultivation and to property in land, had they been themselves aware of their title to such rights. Such was the revolution in 1688 at which time, surely, an article declarative of the natural right of property in land might have been inserted into the Bill of Rights, had the people at large been beforehand taught to understand that they were possessed of any such claim.[33]

---

33. Perhaps the most important paragraph in Ogilvie's Essay. (See A FEW WORDS at the start, and in conclusion.)

Even the privileged must suffer when the whole country falls into decline. The wisdom of allowing the people without other employment to have *access to the land*. (Paras. 51-53.)

Under circumstances of public distress, even the higher and privileged ranks, awed into wisdom and humanity by the impending gloom, may be inclined to aquiesce in those regulations which tend to renovate the whole body of the State, though at the expense of diminishing in some degree the privileges and emoluments of their own order. They will consider that, unless the numbers, the industry, and the manly temper of the body of the people can be kept up, the fortune of the community must fall into continual and accelerated decline, and the privileges of every rank become insecure.

If, in the meantime, commerce is restrained and manufactures decline, let the cultivation of the soil be laid open, on reasonable terms and without delay, to the people thus deprived of their usual employment; such a resource would convert what they must account a misfortune into an opportunity of finding real and natural happiness.[34]

What more effectual preparation can be made for the most vigorous defence of national liberty and independence, than to interest every individual citizen more immediately and directly in the welfare of his country, by giving him a share in the property of the soil, and training him to the use of arms for its defence. The former of these means of public security and defence is scarcely less requisite than the latter, the propriety of which is so generally understood.

---

34. Considering this paragraph in connection with the feelings of profound hopelessness that engulf so many today who are subjected to periods of prolonged unemployment, here is something that struck me recently in Voices from Earth First, (Prior House, 6 Tilbury Place, Brighton BN2):-

> "Burying our hands in the earth and turning the turf . . . was an amazing experience . . . As Barry Lopez puts it: 'I know of no restorative of heart, body, and soul more effective against hopelessness than the restoration of the Earth. Like childbirth, like the giving and receiving of gifts, like the passion and gesture of the various forms of human love, it is holy.' "

What about the unemployed – and *what about those in our prisons?* . . . who, if any amongst us – and whether they know it or not – are looking for that "restoration" . . . that healing. Should *they* not have a chance to "bury their hands in the earth" ?

Ogilvie would have been the first to say it.

Ogilvie Points the Way Ahead (Paras. 54-55.)

As for the beneficial effects of such a statute, the candid and intelligent are requested to estimate in their own thoughts what these might prove in the district with which they are most particularly acquainted, and to consider whether it would not very much improve the condition and the prospects of the day labourer, the hired servant and the working manufacturer, without imposing on the established farmer or the landlord any unjust inconvenience? Whether it would not lessen the number of the indigent and the idle? After having made this estimate, let them consider what might have been the present state of that district had such a progressive Agrarian law been established there one hundred or even fifty years ago.

Various objects have engaged the enthusiasm and excited the efforts of mankind in successive ages; schemes of conquest and settlement in one age; plans of civil and religious liberty in another; manufactures and commerce have now in their turn; and perhaps in some not very distant age a just regulation of property in land may become the chief object of public spirited endeavours.

"Sic poscere fata, et reor, et si quid veri mens augurat, opto"

"Our destiny points us in that direction, my own reasoning powers tell me that that is where we are heading – and so, too, does my intuition, likewise."

(Translation by S-A H)

A Few Words in conclusion, on Ogilvie's Essay

. . . And so we find – as we turn the last pages of Ogilvie – that a huge burden is lifted from us! We can forget all those time-consuming squabbles about a "tartan tax", because –

THE TRUE TARTAN REVENUE IS RENT!

For Ogilvie has shown us that *only by insisting upon that revenue* shall we ever gain our economic freedom; and that, without that fundamental *economic* freedom, any political freedom won must remain a hollow prize.

But it is worth examining that 50th paragraph more closely. Firstly, we have Ogilvie's apparent insistence that no class of people – *and no government in power* – can be trusted to bring in so radical a reform as that which would restore to every citizen their *equal right of access to land*

How did Ogilvie come to see this so clearly? Ogilvie's great strength lay in the fact that – for all his powerful, his immensely powerful, intellect – in the inner processes of his thinking he allowed the heart-centre, as well as the head, to come into play. (Recent science is reminding us that we think with every atom of our being). Thus Ogilvie, whose heart was pure, drew upon the full range of his wisdom. He knew well that the *people themselves* would have to make their voice heard on this question.

As to the political circumstance that the people would need to make their voice heard: as we have seen, he was quite specific on this. It would need nothing less than an occasion when "the decisive power of the State" would fall directly into their hands. A referendum is, of course, just such an occasion. However, I am struck by a possibly "hidden" hint left to us by Ogilvie concerning just such an event.

In his 53rd paragraph (here), in a few words about the defence of the country – (a *political*, not an economic context, let us note) – the word "independence" is slipped into the sentence. I say "slipped in" because it seems to be superfluous to need, the words "national liberty" being quite sufficient for the meaning.

We have to realize that, in so "prohibitive" a period, when Scotland was more wisely referred to as "one of the northern counties of England"(!), any *direct* statement on the matter of independence would have been extremely unwise. Ogilvie was on dangerous ground enough already in discussing land tenure! So – what was he to do?

At this point I would have liked to re-read the whole of Ogilvie's Essay – to see where else one might find the word "independence" used with this *political,* as distinct from *economic*, meaning. Considering those times – and also that his Essay was centred on the economic question – it might well be that we should discover no other such reference. That would not make this single one less, but perhaps even more, interesting – especially in view of the closing words of his Essay, since the Latin quotation he chose reveals his powers of insight as having been deeply engaged in the field of *fore*sight too!

So it seems to me that Ogilvie, in including the word "independence" where it could be done, was deliberately casting his glance ahead – for the sake of his own people – to remind us, at just such a time as this, that if Scotland is to find her true place among the nations – a final referendum awaits her yet.

This may with certainty be added: that Ogilvie, viewing the power of the establishment based as unfalteringly today on its land monopoly foundations (*under Labour and Tory alike*), and more firmly entrenched than ever two hundred years after his time, would not have hesitated in recognising today that we shall *never get land rent reform from Westminster* – (nor would he have needed to look twice at the Treaty of Rome to know that we shall never get it from Brussels, of course!)

Glancing again at that 50th paragraph, we note Ogilvie's equal insistence upon a second point: that, before the people can exercise their decisive power effectively for freedom, the economics of their situation *must be thoroughly grasped by them.* We would do well to heed him on this! For the experience of Denmark in our own day is salutary. (See Part III.) The Danish people, lacking an understanding of whence their good fortune had come, were unable to retain it. "The error of the most ardent reformers . . . has always been . . . in their eagerness to effect their purpose, (to) let the political movement outstrip the intellectual one", and so "invert the natural order". *First* must come the spreading of *knowledge*, so that those interests which keep society falsely in their grip are "sapped", and their hold upon our thinking is "loosened". So Buckle, in his "History of Civilization in England" (Bk. 2, Ch. 1 . . . from which the English have still, alas, to learn! Denmark's experience has not been fruitless, however, in the extremely interesting history of it bequeathed to us. But Scotland needs not to repeat it!)

How is this thorough grasp of the economic structure that rules us to be achieved? Our general ignorance of the economics of land tenure – so much less obvious than the politics of it! – is a vast legacy from centuries of misrule. For a false social order – dedicated always to its own continuance – naturally subverts education to its own ends. Today's ignorance of land economics bears dreadful witness to that power-behind-the-scenes, which Henry George points out is the real "moulder of our thoughts". As he writes of it: the real power, "the active, energetic power", at work in every country "be its political forms what they may", is "the power of a *vast and dominant pecuniary interest*". (*Progress and Poverty*, ch. 14. Emphasis added. . . . Incidentally, it was the work of Henry George that inspired the Highland Land League that fought the clearances, and through his grand-parentage he links back to Glasgow, too.) This pecuniary interest is woven deep through today's form of *monopoly* capitalism, as we shall see in the notes on Ogilvie's Essay – that monopoly capitalism which is a great part of today's *landed* power.

Another factor, Henry George points out in the same passage, militates against our understanding. Speaking of how the *workings of land monopoly* are the real reason that labour is robbed, he says: "this simple truth, in its application to social and political problems, is hid from the great masses of men partly by its very simplicity".

Part of the technique of false education is undoubtedly to concentrate us, by contrast, upon *multiplicity* – so that we never find the secret! (And this applies to more than just our education in economics, in fact.) Christ taught us that we must become as little children to enter the kingdom of heaven. Well – we certainly have to, to enter the kingdom of heaven on earth! Let Ogilvie, then, doubly serve us as an educator on this matter; for through his eyes, just as through Henry George's, both simplicity – and *complicity*! – become, if we read attentively, marvellously clear.

Birthright. . .and. . .Scotland Today

Here is a third quotation from Henry George – understandably a general favourite!

> "We cannot safely leave politics to politicians or political economy to college professors. The people themselves must think, because the people alone can act."
> (*Social Problems*.)

So we return to the great question: how is such a mighty grass-roots educational effort to be achieved? The Scots – who have left their mark upon the world in such a diversity of ways – are not lacking in ingenuity! *They will find their own way to it*!

. . . And out of their findings, upon that way, they can carve a true pathway forward for Scotland – that pathway which *has to spring out of themselves*.

There is something yet to say about Ogilvie at a more personal level, if we would appreciate fully his place in the history of our land.

Not many are those who discover the highway of economic justice for themselves. It seems that Ogilvie, however, did so.

What is the reason we can be so sure that Ogilvie made his discovery independently? We find it in his own words. In his Introduction to his Essay, he speaks of the principles he holds as being "coeval with" his own free-thinking enquiries. It is impossible that someone of Ogilvie's innate truthfulness should have used so distinct a term as "coeval with," had the principles he arrived at been "coeval with" their discovery in another's writings. He was too upright a soul to have hidden any debt he owed to another for his work, and even in those difficult times would have found some way of hinting at "other occasional writings" he had some across. But he says nothing of this, and no doubt lived through many years feeling himself quite alone in his discovery.

From a fascinating bit of reading, "Forerunners of Henry George", (see Reading-List), here is the opening passage:-

> " 'When you have seen a truth that those around you do not see, it is one of the deepest of pleasures to hear of others who have seen it.' Thus Henry George wrote on learning that his proposal for a Single Tax" – (as the "tax" upon land rental values is sometimes, although inaccurately, referred to) – had been evolved by men before his time, dead and almost forgotten."

No doubt it must have been this same "deepest of pleasures" that William Ogilvie experienced, in reading from Thomas Paine's "The Rights of Man" – the book found by his bedside at the end. (Paine, a contemporary of Ogilvie's and apparently independent discoverer also of the Law of Rent, whose work was published shortly after Ogilvie's, is quoted from elsewhere here.)

Not many, indeed, make the discovery of the Law of Rent for themselves, and it is yet another indication of the stature of William Ogilvie, and our need to listen to him at this juncture in our history.

It has been impossible to spend time in the presence of Ogilvie, as I have done over the past two years, and not come deeply to love him – as one does those great souls in whom an innate nobility, and the profoundest human compassion, are combined. . . . So I have sometimes imagined myself, sitting of an evening in his family circle, taking up one by one the sheets that fall from his hands, to appraise his latest work focused on the welfare of mankind, or – dealings with those Seven Wise Masters, on a slightly sterner note!

But Ogilvie had no family circle, of course – not in the way of a wife and children, that is. No doubt he remained dedicated to the welfare of his sisters, who fell to his early care when all were orphaned so young. His compassion stretched equally, as we know, to the impoverished of the "third world", where the servants of the East India Company, *et al.*, were already making a desolation of "the brightest jewel in the crown". Nor was his concern less for those of Europe's "third world" who were exploited under the system of share-cropping, or *metayage* – another form of the various labour-slaveries that still exist today.

With labour so exploited still in every land, under cruel land tenure laws . . . how many are the oppressed that wait for Ogilvie's country to *shine her beacon of hope across the world?*

Her Saltire! For is our Saltire to speak only for Scotland? – only for a *political* independence, that is? Or is it to carry a broader message? – to blazon across the world, through its national symbol, the possibility of the *economic freedom of every dweller on this earth* – because an economic freedom already made our own, and woven through every strand of our flag? Hence, a national flag like no other – *like no other flag ever flown?*

As a first step: let us take a brief look back at that historic Referendum Day of September 11th, 1997. Did we hear – in the celebrations that went on through September 12th . . . did we hear, on the radio from the streets of Edinburgh, a top-ranking Labour voice proclaim that – "independence is not for the Scots"? Then perhaps there is something that Labour has overlooked!

For is it not possible that that vociferous "YES" of September 11th was celebrating . . . not in fact the concept of devolution, but the *vote for full independence delivered by Wallace?* – the 700th anniversary of whose great victory at Stirling Bridge fell on Referendum Day!

– A flag like no other flag every flown . . .

*

Extracts from:

D.C. MacDonald's

BIOGRAPHICAL NOTES

on William Ogilvie

*

1) The Seven Wise Masters
2) Personal Recollections of William Ogilvie

*

Extracts from the Biographical Notes

1) THE SEVEN WISE MASTERS

*

*

A Few Words . . . . .

on

The Seven Wise Masters : Ogilvie wields his pen

It may be wondered why I have headed this section ". . . . Ogilvie wields his pen", when we have already seen how formidably he wields it in his Essay.

In that Essay, however, Ogilvie had to remain ***incognito*** – "was coerced to conceal himself as a smuggler in a cave", as MacDonald puts it in vivid phrase. The account of his battle with the "Seven Wise Masters" – (the ironic appellation which they acquired in the course of these events) – affords, then, an entirely special view of Ogilvie wielding his pen *under his own name.*

Of additional interest, in this correspondence, however, is the matter of the "jousting".

For where, one may well ask, is the virtue of being able to wield a pen in public matters, if one shies away from tackling affairs of equal challenge in life's more personal arenas? Justice is not only a matter of land rent; it is a matter involving *all* our relationships with one another. And if we did all in our power to ensure its establishment on "home ground", it might be that land rent justice would not be so hard to come by . . . .

Let us, then, salute the Master of Pittensear, that in the more personal areas of life he acquitted himself so formidably likewise.

*

The battle with the Seven Wise Masters – or the Sapient Septemviri, as they were neatly described – opens our eyes to another aspect of Ogilvie, however – one of particular interest, and of which we are afforded here a deeper glimpse than his Essay allows. It shows him to have been a pioneer not only in the social and economic sphere, but in the ecological as well – that which has become the crying issue of our time, and is equally rooted in land monopoly.

In making the selections here from the issues that arose between Ogilvie and his colleagues, I have therefore given particular space to one of environmental content. In form, it is a damning indictment by Ogilvie of their proposal to sell off . . .yet *another* piece of University land! But this time it happened to involve an area that Ogilvie, with characteristic vision, had recognised as an ideal site for a botanic garden for the University. Nor was this all. There was a well of water involved – a resource which Ogilvie again was alone in recognising the worth of. Moreover, with his unfailing championing of the ordinary folk, he spoke for the garden space that the area would also lend itself to, for new houses built in that area.

All-in-all, the ground concerned had considerable what wc would call *development potential*, and Ogilvie's brilliant and down-to-earth (meticulously calculated!) exposure of the community land values being virtually given away – (to the son of one of the Septemviri, of course!) – reveals peculiarly starkly what he was up against. These Septemviri conjure up the Cree Indian saying:-

"Only when the last tree has died, and the last river been poisoned,
and the last fish been caught, will we realise we cannot eat money."

Ogilvie stood to the end the *sole* opposer of the sale.

Ogilvie's vision for the University was not just, however, for a botanic garden. He proposed also – something that would have been uniquely ahead of its time – an endowment for a lecturer on "Practical Husbandry, and the best method for improving a farm". This he proposed as being "of more real service to the community" than many other more "frivolous" pursuits – (and he let himself go a tiny bit in including "spouting, declamation, and the like"!) – yet, as he pointed out, all these had schools or professorships, whilst practical husbandry had none. (Note: I stay with Ogilvie's more exact term "practical husbandry". Agriculture, form Latin *ager* – a field, conjures up today mainly a vision of large treeless areas: the false path that land husbandry has taken since Ogilvie's time. See on, the work of Dr. G.T. Wrench.)

We can imagine Ogilvie's proposal here sank without trace! His colleagues' annual published advertisements for applications to the University – couched in outrageously snobbish terms – had no place for humble farm-workers! – (though the original endowment of the University was the very opposite of exclusionary).

It is the Latin words quoted by Ogilvie at the end of his proposal, however, that are of such special interest for us. The study of this down-to-earth matter of "practical husbandry" stood, in his eyes, as "the next thing to wisdom and practically of blood relationship with it".* It is here that we see the deeper divide between Ogilvie and the Seven Wise Masters, just as the yawning gulf between Ogilvie's and our society's view of "agriculture" is seen also in that same statement. It turns upon the word "*wisdom*".

How *could* Ogilvie have approved today's agricultural methods, based as they are on a knowledge from which wisdom is completely divorced? – knowledge of the soil as of a chemical compound, with no thought of its carrying a life-force beyond our ken that our chemical practices are playing havoc with? Ogilvie, many-gifted, had a great taste for poetry. No doubt he would have enjoyed T.S. Eliot's lines:–

> *"Where is the life we have lost in living?*
> *Where is the wisdom we have lost in knowledge?*
> *Where is the knowledge we have lost in information?"*

Just to pursue the matter to the end – (which I think Ogilvie would have approved): where does the "information" come into the picture, capable of drowning out even "knowledge"? Why – all those *directives* from Brussels, of course! Directives proliferating on through Whitehall, and indeed through St. Andrews House: directives telling farmers how to behave with the soil (not to mention the rest of it) – the soil which they alone actually handle! We are totally upside-down – and the best evidence of this is that we do not even see it!

"Bureaucracy always betrays", Simone Weil wrote, and there are deep reasons for this.* but suffice it here to say that, since indeed "bureaucracy always betrays" – the soil wants out of the hands of Brussels, out of the hands of Whitehall – out of the hands of St. Andrews House – and *back into the hands of the people.*

---

* *"Sola res rustica, quae sine dubitatione proxima et quasi consanguinea sapientiae est, tam* ***discentibus*** *eget, quam* ***magistris****."*
"Only practical husbandry – which is without doubt the next thing to wisdom and almost of blood-relationship with it – is as much in want of ***students*** *as it is of* ***teachers****."* (If this is not a DCM translation, it must have been mine. Hard to recall from nearly 2 yrs. ago now! SAH)

---

* ***Imprisoned Ideas****, by W.M. Brown. See* Part III.

Thus Ogilvie would today have championed radical land reform, not only for the sake of the people, *but for the sake of the soil.* For it was through land monopoly that the people were forced onto the chemical pathway. See the work of Dr. G.T. Wrench, under "Goliaths Unmasked", in Part III.

We may be sure that, were William Ogilvie in a Chair of Agriculture today, he would make the work of Dr. Wrench *elementary and essential reading for every one of his students.* But we may be equally sure, of course, that Professor Ogilvie would not find a Chair in Agriculture today! (And that is some reflection on the "development" of education, as well as of agriculture, in the interval!*)

The real interest of this section concerning the Seven Wise Masters, is that it reveals to us that that land monopoly, which Dr. Wrench shows us so clearly as destroying the soil of the Earth, equally effectively destroys the "soil", as it were, of the soul ...

The Seven Wise Masters have not disappeared from our midst. They have found themselves better positions of power. They now rule in the board-rooms of the multi-nationals, (simply – the more sophisticated outgrowths of land monopoly), in the myriad offices of the Whitehalls and Brussels of this world, and in particular – because deeply linked with the *control of people* – they have, from positions well behind-the-scenes, set up such fronts for their work as various "health" and "water" bodies, since these offer some of the best short-cuts to that very end.

As we note from the further Protests by Professor Ogilvie in this selection, there was practically no sleight of hand to which our famous Seven did not give themselves, in order to achieve their intended *take-over of power* in all their dealings. While enjoying the account here of Ogilvie's catching of them so red-handed, let us not fail to allow the reading of it at the same time to sharpen our contemporary gaze, that we may come to recognize some of the features of the Seven Wise Masters ... abroad in our world today.

And now, from the pages of D.C. MacDonald's *Biographical Notes* – let us enjoy the jousting!

*

D.C. MacDonald's *Biographical Notes*: The Seven Wise Masters

In the year 1786 Professor Ogilvie took the lead in an attempt to reform the system of higher education in the North of Scotland. "There were then two Universities in Aberdeen, and there were also", it used to be ludicrously remarked, "two in England!" King's College, founded by Bishop Elphinstone, was sanctioned by a Papal Bull dated 10th February, 1494. Marischal College was founded by George, fifth Earl Marischal, by charter dated 2nd April, 1593.

The older seminary regarded her younger sister as a new danger, which might possibly disturb the *ancient foundations of Learning*! An unhealthy rivalry was developed, from which both colleges suffered; but King's College, which had closed its gates against all *innovations*, was the greater sufferer. In Professor Ogilvie's time it was much afflicted with the evils of a supposed state of perfection. Whenever such a

---

* ***Dumbing us Down: the Hidden Curriculum of Compulsory Schooling**, by John Taylor Gatto.*

state is reached, in the case of any institution, it is an undoubted sign that a very radical change is urgently wanted.

But Professor Ogilvie had other evils to put up with as a member of King's College. His colleagues not only alienated some of the lands belonging to the College, but they misapplied and "misappropriated" College funds. They also disposed of the patronage of no less than fifteen churches, and worse still, the right of presentation to twenty bursaries.

The great landlords were the purchasers of these *saleable commodities*, and in this way they became the private owners of rights *and duties* which, until then, were held by the Professors *in trust* for the public. The money received for Church patronage has been accounted for, but the price of the other articles of commerce was appropriated by the Masters as their own private property. It became "money in their purse"!

The Masters who were guilty of these "dilapidations" doubtless believed that, *by law*, they were the private owners of the University and all its belongings, in the same way as some landlords now believe that the land is theirs, and as some feudal monarchs believed in days gone by that they were the private owners of *all they surveyed*!

The Masters objected to being *tyrannized over* by the Sovereign, the Government of the Legislature! They forgot that the Sovereign was the real as well as the *nominal* chief patron and head trustee of *King's* College, and in their zeal for *liberty* for themselves forgot that the University was instituted as the King's common highway to knowledge, for the special benefit of the "inhabitants of the highland country and northern islands". (*Letter*, King James IV to the Pope in 1493.) They, however, converted it into a private academy solely for the benefit of the sons of the "private gentry, the clergy, and the richer farmers". And notwithstanding that several bursaries were left by the good and pious Bishop Elphinstone, the founder, for the *free* education *and maintenance* of indigent scholars, the following advertisement used to be published annually in Ogilvie's time:-

> "The Masters, being determined to admit none as candidates for the Bursaries but such as are above the lowest rank, and can appear in a decent way, both as to dress and behaviour, and have some reasonable prospect of money and friends to enable them to prosecute their education, and bring them into some respectable profession in life, do give this public intimation of their resolution and desire – that such as intend to be candidates at the ensuing competition may bring proper certificates for this purpose, without which they will not be admitted to trial."

It is superfluous to mention that Professor Ogilvie was not a silent witness or a consenting party to such proceedings. He was now in his fiftieth year, and finding that he had protested in vain as a member of Senatus for the long period of twenty-two years, he resolved to carry his appeal to the bar of public opinion.

Professor Ogilvie looked upon Universities as public institutions, and he considered that Professors were merely public servants as regards teaching, and Trustees for the public as regards endowments, buildings, libraries, etc. The Masters of King's College who obstructed the proposed University reforms held very different views from Ogilvie. They not only scorned the idea of being considered public servants, but they unblushingly claimed the University and its endowments as their own private property.

As soon as Ogilvie and his party published their scheme of Reform, the "*seven wise Masters*" of King's College (as they were called) published the following "advertisement" in the *Aberdeen Journal* newspaper:-

"THE Principal and six Professors of the King's College of Aberdeen, having learned that a petition has been for some time handed about, by direction of the members of the Marischal College, to be subscribed by the Noblemen and Gentlemen in this country, for procuring an Union of these two Colleges, find it necessary to give this public notice, that the said petition has been framed and circulated without their knowledge, or any communication with them, they being still ignorant of its tenor; that the first intimation they had of it was a very few days ago, that a single copy of a printed plan of the Union, to which they suppose the petition to refer, has been still more lately transmitted to them, long after it had been communicated to persons much less interested in it, a plan which they conceive to be in many respects *improper, impracticable, and attended with a very imperfect representation of facts relating to their conduct*; that they cannot but consider this as an attempt to surprise persons to whom the petition is presented, into a subscription, on a representation by one party, or perhaps under an idea of its being agreeable to the sentiments of both Colleges."

In answer to this "advertisement", Professor Ogilvie wrote as follows:-

Tuesday, July 25, 1786.

"PRINCIPAL CHALMERS having asserted, that six Professors of King's College join with him in his advertisement of yesterday, without mentioning their names, I find it necessary for me to declare that I am not one of that number. I know that neither Professor Ross nor Dr. Dunbar can be included in it. There remain, therefore, just those six Professors, most of whose proceedings of late, in College affairs, it has not been in my power to approve.

"In nothing have I ever differed from them more widely, that in that opinion they have just delivered concerning the Plan of Union so lately submitted to the public.

"They say, *it is improper*: to me, it appears highly beneficial; in most of its parts unexceptionable, and far, very far, to be preferred to that comparatively selfish and illiberal plan, which the Principal, with four of his six Professors, are known to have supported very strenuously in 1755.

"They say, it is *impracticable*: I hold it to be very easily practicable, if only 'the parties having concern will lay aside their confined and interested views, and give way to a more general and public good'. I quote, with pleasure, the Principal's very pertinent expressions in the beginning of his Memorial, dated Feb. 5, 1755.

"These are certainly the only obstructions which have prevented the proposed Union from taking place. Time hath removed those prejudices, and confined views, which formerly prevailed; but interested views may, perhaps, still remain.

"They add, *that the plan is accompanied with a very imperfect account of their conduct.* Agreed: many particulars of their conduct, relative to the Union both in 1770, and of late, have been omitted; and others seem to be touched with a gentle hand; probably, lest a more perfect account might give, to some of them, more vexation.

"The whole of this advertisement is calculated to convey an idea that the two Colleges are, on this occasion, entirely opposed to each other. This is not so: the Professors of Marischal College are, indeed, unanimously engaged, under the direction of their Chancellor and Rector, in endeavouring to promote this desired

Union. But Principal Chalmers, with the six Professors who oppose it, are a Party only. They are not the University of King's College.

"WILLIAM OGILVIE."

This controversy between Professor Ogilvie and his colleagues took place four years after he finished *The Right of Property in Land*, and probably *after* the work had been suppressed – a circumstance which must have ruffled his temper. He was, however, exceedingly good natured, and was able to conduct the controversy with remarkable magnanimity. Like all true lovers of mankind, Ogilvie had a considerable share of wit and humour in his composition. And sometimes these qualities came near the surface, in the shape of a peculiar and kindly irony or sarcasm of the softest possible fibre, by which he was able to handle disagreeable truths in a straightforward manner without torturing his opponents. His aims were just, and his ways benevolent. He used a sharp weapon, and could afford to deal gentle strokes.

The seven Professors, instead of accepting an open challenge, preferred to keep behind the double hedge of Presbyteries and Landlords. (Among the latter, it is right to mention, a large majority of the great noblemen warmly supported University reform.) Notwithstanding all the difficulties Professor Ogilvie had to contend with, he carried out his determination to inform the public of the scandalous mismanagement of King's College. "COPIES of MEMORIALS, and REASONS of PROTEST, inserted in the RECORDS of KING'S COLLEGE, in the years 1783 and 1785", were published by him in 1787, along with "*A Complete Collection of the Papers relating to the Union of the King's and Marischal Colleges of Aberdeen*", (Nos. I and II of which refer to a Botanic Garden):-

No. I. ***Representation to the College Meeting, February 16th, 1784.***

Mr. Ogilvie represents to the meeting that he has many objections to the proposed sale of the washing-green and croft, and wishes to call their attention to one in particular.

That spot of ground is uncommonly well adapted for a Botanic Garden, by the variety of soil it contains, its command of water, its sheltered situation, and its nearness to the College.

Although we are not able, or willing to set a Botanic Garden on foot at present, our successors will probably soon find it necessary to have one.

It is not the pecuniary interests of the College which ought to be regarded in this matter, for that is a trifle, but its interests and accommodation as a seminary of Learning, and the reputation of its present members.

Certainly it will be accounted great ignorance of the progress of Science in the present times, or great disregard of what other learned Societies are pursuing for an University, having the property of a spot of ground so singularly well adapted for a Botanic Garden, and so contiguous, to part with that property, either for money or for favour.

No. II. *Reasons of Protest against the proposed Bargain with Mr. Hugh Leslie,* given in on April 17th, 1784.*
(Extracts. S-A.H.)

(1st.) It tends to the disadvantage of the College –

By stopping a very convenient road which communicates with the country on the south-west side, and leads directly from the new houses to the open fields;

By shutting up a well of excellent water, better than any in the neighbourhood, and which continues during the summer months, when they are apt to fail;

By giving a more convenient washing-green that any that can be provided in its stead;

By giving away ground which, lying so near at hand, may be much wanted by the inhabitants of the new houses, and of those which are afterwards to be built, for additional gardens, for pleasure ground, or pasture;

By depriving the College of the command of a spot of ground which, by its variety of soil, its command of water, its sheltered situation and vicinity, is so remarkably well adapted for a Botanic Garden, which some time or other the College will have occasion to establish.

(2nd.) It is contrary to the intention of our Founder . . .

(3rd.) It is an evil precedent. – About 15 years ago we first began to feu off land within the College bounds; about two years ago part of the Humanist's glebe was feued off, a third alienation seems now to be determined upon, and others are thought to be in contemplation; these instances follow so fast on each other, that it is time to stop and consider where the practice may end . . . .

(4th.) The bargain is unequal. – Little notice might have been taken of this, had it not been extolled as extremely advantageous for the College, and had not that reason been alone given for concluding it so unadvisedly. Let us see then how the matter stands. – Land lying within a hundred yards of a street derives value from its situation whatever be its quality. Some part of this is very good, and the whole very tractable: £4 per acre is a moderate average rent of land lying so near the Old Town street on leases of 19 years. Thirty years' purchase is the lowest price which a proprietor of land will accept when he is not constrained to sell. Thirty years' purchase of £4 converted into a feu-duty gives £6* per acre instead of £3.10s. as the simple value of the ground, without taking

---

* *This Mr. Hugh Leslie was a son of one of the Professors. He got the ground in spite of Professor Ogilvie's protest, and his representatives still hold it seemingly unchallenged. It is somewhat amusing to note that about the year 1808 Mr. Leslie and the Professors of King's College had a desperate quarrel about a road, which led to their taking* ***criminal*** *proceedings against him. He in return published a work of 335 pages 8vo, bearing the title* "The Doctors outwitted", *in which they are painted with touches from Rabelais, and as black as ink could make them. He wished them all "kicked out of their situations, with the exception of Professor Ogilvie,* ***who***", *he adds, "seldom takes part in their deliberations".*

---

* *£4 x 30 = £120 @ 5% = £6.*

into consideration the conveniences which the purchaser acquires, and the inconveniences to which the sellers have submitted. In this case the purchaser acquires a desirable addition to his pleasure ground, and gets rid of a troublesome road; the sellers are deprived of a commodious access to the country, of an excellent well, and ground very valuable to them for academical purposes and others. These considerations ought to have raised the price far above the moderate feu-duty proposed. Everyone must see this: Mr. Leslie with great candour acknowledges that his son gets the ground somewhat below its full value, and mentions 10 or 20 shillings a year as the abatement. The mere loss of this value may be accounted a trifle, but the stopping a road, the shutting up a well, and depriving the College of ground which may be so much wanted for purposes the most creditable for an University, are considerations of some importance.

(5th.) It is at least doubtful whether we can legally alienate for ever lands lying within the precincts of the College . . . .

But whatever our powers shall be found to be, it certainly behoves us to keep at a distance even from the suspicion of abusing them.

With regard to this transaction, in which we act as life-renters and trustees for our successors, it will perhaps be asked whether the majority would have feued off these subjects to a stranger on the same terms, or almost on any terms whatever.

It may likewise be asked whether any individual of the Society, if proprietor of the new houses and the subjects in question, would have allowed the road to be stopped, and the well to be shut up, or consented to part with that piece of ground on these terms, or almost on any terms whatever.

*

No. V. *Reasons of Protest against the Resolutions of the College Meeting, April 9th, 1785.* (Extracts. S-A.H.)

(1st.) Because the majority have rejected my proposals as improper, without venturing to deny the reality of those abuses to which they refer, and without suggesting any less improper in their stead . . . .

(2nd.) Because, by requiring that hereafter all Reasons of Protest should be communicated to a College meeting previous to their insertion, the majority have prescribed a form which, if it is not frivolous, must have a pernicious tendency.

They have also found that the insertion of my last protest, by my own hand, was irregular. How could I suppose any irregularity in that which is so consonant to the practice of the Society? How many minutes are there inserted by private members, in their own hand, without any formal notification to a meeting? No later than ..... the very gentleman who moved for those resolutions against which I protest, inserted with his own hand, and without the least communication to the College meeting, a minute purporting to be their resolutions, and assigning certain payments of money in their gift. If it be competent to a private member to insert minutes in this manner, how much more must it be so to insert his own Reasons of Protest, Reasons over which, if communicated, the Meeting can have no power to alter or reject them. For that they have, even this majority will not assert.

Amid their zeal for frivolous and pernicious forms, let them be reminded of that facility, with which on a late occasion they chose to trample under foot forms truly salutary and essential. I mean those forms which require that all our resolutions on business should be recorded in the minutes at the time, and signed in presence of the meeting.....

WILLIAM OGILVIE

(N.B. No.V included also proposals made by Professor Ogilvie at a College Meeting to augment the extremely depleted library fund. S-A.H.)

(Further regarding the matter of the recording of the minutes. S-A.H.)

(1st.) Because on this occasion an inconsiderable majority, viz., Dr. Gerard, Dr. Chalmers, Professor Gordon, Professor Leslie, arrogate to themselves a power which cannot belong to any majority, however numerous or respectable.

Will they presume to say that any member has not a right to make in the College meeting such proposals as he thinks may tend to the advantage of the Society, and to have them inserted in the minute as part of the *Res Gestae* of that day? Or will they say that matters of a frivolous nature were suggested to their attention, when it was proposed that the scanty income of the Library should be improved by increasing the fees which are now usually paid on degrees?.....

That the Library fund should receive compensation for certain sums which had been improperly taken from it .....

(2nd.) Because of late a system has been adopted of eluding inquiries, and suppressing all free discussion of questionable points. On various occasions this system has betrayed itself, and in the meeting of October 23 it was pretty openly avowed. The present resolution of the majority manifestly flows from it, and being of small importance in itself is probably intended to form a precedent. In that light it seems important and pernicious, and deserves to be resisted to the utmost.

WILLIAM OGILVIE.

*

These *Letters* and *Extracts* furnish the only instance in Professor Ogilvie's life, where we find him revealing himself in his true character, as defender of the rights of the people; excepting another glimpse in 1764, when his name prominently appears in connection with a scheme for a Public Library in Aberdeen, which was to embrace the libraries of the Universities.

With the exception of these two glimpses, Professor Ogilvie, as far as known, never disclosed his name to the public in connection with anything he did, or attempted to do, during the whole course of his long life.

We are therefore indebted to the *Seven Wise Masters* for being instrumental *in bringing him out* in 1786, and as a token of gratitude for that service, their portraits, from a sketch made by a local artist at the time, are given in this volume. The original

The Sapient Septemviri
1
8
7
6
5
4
3
2

*

plate (engraved by the well-known John Kay of Edinburgh) has the following explanations at the foot – the words in italics being now supplied as an additional key to the picture –

1. The Beauty of Holiness Lecturing: *The Rev. Skene Ogilvie, D.D., minister of the First charge, Old Aberdeen.*
2. Had you not sold your Patronages, First minister might have been annexed to my Divine Chair of Verity and Taste: *A. Gerard, Professor of Divinity.*
3. Annually for forty-five years and upwards I have beat up, even to the Ultima Thule have I recruited our University: *Rodk. Macleod, Regent.*
4. I have rendered Vernacular the Greek Language from Aberdour to Aberdeen: *John Leslie, Professor of Greek, Tutor to Lord Aberdour.*
5. Agriculture is the noblest of Sciences, Mind your Glebes, the Emperor of China is a Farmer: *Jo. Chalmers, Principal.*
6. Has not the Effulgence of my Countenance been a Light unto your Feet and a lamp unto your Path: *Thos. Gordon, Regent.*
7. College Property, Patronages are unalienable, so says the Law, the Noble Patron has rewarded most justly your Rapacity: *Wm. Thom, Civilist.*
8. Degrees Male and Female, in Medicine and Midwifery, sold here for Ready Money: *Wm. Chalmers, Mediciner.*

The rough outline of Professor Ogilvie's brow does not belong to the original plate. It is from a scrap found with his miniature. It is now added as a sort of key to the portrait as regards the formation of the forehead, to which the wig, unless closely scanned, gives the false impression of a receding forehead.

The controversy between Professor Ogilvie and his obstructive colleagues in connection with University reform, was carried on with much vigour and sanguine hope of success, until the Pitt-Dundas administration gave its word of command – *as you were*. The Reforming Party, it may be noted, acted all along with remarkable magnanimity; and, as occasion offered, indulged in some sparks of humour. Professor Ogilvie, along with Professor Stuart of Marischal College, was the joint-author of some of the spiciest contributions. A rhyming lawyer, Jo. Marschal, who appreciated the situation, advocated the cause in the following lines:–

"To The Members of Marischal College.

"Since Solomon told us, as sure as a gun,
That nothing at all is NEW *under the sun,*
We're bound to believe that all *new* things are evil,
And come from that Prince of the Air called the D—–l,
From that subtle spirit, without any question,
Springs every *new* notion, and each *new* suggestion.
What else could inspire you Reformers to aim
At an Union of Colleges here – O for shame!
Retract, and avoid all the dismal disasters
Foreseen and foretold by
"The Seven Wise Masters!"

*

*

A Few Words – Concluded

It seems that the brightness of Ogilvie's shining was of offence not only to the Seven Wise Masters.

D.C. MacDonald recounts how the "College Reformers", who carried on his work towards union of the colleges (achieved in 1860), in quoting – to support their case – from Ogilvie's *Protests* and *Dissents*, carefully avoided using his name while making full use of his work!

Did they perhaps feel a certain need to shield themselves from a still too powerfully lingering presence? Why so?

The following extracts, from "OUTLINES OF A PLAN for Uniting the King's and Marischal Universities of Aberdeen, with a view to render the System of Education more complete", may offer us a clue:–

> "(11) Systems of pretended science the most chimerical . . . and a superstitious theology which inculcated tenets subversive of the Spirit of Christianity, and degrading to human nature, were long the only objects of study in the Universities, and some of them are not yet entirely exploded.
>
> "(12) An attachment to old rules and customs is a principle of powerful and general influence. They have the advantage of present and long possession, and are not easily overturned. Improvements of undoubted utility have often been long postponed after the circumstances of the times required them, and in some instances altogether neglected."

MacDonald speaks of "strong internal evidence" that these OUTLINES OF A PLAN are from Ogilvie's pen. How, indeed, can one fail to detect here those well-known "gentle strokes", from the "sharp weapon" wielded by a master hand? And how tellingly worded are those indictments of the *on-going false worship, via our own educational system, of both the State, and of Science – today's new 'church'!*

There is no mystery at all in MacDonald's recounting how "both Whig and Tory *reformers* systematically boycotted Professor Ogilvie's name, not only while he lived, but also after his death" – no mystery as to why those "*reformers*" found it necessary still to avert their eyes from his too steadfast gaze!

And can our educational system YET look Ogilvie in the face?

Or our 'pulpits' – political, scientific or religions – ?

The SEVEN WISE MASTERS are as fully in business today as ever!

*

"Only when the last tree has died, and the
last river been poisoned, and the last fish been
caught, will we realise we cannot eat money"

– comes sighing to us on the wind . . .

And "*Oh – where is the wisdom . . .?*"

– comes murmuring after . . .

Birthright. . .and. . .Scotland Today

Extracts from the Biographical Notes

2) PERSONAL RECOLLECTIONS OF WILLIAM OGILVIE

*

A Few Words ... by S-A.H.

The Personal Recollections

*

A Few Words . . . . .

What presentation of Ogilvie would be complete without allowing some more personal glimpses of this great soul, both in the wide range of his accomplishments, and as friend of the young.

Let the following recollections, gathered from the pages of D.C. MacDonald, speak for themselves.

MacDonald's Biographical Notes

Special Extracts

Personal Recollections of William Ogilvie

*

For the following interesting sketch of Professor Ogilvie, we are indebted to Pryse Lockhart Gordon, a son of the minister of the parish of Ardersier, in the county of Nairn, who entered King's College, Aberdeen, in the year 1776. He says in his Memoirs:-

"We attended the lectures of Mr. Ogilvie, Professor of Humanity, three times a week. He was esteemed the most elegant scholar in Scotland of his day; and his translations of Horace and Virgil have, perhaps, never been surpassed; they ought to have been printed *in usum Delphini*. Ogilvie was also a man of great general erudition and critical knowledge, especially in Natural History and the fine Arts. He was a profound antiquary and medallist, though his opportunities of acquiring this taste were so limited. He had, however, collected a little museum, and was rich in rare prints. . .

"On my return from Italy in 1800, I paid my old master a visit; and though then at a very advanced age, he was in complete possession of his mental faculties, but a cripple with gout. I presented him with a few Greek and Roman coins, which I had picked up in my travels, and also some fragments from Pompeii, and a small genuine Greek vase. It was delightful to see how the eyes of the old antiquary sparkled (or rather squinted), when I laid before him these treasures as a *ricordanza*, and the pleasure with which he examined them. I was much surprised to find in our conversation the minute acquaintance which he had of every work of art in Italy, the correctness of his taste and wonderful memory.

"He shewed me a large collection of castes in sulphur, which my uncle Mr. C. Morrison, had presented to the college where he had been educated. They probably would never have seen the light, had they not been committed to the especial care of Mr. Ogilvie . . ."

From the recollections of this pupil, it seems that he had not the faintest idea of Professor Ogilvie's advanced views on *politics*. If he had, he, with the fillal regard of a devoted pupil, conceals, what to his understanding, was seemingly a dark spot – "imprudent in politics" – on the otherwise unblemished character of his favourite professor. He mentions that the 4th Duke of Gordon visited Italy in 1761, and stayed for a considerable time in the country of the Grand Dukes of Tuscany*. Professor Ogilvie, who, as already mentioned, was travelling tutor to the Duke of Gordon, had then a right royal time of it, and it is no longer a matter of conjecture how he utilized his continental rambles.

(In his original unedited *Essay*), we find Professor Ogilvy referring to the pernicious effect of the "hospitals and almsgiving of the Italian cities". In the ruins of the house of Medici he must have read an object-lesson of deep interest. The last branch of that renowned family "found Tuscany a prosperous country where art, letters, commerce, industry, and agriculture flourished, and left her (in 1737) poor and decayed in all ways, drained by taxation, and oppressed by laws contrary to every principle of sound economy, downtrodden by clergy, and burdened by a weak and vicious aristocracy".**

*

The Rev. Donald Sage, of Resolis, in the county of Ross, who knew several of the students who studied at King's College, has left us the following notice of Professor Ogilvie:–

"Wm. Ogilvie, the renowned Professor of Humanity and Natural History at King's College, was fresh in the memory of all my contemporaries at Aberdeen College. They never wearied talking of him, and of his unrivalled translations of Virgil's Ecologues. It is much to be regretted that these were not published. He devoted nearly every third hour of his literary life to the study of these magnificent specimens of ancient pastoral poetry."***

*

On Monday, 23rd August, 1773, the celebrated Dr. Johnson visited Aberdeen. He saw some of the *"wise mast*ers". *Vir Sap*it, etc., was their moto.**** The doctor was in a conversational mood, but Boswell tells us: - "The professors were afraid to speak". Professor Ogilvie must have been from home, otherwise the faithful Boswell would have said something about him.

---

* *Cosmo the 3rd Duke of Gordon, was called Cosmo, in compliment to Cosmo de Medici III, Grand Duke of Tuscany, "with whom his father was on the closest habit of friendship".*

** *How many syllabuses on the Italian 'Renaissance', undertaken by our universities and colleges of art, open the eyes of their students, **via Ogilvie's** observations, to the simultaneous **decline** going on – and to **the reasons for it** ("laws contrary to every principle of sound economy", etc.)? Time for them to catch up on Ogilvie – Henry George – Patrick Edward Dove, and others! Not even the study of the history of art of any country can ever be complete without an interwoven study of how far it has departed from the observance of **natural economic law**. As one who did the "Corso per Stranieri" (Course for Foreigners) at the University of Florence in 1949-50 – with **plenty** of study of the Renaissance included in it – I speak with feeling How enthralled I would have been to have had my own Scottish **Ogilvie's** first-hand observationsof that Renaissance scene woven into our Course! (Scottish seats of learning – take note!) S-A.H.*

*** *Memorabilia Domestic, Wick, 1889.*

**** *This Latin motto clearly has some ironic bearing on the reluctance of our Seven, on this occasion, to speak! If any reader can furnish the complete motto – (with or without translation) – I shall be very happy to have it, having applied to Aberdeen University library without success, despite their kind searches. S-A.H.*

*

Francis Douglas, another literary tourist, visited Aberdeen in 1780. He wrote a minute account of the Universities, and the reader is indebted to him for the following extract:–

"About eight years ago, Mr. William Ogilvie, Professor of Humanity, began of his own accord to put together a collection of specimens for a Museum of Natural History, in the King's College, and has now fitted up, and furnished three apartments for their arrangement. The Professor recko he has already nearly obtained the first object he had in view, which was to procure such an assortment of specimens of fossils, and in the various branches of Zoology, as might serve to excite the liberal curiosity of youth, and make them, in some measure, acquainted with the immense variety of the works of nature . . . One is astonished to find so large a collection of birds, fishes, marbles, spars, &c., accumulated in so short a space."*

*

We extract the following brief notice from another literary tourist, who came after Douglas: The Rev. James Hall, in recording his visit to Aberdeen, says:–

"Professor James Beattie, of the New Town College, nephew of the late Dr. Beattie, seems to know more of Natural History, and the important and now fashionable branches of knowledge connected with it, than any other person I know in any part of Scotland, excepting the accomplished Professor Ogilvie, of King's College here".**

*

Sir James Mackintosh, another pupil of Professor Ogilvie, did not neglect to add *a stone to the cairn*. He entered King's College in October, 1780, and a quarter of a century afterwards we find him making the following note in his Memoirs:-

"The lectures of Mr. Ogilvie, Professor of Humanity (as the Roman literature is called in the Scotch Universities), I still remember with pleasure. This most ingenious and accomplished recluse, from whom I have received a letter within this month (June, 1805), is little known to the public. He published, without his name, 'An Essay on the Right of Property in Land', full of benevolence and ingenuity, but not the work of a man experienced in the difficult art of realising projects for the good of mankind. Its bold *Agrarianism* attracted some attention during the ferment of speculation occasioned by the French Revolution.*** But what I remember with most pleasure of Mr. Ogilvie were his translations of passages in classical writers."

Sir James Mackintosh was considered, in his day, as being rather in advance of his time, but in regard to the *Land Question* he was at least a full century behind Professor Ogilvie.

---

* *A General Description of the EAST COAST OF SCOTLAND, by Francis Douglas. Paisley, 1782. Aberdeen, 1826.*

** *Travels in Scotland, by Rev. James Hall, A.M., London, 1807.*

*** *J.R. M'Culloch, in his **Literature of Political Economy**, (London, 1845), after quoting these words, adds: "But in truth, the author's schemes, however well intended, are not impracticable only, but mischievous; and his principles and reasonings are alike false, shallow and sophistical. Probably, however, it was hardly necessary to say so much of a work that never had any influence, and which has long been forgotten". N.B. Poor J.R. McCulloch had no idea that he was writing his own **certificate of character** when he penned this criticism of **The Right of Property in Land!***

The following letters from a grateful pupil will be perused with some interest by every intelligent reader of *The Right of Property in Land:-*

Letter from John Garvock to Professor Ogilvie. (Extracts S-A.H.)
"Horse Guards, 6th November, 1812.

"MY DEAR SIR, – Major Tod did me the favour of calling upon me this morning, as he informed me by your desire, and I need not tell you what gratification it afforded me to find that I was not forgotten by you. I was much pleased to learn from the Major that your health is tolerably good, and that you are still enabled to continue your attention to your favourite pursuits . . .

"It is now very long, indeed, since I had the pleasure of any communication with you, but this I must attribute entirely to my own negligence . . .

"You have, I presume, just commenced your session, and though my mind has long been necessarily too much estranged to literary habits, *Alma Mater* at this moment rises distinctly to my view. I feel the former fires – *veteris vestigia flammae* – and all those impressions (never to be obliterated), which I received from your tuition and of the college now, but while you remain a member of it, the true interests of literature and liberal knowledge, I am sure, will never be forgotten. I well remember, however, that your corporation formerly possessed a due proportion of that salutary dread of innovation, I will not say reform, which has long pervaded the nation at large; and such feelings are too apt to gain instead of losing ground by time . . .

"With sentiments of the truest respect and attachment, and with every good wish, believe me to remain,

"My Dear Sir,
"Your ever obliged and faithful,
"JOHN GARVOCK".

Letter from John Garvock to Dr. Kerr, Aberdeen.
"Horse Guards, London, 23rd February, 1819.

"Sir, – Having understood that you were the professional attendant and intimate friend of the late Professor Ogilvie, whose death I have seen announced in the public papers of this day, I venture, though an entire stranger to you, to request the favour of your making me acquainted with the circumstances of his last illness.

"I have no correspondent in Aberdeen, to whom I could look for such information, and that I should feel no ordinary interest in this melancholy event, would not surprise you, if you were aware of the unbounded kindness I experienced from Mr. Ogilvie at an early period of my life.

"His uniform partiality to me, for many years before I left Aberdeen, was indeed well-known to others, but myself alone could know the full extent of his goodness, and of my own obligations, the sense of which has continued to increase as I have become better able to appreciate the value of his friendship, and the unrestricted intercourse to which he admitted me. How much a young man must have been indebted to that intercourse, I need not tell you, sir, who have enjoyed his society. From him I imbibed principles and tastes, which will abide with me through life, and always prove, as they have hitherto done, their own reward.

"Thus thinking and thus feeling, you will, I am sure, allow for my anxiety on the present occasion, and I trust it will afford yourself a melancholy pleasure to give some account of your lamented friend to a person who must ever take a lively interest in every thing connected with his memory.

"Will you have the goodness to inform me whether any portrait of Mr. Ogilvie is in existence,* and how his papers, which must be numerous, are to be disposed of?

"I remain, with much respect, sir,

"Your very faithful and obedient servant,

"JOHN GARVOCK".

Who was John Garvock? will naturally be asked. Well, it is to be hoped some representative of his will answer that question, and perhaps, at the same time, furnish more particulars about the life and work of Professor Ogilvie.

With regard to the important question of Professor Ogilvie's MSS. – What became of them? – It is impossible at present to say. This is to be regretted, not only on account of his famous translations of Latin authors, but also on account of his own original productions – 'his contemplations and schemes for the general welfare of mankind'. The reader, doubtless, would like to see his HISTORY OF PROPERTY IN LAND – "treating more at length of the Mosaical Agrarian, considered as an economical regulation" – unearthed, and offered to the public".

We may assume that many anonymous contributions from his pen appeared in periodicals, in pamphlets, and in the Press, during his life, but without his MSS. it is now difficult to trace such works with certainty to him. It is, however, the loss of his unpublished works that we deplore most. Shortly after his death, the whole of his MSS. were "*nailed up*" – "in six or eight large boxes" – to await the return of one of his nephews, James Ogilvie Tod, an Indian Judge, who was thought to be in possession of the author's own instructions regarding their disposal.

Their interment by his next-of-kin was, perhaps, justifiable in those days, but if cremation was latterly adopted, one feels very much in need of praying for a double share of the author's own spirit of magnanimity, to be able to touch the subject with a "gentle hand". The children of that period may be excused. It was their misfortune to have been born and brought up under a reign of tyranny, bigotry and hypocrisy.

---

* *On this point, see passage quoted under the portrait of Ogilvie, at the front of this volume.*

WILLIAM OGILVIE

A BROADER SWEEP

by Shirley-Anne Hardy

*

Pathways Travelled –

1) Land or Capital?

2) Threefold Robbery -
   or True Social Fund?

3) Whom the God's would Destroy. . .

*

Ogilvie's Searchlight – A Broader Sweep

"But if the intelligent, and the friends of mankind, will take some pains to inquire into the nature and extent of that oppression, under which the industrious groan, and the force of that exorbitant monopoly, from whence their grievances proceed; and if such men will employ the talents which nature hath given them, in explaining these grievances, and the rigour of that monopoly, to the whole world . . . "

(Para. 42 of Ogilvie's Essay here.)

*

Dear William Ogilvie – your welcome words above have set me free!

I was just wondering how I could possibly fit the longer notes here, inspired by you, into the Essay pages. Then, as I was looking at some words in one of your paragraphs, my gaze fell on others just above. . . . And so I found a hidden doorway, beautifully placed in that very paragraph – a doorway through which I found myself freely invited to walk into this wider spacing!

For what you say strikes a very deep chord with me. We do have to "take pains" to enquire into these things: into the "nature and extent" of the oppression suffered under this fundamental monopoly, and also – into the "force" and "rigour" of it, because these are not so easily seen.

And now – two hundred years on since you lived – the task is extremely urgent. Orthodox economics has left us in a cul-de-sac – unable to explain how it is we can fly to the moon, yet still not house ourselves properly. And this unresolved enigma has very damaging repercussions on society. "Man is greedy", we hear as the excuse for it all – and upon this fragile proposition are invited to dump our social ills! Even school-children are given "projects" upon this truly awful theme! But of course, if "man is greedy", then we can also teach our children that it's vital to have all those guns and prisons and things. The only difficulty is that, if man is "greedy", then the "greedy" ones are also going to be in command of those guns and prisons. Now *there's* a thought!

Why not get the children to take a look, instead, at that conversation between Jesus and Zacchaeus – (Zacchaeus who had climbed up into the sycamore tree to get a better look: Luke 19) – and then ask them to work these things out for themselves? Children so often see with clearer eyes than we do. Any why not hang the Law of Rent chart up in the school-room too? – and let the children embellish it with drawings of apple-trees, houses, streets with corner-sites and those shopping-special zebra crossing-points – with their lollipop ladies and all! . . . ?

Few people know that the game of monopoly – (a game that was a craze in my own childhood) – was devised by a *Henry Georgist!* – precisely to draw attention to this crazy environment we have made for ourselves. So how about a Mary Poppins edition of Monopoly for the very young? – now there's another thought! It is highly doubtful if it would remain hidden from children's eyes for very long that we have a "flaw" in our system somewhere – and a flaw which positively inculcates that "greed" we are all so obsessed about. Sows it broadcast – in rich and poor alike, because it sows broadcast in the first place – *fear.*

Fear certainly has fertile ground for play in a society built on INJUSTICE . . . So would it not be better to get rid of the injustice, and the fear – and then see that false "greed" vanish with them?

. . . Just as might have happened with the burghers of Hamelin – but instead it was the children that vanished. Ah yes, it has now leaked out who were the original "rats"! You can read the story of it in Part III – a story for children of *all* ages. And just in the same way as with those invented "rats", so the invention that "man is greedy" is made the scapegoat for society's ills today.

How wisely you urged it, William Ogilvie! The scene requires a *deeper scrutiny* ...

*

William Ogilvie

A Broader Sweep

*

Pathways Travelled

1) LAND OR CAPITAL

*

PATHWAYS TRAVELLED

(1) Land or Capital?

"But that class of men in whom the strength of every government resides, and in whom resides also the right of making laws – (or the power of influencing and controlling those who possess the right of making them) – have generally been borrowers of money and proprietors of land." (Ogilvie, para. 16.)

*

The power of those who "roam the world of the Seven Wise Masters" is tellingly summarized by Ogilvie in this paragraph; and the features of that power are very familiar to us today!

Here are the pathways by which corruptive power may operate, under which the people will then be held. And held by whatever government, as Ogilvie points out, since the operations of every government hoisted on the pillars of land monopoly are inevitably involved with that underlying corruptive power.

Even in Ogilvie's time, the basis of such influence was not, however, just landed power. As he points out in the phrase "borrowers of money", (see note 12), it was power over capital too. In his preceding two paragraphs, however, (paras. 14 and 15), he makes plain which he views as the more truly foundational – *and why*.

Today it is the power of what Ogilvie regarded as the less foundational that mainly grips people's imaginations. *Capital* is the great enemy of labour. *Capital* is the great wickedness. The difficulty is that capital is so much more visible than land – so much more voluble! It shouts at us from all those glass-and-concrete blocks. In the cities, where capital shrieks loudest, land is silent – almost invisible. We see the concrete – but not the rental-values! Yet there is a certain saying, is there not, about the one this lies *under* have power *over* . . . ? – and life sometimes throws up amazing parallels – ? (And let us remember that there is a woman involved here too – *Mother* earth . . . under all that more superficial masculine stuff!)

Marx became waylaid by the more obvious appearance of things – and it may be that his day had to be, before Ogilvie's could dawn. However that may be, the Scots, on the whole, have been apt to hold Ogilvie's rather shrewder view of the matter.

For our good neighbours south of the Border, it is of course many centuries ago that they suffered the massive enclosures of *their* common lands. The Clearances of the Scottish Highlands, by contrast, are still practically on the fringes of living memory. Thus any insights they held that the roots of economic power lie in landholding could not possibly have faded from the memory of the Scots. But to discover that such insights were just as vividly alive, at the time of their cruel dispossession, among the English peasantry . . . is another matter. For who has ever heard any whisper of this? Yet if we turn to a book such as Hoskins and Ward's "The Common Lands of England and Wales",* we will read there of the heroic stand taken by those peasants, equally as by their Scottish counterparts: those peasants who equally knew that the root of

* *See also Henry George's Progress and Poverty, ch. "Property in Land Historically Considered".*

economic power lay in landholding. They knew that the taking of the common lands they depended upon for their living – a place to attend the pig and gather winter fuel – meant the *end of their economic independence and* beginnings of their slavery. We only need to read, too, of the terrible punishments meted out to those desperate peasants taking their last stand . . . to realize that the ruthless land-enclosers *knew it just as well.**

The myth of the English peasants "flocking to the factories for the good wages to be found there" reveals the same technique of cover-up so familiar to ourselves – utilized in the hope that a people will eventually forget their history, forget how they came to be where they are, and so – most hopefully of all – live resigned to an unjust lot. This technique having virtually succeeded in the case of the English, it is as well to revive the history of the English people, along with our own. Those peasants did not of course "flock" to the factories. They were driven – as men are finally driven. By hunger. By desperation and despair.**

Here is something else. It was at the time of these enclosures that the first Poor Laws came in. To deal with the new "problem", of course, of all those *vagrants*! All those tramps and beggars who had no *work*.

All those men cut adrift . . .

Can we still not understand it?

Of course, those who made the Poor Laws made first the Enclosure Acts! – exactly as Ogilvie points out in his paragraph quoted at the head of this note. But not many were pointing it out so clearly . . . And need it be added that our boasted Welfare State is but the modern successor of those Poor Laws. So no wonder if it is failing us. For *nothing* has changed regarding the fundamental crime of the dispossession of the people from their land. As Dr. Wrench points out, laws passed as palliatives, to try to ameliorate an *un*-righted underlying injustice, cannot succeed.

It is good to remember these things, that we may be reminded, by them, that any quarrel the Scots may have lies not with the English themselves. Indeed, ordinary people are much the same the world over. It lies with the *Establishment*! And this Establishment, it must be said, overflows into a *Scottish* Establishment, just the same!

The Scots, then, have been more fortunate than the English, in their history. That economic power may still be rooted in landholding, despite appearances to the contrary, is something they intuitively grasp and understand.

Ogilvie certainly was not taken in by the appearances of things in his time, and we may be sure that he would have remained as unshaken by any such mere appearances in ours. Both Ogilvie's view, and the intuition of the Scots, on this matter,

---

* *Karl Marx did in fact, later, realize and clearly state that the root of all capitalist expropriation lies in the expropriation of the peasant from the soil. However, this is not in the edition of Das Kapital in general circulation.*

** *The English poet, John Clare (1793-1864), has recorded something of the heart-rending destruction wrought to the lives of the peasant people by these on-going enclosures. His poetry is deeply moving, and I was not surprised to hear him described on a radio programme recently as in some respects the English counterpart of Robert Burns.*

would certainly seem to be strongly validated by a book of title, "History or the Great American Fortunes", by Gustavus Myers, and the following is one of many interesting passages from it:-

> "This large . . . fortune, as that of . . . other extensive landlords, is not, as has been pointed out, purely one of land possessions. Far from it. The invariable rule . . has been to utilize the surplus revenues in the form of rents, in investments in a great number and variety of corporations. The rent-racked people of the City of New York . . have sweated and laboured and fiercely struggled, as have the people of other cities, only to deliver up a great share of their earnings to the lords of the soil, merely for a foothold. In turn these rents have incessantly gone toward buying up interests in rail-roads, factories, utility plants and often more and more land."

Since this book appeared in America in 1907, published by the (then!) Modern Library of New York, we are almost a century further into that scene – and one might say, fully deserve to have inherited the devastating power of today's multinationals in their plundering of the planet and its inhabitants, for having so steadily ignored their origins. The multinationals are simply, of course, the *multi-monopolists* – and we should refer to them more precisely as such, if we would embark upon the essential dismantling of their power via *radical land rent reform.*

But we must hurry up and do it. For here, at the cross-roads of the economic power with the political, is the key to the environmental disaster that has overtaken us – to the whole saga of our planet's depleted and vanishing resources. Yes, we must be quick. For now this addictive game of monopoly betakes itself to pastures new – to seeds, and genes, and clones, (all strictly patentable, of course, under the necessary legislation!) For this is the new monopoly game – the one for adults – the one for real. In short, the Seven Wise Masters have once more "diversified their portfolios" – that is all. *Of course* the planet goes cheap under the "force" of this fundamental monopoly – as "cheap", it may be, as bulldozing indigenous peoples off their land. And *of course* that land is re-let, (or its products sold), at the highest market price . . . in our ever more and more similarly monopolised market-places.

People are so wound up about the so-called "multinats", that they can't *un*wind enough to see where it all **comes** from! But when they do, the earth-carers, the planet-carers, the animal-rights carers, the seed-bank carers – all of those struggling for the planet today – will finally awaken to the fact that the real enemy all along has been THEIR OWN IGNORANCE. They will then recognize that radical land reform is not mere land reform, but is, in fact, *wholesale economic reform.* And this is the great reason why land reform has to be RADICAL – has to be land rent reform: because it will reach to the roots of the multi-monopolists, who are *the* landed power of today.

How right Ogilvie was – and is!

And those intuitive Scots are his worthy successors, surely.

But all this does not mean, of course, that we are not afflicted by the large-landholding syndrome in its plainer features and homelier settings. But what is all this about Assynt . . . then the Isle of Eigg . . . and now Scottish National Heritage with its "dream ticket" to buy up the abused Glenfeshie estate for the nation?* What kind of *dream folly* is this that we are reduced to buying back our own land? Collect rental

---

* *17 Nov. 97. The new owner of Glenfeshie is Danish. The dance-and-song goes on!*

values – and so end the whole abusive system which has abused Glenfeshie *not alone.* COLLECT RENTAL VALUES – and so pull the rug out from under the feet of these huge capital accumulations – (in reality, as we have seen, land-and-resources monopoly values) – through which Scotland is meta-morphosed into an investor's plaything. But cease from this ridiculous solemnity of buying back Scotland for the Scots!*

In the enormous mushrooming of State power since Ogilvie's time – (something Ogilvie precisely warned us so strongly against** . . . how he would have enjoyed A.J. Nock's "Our Enemy, the State"!) – there have grown up alongside that mushrooming, not unexpectedly, various "variations" on the above theme, in the many further opportunities laid open for the collusion of the State with the landed interest. Thus public utilities, including areas of "the people's" land, are sold off at less that true value, whilst less accessible acres go cheap to adjacent landholders – as the only people with ready access to them! Of course, the true value turns up somewhere in the end – only not in the people's pocket!

Similar games are open to those who hold the cards of such things as – say, trusts in the welfare scene? – or the land involved in the winding down of Britain's industries? Land deals are easily secretive affairs in our land-innocent-pretended society, and the public is usually left to form its own conclusions. But concerning certain deals in the industrial scenario – and recalling the warnings, at the time of our entry into the (then) Common Market, that its purpose was indeed to wind Britain's industry down and turn us into an off-shore island – let me quote from NEW EUROPEAN, Vol. 97, No. 1, (14-16 Carroun Road, London S.W. 8): "The first true Europeans, men and women who totally embraced the concept of a frontierless, free-market union, were not politicians with a vision of a European Community: they were crooks."

How long are we going to allow ourselves to be made fools of by these masked plays – with their lucrative land rental values as the lucrative playing-cards? Land, as Ogilvie repeatedly emphasised, is the fundamental stock of a country. The *only* people to be rightly endowed with responsibility for it, are therefore THE PEOPLE THEMSELVES. Land rent reform, taking back the rental values for the community, de-capitalises land, so under land rent reform ALL LAND DEALS CEASE. Moreover, the assessed valuation rolls are placed, in every area, on permanent public display – bringing the valuations under full public scrutiny and challenge by the people themselves.

In view of the endless scandals over land deals by the State, by local authorities, and by "trusts" alike, all in the name of "the people", it becomes obvious that the people – no longer just in name, *but in actuality* – must now take direct charge of their land; which means in the first place taking charge of its *rental values*, so to bring to an

---

* *As for New Labour's more recent proposal, regarding such estates, to step into the scene with legislation where* ***asset stripping*** *is seen to be going on: it would be hard to imagine a more naive proposition! Asset-stripping is going on all the time – under every land title-deed: the "stripping" from the community of the "asset" of the land rental values that arise, and are being diverted form the community to private pockets.*

** *Para. 37 of his Essay.*

end the shameful careers in these currently marketable, and hugely sought after, assets – which include Scotland's living soil. And surely the Scots are capable of doing that!

How it is to be done, in the broader sense, Ogilvie has shown us: by instituting, (necessarily as a fully independent people), a Bill of Rights, ensuring, as its primary clause, the right of the people to their land *in perpetuo* – i.e., for the present generation, and those to come – by taking, for the social revenue, the full rental value of their land.

As to how a community might, in a more particular sense, take charge of those values, and how it might, by this means, build itself into something truer and stronger than has hitherto been possible with wings pinioned by land monopoly and the centralized power that that invokes: to this, another part of this book gives some thought. But surely the Scots, who have never lost sight of their land – not ever even, quite, of those more hidden rental values – surely the Scots, if any people, are well endowed to build that truer community.

S-A.H Nov. 97.

*

William Ogilvie

A Broader Sweep

*

Pathways Travelled

2) THREEFOLD ROBBERY - OR TRUE SOCIAL FUND?

*

PATHWAYS TRAVELLED

(2) The Real Scottish Enlightenment

"Europe, enlightened Europe, will not be able to endure it much longer. . ." (Ogilvie's, para. 42.)

What is it that Scotland "endures" – and not Scotland alone – ?

*

THREEFOLD ROBBERY – or TRUE SOCIAL FUND?

(a) Threefold Robbery

No! The Scottish Enlightenment of the 1700s was *not* enough! For Scotland still "endures"! But Ogilvie did not expect Scotland to go on enduring. As we know from his 42nd paragraph, he looked ahead to a time of true enlightenment when Scotland would *wake up*! – Knowing full well, as he did, that (in Tolstoy's picturesque phrasing of it) when all ordinary people come to understand the iniquity of the system they live under, it will fall like a pack of cards, because it hasn't got a leg to stand on. Tolstoy was an ardent admirer of Henry George. They corresponded, and would have met but for George's untimely death – (but I didn't get *that* in my Hons-Russian-degree-course-specializing-in-Tolstoy, I can assure you!)

Investigating the role of capital in a society built on land monopoly, we took a look at the history of today's mega-fortunes, and saw that these were in fact rooted in multi-monopolism. (The multinats are multimops – mopping up land-and-resources as fast as they can!) But the multimops are only an extreme form of the monopoly power over capital so readily captured in a land-monopoly-based society.

What are the more homely features of this naturally self-aggrandizing mechanism? What effect does it have on the lives of ordinary men and women – the great mass of those who have only their wage-packet or salary to look to for a living?

Reaching right to the root of human necessity, the monopolistic underpinning of land is reflected in a *monopolistic setting of rents*, since under a land monopoly structure the *land* component is heavily involved in rent or price.

So here – in the weekly or monthly rental of living-space – is the first robbery endured by millions. A robbery involving an elementary human need – SHELTER.

But a second robbery is at once tied in with it. For the rents, (the true social payment), having been skilfully diverted into private coffers instead of being paid into the public one – (for even housing officers are simply managing land, and bricks-and-mortar, like any private landlord – in the people's name: see note 27, Ogilvie's Essay) . . . . . the people had then, somehow, to be successfully persuaded into *re-imbursing that social fund.*

Since the plunderers of the people were also those who passed the laws, the solution was simple – an age-old remedy. "And it came to pass in those days, that there went out a decree from Caesar Augustus that all the world should be taxed." (And so also went Joseph, up out of Galilee, to Bethlehem in Judaea, "with Mary his espoused wife . . . to be taxed". Luke ch. 2.)

Hence an ancient ploy came to the aid of the plunderers. Let the people dig into their wage-packets, and taxation supply the social fund. This was fine for the plunderers since taxation weighs but lightly on the rich – (partaking, as they cannot *but*, of the underlying monopoly, which gradually gets woven through the entire economy). But for the poor – for those who have no handle on monopoly – taxes invariably add to life a heavy burden, not to say a dreaded one. (Quite enough for many to vote No to the second Referendum question. But as we shall come to see, taxes are an entirely false source of social revenue. Wage-packets should remain intact, in the hands of their earners.)

Hence the people are now pinioned under a two-fold robbery. They pay monopolistic rents – and they pay taxes. But even this is not enough. Even this is not the whole picture. Let us take a closer look at that paragraph of Myers':–

> "This large . . . fortune, as that of . . . other extensive landlords, is not, as has been pointed out, purely one of land possessions. Far from it. The invariable rule . . . has been to utilize the surplus revenues in the form of rents, in investments in a great number and variety of corporations. The rent-racked people of the City of New York . . . have sweated and laboured and fiercely struggled, as have the people of other cities, only to deliver up a great share of their earnings to the lords of the soil, merely for a foothold. In turn these rents have incessantly gone toward buying up interests in rail-roads, factories, utility plants and often more and more land."

So the illicitly pocketed land rents have gone not only to tightening the screw on the land monopoly by buying up "more and more land" – they have also, (as we have already noted), been used to buy up, and increasingly monopolize, the country's increasingly capital-intensive industry.

However, there is something that Myers hasn't quite seen here. He says: "in turn these rents have . . . gone towards buying up . . . often more and more land". But *is* it, in fact, just "often" more and more land? No! It's *always* more and more land! Because all those "railroads, factories, utility plants", etc., are caught up in the land monopoly too, that being their fatal inevitable "grounding". We may be sure that this point was not missed by Ogilvie! (See again his para. 15.) As Ogilvie recognized, land is always, and fundamentally, involved in capital undertakings.* And we may be sure that our land-wise magnates perfectly understood this also, and were careful to arrange that **they** weren't going to be the ones paying rents!

In buying up such capital ventures, therefore, the thing to do was always to *buy up the land under them as well*. It is this investment in the land involved, and hence exemption from rental payments – (except, it may be, on the *other* side of the fence, as rental recipients from their own investment sin land) – it is this which is the real power of the supermarkets that oust the corner-shops, just as it is the "real" business in many a take-over too. Equally, it is the system that most of those venturing forth into the small

---

* *__Land__ is the term used in classical economics – (referred to a few paragraphs on) – to include __all natural resources__. Hence it includes such things also as the air-waves that come into the picture today – and of course the sea and its resources too. It is not perhaps an ideal term, but land inevitably remains our primary concern since – bar the fractional population that lives on house-boats – it includes our essential living-space. In fact, so long as we stick with clear definitions – (see first sentence of this footnote) – so that we know what we are talking about, that is the all-important thing.*

business world of today do not fully realize that they are up against, since it is not a part of all those helpful curriculums that are offered them, to point it out.

Now – what about this capital-intensive industry that Myers' land magnates were engaged so busily in buying up? What exactly *is* capital?

Since it is the classical economists, as they are called, who alone have delved to the bottom of the land monopoly business, and been able to expose it as essentially a monopoly of rental values, let us turn to them for a look at capital too.

But firstly – what is it that is so essentially different about the classical economists? How is it that they were able to uncover the land racket in this way?

It is because they base the study of economics upon a definition of terms – a definition unique in being not only clear, but unchallengeable, because reaching down to the very "bones" of our situation. No other school of economists does this; and this is why it is so important to go to the classical economists – such as Henry George, author of that best-seller on economics, *Progress and Poverty** – if we want to understand our situation aright. For we must understand it aright, if we want to change it aright – and not just jump from the devil into the deep blue sea! – which is, unfortunately, what the Eastern bloc countries did . . . some now, inevitably, trying to jump *back* again . . . Needless to say, Ogilvie is of the classical school.

So let us briefly pause with these classical economists, that we may find a clear definition of capital. For in finding this clear definition, who knows what else we may discover?

What are the fundamental terms used by the classical economists? Economic activity is concerned with getting our bread in this life. – With getting all the other things we need and want too, but bread is the bottom line. Where that "bread" is not hanging ripe on the bough for us just to stretch forth and pick – (and even then it would need to be on unclaimed land!) – we can only satisfy our need for food by labour of some kind, and the absolute requisite for labour is *access to land.* So, in classical economics, the two fundamental categories are *land* and *labour*. And the fundamental proposition of classical economics – the psychological background against which the economic activity takes place – is the simple and fairly obvious one that "man seeks to satisfy his desires with the least possible exertion". (Hence the scramble for those rental values!)

In today's orthodox – (but totally "unanchored", of course!) – economics, land is classified as capital. but we also apply the term *capital* to the things man has made. Can both really belong to the same category? Land, (a term used in classical economics to signify the whole world of natural resources – see earlier footnote), clearly stands in a category of its own, being neither made by man, nor able to be added to by him – (even exceptional drainage works do not *add* to natural resources, only convert them). Land may be God's capital – it certainly is not man's!

Does not this recognition, by the classical economists, of the uniqueness of our whole world of natural resources, in turn place *them* in a category of their own – leagues ahead of any other school? For surely they are the only school of economics thinkers with an essential appreciation of what we are all waking up to, in the new ecological era we now stand in: that is, the unique and precious nature of this planet we call "home". For this reason alone, let us betake ourselves to the classical economists, and look askance at the "orthodox" school – (which indeed just about measures up to the mess they have made of the planet today!)

---

* *See Reading List.*

But let us pause a moment to consider what happens when land is placed in the same category as *capital.* What happens is this. That which is beyond man's powers to create (the natural world), but which – given access to – man can create what he needs *out of*, is now equated with . . . those things which he creates *out of it*! What could be more absurd? But it is also very dangerous. for in refusing to "notice" that access to land is a pre-condition of man's being able to support himself on this planet, we have carelessly disempowered the vast majority of our children . . . from being able to do just that. The blurring of *land* with *capital* has set up an embargo on labour – a hidden condition against who, AND WHO IS NOT, permitted to work in this world. – Against who is permitted to feed and clothe themselves, not to mention – to exercise the various special gifts and talents that were bestowed upon them for use here.

For a society to let itself become entangled in such an "overlooking" is scarcely a trivial matter. That nation which fails to establish, at its base, the *equal right of all its children to access to land,* but instead allows some to pocket that access at the expense of others – such a nation has succeeded in building, right into its foundations, a platform of grossest injustice. In placing this embargo, right at the floor of life, upon the ability of the great mass of its children to support themselves, what that nation is virtually saying to that excluded mass is this: You have no right here. You are not fit for this land. You are fit only for the gutter.

Is it any wonder, then, if that is just where countless of our children end up? In the gutter. On pavements – in doorways. The castaways . . .the expendables. *The pride of a nation – her children*!

Are we blind? Life ultimately is founded upon *law.* Not human law. NATURAL LAW. The law expressed in those ancient sayings that are a part of the wisdom of a people – of *every* people, every culture, every language. Such sayings as – As you sow, you shall reap. Or how about: Sow the wind – reap the whirlwind? . . . Sayings which we have forgotten to teach to our children, because we are out of touch with them ourselves. We ourselves have forgotten them. But of course – we shall not be allowed to forget. That nation which sows disaster for its children reaps that disaster itself. And in double measure. Need one say more? The signs are all around us. – While Scotland remains eaten up with concern about things like *tourism*!

Such are the fruits of the confusion of *land* with *capital* . . . Such are the fruits of the corrupt, decrepit economics of the school of the *Seven Wise Masters.* Time, methinks, we threw their economics OUT.

To summarize, then: LAND IS NOT CAPITAL. It stands in a unique category of its own, as something we must find a way of sharing. The return to land, rent, equally then becomes SOMETHING WHICH WE MUST SHARE. (Note: In classical economics, the full term for this return to land is economic rent, to distinguish it from rent of any other kind.)*

---

* *A question. How do we discover this separate rental value of the land* ***alone****, when buildings are so often involved? It is discovered by assessing each area of land as though bare of all improvements – (the term used for* ***man-made*** *works) – so that it reflects only the value it receives from the presence and activities of the surrounding community. (As we know, even bare land, in any occupied area, has a price today well beyond the reach of most – if, indeed, there is any available.)* ***Note****: there is no difficulty in assessing land as distinct from improvements. some countries do it already for local rates, and valuers in fact assess land like this every day in assessing the improvements separately for insurance purposes. Only – the values of land and improvements are not usually presented separately. Obviously not, under a system whose idea is to hide up the worth of the rental values! – which was the original idea in mixing* ***land*** *in with* ***capital****, of course. And so, under our "orthodox" economics system, there is utilised a magical umbrella term, "property" which skilfully entraps the scene whole – land and improvements in one!*

Reaching forward to our definition of capital, we now have *land* – in its distinct and unique category; and the return to land – *rent*, our equally distinct social fund.

In tracking the meaning of capital, we come, then, to the second of the two fundamental categories in economics: that is – *labour*. The return to labour, as we know, is *wages* – although we have now seen that this "return" is not exactly the thing it should be. We have found there is a "snag" or two in the system, on account of the monopoly of land.

Could there be a third "snag" arising out of the part capital plays in the system – in view of this attempt to confuse capital with land? There's an interesting possibility! But let us not jump ahead! First let us find the classical definition of capital.

This is simple.

In classical economics, the full product of labour applied to land* is wealth. Note first, then, that wealth, in classical economics, is always something *real*. It is some fruit of labour – (not, therefore, land) – having *value in itself*, as well as any exchange value it may have. It is not something having just exchange value – like money, like all that "wealth" so-called which suddenly blew away in the overnight whirlwind on the stock markets around the world, in the last days of October 1997! No! Wealth in classical economics stands for something real and tangible. And only for that. (Money is not therefore, of course, wealth either, according to classical economics. It is simply a useful counter, exchangeable *for* wealth . . . wealth which, in our society, may of course – (as we can see from these dramatic events on world stock-markets), just as easily be counterfeit wealth as the real thing. For our society does not confine its use of the term "wealth" to the classical economists' definition of that term.

To return to our tracking of real capital. The labourer, in classical economics, out of the product of his labour – *wealth*, pays first to the community – (for the use of the land) – *rent*; and the balance is his *wages*. But any part of his wages that is not at once consumed, but is put aside, (for re-investment in the work, or for whatever other purpose), is termed his *capital*. Capital, then, is always some part of *real wealth*. It follows, then, that to the lending only of this genuine form of capital, can genuine interest be returned. But we will return to the matter of interest later.

Real capital, then, is simply a part of the output of labour's application to land. It is a part of wages – where the labourer finds there is a surplus that can be put aside; and there is nothing else that is real capital. Hence all capital, following from this sound definition of wealth, is not only something real in itself, but belongs in its entirety to *labour*. To whom else, indeed, could it belong? – except by robbery . . . . .

But what of capital as it is generally spoken of today?

Let us track what happens to capital in a society which allows land to become monopolised.

Our failure to collect annually the rental value of land as our social fund – (more fairly put: the high-handed pocketing of it by those who made the laws) – resulted in the "creation" (robbery) of a useful *asset* in the hands of the landholders: an asset *visible* as land, but essentially, (as an economic asset), the visible outpicturing of *pocketable rental values for years to come*; and naturally, highly marketable – highly saleable – as a result.

---

* *More completely stated, we should add: or, of labour applied to things that are* ***already*** *the reaping/fruits of labour applied to land – such as the office buildings we work in, the stage on which a theatre company performs, or the aircraft that is piloted across the world, etc.*

Now, since *wealth*, as we have seen is in its true definition an entirely honest product and possession, so, to those dealing in land rental values, it was highly desirable that their asset should be covered by that same term – so to be thought of by people in general as an *honest* asset, a form of wealth-the-real-thing. Hence, through this "pressure from above", land came to be slipped into the category of "wealth", as a part of capital.

Now although land has in this way been taken out of its true (classical) category of uniqueness, and got cunningly slipped in with capital instead – and as such is spoken of and generally regarded today, nevertheless the *monopoly* element in landholding remains rather too uncomfortably visible. It fits ill with the true idea of capital : something that man creates, and which can therefore be added to. It is this glaringly *monopoly* element which the attempt to class "land" with "capital" has never quite got away with. Thus there remains something instinctively "wrong" to us about vast landholdings – because there remains something instinctively wrong to us about classifying land as capital. No – attempt it as they may, the neo-classical economists – (as they are called, who have tried to dispense with the classical school) – attempt it as they may, they have never completely got away with classifying land as "capital". Not at any rate, I think, with the Scots. For there is no *real* element of capital in land.

However, in the case of the land monopoly element that has got *mixed in with* real capital – (all that ground lying under the factories, etc., which Myers wrote of, neatly included *with* the factories in the umbrella word "property"): this land monopoly element, once mixed in with that real capital, became thereby extremely successfully "screened". – Such that this form of "capital", now combining *real wealth* and *land rent monopoly* together, has far more easily gained acceptance in people's minds as capital-the-real-thing; and as such is spoken of in today's world – frequently in terms of "stocks" and "shares".

However, this surreptitious sowing of the "tares" among the "wheat", in the element of capital, will one day have run its course, and the good time of harvest will be at hand, when the false and the true are firmly and forever separated – and hopefully that time is not too far off.

But let us return to today's scene, and to someone living off a wage-packet in our thoroughly befuddled economy. What if he begins to feel somewhat pinched as to his livelihood – (pinched, indeed, much has been!), and is unable to get a wage-rise – (because his trades union has not yet caught up with the *Law of the Depression of Wages* as the other side of the Law of Rent: see chart in Part III)? What, then, if he tries for a loan, and goes off to the bank to borrow some capital?

He now finds that it is, of course, an ersatz object he is faced with having to borrow. For he is having to borrow not just *real* capital (such as he has helped create), but he is having to borrow also monopoly land values that have got woven into it.

A double ill, for he does not in fact want to borrow land – or to borrow monopoly. So why should he have to borrow *monopoly land values*, when all he wants to borrow is capital? Because that is capital, as it has come to be in our society. A very ersatz, mixed-up thing. So naturally, the *interest* asked of him upon his borrowing will be a very ersatz and mixed-up thing too.

How is the simple wage-earner to cope with paying such interest? There is a saying in Proverbs that "the destruction of the poor is their poverty". A very pithy saying – and perhaps it is the ultimate comment on a corrupt society, too.

Here, then, is the third "snag" – here is the third robbery: the interest that is asked on borrowings. As already pointed out, it is those who have no handle on monopoly who are the really hard hit – that is, the huge preponderance of dwellers on this planet. By the same reasoning, the interest paid *out* on capital is also a very ersatz and mixed-up thing, (but we shall go into that further presently).

It must be said that certain banking practices form part of the scene here, but it is not my purpose to go further into them. Firstly, because the root of the falsity lies not in banking, but in the system of *false values we have created by allowing land rental values to become a private monopoly* – hence to be capitalised, and hence designated "wealth" – and so, offered in exchange for wealth, the real thing; and secondly, because these matters are already sufficiently discussed in what seems to me a quite excellent booklet by Graham Hart, *Banking, Currency, Credit and Inflation*, which I have placed in the Reading-List.

Now let us pause a moment on this false concept of wealth that is so current today. Wealth sprung of monopoly values is not – (as we have seen from the classical definition of wealth) – *real* wealth at all. No matter how high it is recorded in the books, it doesn't stand for anything real. Its substance is purely privilege – monopoly. Hence a sudden economic catastrophe may land a nation in bankruptcy, whose situation had appeared, on paper, to be stable – (however unjustly founded . . . But then, is anything founded in injustice ever really stable?) At any rate, the "whiskering" of the stock-markets in late October 97, followed by the Japanese "event" of November, surely reminded us just how ephemeral the "wealth" they register is.* But a far more solemn warning is delivered us in the book, *Why the German Republic Fell*, by Bruno Heilig – an Austrian journalist who charted Hitler's rise to power, and survived the experiences of concentration camps to make his discovery of Henry George:–

> "The Nazi regime is not Hitler's, the man's, achievement. Nazidom has grown organically out of a rotten democracy, and the rottenness of that democracy is the natural consequence of unequal economic conditions; and unequal conditions obtain all over the world owing to the instituted private appropriation of the rent of land . . . . . there can be no lasting peace even after the defeat of Nazism if the present economic structure of the civilized countries remains. The private appropriation of the rent of land is the deadly enemy of mankind." (See Part III for further extracts; also Reading-List. Heilig's book *Men Crucified*, a deeply moving account of his experiences in the concentration camps, is available from the public library.)

How much I should have liked – (had he not already passed from this world) – to have sent a copy of this small booklet of Heilig's to Primo Levi, whose unforgettable accounts of his experiences in Auschwitz include sections dedicated to a deep probing of this very question: WHY?

But do we really need such grim warnings as the above to re-possess ourselves of our wits, and so re-possess ourselves of our land rental values? Meanwhile, could we present a more ridiculous picture – three times over stabbing ourselves with a three-fold robbery! There was a book written in recent times called "The Thornbirds". The human race are the thornbirds *par excellence* – the original thornbirds of them all!

---

* *A renowned economist, on the news just after the Japanese crash spoke of the world stock-markets as having "a very substantial level of insanity". Yet that there is apparently nothing we can do about it.* ***We create the system!*** *Could there possible be a more insane* ***attitude****?*

Meanwhile we continue to accept all the political mumbo-jumbo that goes with our incredible system – such as that the wealth ("wealth") in our society is hopefully going to "filter down" from the top to the more needy ones below – when it's already been well filtered *up* in the first place . . . . . or rather, carefully siphoned off!

Let us collect our wits and display some real I.Q. Let us collect those rental values annually, for the community. We shall then see true capital emerging from the folds of the false, to remain in the hands of those who made it; while the false will – evaporate! – much like the wicked magician in the fairy-tale . . . to be replaced by the true prince re-appearing in our midst: our handsome social (land rent) fund – its peculiarly ugly feature of monopoly *gone*!

In that good day we shall see that the interest we were duped into paying on capital was due to a falsely created "scarcity" value built into it by an underlying monopoly force that is not related to capital at all. Once this false "scarcity" value – (stemming from the land-and-resources monopoly) – is done away with, via the collection of the land's rental values, how can there any longer be an international market in stocks and shares, or even a national one? On this, I cannot but find myself in accord with W.L. Sinton, a page from whose book *Economics and Spiritual Law Harmonized* will be found in Part III.*

It is worth pausing a moment at this point to remind ourselves that what we call interest on capital today really amounts to *usury*. That was the old name for it. But when respectability was desired for it, no wonder that name was dropped! A remarkable "live" sermon against usury – with all the essential features of it that we know today – is to be found in the 5th chapter of Nehemiah, in the Bible. It is not a sermon likely to be heard from our pulpits today, however, for the practice of usury has become so cloaked with that desired "respectability" – and so woven into the very fabric of our society, (interest being paid even on the smallest savings, and our very State-support systems being hugely financed out of it) – that few people think of it in its original "usurious" terms. The 5th chapter of Nehemiah is a marvellously refreshing read – and as we read it, let us picture Jesus in the midst of that scene, and just where he would be standing.

It is interesting to reflect briefly, at this point, on Ogilvie's words quoted in the introduction to these longer notes – about the "force" of that "monopoly" (land) being something "exorbitant"; for "exorbitant" is a word particularly closely associated with excessive interest rates, or "usury". The earlier law against usury had been over-turned before Ogilvie's time, and his extremely astute mind could not have failed to recognize how the interest paid on capital, even then, represented in good part a *monopoly of rental values*. Ogilvie would not, I think, have been averse to some examination of this matter of interest on capital!

Let us review the scene once more, for its findings will be quite startling to most of us.

---

* *There are those who will readily point out that – whatever Scotland does on her own will not end stock-markets that are international.*

– And the Scots are so proud of their achievements ***across the world!*** *– (including their prowess in matters of finance!) What Scotland does, will undoubtedly be looked to by others – and amidst so many nations careering to destruction through land monopoly, let us reflect that: we can at least save ourselves by our exertions, even if we cannot save others by our example!*

Let us take heart, then, from that delicious postcard "Wha's like us!", (hopefully to be placed in Part III). It is up to the Scots to chalk up another "first", methinks!

If the land rents are re-routed to a social fund, bringing to an end the monopoly of land, and also the false "scarcity" value with which it has masked capital – so that capital is left as its original real self, a part of real wealth: what inducement will there then be to send it roaming the stock-markets of the world for a taker? *Real* capital surely, will be utilized where it is made.

The real reason that capital roams abroad today – (in its false form, as mixed up with land values) – is that, owing to an unjust land dispossession system, those who make capital – the real thing – are *unable to keep it in their hands.* Once this *real* capital can be put to use by those who have created it, why should it go looking abroad for takers? Is there any country in the world today where those who live only from wages have actually got all the basic necessities of life – let alone a few further things they might choose to have, to live more fully? People living only on wages never have the living they have earned. Even if they have homes, these steal from their wages on account of their rents or mortgages – (i.e., the land rental values factor *monopolised*). Once capital is freed to stay in the hands of those who make it – by the removal of land monopoly – there will be plenty of use for it right on the spot where it is made.

The stock market transactions on capital are recorded on paper in terms of money. But as we have already seen, money does not stand up to the classical economists' definition of wealth – (something the October 97 stock-market shaker drove home to us). Being only a representation of something, and used solely to facilitate exchange, money still faces us with the question: does it represent true wealth, or fictitious? As Sinton points out, the money that goes abroad looking for takers today in the name of stocks and shares, represents in reality a *monopoly claim upon production* (because of the huge part played by monopoly in the system); hence, not real wealth at all. Were land de-monopolised, then that capital that has travelled abroad would be shown up as false – as having been part of that monopoly now done away with. No wonder, then, the tremendous hide-up, by the Establishment, of the role played in the economy by land monopoly – the role of those land rental values of which society has been robbed! Meanwhile neither Left, Right nor Centre of the political arena reveals the smallest interest in this huge cover-up . . .

When we consider *real* capital and its workings, we can see that there is no need for the question of interest to arise, for it to function properly. It is enough if, (as Sinton points out), such capital earns its replacement value.

Many businesses exist which not only make use of, but hire out, real capital equipment of all kinds – everything from heavy machinery to special-occasion clothes to theatre-props. Such businesses, like every other business, certainly need to earn enough to cover repair and replacement of their stock, (in addition, of course, to wages or salaries, and rent due on the site). But, regardless of how such businesses may be constituted in our land-monopoly-based society – whether, that is, they have shareholders or not, who expect to receive interest payments – it is plain that payments – out of interest are *not* an actual requirement for them, in order to operate.

It is hard for us to imagine a society in which whoever wished to, was capable of putting together their own capital stock, out of full earnings. We are too attuned to depletion in our society – to the syndrome of rich and poor, with the vast majority of the population numbered among the latter and the gap between the two groups ever widening. Sinton writes that, with the taking over of land values for public use, "rich men, as we now think of them, cease to exist. All men become working men". It is hard to argue with this – or to regret the passing of a system so contrary, which denies to the vast majority their proper living – or even any living at all.

No wonder, then, that Sinton adds that this reform "is so revolutionary it will make the Reds look White". What Labour government has ever envisioned – let alone actually *envisaged*! – a society in which all are free to work, (the land unlocked), and none live in idleness off others? Well, Henry George did. And so did William Ogilvie. No wonder their vision is such as to turn the Reds pale!

For a political party, of whatever shade, the primary pre-occupation is *power* – not poverty. If poverty were actually dealt with – eliminated, rooted out – most of politics would disappear with it, since what most of politics is embroiled with is simply the grim reapings of *poverty institutionalised.*

Sinton – who published his work in 1930 – has not been alone in digging down to the roots of this question of interest paid on capital. More recently, Bill Pitt of Australia has brought to light the similar conclusions of one, Michael Flurscheim, a German industrialist of late last century, who was similarly inspired to think through this matter by coming across the writings of Henry George.*

Henry George, like Ogilvie and others, gave us his great work; but none of these would have wished – or expected – us to stand still and mark time in their footprints. Ogilvie specifically pleaded – (his words quoted at the start of these Notes) – that his investigations should be carried deeper and further, and who was he addressing if not posterity? Of land rent robbery's role in creating a modern form of slavery, Henry George, a hundred years after Ogilvie, has acted as the great spokesman for our time. His was a colossal work – a colossal task. In his chapter "Interest on Capital" in *Progress and Poverty*, George does in fact point to the enormous constituent of capital which in our society is formed of land values, and hence is not real capital at all – with the corollary that that constituent's part in "interest", is not interest either, but rent. Elsewhere in his writings also, he does not hesitate to emphasise that big fortunes in capital are rooted in land monopoly.

That Henry George concentrated, in his work, on the exposure of that monopoly in its more primitive form of *land rental values* seems to me, on reflection however, possibly just as well. In his era, this was in itself so great a revelation, that it was perhaps enough for people then to take in. But then it is unquestionably our task in turn, today, to take up this closer examination of the role of capital – capital as it functions caught up in a land-monopoly-based structure; and equally unquestionably, it is a task of urgency, with errant capital now devouring our very planet-base.

As to whether Sinton and Flurscheim, (and possible others yet, of whom we have not heard), will prove to have been one hundred per cent correct in surmising the disappearance of interest in a justly-based society – the reality of a justly-based society will soon enough sort the matter out! Theorizing is purposeful within limits, but it can be over-engaged in – especially by those . . . not actually wanting to exert themselves to bring necessary change about! – Like those other non-exerters who say: "It sounds fine, but it wouldn't work", when what so glaringly obviously does not work is our present system! Serious questioning starts when people start asking the questions seriously of **themselves**, and so making their own journeys of exploration and discovery. My main purpose here has been to open the matter up.

However – whether Sinton, Flurscheim *et al.* prove fully a hundred per cent correct, it is at least unquestionable that they are majorly so: that the monopoly element

---

* *An article by Bill Pitt on this was published in* ***Progress****, Australia, in 1997. See List of Addresses.*

of capital, along with its "usurious" returns, it very tightly tied in with the monopoly element in landholding, which has *co-opted capital to itself.* And I am convinced that a major reason for the Establishment's resistance to radical land reform – (a resistance that holds Labour as fast as it does the Tories: see "New" Labour's concept of *Land Reform* in Part III). – is due, in fact, to the awareness, whether dim or acute, that the role of capital, under this reform, will undergo a very profound change; a change which the Establishment, whether under Left or Right, feels unable to face.

Fortunately, this aspect of the matter has a happy reverse! Once the people themselves are able to see the radical nature of this reform – are able to see how it is the monopoly element in land which lies at the root of the monopoly element in capital (due to the fact that capital must use land) – and so are able to see also how the monopoly of land rents is the underlying reason for the great gap between rich and poor – then the people themselves will set about the bringing in of this reform. The tragedy of Labour's – (*real* Labour, the people's) – long confrontation with Capital, and the belief that Capital is the exploiter of Labour, will at last be seen for the delusion it always was. LAND RENT REFORM is what Labour should have been tackling all those years ago.

*

(b) True Social Fund

Capital, the real thing, is so necessary to us – and capital, the errant, so *un*necessary!

But there is a function of our society in which that errant capital is involved, which is a legitimate one in itself. It is the idea of savings. How will the idea of savings work out, in a just society dealing only in real wealth?

We will still be able to put by savings into a savings account, of course. Our savings will not receive interest – (if Sinton proves a hundred per cent correct) – but they will be far securer than today's savings, because, being backed only by *real* wealth, they will NEVER BLOW AWAY!

But I am thinking of something else – times of emergency that can overtake any of us, when we might suddenly need to borrow in excess of what we had saved. Despite what Sinton says – about the abundance of capital making the idea of interest impossible – that "abundance" could still operate very unequally in the lives of all of us, in the way that life's journey can throw up, for any of us, times of sudden fortune and misfortune – times when we need to lean heavily on others, just as times when we can in turn lend others our support.

Now, if there are a variety of banks operating, each vying for customers, it is hard not to see that idea of interest creeping back into our lives, as each bank sought to attract customers by more favourable terms.

It is here that, on pondering the matter, I have felt drawn to the idea of a *unified* community savings bank – (with as many branches, of course, as are useful) – for it would rule out competition of that kind.

Henry George, in considering what matters the land rent fund should deal with, termed as "natural monopolies" those few things in a society which are better dealt with on a unified basis, rather than left free to the members of that society to carry our for themselves – (individually, co-operatively, or however they please).

It seems to me that the operation of savings, in a just society, might well best come into that category of "natural monopolies". True – the reason for its being unified in this way is not the usual one, not the kind of thing Henry George actually had in mind in using that term – the concept of achieving any superior *business* efficiency thereby. But it has to do with something very vital of another kind – for any society that wishes to build itself into a true community, a buzz-word today sorely lacking in substance. For the concept of a unified savings bank has to do with the way we relate to one another: namely, that we *cannot* act so as to profit ourselves out of one another's needs.

We are so used, today, to living in a painful isolation from one another, each struggling separately to provide for ourselves and our families – against an uncertain background, the background, as Heilig reminds us, of a rotten democracy. But we are assuredly not meant to live in this way. There is a better way to live. – A way which tells us: I can draw upon your strength, in my time of need, because I can give of my strength, for you to draw upon, in yours. (And a bank encompassing the savings of *all* its members would never lack the practical means of realizing this.) Would this not be a way that would sow happiness in the hearts of our children? Would it not bring alive to us again that ancient Celtic saying – "it is in the shadow of each other that the people live"? Today's economic structure does not allow this. But we can *break through* that structure – break through in the words of the song sung by Paul Robeson in *Sanders of the River*:–

Each for all,
And all for each,
Until we reach
Our journey's end.

Yes – for so long as our journey through this life takes us, we know that we are sustained not just by our own strength, but *by one another's*. The idea of "community" has suddenly flowered.

*

It may be, of course, that in a free society things will work out differently – and I am all for the fullest possible freedom in a society from which fundamental economic exploitation has been removed.

It may be that there will be no need to think in such terms as above, for perhaps there will be no way interest on capital can resurrect itself. On the other hand, perhaps it will be there, but in only so minimal a way that it will bother no one, in a society that is flourishing. Or perhaps again, our own sense of values will have changed so greatly that the idea of interest on capital will have lost its appeal.

However, a cruel, corruptive and exploitative ethos, such as has held our economic life in its grasp for several centuries now, will not at once give way universally, and so it is perhaps as well for us to have a few ideas on how to help ourselves forward, at least in the initial stages.

What is interesting to ponder is how the change to a fundamentally just society will enable us not only – *all* – to make a comfortable living, but will lift us higher in the scale in other dimensions of our life too.

One thinks of the saying, "in the diminishing of another, we ourselves are diminished". In a society based on exploitation, many who hear such words are so driven themselves, just trying to keep going on society's exploitative terms, that – apart from the immediate circle of family and friends – such a saying can only be thought of as something beautiful from a far-off realm . . .

So it has been interesting to picture the idea of that savings bank – even if just as a practical, down-to-earth example of the kind of change in our inner lives, that would have space to flourish, in that new society.

One thinks of entering the premises of such a bank – a building that vibrates, in subtle ways, with the joys and sorrows stemming from a whole community. Will not our inner life, every time we cross that threshold, be drawn up, in subtle ways, into that higher level of vibration that fills it? – a vibration of interconnectedness with *all*.

"All things
by immortal power,
near or far,
hiddenly
to each other
linked are,
that thou canst not
stir a flower
without troubling of
a star." (Francis Thompson)

These are not impractical or dreamy words, but are of the very essence of our day and age to grasp and understand. Some have warned that, so far has the destruction of this planet reached, a very major transition time lies ahead if it is to be saved, and that such a time will require a very heightened level of vibration by dwellers on this planet to survive it.

Freed from this terrible, destructive rat-race, will not our very perceptions be heightened and renewed? Even to sense "the troubling of a star" may become something of common occurrence. In such a day, the Planet itself will begin to flower again.

*

Having looked at the idea of a savings scheme operating through the same broad field as that brought into being by the land rent fund, let us take a further look at that fund itself. For in fact there are aspects of it which suggest that such a savings scheme was something looking at us – even staring at us – in the face, from the very start . . . (whatever banks we might choose to set up to operate it).

Firstly: in the last part of the chapter "The Unbounded Savanhah" in *Progress and Poverty*, Henry George points out that, as society advances and becomes more productive, there is not only as a result an increase in the rental fund – there is an increase also in the *proportion of* wealth which goes to that fund, as against that which goes to labour and capital – (Henry George was, of course, writing also of a return to capital).

This is easy to see in our *un*just society – (see Part III, the Law of Rent) – where rents are at a monopolistic setting, (the tendency of rent to overreach its asking, in its demand on labour and capital, is what lies at the root of the cycle of boom and slump). But even in a just society, where that monopoly was done away with, we can in fact understand how rent would still draw the greatest proportion of the wealth created, since land is the absolutely primary factor in all production, and itself beyond value and beyond price – to us all. (Hence the anomaly, strictly speaking, of the term, *land value taxation*. It is really the land's *rental* value that is referred to.)

That we should owe the earning of our bread, in a just society, more to the life of the community as a whole than to our own personal exertions – (reflected in rent's drawing a greater proportion of wealth than wages would do) – seems reasonable, when we consider how different it would be if we were living in a wilderness, on our own. How stark a contrast this is to the situation in our present society, where it is the isolated individual – each in their own isolated situation – who has to struggle so hard . . . just to *keep* a job in the first place. It is exactly as if each of us was living in our own wilderness; and Henry George's discernment here as to how a true society operates provides a telling yardstick with which to measure not only the injustice, but the *unnaturalness*, of our own.

So the social fund – once society has advanced to a certain stage – actually draws to itself a greater proportion of wealth than that which goes to wages. Is it surprising then, that the idea has begun to be voiced here and there among Georgists in recent years, that the land rent fund might well afford a basic income for every citizen? The chief proponent of the idea, to my knowledge, has been the American Georgist, Jeff Smith, who has coined for it the neat term "ci-di", or *citizens' divided.* (This was something included in my own *The Land Question*, 1981.)*

---

* *I first read of the idea in* ***The True National Dividend****, by W.R. Lester, and subsequently in an article by Fred Foldvary in* ***Land and Liberty****.*

The distribution of a ci-di to every citizen carries with it the possibility of its being left on deposit, in the fund, in that citizen's name. Hence we could say that the idea of a natural citizens' savings bank was something perhaps woven, from the start, into the idea of the true social fund.

I am the more persuaded regarding the naturalness of this idea of the ci-di, from other words of Henry George's in that same chapter, "The Unbounded Savannah". For he speaks of what we add to each others' lives, not just by formal labour inputs or the useful social infrastructure (roads, etc.), which together we bring into being, but also of more intangible things: the "sense of companionship", "power of sympathy", and stimulation, too, from the variety of characters and tastes around us. That such things can add to our actual work output, we all know; hence, then – to the wealth we create, *and hence, in turn, to that very social fund itself.* So it would seem there are very practical grounds for the idea of that ci-di.

Such a payment, arising from our sense of indebtedness to one another, would certainly be worlds away in idea from the out-payments of "State welfare" – which too often leave their recipients with a sense not of gratitude, but of grudge! This leads us naturally on to the thought that a society which arrived at the freedom and happiness of funding itself from its true source of land rent, might well choose to set aside a day each year to celebrate this. – A day to give thanks for one another; to remind ourselves of the necessity, for a community, of anchoring itself *in justice*; and a day to serve annually, above all, for a *re-dedication of ourselves* to that essential foundation on which we all stand.

And so it seems to me that Henry George, in pointing to this natural twofold growth of the land rent fund, has – possibly by unconscious inspiration – done a remarkable thing for us. For he has opened the way for us to see how the true social fund has, incorporated into it, in this way, a true *socially caring* factor: something that is not only a positive discovery in itself, but one that should certainly ease the transition stage to a new and juster society.

*

Now, to take a look at the land rent fund in contrast to taxation, as a source from which to draw our social revenue: there would be so many aspects of our present life stood on their head in a just society, that it is hard to know where to start! For instance, can any of us imagine just what it would be like to live in a society where there was never any question of being *out of work?* To picture such a situation, we have to turn to what are generally called "primitive" societies – those living in a decidedly more natural state, in which no such problem as "unemployment" arises. So much has "civilization" done for us!

From this transformation – from a massively workless to a fully working society –a society, in short, that *works!* – three huge economic unburdenings at once follow.

Firstly, every member of society of working years would be contributing to the land rent fund – bar the fractional number living on marginal land, (land, that is, which would support a living, but no more).* So here we are brought face to face with the first enormous loss society today sustains – the revenue from those who make up the huge numbers of the "workless", (simply – the fully dispossessed).

On the heels of this comes, secondly, the further huge loss from our revenue in

---

* *See Law of Rent chart in Part III.*

the payments out that must be made to support – not just the unfortunate individuals who are out of work, but the entire families left as a result desperate, without a breadwinner. – And let us not forget that these social payments must include the rents at those monopolistic settings which we have already mentioned earlier, too.

Thirdly, what of the huge further expenditures incurred by the armies of State operators required to operate these "benefits" schemes? Another enormous drain from society's tax revenues – which must of course pay the salaries of *all* State employees.

But there is a great deal more to it than just this. As already pointed out, the only reason that the State is involved in spheres such as housing, health and education, is because the huge majority of the population are *dispossessed*, and as a consequence are so impoverished that they are unable to do those things for themselves that it would be most natural for them to do – *and* that they would do far better for themselves than the State can ever do for them. Just think of the failed, inhuman housing schemes, for a start – and of the ruin of the nation's health under a State "national health service" – (something we shall look at more fully in Part II. It is true that Henry George believed education might be a proper function for the State, but that corruption of public morals he so vividly foretells – (see "How Modern Civilization May Decline" in Part III) – has long ago disqualified any such idea. We only need think of how the State has *consistently*, under Left and Right, for the best part of half a century, been teaching our children that fluoridation is simply a "scientific" measure – oh, and of course, a hundred per cent safe! – to realize just how many other lies it is filling our children's heads with. Can we doubt that Henry George would be the first to declare it?

Then there are the equally improper spheres of State "management" – (*mis*management would be the more proper term) – that have followed from . . . what we might call the other half of this picture: that is, the spheres of interest taken over, not on account of the impoverishment of the dispossessed, but at the instigation of the *dispossessors*. Such are the State departments of agriculture, fish, food, forestry – (or forestry, rather, farmed out to a "forestry commission"), various "development" and "environmental" agencies, and a recent proliferation of those State bodies called "quangos" – but more truly "quagos" being *qua*sier *g*overnmental that *n*on-governmental *o*rganizations by a long chalk. Quite a number of these have co-opted the word "Scottish" to their titles, but performance would indicate that they represent less the Scottish-people than the Scottish-Office – or even say just, the "State", that sphere of spheres in which the *Seven Wise Masters* are so truly at home. (The "S" of "State" stands excellently also for those "Seven" themselves!)

The wastage of tax-payers' money in all this falsely State-adopted business is probably incalculable. But here I would have to state my considerable obligation for any insights I have gained to that masterly small volume (just 109 pages), *Our Enemy the State*, by A.J. Nock, (see Reading-List), who, like others amongst us, early stumbled on the writings of Henry George. I must mention also my particular indebtedness to a certain passage which I came upon, many years ago, in Henry George's *A Perplexed Philosopher* – (a superb taking-apart of the renowned Herbert Spencer's attempt to back-track on his former pro-land-reform stance). Towards the end of the chapter entitled "This Apology Examined" there occurs the following passage:-

> "For this letter to *The Times* not only shows Mr. Spencer's intense desire to be counted on the side of 'vested interests' in the struggle over the land question that was beginning, but it also shows how he was intending to join formally the ranks

of the defenders of private property in land without the humiliation of an open recantation of what he had said in Social Statics . . . (The) new matter in this apology in The Times consists in . . . boldest of all . . . the *assumption that the recognition of equal rights to land means the administration and management of land by public officials*." (Emphasis added.)

It is perfectly clear that Herbert Spencer was in deepest cahouts with the landowning contingent by that time – (desperate as he was to escape the pen of Henry George!) – and that passage above from Henry George's book quoting Spencer's words has consequently remained one of the highlights of my self-educational pathway. While I could write quite a few paragraphs upon it, let me simply leave it with the pencilled note made at the time – (probably nearly forty years ago): "Key to today's whole mumbo-jumbo about land-use/management! It *did* come direct from the landowners then, this socialist rhetoric!" – To which, as today's, I might just add: The landowning establishment have proved well capable of scooping up socialism into their net! But they could not scoop up Henry George!

Hence – to apply Heilig's words: Labour, likewise, "has not touched the land problem". (See extract from Heilig in Part III, and Labour's programme for Land Reform.) It is solemnizing to realize the relevance of that statement of Heilig's – that "therefore every country is potentially a Fascist country". Even under Socialism? The history of fluoridation – a test case if ever there was one – *points in an identical direction.*

From this brief look at the question of just how far today's realm of State activity has been permeated – even positively launched – by the landowning establishment, we can each perhaps do some pondering for ourselves as to just what a burden on public revenue would be lifted by the ending of land-rent-robbery . . . as that huge load of parasitical State officialdom found itself suddenly without its most powerful backer – and without *raison d'etre.* As Henry George points out, the State should confine itself to those few things which the people together, in free co-operation, cannot so successfully do for themselves.

At this point I am prompted to suggest a look at Lindy Davis's enjoyable and down-to-earth *By the Way*, in Part III, as a reminder of just how impossible it is for any of us to depict, ahead, the specific details of such a transition to justice and liberty. But Henry George does say in *Protection and Free Trade* – (a book written after *Progress and Poverty*, and therefore containing his yet maturer reflections . . . granted that these are a hundred years ago) – that the land rent fund would far outstrip the taxation one. In fact, there is a school of Georgist thought which holds that *all* taxes in any case *come out of rent* – and if one looks at the Law of Rent chart (Part III), it is possible to understand why.

There is a further very enormous "plus" for the land rent fund, and that is the absolutely minimal cost that it would be to collect. Compare this with the buildings full of offices required to administer taxation, and the quite unquantifiable paper consumption that it requires too. How planet-friendly in this latter respect alone the rental fund would prove by comparison! Land – unlike people and possessions! – cannot move, hide itself or run away, and – the scheme once set up – up-dating of the valuations, even annually, with today's computers would be virtually child's play. But all this was verified in any case by a pilot scheme carried out in Whitstable in Kent, under the auspices of the Rating and Valuation Association (in existence then) and reported to the international Georgist conference of 1973. The valuer employed was himself totally won to the scheme, on account not only of its fiscal good sense, but also its obvious justice.

Regarding the multitudes of people in State employ today, no observation of mine concerning State activity is ever directed at the individuals involved. As with landholding it is the *structure* that is wrong, not the people. State departments are full of those doing their best with a structure many doubtless find extremely unsympathetic themselves. One notes the growing number taking early retirement.

A word was said earlier on the point that a justly-based society does not deal in taxes, so let us return to it briefly. Once the economic rent – his due to the community – is paid by the labourer, out of the (*real*) wealth he has created, the balance of that wealth being entirely due to his own exertions, *belongs entirely to him*. Classical economics has no quibble about this. Any attempt by the State to appropriate any part of wages – (or any *real* return on capital; i.e., should it turn out, under this reform, that it earned any slight amount above its replacement value) – falls, as the classical economists point out, into the category of *robbery*. Precisely that second category of robbery we have already noted, (since capital arises out of labour), with the State acting as the agent of the original robbers of the land rent.

It is not the business of the social fund to rob from the individual one – any more than it is for an individual to rob from the social fund – (as happens inevitably now, with rent's privatisation: both in its direct appropriation, and in its appropriation via false capital values). *Both* funds belong, by definition, to different spheres of operation and of use. In any healthy society, it is obvious that the State must "cut its coat to fit its cloth". Indeed, we insist on this for the private citizen, so why not for the State? It is a measure of the fairy-tale world of economics we inhabit, that we imagine it should be otherwise. Society, rightly, does not allow the individual to run up debts he cannot pay. It is extremely foolish of us to allow *the State* to do so, for if the State goes bankrupt, then – living in the extremely vulnerable kind of society we live in – (based on huge inputs of bogus wealth, formed of paper money, land rent *monopolistic* values, confusion and dishonesty) – we will *all* go bankrupt with it.*

* *A word on "pollution taxes", which have come into vogue in recent years as a proposed measure to deal with the appalling environmental destruction wrought by our system of land monopoly. It may be that, so far have we travelled down this destructive pathway, society will wish to weave in certain anti-pollution taxes at the beginning, even under this reform.*

Standing a little further back from the scene, we can only view these as a temporary measure. It is not natural for any species to "foul its own nest". But how are we to expect the dispossessed to regard it as ***their*** *nest? They are only here on* ***sufferance****. Let it* ***be*** *their nest – and be felt to be their nest – by local re-empowerment based on local rent collection, and the fouling will gradually be exposed for what it is: a part of the baggage of an unnaturally constructed society.*

*As for the major fouling accomplished by today's dispossess****ors*** *– majorly built, as we have seen, on their dominance of capital, which will not longer be theirs to command: this fouling will automatically decline on account, also, of the premium placed, by this reform, upon the utilisation of land and resources – which will no more be able simply to be bought outright and done-as-you-please-with, as now, but will be required to be maintained to a sustainable, ecological standard; while, correspondingly, the taxes at present placed upon labour are done away with, encouraging the intensive use of manpower rather than of resources, to the benefit of both.*

What can one say of the kind of agreement to emerge from the Kyoto conference of winter 97-98, whereby pollution limits are recognized as ***marketable commodities****, with the right to pollute to such-and-such a degree a saleable asset? It may be part of the still corrupt pathway we have to tread out of our illimitable corruptions. But a fully self-respecting society, such as can only build itself out of a full rspect for the Earthly Mother, must regard the concept of* ***tradeable pollution rights*** *with disgust.* (This final para added Jan. 99 S.A.H.)

Perhaps we can see now how far we have become benumbed and brainwashed in our thinking. Elsewhere in this volume are placed some powerful words by Professor Mason Gaffney, on precisely the brainwashing that goes on apace in our universities (Britain being no different in this respect from the U.S.A.) No wonder one frequently finds clear thinking and the ability to grasp fundamentals far more evident amongst those who have had *no* university education at all! But of course it is the university-educated ones that "guide" the economy! Hence the dire situation we are in today.

A further enormous reduction in social costs is the reduction in both prisons and hospitals that would follow on this reform. But that is something we shall look at in Part II. The final reduction in costs to the economy to be mentioned in this section, is one that I find a cause of endless mirth. So let's share it! The taxes we fund ourselves with are already, of course, a self-defeating device – hitting the productive worker on the head and penalising production in a nice variety of ways. But Graham Hart, in his booklet already referred to, points out something else. Namely, that the State, as the biggest purchaser of society's goods and services – (now there's a thought in itself!) – has to spend a huge part of that tax-payers' money which it has collected *in*, in buying *back* again, along with the goods, those very taxes which it has levied! As one might say – *some levity!*

We have already pointed out, too, how the State's obligation to support jobless families lands it with paying those rents-at-monopolistic-settings . . . which those families are in the first place saddled with paying precisely on account of the State's support of land-rent robbery! Just how many more of these shootings in the foot – slammings of itself on the head – scoring of own goals – our State tax system has managed to "decorate" itself with . . . might well furnish a thesis for a doctorate in comedy! We are clearly swallowing our social fund in double gulps – so high on the mon(k)ey tricks of the taxation ride, that the proverbial visitor from Mars wouldn't know where to make head or tail of us!

*

To saner scenes! Of a society based on justice – and not on the terrifying departure from justice that is the mark of ours – Henry George wrote once that even the richest man, on hearing of it, would gladly sell *all* his possessions to buy entry to it for his children. And surely this is no surprise – particularly in view of Heililg's warning words; who, as an investigative journalist, and forced to endure the horrors of Hitler's regime, reached through to a profounder understanding of today's scenario, by far, than any of our politicians have done.

Let us then look at the situation of those who are today's rich, and whom Henry George's words above might be addressing. We are all human beings – we *all* bear responsibility for our rotten democracy – and drastic changes can be difficult for anyone to meet. Let us look with an impartial eye.

Firstly – what of those who live largely, or in part, on land rents, but on such a tight margin that they are not, (as the large rent receivers are), involved in the capital investment scene of stocks and shares? What of those who struggle to maintain large estates, the costs of which the rents hardly meet?

The good news, surely, is that their days of struggle will be over. No longer will they feel obliged to struggle to uphold the long-standing family tradition of a long-standing family estate – (which the payment out, of the rental dues, might well now make impossible). For the new ethos abroad tells us plainly that the whole of this Planet is really but one large "family estate", for sharing by *all* of its children.

But such people are usually, in any case, those most heavily involved in the land *not* just as landholders, but as workers themselves – heavily investing both mind and muscle to make a go of it. Surely they are the very ones to be drawn towards this reform; and to be drawn, also, to the burgeoning "permaculture" school of land-use – (see Address List) – with the chance of working out their own applications of its principles to some challenging Scottish terrain. As these principles are apt to be labour-intensive, it might make sense for the present landholder to concentrate on the more "home-ground" part of such an estate – (most probably the part to which the strongest attachment is in any case felt); whilst others, no longer in the rank of tenant, took on the care of other parts similarly. Or perhaps, by agreement, the whole could be run co-operatively, amongst people who already know each other so well. A better life for all would surely result.

And what of those who live heavily off capital-invested income – (whether or not *direct* receivers of land rents)? Very many of those who do, and who are not of retirement age, are very probably engaged in an active occupation of some kind, in any case, even if it does not qualify as "paid" work in our society. But then, our society has some funny ideas as to what work deserves "payment" – (not to mention what kind of "work" is actually fit for human beings at all . . .) Let us remember, that it will not be today's bleak work-place scene that we face, where opportunities to "do our own thing" are locked up with the land. C.M. Hussey – (see the outstanding article on Ireland, *Ireland – Land and Peace* in Part III) – has imaginatively captured something of the change that would occur, in writing of it – "A free land system has a constantly renewed internal frontier of opportunity". The stranglehold on job opportunity today, exerted mainly by the giant companies, is – like the stranglehold on real capital – at bottom a *stranglehold on land.*

It is difficult to think of anyone – even anyone who today chooses idleness – not *wishing* to contribute to such a different society. Similarly, it is hard to imagine those today working in frequently dead-end jobs of State employ, (and of course liable to sudden redundancy, as with every other mass employment agency), or indeed, to think of any enterprising individual – including the many who earn their living today on the stock-markets – *not* preferring that "constantly renewed internal frontier of opportunity" offered by a society basing itself on justice, and on real wealth.

We should reflect, in addition, that such a society will gradually develop a very different outlook. Not – How much can I get?, but – How much can I give? – is likely to become its watchword. Just how possible will it be for anyone to live in such a society, with any esteem, who is not making their fair contribution to it?

*

I realize that the scene of the just society is far more complex than would of course appear, from what I have here written. It cannot be otherwise. To refer again to Lindy Davis's *By the Way*, already mentioned – (see Part III): "It's complex out there." For – "It appears to be a universal law that truth is simple, and the further we stray from the truth the more complex things become". (Mark Hassed, in *Progress*.) The thing for us to do is to hurry back to simplicity – the good foundation of simplicity offered us by this reform. The thing is – to make the adventure. For the adventure, being dedicated to a fundamental right, cannot but bless us; and will doubtless of itself teach us, as we go, the accompanying steps that we should take.

I realize, of course, that today's stock-markets are international, so, unless there should occur some sudden general economic catastrophe, Scotland's reform of her own rotten democracy would not find their overnight demise. So the land dues that would be paid into Scotland's – (*hoped-for* 100%-real-wealth) – land rent fund, would also be coming in part, doubtless, from wealth reaped in those overseas markets, where monopolised land rent and its ersatz from of capital still parade. But mark what Outhwaite – (fuller paper in Part III) – has to say upon this:-

> "The land monopolists, laden with tribute rendered up by the citizens, utilize it to acquire tribute rights over territories abroad; so, too, the capitalist slave-masters. The wage-slaves not being allowed to consume what they produce, the capitalist employer seeks markets abroad."

So – just as we saw with capital: the "wage-slaves" are too impoverished to be able to keep in their own hands – and exchange with one another – the *real* wealth that they produce. The elaborate competition for overseas markets is all a charade! The home market is crying out – the purchasing will is there – but, on account of the robbery of labour, it is *robbed of its economic clout.* (And we can crown this from Ogilvie himself, paras. 18-22.)

The answer is wide open to us. Once rid of these robberies at home, Scotland could see that bogey of "foreign competition" out! And in addition to the ending of all that false struggle, the rental dues paid over to the community from that *home* market would bless our social fund with an intake of *real* wealth.

Of what incredibly beautiful working-out are the ways of Providence! One is reminded of the saying: for every step you take towards the Highest, *It* will take a hundred steps towards you. Nor are these by any means fanciful words. The same truth is powerfully expressed by the German poet, Goethe:-

> "Until one is committed, there is hesitancy, the chance to draw back, always ineffectiveness. Concerning all acts of initiative (and creation), there is one elemental truth, the ignorance of which kills countless ideas and splendid plans – that the moment one definitely commits oneself, then providence moves all. All sorts of things occur to help one that would never otherwise have occurred. A whole stream of events issues from the decision, raising in one's favour all manner of unforeseen incidents and meetings and material assistance which no man could have dreamed would have come his way.
>
> Whatever you can do or dream you can, begin it. Boldness has genius, power and magic in it. Begin it now."

*

Are we then at the brink of a *real* Scottish Enlightenment at last? – Not that one which percolated *downwards* from an intellectual élite, but one which travels *upwards?* Nor just from the intellect, but from the heart and guts of a *whole people*, and enters into the whole land . . . ?

Let us turn again to Ogilvie and remind ourselves of what it is we "endure" – Ogilvie who saw so clearly the destruction spawned by our system of legitimized, legalized robbery: joblessness, homelessness, the consequent breakdowns in health, mental and physical, and the further twists of the dreadful, downward spiral into vandalism – drugs – crime – suicide . . . Henry George points out that a society can still be preening itself on its advances when the ebb-tide has *already set in.* (See Part III.)

Let not those who happen to be particularly involved in monopoly – whether through land or capital – feel that they bear any peculiar burden of guilt for our situation today. The guilt and responsibility for this situation, as Ogilvie pointed out, belong firmly to us *all* – who have ignored and tolerated the present system far too long – too often just concerned with finding our own niche in it. It must be said, in addition, that most are quite ignorant as to how the system works.

Finally, people can be locked into their positions, in such a society, on the upper just as on the lower side. There is a saying of the North American Indians: before judging another, it is well to walk ten miles in his moccasins. Let us delay not, therefore, in foolish fields of guilt or blame. *All* are needed, for the task ahead will require of us a united effort.

In fact, it is not only the exploited who are the unhappy ones. Those who are positively occupied in the exploitation of others are unhappy too, whether they know it or not. Why? Because their self-preoccupation has cut them off from the human family. Peel away enough layers, and even the *Seven Wise Masters* will be found to have the same human needs as all of us – needs which all their material splendour and glory can *never* supply.*

To Ogilvie, the self-destruction built into our system was plain. Quietly as he phrases it, he refers to a "sinking state" (para. 9). Well he knew that a society founded on land monopoly *must sink*. Let us attend to his words, then – for it may be that, in speaking them, he had cast his mind forward prophetically to our very time – a time when the power of that monopoly would be bringing forth those "maturer fruits" which would finally bring it down.

Amidst this fateful jumbo-jamboree in which we are all involved – stretching planet-wide – have the Scots got it in them to establish an island of sanity somewhere? Economic sanity is rooted in *land sanity*, and it is an extraordinary thing that a knowledge of land sanity should have formed so special a part of the history of the Scots. It was my own amazed discovery when, in the early 1980s – (from someone into whose hands *The Land Question* had fallen) – I received, from across the Atlantic, a book carrying in it a chapter entitled "Forerunners of Henry George".** It was my reading of this which first made me aware that a grasp of land economics is something in our very blood. If this be so, then no matter how long we have been turned away from it by those who would have us forget, *we were bound one day to remember again.*

Scotland holds in her bones some of the world's most ancient rocks.*** The subtle power and vibration of rock should never be discounted. Did not Jesus say, "if these should hold their peace, the very stones would cry out"?

The "lost" knowledge and understanding of a people, along with their emotions – and especially those emotions born of great suffering such as land clearances – are assuredly stored up in the rocks of their environment. And that stored-up knowledge and emotion assuredly waits there – a battery of power, yet undischarged, awaiting its time . . .

We have only to cultivate the quality of *listening* – that deep, inner listening native to us all – and we shall understand again the power that is within us – the power of a people to fulfil their destiny – that destiny which Ogilvie so powerfully, a*nd not alone*, foresaw.

S-A.H. Nov. 97.

---

* *I am reminded of the syndrome, in Russian literature of the nineteenth century, of the "superfluous man" – a depiction of those rarer, unhappy, questing souls of the Russian aristocracy, who felt themselves to be unaccountably "unnecessary" to society – cast, as it were, upon an elevated and sumptuous kind of rubbish dump. They could never work out just* ***why*** *it was they were so "unnecessary", or how to deal with it . . . Yes, how much the Russian upper classes, as well as the lower ones, were in need of Henry George!*

** *From: The Single Tax Year book, edited by Joseph Dana Miller. (The Single Tax Review Publ. 6., New York, 1917.) A copy of this chapter will be placed with the National Library of Scotland.*

*** ***The Holy Land of Scotland****, by Barry Dunford. (Brigadoon Books, Aberfeldy, 1996).*

William Ogilvie

A Broader Sweep

*

Pathways Travelled

3) WHOM THE GODS WOULD DESTROY . . .

*

(c) "Whom the Gods Would Destroy . . ." *

In probing the meaning of wealth we have found that, even as "all that glitters is not gold", so – *all is not wealth that so parades!*

There is another way – apart from economic catastrophe – in which planet-dwellers are made aware of this from time to time. An uncomfortable way! The gods have kept a special card up their sleeve for any society that shows itself in too hot pursuit of wealth of the ephemeral kind – those monopolised rental values!

There is something that a society which is too pre-occupied with the "pseudo" gradually loses sight of. . .and so loses control of. *Loses control without noticing.*

Yet it is the very thing that above all else it *should* be noticing. Because it involved that thing that above all else man on this earth has need of, (and so – need of *access to land* for, of course), and that is FOOD!

Man is in love with his own inventiveness. Just think! After *Dolly* – our cloned sheep – we've produced. . .a *Polly!* So resistant are we to thinking there is anything we haven't got real control over – the thought of it so appals us – that our very vocabulary is marvellously adjusted to hide the fact from us. Thus – one no longer hears speak of agriculture today. It is always the *agriculture industry!* (Oh and – the *water industry,* most certainly, of course!)

Because, with industry, *we* do it, you know. *We* are the magicians that do the producing! There – Dolly and Polly!

The thought of "agriculture" without "industry" frightens us. Can it really be there is something out there that is *not* due to our "industry" – *not* subservient to our manipulations – and that one day could even expose the awful pseudo-ness of the pseudo concept of wealth we are locked into?

Afraid so! There's *soil* out there! And man – agricultural industry man – hasn't a notion how it works, what its real needs are, or what – the secrets of its fertility.

. . .And so the day arrives which the gods have kept up their sleeve – the day when a sackful of bank-notes won't buy a loaf of bread. . .

Soil – soil that's mistreated – *strikes back.* The difficulty for us is that soil is silent. It doesn't audibly cry. Nor does it visibly move or alter. Not, that is, unless we look hard. And unless we listen hard. But we are not accustomed any more to such looking and listening. . .in this ear-assaulting environment we have created for ourselves, with its flashing T.V./video screens. Along with a number of other things, soil is something that we just don't notice any more. . . Even when it is blowing away...

But in the "great and good" books - the kind of books that are now out-of-print – there are plenty of warnings for us:-

> "Money and mechanism are the character of the civilization in which we live. They ... are the power of our present day; we ourselves are their offspring; to imagine anything else is a mere attempt to escape from their reality. But a yet greater reality than they is the soil. Historical periods of culture and civilisation come and go, but the soil, the producer of life, is lasting ... And, if a civilization is such that it degrades the soil, then it is the civilization, and not the soil, that comes to an end." *Such a danger threatens our present civilization."* (Dr. G.T. Wrench. Emphasis added. See also Part III.)

It is already half-a-century now, since Dr. Wrench wrote those words – and it is just as well for us that there are a few copies of his book still to be found lying around here and there ...

---

* *For those not familiar with the saying, its concluding words are* – ***they first drive mad!***

But then Dr. Wrench goes on to say an extraordinarily interesting thing. He says: "It is from the pivot of that threat" – (i.e., of the destruction of our soil) – "that thinkers send their encircling gaze. . .with such a change of values, *and not with political, social and economic alterations without any transvaluation of values,* that (they) are concerned". (Emphasis added.) *

How remarkable a statement from Dr. Wrench! For have we not just been looking at this very thing? We have seen the false transvaluation that we have made – of our original social land rent fund – from being a social asset to being a personal one. We have seen the havoc that this has caused in our lives. And finally, we have seen the need for a transvaluation *back*, of those false values we have adopted – (the need for a *re-cognizing* of that fund as our true social revenue) – as the first and necessary step to re-claiming it, and so, taking at last the essential path back to justice – and solvency.

But it is no surprise that Dr. Wrench should have spoken to us in this way, for he was well acquainted with the work of Henry George.

Both Dr. Wrench and William Ogilvie, like Henry George – (and so many others kept from our knowledge) – understood the destruction to a society that follows from the privatising of land rent. They saw very clearly that that false step had to be *undone*, and that, this once accomplished – once the rental payment was collected again, annually, for the community, from every landholder – the role of land in our society would suffer a radical change. No longer able falsely to parade as capital, (on account of the rent's being *annually* collected), land would at once become a liability to hold, instead of an asset. A radical re-distribution of the land would then take place naturally, of itself.

This is why neither Ogilvie nor Dr. Wrench – nor any other writer on this reform – would have anything to do with futile attempts to re-distribute land *physically*. Such individuals fully understood that the real attraction in landholding lay in the accruing rental convertible-to-capital values. All the rest – the "glamour" of the highland chieftain scene – followed upon *that*. Land, once converted to a capital asset, was a *business proposition first and foremost*; and such has remained. Once the business profitability disappears from the scene, the "glamour" will disperse as the charade it is.

That charade has mesmerized us for so long, that we find it difficult to believe it can ever go. But let us remember that the real glamour drawing people to highland estates, is the glamour of being regarded as people who *know where to invest money* – i.e., who are not fools! That is the way round it is, and not vice-versa. And that ideawill be stood on its head, once the community decides to ask for its land values back. Those who genuinely love, live on, and care for the land, will assuredly not be deprived of land to care for. They will have land – the land they can genuinely care for; having regard, that is, to the rental that must be paid annually to the community for it. And those thousands who long to do so, but have never had a chance, will be able to love, live on, and care for land too – in a *direct relationship*, not as someone else's tenant. For such the land is crying out.

If any of us still harbours any doubts as to whether it is land regarded *physically*, or land as a *producer of rental values*, that is the more fundamental and desirable feature of land monopoly – and hence the one that society is really required to deal with – these doubts will readily be removed by a reading of A.J. Nock's remarkable book, "Our Enemy the State", an extract from which is included in Part III.** It is interesting that, in the following summary of the matter – (the words to which emphasis has been added) – Nock does not actually include the word "land" at all. He is here writing of the land-grab that followed America's War of Independence, when previously British-held land fell into the lap of the victors:-

> "Professor Sakolski observed drily that 'the early land-lust which the colonists inherited from their European forebears was not diminished by the democratic spirit of the revolutionary fathers'. Indeed not!. . . The primary

---

* *Dr. Wrench, writing in the earlier part of this century, referred to "thinkers" and "agriculturists" as separate groups – which was truer of that time. Today, agriculturists and thinkers are likely to be the same people – and all the better for that.*

** *See also Reading-List.*

monopoly, fundamental to all others – *the monopoly of economic rent* – was sought with redoubled eagerness." (*Note*: the term "economic rent", as already noted, is used by classical economists to denote the *rental value of land*. S-A.H.)

We might also reflect upon the dramatic transformation of Denmark's entire economy, during the merely three years (1957-60) in which she enjoyed *merely a portion of* the full capture of her land rent, (see Part III). . .and reflect that this was scarcely due to the placing of geographical limitations upon some country land-holdings!. . .and reflect, also, upon the fact that land cannot be dealt with simultaneously extent-wise *and* value-wise, since the two methods are inherently contradictory – (see Part III, The Law of Rent, and note thereto) – and that it is only by the method which assesses land *value-wise* that the community can collect back its rents.

It is difficult for us to shake off the idea that it is the land as a geographical entity that must be gone for, and that some attempt must somehow be made to take hold of the land physically and divide it up – (an absurd proposition in any case, with people perpetually coming and going, and new arrivals on the earth each day too). Land rental values are the invisible "other side" of the land coin – which is carefully omitted from our educational syllabuses. But they are by far the most potent one. People may perhaps have wondered to themselves whether the land will really allocate itself under this reform. Our difficulty is that we do not pause long enough. . .to consider fully enough. . .what is really involved in this very fundamental, radical measure. Once we do this, however, we will gradually come to see the way that this measure will operate: that the rental values will re-distribute themselves – to the community, away from private coffers; and that the land – once shorn of its "asset" attributes – will find its natural re-distribution, following upon that.

Let us remember, too, that those like Henry George and William Ogilvie, who came to write so clearly and forcefully upon this matter, themselves spent many years probing it to its depth. (See Ogilvie's Introduction to his Essay here.) Moreover, not only did they give their minds to it. The hearts of both were equally dedicated to the task. For both – like so any others who have written on this matter – were profoundly moved at the amount of human suffering they saw around them; and it was *this* that, in fact, initiated their searches. Those who have invested both heart *and* mind in such a task, and over so long a period: such are worthy of our attention. You have a portion of Ogilvie's text here, fully evidencing his feelings for those he saw as victims of an unjust and oppressive system, and I am reminded at this moment of Albert Einstein's words on Henry George:-

> "Men like Henry George are rare, unfortunately.
> One cannot imagine a more beautiful combination of
> intellectual keenness, artistic form, and fervent love of justice."

To return to Dr. Wrench and his insistence upon a transvaluation of those rental values: what did he see as its connection with *soil husbandry*?

The extracts from Dr. Wrench's work, (written in the earlier half of the century) – included here in Part III, trace the tragedy of the soil's role as a community asset being, under this system, sacrificed to its role as a source of personal and private enrichment for its "owners". For a while (as will be seen from these extracts) the impoverishment was mainly of the peasants, and less of the soil – though the goodness was stolen from much of the land to be concentrated upon that of the lord of the manor. But in Ogilvie's 23rd paragraph we find a pointer to soil destruction that is particularly relevant to our day. Ogilvie noted how the land used for commerce, being more intensively used than that in use for agriculture, made for a considerable *increase in the rental values* of the land so used – and therefore also in the rents pocketed by its landholders.

So it will always be. The more intensive the use of an area of land – the greater the production that can be reaped from it – the higher its rental value will inevitably stand; and this tendency – where rents are for private pocketing – will tend inevitably, in turn, to the herding of the people *off* the soil, and *into* the industrial areas, in order that those higher rents may be extracted from them. . .while the soil-industry that remains, (since people must be fed), is in turn made progressively more intensive, so that *its* rental values – (hence in turn – capital values, and hence collateral at the bank) – will similarly rise as high as possible.* And here we have the *raison d'etre* of today's *intensive farming*. It has nothing to do with agriculture as such, but everything to do with the *enhancement of land rental values under land monopoly*. We note in Ogilvie's Essay how he spoke of agriculture remaining in the doldrums, while manufacturing industry was steadily advancing. They had not yet, of course, in Ogilvie's era, discovered our "progressive" techniques of intensive farming – nor yet stooped to the cruelties to the animals involved in these "intensive" systems, which are basically *land-rent-intensive* systems, as we now see.

---

* *It is sometimes queried whether the collection of land rents for the community will not cause land to be exploited. As we can see from the above, the situation is the other way round. The utiliser of land in a just society is not concerned with* ***raising*** *the rental value of his plot. Far from it! He is concerned solely with meeting the rent due, according to the assessment placed on it by the community. It is entirely open to – and up to – a community not to assess their land at an exploitative level; and this applies particularly, of course, to agricultural land, which should always be assessed according to its best* ***sustainable, ecological use****. As the valuation rolls will be permanently on public view, and hence open to public challenge, the assessments will reflect the* ***community's consensus*** *on this.*

Just the reverse of this system operates, of course, when the rent is not something the individual has to pay out, but is able to pocket – (and more particularly when one considers how higher rental values make for a higher capital value of the land, and hence – as already pointed out – greater "collateral" at the bank). What greater incentive to exploitation of the land – and of its labourers – than under such a system, could there possibly be? Note also that he who despoils land, under the community revenue system, will still (if that community treasures their land) be required to pay a rent reflecting its ***previous sustainable ecological use****. In short, there are a number of ways in which the community's collection of its land rents can be used as a tool for the benefit of the land, as well as of the people.*

Finally, it would get rid of the almost unbelievable stupidity we at present indulge in, of paying out thousands, even tens ***and even hundreds*** *of thousands of pounds to landholders (frequently the already very well off) . . .* ***not*** *to utilise their land. . .for whatever reason. Under community land rent collection, what will the situation be? Simply: the rent which would have been required will be foregone by the community – not asked of the landholder. And that will be that – full stop. No question of any payments* ***out****, from the community to the landholder, can possibly, under this system, arise. And the day will come when people will ask themselves how they could possibly have allowed successive governments to rook them for so long, for obscene payments like these.*

When one considers, on the one hand, the munificent hand-outs to people. . .to do nothing – people already possessed of that primary human necessity which money can scarcely buy nowadays, LAND; and considers, on the other hand, the impoverished DISPOSSESSED masses, whose "benefits" (such we term them) are being cut to shreds: the ***immoral groundwork of our society is surely placed on full display****.*

When one considers, further, that ***all of*** *that "set-aside" land (bar maybe a few SSSIs) could be put to a 100%* ***people-friendly, soil-friendly*** *use under permaculture (see on), providing work, and homes – (self-built, why not?) – for countless families at present deprived of both: we surely show ourselves as a country with assets on all sides we SIMPLY DO NOT KNOW WHAT TO DO WITH! – except to throw away. Land into idleness, and people onto the streets!*

It is this kind of madness – (now what was the heading to this note?) – this kind of craziness and corruption combined, operating shamelessly in our midst – helped forward by the dulled acceptance of a people ***totally disempowered:*** *it is this kind of scene, (paralleled in too many other departments of our life), that has prompted – (small wonder!) – the later chapter in this book, "Community and Re-empowerment". And let it be suitably capitalised at this point: COMMUNITY AND RE-EMPOWERMENT. Of suitable acronym – C.A.R.E., too!*

It will be as well for us to take a deeper look, while we are about it, at this matter of agriculture, and the rental values that get so destructively mixed into it, under land monopoly. Let us recall that initial master-stroke that pushed off the Common Market boat in the early 1970s: Sicco Mansholt's grand design that pushed off five million peasants – off the land. Off those more peasant-intensive farms that hadn't quite caught up with our more machinery-intensive ones yet. To be "absorbed" into industry, of course. . .

> "The plan's basic premise was that the community's farming population of 10.6 million should be reduced by five million. . .
>
> "The plan provides for the possibility of enlarging individual farms as well as for amalgamations. . . at the same time, anyone who wants to carry on alone with an uneconomic smallholding can remain an 'independent yeoman farmer', at the cost of living poorly. The choice will be up to the individual. For a while, some farmers will keep their smallholdings out of sentiment, and because they know no better. But not many will be left by 1980, if only because of fuller information through the mass-media and education. (Extract from an article on the EC's agricultural policy by Sicco Mansholt, its main architect. Published in "European Community", Nov. 1970. EEC Press and Information Services.)

So – if you don't make the right choice, my friend, you'll be brainwashed till you do! Now we know the real interests that "education" serves in the EU – (as in any land-monopoly-based State – or mega-State). And now we know what interests the "mass-media" and "information" serve also! (And how right the Scots are to take exception to that decision of Westminster to retain control of our media!)

Yes, this is the bullying, arrogant – and of course thoroughly anti-sustainable-ecological – set-up we joined back in the 1970s. An interestingly naked statement of its aims from nearly thirty years ago. Things have moved on since, of course. Ecology has arrived in a big way, and the public is more aware. We wouldn't have such a raw statement of the matter today! It would be more sophisticatedly *dressed up* for us. But that is why it is so good to look back to this plainer statement, at the start of this business. For *business*, of course, it was. No matter how idealistic the individuals may be that serve in those Euro-ranks, it alters not one whit the basic concept, and intent, of the Euro set-up, now known as the *European Union*, whose structure still essentially serves those vested interests it was set up to serve: a set-up arrogant, bullying – and primarily fixated, (as Nock pointed out, of the American revolutionists *following in the steps of their European forebears*), on all the profits possible to be made out of monopoly. For a closer scrutiny of this mega-State, A.J. Nock's "Our Enemy, the State" provides, indeed, an incomparable study. (Let us note something else: *Common* Market into *Com*-m-*unity* into *Union*. A clever and deliberate progression – the merely economic transformed by gradual stages to the supremely political!. . .while the prefix "European", becoming dominant as the first word, ensures that this progression is barely noticed! . . All nicely pre-planned and pre-packed. *We're suckers for it!*)

Yes – that was the racket we joined! But only the beginning of it, of course!

Next came all those "intensive" butter and beef mountains that couldn't be sold. . . (produced by all that *land-rent* farming) – and all those refrigerators a nice little added bonus too – (assembled, no doubt, by those lucky peasants "absorbed" into industry!) For don't say those *poor farmers* are going to have to pay for all this? Certainly *not*! It wasn't for *that* we set up the Euro-thing! Forward the tax-payer! (Well – wasn't that what we pocketed the rents for?) Subsidies – *subsidies to the rescue*!

Is this a joke? Is it the Mad Hatter's Tea-party we've paid entrance to?. . .a tea-party held in some new kind of milking-parlour. . .quietly set up for another kind of "milking" alongside the cows? – with the stuff that's siphoned off in it. . .kind of gravitating back to that field of land values again. . .?

Can we not just hear Ogilvie say it! – "U.K. in – SCOTLAND OUT!"

Ogilvie knew, just as Wrench did –(although it did not appear so vividly yet in his time)– that the disaster of land monopoly was **dual**: for the destruction of the people, and driving of them from the land, would mean the destruction of the nation's soil.

Why so?

Because soil happens to be *alive*. How would you, a human being, like to be tended by machines instead of human hands? Well, neither does the soil like it, either – and nor does its offspring – *which becomes our food.*

It is not only we who are needing to "bury our hands in the soil", as Barry Lopez said. The soil needs us to bury our hands in it, too. And unless we do, we won't be able to get the food we need to keep us healthy – because the soil won't be able to give it to us. (And note that trio, "health, wealth and happiness". Is not health placed at the front?) Then finally, by this progression, the soil won't be able to keep us at all, either healthy or unhealthy.

What, then, of our vaunted tourism? Where are those tourists who will be able to fill our bread-baskets. . .when they are themselves at home looking for bread? The true riches of a nation are *its land and its people* – and should a nation forget this, a sharp reminder may very easily arrive in unwished-for ways. How clever of the gods to have anchored man's absolute needs so absolutely in what is beyond his control! – to have anchored man so firmly to *reality*, notwithstanding all his desperate attempts to occupy himself elsewhere!

Meanwhile the "silent" soil is crying, dying, under artificials, poisons and heavy machinery – bereft of human hands. . . Bereft of human hands, its structure destroyed – blowing away in the winds. . . It is not intensive farming, but intensive loving, that the soil is asking us for. The topsoil is blowing away planet-wide – *that topsoil which alone is capable of growing our food.* Let the wisdom of Ogilvie remind us that, in the absence of land monopoly, the tendency would be for a country to carry "the greatest number of independent freehold cultivators" possible, (para. 45). This being so, in the event of catastrophe either economic or ecological, that nation which had given top priority to the nurturing of its soil might then have some chance of feeding itself – and of feeding others too.

Could Scotland survive outside of Europe? Let us pause a moment to recollect that free trade (world-wide) is the entirely natural concomitant of free-ed land. But as Henry George so clearly states in "Protection or Free Trade", free trade – the original, totally natural, activity of human beings trading freely with one another across the world – does not stand a chance under land monopoly. Hence the inevitable magnetism of Europe for an *imperialist land rent robbery set-up*. In short – like is drawn to like! As we saw in the previous Note – (and ref. Outhwaite, Part III) – the endless cry for overseas markets is false in origin, stemming only from nations whose peoples, under the intolerable yoke of land monopoly, have been to such an extent impoverished that their own naturally buoyant *internal* markets cannot operate – since the people have not the wherewithal to buy the goods that they themselves produce – or to pay for that they might, in freedom, choose to import. *Remove the restrictions at home* – and cease to cry for overseas aid! In taking this step, we shall not only survive in a market world-wide, we shall resurrect ourselves from our present calamitous state. To anyone who reads Henry George's masterly book, *Protection or Free Trade*, it is plain that the true solution to the European question is: let the Scots take back their land, and be no more a slave to the European land monopolisers than to those at home!

In the sphere of the production of that basic necessity, FOOD – in the sphere of agriculture – the growing permaculture movement of the latter part of this century is fortunately demonstrating how entirely practical a people-intensive form of production can be, even in this "modern age". Permaculture – (started by Bill Mollison in Australia some twenty years ago – see Address List) – teaches how to weave human needs in with the land – human needs for food, shelter, fuel and other necessities –whilst making use of the environment in an entirely sustainable, ecological way. Planet-friendly and habitat-friendly as well as people-friendly, permaculture must surely be *the* land-use of the future for the human race; in particular since trees – which we have need of absolutely for *breathable air and water alike*, (see further in Part II), are fundamental to any permaculture design.

People-intensive permaculture, like any other movement of sanity on this planet today, requires of course the *de-monopolization of land*, to allow the re-occupation of the land by the people. But the land monopoly set-up is so frightened of seeing *people* back on the land that they are promoting every other idea possible for farming, from deer to llamas to ostriches. Soon it will be zebras and giraffes! That "agricultural-industry" business (whether Euro or U.K.), being an entirely land-rent-robbery specimen, is the most unsalubrious set-up concerning land use, in every way, that could be devised. Its achievements were once brilliantly described by Aldo Leopold, author of *Sand County Almanack*, as "improvements to the pump – not to the well".

These words of Aldo Leopold's have come peculiarly true with the news, in early November 97, that the underground water level in England has now fallen to an unprecedented and alarming low – such that people are being requested not to pump out of bore-holes any more. So "improvements to the pump and not to the well" is coming home to roost in a very literal way! Once upon a time people looked to the land and learned from the land – but then we invented "agricultural colleges", deserting our one and only real one – and since then we have understandably lost our way. But does not Aldo Leopold's saying also well sum up our entire *soil*-destroying, *soul*-destroying monopoly-and-taxation structure, now bringing us down to the inevitable bankruptcy of *its* bore-holes too? – to the inevitable bankruptcy that always lay at the bottom of that distorted delving after. . .a lost social fund?

It is trees which raise the water-table. They are our incomparable water-resource against both drought and flood. But *agricultural-industry man* pays scant attention to trees. We have no need to mourn the passing of that "agricultural industry" in any respect. Its tendency has been, inevitably, to de-sensitize those engaged in it. We can scarcely blame the farmers – crushed as they have been for decades under "economic necessity" (so-called). But it cannot escape observation that the movement to retrieve, from often appalling sufferings, the animals involved (crusades such as that against live export and battery-rearing, Market-Watch, etc.), have all had to be initiated by ordinary people, not engaged in farming at all.

It is in this matter of values that the conversion of rent – *downwards*, from a social to a personal asset – has been so particularly tragic for us. For it seems that, once we moved away from a sane dealing with the rents, a whole tribe of insanities – for which the gods might indeed wish to destroy us – have followed on our heels.

In contrast, we turn to the sanity of the classical economists – that placing of land in a category of its own. We have noted the ecological statement made by that placing – but it goes further than this. Science is more and more catching up, today, with the view of the earth as a living being. (See Fritjof Capra in Part III.) So would not this put the buying and selling of the earth into the same category as the buying and selling of human beings? Indeed – into a yet worse category if the Earth is *our mother*? It is soleminizing to read the words of the Essene teacher in Part III, and find that all man's foreseen terrible destructions of the earth have, as their terrible precursor, that man "shall sell his Earthly Mother into slavery". Can it *ever* drive home to us, as we go about our fields and gardens – our roadside verges and tourist-orientated landscapes – that in our casual poisoning and polluting of them, it is OUR MOTHER that we are polluting and poisoning?

Much can be learned about a society from the way it treats its land rents. As Dr. Wrench points out, it is not just an outward change that we are asked to give our attention to here. A "transvaluation of values" takes place on the inner side also – and *that inner change always comes first.*

It is those who seek a society based on different values who will bring this reform about.

*

WILLIAM OGILVIE

AND THE

STATE OF SCOTLAND TODAY (1996)

*

A Word on the 1998 Revision of

WILLIAM OGILVIE AND THE STATE OF SCOTLAND TODAY (1996)

*

This chapter remains essentially as written in 1996 for the proposed Scottish Ogilvie Society publication (as recounted in the chapter *The Making of This Book*).

Some restructuring of it was found necessary, however, in extracting it from the different layout of that book; and that work allowed some other small revisions of the text as I went along.

*

William Ogilvie and the State of Scotland Today (1996)

William Ogilvie (1736-1819), Aberdeen's 'Rebel Professor', was one of Scotland's remarkable succession of proto-Georgists – men whose work preceded by a considerable period the great work on land reform of Henry George, the famous author of *Progress and Poverty*, published in 1879.

At the time when Ogilvie lived, Scotland had long lost her freethinking liberties, along with her parliamentary ones, and was well under the strictures of the Parliament at Westminster. This had made it a 'penal offence even to question the land laws'.[1] That Ogilvie managed to write and publish his remarkable work (most copies anonymously) and *still survive*, was due solely to his displaying, in his own sphere, something of the battle skills of William Wallace Braveheart. Outside of his teaching work at King's College, now part of the University of Aberdeen, where he won both the affection and high esteem of his students, Ogilvie played the role of 'an ingenious recluse', while yet being involved with the great men and movements of his time, both in Europe and America and even in the East.

The edition here of his work *Birthright in Land* omits certain sections of less relevance for us today. But even the omitted sections have considerable interest, for in showing how strenuously he attempted to persuade a passageway for his radical ideas through the stultifying contemporary scene, they reveal the great generosity of Ogilvie's spirit. For here was a man resolved, by whatever means possible, to better the condition of the humblest and poorest of his fellow men. His work reveals him as equally capable of having followed a career in law, or in agriculture, and since he was equally highly regarded for his knowledge of the natural sciences, and of art, his great versatility can only be wondered at. Of agriculture he had plentiful first-hand experience, since – all the more credit to him for his work on land reform – he came from a land-owning family.

As for the passages here presented: the marvellous range of Ogilvie's 'speculative enquiries' (as he called them) added to the profundity of his penetration into every question that came under his gaze, must mark him as truly a Gulliver among the Lilliputians of his time – or any time, including our own, as we shall see. No wonder then, if he and Robert Burns sought solace in each other's company (incognito to the world, of course, for as to the times and places of such meetings, the wit and wisdom of an Ogilvie and Burns combined would almost certainly have ensured the covering of all traces).

Ogilvie possessed – doubtless in secret, like Burns – a copy of Thomas Paine's 'forbidden' *Rights of Man*; and how those two great empathisers with earth's downtrodden must have rejoiced in Paine's masterly summary of the land question thus: "The Earth being the birthright of all mankind, its rental is the natural property of the people ... Every proprietor owes to the community a ground rent for the land which he holds". (see D.C. MacDonald's *Biographical Notes* for a fuller discussion of Burns and Ogilvie.[2]) As we shall see, Ogilvie's views are fully applicable to our own time, capable of resolving a host of economic problems – on which to this day we remain tied in painful knots.

It was D.C. MacDonald who, in 1891, re-published Ogilvie's *Essay on Property in Land*. He made of it a composite volume, entitling it *Birthright in Land*, and providing for it his own preface to the *Essay*, along with some remarkable biographical notes on Ogilvie – (both included in this present volume). D.C. MacDonald must have

---

[1] *Professionalism and History by Frank Dupuis. Land and Liberty Press Ltd., 1962.*

[2] *Also: A FEW WORDS on the Strathconon Chronicle, S-A.H., April 1998.*

been a most interesting man himself. He lived, moreover, at a time when anecdotes and memories of even the time of Burns and Ogilvie could have been passed down by word of mouth[3] with a still living resonance – (something that the din of today's media would have done much to obliterate). Both his knowledge of, and insights into, the times of Ogilvie and Burns – (as into his own times indeed, *and ours scarcely less!*) – along with his insights into the links between Burns and Ogilvie, make fascinating reading.

The Biographical Notes on Ogilvie open with a veritable drum-roll on the law, and more particularly on the Instrument of Sasine. Thus we discover that one of the highest and most sacred of all Scotland's laws handed down to us is one that enshrines an act of brigandage! *The origin of the word Sasines is Seizings*![4]

Here is how MacDonald, writing at the turn of the century, sums up the consequences for society of this Instrument of Sasine: "The law is not administered by the judges in our law courts, because they are only the agents and nominees of the landlords. They administer only landlord-made laws." Here is the scene in its broader historical context – (I quote again from Dupuis): "During the earlier period of constitutional monarchy, 1688-1833, the landlords as MPs and magistrates governed England openly and directly" – (Scotland too, of course, after the Act of Union, 1707). "Thus all our 'traditional parliamentary liberties' developed safely for landlordism. To question the land laws was made a penal offence. For a moment, after 1832,[5] landlord power trembled", but as the extension of the franchise brought no reform of land tenure in its wake, so the *in*direct power of landlordism, still operating in society through multifarious channels, "*has proved just as effective as direct power.*" (Emphasis added.)

Of peculiar poignancy for our times is the account given, in the Appx. to the *Biographical Notes*, of the stand taken by the Skye crofters – inspired by Henry George – at the time of the Battle of the Braes. Would that we might hear from the crofters of today words of equally generous longing extended to their fellow men! – not to say, words of equally penetrating perception as to the *root cause* of their sufferings. Alas, how is the spirit of Scotland diminished since that time![6]

Let us now turn to a closer appraisal of Ogilvie, and review his Essay in the light of today. Of how great relevance is his work for us?

Ogilvie wrote for a mainly agricultural society; yet the full round of his gaze encompasses practically every problem with which our society is right now so befuddled, and in every case shows to us its roots. *These roots lie invariably in the structure of land monopoly* – the continuing curse of our times, as it was of Ogilvie's.

Consider simply the following points, culled from the pages of Ogilvie published in this volume:-

1. That it is more important to control the monopoly of land than the monopoly of money. (Cf. "It is easier to do without money in a time of land shortage, than without land in a time of money shortage.")

---

[3] *Indeed, see the words accompanying the portrait of Ogilvie at the front of this volume.*

[4] *The Register of Sasines – a register of transactions affecting land and property in general – may be inspected at Meadowbank House, Edinburgh.*

[5] *The Reform Act of this date.*

[6] *Since the writing of this chapter, I have added from MacDonald's work a chapter on the Seven Wise Masters. S-A.H. April 1998.*

2. That it is not the *amount* of land held that counts, but its *value*. (Yet discussions on land reform today still get bogged down on the question of amount!)

3. That it is the landowners who benefit all the way from the development of commerce, moving easily from land monopoly into *monopoly capitalism* – for the poor must always rent land for houses and work. (Yet we still overlook that today's great capital accumulations – including those of the multinationals – stem from land monopoly. Hence we fail to understand that our society is not a *capitalist* society, but a *monopoly capitalist* one.)

4. That the burden of taxation falls always on the poor – the rich escape it. (Just as we see today!) Then how on earth do we think we can go on funding our social services from taxes rather than rent – killing the goose that lays the golden egg, whereas *rent simply removes a windfall gain*. We are so obviously on the high road to bankruptcy – yet most people, or even groups, still cannot reach beyond the persistent determination to better their own slice ... of a disastrously diminishing cake. By contrast, it is generally assented, by those who have studied the matter that, were the rent of our land used as revenue, there would be sufficient surplus from it also to pay a basic income to every citizen.

5. That it is folly to blame mechanisation for putting men out of work. (Trades Unions struggling with redundancies from today's high-powered technology – *take a look at what's underneath you*!)

6. That it is immoral to impose wage restraint on the labouring classes. (Trades Unionists again – you've missed your great champion!)

7. That in times of unemployment people should be given access to land to employ themselves. (Could there possibly be a more crying need for this policy than there is today? And in this very direction, the people themselves, who best understand their own situation, are already moving forward *ahead* of government, turning into productive permaculture gardens the cheerless emptiness around city blocks and other derelict and unused sites, and turning hooligans into horticulturists on the way. As Henry George urged it, *the people themselves must think, because the people alone can act*.)

8. That it is a great mistake for a nation to tax its commerce. (Surely the small businesses of today should be pricking up their ears at this, even if the big businesses – which are involved always with *land* business – are less keen. And does not this suggest also that the conflict between labour and capital – *true* capital, not that propped up by land investment – is false? ... as also, of course, that continual 'creation of jobs' refrain, in a land still lacking in basic housing?)

9. That our present desperate search for overseas markets follows a deluded pathway. (Free trade is the natural concomitant of a society whose land rental values are returned to the people – the people themselves being the natural beneficiaries of both)

10. That the chief obstacle to the rapid improvement of agriculture is the monopoly of land. (Yet we still remain focused on land *use*! Moreover, as to this 'land use' and 'improvement of agriculture': what *would* someone of Ogilvie's penetrating eye have to say about today's soil-destructive chemical practices? Or – a man of his compassion – about our modern methods of livestock farming? Both of these, of course, offspring of the same *monopoly capitalism*, arising from land monopoly, which rapes the land – and landscape – of Scotland, just as it does the people.)

11. That short leases stifle cultivation of the land. (So – what of Scotland's latest legislation on this? Could it be that it is farmer *landlords* who shape the policies of our National Farmers Union?)

12. In a society heading downhill, even the rich and powerful are not impervious to misfortune, so that it would be very much in their own interest to help better the situation of *all*.

13. That the flaws in state charity are inherent and irremediable. Ogilvie's observations on the social outworkings of the Poor Laws of his time constitute a no less damning indictment of our own Welfare State: both having equally arisen as false answers to the *underlying injustice of land monopoly*.

As we see, Ogilvie has *considerable* relevance to Scotland today. But then, like Henry George, he was a man of *vision*. And always it is the same issue *underlying* all these observations upon which he focuses our gaze. He compels us at last to see that land monopoly is an issue our society *has* to face, if it is ever to break out of the system of feudalism which holds us, today, as ever, in its grip.

With Scotland now moving towards some form of self-government, the question will surely arise, sooner or later, of making our own laws – and what more fundamental than the laws on land tenure? But if we are going to get it right, we will have to start studying *now* Scotland's own radical thinking on this matter. If we do this, we will discover that we do not need to look beyond our own borders – beyond the message of Ogilvie himself – in order to satisfy the aspirations of our people to a just share in their own land.

Finally, with all the scorn being poured out on Scotland about a 'tartan tax' – just let us see how Ogilvie allows us uniquely to wipe the floor with our mockers. A tartan tax, indeed? The nation that produced a William Ogilvie? For that matter – a tax of *any* kind! -? Why, we Scots are not so ignorant as not to know very well that taxes are born to enrich the rich and impoverish the poor. Rather we will rid ourselves of these taxes altogether, and take our revenue instead from the rents of our lands, as the Scots of old have taught us.

The light cast by William Ogilvie upon Scotland today is a powerful one. It is impossible to read Ogilvie's words and *not* to understand that a mere tinkering about on the surface of things will achieve nothing. We must go to the *root* of the matter, and free the land – as he has shown us how to do. We must cease to be deceived that we can cut any pathway forward for ourselves, without examining the underlying structure of our society: that rotten structure of land monopoly which underlies *all* our social – and environmental – ills.

In this great task, there is no reason why the 'highest' in our land should not join with the 'lowest' – inspired by that amazing example set by the Duke of Gordon and other nobility, in William Ogilvie's time, in the North East of Scotland – (undoubtedly considerably influenced by Ogilvie himself) – of whom MacDonald gives us fascinating glimpses of his *Biographical Notes*. For those earls and dukes, along with Ogilvie and Burns – (nor let us forget the exceptional 'Reverend', John Skinner, amongst them) – were, as MacDonald tells us, practically the *only* radicals in Scotland at that time.

That these members of the nobility should have championed the work of William Ogilvie – both in his attempts to free Aberdeen University from exclusiveness and bigotry, *and* in his radical thinking on land reform – surely betokens that truly generous democracy of spirit which has at times, here and there, illumined our past.

Those in positions of power or privilege today, in *any* sphere, are free to show an equal magnanimity. They no less can help to forward the tides of change. It needs the 'highest' as well as the 'lowest' in the land to build that happier state where man to man shall brothers be.

So the human heart longs ...

So Burns has foretold it ...

And already we can sense it –

- *Comin' Yet For A' That*!

*

WALLACE TO HENRY GEORGE :

SCOTLAND SPEAKS

(1996)

*

A Word on the Revision of

WALLACE TO HENRY GEORGE - SCOTLAND SPEAKS
(1996)

*

This chapter remains essentially as written in 1996 for the proposed Scottish Ogilvie Society publication, but – as with the the chapter *William Ogilvie and the State of Scotland Today* – some minor re-structuring was necessary in extracting it from that earlier context, and this allowed some other small revisions of the text as I went along.

The opening part of the chapter will be familiar to some readers from the article I wrote in September 1995, and which was published by the Scottish Ogilvie Society under the title *Braveheart*.. When a 'modern commentary' was sought by the S.O.S. for its book, it was proposed that this should be supplied by my writing an extended version of the *Braveheart* article; and that is how it came to be developed into the present chapter.

*

... *Scotland Speaks* (1996)

We all equally arrive on this planet from some mysterious Beyond. Yet, upon arrival, some find themselves having to pay others for living space. We pray, "Thy will be done on earth as it is in heaven". What a mockery of Christianity!

Let us enquire: to whom did the *first* man to stake out a claim to land pay money for it ...? Well then, what is he doing *taking* money for it from someone else -? Isn't it obvious that the name of the game is power? – the power of the few over the mass of the dispossessed.

The outcome of this game is inevitably an increasing number of those who, having no right of land upon which to work their skills, become the 'unemployed'; looking to others for the opportunity to labour – and beating down wages against each other in that bitter, bogus struggle for work. But the existence of a cheap pool of 'unemployed' to call upon has ever been one of the winning aces of those who hold the cards of power.

Any attempt to deal with the land question, therefore, which fails to deal with *dispossession as a whole*[1] is manifestly but skating on the surface of things – betraying the real claims of the dispossessed, and turning a deaf ear to those growing hordes now clustering in our cities without a roof. In the words of Solzhenitsyn: "And while some danced happy and carefree with songs and music, others shed tears which no hand could wipe away ... How did this happen? How could such a gulf have opened out?... Why is it that some words, even though spoken distinctly and out loud, are incomprehensible to some human beings? The words fade away and disappear like water – without taste, without colour. Without a trace."

To restore to the dispossessed their minimal right of *justice upon earth* – to remove the monstrous power obtained by some over others through pre-empting earth's living space – we must remove, in its entirety, the bogus selling-price of land. That is, we must remove its *capital value*, this being the base upon which the right to monopolise land is founded. How shall this capital value be removed? There is *one way and one way only*, and that is: by society's collecting the full rental value of its land, site by site – or holding by holding – from every occupant every year. For it is *this* value (entirely community-created) which – left lying upon the land uncollected – then yields to the claim of ownership by the 'owner' of that land; and it is purely the on-going expectation of this privately collectible rent which builds on to land its false capital value, its lucrative selling price ... which in turn makes an investment asset of land, yet further encouraging monopoly.

What then, are we doing with conferences on land reform that propose, for example, merely restrictions on the buying of land by foreigners? What can this possibly achieve except a larger field of expectations for our own grandees? – while the poor wretched rent payer remains trapped precisely as before? Or why focus reform on areas of land above an acre? Phew! – what price half an acre of prime *city* land? It is the *entire bogus apparatus of our present land ownership system* that needs to go.

We have recently been re-awakened, by the film *Braveheart*, to the courageous life of William Wallace – 'Guardian of Scotland' deservedly named. What we now need is another film, linking William Wallace's great endeavour with that of another William –

[1] "Expropriation must precede exploitation" – A.J. Nock in Our Enemy the State. (see Reading List) This book reveals the role of the state as a fundamental supporter of land-monopoly-based power.

William Ogilvie of Aberdeen, who 500 years later dedicated himself no less to the freeing of the Scots, by his radical writings on land reform.

For Wallace also gave attention to this matter. Issuing a *direct* call-to-arms to every able bodied male between the ages of sixteen and sixty, he cut straight through the bonds of vassalage which held tenant subservient to landowner – and the people flocked to his standard from all parts. Thus by a bold act of supreme statesmanship Wallace called into being, at one stroke, an independent body of people – a body standing in stalwart opposition to the unscrupulous power of the nobles, and calling itself (in the legal Latin of those times) *Communitas*. (It may be asked: where is there any comparable *Community*, to this day?) Those were the days before political presidents. But how could Wallace, at its head, ever have been called anything but Guardian? – a title which has ever remained unique to him.[2] And something else: the Scots referred to their kings only as 'Kings of the Scots' – they were not trusted further. But Wallace was made Guardian of Scot*land*.

Thus did Wallace place his country an incalculable stride beyond her contemporaries, by establishing for a brief period the *first true democracy in Europe* – democracy, a word whose Greek origins mean literally 'people-power'. (Demos – people + kratos – power) People-power, the real thing – that is, the decentralising of power and placing it back into the hands of the people – has, of course, no possible place where the centralising power of land monopoly operates ... assimilating so easily to itself as it does, in turn, *State* power. For this reason, democracy in Britain today, as in Europe, remains but pretence. (What do we really think can be hoped for from our *European Community*? – mockery of that earlier *Communitas*, indeed!)

It is undoubtedly the spirit of Wallace which shines through the most powerful passages of the Declaration of Arbroath, and who knows if some of the words of it did not come straight from the heart of the founding document of Wallace's *Communitas* (Paisley, 1292), of which all records have been lost – or rather, await our rediscovery ... ?

What tragic decline of Scotland has followed upon those earlier times! – the joining of her Crown with that of England in 1603, and the Treaty of Union that followed in 1707, being the main stepping stones thereof. For no 'upper house' ever stained the democratic principle while Scotland had her own parliament – ("that folks might not be bothered with the same blethers twice told", as it was more humorously put!) – and her single chamber enjoyed a remarkably democratic representation for those times, the Elected element in it having roughly 147 seats, to the nobles' 67. Thus, settled in our own parliament, "the final word on the vital Land Question would have been spoken, not by title-inheriting English Peers in London, but by elected Scotsmen in Edinburgh; in which case the ruinous depopulation of Caledonia could never possibly have occurred. The Scottish peers could never have long held up any ardently desired Small Holdings Bill, because they would have been routed in every encounter by Scotland's Elected Persons.[3]

---

[2] *Following Wallace's great victory at Stirling Bridge on 11th September 1297, he and Andrew Moray (who had rallied forces from the north towards that victory) were made joint Guardians of Scotland. Sadly, however, Moray died from his wounds within two months, so that, for all practical purposes, the title has belonged to Wallace alone.*

[3] *See Leaves from the Book of Scots by Morrison Davidson, the Scots Secretariat, formerly of Carlops by Penicuik, undated. Contents suggest the early years of the twentieth century. (See Reading – List)*

... Scotland Speaks (1996)

During the darker days that followed the Treaty of Union, however, the torch of Scotland's liberty was still kept alight, if in quieter ways. For William Ogilvie was not alone in grasping that the question of land tenure – which is, as he realised, the question of the *right to the pocketing of land rents* – reaches to the very heart of the question of liberty. Because of the strictures placed by the parliament at Westminster upon the free discussion of such matters - ultimate insult indeed to a free thinking people like the Scots! – so Ogilvie remains exceptional in his far-reaching and brilliant treatment of the subject, until those strictures were lifted with the Reform Act of 1832.[4] But let us at least record here the names and dates of those others – *so far known* (for much is silence in Scotland's history) – who were familiar with the arguments concerning land reform as centring upon the question of *Land Rents*.

There was Cadwallader Colden (1688-1776), from Duns, who went out to America; Kirkcaldy's Adam Smith (1723-1790) who, D.C. MacDonald assures us, had to cut chunks out of his *Wealth of Nations* as being far too outspoken on this matter; from Fife, Robert Fleming Gourlay (1778-1863), known as Scotland's Greatheart, whose political career was in Canada; from Fife also Thomas Chalmers (1780-1847), author of *Political Economy*, whose funeral was attended by half the population of Edinburgh; and Dr. James Anderson of Edinburgh, who, Henry George himself tells us, was the *first* to formulate the Law of Rent – (that natural law, whose first statement is usually attributed to Ricardo, hence known as Ricardo's Law of Rent), Finally, Patrick Edward Dove (1815-1873), from Lasswade near Edinburgh, writing after 1832, was at last able to do so openly, and to put his name to his writings, giving us his scholarly work *The Foundation of Social Justice*, passages from which show him plumbing the matter as clearly as Ogilvie.[5] Will research ever reveal, I wonder, whether Ogilvie's book came at some time into his hands?

Like Ogilvie, Dove wisely appealed, in his writings, to the *best* in the nature of those he addressed, including the land owning element – and indeed there were land owners in their times with fully enough honour to acknowledge the justice of this reform. It should be pointed out that Dove's references to England in his text, rather than to Scotland – which seems strangely puzzling at first (and echo Ogilvie's silence on Scotland) – simply reflect the familiar pattern of those times. Thus was the well known hotel at Edinburgh's Waverley Station (as a scattering of such hotels throughout Scotland) christened The North British, the endeavour of the establishment being to obliterate as far as possible the Scots' recollection of their own distinctiveness and individuality!

Patrick Edward Dove was the more remarkable in that, like Ogilvie, he came of a land-owning family. His nature, too, was of the same nobility as Ogilvie's; a landowner who never recognised the concept of trespass, and who was greatly loved and respected by all.

Finally, Scotland is not without her share in the genius of Henry George. For he who was the moving force behind the Highland Land League that fought the Clearances of that time – (has even *this* fact reached our classrooms today?) – and who inspired those

---

[4] *See ch. William Ogilvie and the State of Scotland Today.*

[5] *This information has been gathered from the chapter 'Fore-runners of Henry George' in the Single Tax Year Book (Quincentennial), edited by Joseph Dana Miller. The Single Tax Review Publ. Co., N.Y., 1917. See Biographical Notes for mention also of Thomas Spence. An extract from Dove's work is published in this volume.*

brave and generous words of the Skye crofters at the Battle of the Braes – tells us himself that "my mother's father was a Glasgow body". Perhaps, in view of Scotland's pre-eminence on this matter, it was inevitable that Scottish blood should have flowed in the veins of the man who fathered the twentieth century movement for land reform. (His book *Progress and Poverty* has been translated into numerous languages, and sold more copies than any other book of its era, except the Bible) Was it not perhaps inevitable too that the movement in Britain, inspired by Henry George's visit at the end of the last century, should have taken off first *north* of the Border?

More recently, the influence of Henry George has been at work in Russia. For representatives of the Georgist movement, coming together from across the world just after the fall of communism, have been working with some of Russia's top land policy makers, and have already played an important part in helping to prevent the passage of land legislation false to Georgist (i.e., *justice*) principles. In turn, Russia has been re-discovering her own legacy of thought on this matter, in the writings of Leo Tolstoy, through David Redfearn's fine book.[6]

Naturally, not a whisper of such top battles on land policy in Russia has been relayed through the West's media. Nor do we have the faintest inkling of such a fascinating bit of history as that, following the February 1917 Revolution in Russia, "the Kerensky Government planned to introduce Georgist land and tax reform. The plans crystallised during the summer – but too late; the Bolsheviks struck in October, before the reform could receive a full public hearing." (Fred Harrison, *Land Policy Council*, 1993. See Address – List)

Such a libertarian reform would naturally have been anathema to the Bolsheviks. *It would also have been anathema to the land-monopoly-based powers of the West.* Now we can begin to understand the saying that the Russian Revolution was financed in part by Wall Street. Yes! Far from being a 'defeated nonentity', Henry George has been a shaper of world history – to some effect! Nor is this Russian saga the only example of it.[7]

Thus we can see that the work of William Ogilvie in Scotland two hundred years ago stands in the *direct* line of mankind's advance, right up to this century, in this continuing endeavour to establish at last radical economic justice on earth, via enlightened land reform.

Is it not then pitiful that, having so many illustrious souls among our forebears, Scotland should have reached such a state of decline today – indeed, of social collapse, with the scale of homelessness, drugs and crime? A mass of people are eagerly at work, trying to tackle these social problems. But how many of them can see clearly what it all links back to: that profound alienation and hopelessness – aggravated by sheer poverty – which is rooted in the first place in our *dispossession from the land*? It is this – *this* – that we must bring our understanding to bear upon, if we would tackle our 'intractable social problems' at root.

---

[6] *Principles of a New World order, by David Redfearn. (Obt. From the Henry George Foundation. See Reading – List)*

[7] *See Reading – List. (March 1999. I had intended to add further material re this – but am defeated by time! Readers will no doubt enjoy making their own explorations.)*

... *Scotland Speaks* (1996)

How is this to be done? We must regain the knowledge of where we came from. We must take to ourselves – and to our hearts – those chapters of our history which have lain too long shamefully buried from our sight. For in order to re-awaken hope, it is not enough to resurrect a knowledge of our past's *tragedies*. We must resurrect also that *knowledge of the teaching of liberty* which has burned as a small brave candle through all our darkest times: that is, the clear perception of our direct relationship to the land as something striking to the very core of our existence – because it lies at the heart of freedom and happiness, something which Wallace understood so well. Once we have come to understand this, we shall then begin to see that what Wallace began is OUR TASK TO COMPLETE, and that it is a task for every single one of use. For from our hidden-up history we shall discover that our forebears unfolded a practical reform for society today – one capable of carrying forward Wallace's great first step.

But that vitally important teaching bequeathed to us by our forebears remains still hopelessly under cover – and so will remain for as long as our educational system is in its present hands – that is, in the hands of a *monopoly-structured establishment*.

How then cut a pathway forward, if we are forever brought back to the same place? We can set up our own educational workshops. We can take the initiative in *educating ourselves* on our hidden-up past. So shall we re-learn the only true basis of democracy – of *people power* – and be able at least to expose today's sham of a democracy for what it is. So, gaining an understanding of the false road by which we have come to where we are, we can at last fit ourselves to take matters into our own hands: to remake our history, and this time to *make it aright* – after the pattern that Wallace would have had. Yes – that same pattern of FREEDOM for which he struck so great a blow.

For we will take to ourselves again our land. We will all, even the humblest among us, find our original and inalienable stake in it – empowered by the recognition gained from the study of our past that the *land is fully ours to take*. We have to reclaim, *for* the community, those rental values which are *community-created*, and so set in motion the workings of a powerful, natural law. Once we do this we will come to discover in our own experience how both land and wealth undergo, of themselves, a radical re-distribution – rendering superfluous any proposed bureaucratic apportionments of land, along with the whole falsely based structure of taxation besides. In this way we shall bring to an end our present state of economic serfdom, and inherit instead that inspired vision of a true society which Wallace saw and held out to us – seven hundred years ahead of his time.

What is the practical requirement for establishing this pattern, once the educational work is done? We have to *change the laws of land tenure via land rent reform*. We must free ourselves from the present falsely created system of land ownership, which is both a shame and an affront to us. We must rid ourselves of that *Sasine law of brigandage*, which holds the land of Scotland in servitude even as it holds her children too. Then, and then only, shall we honour him who was truly Guardian of ScotLAND.

But, as our painful history has made fully plain to us, we cannot hope for any alteration to those laws – nor for any alteration to Scotland's sunken state – until *out of full independence* –

SCOTLAND SPEAKS AGAIN!

D.C. MacDonald's

PREFACE

to Ogilvie's Essay

*

D.C. MacDonald's

PREFACE

To Ogilvie's Essay

*

This work was written between 1776 and 1781, about a hundred years before Mr. Henry George wrote his *Progress and Poverty*.

Both authors traversed the sorrowful jungle of Political Economy, and both discovered "the central truth". The independent testimony of the one is corroborated by the equally independent testimony of the other.

The same truth was revealed to John Locke between the years 1680 and 1690. And is there any doubt that it was seen by Moses, David, Socrates, and a host of prophets, poets, and philosophers, ages and ages before?

Do we not find the *Birthright of Man* stereotyped in the words "OUR FATHER"? The Faiths of the world, ancient and modern, whether considered natural or revealed, have all something in them, in common with genuine Christianity, which declares "*Equality of Rights*" between man and man.

"Whether," says Locke,* "we consider natural reason, which tells us that men, being once born, have a right to their preservation, and consequently to meat and drink and such other things as Nature affords for their subsistence, or 'revelation,' which gives us an account of those grants God made of the world to Adam, and to Noah and his sons, it is very clear that God, as King David says (Psalm cxv., 16), *'hath given the earth to the children of men,' given it to mankind in common.*

"As much land as a man tills, plants, improves, cultivates, and can use the product of, so much is his property. He, *by his labour*, does, as it were, enclose it from the common.

"God gave the world to men in common ; but since He gave it for their benefit and the greatest conveniences of life they were capable to draw from it, it cannot be supposed He meant it should always remain common and uncultivated. He gave it to the use of the industrious and rational *(and labour was to be his title to it) ; not to the fancy or covetousness of the quarrelsome and contentious*." And adds Professor Ogilvie : "Nor yet that it should be appropriated in such a manner as that, when not more than half cultivated, the farther cultivation and improvement should be stopped short, and the industry of millions willing to employ themselves in rendering the earth more fertile should be excluded from its proper field, and denied any parcel of the soil on which it could be exercised, *with security of reaping its full produce and just reward*". "This title to an equal share of property in land" is declared by Professor Ogilvie to be a "BIRTHRIGHT *which every citizen still retains*." We shall see how far he advanced the question towards the standpoint of *Progress and Poverty*.

"The reform," says Mr. Henry George, "I have proposed . . . is but the carrying out in letter and spirit of the truth enunciated in the Declaration of Independence – the'self-evident' truth that is the heart and soul of the Declaration – 'That all men

---

* *Essay on Civil Government.*

are created equal ; that they are endowed by their Creator with certain inalienable rights; that among them are life, liberty, and the pursuit of happiness!'

"These rights are denied when the *equal right to land* – on which and by which alone men can live – is denied. Equality of political rights will not compensate for the denial of the *equal right to the bounty of nature.* Political liberty when the *equal right to land* is denied, becomes, as population increases and invention goes on, merely the liberty to compete for employment at starvation wages. This is the truth that we have ignored."

Such being the disease, what is the cure?

"It is necessary," says the Philosopher of Pittensear, "that the object to be aimed at, and the means by which it may be obtained, should be again and again stated to the public in a variety of speculative views, and so rendered familiar to the understandings of men.

"Internal convulsions have arisen in many countries by which the decisive power of the state has been thrown, for a short while at least, into the hands of the collective body of the people. In these junctures they might have obtained *a just re-establishment of their natural rights to independence of cultivation and to property in land,* HAD THEY BEEN THEMSELVES AWARE OF THEIR TITLE TO SUCH RIGHTS, *and had there been any leaders prepared to direct them in the mode of stating their just claim, and supporting it with necessary firmness and becoming moderation. Such was the revolution of 1688, at which time, surely, an article declarative of the* NATURAL RIGHT OF PROPERTY IN LAND *might have been inserted in the Bill of Rights,* HAD THE PEOPLE AT LARGE BEEN BEFOREHAND TAUGHT TO UNDERSTAND THAT THEY WERE POSSESSED OF ANY SUCH CLAIM. *Such also was the late convulsion in America (1776), the favourable opportunities of which are not yet exhausted.*"

It is interesting, as well as instructive, to notice the harmony that pervades the writings of these three Apostles of *Man's natural right to independence, his liberty to labour, and his Birthright in land.* John Locke stirred up the English Revolution of 1688, and in doing so he set a good example to the rest of the world, and raised his country to a glorious position among nations. We are only beginning to see this now. William Ogilvie was neither an idle spectator of the French Revolution of 1789, nor of the American Revolution of 1776. The man who regarded Revolutions as "favourable opportunities" for restoring the natural rights of mankind was, like John Locke, a practical philosopher.

Mr. Henry George, as a political philosopher, is equally practical. He is a child of 1776, *in spirit and in truth!* He is a Lockist as regards the right of labour – labour being the title and also the measure which alone can give to the individual an exclusive right of property in natural products. And he is an Ogilvist (which is only a logical development of the Lockist) as regards man's BIRTHRIGHT IN LAND – the basis of the SINGLE TAX, and the door through which LABOUR may freely enter into possession, and enjoy, not a mere portion of its fruit, which some tyrant may set apart, but "its full produce and just reward".

Sad and strange to say, amidst our boasted civilisation, our profession of the Christian Faith, and our avowed belief in one impartial God, all knowledge in regard to the just and equal right of mankind to participate in the bounties of Nature, has hitherto been systematically boy-cotted. Until recently, the teacher of such principles was treated by *Law and Order* as a dangerous criminal. John Locke had to take shelter in

Holland. William Ogilvie had to conceal himself under a bushel in Scotland. Many a noble son of Erin had to mount the gallows, while thousands suffered imprisonment, and millions were exiled from that unhappy country – a country which is still held like a mangled corpse in the crocodile jaws of commercial landlordism ; and the monster will not let go its hold except on one condition, namely, to be allowed to gorge itself with British *blood.*

But why not utterly destroy this monster? What better service for our soldiers, blue-jackets, and policemen, than to employ themselves in destroying this common enemy of mankind? Parliament could do it, a royal warrant could do it, the sufferers have a right to do it, nay "every man hath a right" to destroy such monsters.

"In transgressing the law of Nature," says John Locke, "the offender declares himself to live by another rule than that of reason and common equity, which is that measure God has set to the actions of men for their mutual security, and so he becomes dangerous to mankind ; the tie which is to secure them from injury and violence being slighted and broken by him, which being a trespass against the whole species, and the peace and safety of it, provided for by the law of Nature, *every man upon this score*, by the right he hath to preserve mankind in general, may restrain, or where it is necessary, destroy things noxious to them, and so may bring such evil on any one who hath transgressed that law, as may make him repent the doing of it, and thereby deter him, and, by his example, others from doing the like mischief. And in this case, and upon this ground, *every man hath a right* to punish the offender, and be the executioner of the law of Nature."*

The benevolent and magnanimous Professor Ogilvie had this passage before him when he wrote the first section of his Essay. In a foot-note he says: "It were unjust to censure the proprietors of land, however, for retaining and exercising, as they do, a right whose foundations have not been inquired into, and whose extent no one as yet controverted". Then he goes on to explain that ignorance is the root of the evil. There were many cases to which the modified doctrine of Professor Ogilvie would apply, *e.g.*, the "humane landlords of England" of his own time, and some of the princes of ancient times, "who lived for the happiness of their people". The *commercial* landlord, who, he tells us in the same note, is "of all citizens the most pernicious," who burkes all inquiry into the foundations of his right, and who with the aid of lawyers and priests, fills the eyes of mankind with the dust of ignorance, he would leave to be dealt with in accordance with the principles approbated by Locke. We should not degenerate from these principles, and it is to be hoped that few readers will grudge the references here made to the once famous, but now forgotten – strangely forgotten – writings of one of the best of men, and one of the greatest philosophers the world ever produced, namely, John Locke.

Professor Ogilvie, who came after Locke, devotes himself in this treatise to one subject – *Birthright in land*, it may be called. And the Author may be justly styled – *The Euclid of Land Law Reform.* He was left little or nothing unsolved in connection with the Land Question. He has given us a true base line – man's equal right to the raw material of the earth, to the air, to the water, to the rays of the sun, and all natural products – from which we can work out any problem, and by which we can test the "title and measure" of every man's property.

---

* *The renowned George Buchanan, the great-grandather of British Liberty, puts it even stronger than this. (See Biog. Notes).*

Resting on this base line – man's natural rights, – Ogilvie represents to us the perpendicular line of *man's right to labour*, "with security of reaping its full produce and just reward". Here we have the question in a nutshell. Take away the base line, and you have *no right to labour*, and *no produce or reward*, except what may be meted out by the usurper of your natural rights. You have to beg for leave to toil! We thus see clearly how the robbery of labour may be prevented, and how impossible it is to put a stop to such robbery while the industrial classes neglect to claim and exercise their natural right – their right to an equal share in the earth, and all its natural products.

Strikes against low wages, high rents, unjust taxation, absurd conflicts between capital and labour, rebellions against this or that form of government, are futile skirmishes, and very frequently are of the suicidal cock-fighting order, at which the real enemy, elevated on a grand stand, simply laugh. To contend successfully with these evils, society must learn to begin at the source thereof.

While labourers are content to remain deprived of their natural rights, they must pay whatever ransom the brigands who have seized these rights choose to demand. Not only is industry robbed, taxed, and crippled, but the brigand, as dog-in-the-manger, very often puts an entire stop to it, and thus the happiness and comfort of millions of mankind, who are willing to work, are curtailed or wholly sacrificed, and misery and starvation reign instead. I am somewhat afraid to say hard things against brigandage. An institution that is still propped up by *Law and Order*, and supported by (or winked at) on almost every hand by the avowed servants of Jesus Christ, must be touched with a "gentle hand". William Ogilvie has done so in the *Essay* now before us. Although a landlord himself, he did not disregard the truth, and it will be found that his pen was guided by an impartial and benevolent spirit. I do not require to introduce the author to the reader. He has written his own Introduction.

It may, however, be noted that the practical schemes propounded in the *Essay*, were intended only as "examples and beginnings of reformation," to use the author's own cautious language, and should be read as such, and in the light of the circumstances of his own time. Let the reader then peruse once more the closing sentence of the *Essay* and the author's note thereto, and ponder over the contents of the work, comparing his own ideas with those of the author, before coming to a hasty decision, and let no scheme for the happiness of mankind be rejected without at least attempting to substitute and promote a better one. The reader, in applying the author's principles to the present time, and having regard to present and future circumstances, will find that these principles are not of the hard and fast kind, but that they are in accordance with Natural Law, and therefore may be accepted as eternal and universal in their application.

When a child is born, we recognise that it has a natural right to its mother's milk, and no one can deny that it has the same right to mother-earth. It is really its mother-earth, *plus* the dew and sunshine from heaven and a little labour, that supplies the milk and everything else required for its subsistence. The monster that would deprive a babe of its mother's milk, or would monopolise the breasts of several mothers, to the exclusion of several children, is not more deserving of being destroyed than the monster who seizes absolute possession of more than his share of the common mother of mankind, to the exclusion of his fellow-creatures.

Now, as these monsters are comparatively few, and were always a very small minority of the human race, the question naturally arises, Why the vast majority submit – why, in short, they do not destroy such monsters without a moment's consideration? How are the monsters guarded? By policemen? – No. By soldiers? – No. By gunboats and blue-jackets? – No. By Law Courts and bailiffs? – No. By the magical of the sovereign? – No, we do not now believe in the divine right of kings. By what then?

In order to perpetuate landlord serfdom, it is necessary to keep our mothers systematically ignorant of their children's birthright. A theology is invented. By a most unchristian system of law and theology woman is regarded as an inferior being, while man is elevated to the position of a God – a Creator!* Thus robbed of her natural position, and of her equal rights in her own sphere as a parent, she brings forth her children; and her children are treated as bastards, denied the right to draw one breath in their native land, unless the parents beg permission of the landlord. They have to pay for the right to live on *his* land. They are victims of humiliation and extortion from the cradle to the grave.

The strongest force connected with human nature is maternal affection. The pagan priests knew this – hence the reason why they always made it their chief business to subject womankind to ignorance, superstition and slavery. The Jewish priests treated women very much in the same way, notwithstanding the distinct commandment of Moses, who, by the way, must have *honoured* his mother fully as much, and deservedly so, as he did his father.

Were we to probe history properly, we would find how much the influence of women has had to do with all the great reforms – the great revolutions by which the world has been blessed. Jesus Christ attempted to raise woman to her natural position, but His followers have discarded His doctrines. The Apostle Paul seems to have been more of a Jew than a Christian in regard to the status of woman; and it suited European feudalism to follow the Apostle rather than Christ. Hence woman's position in the Christian Europe of today is much lower than it was among the pagan Celts and Goths, who, as Plutarch tells us, *honoured their mothers*, as well as their fathers, by giving them a place and a voice in their legislative assemblies.

Is it for the benefit of society that we have excluded maternal instinct and its immediate influence from our legislative Councils? Our brutal, unjust and unnatural laws will answer this question. Take, for example, our "Reform Acts", passed since 1832, as they now stand, and imagine if anything so hopelessly jumbled could be put together by an assembly of crazy old women. Our Land Laws, looked at as a sample of legislation by males, present to us a dense jungle of iniquity, full of thorns, briars and bitter fruit. What hold has an Englishman of his house while some lord owns the ground on which it stands? Our Land Laws furnish ample evidence that one section of humanity cannot adequately perform duties which naturally belong to humanity as a whole. To clear that jungle, to reclaim the land, and to settle the question of man's birthright, society must utilise the full strength, genius and natural instincts of undivided humanity, without distinction of sex. If men, in common with the males of other animals, are characterised by boldness and strength, do we not find that women, in common with the females of other animals, are in some respects superior to men in sagacity and instinct? Even in regard to boldness and strength the female should not be despised. The world has produced more than one Joan of Arc.

These thoughts are placed here before the reader because it is "devoutly to be

---

* *This is a relic of paganism – the worship of males. The worship of the sun* ***(on sundays!)*** *had its origin in the belief that "he" pro-created new life every Spring. This very ancient religion is not British. The* ***grian*** *(sun) of the Celts is not a* ***he****, but a goddess with "golden locks", and so – with the* ***Bard of Avon*** *– Juliet is the sun!"*

wished" that every girl as well as every boy, every woman as well as every man, and especially every mother, should read and carefully digest such works as Professor Ogilvie's "Essay on the Right of Property in Land". No social movement can be carried to a successful issue either by evolution or revolution unless woman joins heartily in it, and becomes a spur in the march of civilisation.

"Auld Nature swears, the lovely dears,
Her noblest work she classes, O:
Her 'prentice han' she try'd on man,
An' then she made the lasses, O." *(Robert Burns.)*

Professor Ogilvie's *Essay* is a pastoral prose poem, through which we can realise this beautiful world, with it ample provision for satisfying man's instinctive and rational faculties of enjoyment. The "Sovereign Power" from which all blessings flow is manifested as a wise, just, and impartial Creator, who invites us to make His laws our laws, and who in these latter days has delegated to us some wonderful powers, by which – with equality of rights and freedom of labour – the comforts of this life, and the products of the world, may be multiplied more than a thousand fold, *purposely* (shall we not say?) to increase the happiness and virtue of mankind.

The sun never sets, and when one group of workers are retiring to rest, on his "going down," another group are rising with him. Light and labour thus go their incessant rounds ; and so it is with the seasons of seed-time and harvest – the eternal law of revolutions seems to regulate all things! Human speech, borne on the mysterious wings of thunder, revolves round the earth, and "man to man the world o'er" can hold instantaneous converse. Man himself revolves round the world, carried by his fire-souled amphibious steed from places where he lacks food, raiment, or enjoyment, to more hospitable regions. Or he can, with magic-like power, cause the superflous granaries, larders, and wardrobes, to move from one side of the globe, to feed and clothe the hungry and naked on the other. Nature seems to have decreed – "There shall be no more famines!" But although the sun shines ceaselessly, and man's labour follows him steadily in his course, the flow of blessings which such evolutions naturally produce is polluted and diverted by the influence of landlordism, which, like a upas tree, poisons the surrounding atmosphere, spreads desolation in the country, and crowds the town with vice, want, disease, misery, and crime, far beyond the power of churches, charities, hospitals, divorce courts, and police courts to cure. There is only one cure – "Cut it down : why cumbereth it the ground?

Aberdeen, May, 1891. D.C. McD.

D.C. MacDonald's

BIOGRAPHICAL NOTES

on William Ogilvie

*

D.C. MacDONALD'S

BIOGRAPHICAL NOTES

on

WILLIAM OGILVIE

*

"See yonder poor, o'erlabour'd wight,
So abject, mean, and vile,
Who begs a brother of the earth
To give him leave to toil;
And see his lordly *fellow-worm*
The poor petition spurn,
Unmindful tho' a weeping wife
And helpless offspring mourn."

Robert Burns (says his brother Gilbert) "used to remark that he could not well conceive a more mortifying picture of human life than a man seeking work". The life problem of the present day was clearly seen by Burns more than a hundred years ago, and he then pointed out that monopoly in land was the main source of human misery. He looked up to heaven and called as his witness –

"The sun that overhangs yon moors,
Out-spreading far and wide,
Where hundreds labour to support
A haughty lordling's pride".

This miniature sketch was drawn from real life in his *own* country. Then, casting his eye beyond Scotland, and seeing landlordism rampant everywhere, he exclaimed -

> *"But, oh! what crowds in ev'ry land,*
> *All wretched and forlorn".*

William Ogilvie, who was a compatriot of Burns, was born in the year 1736, and was thus twenty-three years older than Burns. The scenes from which Burns took his pictures must have been familiar to Ogilvie. Both were lovers of mankind, and there was a very strong mental affinity between them. Ogilvie was known as 'the *gentleman an' scholar*", but never (except within a very limited circle) as a Land Law Reformer. This is a regretful circumstance. It is equally regretful that Burns is more known as 'a *rhyming, ranting, roving billie*' than as a pioneer and great thinker, in regard to reforms for the benefit of mankind. If we study his epic of the 'Twa Dogs' and his other writings in prose and verse relating to the Land Question and Man's Natural Rights, not only in the light of his own time, but also in the fierce light of the present day, we shall not be surprised at anything we find in Ogilvie's book. Even the seemingly modern-looking Single Tax proposition, so clearly laid down by Ogilvie, will not astonish us. A look at the 'Twa Dogs' shows us how *Caesar* was able to take a more advanced view of the situation than *Luath*. No doubt if William Ogilvie had been a poet instead of a philosopher, he would have expressed the thoughts he has given us in his book somewhat after the manner of the lines above-quoted.

Ogilvie and Burns saw eye to eye: but while Burns roused up his fellow-men from the gutter of serfdom, Ogilvie reasoned with them as to the causes which brought them to such a low condition, and also as to the means of reclaiming their natural rights. Ogilvie considered the whole question from a magnanimous, impartial, and truly scientific point of view. He pleaded for 'free inquiry'; he sought after truth; he was not one of those rough-and-ready reformers who would simply say, "Abolish landlordism and all evils will vanish". No. He looked upon modern landlordism not as a cause but as an effect. The primary and fundamental cause of all the evils under which humanity suffers is traced by him to man's want of knowledge; and landlordism, with all its consequent evils, under which humanity groans, according to him, is directly owing to man's ignorance of his natural rights. It is this ignorance which begets slavish submission and breeds oppression. Ogilvie considered the situation logically. In his view IGNORANT HUMANITY MUST NEGLECT ITS RIGHTS, AND WITHOUT ITS RIGHTS CANNOT PERFORM ITS DUTIES. Rights and duties are co-relative. Ogilvie recognised this very old maxim of Natural Law. He saw the dishonest and absurd position which the landlords take up in every country. They first rob their fellow-men of their natural rights, and then they add insult to injury by accusing them of neglecting their duties. They call them poor and lazy, while at the same time they, as a rule, do no productive work themselves, and their whole wealth consists of property created by the labour of others. And these 'freebooters', as Ogilvie calls them, are styled noblemen and gentlemen, and have arrogated to themselves the position of rulers and legislators in almost every country under heaven.

The people's ignorance of their natural rights is not only the primary, but it is also the sustaining, cause of landlordism. In a note of Ogilvie's (omitted in this edition), reference is made to the ignorance of mankind thus: "In no article are they more ignorant than in respect to property in land, the established rules of which are in every country accounted permanent and immutable". The divine right of kings was until yesterday accepted as an article of faith, and we in Britain are still foolish enough to recognise grants of land signed by authority of *such* 'divine' mandates! We do not now recognise the right of living monarchs to do such things, and yet we confirm, acknowledge and practically homologate the musty parchments of King Tom, King Dick, and King Harry. "These be thy Gods, O Israel!" Their charters to the landlords, and the sub-charters by these landlords to others, including conveyances for borrowed money, are the *only* Sacred Writs recognised in our Courts of *Law*. Mark the word 'Law'. Justice has to take a back seat whenever one of these Sacred Writs is produced.

All titles to land are fetishes. In this country they are the fetishes of discarded and dead divinities. But such is the power of ignorance and superstition when established and maintained by Law and Order that these fetishes are held much more sacred now than in the so-called dark ages.

Our Judges are *specially paid, and sworn in*, not to question these Sacred Writs. Our *National* Clergy are also *specially paid, and sworn in*, to instruct us about the SACREDNESS OF THESE WRITS. There is no water in the sea, and there is no bribery and corruption in the British Isles! No! We thank Heaven that we are not governed like other countries, where, as in America, bribery and corruption are *sometimes* investigated, and even exposed and punished. Our 'permanent official' keeps all these things *square*! We British are a 'Christian Nation'! If 'agitators' would only keep away, the people would be contented and happy with their hope of glory in heaven. Why should *they* care about this earth, 'this wicked world'? Why should they rebel against Law and Order? If they do not suffer oppression, misery, injustice, and poverty in this world, where do they expect to go when they die?

Somehow the rich do not act in accordance with a belief in our Creeds and Catechisms, but they nevertheless support by endowments and otherwise the establishment and spread of that *unearthly Gospel for the poor*! Ogilvie, by the way, makes a mild suggestion about an endowment for 'the independence of the plough' - an endowment leading to 'virtue and happiness *in this world*'. He believed a little in that sort of thing.

Knowledge is no longer a *civil* crime. We can, for example, glance at the *style* of Fetish by which the land in Scotland *was seised*, and 'by virtue of' which it is *now* held by the landlords. It is called an 'Instrument of Sasine' or (Seizin', from the verb 'seize'. It begins with the words: 'In the name of God, Amen!' and then narrates the *sacred* ceremony by which the landlords *required* 'to complete their title'! The sole purpose of this ceremony was to declare and promulgate the doctrine of the 'divine right of landlords': a doctrine which was superinduced upon Feudalism by the aid of Priestcraft sometime during what we call the dark ages. And it is more then probable that it was during these dark ages that the same pernicious doctrine was ingrafted upon the faiths of *Christian* Europe. It was this that barred the doors and windows of men's minds against the smallest possible ray of knowledge 'In respect to property in land', and hence the ignorance and superstition of 'the bulk of mankind in every country', as Ogilvie truly states in his book. The doctrine of the 'divine right of landlords', when fully established as an article of Faith in the minds of a people, notwithstanding its ridiculous monstrosity, its opposition to natural justice, and its poisonous effect on the natural feeling of patriotism and love of one's home, is as difficult to dislodge *as any other article of Faith.*

We get a very bright glimpse of Ogilvie's character further on, where he deals with the '*divine* rights' by which Landlords and the Clergy levy rent and tithes. He puts these '*divine* rights' in one basket, and thus disposes of them: "The foundation of both rights, notwithstanding prejudices on either side, is precisely the same, viz., *the improvident regulations of municipal law*". Not only was he before his own time, but his views are about a century in advance of even the present day. But we can see this only after a careful study of his book, and by reading between the deep furrows which he has turned up for us. He knew from history that it is not by the sword that doctrines and beliefs are instilled into the minds of men. William the Conqueror introduced what is *called* Feudalism into England, *by the Pope's authority*. 'In the name of God, Amen!' His successor, Henry II, introduced it into Ireland, *by the Pope's authority*. 'In the name of God, Amen!' It was somehow smuggled into Scotland, whether by the Pope's express authority is not known, but that it was done 'In the name of God', and that the Priest said 'Amen!' there cannot be a doubt; and on that blasphemous and fraudulent basis it now stands in Democratic, Presbyterian, and Protestant Scotland. It took many centuries to develop itself in the little country of the Scots. Strange to say, the overthrow of the Church of Rome, and the establishment of Protestantism at the *Reformation*, largely contributed to the establishing of the doctrine of the *devine right of landlords* in the Scottish mind*. The Landlords then made themselves the Patrons of the Religion of the people, and they not only 'grabbed' all Church lands, but they also 'grabbed' all the tithes, allowing only a pittance to the clergy.

---

* Note also that another *Reformation* - the Revolution of 1688 - was utilised in the same way by the *Divine* Party. The 'False Argyll' reported that the people of Glencoe refused to discontinue the ancient Scottish tenure, and this was the *excuse* which led to the massacre in 1692. These little bits of history are carefully slipped over by the majority of our so-called historians, like all other facts relating to the people's right to the land. But the most extraordinary thing connected with Scotland and the *divine right of landlords* is to be met with in connection with the last *Reformation* - the 'Disruption' of 1843, when the *Free Church* was instituted. A very large section of the Scottish people, and *all* the Highlanders, then revolted in regard to the landlord's *divine right of property in Church Patronage*. The 'Auld Kirk' was deserted. But the clergy of the New (Free) Church have done more in the Highlands of Scotland towards getting the doctrine of the *divine right of landlords* TO THE LAND, *into the minds* of the people, than had been done by *all other forms of Priestcraft*, from William the Conqueror's time to 1843. This strange fact, and its sad consequences will be (p.t.o.)

We should not forget that all grants of land were originally given *in trust for the people*, and that the rents were originally levied for public purposes. The landlords were all public officers, but as they by degrees became sole legislators they legalised the embezzlement of all revenue from land. Then they taxed *the landless people*. They schemed many taxes. But the SINGLE TAX *restored* would put an end to all these!

It is the right, the duty, and the *interest* of every citizen to demand the just occupation and taxation of the land, and to insist that the dishonest and criminal administration of private *unlimited* ownership of land should no longer be tolerated.

The ignorance which deludes the people - the whole people - from making this claim was seen by Ogilvie, and he honestly and resolutely set himself to remove it. He saw with disgust that "the farmers and cultivators have no clear perception of the injustice and oppression which they suffer". Even those who thus come in direct contact with landlordism (not to speak of the outcasts in great cities), he says, "do not understand, or dare not consider steadily, from what cause their grievances take their rise".

The declared object of his book*, is to show how "property in land might be rendered more beneficial to the lower ranks of mankind". A somewhat dark, unwritten page in British history relates the disgraceful fact that both author and book were boycotted, and that up to this time (1889!) the lower ranks of mankind in England, Scotland, Wales, Ireland, and the British Colonies never heard that such a man lived, far less that he left them such a legacy. "The worthy and humane English landholders", whom he appointed" as his literary trustees, evidently neglected their duties to the intended beneficiaries. We may guess that the French Revolution gave these worthies a scare, and that the author was regarded in those days as rather a dangerous man. It would be said that he was dangerous to the community, dangerous to society, and dangerous of course to the NATION - *that is*, the landholders. He himself anticipated all that: see his *Essay* as to what constitutes "any nation"! But I must leave the reader to find out for himself to what extent the work is based upon truth and justice, and how much the author was prompted by love for mankind as the ruling spirit or chief feature of his character.

The facts known about Ogilvie's life are exceedingly scanty, and would of themselves be of little importance; but when considered along with the conception we form of the man as displayed on every page of his book, the smallest scrap of authentic information will in these days be of some interest, not only to "men of enlarged and inquisitive minds", but also to readers in general. It is in the

---

(Continued from overleaf.)

referred to further on. If these (dissidents' had taken up Ogilvie's cue of favouring a just and independent land reform in 1843, the *Free Church* and Scotland would be in a better position today.

* As stated in the *Essay's* original introduction.

book, however, and in the book alone, that we meet face to face with the author. Ogilvie instilled his soul into it, and he left us evidence that it was the chief aim of his life. We therefore, should as soon think of separating the man Isaiah from the Book of Isaiah, as we should of separating the man Ogilvie from the book of Ogilvie.

By way of cautioning the reader not to look for a sketch of Ogilvie, necessarily made up of disjointed fragments, it may be stated that the order in which these fragments happened to unearth themselves will be followed as far as possible.* The Scotch newspapers and periodicals, published at the time of his death, tell us the bare fact that he died. The reasons for such neglect are obvious. In the first place, Scotland is not peculiar in her dealings with native prophets; and, secondly, Ogilvie was too advanced in his notions of reform to be considered worthy of any notice in those days. England behaved better. The *Times* of 23rd February, 1819, in recording the fact of Ogilvie's death, records also this:-

"Mr. Ogilvie was one of the most accomplished scholars of the age. His talents were of the first order. His taste was of the most refined and correct nature, and the whole of his very prolonged life was passed in the ardent pursuit of knowledge. He died universally admired for his valuable acquirements, and esteemed by all who knew him in private life for the benevolence of his heart and the faithful discharge of every social duty."

He is buried in the south transept of the Cathedral in Old Aberdeen. A small tablet in the wall describes him as 'William Ogilvie, Esquire of Pittensear, in the County of Moray, and Professor of Humanity in the University and King's College, Aberdeen, who died on the 14th February 1819, aged 83 years'. This tablet is enough to make us think that we are unearthing the wrong man. Here we have a landlord who is also a University professor. We know what landlords in general are, and we also know what no less an authority than Adam Smith said about Universities - that they were "the sanctuaries in which exploded systems and obsolete prejudices found shelter and protection after they had been hunted out of every other corner of the world". When, however, we find Ogilvie hurling this very quotation at his fellow-professors in connection with a University reform he advocated in 1786, and when we also discover that his views and proposals regarding such reform were fully as advanced as his schemes for dealing with property in land, the doubts suggested by the tablet became less formidable.

There was no expectation of meeting with any direct evidence of the authorship of 'THE RIGHT OF PROPERTY IN LAND', but luckily the discharged account for printing the work was recently discovered along with some of Ogilvie's private papers. The same bundle of papers also contained the following letter from his friend, Thomas Reid, the author of *An Inquiry into the Human Mind*:-

---

* A rough cairn is all that can be attempted.

"GLASGOW COLLEGE,
"April 7, 1789

"DEAR SIR,

"The bearer, Mr. George Gordon, a preacher, wished very much to be introduced to you. As he has been long of my acquaintance, and a young man whom I esteem, I could not refuse him that favour. He is much pleased with An Essay on Landed Property, and cannot see a reason (neigher can I) why it should go about like a foundling without its father's name. Men seem by degrees to improve in the notion of liberty, and I hope likewise will in that of property. But though this earthly globe should be monopolised by a few to the exclusion of others, I hope the intellectual Globe will always be common, and that those who possess the largest share will be still ready to impart to such as are willing to improve it. The bearer professes to belong to this last category, and hopes to increase his stock by a visit to Aberdeen.

"I am, with much esteem and affection,

"Dear Sir,

"Your very humble Servant,

"THO. REID."

Thomas Reid, it may be mentioned, was a Professor of Philosophy in King's College, Aberdeen, previous to his being chosen, in 1764, as the successor of Adam Smith in Glasgow University. He met Ogilvie in King's College first when Ogilvie was a student there, and subsequently (from 1761 to 1764) as a fellow-professor.

Let us look for a moment at Reid's letter in the light of its own time. The French Revolution burst forth within two weeks of its date. The fall of the Bastille followed quickly on 14th July. The 'father' of the 'foundling' was, no doubt, considered a very dangerous man! He advocated 'free inquiry'! He stirred up, and even predicted this Revolution. He pointed out that the wrongs and sufferings of the cultivators of the soil had reached a pitch *never dreamed of in the philosophy* of those times. "But," says he, "if the intelligent, and the friends of mankind, will take some pains to inquire into the nature and estent of that oppression under which the industrious peasants groan in secret, and the force of that exorbitant monopoly from whence their grievances proceed; and if such men will employ the talents which nature hath given them, in explaining these grievances, and the rigour of that monopoly, to the whole world, Europe, enlightened Europe, will not be able to endure it much longer; and the subversion - nay, even the abatement - of this monopoly, with the abuses flowing from it, may well deserve to be accounted the best and most valuable fruit of all her refinements and speculations."

Ogilvie finished his *Essay* in 1781, eight years before the French Revolution broke out. He was "well aware that great changes suddenly accomplished are always pregnant with danger", and he said so, as a warning to the "friends of mankind". He studied the question in his own careful way beforehand, and, as we have seen, foretold what would happen. But the oppressors and their tools turned a deaf ear to all warnings. Every page of his book is full of humane wisdom, and while he manifests great sympathy for the oppressed, his feelings regarding the oppressors are mingled with a kind of sympathetic pity, rather than pure indignation. His very strong sense of justice was balanced and kept within reasonable bounds by his knowledge of the world's history and his study of the Laws of Nature, and especially his study of human nature.

The present state of 'Enlightened Europe', with its growing evil of military despotism, its heaps of wealth in the hands of a limited number of individuals or syndicates, the terrible increase of public debts, the growing struggle for existence, the appearance of old-world evils in new countries, all mainly due to the general neglect of the natural rights of mankind in this matter of property in land, must suggest to the dullest reader that we are still far from realising what the author looked forward to in the last paragraph of his book, and what his compatriot Burns prayed for, and prophesied thus:-

"THEN LET US PRAY THAT COME IT MAY,
AS COME IT WILL FOR A' THAT,
THAT MAN TO MAN THE WARLD O'ER,
SHALL BROTHERS BE FOR A' THAT."

It is impossible to say that such a lover of mankind as William Ogilvie kept himself willingly behind the scenes during his whole life. It is perhaps more correct to say that he did not; and that it is only now that the curtain of error and prejudice is being raised. When we know that even Burn's bright star was almost totally obscured in those dark days, what chance could the like of Ogilvie have had? Burns died of hard work and starvation. He carried about with him a broken heart and a shattered frame from the time he was a mere boy, when he was compelled to overwork himself at the plough, at the scyth, and at the flail, trying to assist his struggling parents to pay an impossible rent. He saw his father murdered - sacrificed on the altar of landlordism, in 'Christian', 'Bible-loving', 'pious', but, *then*, laird-worshipping Scotland. Burns never recovered from the effects of this landlord oppression to which he was subjected in his youth, and especially the shock of his father's death. Scenes like the following picture of wretched Scotland in those days may have prompted Ogilvie to write his book. It is the 'gentleman an' scholar' speaking in the 'Twa Dogs':-

"L--d, man, our gentry care as little
For *delvers*, *ditchers*, an' sic cattle;
They gang as saucy by poor folk
As I wad by a stinkin' brock.
I've notic'd, on our Laird's *court-day*.
An' mony a time my heart's been wae,
Poor *tenant bodies* scant o' cash,
How they maun thole a *factor's* snash;
He'll stamp an' threaten, curse an swear,
He'll *apprehend* them, *poind* their gear;
While they maun stan', wi' aspect humble,
An' hear it a', an' fear an' tremble!"

It was in 1775, when Burns was sixteen years of age, that his soul was impressed by this painful experience. In his autobiography he says: "My father's generous master* died; the farm proved a

---

* *This is the language of serfdom. In the Court of Session (ultra vires), Act of Secerunt of 1756, anent Evictions, the terms used are 'masters and tenants'. Thus qualified, the word 'tenants' legally meant serfs. The bond was called 'a lease'. Mark the words 'freedom from his lease'. The 'tenant-at-will' was a mere slave.*

ruinous bargain; and, to clench the misfortune, we fell into the hands of a factor who sat for the picture I have drawn of one in my tale of 'The Twa Dogs'. There was a freedom from his lease in two years; we retrenched our expenses and lived very poorly. A novel writer might perhaps have viewed these scenes with satisfaction; but so did not I. My indignation yet boils at the recollection of the scoundrel factor's insolent, threatening letters, which used to set us all in tears." These words were penned in August 1787, and the scene of 1775 was still burning in the soul of the poet. In the interval Adam Smith published his great work, *The Wealth of Nations*, in 1776, and Ogilvie's book followed. But we should also notice that another Scotsman was before them, namely Thomas Spence, who, on 8th November 1775, delivered a lecture before the Philosophical Society of Newcastle, in which he declared, in the strongest terms, that all men "have as equal and just a property in land as they have in liberty, air, or the light and heat of the sun": and for the printing of that lecture, the Newcastle philosophers, he tells us, "did him the honour to expel him" from their society.

Burns and Spence belonged to what the world calls the *lower orders*, whereas William Ogilvie of Pittensear was a born and bred patrician, and was lineally descended from Gillecrist who was the last *Maor Mor* of Angus, one of the seven provinces of Celtic Scotland.* This Gillecrist having in the reign of Malcolm Canmore dropped the Celtic official designation of *Maor Mor* for the feudal title of Earl, thus became the 1st Earl of Angus. His son Gilbride succeeded him as 2nd Earl. Gilbert, the third son of this 2nd Earl, became the progenitor of the Ogilvie family. On account of having distinguished himself at the Battle of the Standard in 1138, he obtained from King William a grant of the lands of Ogilvie and others in Angus, and thence assumed the surname of Ogilvie. From this Gilbert Ogilvie no less than three Scotch earldomes have sprung - namely, Airlie, Findlater, and Seafield. The Ogilvies of Pittensear belonged to the Findlater branch, which branch originally held the two earldoms of Findlater and Seafield. The Seafield peerage on the failure of males, passed, through a female, to the Grant family in 1811; but the Findlater peerage, being limited to males, then became dormant. The kinship between William Ogilvie and the Earls of Findlater and Seafield was more real and substantial than a mere matter of pedigree. It was through the Earl of Findlater and Seafield, he himself tells us, that he was appointed Professor at King's College, Aberdeen. In writing to a friend at the time (1761) he says: "I must not forget to tell you that I owe it entirely to Lord Deskfoord, who is certainly of all patrons the most unwearied and generous". Lord Deskfoord was then Chancellor of the University and Kings College. He became the 6th Earl of Findlater and 3rd Earl of Seafield on the death of his father in July 1764.

---

* *"Or, it may more correctly be said - of Pictish Scotland, since it was the Picts who originally divided Scotland into seven provinces."*

Ogilvie, like his more distinguished compatriot, Burns, was by birth and lineage an anti-Whig, and, as a man, he must have despised the wirepulling *Scotch* Whigs of his time as *"but a pack o' traitor louns"*! He was the only son of James Ogilvie of Pittensear, Morayshire, and of Marjory Steuart of Tannachy, in the neighbouring county of Banff. There is no authentic account of his boyhood, but it may be assumed that he was brought up in the little mansion-house of Pittensear, and that he attended the Grammar School at the county town of Elgin until he left home for College. Pittensear House is within five miles of Elgin.

At the age of nineteen he entered King's College, Aberdeen, as third bursar of his year, 1755-56. He graduated in 1759, and was then appointed Master of the Grammar School at Cullen. He remained in Cullen only for a year. We find him attending the Glasgow University during the winter session of 1760-61, and the Edinburgh University during the winter session of 1761-62. In Glasgow, he studied under Dr. Joseph Black, at the very time that eminent chemist was expounding his great discoveries regarding 'Latent Heat and Specific Heat', and when James Watt was busy in his little workshop in the College buildings making *his great discoveries*. We may safely conjecture that Ogilvie paid many visits to that little shop along with Joseph Black and other frequenters, and we may put it down as a certainty that he did not miss the lectures of Adam Smith, who then occupied the Chair of Moral Philosophy. Among the eminent professors in Edinburgh whose lectures he presumably attended were Dr. Blair, Professor of Rhetoric, author of *Lectures on Belles Lettres*; Dr. Adam Ferguson, then Professor of Natural Philosophy, afterwards of Moral Philosophy, author of an *Essay on the History of Civil Society*, and a *History of the Progress and Termination of the Roman Republic*; and Dr. Cullen, Professor of Chemistry, famous for being the first in Britain to teach chemistry as a science.

Ogilvie was, on the 29th of November, 1761, appointed an Assistant Professor of Philosophy in King's College, Aberdeen, "upon the assurance which the members (of the College) gave Lord Deskfoord that he should be chosen into the first vacant office that might happen of a Regent's place". Some letters between him and the University authorities contain several interesting biographical glimpses of Ogilvie, and they also show the extremely careful diplomacy which had to be exercised in those days in regard to the introduction of any *new light* into universities. The first vacancy occurred on the 16th of October, 1764, when Thomas Reid, Regent and Professor of Philosophy resigned.

Ogilvie did not begin to teach as a 'Professor of Philosophy' in King's College until November 1762, when an engagement under which he was at the time of his appointment, as tutor to a Mr. Graeme, expired. It was also his own desire 'not to leave Edinburgh' during the winter of 1761-62: "and further", says Lord Deskfoord, "he apprehends that his attending the most eminent professors at Edinburgh for this session may qualify him better than he is at present for teaching afterwards in the College of Aberdeen".

It was still the old system of teaching in Aberdeen, and Ogilvie, as a 'Professor of Philosophy', was expected to teach the whole circle of the sciences - 'the sciences of quantity, of matter, and of mind'. There were no separate Professors of Mathematics; of Natural Philosophy, Natural History, Chemistry, or Botany: of Logic or Moral Philosophy, in King's College in those days. The three Regents (who were generally styled 'Professors of Philosophy') were expected to teach all these subjects, and also to give lectures on Geology, Meteorology, Astronomy, Natural Theology, Rhetoric, Economics, Jurisprudence, and Politics. The students, under the old system, did not change from one professor to another; but each Regent, in his turn, took the second year's class, and carried on the same students continuously for three years.

In 1765, the year after Ogilvie's appointment as full Regent, he exchanged offices with the Professor of Humanity. This gave him greater scope, as all the students attended the Humanity Class.

On the 23rd of September, 1765, the Masters approved of the proposed exchange, and from this date Professor Ogilvie taught the Humanity Class until 1817, when, at *his own request*, an assistant and successor was appointed. "For upwards of half-a-century Prof. Ogilvie was perhaps the most energetic member of Senatus, his decidedly progressive views bringing him not unfrequently into conflict with his more conservative colleagues. The pages of the College Minutes during his incumbency bristle with protests against, and reasons of dissent from, the decision of the majority."*

During the period from April 1759, to November 1762, we may take it for granted that Ogilvie lost no opportunity of acquiring such knowledge and accomplishments as he deemed a professor in those days should possess. Besides his attendance at the Glasgow and Edinburgh Universities, it is most probable that he visited England and the Continent, and made himself acquainted with the various systems of teaching carried on in the principal seats of learning in Europe. He was travelling tutor and companion to Alexander, 4th Duke of Gordon, and the fact of the Duke's having visited the Continent is well known, but there is an uncertainty as to the precise date. It may be mentioned that Adam Smith resigned his professorship in Glasgow about the year 1763, on account of his engagement as travelling tutor and companion to Henry, 3rd Duke of Buccleuch, and as Gordon was Buccleuch's senior by three years, it is not improbable that Gordon and Ogilvie visited the Continent about the years 1760-61, or '62. But be this as it may, the reader will not fail to see from *The Right of Property in Land* that its author not only visited the Continent of Europe, but that he also made a special study of the condition of its people about the latter half of the eighteenth century. He saw the French Revolution coming, and the causes leading up to it: "The widow is gathering nettles for her children's dinner; a perfumed seigneur, delicately lounging in the Oeil de Boeuf, hath an alchemy

---

* *Note by Mr. P.J. Anderson. Secretary to the NEW SPALDING CLUB. in Scottish Notes and Queries for June, 1889.*

whereby he will extract from her the third nettle, and call it rent."*

In Ogilvie's time landlordism was most rampant in his own country. He witnessed the passing of the Act 1747, by which military tenure in all Scotland, and the ancient clan tenure in the Highlands, were respectively abolished; and he must have noticed with much pain the establishment of serfdom which followed. He saw oppression, poverty, and misery introduced by 'THE REIGN OF LAW AND ORDER' which then prevailed; and, worst of all, he saw the Scotch peasantry not only submitting to the lawless oppression of the tyrant, but also cringing before the very parasites of squirearchy.

The soul of Justice as well as the soul of Freedom had fled from Scotland in Ogilvie's time, and he himself was compelled to live as a sort of exile *in his own country*! Reader, do not, therefore, wonder that in his book on the Land Question, while he referred to almost every country in the world, he was obliged to draw his pen through Scotland and its people. He refers to England like an Englishman, to Ireland like an irishman, and he even stands up as a patriot for Orissa and Bengal; but he draws the line sharp and clear when we find him referring to England, Bengal, Egypt, Ireland, "or the northern counties of England"! At first sight, with the suspicion that Ogilvie was a good old Radical, and certainly not a *Scotch* Whig whatever he was, I thought that this was a sarcastic reference to Scotland; but on consulting his compatriot and contemporary, Burns, I am satisfied that the omission of all reference to Scotland proceeded from sheer disgust at the utterly slavish condition of his countrymen at the time he wrote. His only hope lay in the adoption by Scotland of the *English* Revolution principles of 1688. If the Scots, the Irish, and also the French had joined in that Revolution and assisted the English in selecting A MAN, instead of a Prince, as chief trustee of those rights and liberties which the Revolution gave birth to, it would have been better for all. Peace and Reform, instead of war and tyranny, would have followed.

It was the Prince of Orange that, in 1692, granted the warrant for the Massacre of Glencoe. He, and the intriguers who procured, and the savages who executed, the royal mandate, ought to have been *suspended*. Scotland was evidently denied *English* justice as well as *English* liberty. The Revolutions of 1715 and 1745 were natural consequences. Some time after 1745, Scotland was made a recruiting ground for an army and a navy used in maintaining the slave trade, and also in fighting against American Independence. Add to this the effect of internal strife between creeds and factions, a corrupt executive government, not to mention landlord oppression, and the words knavery and slavery will suggest themselves as applicable to the condition of the inhabitants of Scotland then. In Ogilvie's time many thousands *were forced* to emigrate 'In search of their natural rights'.

Thomas Muir, Younger of Huntershill, a member of the Scottish

---

* *Carlyle's Past and Present, inspired by Byron, see AGE OF BRONZE XIV. 'The grand agrarian alchemy, high rent."*

Bar, but better known as the 'Political Martyr of 1793', was on the 30th August of that year tried before the High Court at Edinburgh, for the *crime* of having attended one or two public meetings in connection with the extension of the franchise, *which was then strictly limited to landlords*. For this heinous *crime* he was sentenced to fourteen years transportation - *to death*, it may be said, for the sentence directly led to a premature grave. The trial was conducted in the most insulting way possible, not to speak of the treasonable manner in which a landlord judge and jury (a servile Bar aiding and abetting) trampled the British Constitution under foot. As for justice, there was not even the *form* of it observed. The jury was a packed one. It consisted of nine landlords, one bookseller, two bankers, and three Edinburgh merchants; and when one of these merchants (Mr. John Horner) was passing the bench to get into the box, Lord Braxfield, in a whisper, addressed him thus: "Come awa, Maister Horner, come awa, and help us to hang ane o' thae damned scoundrels". The same judge was in the habit of saying, when any legal difficulty occurred in framing libels against such *criminals* as Thomas Muir, William Ogilvie, or Robert Burns: "Let them bring me prisoners and I'll find them law".

I should have preferred not to soil these pages with the name of Braxfield, but as I believe he betrayed his knowledge of Ogilvie's book, by making the worst possible use of it at Muir's trial, I am disposed to return good for evil by doing his Lordship the honour of giving a quotation from his speech on that occasion, and placing it alongside Ogilvie as a first-rate argument in favour of the SINGLE TAX.

BRAXFIELD: "A government in every country should be just like a corporation, and in this country it is made up of THE LANDED INTEREST, WHICH ALONE HAS A RIGHT TO BE REPRESENTED. AS FOR THE RABBLE, WHO HAVE NOTHING BUT PERSONAL PROPERTY, WHAT HOLD HAS THE NATION OF THEM? WHAT SECURITY FOR THE PAYMENT OF THEIR TAXES? THEY MAY PICK UP ALL THEIR PROPERTY ON THEIR BACKS AND LEAVE THE COUNTRY IN THE TWINKLING OF AN EYE, **BUT LANDED PROPERTY CANNOT BE REMOVED"** - *The Martyrs of Reform in Scotland, by A.H. MILLER.*

OGILVIE: "It is indeed *the landed property of the nation that is ultimately and solely engaged for all national debts; every other species of property may be concealed, transferred, or withdrawn, when the demand for payment is apprehended.* It is therefore to be wished, for the security of public credit ... that property in land were exceedingly divided; so that every person had a share ... It becomes even the interest of the great landlords, that such a distribution of property in land should take place ... *So that every member (of society) may be rendered responsible for the public debt*". (from a section of Ogilvie's *Essay* omitted in this edition.)

"When mention is made in political reasonings of the interest of any nation", says Ogilvie, "and those circumstances by which it is supposed to be injured or promoted are canvassed, it is generally the interest of the landholders that is kept in view." How true! And ought we not to thank Braxfield for giving us such confirmation and admission of the truth stated by Ogilvie? Braxfield *played the villain* so well that the dullest *among the gods* cannot now fail to understand the *Play of Landlordism*.

It is interesting to note that Burns wrote his Revolution song, "Scots! wha hae wi' Wallace bled", in September 1793. Immediately after the sentence of Thomas Muir. On the 30th of the same month he presented to the Subscription Library of Dumfries a copy of *De Lolme on the British Constitution*, on which he inscribed the following words: "Mr. Burns presents this book to the Library, and begs they will take it as a creed of British Liberty, until they find a better. - R.B.". The significance of this present at the time he composed 'Scots! wha hae', and when Thomas Muir and other worthy 'sons' were in 'chains', will be clearly understood from the following passage which DE LOLME quotes, in Chapter XIV of his book, from Blackstone's Commentaries on the Law of England (Book 1, Cap.1). In reference to the lawfulness of Revolution, whenever the rights of the people are trampled upon.

Blackstone says: - "And lastly, to vindicate those rights, when actually violated or attacked, the subjects of England are entitled, in the first place, to the regular administration and free course of justice in the courts of law; next, to the right of petitioning the King and Parliament for redress of grievances; and lastly, TO THE RIGHT OF HAVING AND USING ARMS FOR SELF-PRESERVATION AND DEFENCE".

These were the principles of the English Revolution settlement of 1688, and upon which the British Constitution were based. Considering the very complete knowledge of the *legal* rights of British citizens, that Burns possessed through his study of De Lolme's admirable book, and his own very keen sense of man's natural rights, together with his extreme abhorrence of all forms of injustice, and especially when such injustice is perpetrated in the name of LAW AND ORDER, we need not waste much time in speculating as to how he felt on hearing the result of Thomas Muir's trial. It is enough to say that he there and then composed a war song for Scotland - a *Marseillaise*!

He himself has not left us in any doubt. Here are his words: - "I showed the air ('Hey tuttie taitie') to Urbani", who was highly pleased with it, and begged me to make soft verses to it; but I had no idea of giving myself any trouble on the subject till the accidental recollection of that glorious struggle for freedom, associated with the glowing ideas of some other struggles of the same nature, *not quite so ancient*, roused my rhyming mania".** Mark the

---

* *Pietro Urbani, an Italian musician, who met Burns at St. mary's Isle, the seat of Lord Selkirk, on 31st July, 1793, the day before Burns's ride with Mr. Syme "In the middle of tempests over the wildest Galloway moor", when 'Scots! wha hae' was thought, through the suppression of the correct date, to have been composed.*

** *Letter, sending 'Scots! wha hae', to Mr. Thomson, dated 'September, 1793', received in Edinburgh on the 3rd or 4th, and replied to on the 5th. Referring to the old air 'Hey, tuttie, taitie', Burns says, "There is a tradition, which I have met with in many places in Scotland - that it was Robert Bruce's march at the Battle of Bannockburn. This thought, in my yesternight's evening walk, warmed me to a pitch of enthusiasm*

words, *not quite so ancient*, which Burns himself puts in italics. Then let us ask ourselves whether this soul-stirring Ode was not a real cry to arms against Braxfield and Company? Let us look at the Ode itself and the short prayer to God with which it concludes, and ask ourselves whether Burns had the English Edward or the Scotch landlords in his mind's eye at the time he wrote it, and let us not forget that he thoroughly approved of adopting the *English* Constitution in Scotland, and that he by no means wished to revive old national feuds.

"By Oppression's woes and pains!
By your Sons in servile chains!
We will drain our dearest veins,
But they *shall* be free!
Lay the proud Usurpers low!
Tyrants fall in every foe!
LIBERTY'S in every blow!
Let us Do - or Die!!!"

"So may God ever defend the cause of Truth and Liberty as He did that day! Amen! - R.B."

Here we have Burns at bay. There were then only 2652 Parliamentary voters in Scotland". This number included all the landed gentry and their faggots. These were undoubtedly the 'proud usurpers' who caused the "oppressions, woes, and pains", referred to by our patriot bard.

** *on the theme of liberty and independence, which I threw into a kind of Scottish ode fitted to the air, that one might suppose to be the gallant royal Scot's address to his heroic followers on that eventful morning". The words "my yesternight's evening walk", were changed by Dr. Currie into "my solitary wanderings", and this error was not discovered until shortly before Mr. Robert Chambers of Edinburgh published this edition of Burn's works in 1857. Dr. Currie's edition was published specially for behoof of Burns's widow and children, and many things were suppressed through fear of being boycotted by the 'classes'. It will be seen that the news of the brutal sentence passed on Thomas Muir would reach Dumfries, in those days, on 31st August or 1st September, 1793. The 'yesternight's evening walk' which produced 'Scots wha hae' must have been on Sunday the 1st or Monday the 2nd, and Burns must have despatched it on the 2nd or 3rd, more probably the 2nd, as Mr. Thomson says he read it to some friends in Edinburgh on the 4th.*

Mr. Thomson wanted Burns to alter this ode, but Burns refused. He writes on 15th september, in reply to Mr. Thomson, stating that the proposed alterations would "make it tame". "I have (he said) scrutinised it over and over; and to the world, some way or other, it shall go as it is". The world's verdict is in favour of the poet. "So long (says Carlyle) as there is warm blood in the heart of Scotchman or man, it will move in fierce thrills under this war ode; the best we believe that was ever written by any pen".

We must not forget another circumstance. When Thomas Muir was apprehended on 2nd January 1793, Burns was at that very time being court-marshalled by the Board of Excise for a similar *crime*! On 5th January, in a letter to his friend Mrs. Dunlop, he says: "The political blast that threatened my welfare is overblown". On the same day he writes to Mr. Graham of Fintry, who was mainly instrumental in shielding him from that 'blast', making the solemn promise - "henceforth I seal my lips".

What happened in the interval between the 5th of January and September 1793, the reader already knows. He also knows that Burns broke his vow. The soul of Burns could not be caged. The theme of LIBERTY was a part of it, and death only could close those lips. He was not a coward. The man who wrote -

"Wha will be a traitor knave?
Wha can fill a coward's grave?
Wha sae base as be a slave?
Let him turn and flee!"

- in September 1793, *meant what he said.* He meant Revolution. We must not go about the bush in stating this. To do so would imply a cowardly slander on Burns. Alas! Caledonia -

"Where is *thy* soul of freedom fled?"

For nine weary months Burns waits in vain for a response to his song of war: Scotland was no longer *the land of the free*. To the eye of Burns it was now the very burying ground of liberty. The great soul of the poet is then borne away on its own soliloquy:-

"Swiftly seek, on clanging wings,
Other lakes and other springs;
And the foe you cannot brave,
Scorn at least to be its slave."

TO HIS COUNTRYMEN HE BIDS THIS FAREWELL:-

"Avaunt! thou caitiff servile, base,
That tremblest at a despot's nod,
Yet, crouching under the iron rod,
Canst laud the arm that struck the insulting blow!
Art thou of Man's imperial line?
Dost boast that countenance divine?
Each skulking feature answers, No!"

AND HE HAILS THE AMERICANS THUS:-

"But come, ye sons of Liberty,
Columbia's offspring, brave as free,
In danger's hour still flaming in the van,
Ye KNOW, and dare maintain,
the ROYALTY OF MAN!"

These lines are quoted from the Ode to LIBERTY already referred to, a stanza of which was sent by the poet to Mrs. Dunlop in June 1794. The remainder was *im*MUIRED until 1872 (!), when Mr. Robert Clarke of Cincinnati purchased the original manuscript in London, and to him the world is indebted for its first publication. This Ode forms a key to the real intention, feeling, and purpose of 'Scots! wha hae'. They should be read together. And if the reader wants to see further into the soul of Burns, in regard to the theme of LIBERTY, from and after September 1793, he will find Scotland dealt with precisely as in Ogilvie's book. His 'TREE OF LIBERTY' composed in 1794 (but boycotted until 1838)*, ends with these lines:-

"Syne let us pray, AULD ENGLAND may
Sure plant this far-famed tree, man;
And blythe we'll sing, and hail the day
That gave us LIBERTY, man."

And in the eighty-four preceding lines, the word 'Britain' occurs twice, while, *as in Ogilvie's book*, Scotland is *CONSPICUOUS BY ITS ABSENCE*! But this is not all - precisely like Ogilvie, *he draws the line sharp and clear*, thus:-

"But seek the forest round and round,
And soon 'twill be agreed, man,
That sic a tree can not be found
'*Twixt London and the Tweed, man*".

In the next verse a painful view of Scotland appears *between the lines*:-

"Without this tree, alake this life
Is but a vale o' woe, man;
A scene o' sorrow mixed wi' strife,
Nae real joys WE know, man.
WE labour soon, WE labour late,
To feed the titled knave, man;
And a' the comfort WE'RE to get
Is that ayont the grave, man."

In the year 1795 the lessons of the French Revolution were beginning to make some headway in Scotland. An invasion was imminent. The NATION then evidently saw that although '*landed property cannot be removed*', the *removal* of the landlords presented very little difficulty. What a pity the 'rabble' did not see eye to eye with the 'NATION' at that time! The rabble were then invoked to defend their king and country. Mark the words '*their* country'.

---

* *This and other Odes by Burns expressing similar sentiments are still boycotted. W. Scott Douglas and A. Cunningham found fault with Robert Chambers for publishing such Odes. Robert Chambers himself says, that - "Is there for honest poverty" embodies "all the false philosophy of Burns' time, and of his own mind". These cringing editors have done much injustice to the 'honest fame' of Burns. They should have seen themselves as others see them, in the Poet's letter of 13th April, 1793, to Erskine of Mar, where he says - "I have often, in blasting anticipation, listened to some hackney scribbler, with the heavy malice of savage stupidity, exulting in his hireling paragraphs". These editors knew about the real date of 'Scots! wha hae', as far back as 1839.*

THE LAND FOR THE PEOPLE
GONE to a Better
EMIGRAVIT
Death is the lord of all. Nay! false opinion. He only holds On lease his dark dominion
6 ft allotments perpetual lease
KEEP OFF THE GRASS
Your portion! make the best of it
The Landlords have the rest of it.

*

Volunteer(?) corps were formed in mahy districts in Scotland, Dumfries included. Burns *had* to join, and was forced to incur a deathbed debt in buying a uniform. In a ballad headed 'The Dumfries Volunteers', composed in 1795, Scotland is again conspicuous by its absence:-

"Oh, let us not like snarling curs
In wrangling be divided,
Till, slap, come in an unco loon,
And wi' a rung decide it.
Be Britain still to Britain true,
Amang oursel's united;
For never but by British hands
Maun British wrangs be righted."

These lines also form a key to 'Scots! wha hae'. Numerous keys can be had. Take, for instance, the following lines written by him in 1794 in a lady's pocketbook:-

"Grant me, indulgent Heaven, that I may live
To see the miscreants feel the pains they give:
Deal Freedom's sacred treasures free as air,
Till slave and despot be but things that were."

These, it is obvious, were *living* miscreants, not the followers of 'Proud Edward', and it is to them, *and them alone*, that he refers in September 1793, when he uses the words:-

"Lay the proud usurpers low!
Tyrants fall in every foe!
Liberty's in every blow!
Let us Do - or Die!!!"

Burns, like Ogilvie, was a philosophical admirer of English freedom as well as an ardent believer in the Revolution principles of 1688. He was not the man to revive Border feuds. The reference to Wallace and Bruce in 'Scots! wha hae', doubtless was intended to rouse and stir up the '*rabble*' of 1793. The 'woes and pains' and 'servile chains' have nothing to do with England or 'Proud Edward'. Burns was thoroughly loyal to the *British Constitution*:, at a volunteer festive gathering in 1795, when asked to give a toast, the following are the concluding lines of it:-

"And here's the grand fabric, Our FREE CONSTITUTION,
As built on the base of the GREAT REVOLUTION;
And longer with politics not to be crammed,
Be anarchy cursed, and be tyranny damned;
And who would to LIBERTY *e'er prove disloyal,*
May his son be a hangman, and he his first trial!"

These are brave words; and we can almost see not only the Dumfries *gentry*,* but also the Edinburgh *gentry*, 'Old Braxy'

---

* *There is reason to believe that, in his latter years, the Dumfries Aristocracy had partly withdrawn themselves from Burns,*

included, cringing under the truth, justice, and heroism which inspired the soul of the author of 'Scots! wha hae'. In a country under tyrannical rule, as Scotland was then, it was only natural that about one half of the people should be Government spies and the other half cowards. Burns, although he was an excise man at £50 a year, and only £35 when off duty on account of ill-health, was not a spy. Various attempts were made to coerce him to join the other *party*; and his *faith* was often put to the test in connection with 'Loyal' toasts. On such occasions he took the opportunity of trampling on the maggots and flies which were then changing the British Constitution into a veritable mass of corruption. These parasites gloried in toasting '*King and Country!*' *Their* Country! and *their* King! Yet they expected the 'rabble' not only to respond to such toasts, but, when any battles had to be fought *on behalf of the* 'NATION', the 'rabble' were expected to do this also. Nay, the 'rabble' were, as a rule, coerced to fight the 'NATION'S' battles. In the West Highlands, men were hunted, caught, and, if they refused to be sworn in, they were bound hand and foot, and thrown into a dungeon in the laird's house. They were dragged out of this dungeon once a day, and the soles of their feet, after being first rubbed with grease, were held up to a roasting fire. This repeated ordeal, as a rule, led to all the swearing-in required, even in the making of a dragoon. In the Eastern Highlands (Aberdeenshire), 'hanging by the heels' was sometimes resorted to as a preliminary to swearing-in.

Auld Willie MacPherson of Loch Kinnord, an octogenarian, who died a few years ago, used to tell of a widow's only son, who was murdered by the laird in that way. An eye-witness had described to him "what a terrible thing it was to see the poor fellow hanging by the feet, and the blood pouring out of his nose, eyes, and ears". This sight was, doubtless, *intended* to be a 'terrible' one. Yes, to serfs and cowards. But to the human beings worthily called *men or women*, such a sight would be *revolting*, and we may assume that atrocious spectacles of that kind are possible only in countries where the inhabitants are brutalized by tyranny, and the human soul is steeped in the ignorance and superstition of priestcraft. We may safely conjecture that the parish clergyman dined with the laird the same day the murder was committed, and that he afterwards visited the sonless widow, and lectured her from *The Larger Catechism* "as to the great sin her foolish and wicked son had committed in rebelling against God's authority, of which the laird was only the instrument".

Burns and Ogilvie could not possibly be anything else than

---

* *as from a tainted person. That painful class, stationed, in all provincial cities, behind the outmost breast-work of gentility, there to stand siege, and do battle against the intrusions of grocerdom and grazierdom, had actually seen dishonour in the society of Burns and branded him with their veto, had, as we vulgarly say, cut him! Alas! when we think that Burns now sleeps 'where bitter indignation can no longer lacerate his heart', and that those fair dames and frizzled gentlemen already lie at his side - where the breast-work of gentility is quite thrown down - who would not sigh over the thin delusions and foolish toys that divide heart from heart, and make man unmerciful to his brother!" - Thomas Carlyle, 1828.*

Revolutionists. They were not, however, tried before an Edinburgh jury; neither was Moses tried before an Egyptian Braxfield. Poor Thomas Muir did not grasp the nettle firmly enough. He was only a Reformer, and, being somewhat lamb-like in his ways, he was considered a tender morsel by the "hounds which growl in the Kennel of Justice", as Burns describes the Scotch Executive of *Law and Order* of his time.

Thomas Muir wanted to extend the franchise - to give people a *paper* vote - a phantom reform - which, compared with Ogilvie's scheme, may be described as a system of political tinkering, giving rise to disappointment on the one hand, and dissatisfaction with increased discontentment on the other. Ogilvie's equal-share-in-the-land would carry with it, as the law of representation then stood, not only manhood suffrage, but womanhood suffrage also. And why not?

Ogilvie's single and simple remedy was quite ample for sweeping away the double and compound evils of modern landlordism, and we now see what a wise and practical radical reformer he was. But how sad to think that we, in the British Isles, who boast so much of our civilization, are still kept in ignorance of those elementary truths regarding our natural rights. *Yes, kept*! it seems to be the special duty of those who 'fatten on the wages of servility' to keep the people as ignorant as possible. And until recently any '*agitator*' who dared to instruct his fellow-men, in regard to their rights, was held guilty of high treason and sedition. This, by the way, is still a crime, not only in Ireland, but also in England and Scotland. Have we not lately witnessed the degradation of these so-called 'free countries' by the arrest of Irish refugees on British soil. These things act as a spur to the slow but sure Revolution now going on in Ireland, and partly in Scotland; and no one can wisely grudge a *little spurring*. The BRITISH CONSTITUTION is no longer 'the glory of Britons and the envy of foreign nations', as our parochial essayists used to tell us. Even England - 'Merry England' - the 'home of freedom' - is not now so merry or so free as she once was; but it requires no prophet to foresee that her time of wakening up, and reverting to the Revolution principles of 1688 as a basis of restoring the Rights of her People, and the happiness of their homes, cannot be far distant.

Let us now look at the contents of a small but interesting manuscript - *interesting to the reader of* THE RIGHT OF PROPERTY IN LAND. It is unsigned, but it is undoubtedly in the handwriting of Professor Ogilvie:-

"PITTENSEAR, September 12th 1776

> "It seems highly probable that this distemper, whatever be its nature, will remove me from the present scene.
>
> "I ought surely to depart without reluctance and repining, having abundant reason to return thanks for that portion of life and that measure of good which I have already enjoyed, which seems to have exceeded, at least in tranquility and contentment, the common standard of what is allowed to man. I have only to implore that some time may be allowed for the settlement of the affairs I leave behind me, and, if possible, to reduce into some form a synopsis at least of those contemplations and schemes which have

occurred at various times to my mind, as of importance to the general welfare of mankind and the improvement of their present state.

"It ought to be my care to apply with assiduity whatever time is given to these respective purposes, but without anxiety or repining, because both these must necessarily be left very incomplete; to turn away my thoughts from all that is probable to take place in my affairs when I am here no more, except so far as may be useful in suggesting useful direction to my nearest friends to be left them in writing, but without subjection to any positive commands. May it please that Sovereign Power, from whom I have received so many good gifts, to grant me now euthanasia, an easy and tranquil dismission from this mortal stage, or, if that may not be, at least may He vouchsafe that amid the pain and agonies through which I am to pass my patience may be sustained and the use of my reasoning powers remain undisturbed to the last parting pang."

Pittensear, the reader already knows, was Professor Ogilvie's ancestral home. The date suggests many digressions which must be brushed aside. But one or two may be glanced at. The 4th of July 1776, had just given birth to the great American Republic, and the news of the event was creating some stir in the Mother Country. The domineering British landlords - the NATION! - were busy *enlisting* the sons of the British 'rabble' -

"To cowe the rebel generation,
and save the *honour* o' the NATION!"

The ignorant 'rabble' *enlisted* and agreed to cut the throats of their cousins in America. It was *Law and Order*, and they are sworn by all that's holy to fight *for their King and Country*! But in reality they fought for the purpose of coercing the Americans to pay a tax upon tea, imposed by British landlords, to enable themselves to pocket more of the rents earned by the cultivators of British soil.

"Safe in their barns, these Sabine tillers sent
Their brethren out to battle - why? - for rent:
Year after year they voted cent, per cent,
Blood, sweat, and tear-wrung millions - why? - for rent!
They roar'd, they dined, they drank, they swore, they meant
To die for England - why then live? - for rent!"*

Witness the great American Republic! Is not her 'independence' now used as a taxing machine? Where is George Washington now? Where are those ancient tea chests? Frailty, thy name is '*American Independence*!' And where are the British feudal landlords now, who got the land *in trust* for the people? They are levying a tax *on the people*. They call it 'rent', and give no account of their stewardship.

It is quite plain that the *Wealth of Nations* (published in 1776)

---

* *Byron - 'A Country Ruled by Rent'*

did not come up to Ogilvie's expectations *in regard to property in land*. There is no doubt Adam Smith was boycotted by the *Law and Order* of those times, and coerced to modify and delete whole chapters referring to the landlords, as being seditious and unfit for publication. Ogilvie, as we have seen, had regard to a higher 'power' than the *Law and Order* of a set of petty tyrants, when he formed his resolution to publish his 'contemplations and schemes'. His book is a monument of truth, wisdom, and courage. His magnanimity was unbounded; his heart overflowed with love and genuine sympathy towards mankind. Like Moses, he set himself to free an enslaved people; enslaved, because ignorant of their natural rights; powerless, because wanting the source of all power - knowledge. Like Moses, he advises mankind to take their stand, *upon the earth*, by practically adopting the *First Commandment* - Thou shalt have no other gods, dukes, earls, lords, landlords, or other land-grabbers, coming between you and the Creator of the earth, as regards the birthright of every human creature. He regarded not the alleged heavenly rights of earthly kings of their vassals. The golden calf of commercial landlordism he detested even more than all the superstitious kingcraft and priestcraft of ancient Egypt.

It is evident that *The Right of Property in Land* was the great aim of his life. Nay, more, we can see that it came forth from his soul as the fulfilment of a sacred undertaking with 'that sovereign Power, from whom', he acknowledges with overwhelming gratitude, he 'received so many good gifts'. He was then in his fortieth year. His health had utterly broken down through over-study and sedentary habits*. He recovered his health, and lived for upwards of forty-two years after this. He, however, did not allow much time to pass before he *reduced* 'into form those contemplations and schemes which *had* occurred at various times to *his* mind as of importance to the general welfare of mankind and the improvement of their present state'. The receipt for the cost of printing '*The Right of Property in Land* ... and The Regulations by which it might be rendered more beneficial to the lower Ranks of Mankind', is dated 25th August 1781.

It is interesting to consider the manuscript of Ogilvie's *Essay* and the 'synopsis' to which it undoubtedly refers. From the title page we can go to the *introduction*, and there we find more of the *Pittensear Schemes* 'gradually unfolded'. These schemes, it is of some importance to note, are the result of the author's '*own opinions, thinking freely and for himself*'. He tells us that 'the leading principles of that system, which he now holds, respecting property in land have been coeval *in his mind with the free exercise of his thoughts in speculative inquiries*; they have recurred often, they have been gradually unfolded, and for some years past he has been accustomed to review them frequently, almost in their present form, with still increasing approbation'.

Here we have a candid and straightforward author whose opinions, he himself tells us, are *new*. 'All that he would request in their favour (and the candid will readily grant this) is, that they may not be rejected on a first disgust, and that those who cannot adopt the

---

* *Letter from his friend and colleague, John Ross, Professor of Oriental Languages.*

opinions here advanced *may at least bestow some pains in ascertaining their own!*'

There is a gentle touch of humane irony in these concluding words which is characteristic of the author. Other *gentle touches* will be met with throughout the work, but they are sometimes so very gentle that it is even possible to misapply them, as in the case of the words. 'The poor you have always with you'. For example, how seldom these words are interpreted thus: 'The poor *you* have always with you ...'

In the year 1786 Professor Ogilvie took the lead in an attempt to reform the system of education in the North of Scotland. Nothing could have surpassed in *perfection* the system of graduation which the Masters of King's College carried on in Ogilvie's time. Three days before the examination day, the questions, *and also the answers thereto*, were dictated by the masters to the students. This scientific mode of incubation, together with *the laying on of hands* and the incantation of the 'graduation oath' could scarcely fail to bring forth a fully-fledged M.A. from almost every egg in the academic nest.

It is superfluous to mention that Professor Ogilvie was not a silent witness or a consenting party to such proceedings. He was now in his fiftieth year, and finding that he had protested in vain as a member of Senatus for the long period of twenty-two years, he resolved to carry his appeal to the bar of public opinion.

A paper which was printed and circulated at this time, bearing the title 'OUTLINES OF A PLAN *for Uniting the King's and Marischal Universities of Aberdeen, with a view to render the System of Education more complete*', contains strong internal evidence that it came from Ogilvie's pen. It proposed various improvements, and, among others, that all sinecures should be abolished. The whole of the Professors of Marischal College were favourable to the scheme, but seven out of the ten Professors of King's College, the '*seven wise Masters*' (or *The Sapient Septemviri*) as they were called, opposed it; and the reforms planned by Ogilvie in 1786 were not carried out until 1860.

His letters concerning the affairs of the University furnish the only instance in Professor Ogilvie's life, where we find him revealing himself in his true character, as defender of the rights of the people; excepting another glimpse in 1764, when his name prominently appears in connection with a scheme for a *Public Library* in Aberdeen, which was to embrace the libraries of the Universities. With the exception of these two glimpses, Professor Ogilvie, as far as known, never disclosed his name to the public in connection with anything he did, or attempted to do, during the whole course of his long life. He loved tranquility, and avoided publicity. It is not improbable that, after due deliberation, he came to the conclusion that his contemplations and schemes for the general welfare of mankind would have more effect if published anonymously than otherwise. His *Right of Property in Land* was read on the continent of Europe, as the work of an Englishman, who advocated the abolition of serfdom, and who was able to say: 'Look at us *English*, how we have prospered since we became a free people - you French, Germans, Poles, Russians, etc., want a revolution very badly, we had our last one in 1688; you are a full century behind us'.

Professor Ogilvie must have rejoiced in the abolition of serfdom in France. The Revolution of 1789, ghastly in some respects, was only the natural outcome of what preceded it. Its ruffians were the immediate offspring of serfdom, bred and trained in the schools of tyranny, oppression, corruption, and cruelty.

He also lived to rejoice in the still more sweeping land tenure reforms carried out in Prussia. "Nothing probably", says Professor Fawcett, "has so powerfully contributed to promote the extraordinary progress of Prussia as the reforms which were carried out in her system of landed tenure, at the commencement of the present century, by Stein and Hardenberg. A feudal tenantry was transformed into cultivating proprietors, who have, probably more than any other class, contributed to the social and material advancement of Prussia."* These reforms were doubtless planned by Frederick the Great, and no reader of *The right of Property in Land* would be surprised to learn that a copy of that work, marked 'with the author's compliments', was found *inter alia* in the repositories of that famous monarch. Such a discovery would not be more surprising than that Professor Ogilvie had something to do with the land tenure reforms carried out by Lord Cornwallis in Lower Bengal, in the year 1793.

The following memorandum, in the handwriting of Professor Ross, found among Professor Ogilvie's papers, gives us a suggestive glimpse:-

June 15th, 1790

> "Mr. Ross has got some *Calcutta Gazettes* which he will send to Mr. Ogilvie in a day or two hence. The Calcutta publications were stopped at the India House, but Dr. Dunbar says that they will be sent to Mr. Ross soon. When he receives them he will send them to Mr. Ogilvie, at whose desire Colonel Ross sent them."

Dr. Dunbar has been alluded to already as one of Professor Ogilvie's radical colleagues. He was the author of *Essays on the History of Mankind*, published by W. Strahan, London, in 1780., He was also the author of a Latin pamphlet on the American War of Independence; and, for having taken the side of the Americans, he is described as "being somewhat imprudent in politics".** Colonel Ross was evidently a brother of Professor Ross, and very probably, either an old pupil or a fellow-student of Professor Ogilvie.

The following letter gives a fuller glimpse of Professor Ogilvie's connection with the *Regulations* which Lord Cornwallis***

---

* *Manual of Political Economy, London, 1874, p.201.*

** *Personal Memoirs by Pryse Lockhart Gordon, London, 1830.*

*** *Lord Cornwallis wanted to give the Khoodkhast Ryots - that is, the original cultivators, or their descendants - a proprietary*

attempted to carry out, but which the 'permanent official' took very good care to render not only useless, but in many cases oppressive and tyrannical, until the misery of the Native cultivator could find a comparison nowhere on the face of the earth, *except in Ireland*:-

"Aberdeen
"4th July, 1972

"MY DEAR SIR,

"On my return home from the country last night, I had the pleasure of your letter of the 2nd inst., together with the books. Your remarks on Mr. Law's book seem to me perfectly just. Some of them occurred to myself on reading it. If you will take the trouble to send me a copy of the remarks you mention, along with your extracts from the *Essay on Property in Land*, I will take the very first opportunity of forwarding them to my brother. I know he will be very happy to receive any communication of that sort, and perhaps, if Lord Cornwallis remains in India long enough to consider them deliberately, they may be productive of good effects to the peaceable, industrious

---

*** *right. They got Fixity of Tenure and Fair Rent by his Regulations. The Zemindar, or Landlord, could not evict them, or extort from them a higher rent than the Pergunnah neerik, i.e., the rent common in the district. This Law, however, was generally violated, and the following is a flagrant example of such violation:- "The Zemindars of Rungpore, Bogra, Mymensing, Dinagepore, and other surrounding jute districts have raised the rates of land rent on jute crops from one rupee per Beegah to seven, eight, and ten rupees". Dacca News, 12th June, 1858.*

Other Ryots, who were only tenants at will, were the victims of extortion, or eviction, at all times. The Khas (Government) Ryots of Madras were not better off than the Ryots under the Zemindars of Bengal. "Madras", says the Dacca News, "we believe maintains an army of 45,000 Cormorants and Vultures under the name of 'Rent collecting peons'." The East India Company boasted that the Khas Ryots of Madras had equality. So they had; but it was like the equality of 'frogs under a flagstone'! "The Company's servants resembled the French nobility." The Sepoy Revolt of 1857 was in obedience to Natural Law. The British Government realised this, and the East India Company was wound up in September, 1858. Those who had the use of their eyes saw the end coming.

The Land Company of Scotland carried out the 'clearances' in the Highlands and Islands chiefly by the aid of the Protestant and Presbyterian clergy. These oracles said to the people: "This is God's own work"; and the people succumbed, as they used to do when told that God sent a plague. Innocent children wondered, deluded women wept, and men otherwise brave behaved like sheep. To rebel against God was considered not only sinful, but utterly hopeless, and the power of describing the vengeance which would await such rebels in the next world, was recognised as a heavenly gift among the clergy of those days.

inhabitants of Bengal.

"In the meantime, it occurs to me that, as you are so much master of the present state of that country, and of the proposed plans for the management of it, you might give to the *public* a short essay on the subject, which I am certain would be well received, and might be very useful to those who wish to render the numerous inhabitants of Bengal independent and happy. Your suggestions and ideas might be put in execution there, under a wise and steady government, and in my opinion it is the only country in the world, at present, in which trials might be made, either on a small or large scale, according to circumstances.

"You know I am, with invariable esteem,

"Entirely yours
"JOHN ROSS."

The 'short essay', if published, remains to be unearthed. Meantime the brief diagnosis of the distresses of India and Ireland which the author gives in his *Right of Property in Land*, coupled with the remedies he suggested, may be accepted as a miniature sketch of a true lover of justice, whose principles, although rejected and despised by the wiseacres of his time, were based upon wisdom and truth. His foresight suggests to us wide and accurate knowledge as well as the possession of a very remarkable intellectual crucible.

Thomas Muir had a copy of *The Rights of Man* in his possession, and this was made the principal *crime* for which he was banished. Burns, in order to escape a similar fate, had to hide his copy, and *The Age of Reason*, with the blacksmith of Dumfries. Professor Ogilvie's works would be considered more criminal than these. The man who dared to deny the divine origin of rents and tithes, and, moreover, who boldly defined them as 'the improvident regulations of *human* law', and who was able to cite Moses as his authority, would, doubtless, be considered more dangerous than the renowned Thomas Paine. It was, perhaps, on this account that no lair could be found in the Aberdeen University Library for a copy of *The Rights of Property in Land*, while *The Rights of Man* did find a place in that consecrated ground. One of the books which Professor Ogilvie had beside him when he died, was the University Library copy of *The Rights of Man*; and it is not improbable that the very last stroke of his pen was employed in reviewing that book, or in revising a new work on *The Rights of Man to the Land - how lost, and how to be regained.*

The schemes of Ogilvie, this 'ingenious and accomplished recluse', pointed towards the possibility of *Paradise regained,* even on this earth. He had no grudge against the Creator for having made the earth as it is. Examining human nature, he compared the happiness, health and virtue of mankind in town and country. He declared in favour of the latter, and against monopoly in land. His 'projects for the good of mankind' will stand the test of time. When *Macaulay's New Zealander* visits England, it is not the ruins of her edifices that will engage his thoughts, but her neglected fields. It is there he will read the story of her decline and fall. The game is the same everywhere. A corrupt dog-in-the-manger governing class is formed, and idleness and taxes are enforced on a landless people, with the usual and consequent miseries, vices and crimes.

This lesson is being learned even in America and Australia, with their millions of acres lying waste, while thousands of men and women are starving in the large cities, and compelled to

- 'beg a brother of the earth
To give them leave to toil'.

Tasmania furnishes a striking instance of a new country ruined by landlordism. "Within five miles of Hobart is an estate that was once called the granary of Tasmania. It is now a sheep run. First came the absentee landlord who, living 12,000 miles away, cared nothing for his estate, but to suqeeze all he could out of it. Next came a landlordship of trustees, in which the very possibility of a personal interest was destroyed, and under which the estate fell into worse and worse condition, houses in ruins, fences falling to decay. Last came the kind of landlord on whom so many pin their faith, the occupying landlord, and he swept all the farmers off the land and turned it into a sheep walk."* The occupying owner of this kind, the rack-renter, the middleman, the large grazier, and, as in the Highlands of Scotland, the deer forest monopolist, are among the worst plagues of society. They destroy the most important of all industries, and drain the last drop of the best blood of a nation.

The Land Question lessons occurring in Holy Writ are systematically ignored and misrepresented by the majority of the clergy, bribed and corrupted by despots and politicians. Even the immaculate Joseph made the priests of Egypt his friends, by not touching their glebes, when he relieved the Egyptians of their money, cattle, horses, asses, and also their land and their liberty, made Pharaoh a tyrant, and, for the first time in the world's history, invented landlordism and rent: "so the land became Pharaoh's. And, as for the people, he removed them to cities, from one of the borders of Egypt even to the other end thereof; *only the land of the priests bought he not.*"

These particulars we get from Moses, but never from the pulpit. Joseph *gathered* the corn. (Gen.xli) It is not said that he bought it. It is, however, narrated (Gen. xlvii), that he sold it at a most extortionate price. He was not over scrupulous as to compensating the claims of the landlords. He did it *commercially*. For their land, and for themselves as slaves, he gave seed corn for one year's crop. Moses, with severe sarcasm, puts the following words in his mouth:- "Behold (said Joseph unto the people), *I have bought you this day, and your land*: lo, here is seed corn for you, and ye shall sow the land; and ye shall give one-fifth part of the crop to Pharaoh", your landlord, as rent.

---

* *Pamphlet by Mr. A.J. Ogilvie, who is himself a considerable landholder in Tasmania, and who holds similar views with his namesake of King's College, including the SINGLE TAX scheme. Landlordism he defines as 'legalised robbery'; and with regard to Ireland he says "what we want is not to change the robbers, but to stop the robbery".*

When the *feudal* Pharaohs in other countries *relieved* the people of their land, they did not even give one year's seed corn as the price thereof. The modern Joseph is also different: He pockets all the money he can lay hands on, and is thus guilty of swindling Pharaoh, as well as the people. In regard to the fixing of rent, old Joseph was quite a model land steward, but unfortunately his virtue in this respect is never held up for imitation. The morality of expositors, somehow, cannot get beyond the charms of Potiphar's wife.

In THE CONFESSION OF FAITH and CATECHISM, formulated by the English *divines* of 1643, and adopted by the Scotch landlords in 1649 and 1690 as the 'CONFESSION OF THE CHURCH OF SCOTLAND', we can study the relation between the English divines (of Westminster) and the Scotch landlords. It is significant to note that the latter, in Parliament assembled, on 5th February, 1649, proclaimed Charles II King and Pope of Scotland: and, two days thereafter, they adopted this English *Confession and Catechism* - this weapon of extortion and eviction - this device by which the *Divine Right of Landlords* has been made an article of the *Christian Faith* in Scotland. The CLERGY GOT A LITTLE BRIBE AT THIS TIME. The landlords gave up Church Patronage. But the Merry Monarch restored this *Divine Right* to the landlords after he was made King, Pope, and god of England. Again, and accompanied with the very same bribe*, the Scotch landlords, in 1690, re-adopted this *English Confession and Catechism*, as the '*Confession of the Church of Scotland*'.

The English had a Revolution in 1688, and one can easily see why the landlords of Scotland resorted to this ecclesiastical dodge of humbugging the people:-

> "Q. *What is the honour that inferiors owe to their superiors?*
>
> A. All due reverence ... *imitation of their virtues and graces*, willing obedience ... due submission ... maintenance of their person and authority ... and so to preserve that authority which God hath put upon them ... For there is no power but that of God: THE POWERS THAT BE are ordained of God: whosoever, therefore, resisteth the power resisteth the ordinance of God: and they that resist shall receive to themselves damnation."
>
> From the 'CONFESSION of the CHURCH OF SCOTLAND'

The clergy were made to subscribe this Confession, and if they did not preach up to it, they perjured their souls. The Confession enjoined that the '*Powers* are ordained of God', and that the 'virtues and graces' of Charles II, George IV, and the absentee landlords, described in *The Twa Dogs* are to be imitated by the people! It is

* *In 1712, there was another shuttle-cock restoration of Church Patronage, after which the landlords held it until 1874, when the author of Coningsby allowed them £250,000 in name of 'sacrilegious spoil', for once more relinquishing their 'unhallowed booty'!*

impossible to estimate the amount of evil wrought in Scotland by this document.

Professor Ogilvie recognised the vast influence of the Church. He warned the clergy, '*for their own safety*, to "attach themselves more particularly to the inferior and laborious classes of men"; for, says he, "it may be apprehended that a crisis of great danger to their (the clergy's) temporal rights and privileges cannot be far distant".

The facts teaching the relationship between religionism and landlordism, placed here for the contemplation of the reader, have suggested themselves between the lines of Professor Ogilvie's *Essay*. His profound knowledge of the question, combined with the masterly scientific way in which he solved its problems and explained its principles, enabled him to foresee all that has taken place since 1781. There is nothing new to add. He is still abreast of the times. Will the clergy now act on his advice, and aid in breaking the seal of ignorance which is the primary cause of so much poverty, misery and crime? Or will they still continue to use the pulpit as the citadel of oppression, slavery, robbery, error, ignorance and superstition?

In 1844 Mr. Disraeli was evidently a formidable Land Leaguer, but, owing to the worship of landlordism by *all 'sects'* of 'religionists' at that time, he was powerless. Even a "respectable body of dissidents" like the newly-instituted democratic *Free Church of Scotland*, although the undoubted offspring of a revolt against a "factitious aristocracy", would not give him the least support. No wonder he, in 1849, when famine and eviction were doing their cruel work in Ireland and Scotland, "recognised in the Church the most powerful agent" of landlordism! The clergy then declared that famine and eviction were "visitations from God, sent as trials on the Faith of His own people"! The poor people - *poor devils* - "believed and trembled"! The *League* between religionists and landlords was a powerful one.

The roof of the evil is landlordism. It is with its 'spoil' that sovereigns, priests, judges, landlords, professors, policemen, soldiers, and other public servants are debased, corrupted, and bribed. The higher education of the mothers of the coming race will, it is to be hoped, grapple superstition by the throat. Woman will then be educated and trained to exercise her divine instinct - maternal affection - and will bestir herself in claiming and maintaining the birthright of her children in regard to all the productive forces of nature. Sons and daughters will be born free. And as they come forth from the womb of Nature, they, each and all of them, will be acknowledged to be the children of the same Almighty and Impartial father, and therefore entitled to an equal share of His property, mother earth. This doctrine is the aim and end of the gospel of Jesus. It contains a rational notion of a HEAVENLY FATHER.

"That exclusive right to the improvable value of the soil which a few men are permitted to engross", as defined by Professor Ogilvie is "a most oppressive privilege, by the operation of which the happiness of mankind has been for ages more invaded and restrained, than by all the tyranny of kings, the imposture of priests, and the chicane of lawyers, taken together, though these are supposed to be the greatest evils that afflict the societies of human-kind".

We pause at these words, and as they enter our souls we get a glimpse of the sage that penned them. We realise his animated presence within ourselves, in combination with the quickening truth presented to our understanding. Here we have the essence of Political Economy - the Land Gospel - compressed within the small compass of seventy-two words; and in one word - the word 'permitted' - he has revealed to us both the diagnosis and the cure of the "greatest evils that afflict the societies of humankind". "A few men are *permitted* (by the many!) to engross a most oppressive privilege - *the exclusive right to the improvable value of the soil*." This is the real cause why the happiness *of the many* has been invaded and restrained for ages! Kings, priests, and lawyers are merely scare-crows and puppets, and "a few men are *permitted*" to pull the strings! We have this fact on the undoubted authority of a man who was himself one of the 'few', namely Professor Ogilvie.

In withdrawing the *permission*, which is the simple cure suggested, there is no word in his teaching about the question of compensation - not even as a temporary obstacle. In the case, however, of *real* property, *created by labour*, he would fully compensate the real labourer for all loss sustained in connection with any of his benevolent schemes of land reform. The landholder has a right only to the 'improved' - the created - value of the soil. He has no right to the "original and contingent value". "That must still reside in the community at large, and, though seemingly neglected or relinquished, may be claimed at pleasure by the legislature, who is the public trustee."

The land belongs to "the community at large"! We must not narrow the Land Question, as merely affecting the labourers or tenants of the soil, and their Lords and masters. Those who are not directly connected with these *Lords of Creation* are equally interested. The robbery which the landless labourers *permit*, in the shape of indirect taxation and expatriation, is more fraudulent, more pernicious, more cruel, more extensive and widespread than the robbery of rent. 'and rent, however, we must not forget, is the root of all the robbery - the taxation of the landless people being merely the outcome. This is so very obvious, that I feel a kind of shame in mentioning it. Yet it is a fact we steadily ignore.

We forget that the land belongs to the Nation - to the People - and that its rent is a national fund which should be used for national purposes - for the equal benefit of the whole People. We forget that the mere withdrawal of our permission of the abuse of National funds would leave us with a handsome surplus every year, after providing for free libraries, free schools, and free universities; and that all taxes and excise customs on industry or articles of consumption would cease to be necessary. We forget about the numbers of widows, orphans, aged or disabled workers, and other fit subjects of benevolence, who ought to be provided with pensions out of such a surplus in a country which boasts of the Christian Faith.

Why is it that the laws of Moses have been disregarded as to *Property in Land*? Why is it that the gospel of Jesus has been topsy-turvied, perverted, and made subservient to landlordism and slavery?

Why is it that such works as George Buchanan's *De Jure Regni*, John Locke's *Civil Government*, Professor Ogilvie's *Right of Property in Land*, and Henry George's *Progress and Poverty* are not read in every cottage, and *authorised* to be taught in every school in the three kingdoms? And why is it that '*A man's a man for a' that*' is not sung as a sacred song, in every Church, Chapel, and Sunday-School, not only in the 'Land of Burns', but in every land where the English language is spoken?

Submission to ignorance is a breach of Natural Law, and every breach of Natural Law is duly followed by its appropriate punishment. Such a transgression on the part of an individual, and most certainly on the part of a community, is followed by slavery, poverty, and misery.

It is not strange that Professor Ogilvie desired to revive the Agrarian laws of Moses; neither is it strange that he touched the clergy *with a gentle hand*, knowing, as he did, the polluted fountains of their *inspiration*. He, with Adam Smith and other distinguished contemporaries, regarded Universities as the sanctuaries of ignorance, and the seminaries of "a superstitious theology which inculcated tenets subversive of the spirit of Christianity, and degrading to human nature".

Can the example of Moses help us here? Emphatically, Yes. He was not only the Prince of Revolutionists, but he was also the Prince of *Free Thinkers* and *Free Inquirers*. When "the angel of the LORD appeared unto him in a flame of fire out of the midst of a bush", what did Moses say? - "And Moses said unto God, Behold, when I come unto the children of Israel, and shall say unto them, 'The God of your fathers hath sent me unto you'; and they shall say unto me, 'What is his name?' what shall I say unto them?" Moses was not to be satisfied with the '*God of his fathers*', or the 'God of Abraham!' he must have a God *for himself*, namely, the I AM. "And God said unto Moses, I AM *that* I AM: and He said, 'Thus shalt thou say unto the children of Israel, I AM *hath sent me unto you*'," "And God said, moreover, unto Moses: 'This *is* my name for ever, and this *is* my memorial unto ALL GENERATIONS!'" It is not I WAS, or *my Fathers were*, but I AM!

Reader! have you got an I AM? Because, if not, Nature has made a mistake; you should have been born with four feet, a long nose for smelling along the ground, and a tail which you could occasionally wag by way of expressing your reverence and homage for some *Master*, whose will, even when he is kicking you, *must be your pleasure*! The fossilised '*Jehovah*' of modern Theology is the God of the British House of Commons, and has been the God of that House for centuries, when making many anti-I AM laws; laws of oppression, coercion, slavery, wars, and murders, including the murders of starvation caused by the monopolising of land - preventing its use and cultivation. The landlords - murderers(!)? Yes. ST. GREGORY THE GREAT said so, more than twelve hundred years ago, long before Buchanan, the Saint-Andrews, Oxford, and Spanish Inquisition '*damnable heretic*', was born:-

"Let them", said he, "know that the earth from which they are created is the common property of all men; and that, therefore, its products belong indiscriminately to all. Those who make private property of the gift of God pretend in vain to be innocent. For in thus retaining the subsistence of the poor they are the murderers of those who die every day for want of it."

Next to the I AM creed of Moses, who was the Greatest and grandest of all *Spartans*, we have here, perhaps, the most clear and the most concise economic creed ever uttered or penned. But it is only an amplification of the I AM creed. The *First Commandment* is only an amplification of that same everlasting creed; and, as a *Declaration of Independence* - the independence of an enslaved people - the inspired and inspiring God-given words I AM are unsurpassably comprehensive, unsurpassably tyrant-proof, unsurpassably laconic.

From the *First Commandment*, the amplification proceeds in the *Second* and enjoins the prevention of sham gods, sham dukes, sham lords, and '*dummies*' of all sorts; and implies the exclusion of all sham creeds descriptive of spurious gods recommended for 'homage', 'reverence', or 'worship', in room of the I AM genuine God of mankind, the GOD of Liberty, Justice, and impartiality.

From the *Second Commandment* the amplification still proceeds in the *Third*; and urges practical manliness on the part of mankind. "Thou shalt not take the name of THE LORD *thy God* in vain". Any man who has the I AM spirit in him rebels at once against all forms of tyranny.

There was much need of the *Third Commandment* in Scotland when Burns wrote his War Song -

"Scots! wha hae wi' Wallace bled".

And it is not to be wondered at that William Ogilvie took his *Political Economy* from the Books of Moses. He had the I AM spirit -

"Let us Do - or Die!!!"

William Ogilvie and Robert Burns recognised only one divine Law and Order, only one Sovereign Power - that which governs the Universe, and guides the circling spheres. Examining the *Law and Order* of 'divine' Kings, 'divine' Ecclesiastics, 'divine' Men of Rank, 'divine' Olivers, and even 'divine' Landlords *in Del nomine,* what did they see? They saw a reign of usurpers, hypocrites, murderers, and robbers who had disfranchised the bulk of mankind, contrary to Natural Justice. The *Spectre of Democracy* was no terror to them. They assiduously prayed - *Thy Kingdom come: Thy Will be done ON THIS LITTLE EARTH as it is in Heaven.*

The fact of Professor Ogilvie, when verging on the allotted span of three score and ten, being still in the van of Land Law Reformers, agitating his benevolent schemes with "unabated fervour and vigour", amidst the storms and disasters of the French Revolution, and the despotic cyclone which was then raging, is a remarkable spectacle which even the eye of opposition cannot behold without a sense of admiration. Professor Ogilvie loved mankind and wished to see justice done all round; he *preached and practised* genuine christianity during the whole course of his life, and he continued faithful even unto death. How very different is the nominal Christian, who is goody-goody enough to admit the justice of abolishing slavery, oppression, and the legalised robbery of landlordism, but who, with a wise shake of the head, asks you, "What's the use of agitating, seeing that YOU and I will be dead long before any Parliament will pass a measure of that kind?"

In the year 1773 William Ogilvie purchased for £1,500 the property of Oldfold and Stone-Gavel, situated on Deeside, about six miles from Aberdeen. He held it for thirty-five years, and when he sold it, in 1808, the price he received was £4,000. But the difference was not all profit. About the year 1798 he borrowed £2,000 from his old friend, the Duke of Gordon, and of this sum he expended £1,910 in draining, trenching, and blasting, and more than the balance was paid away in connection with the valuation and purchase of tithes.

In the year 1802 we find him carrying through a Process in the Court of Teinds, by which he saved the property from being plundered by increased tithes on the increased value arising from his improvements. He got the tithes valued according to the old rental. The tithes of teinds were then fixed at £9.10s. of which only £1.8s.8d. reached the Parish Minister, the balance going to the tithe-owner, which happened in this case to be the Crown. He knew how to prevent the tithe-owner, and also the parson, from robbing the labourer of the value of his improvements on the land, and he adopted the proper precaution. The Process he raised, besides fixing the value of the tithes, concluded for a sale of the surplus to himself, and decree was obtained accordingly, for the sum of £68.5s., being at the rate of nine years' purchase of the amount of surplus or 'free teind'.

We see that "our accomplished recluse" was not a mere theorist who allowed his mind to run after what is called utopian fancies. The practical knowledge displayed in the *Essay* he manifested in a material manner on the barren lands of Oldfold and Stonegavel. "There is", says he, "no natural obstacle to prevent the most barren ground from being brought by culture to the same degree of fertility with the kitchen garden of a villa or the suburbs of a great town." And he tells us how to do it. But those readers who are not acquainted with the principles of agriculture, and who also are strangers to the principles of morality and justice, cannot be expected to appreciate the author's knowledge, unless we drag them to the very ground upon which he carried out his experiments, and there show to them the fruit of his labours, in the shape of an extra-ordinary increase in what we shall call *earned* increment.

The property of Oldfold and Stonegavel changed hands about thirteen years ago, when the trustees of a Widows' Fund in Aberdeen purchased it at £12,000, as an agricultural subject, and merely as an investment, without any mansion house, or woods, or any value for sport. Prior to 1757 it only yielded a yearly rent of about £12, being then in its natural state, and let to a sheep farmer. The yearly rent it yields now is about £410, and the gross annual value produced, let us estimate at, say, £1,640, when we take landlords (freeholder and feuholder), farmers, labourers, tradesmen, and merchants, etc., who all get a share, into account. Its gross annual value, produced from a stock of sheep and the labour of one miserable herd boy, up to the year 1757, would not exceed £36.

It will be seen that the rise in the producing value of this property is much greater than the rise which has taken place in its selling price. The rise in the price, let us observe, was a direct benefit to the owners, while the rise in its producing value benefited the whole community; a fact, by the way, which the advocates of absolute private property in land should note, in regard to their dog-in-the-manager doctrines about waste land, game preserves, and pastures, while there is one idle Briton who is *willing* to work, and who wants land for cultivation and improvement.

The facts and figures connected with Oldfold and Stonegavel embrace an object lesson, apart from their interest in giving us a glimpse of the author of *Birthright in Land*, successfully putting in practice the principles laid down in his *Essay*.

Trade Unionists and *blacklegs* war against each other, and both parties are equally ignorant of the real cause why one man has to beg of another "for leave to toil"! and they blindly *tramp* the remedy under their feet.

Professor Ogilvie addressed himself in accordance with the Revolution principles of 1688, to "the sovereign, the legislature, or the real patriots of a country". We have seen how he deplored that the British patriots of 1688, and the American patriots of 1776, failed in securing their "natural right of property in land" - to "*establish*", he says, "*an arrangement of the highest importance to the general welfare of their fellow-citizens*". And we have seen how he deplored that the French patriots of 1789 stopped short at peasant proprietorship - "whose labours", he says, "now (1805) seem to have subsided in the dregs of mere despotism".

But what did the British patriots get? Did they improve their position at Waterloo? For whom, and for what, did they shed their blood there?

The Highlanders who responded to the trumpet of war in obedience to their chiefs, how were they treated after Waterloo? We know that on landing in England the remnants of the Highland Brigade were received in every town they marched through with perhaps as much real patriotic pride, honour, and kindness as ever fell to the lot of brave and victorious men; and as they proceeded Northwards to what, once upon a time, was *their own country*, the feelings of warm welcome seemed rather to increase than diminish, until, Alas! they came to one spot:-

"*A dearer, sweeter spot than all the rest*".

"That", says *an applicant under the Scottish Crofters' Act of 1886* - pointing to a glen - "Is the place where my father was born and brought up". Like some other young men he was forced into the army, but it was on the express condition that his parents, and their posterity, should never be disturbed in the possession of their land. On his return home after the Battle of Waterloo, instead of his home - the home of his ancestors - there was nothing but roofless walls, thresholds overgrown with grass, and the nettle and thistle in full possession, rooted round the old hearth stones. He, for a moment, distrusted his eyes. The unexpected sight of such desolation pierced his heart, and he felt stupefied. How cruel of the French bullets to have spared him for such refined landlord torture!

It was a complete *Highland Clearance*; not a living soul was left in the glen to tell what had become of the people.. This was the work of the Commercial Landlord - the *Commercialised* Highland Chief, or, more properly, thief! the advocate of Freedom of Contact - freedom to do what he likes with the land, and to kick the people about, or away altogether, in accordance with his caprice, avarice, or pleasure. The same story, with sad variations, may be told of many a Highland Glen. And, with equally sad variations, it could be extended to the Lowlands, to England, to Ireland, and, without any doubt, to British India. The British *nabobs* excelled all other freebooters, barring, perhaps, the Spanish Christians who plundered and murdered the natives of Mexico. The East India Company was a huge syndicate of *Commercial* landlords, the undoubted scum and dregs of British despotism; but, nevertheless, it was approved of and supported by the '*Christian*' Churches of Britain and their Missionaries under the pretext of carrying the Gospel to the downtrodden races of the East.

When the real duties of a Sovereign are systematically neglected, and when a 'factitious Aristocracy' have entirely forgotten the rights of the people, by whose mandate alone they act as legislature, it is then high time that "the *real* patriots of any country" should waken up. The real *Trafalgar* when "England expects every *real patriot* to do his duty" has yet to be fought.

Sir James Mackintosh, who vindicated the French Revolution, vindicated also, by anticipation, the Indian Revolution of 1858. But the mild and amiable Sir James, although a *vindicator* of Justice and Reform, was an exceedingly frail and timid *agitator*. He was somewhat like JEREMIAH, while his old *Master* was fashioned after the *ancient model* of MOSES.

To Professor Ogilvie's proposals of land law reform, Sir James furnished this *wet blanket* - "Practical effect here (in India) you must not hope!" He was only beginning to see that his old *master* really intended his *schemes*, not as mere 'speculations', but rather to be adopted *practically*, "as of importance to the general welfare of mankind, and the improvement of their present state". In a letter to Professor Dugald Stewart of Edinburgh, dated 'Bombay, November 2, 1805', the following reference occurs: "A nephew of Dr. Reid, a young gentleman of the name of Rose, has lately come out here as a cadet, recommended to me by a very ingenious and worthy person, though not without the peculiarities and visions of a recluse. Mr. Ogilvie of King's College, Aberdeen."

We We (have already seen) how imperfectly informed Sir James must have been, in regard to "this most ingenious and accomplished recluse". He seemingly had no idea that Professor Ogilvie was possessed of more practical knowledge of agriculture, and the true relation of landlord and people to the land than perhaps was possessed, in the aggregate, by all the political philosophers of this time, the celebrated Adam Smith being thrown in along with the rest. He was by far too honest a man to attempt to write on any subject until he had first mastered the facts. The *Essay* itself is the best proof of this, and it would be impertinent to assert that the author was a practical and scientific man unless his work could stand the test of cross-examination. But nevertheless, the notion that he was only a *visionary and speculative recluse* was prevalent. That was one way of opposing his admittedly just and benevolent schemes. "What is the use", some would say, "of any schemes, however good, however benevolent, if they are not practicable *in this world*? The *next* is the place for these things! Therefore, any advocate for happiness *in this world* must be treated as a very dangerous heretic." We may guess the reason why Professor Ogilvie was a 'recluse'!

The renowned George Buchanan was not a recluse, and consequently he was put in prison; and to escape being burnt alive, he had to fly from his own country. Like the Damascus heretic, he made his escape 'through a window'. Whether he was let down 'in a basket', or had the benefit of a more modern fire-escape(!) history sayeth not.

Where is Buchanan now? Where is our Great Grandfather of British Liberty and true Radicalism, the hater of cant and tyranny? "A tyrant", says Buchanan, "is one that rules by his own will, and contrary to the interests of the people." The "opinion that a tyrant must be obeyed is wrong. For the people may justly make war against such a ruler, and pursue him till he be slain."

Is not the birthright of every Briton, a share of the 'National Debt?' But what has become of every Briton's corresponding birthright share in the Country - in the Land? the protection of which from invasion formed the main pretext of incurring this debt, and of allocating it indiscriminately on the shoulders of a defrauded population.

It is a huge fraud, and the most impudent, the most criminal, as well as the most extensive, ever committed since the creation. Think of it for a moment. The landlords abolished military tenure, and substituted money payments for military services. Then they pocketed this money for their own private use, and raised other money by taxes on the landless people, and by loans, *to pay for military expenses*. The most of the military money, by the way, was paid to themselves, their sons, and sons-in-law, in the shape of *military pay and pensions*. No wonder Lord Byron exclaimed: "War was rent!" Yes! they not only raised the price of the fruits of the earth, and thereby raised rents, which they, by a show of law, pocketed, but they also pocketed the bulk of the war taxes and war loans, and, on this account, they schemed and carried on war as a most profitable business:-

> "*Farmers of War! dictators of the farm;*
> *Their ploughshare was the sword in hireling hands,*
> *Their fields manured by gore of other lands.*" *

The Lords of the soil, let us repeat with emphasis, abolished the *only* tenure, the *only* alleged right *they* had to the soil - they abolished *military tenure*. They did so in England in 1672, and in Scotland in 1747; and they have had no tenure of any kind ever since, barring the self-established tenure of Freebooting, which they term *Fee-Simple*! The word '*Fee*' means an estate in land held of the sovereign as trustee *for the people*, or held of some royal sub-trustee, also *for the people*, and for which the holder, in the words of Camden, has to *do service or pay rent*. The word '*Simple*' means silly, and qualifies *people* - the people who are *simple* enough not to

* From Byron's "The Age of Bronze", already quoted from by D.C.M. earlier. S-A.H.

call the landholders to account. How the people have been *whiggled* by the whig commercial landlords is a problem not to be lost sight of by modern reformers, who should put no trust in the *fishy* arm of *party* names. Let us not forget the things done even in the name of Christ!

"How preposterous, says Professor Ogilvie, "is the system of that country which maintains a civil and military establishment by taxes of large amount without the assistance of any land-tax at all! In that example may be perceived the true spirit of legislation as exercised by landholders alone". He also points out that "their large incomes (from land rents) are indeed pensions and salaries of sinecure offices!" He was an eye-witness to the robbery which was perpetrated in Scotland in 1747, when military tenure was abolished, and the land, with all its rents and royalties, finally taken from the people by the darling Whigs, the Tories agreeing, the Courts of Law agreeing; and, let us note, that the 'Protestant' Clergy have not to this day made any *protest* against that robbery.

Let the reader imagine that all the excisemen in the British Isles somehow got all political power into their own hands, that they then demitted their offices and put in a claim for compensation for giving up the pleasure connected with smuggler-hunting, including occasional bribes for *letting people off*. (The landlords took *fines*, which is only another word for *bribes*) These retired excisemen then vote public money to pay this 'compensation', a puppet King gives the necessary assent, the Bishops in the House of Lords say *Amen*! and all curates and clergy throughout the country echo *Amen*!

Then these excise *lords*, let us say, keep all the excise duties to themselves; they manage all the distilleries and breweries as their own private property; they raise the excise duties to any rate they like; being proprietors *by law established*, who can interfere with them "to do as they like with their own"? They '*impose*' duties on other things; they tax everything ujnder the Sun except distilleries and breweries; they tax the Sun itself for several years (the window tax); and they make the people pay the salaries of the new excisemen, who, by the way, are kept as mere flunkies to these idle lords. This imaginary swindle is only a drop in the bucket as compared with the appropriation by the landlords of all the land - all the productive powers of Nature, necessary for the sustenance and enjoyment of the community - *Community*! Verily the bigger swindle has actually been perpetrated, and we still assert that *the age of miracles and witchcraft has gone by*. What meaning has the word 'community' now?

The history of Scotland, if written with the pen of truth, might be made most instructive to the whole human race. How did Scotland stand in Professor Ogilvie's time? We have mentioned that he witnessed the sleight of hand - to borrow that view of it from the language of Lord Salisbury - by which military tenure and 'clannish tenure' were 'slipped' into the present tenure of *commercial landlordism*, "entirely to the advantage of the landlords". The people were indiscriminately robbed. The rank and file who fought *for George*(!) at Culloden were robbed as well as the so-called rebels of those days.

Let us here *note* that every man, woman, and child killed by the

Royal Army after the Battle of Culloden was a clear case of murder. Every tenant was bound by the *Law of the land*, until 1747, *to follow his feudal/chief to the field*. And the so-called *rebels* who followed their *feudal lords* under the banner of Prince Charlie in the '45, did so in accordance with the *Law and Order* then in force. Had they refused, they would then have been *real* rebels. Consequently, we find that not a single individual *of the rank and file* of the 'rebel' army could be tried in a Court of Law, hence the necessity of shooting and hanging them without the ceremony of a trial. The Duke of Cumberland, upon the whole, seeing that he was only a mercenary soldier, who took his orders from the Duke of Argyll, the real ruler of Scotland at the time, did his part of the work with as much humanity as could be expected of a professional master 'butcher' of human beings. We have this on the authority of the Scottish, and also of the English Protestant clergy, in the praises and prayers they *sent up* (!) in favour of his good deeds.

But there was, at least, one noble exception, the Rev. John Skinner, who in the last verse of his 'Song of Songs' - *Tullochgorum*, cursed the *fig-tree* Christians of his time in the following manner:-

"*But for the sullen, frumpish fool,*
That loves to be Oppression's tool,
May envy gnaw his rotten soul,
And discontent devour him;
May dool and sorrow be his chance,
Dool and sorrow, dool and sorrow,
Dool and sorrow be his chance,
And nane say, 'Wae's me for him!'"

The clergy after the '45 did their utmost to extinguish the *soul of freedom* in Scotland, while they themselves, especially the State clergy, held a high old time of it, domineering over the people and wallowing in whisky punch. If anyone mentioned injustice, oppression, or tyranny, he was instantly gagged.

Military tenure, we have seen, was abolished in 1747. As a youth Ogilvie witnessed that *juncture - that favourable opportunity* - whereby the Scots might have got their natural rights restored "had they been themselves aware of their title to such rights". A large portion of Scotland was then 'nationalised': the estates of the rebel chiefs were forfeited to the Crown. But how much of these lands was given to the people? Not one square inch was given even to the '*loyal* men' who fought and conquered the 'rebel' army at Culloden!

By-the-way, the Rev. John Skinner was a sturdy Land Leaguer in his day, who used his pen in prose as well as in verse in favour of the people's cause. And it is not improbable that he and Professor Ogilvie *compared notes* on the Land Question as well as other things. But like the *Twa Dogs*, this must be left to the reader's own conjecture, for want of direct evidence. It is, however, worth noting that these three Land Leaguers, *Tullochgorum*, *Luath*, and Ogilvie, *alias Caesar*, were all closely connected, and *associated*, under the genial patronage of one man, namely, Alexander, fourth Duke of Gordon. It is also worth noting, as a special feather in Professor Ogilvie's cap as his tutor, that this nobleman was a model landlord, whose example and influence in the North of Scotland in those dark days cannot be over-estimated. Notwithstanding this, the memory of Duke Alexander, '*The Cock of the North*', and the author of the most popular version of the song '*The Reel of Bogle*', has been buried in oblivion almost as completely as the memory of his accomplished tutor.

Thanks, however, to Burns for his picture of *Bonie Castle Gordon*. We there get a view of the 'princely' manner in which Professor Ogilvie's pupil performed his duty and office of landholder. He was not a sinecurist, neither did he belong to the *commercial* or '*guinea's stamp*' tribe of landlord. Burns visited Gordon Castle on September 7, 1787, and made the following *note* in his Diary: "Fine palace, worthy of the noble, the polite, the generous proprietor: The Duke makes me happier than ever great man did - noble, princely; yet mild, condescending and affable, gay, and kind - the Duchess charming, witty, and sensible - God bless them!" These everlasting words have embalmed the memory of one of "the worthy and humane *English* landholders", who resided in the so-called '*Northern Counties of England*', to whom Professor Ogilvie dedicated his *Essay*.

Burns draws a comparison between the management of India's plains, under *The Company*, and of the *Bonnie Castle Gordon* domains, under the pupil of Professor Ogilvie. The reader already knows that Professor Ogilvie took a keen interest in Indian land-law reform. Did he meet Burns at *Bonie castle Gordon*, and did *they twa* then discuss about Indian landlordism? If they did not, it then becomes even more interesting to trace the strong affinity which existed between the contemporary souls of these two remarkable men. But regarding probabilities, it is right to add that one of Professor Ogilvie's sisters was married to William Tod, the Duke's Factor at *Bonie Castle Gordon*, and that the Professor was a frequent visitor there. Dr. Currie might have assisted us here, but we know why in those days he had to hide the date of

"*Scots! wha hae wi' Wallace bled*".

Perhaps for a similar reason he kept his thumb on the name of that *anonymous* 'gentleman' he describes as "a particular acquaintance of the Duke", who delivered the Duike's invitation to the Poet's fellow-traveller "in all the forms of politeness", in order to prolong the Poet's visit at *Bonie Castle Gordon*.

It is a most pleasing retrospect of those dark days to know that almost the whole of the nobility of the North of Scotland rowed in the same boat with Professor Ogilvie in connection with his scheme for the reform of University Education.

Ogilvie tried hard to prevent Universities being utilised for the promulgation of positive ignorance and that form of superstition which fosters the doctrine of commercial landlordism. We are now accustomed to the *land merchant* in the same way as our ancestors were accustomed to the *slave merchant*. The present proposals to redeem the land and compensate the owners are on all-fours with the slave question proposals of the past. Some 'owners' are now selling out, and some *slaves* are buying in. The latter should study the SINGLE TAX question.

Among the ardent supporters of Professor Ogilvie for University Reform we find the following, viz.: The Duke of Gordon, the Earl of Buchan, the Earl of Kintore, the Earl of Aboyne, the Earl of Aberdeen, Lord Adam Gordon, Lord Gardenstone, Sir Alexander Ramsay, Sir David Carnegie, Mr. Baillie of Dochfour, with the Earl of Findlater and Seafield, *Chancellor of King's College*, and the Earl of Bute, *Chancellor of Marischal College*, as pioneers.

All the noblemen above-mentioned openly gave their names in favour of Professor Ogilvie's scheme of educational reform. They also pulled with him as *real* land reformers; and other landlords could be mentioned, who were equally keen for education and land reform. These truly noble men were, with Burns and a few other exceptions, the *only* radicals of those days.

Here is a wonderful picture of landlordism, is it not? To find all these noblemen pulling together in the same boat with the author of *The Right of Property in Land* at the helm, is a fact well worthy of a corner in history.

There is ample evidence that it was these self-same truly noble men who gave the first impulse to Agricultural industry in the North-East of Scotland. The counties of Aberdeen and Banff - the district of Professor Ogilvie's landlord associates - form a distinct small-holding sanctuary on the map of Scotland to this day.

The same Act of Parliament which abolished military tenure in 1747 abolished also the feudal hereditary jurisdiction of all the landlords in Scotland. Until then we must not forget that the landlords had the power to hang, drown, or dungeon the people as they liked, just as they now have the power to shoot grouse, deer, and other wild animals; but with this difference, that there was no close time - they could hang people all the year round! It was a great privilege, and one upon which the majority of the landlords put some value; and, of course, they lodged a claim for compensation !! The matter was decided in the Court of Session in the year 1748. They claimed the sum of £1,587,090 sterling, and that Court allowed £152,037 12s. 2d. as a redemption price of the sole right and privilege of that form of Scottish landlord sport in all time to come.

The *poor* Scot in those days had to cringe under tyranny, with an alternate choice of starvation at home or slave-driving abroad. We know that even Burns was only prevented from becoming a slave-driver by "the accidental delay of the vessel in which he had taken out his passage for Jamaica", and the almost equally accidental friendly intervention of the Rev. Dr. Blacklock. "I had", says the Poet in his letter to Dr Moore, "composed the last song I should ever measure in Caledonia - 'The gloomy night is gath'ring fast', when a letter from Dr. Blacklock to a friend of mine* overthrew all my schemes, by

---

* *The Rev. George Lawrie of St. Margaret's Hill, Kilmarnock. Is it not remarkable that Providence made use of two divines to prevent Robert Burns from leaving Scotland in those days? Scotland should not forget these two men. They should be entered as St. Thomas and St. George on the roll of Scottish Saints.*

opening up new prospects to my poetic ambition."

This was in the autumn of 1786. At this time, precisely, Professor Ogilvie was in the thick of his fight for the Light and Truth in Aberdeen. The year 1786 marks a period of contemporaneous radical reforming eruption of the I AM spirit of these two men. It is perhaps not strange that their meetings, or correspondence, have been kept from the public eye to this hour, after all.

Has *British Christianity* in any way changed its creeds or tenets since those days of '*respectable professions*?' No! not one iota. And hence we have waste wildernesses under sheep abroad, and under deer, sheep, and game at home, while we breed human sinners *for* the slums of towns, and *in* the slums of towns, to a most alarming number. Why call it 'Christianity?' Herodianity, Pharaohianity, or Neroianity would be much nearer the appropriate name. Let us think for a moment about the idea of Jesus Christ *being in the flesh* in Britain at the present time, and holding His tongue about the doings of landlordism, with its evictions and rack rents! Or think of Him on a platform supporting Mr. A.J. Balfour, or His Grace the Duke of Argyll!

The Duke of Fife is, perhaps, the only Duke in the British isles, or any other country, who can say: "My ancestors purchased all the lands I possess, with the exceptions of some commons, such as Cairngorm or Benmacdhui, acquired merely as their share of the spoil when the other landlords were having a general scramble for all the hills and glens in Scotland".

How did the *House of Fife* rise so very rapidly? Besides the possession of land, and the influence invariably associated therewith, there was something else. The *House of Fife*, we find, attached to itself not less than twenty-three Church Patronages!

The so-called *natural or divine homage* towards landlordism, the Earl of Fife knew to be a College manufactured article, and a saleable commodity: He knew that the *House of Argyll* was maintained by the dexterous manipulation of ecclesiastical influence. He purchased from the *Seven Wise Masters* several Church Patronages in Aberdeen which had belonged to the University from its foundation. He was, therefore, bound to join in the crusade against the proposed educational college reforms of 1786 for reasons too obvious to require any explanation. If his *shepherds* were to be taught any new notions about his *sheep* having any right to the land, or even to their own *wool*, that would be a most dangerous doctrine!

The reader cannot fail to see the thing. Christianity, like all other forms of religion which preceded it in this world, once taken up by an aristocratic class, was bound to become an instrument of oppression. We know what the Church did in the past, and we can catch her red-handed at the same *game* now if we like. But as Christians, we wink at the monopolising of land - nay, we are the pioneers of that system in this world.

Nevertheless, the Duke of Fife does not feel free from risk. He is, therefore, selling his lands in Scotland as fast as he can. He knows that his title deeds are worse than useless. They prove that he is in possession of stolen property - the property of the People!

They prove that all his lands are liable for the *National Debt*! They prove that the People, or, to put it technically in order to drive the fact into the thick skulls of ignorant lawyers, *that the Crown, the feudal Superior of all landlords, as Trustee for the People*, can legally and justly impose the SINGLE TAX, *and tax all lands to their full value*. And it is no answer to the People's claim that a landlord, or his ancestors purchased the land; otherwise the Duke of Argyll and a few other dukes and lords might at any time sell England, Wales, Scotland and Ireland to Mr. Winans, or to the Emperor of Russia.

The following paragraph is taken, word for word, from a boycotted book, written by Sir George MacKenzie of Rosehaugh, and published by *Royal Authority* in the year 1678, bearing the title; 'The Laws and Customes of Scotland in matters Criminal'. Sir George is referred to as a believer in the *divine right of Kings*, but it is quite clear that he did not believe in the *divine right* of "Oppressors, thieves, *and other great men*!" This passage, be it observed is taken from his Chapter on ROBBERY:-

"The Crimes answering in the Civil Law to oppression were *vis publica, vis privata and concussio*. Those were punishable, *I. julia de vi publica*, who raised arms, or did violently eject men out of their houses or lands; those who assisted the Oppressors with men are guilty thereof, and the punishment was *aquae et ignis interdictio*..."

George Mackenzie was 'a gentleman'. When the judges of the Court of Session banished all the members of the Scottish Bar from Edinburgh, in obedience to a letter from Charles II, George Mackenzie appeared before them as 'a gentleman', he said, and he made these obsequious functionaries and also their royal master sprawl under his feet. He, notwithstanding his weakness for the divine right of Kings, on that occasion manfully vindicated the divine right of every man to defend himself, and to oppose tyranny, injustice, or impudence in a King as in a beggar.

Sir George is almost the only Scottish Lawyer ever known to have done anything for Liberty and Property, hence the reason he and his books have been systematically boycotted to this hour.

Sir George was obliged to leave his own country and take refuge in England.

No country in the world can boast of better laws than Scotland. It is, however, not necessary to reiterate how these laws were broken, and by whom; or to make any comment regarding the punishment which might and ought to be inflicted on the breakers of these laws.

The 'aristocratical spirit', and the belief therein, forced upon the people by courts, colleges, churches, and schools, reigned supreme in the British Isles, and in Scotland in particular, during the whole period of Professor Ogilvie's life.

What an exposure he has made of the various institutions and orders whose chief aim is to conceal the truth and to perpetuate injustice, namely, Universities, Colleges, Courts of Law, Religious Sects, Political sects, and the whole fraudulent fraternity of human parasites which hang around *The Powers that be*!

There is more than one reason for giving a place in these *Notes* to (some extracts from) a letter, written to GENERAL WASHINGTON by the Earl of Buchan, the mutual friend of Burns and Ogilvie:-

"DRYBURGH ABBEY,
"28th June, 1791.

"Sir, - I had the honor to receive your Excellency's letter ... may that Almighty Being, who rules over the universe, who presides in the councils of nations, and whose providential aid can supply every human defect, consecrate to the liberties and happiness of the American people a Government instituted by themselves for public and private security, upon the basis of law and equal administration of justice, preserving to every individual as much civil and political freedom as is consistent with the safety of the nation ... I have entrusted this sheet, inclosed in a box made of the oak that sheltered our great Sir William Wallace after the Battle of Falkirk, to Mr. Robertson of Aberdeen, a painter, with the hope of his having the honor of delivering it into your hands ... I beg leave to recommend him to your countenance as he has been mentioned to me favourably by my worthy friend Professor Ogilvie of King's College, Aberdeen ...

"I am, with the highest esteem, Sir,
"Your Excellency's most obedient and
obliged humble servant,

"BUCHAN"

It would seem from the words now italicised that Ogilvie and Washington were not unknown to each other; and it is highly probable that the latter was presented with an early copy of *The Right of Property in Land*, and with some manuscript notes besides. The reader will remember that he refers to *North America* as having "lately enjoyed an opportunity of new modelling the establishment of landed property, even to theoretical perfection".

If Professor Ogilvie visited Dryburgh Abbey in June, 1791, he would then be within a day's ride of the abode of Burns. Trying to catch the *Twa Dogs* together, oddly enough we again come upon a suppression of dates and names.

"*In the summer of 1791*", says Dr. Currie, "two English gentlemen, who had before met with Burns in Edinburgh, paid a visit to him in Ellisland. He received them with great cordiality, and asked them to share his humble dinner - an invitation which they accepted." They did not leave before midnight - they "forgot the flight of time and the dictates of prudence". No wonder; for Burns, as described *by one of the party* to Dr. Currie, "was in his happiest mood, and the charms of his conversation were altogether fascinating. He ranged over a great variety of topics, illuminating whatever he touched. He related the tales of his infancy and of his youth; he recited some of the gayest and some of the tenderest of his poems: in the wildest of his strains of mirth he threw in some touches of malancholy, and spread around him the electric emotions of his powerful mind."

Who were these two '*English* gentlemen', and in particular what name shall we call the one who gave the information to Dr. Currie; and why should Dr. Currie suppress the name of any real Englishman? One thing is clear - *Twa* sympathetic souls - whether they were *the* 'Twa Dogs' or not - did meet and spend a happy night together.

Considering the state of poor Scotland then, and the watching by 'epauletted puppies' and other spies of all the movements and meetings of persons suspected of being possessed of any genuine I AM spirit, Professor Ogilvie, no doubt, found it necessary as a rule to travel *incognito in his own country* - most likely as an *Englishman*, keeping his thumb upon the meaning of his own phrase - '*the Northern Counties of England*'. He wrote his *Essay* as an *Englishman*, and inscribed it to *Englishmen*!

We can hardly realise now-a-days the dangers and difficulties that a reformer like Professor Ogilvie had to contend with in his time - a time when the Soul of Freedom had, in truth, fled from Scotland. There is no doubt whatever of this, that if his notions of land-law reform had been fully known to the landed *gentry* and clergy, his life would have been taken either by a paid assassin, or by a stirred-up mob. He was an 'ingenious recluse', and thus escaped more successfully than his renowned contemporary Dr. Priestley*, whose house was burnt by a Birmingham mob, his books and manuscripts torn and strewed for miles along the public road, while he himself had to run for his life.

A military rabble, led by 'epauletted puppies', to use the designation handed down to us by Burns, sacked the house of the Rev. John Skinner of *Tullochgorum* fame, carrying with them his books, manuscripts, and 'everything'. They spared his Manse, but they burnt his Church to the ground. More than once *Tullochgorum* saved his life by 'skulking' in some hiding place, or "attiring himself in the garb of a miller, to escape the observation" of the military miscreants of those times.

We can imagine the pangs felt by the highly sympathetic soul of William Ogilvie for the "woes and pains" of others, in those days. As regards his own personal sufferings, his *weep-not-for-me* spirit almost arrests us from referring to them in these pages. In his soliloquy of 1776 we see a man who could bravely and contentedly face death itself, "without reluctance and repining". "Having", says he, "abundant reason to return thanks for that measure of good which I

---

* *The Rev. Robert Hall of Cambridge, who defended Dr. Priestley and vindicated the French Revolution as well as British Liberty, was an ardent disciple of Professor Ogilvie. He attended his lectures during four sessions (1781-86), and was charmed with his translations of the Roman poets, which, in a letter to a friend, he described as "extremely elegant". It is well known that Robert Hall and Sir James Mackintosh were fellow-students, but few are aware that they studied under such a teacher as the author of* <u>*Birthright in Land*</u>.

have already enjoyed, which seems to have exceeded, at least in tranquility and contentment, the common standard of what is allowed to man".

We, however, cannot skip over another 'rude' and equally 'unseasonable visit', as a companion picture of the period. When the so-called *Royal Army* was passing through Morayshire in 1746, a short halt was made at Pittensear House, and three cannon shots were fired at it. One of these shots struck the front wall close to the dining room window, and, we need not say, caused the inmates much alarm. William Ogilvie, then about ten years of age, in all probability witnessed that scene - a sad example of what even a *Whig* Government may do at the head of a mercenary army. He, without any doubt, surveyed the wreck after the storm had passed. We have it on the authority of old people still living near Pittensear, that his mother, who happened to be in childbed at the time, never recovered the shock of that day's proceedings, and that shortly thereafter she was laid in a premature grave. And a few years later, when his disconsolate and broken-hearted father had quitted life's stage, he was left alone, in place of both father and mother, as guardian to four orphan girls.

Here we may trace the way in which, what we may call a *motherly feeling* towards all the children of men, was developed in his breast. His *Essay on the Right of Property in Land*, in every line of it, says: *Suffer little children to come unto me*, and I shall teach them that *God is no respecter of persons*; that all *the children of men* are entitled indiscriminately to an equal share in the soil, in all wild animals, game, fish, and the whole products of nature, necessary for man's subsistence or enjoyment; and that anything contrary to this doctrine is a gross and blasphemous slander on the Creator, as well as a most iniquitous fraud on the bulk of mankind.

Vive vale. Si quid novisti rectius istis,
Candidus imperti; si non, his utere mecum.

Farewell, then -

And if you can propose anything
more just than what's here said,
tell me frankly what it is.

If not,

See you make good use of this,
Even as I do.

(Translation by 8-A.H.)

APPENDIX

Resolutions of the Skye Crofters

The following benevolent principles of **Land Reform**, so much on Professor Ogilvie's lines, were adopted in Skye, as preached by Mr Henry George, before the **Essay** now re-published was unearthed:-

"Resolutions by the Skye Crofters, passed at Meetings addressed by MR HENRY GEORGE in January, 1885.

"Whereas the land was made by God, who is no respecter of persons, for the equal use and enjoyment of all the people whom He brings into life upon it, we hereby declare, that any system which compels the people to pay rent to other human creatures, for the privilege of living upon God's earth, is a robbery of labour, and a wicked violation of the benevolent intention of the Creator.

"**Resolved.** - That while we shall thankfully welcome * any measures that will lessen the tyrannous power which the so-called landlords of Skye have exercised over us, we will not consider any measure as a settlement of the land question which does not restore our Gof-given rights in our native soil, <u>and does not restore the same full rights to our brethren of the cities, towns, and mineral and agricultural districts of England, Scotland, Ireland, and Wales</u>, by taking all rent for land for the common benefit of the whole people, putting an end to the wicked wrong which compels labouring men to want, suffering, and untimely death, in order that idlers may live in luxury.

"**Resolved.** - That we call upon our brethren, <u>the working men of the whole country</u>, to give us their support in obtaining our natural rights, as we shall give them ours in obtaining theirs, and especially we call upon them to enter their strongest protest against the invasion of Skye by armed forces from the mainland, with the object of enabling the landlords to deprive us of the means necessary for the support of our families, by virtue of laws in the making of which we have had no voice.

"Resolved. - That the attention of the Right Hon. Sir Wm. Vernon Harcourt is hereby called to the unconstitutional manner in which the Sheriff and Procurator-Fiscal of the County of Inverness have acted with regard to the people of Skye, and that he is hereby requested to institute an open inquiry into their proceedings, with a view to their impeachment, removal, and punishment, and that the present Commissioners of Police of the County be at once suspended, and a measure introduced into the next session of Parliament abolishing all such hereditary-landlord-authorities* not founded on the voice of the people.

"Resolved. - That this meeting tender heartfelt thanks to the Right Hon. W.E. Gladstone for having successfully carried through Parliament an Act which enables crofters, for the first time, to exercise their right in the making of laws which affect their interests."

It is from little insignificant facts, observed here and there, that we are sometimes able to discover the course of human affairs, and those movements which now and again lead to the overthrow of long-established systems of despotism and slavery. We discover the currents of the sea by watching the ripples on the surface, and the mere straws which float in it.

* The Local Government (Scotland) Act, 1889, gave partial effect to this suggestion, but owing to the sickly condition of the children of Liberty in Lowland Caledonia, Scotland is still held under Landlord thraldom, excepting that the Crofters' Act, 1886, has produced an effect something like the taking of the Bastille. Rents in the Lowlands came tumbling down without any Land Court.

Extracts from the Biographical Notes

THE

STRATHCONON CHRONICLE

*

A Few Words on the Strathconon Chronicle,
by S-A.H.

The Strathconon Chronicle

*

as being, underneath all the veneer, a pretty well fully-fledged Land League reformer himself! I chose, then, to let this better part of Maister Whatefer have the final word. I think **we** can do with it too.

*

The edition of the **Strathconon Chronicle** which appears here, (running together the two sections that appear separately in D.C. MacDonald's work), is exactly as produced by me in 1996 for the Scottish Ogilvie Society - concentrating much on the Burns section, since part of our aim at that time was to keep the book as compact as possible. (Note: I see that the edition of the **Strathconon Chronicle** which appeared in the Othila Press publication of 1997, chose to retain my re-siting of this verse, along with my original 1996 editing of the ending, as here.)

* * *

Mid-March 1999.....Now what did I say about those computers wanting to teach you how to speak? - ! It's D.C. MacDonald who's got fairly rapped on the knuckles this time - **all** the way through! Yes - there must have been a spell-check on, for it has **expunged ALL** of the soft highland speech of Maister Whatefer from end to end - starting with his name! **He**'s Maister Whate**ver now** - **whatever!**

As there is not the smallest question of my starting, at this date, to check through seven pages of those "rappings" in the new typesetting, I am thankfully returning to the one it was copied from - (with acknowledgements to the Scottish Ogilvie Society typesetting of 1996, which takes over from the next page)...!!

*

D.C. MacDonald makes a telling and humorous Addition to his Biographical Notes, with-

The Rev. Maister Whatefer's

CHRONICLE
OF STRATHCONON

Recorded by D.C. MacDonald
and edited by Shirley-Anne Hardy

...And as his musings unfold, the suppressed thoughts of this 'Wee Free' Minister, despite himself, gradually surface - until we sense him positively smacking his lips at the goings-on of the 'agitator' Land Leaguers. We also discover that he knows a good deal more about Professor William Ogilvie than he at first lets on...

"And it was these pad landlords who refused to kive a stance to puild a Free Church - themselves and the Teffil together - that kindled the Highland Crofters to so much wicket 'agitation' in recent years, until, like the foolish Galatians, they were pewitched by ungodly Land Leaguers apout more land, fair rents, and other worldly affairs instead of always minding the salvation of their souls.

as being, underneath all the veneer, a pretty well fully-fledged Land League reformer himself! I chose, then, to let this better part of Maister Whatefer have the final word. I think we can do with it too.

*

The edition of the **Strathconon Chronicle** which appears here, (running together the two sections that appear separately in D.C. MacDonald's work), is exactly as produced by me in 1996 for the Scottish Ogilvie Society - concentrating much on the Burns section, since part of our aim at that time was to keep the book as compact as possible. (Note: I see that the edition of the **Strathconon Chronicle** which appeared in the Othila Press publication of 1997, chose to retain my re-siting of this verse, along with my original 1996 editing of the ending, as here, (although without ascription), inserting a few extra words. S-A.H., Apr 98.

* * *

Mid-March 1999.....Now what did I say about those computers wanting to teach you how to speak? - ! It's D.C. MacDonald who's got fairly rapped on the knuckles this time - **all** the way through! Yes - there must have been a spell-check on, for it has **expunged ALL** of the soft highland speech of Maister Whatefer from end to end - starting with his name! **He**'s Maister Whate**ver now - whatever!**

As there is not the smallest question of my starting, at this date, to check through seven pages of those "rappings" in the new typesetting, I am thankfully returning to the one it was copied from - (with acknowledgements to the Scottish Ogilvie Society typesetting of 1996, which takes over from the next page)...!!

*

D.C. MacDonald makes a telling and humorous Addition to his Biographical Notes, with-

The Rev. Maister Whatefer's

CHRONICLE
OF STRATHCONON

Recorded by D.C. MacDonald
and edited by Shirley-Anne Hardy

...And as his musings unfold, the suppressed thoughts of this 'Wee Free' Minister, despite himself, gradually surface - until we sense him positively smacking his lips at the goings-on of the 'agitator' Land Leaguers. We also discover that he knows a good deal more about Professor William Ogilvie than he at first lets on...

"And it was these pad landlords who refused to kive a stance to puild a Free Church - themselves and the Teffil together - that kindled the Highland Crofters to so much wicket 'agitation' in recent years, until, like the foolish Galatians, they were pewitched by ungodly Land Leaguers apout more land, fair rents, and other worldly affairs instead of always minding the salvation of their souls.

And instead of attending prayer meetings and sermons, they follow after false prophets like Henry George, going to Land League meetings, and packsliding ferry fast to the old wickedness of the pagpipes, and worldly songs of many ungodly poets like Purns, who was a ferry pad man when he was alive, and more so after he was tead. For his sinful song-book is still read out of sight in many places, which has a ferry 'unsettling tendency' for putting the poor against the gentry and the clergy, and making them forsake the *Confession of Faith*, which must be obeyed whatefer.

"But Oichi Hoichi where will the Land Leaguers, and 'Agitators', and Purns, and Henry George, and Parnell, and poor Gladstone if he toes not repent, go to? There will be plenty of primstone, and weeping and wailing, and knashing of teeth in that place whatefer, and they will get more than plenty of Home Rule from the Teffil, for all eternity, and for efer and efer Amen! For the Teffil was the first Home Ruler, and the first rebel, when he rebelled against God. And it is the Teffil that is now stirring up the people in Ireland and in the Highlands against the '*Powers that pe*', which '*are ordained of God*', as laid down ferry clearly in the *Confession of Faith*, which efery godly man is pound to sign. And all this shows ferry clearly what pig fools the Crofters and the Irish are, when they pelieve what these ungodly Agitators tell them about *fixity of tenure*, *fair rents*, and *free sale*. And who is to rule over them, if the gentry was apolished?

"There was only one agitator minister in the Isle of Skye, and *he was a pachelor*; and although he was a

Moderate, the Free Church people got ferry fond of him, for he preached nothing but Land League toctrines in the pulpit, as well as at Land League meetings. And he is now a *Moderate* minister in the Island of Lewis. And *Free Churchmen* helped to vote him into a ferry goot Parish Klebe and steepend there. And he carried with him the agitation wherefer he went. A little steepend will do ferry well for a single man, and that's the reason that priests and pachelor ministers can afford to join the Land Leaguers, for they are all right if they ket a little cream for their tea from a neighbour, which is quite easy whatefer. Putt what can these pachelors understand apout keeping a wife, and ketting food, and clothes, and shoes, and pooks, and education, for a houseful of children? It is not at all easy for a married minister who has a large family, and only a small steepend, to pe a Land Leaguer, for you see the competition for situations is now so ferry fearful, that, unless one has a letter of recommendation from a landlord, or one of the gentry, it is impossible to get into any post of any kind whatefer, or into a shop or office in Glasgow or Edinburgh or London, or any goot post aproad.

"In the Highlands, we have peen able to keep the people from reading such radical and infidel pooks as Purns, and Carlyle, and Shakespeare, and from singing their own traditional Gaelic songs too, and to confine them to the Psalms, and the Pible, and John Bunyan, and some sermon pooks, and also the *Confession of Faith* and the *Catechisms*, all of which they must not understand except through the ministers, or through *The men* appointed by *The Society for Propagating Christian Knowledge*, or py the Free Church. And *The men* were all ferry safe teachers and kept town all agitation, for they never would discourse apout any happiness except heaven and eternity, and they would not speak apout any Land League affairs, or read any of Ossian, or Purns whatefer.

"In the olden time, when wars were always plentiful, and fighting men much required by the landlords, the assistance of the clergy for enlisting was necessary whatefer; and it was then that they could ferry easily get posts for their sons, in return for such assistance. Plenty of enemies were always made in those tays, to keep the wars koing, in order to maintain the price of krain at a shenteel figure, so that there would pe no risk of the rents of land falling whatefer! For you see the ministers' steepends would fall too, if the price of krain came down, and the gentry and clergy peing in the same poat, you see, would sink together. And the poor, who are always poor, would not pe a pit the petter whatefer, put on the contrary, much worser, pecause the gentry and the clergy would pe less able to kive them the usual *charity!* And it is here one can see ferry clearly, the wickedness of the repeal of the *Corn Laws*, which kave a kreat plow to *charity*, and other forms of holiness!

"If the Radicals get much more of their own way they will pass an Act of Parliament for having efery pody porn into the world with equal rights to eferything, and even the most sacred rights which the landlords hafe to the land will be *controverted!* and all rents, and, may pe, all tithes too, *confiscated* - among the community at large.

"There is no toubt these things are coming fast, for the young clergy are peginning to pe ferry radical whatefer, and they now lay kreat stress on the words: *That God is no respecter of persons*, and such like Piple texts, without modifying them in any way py the *Confession of Faith*. And, in like manner, they fix upon the words Thy Kingdom come: *Thy Will be done ON THE EARTH, as it is in heaven*. For, you see, there will pe no landlords there whatefer! Now this is a kreat *innovation*! as the old ministers were always ferry careful not to meddle much with the "earth", and the rights of the landlords therein, for fear of preaking their vows under the *Confession of Faith*, which enjoined full obedience and subserviency to the landlords, on the part of the common people whatefer.

"It is the wicked *Land Leaguers* that are to plame for kiving such tangerous knowledge to the people, for the 'agitation' has stirred them up to make inquiry apout *all* their rights; and the *Free Church* which stood up for the apolition of Church-lordism in 1843, is put into a strange fix as to the apolition of land-lordism now. The changes that are taking place are ferry extraordinary, when we consider how the landed gentry and the clergy worked hand in hand in times of old.

"Now, although I hafe, as a minister, to keep town all *agitation*, still I must sympathise *in reality* with those who come to look at the land, and at the ruins of the old twellings, from which their ancestors, or maybe their parents, or themselves when children were evicted. It would be a kreat wonder if these were not Land Leaguers whatefer. Even my own poys are krowing up on the side of the *agitation* in spite of me.

The Chronicle of Strathconon

"By the way, it was at King's College, Aberdeen, that my wife's father studied, and he had many stories apout all the Professors there, although I forget their names. If my wife's prother, William, who tied only a year ago, was alive, I am sure he could tell something apout such a man as professor Ogilvie, for he knew all his father's old stories. I remember hearing apout a ferry radical Aberdeen Professor of that time, who had to do with the innovation which spoilt the Universities; py opening the doors to the children of poor men, without kiving any compensation to those who formerly enjoyed the exclusive privileges and endowments of education.

"Look on England - there is no land agitation there whatefer! For they have still *conserved* all the privileges of Oxford and Cambridge for the nobility and gentry, and that's the reason why so many of the English, who ton't pelong to the *privileged* classes, have to send their poys to the Scottish Universities; while at the same time the sons of the Scottish nobility and gentry are enjoying all the endowments and privileges of Oxford and Cambridge.

"Putt things in England may go ferry wrong soon too, for they took in Professor Robertson Smith there, after he was put out of the Free Church College of Aberdeen. For you see, that innovation about colleges and education is the first step of the mischief, and it will pe a wonder if Professor Robertson Smith refrains from writing a Land League pook too. You see clearly how that old radical Professor Ogilvie who pegan the innovations of the Aberdeen Colleges was also the author of a Land League pook.

"Putt he tid a much wickeder thing than that, when he wrote a jubilee treatise on the Land Laws of Moses. And it is a ferry tangerous argument to say that *Jesus came to fulfil those Laws*, and that efery landlord must "return efery man into his possession" *of the land*, all in accordance with chapter xxv. of *Leviticus*. The parable of the Tuke of Argyll - who is a *Campbell !* - having *to go through the eye of a needle*, is also a ferry wicked argument whatefer.

"And, moreofer, it is ferry much against the *Confession of Faith* to say that the clergy, after the example of Jesus, should try to save the souls of the rich py advising them to kive up all their lands to the poor, whose labour *earned* the wrongly-called '*un*-earned increment' of the value of such lands. For this is the Kospel *Notice to quit*! And to the clergy who fail to deliver this *Notice*, and to the landlords who fail to obey it, the Lord says:- "If ye will not be reformed by me by these things, but will walk contrary unto me; then will I also walk contrary unto you, and will punish you yet seven times for your sins. And I will make your cities waste, and bring your sanctuaries into desolation" - all as foretold in chapter xxvi. of *Leviticus*, which raises a ferry difficult point in the minds of all those who pelieve in the Scottish *Confession of Faith*, and in the English and Irish *Faiths* too, more especially on account of the French Revolution fulfilment of that ferry old law*.

" I have seen some nations like o'erloaded asses
Kick off their burthens - meaning the high classes. "

* Lord Macaulay, speaking in the British House of Commons, on Parliamentary Reform in 1831, appealed to the English Aristocracy, to take warning by the fate of the *noblesse* of France. "And why", asked

"Putt, as I was going to say, the story of Professor Ogilvie's *Essay* on the Land Question, written in Scotland apout the year 1781, is ferry strange, and prings to my mind a difficulty my wife and myself always had apout Purns and his *Twa Dogs*. Where tid Purns get all his information apout the *outs* and *ins* of the private life of the shentry, and how they lived aproad too? My wife always pelieved that *Caesar* was a real man, and, moreofer, a real shentleman too, who knew from his own observation all apout the ways of the shentry. She thinks he was a confidential friend of Purns -

" Nae doubt but they were fain o' ither,
An' unco pack and thick thegither " -

and that Purns disguised him as well as he could py saying that:

- " he was nane o' Scotland's dogs,
But whalpet some place far abroad,
Where sailors gang to fish for cod. "

She is of opinion that Dr Currie, when he inquired so specially apout it, must have strongly suspected that there was a real *Caesar* - the most of Purns's characters being from real life whatefer. The answer which his (Burns's)

Macaulay, "were those haughty nobles destroyed with that utter destruction? Why were they scattered over the face of the earth, their titles abolished, their escutcheons defaced, their parks wasted, their palaces dismantled. their heritage given to strangers? Because they had no sympathy with the people, no discernment of the signs of the times; because, in the pride and narrowness of their hearts, they called those whose warning might have saved them, theorists and speculators; because they refused all concession till the time had arrived when no concession would avail."

prother, Gilbert, gave, she thinks, is what might pe expected for several reasons. He was not so foolish, my wife says, as to tell who *Caesar* was, supposing he knew it.

"After that arch Land Leaguer, Henry George, came ofer to this country, I used to say to my wife: 'There's your *Caesar* now. And I myself looked upon his coming from America to *Caesarize* us *à la Purns*, as a sort of prophecy fulfilled, putt the answer I always kot from my wife was 'Fiddlesticks!' Now if I tell her that Professor Ogilvie was a Land Leaguer and a contemporary of Purns, she will at once say that he was *Caesar* whatefer. You know how strange women are for shumping at conclusions!

"Well, shust to try her, I'll not tell her a word, at first, apout what sort of a man Professor Ogilvie was. I'll not say that he was of the real *landed shentry* or that he was the 'shentleman and scholar' who acted as travelling tutor to the Tuke of Gordon on a grand tour of Europe, which tour is so vividly pictured in the *Twa Dogs* as to suggest the pencil of an eye-witness - a philosophical Land-law-reforming eye!

"Of course I'll tell her all these things quietly and py degrees. Putt there is one thing I'll tell her ferry cautiously whatefer, namely this - that it was in the same year (1786) Purns wrote and published his *Twa Dogs*, and Professor Ogilvie wrote and published his *plan of campaign* against the *Highland shentry and klergy*, for the apolition and confiscation of their own College at Aberdeen, which, pefore his innovations, was generally known as *The Highland University*.

Birthright...and...Scotland Today

"Were I to tell her that Professor Ogilvie had a kreat affection for pastoral poets like Virgil, and that he was ferry fond of Horace and Ovid, and that he was 'tinctured with the sublime melancholy of Ossian', she would at once conclude that he, when maturing his *plan*, in that year, 1786, must have visited his academic friends in Glasgow, for it was the Glasgow University he took as his model for the proposed *united* University of Aberdeen. She could ferry easily put me in a corner by asking me, whether I thought any reasonable person could imagine that a Land Leaguer and a lover of pastoral poetry like Professor Ogilvie could refrain from going the length of Ayrshire to visit another Land Leaguer, and a maker, as well as a lover, of pastoral poetry? You see *I* could not say *'Fiddlesticks'* to that whatefer. Professor Ogilvie had his knife ready for the 'Highland Gentry' at that time, as shown by his *Plan of Campaign*, which came out in print on the 20th of July, 1786. And it was 'upon a bonie day *in June*', 1786, that the *Twa Dogs*:

" began a lang digression
About the LORDS O' THE CREATION. "

"For Purns also had his knife in the *Highland gentry* at that time; which comes out ferry clearly in the *Address of Beelzebub* on the Ist of June, 1786, putt kept from being published until 1818; and the true story of it is still expunged from all editions *for the people!* You see the Glengarry men revolted against their Chief in 1786 pecause he took all their lands from them. Eviction was the reward or bounty they received for fighting under the false colours of British Liberty in the American War of

Independence. They fought for the liberty of landlordism - *the liberty to evict* - and they got it!

Other chiefs, on hearing that the Glengarry men resolved to emigrate to America, "agreed to co-operate with Government" to prevent by force these landless Highlanders from emigrating *"in search of their natural rights!"* It was this that moved Purns to write: -

> ' *To the Right Honourable the Earl of Breadalbane, President of the Right Honourable and Honourable the Highland Society, which met on the 23rd of May last (1786) at the Shakespeare, Covent Garden,* to concert ways and means to frustrate the design of five hundred Highlanders, who, *as the Society were informed by Mr Mackenzie of Applecross,* were so audacious as to attempt an escape from their lawful lords and masters, whose property they were, *by emigrating from the lands of Mr McDonald of Glengarry to the wilds of Canada,* in search* of that fantastic thing - LIBERTY '. †

"In the following year, 1787, when addressing the water-fowl of Loch Turrit, the poet's eye was evidently still fixed on the Glengarry *exodus:* -

> " Swiftly seek, on clanging wings,
> Other lakes and other springs,
> And the foe you cannot brave,
> Scorn at least to be his slave. "

* Compare these words with Professor Ogilvie's phrase - 'in search of their natural rights'.

† See *"Address to Beelzebub"*, as cited.

"Were it not that my wife was always ferry fond of Purns, I would pe as ignorant of him as any other Free Church Minister in the Highlands whatefer. For it is always our recognised duty to put in the fire efery copy of Purns, or such pooks, we get a hold of in the hands of our people. Putt this copy of Purns my wife has is a ferry old one that has pelonged to her mother, which was always kept locked up; and my wife got a hold of it when her mother tied. She also keeps it locked up. And we must not read it, except on the sly, so that nopody discovers there is a Purns in the Free Manse whatefer.

"And there is no *agitation* in our district except on the part of some radical Protestant crofters and two or three Catholics, who assert and maintain that the land was originally appropriated by spoliation and robbery, and that the landlords have no right to it whatefer; and they say it is the Teffil, and not Providence, that worked all the mischief; and they call the priest and myself the Teffil's agents too, and they look upon the *Crofters' Act* as real Providence from God in their favour. And they say that the doctrine preached in favour of landlordism is quite contrary to the letter, as well as the spirit, of the Gospel of Jesus. They also say that all those who pray, "Thy kingdom come: Thy will be done on earth as it is in heaven", but who nevertheless stand by, and do nothing to disapprove of rack rents, evictions, and other oppressions *on the earth*, are not much petter than Judas Iscariot; and moreover, that Christianity has been abused as a pretext for war, slavery, and landlordism for a ferry long time."

THE FOUNDATION OF SOCIAL JUSTICE

*

A Historic Statement by Patrick Edward Dove on Property in Land

*

with Dove the Man, by Julia Bastian

*

THE FOUNDATION OF SOCIAL JUSTICE

PATRICK EDWARD DOVE'S HISTORIC STATEMENT

THE QUESTION is upon what terms, or according to what system, must the earth be possessed by the successive generations that succeed each other on the surface of the globe? The conditions given are – *First*, That the earth is the common property of the race; *Second*, That whatever an individual produces by his own labour (whether it be a new object, made out of many materials, or a new value given by labour to an object whose form, locality, etc., may be changed) is the private property of that individual, and he may dispose of it as he pleases, provided he does not interfere with his fellows; *Third*, The earth is the *perpetual* common property of the race, and each succeeding generation has a full title to a free earth. One generation cannot encumber a succeeding generation.

And the condition required is, such a system as shall secure to the successive individuals of the race their share of the common property, and the opportunity without interference of making as much private property as their skill, industry, and enterprise would enable them to make.

The scheme that appears to present itself most naturally is the general division of the soil, portioning it out to the inhabitants according to their number. Such appears to be the only system that suggests itself to most minds, if we may judge from the objections brought forward against an equalisation of property ...

Men must go forward, never backward. To speak of a division of lands in England is absurd. Such a division would be as useless as it is improbable. But it is more than useless – it is unjust; and unjust, not to the present so-called proprietors, but to the human beings who are continually being born into the world, and who have exactly the same natural right to a portion that their predecessors have.

The actual division of the soil need never be anticipated, nor would such a division be just, if the divided portions were made the property (legally, for they could never be so morally) of individuals.

If, then, successive generations of men cannot have their fractional share of the actual soil (including mines, etc.), how can the division of the advantages of the natural earth be effected?

By the division of its annual value or rent; that is, by making the rent of the soil the common property of the nation. That is (as the taxation is the common property of the State), by taking the whole of the taxes out of the rents of the soil, and thereby abolishing all other kinds of taxation whatever. And thus all industry would be absolutely emancipated from every burden, and every man would reap such natural reward as his skill, industry, or enterprise rendered legitimately his, according to the natural law of free competition.[1] This we maintain to be the only theory that will

[1] *We have no hesitation whatever in predicting that all civilised communities must ultimately abolish all revenue restrictions on industry, and draw the whole taxation from the rents of the soil. And this because the rents of the soil are the common produce of the whole labour of a community.*

satisfy the requirements of the problem of natural property. And the question now is: how can the division of the rent be effected? An actual division of the rent – that is, the payment of so much money to each individual – would be attended with, perhaps insuperable inconveniences; neither is such an actual division requisite, every requirement being capable of fulfilment without it.

We now apply this solution to England.* England forms a State; that is, a community acting through public servants for the administration of justice, etc. In the actual condition of England, many things are at present unjust; and the right of the Government to tax and make laws for those who are excluded from representation is at all events questionable. However, we shall make a few remarks on England as she is, and on England as she ought to be; that is, as she would be were the rules of equity reduced to practical operation.

1ST - The State has alienated the lands to private individuals called proprietors, and the vast majority of Englishmen are born to their labour, minus their share of the taxation. (I.e., the share of their wages that goes in tax. S-A.H.)

2ND - This taxation of labour has introduced vast systems of restriction on trades and industry. Instead of a perfectly free trade with all the world, England has adopted a revenue system that most materially diminishes both the amount of trade and its profit. And, instead of a perfectly free internal industry, England has adopted an excise that is as vexatious in its operation as can well be conceived. Both the customs and excise laws, and every other tax on industry, have arisen from the alienation of the soil from the state; and had the soil not been alienated, no tax whatever would have been requisite; and were the soil resumed (as it undoubtedly ought to be), every tax of every kind and character, save the common rent of the soil, might at once be abolished, with the whole army of collectors, revenue officers, cruisers, coast guards, excise men, etc., etc.

3RD - Taxation can only be on land or labour (by land we mean the natural earth, not merely the agricultural soil). These are the two radical elements that can be subjected to taxation, capital being originally derived from one or the other. Capital is only hoarded labour or hoarded rent; and as all capital must be derived from the one source or the other, all taxation of capital is only taxation of land or of labour. Consequently all taxation of whatever kind is; first, taxation of labour – that is, a deduction from the natural remuneration which God intended the labourer to derive from his exertions; or second, taxation of land – that is, the appropriation of the current value of the natural earth to the expenses of the State.

Now, labour is essentially private property, and land is not essentially private property, but, on the contrary, is the common inheritance of every generation of mankind. Where the land is taxed no man is taxed, nor does the taxation of land interfere in any way whatever with the progress of human industry. On the contrary, the taxation of land, rightly directed, might be made to advance the condition of the country to a high degree of prosperity.

4TH - For the expenses of a State there must be a revenue, and this revenue must be derived from the taxation of labour, or from the rent of the lands. There is no other alternative; either the rents of the soil must be devoted to the common expenses of the State, or the labour of individuals must be interfered with; and restrictions,

* Note: The reason why Dove speaks of England in this text is fully addressed in DCM's "Biographical Notes." S-A.H.

supervisions, prohibitions, etc., must be called into existence, to facilitate the collection of the revenue ...

The political history of landed property in England appears to have been as follows:-

1ST - The lands were accorded by the King to persons who were to undertake the military service of the Kingdom.

2ND - The performance of this military service was the condition on which individuals held the national land.

3RD - The lands were at first held for life, and afterwards were made hereditary.

4TH - The military service was abolished by the law, and a standing army introduced.

5TH - This standing army was paid by the King.

6TH - The King, having abolished the military services of the individuals who held the national land, resorted to the taxation of articles of consumption for the payment of the army.

The lands of England, therefore, instead of being held on condition of performing the military service of the kingdom, became the property of the individuals who held them, and thus the State of England lost the lands of England. And the military service of the kingdom, instead of being performed by those individuals who held the national land, was henceforth (after the reign of Charles II) to be paid for by the general taxation of the inhabitants of the country.

Therefore the present system of taxation, and the national debt, the interest of which is procured by the forcible taxation of the general inhabitants of England, are both due to the alienation of the lands from the State, inasmuch as the national debt (incurred for war expenses) would have been a debt upon the lands, and not a debt upon the people of England. If, therefore, the legislature had a right to abolish the military services of those who held the national land, and thereby to impose on the general community all the liabilities of the military service of the kingdom, the legislature has the same right to abolish the general taxation of the community, and to allocate to those who hold the land all the expenses that have been incurred, and that are still incurred, for the war charges of the kingdom.

The alienation of the land from the State, and its conversion into private property, was the first grand step that laid the foundation of the modern system of society in England – a system that presents enormous wealth in the hands of a few aristocrats, who neither labour nor even pay taxes in proportion to those who do labour; and a vast population labouring for a bare subsistence, or reduced sometimes by millions to the condition of pauperism.

So long as this system is allowed to continue it appears (from the constitution of the earth, and of man's power to extract from it a maintenance) an absolute impossibility that pauperism should be obliterated; inasmuch as the burden of taxation necessarily falls on labour, and more especially as the value of labour is necessarily diminished wherever there is a soil allocated to an aristocracy.[2] ...

The abolition of the military tenures, however, did not complete the great evolution by which the lands of England have been transformed into the property of a few thousand aristocrats. That evolution consisted of three great facts.

1ST - The allocation of the Church lands to individual proprietors.

2ND - The abolition of military tenure, and the substitution of the taxation of articles of consumption, in other words, of the taxation of labour.

3RD - The enclosure of the common lands, whereby vast numbers of the peasantry were ruined, deprived of their legal rights, which were quite as valid as the entails of the aristocracy, and, being separated from the land, were sent to propagate pauperism in the towns and villages ... And though the manufacturers of England, taking an expansion altogether unprecedented in the history of the world, were able to consume the redundant population, the time must come when the rate of increase will diminish, when the population shall find no maintenance either in the towns or in the country, and social changes attended with a more equitable distribution of the sources of wealth will result in spite of all that men can do to prevent them ...

No truth appears to be more satisfactorily and more generally borne out by the history of modern Europe than that the progression of men in the matter of liberty 'is from a diversity of privileges towards an equality of rights'; that is, that the past progress has been all in this direction since the maximum of diversity prevailed in the aspect of individual lord and individual serf. And if this be the case, it cannot be an unreasonable conclusion that if sufficient time be allowed for the evolution, the progress of change will continue to go on till some ultimate condition is evolved. And that ultimate condition can only be at the point where diversity of privilege disappears and every individual in the State is legally entitled to identically the same political functions. Diversities of office there may be, and there must be, but diversity of rights there cannot be without injustice.

Such, then, is the theoretic ultimatum that satisfies the reason with regard to its equity, and such is the historic ultimatum that the reason infers from the past history of mankind. Such, then, is the point towards which societies are progressing; and when that point is reached the ultimatum of equity is achieved and the present course of historical evolution is complete.

---

[2] *Political economists have insisted much on the small matters that affect the value of labour. By far the most important is the mode in which the soil is distributed. Wherever there is a free soil labour maintains its value. Wherever the soil is in the hands of a few proprietors ... labour necessarily undergoes depreciation. In fact, it is the disposition of the land that determines the value of labour. If men could get the land to labour on they would manufacture only for a remuneration that afforded more profit than God has attached to the cultivation of the earth. Where they cannot get the land to labour on they are starved into working for a bare subsistence. There is only one reason why the labour of England, Ireland and Scotland is of so little marketable value, and that reason is the present disposition of the soil. Were the soil disposed of according to the laws of equity there cannot be the least doubt that the labour of the labouring classes would at once rise to at least double its present value.*

The foregoing is taken from Patrick Edward Dove's book *The Theory of Human Progression (1850)*. The life sketch of him in the *Dictionary of National Biography* says of it: 'The main principle is that all progress is conditioned by the development of true knowledge; it maintains the doctrines of liberty and equality and argues that rent ought to belong to the nation. It thus anticipates Mr. George who praised it at a public meeting at Glasgow *(British Daily Mail – 19th December 1884)*, though Dove was a strong individualist and opposed to socialism.' The final remark is far from apt; no two men were closer in their social and economic thought than Patrick Edward Dove and Henry George.

Patrick Edward Dove was born at Lasswade, near Edinburgh, in 1815. As young man he travelled widely, and lived for a time in Paris and London. About 1840 he came into the family property in Ayrshire, and lived there until 1848, when an unfortunate investment deprived him of most of his fortune. Shortly after this he married and went to live at Darmstadt, in Germany, where he studied, wrote, and lectured. In 1850, the same year in which Herbert Spencer's *Social Statics* appeared, enunciating similar conclusions, Dove published his *Theory of Human Progression and Natural Probability of a Reign of Justice*. It was the first part of a work entitled *The Science of Politics*, of which the second part, *The Elements of Political Science*, appeared in 1854. The first part was acclaimed by Thomas Carlyle, Sir William Hamilton, Professor Blackie, and Senator Charles Sumner who circulated many copies in the United States, but it never secured general public attention. A second edition, edited by Mr. Alexander Harvey, was published in New York in 1895, and subsequently an excellent abridgement by Miss Julia Kellogg was published by Isaac H. Blanchard & Co., New York. The second part had even less attention, and is now exceedingly scarce. After publishing his book Dove lived for a time in Edinburgh, and later in Glasgow. He wrote extensively on economic, religious and philosophic subjects, and interested himself in military science. In 1860 he was stricken with paralysis and went to Natal in a vain search for health. Returning to Scotland, he died in 1873 and was buried in the Grange Cemetery in Edinburgh. "In his case," says Morrison Davidson *(Four Precursors of Henry George)*, "the adage 'jack of all trades and master of none' was strikingly falsified."

A.W. Madsen

*

Note: A.W. Madsen was Editor, in the earlier part of this century, of "Land and Liberty", an organ of the Henry George Foundation. (See Address List.)

This valuable Historic Statement, extracted from Patrick Edward Dove's work, is kept in print by the Henry George Foundation, and is re-published here by their kind permission. S-A.H.

PATRICK EDWARD DOVE

Julia Bastian

*Julia Bastian has worked as a journalist in London for many years, including a spell with **The Times**. On retirement she took on a part-time job for the Henry George Foundation of Great Britain.*
I am particularly pleased to have Julia's permission to include here her fine and enlightening contribution on Dove, which first appeared in an anthology of Georgist writings published in the U.S.A. in 1998. (See Reading-List for catalogue of the Henry George Foundation.) S-A.H.

Dove the Man

There are clansmen still around in the glens who will pay homage to the man they call the most popular landlord in Scotland. At a time when landlords were hated and feared, Patrick Edward Dove (1815-1873) became much-loved by his tenants, gaining their respect for his fair and honest dealings. This somewhat unusual landlord did not believe in a system where landlords collected the rents from tenants while they did all the work. He maintained that land rent should go direct to the state and be used for the benefit of the nation. Nor did he accept that the game laws of the time were equitable. He employed no keepers on his Scottish estate, and poachers could come and go as they pleased without interference.

Under the old Celtic tenures, the Klaan (children of the soil) had been the proprietors of the land they occupied. Whole counties, Sutherland for example, belonged to its inhabitants. Their chief was held to be their monarch and not a proprietor, and had no more right to expel them from their homes than the king across the border in England. But in 1807, the Duke of Sutherland ordered his agents to clear some 15,000 inhabitants from his land and to burn their homes. Year after year, more of his tenants were forced to abandon their snug farms and find new livelihoods elsewhere, or to seek a new life by emigrating to America. Such "clearances" continued with increasing severity and were not confined to Sutherland. Other parts of Scotland witnessed the tearing apart of the ancient ties which for centuries had bound clansmen to their chiefs. In Bute, the Duke of Hamilton caused the land area rented by twenty-seven families to be converted into one farm, they being deprived of their homes and possessions. The same sorry story was re-enacted in Argyll, Inverness-shire, Ross-shire, Perthshire and the Hebrides, to list but some of the affected areas. Everywhere men gave place to deer, so that Highland landlords might reap their golden harvests in the increase of their rent rolls from shooting and fishing rights.*

It was against this background that on July 31, 1815, a son was born to Lieutenant Francis Dove and his wife, Christiana Paterson. This prosperous aristocratic family resided at Lasswade near Edinburgh, where the young boy, Patrick Edward, enjoyed a loving and favoured childhood. From the earliest days, this precocious lad took an interest in everything around him, and soon expressed a liking for science and logic. His fascination for number, quantity, time and space, unity and diversity, remained with him throughout his life.**

His father was a serving officer in the Royal Navy at a time in history when the British seapower was unbeaten and towered above all rivals, especially with Nelson's victory at Trafalgar in 1805. Napoleon's unquenchable passion for war, and his restless ambition, had inflicted untold harm and suffering on millions of innocent people over a long period. Wellington had just defeated Napoleon, who was soon to be isolated

---

* *John Prebble, **The Highland Clearances** (London: History Book Club, 1966); J.W. Peace, **The Great Robbery** (London: Public commonwealth Press, 1933); and Frederick Verinder, **Land and Freedom** (London: Hobarth Press, 1935).*

** *"Patrick Edward Dove," **Dictionary of National Biography**, vol. 5 (London: Oxford University Press), 1284-1285.*

on the little Atlantic island of St. Helena. Europe was still seething with discontent. But the time was still under the influence of the Age of Enlightenment and the prestige of Britain had never stood higher than in the year of Waterloo – 1815.

The Doves had been rich and prominent landowners for generations. Many naval officers of high rank had given service to the crown, and in due course Patrick Edward's father was promoted to commander and appointed Commissioner of the Navy at Plymouth, at which point the family moved south. Already well educated in Scotland, Patrick Edward continued his studies in France. But here, along with fellow students, he joined in open insurrection against their tutors who evidently had fallen shot of expectations. The Paris Academy saw fit to expel him, as one of the ringleaders, and he was obliged to return home in disgrace. One option now was to follow his father and forebears into the navy, but his father thought otherwise. No doubt he had seen much bloody fighting during the napoleonic wars and had other plans for his intelligent son. He encouraged him to become a gentleman farmer on the family estate. In 1830 he was sent back to learn farming in Scotland.

By the time Patrick Edward was 17, King William IV, the more popular brother of George IV, had come to the throne.* Demands for reform were everywhere in the air, as well as an outcry about the clearances in Scotland. In English counties where the wretched labourers, stung to fury by a combination of injustices such as the game laws, the frequent death or transportation to Australia for sheep-stealing, and the miserable pay they received for long hours, rose up against their masters in revolt. Patrick Edward would have been well aware of their plight.

As a quiet country gentleman farmer, he became a first-rate horseman, a fine shot, an expert fly-fisher, a skilful sailor and an excellent mechanic. He became agricultural adviser to neighbouring farmers and, during the potato famine, exerted himself energetically to provide employment for the many Irish families who came to Scotland looking for work.** Although Dove set himself to learn as much as possible about husbandry, by all accounts he was able to lead a life of comparative leisure, which gave him time to read philosophy and travel widely. He made several grand tours to the continent and lived for long periods in France, which he had come to love.

In 1840, at the age of 25, Dove came into his inheritance, and the following year he decided to purchase a new estate of his own near Ballantrae, Ayrshire. As time went by, running "the Craig" on new, liberal lines won him the reputation of being the "most popular landlord in Scotland," largely, perhaps, because he had absorbed the new ideas in France springing out of the Declaration of the Rights of Man during the Revolution. He firmly believed that the soil of the nation was the inheritance of all people; his tenants could come and go across his land without interference. Thus he grained the respect and affection of his tenants. Until 1848 he lived happily at "the Craig" but, quite suddenly, some of his investments crashed on the stock market and the greater part of his fortune was swept away. It was at this moment that he chose to propose to a young girl as penniless as himself. Anne, daughter of George Forrester, an Edinburgh solicitor, made him a good wife and there were one son and two daughters from the marriage. The couple stayed together until his death in 1873.

The newlyweds left Scotland and set up home in Darmstadt, Germany, where Patrick Edward Dove took a post as lecturer at the University, and pursued the philosophical studies to which he had long been devoted. Here he continued to write about social matters and took time to think out his ideas. It was a

---

* *George IV (1762-1830) ruled from 1820 until his death. William IV (1765-1837) ruled from 1830 until 1837.*

** *From 1845 to 1847 Ireland suffered from a potato famine, forcing many people to emigrate. It has been estimated that 500,000 people either died or left Ireland during these years.*

valuable period for him and the first fruit of this new life was the book, *The Theory of Human Progression.** Initially, he decided to publish anonymously but, finding that it attracted wide interest in academic circles, a limited edition followed in 1850 in London and Edinburgh.

A number of luminaries, including Thomas Carlyle, read *The Theory of Human Progress* and praised the wisdom of its ideas. Sir William Hamilton, the great philosopher, pronounced the book "epochmaking," while Charles Sumner, in the United States, was so impressed with it that he circulated numerous free copies and persuaded Dove, now a writer of stature, to turn his hand to writing in favour of emancipation.** This movement became a torch for Dove.***

Dove was free thinking, blunt speaking and farsighted. He was a man of great physical power, with a noble head. Professor J.S. Blackie, who knew his well, wrote that he "combined in a remarkable degree the manly directness of the man of action with the fine speculation of the man of thought. Altogether, Mr. Dove dwells in my mind as one of the most perfect types of the manly thinker whom I have met in the course of a long life."**** Sir Francis Seymour Haden, the artist, who became his close friend while living in London, was "impressed by his enormous energy, physical and moral."*****

After leaving Germany, the Doves settled in Edinburgh where, in 1853, Patrick Edward lectured at the Philosophical Institution on various subjects. For a while he edited *The Witness* during the illness of his friend, Hugh Miller, and later that year published the second part of his work on politics which he called *The Elements of Political Science.* A third and concluding part was written but never published, and the manuscript was lost.

In 1856 Dove stood unsuccessfully for the chair vacated by the death of Sir William Hamilton, and it is interesting that his rival, who was successful, spoke highly of Dove's "powerful individuality and uncommon grasp of social problems and insight."****** In 1858, the Doves moved on to Glasgow, where he edited a newspaper, the *Commonwealth*, and became general editor of the *Imperial Dictionary of Biography* for the first twenty numbers. He also busied himself with editing the *Imperial Journal of the Arts and Sciences*, and wrote the article "Government" for the *Encyclopaedia Britannica*.

---

* *Henry George praised Dove's book during a public meeting at Glasgow in 1884. It was not until 1942 that the Robert Schalkenbach Foundation of New York published an abridged version by Julia A. Kellogg in a bid to assist the promotion for land-value taxation then in progress. It was hoped that such a volume would help reform land tenure in line with the ideas of Henry George.*

** *Sir William Hamilton (1788-1856) was a noted Scottish philosopher. Charles Sumner (1840-1910), a senator from Massachusetts, was a major exponent of radical reconstruction after the Civil War.*

*** *Julia A. Kellogg in Patrick Edward Dove, **The Theory of Human Progression**, ed. Julia A. Kellogg (New York: Robert Schalkenbach Foundation, 1942), preface (no pagination).*

**** *John S. Blackie (1809-1895) was an eminent educator and proponent of Scottish nationalism.*

***** *Sir Francis S. Haden (1818-1910) was a pioneer physician, writer, and artist, especially noted in the field of etching.*

****** *"William Hamilton," **Dictionary of National Biography**, vol. 8 (London: Oxford University Press), 1111-1116. See also **Glasgow Herald** (May 2, 1873); **Scotsman** (May 1, 1873); and **People's Journal** (May 1 and 8, 1884).*

Britain was the premier industrial power at this time, having taken the initiative during the eighteenth century in the Industrial Revolution. Although she was derisively, but jealously called a nation of shopkeepers, her mills and factories churned out products at an ever-increasing rate and were sent to all corners of the globe, setting the pace for the rest of Europe, and the United States as well. Set against this heightened national prosperity were the degradations of the farmer-turned-labourer and the endless growth of darkened cities. Dove felt that modern manufacture was a monstrous system of misdirected intention, based on a blasphemy against man's spiritual nature:

> The whole system of modern manufacture, with its factory slavery; its gaunt and sallow faces; its half-clad hunger; its female degradation; its abortions and rickety children; its dens of pestilence and abomination; its ignorance, brutality, and drunkenness; its vice, in all the hideous forms of infidelity, hopeless poverty, and mad despair – these, and, if it were possible, worse than these, are the sure fruits of making man the workman of mammon, instead of making wealth the servant of humanity for the relief of man's estate.*

Along with the growth of the industrial proletariat arose numerous problems. Unions and workers' movements began to flourish and visionaries with new systems of thought desired to radically alter the status quo. Being well aware of the socialist and communist doctrines at that time circulating among the workers and in academic circles, Dove advised those in England who heaped contempt upon the doctrines to try to understand the concepts and to seize the fallacies on which they were based.

> Whatever may be true, or whatever may be false, in socialism (using that term in the most unobjectionable sense – Christian socialism, for instance), the principles of equity must first be taken into consideration before we can, by any possibility, proceed to the consideration of those higher principles of action which may come into play, when once the principles of justice are acknowledged and carried into general operation.
>
> This question is perhaps, practically, the most important in modern politics. Insured millions let loose on the world, with vague ideas of fraternity in their heads, with the courage of enthusiasm in their hearts, and with bayonets in their hands, are, at all events, formidable expositors of doctrine. Their energy is exactly what the continent of Europe has so long required; but their ignorance may transform what would otherwise have been a most useful reformation, into a terrible hurricane of vengeance, and a blind exercise of destructive power. Now that the theorist and the orator can raise armed millions, the game of politics has assumed a new character. Theories are no longer barren speculations, nor is oratory mere declamation. It is, therefore, of the first importance that the most cheerful, impartial, and honest endeavour should be made to perfect the theory of politics – to base it first on the immutable foundations of justice – to satisfy the reason before setting the passions in a flame – to evolve principles which can be calmly and soberly maintained by the intellect, before they are given as rules of action to enthusiastic populations, ready to march in any direction that is plausibly pointed out as the right one.**

During these troublesome times, there were also many wars of unification waged in Europe, such as in Italy and Germany; and of liberation, such as in Austria.***

---

* *Dove, **The Theory of Human Progression**, 83.*

** *Ibid., 89-90.*

*** *A united Italy was declared in 1871 with the annexation of Rome; the German Empire came into being the same year. The most prominent nationalist uprising in Europe was in Austria on the part of the Hungarians during the Revolution of 1848.*

The American Civil War (1860-65) was also transpiring, fought, in part, over the slave issue. Dove had always concerned himself with the plight of all mankind and deplored the slave system, whether it was British or American in origin. In the southern states in America, Negro slavery formed the basis of a distinctive aristocratic society. Its economic rationale was the cotton-plantation, and of course England was a major consumer of cotton. But although the Confederacy tried to entice England to its aid in the war, British public opinion, Lord Palmerston's policies,* and the rising fortunes of the North all combined to forestall her entanglement. No doubt Dove helped to form public opinion on this issue at home.

> When the emancipation of the African was spoken of, and when the nation of Britain appeared to be taking into serious consideration the rightfulness of abolishing slavery, what tremendous evils were to follow! Trade was to be ruined, commerce was almost to cease, and manufacturers were to be bankrupts. Worse than all, private property was to be invaded (property in human flesh), the rights of planters sacrificed to the speculative notions of fanatics, and the British government was to commit an act that would forever deprive it of the confidence of British subjects. These evils at home were, of course, to be accompanied by others abroad much more tremendous. The West India islands were, of course, to be ruined past all possible hope of recovery; the blacks were to insurge and to destroy the white population; a moral hurricane, ten times more dreadful than the winds of heaven, was to sweep across the Caribbean Sea; blood was to flow like water; the emancipated slave was to celebrate the first moment of his liberty with rape, rapine, and murder; evils unheard of and inconceivable were to astonish the earth; the very heavens were to fall. And why? Because British subjects were no longer to be permitted by British law to hold their fellow men in slavery on British ground.
>
> The law was a positive enactment armed with power, and the moment the law ceased to exist the negro was emancipated, not by the law, but by nature. The law may make a slave, but it is beyond the power of the law to make a freeman. the only question that can ever be legitimately taken into consideration, with regard to slavery, is immediate and total abolition, and so of all similar cases where injustice is established or systematically perpetuated by law.
>
> The people of Great Britain were taxed by force for the purpose of paying the planters for their slaves. Theoretically, the Commons imposed the taxation on themselves; but nine-tenths of the population have nothing to do with the election of members of Parliament, and so far as they were concerned, the taxation was *ab extra* – forced on them by a government which they had no voice in electing. We maintain that this act was one of downright injustice and oppression, whatever may be said of its magnanimity.**

It was natural for Dove to take an interest in military matters. He was fundamentally a man of peace but he could see the need for strong defence against tyranny. In 1848 he had produced a treatise on the revolver and the handling of firearms in general. A few years later, he published a book, *The Revolver*, with hints to rifle clubs. He also expounded on the defence of the country and deplored the depopulation of the Highlands. He was proud of his invention of the rifled cannon which had ratchet grooves, but although it was shown to have a great range and accuracy, the Ordnance Committee which had examined this weapon declined to take any further steps. In 1859 Dove accepted the command of the 91st Lanarkshire Rifle Volunteers, and later took part in the first meeting of the National Rifle Association at Wimbledon, winning several prizes.

The great prosperity of industrial Britain after 1860 was largely ascribed to Gladstone's efforts to

---

* *Henry J.T. Palmerston (1784-1865), a leading English statesman, was twice prime minister. He championed British interests and pursued liberal policies*

** *Dove, The Theory of Human Progression, 54-55.*

bring about free trade and this became the accepted doctrine of all parties for the remainder of the century.* To this end, Dove wrote strongly in favour of the complete abolition of all customs and excise. This, he said, was a most necessary change that must take place before the country could be free and enjoy commercial liberty, for the labourer, the merchant, and the manufacturer. Besides being adamant in his distaste for customs duties. Dove regarded most taxes as superfluous for the operation of any state. Only a minimal amount of revenue was necessary for the operation of a scaled-down government.

During the mid century Britain's might was nonpareil. Not only was she defended by the world's most formidable fleet, but she was governed by a government of a singular character for the times. Although it suffered from many problems, it was one of the most advanced and modern. Dove, nevertheless, like many of us, was much irritated by state officials and expressed his dislike for officialdom.

From such, there had been a great cry for reform of state and society. Among many orators leading the new generation of thinking people was Jeremy Bentham, who was regarded as the Father of all Reform.** He was the author of a *Catechism of Parliamentary Reform* in which he argued that a more democratic form of government would help to produce "the greatest happiness of the greatest number." This book and those words would not have been lost on the young Dove, whose most important contribution was his great work, *The Theory of Human Progression*. Dove set out in his book the theory of man's intellectual progression. Before a nation can change its condition it must change its beliefs. Dove was a religious man and well understood the ultimate authority of God who made the laws governing Nature. He showed how a country's beliefs determines its conditions and fixes its destiny. Truth, he said, must bring with it a correct and beneficial system of society while false beliefs must ever be accompanied by despotism, anarchy, and wrong. Dove believed that political progress of mankind is a passage to one definite end, to an ultimate condition that requires no further change, to a stable system of law. Part of Dove's theory contained the idea of what we would call a single tax, which he postulated as a most necessary part of historical progress. This initial change, along with other political liberties which Dove saw as integrated parts of an ongoing evolution, could be effected only through a constant increase of knowledge, for this is the only means by which man can work out his wellbeing and ameliorate his condition on the globe. Dove's thesis maintains the doctrine of liberty and equality and, by extension, he argues persuasively that the rent of land ought to belong to the nation and be distributed for the benefit of all. The main principle of his book avers that all human progress is conditioned by the development of true knowledge to achieve these ends. It was vital, in his view, to bring this idea to the attention of scholars.

> Let it be remembered that the progress of mankind in the evolution of civilization, is a progress from superstition and error towards knowledge. Superstition and error present themselves under the form of diversity of credence; knowledge presents itself under the form of unity of credence. Wherever there is knowledge, that knowledge is the same in all parts of the earth, and the same in substance whatever language it may use as the instrument of expression. The progress of mankind, therefore, is a progress from diversity of credence towards unity of credence. There is but one truth, one scheme of knowledge; and consequently, wherever knowledge is really attained, diversity of credence is impossible. Where men differ in credence, they differ because one or all have not knowledge.***

One of the elements blocking this preordained evolution to a higher plane of man's existence was the

---

* *William E. Gladstone (1809-1898) was a noted Liberal British statesman who was prime minister four times and promoted various important reforms relating to Ireland, the civil service, the military, etc.*

** *Jeremy Bentham (1748-1832) was an English philosopher who founded utilitarianism.*

*** *Dove, The Theory of Human Progression, 74.*

present concept of landownership, especially when it is monopolized and sanctioned by statutory law. It perpetuated gross iniquities and generated poverty and starvation in the present. For the future it stymied the best hopes of a more perfected society wherein everyone could have a voice in decision making and a genuine commonwealth.

Given the perilous circumstances of a fast-growing Britain encumbered with so many problems, Dove predicted that the subject of property would become the major cause of strife and contention.

> Property is the rock on which England's famous constitution of king, Lords, and Commons, will suffer its final shipwreck. Such an assertion is, of course, at present a mere opinion; but if the scheme we have advanced be in the main correct, then we do not hesitate to affirm, that if we continue that scheme into the future, we may see that the question of landed property will be the cause of a stupendous struggle between the aristocracy and the laborocracy of Britain, and that its final settlement will entail the destruction of the constitution. and the question lies in narrow bounds, all that is required being an answer to. . .the following: "Is the population to be starved, pauperized, and expatriated, or is the aristocracy to be destroyed?"* Let the political arrangements be what they may, let there be universal or any other suffrage, so long as the aristocracy have all the land, and derive the rent of it, the labourer is only a serf, and a serf he will remain until he has uprooted the rights of private landed property. The land is for the nation, and not for the aristocracy.**

Dove's last years were spent travelling in Natal (in the south of Africa) to experience a change of climate, and he died following a stroke on April 28, 1873. His son, P.E. Dove, became Secretary of the Royal Historical and Selden Societies, and wrote admiringly of his father's work in the years that followed.

---

* *By the destruction of the aristocracy, we do not mean the destruction of the aristocrats, any more than, by the destruction of pauperism, we should mean the destuction of the persons o the paupers. It is to the system that we refer exclusively, and only as either system has been created by the arrangements of men. (Note by Dove).*

** *Dove, The Theory of Human Progression, 114-115.*

ANOTHER HISTORIC STATEMENT ...

*

I had much wanted to include a page at least on the extremely interesting gleanings I made - (albeit all too scanty) - from a dip into Graham Bain's book "The Thunderbolt of Reason", in the summer of 1997.

Its subject is Robert Watson - and I emerged feeling he must surely have been acquainted with Ogilvie - (he was contemporary), for there is a passage from his writings, quoted in Graham's book, which really might have come from Ogilvie's pen. (In my recollection, he refers to the discovery of the land rent principle as the "philosopher's stone".)

This book also includes Watson writing on Fletcher of Saltoun...

I just wish that I could have done more justice to this book, but perhaps readers will make their own discovery of it now for themselves...

(6 Apr 99)

WILLIAM WALLACE

(1272 –1305)

Compiled by Shirley-Anne Hardy

*

... And still the name of Wallace wight,
And the death he died that day,
Breathe upon Scotland the sacred light
That never fades away.

From: Song of the 'Little Peoples'
(See "Leaves from the Book of Scots")

*

1) Contributed by Shirley-Anne Hardy:
   a) In Response to a letter published in The Courier. 28 Dec. '98.
   b) My Own Discovery of Wallace.

2) Extracts from Three Little-Known Histories concerning Scotland:
   a) "Leaves from the Book of Scots", by Morrison Davidson.
      Appendix: An old Scottish custom in Bringing in the New Year.
      (Acks. To Mr. W.E. Scott and The Courier)
   b) "A History of Scotland", by George Buchanan.
   c) Speech of Scottish Chieftain, Calgacus, before the Battle of Mons Graupius – from Tacitus.
      (Translated by Mattingly and Handford. Acks. To Alan Torrance)

3) "On the Trail of William Wallace", by David R. Ross.
   (Acks. To The Courier of 24 Feb. '99)

*

The following letter to The Courier, of 27 Jan 99, was written in response to one that had appeared a month earlier.

I have not seen my letter in print - and it may well have been felt too late to publish. I therefore place it here in full, since I would in any case have wished to place its main content at the start of this section, as an introduction to what follows.

*

The Rocks Pitlochry Perthshire PH16 5QZ

The Editor,
The Courier,
80 Kingsway East,
DUNDEE, DD4 8SL.

27 Jan. '99

Dear Sir,

WILLIAM WALLACE

Let us by all means recognise Andrew de Moray's part in the Battle of Stirling Bridge – but not in a manner which would excite surely the profoundest disgust in Andrew de Moray himself.

I have seen no reply to the letter, so deeply insulting to Wallace, from the Co-ordinator of the Andrew Moray Society (26 Dec. '98). Perhaps its shameful language is the sound reason it has simply been ignored. Nevertheless, the true circumstances of the defeat at Falkirk should be put on record – as also the broader picture alongside. But first – to get rid of the triviality regarding the signatures to the Lubeck letter. Andrew de Moray was of *the nobility* – Wallace, a *commoner*, (which mattered in those days); and even alphabetically W.W. comes after A. de M., (as Dr. James Mackay points out). Rather ask – how *could* Wallace have signed first?

On the chiefer point, however: the strategical astuteness shown by Wallace in a string of guerrilla exploits before the Battle at Stirling stamps the latter very much with Wallace's mark. In particular, at Stirling be it noted: 'From his vantage point Wallace gave the signal to attack by a single blast from a horn, it having been agreed previously that he, and only he, should blow a horn when the moment was right.' The strategic assessing of that 'right' moment was *crucial to the entire battle.* (See *William Wallace*, by Dr. James Mackay, Mainstream, 1995, from whom I quote)

For the same reason (his strategic brilliance) it is impossible that Wallace *chose* to fight the battle that took place at Falkirk – (his famous words quoted on that occasion express to me, in fact, a kind of disgust) – and 'it seems clear that this was never Wallace's intention' (ibid). Even so, Wallace's schiltroms (spearsmen: foot soldiers) – the *commoners*, *Wallace's* men – stood firm and endured to the end on that terrible day. Not so the cavalry – who would be drawn from the more élite – under the Red Comyn. Although held *in reserve* and *at the rear* of the schiltroms, they 'wavered as the English charged the schiltroms, wheeled about and galloped off without striking a single blow' (ibid). (Just imagine any soldier under *Wallace's* command behaving so!) This unspeakably shameful desertion proved critical to the outcome. One may say – Falkirk was lost by the Scottish nobility, not by Wallace; and one may be forgiven for wondering if they were not in fact happy to do Wallace down, from that jealousy of him which was always rife among them.

But Wallace's reputation does not stand or fall by the Battle of Falkirk or even Stirling Bridge. *On his own*, and without any assistance from Andrew de Moray (who was mortally wounded by then): 'less than a month after ... Stirling Bridge ... Wallace had cleared the English out of Scotland and recovered almost all of the castles and other strongholds. By the efforts of one man, with precious little help from the nobility and a great deal of hindrance' (*note*) – 'the power of King Edward had been ripped asunder and Scotland was, for the first time in almost a decade, free from alien domination' (ibid). Bruce? He changed sides when it suited him to do so, and is scarcely worthy to be mentioned in the same breath as Wallace ... who, again, *alone* stood apart, at the wholesale capitulation of Scottish leaders at Strathord in 1304.

As supreme testimony: 'The naming of places after Wallace's deeds ... is crucial to the understanding of the true significance of Wallace. Not even the great saints of Scotland – Andrew, Columba, Ninian and Margaret – have managed to impress their names on the land in this way.' (83 in the present Ordnance Survey Pathfinder series – still more in older historic maps) 'The Wallace place names constitute an unprecedented and populist canonisation of a secular hero.' (Elspeth King, in the Introd. to *Blind Harry's Wallace*, Luath Press, 1998)

"Wallace made Scotland. He is Scotland; he is the symbol of all that is best and purest and truest and most heroic in our national life." (R.B. Cunninghame Graham)

"The Scots memorialised him, by associating his deeds with the landscape and keeping his memory alive through songs and stories. Blind Harry recorded and enhanced, but could not create such a legend." (Elspeth King)

Yours truly,

Shirley-Anne Hardy

MY OWN DISCOVERY OF WALLACE

When we were children, visiting our many cousins in Stirling, our parents used to make sure that we recognised three things on the journey over: the Ochil Hills, Stirling Castle – and the Wallace Monument.

Our parents must have told us the elements of Wallace's story – but that was the extent of my knowledge of Wallace in my childhood; for throughout the days of my (entirely Scottish) schooling, I do not recollect once having heard the name of Wallace pronounced. Certainly, no *Scottish* history 'soiled' the syllabuses I was taught from! - (in those prewar and wartime days). Only plenty about English and foreign rulers!

My first real encounter with Wallace came on a chance visit to Aberdeen in 1981. I suddenly found myself magnetised across a square in the town by the powerful figure of a statue standing there. Presently I realised that I was standing before Wallace. I slowly read the words that were written around the sides of the statue's base. It was an illuminating and deeply moving experience.

There followed a further encounter. A young man on a delivery round came with some goods to the cottage. We fell into conversation, and on that summer's day he sat down in the garden and talked to me. He came from the Falkirk area, and was imbued with a love of Wallace, bound up with Scotland, such that I was profoundly affected listening to him. It was another encounter that engraved itself on my mind ...

Today, when Wallace has 'come alive' in our midst once more (as he was always bound to do), it gladdens me to think how he, by his own power, kept his memory and deeds alive in us, even during the long 'dark age' of the attempt by an alien Establishment to rule him out of our thoughts and consciousness.

Of more recent times I owe a great debt to Alan Torrance, who grew up in Glasgow steeped in the knowledge of Wallace. It was from him that I received my first copy of *Leaves from the Book of Scots* – with quite extraordinary timing, just as I was on the point of writing the extension to my 'Braveheart' article for the Scottish Ogilvie Society book (early 1996. See ch. "The Making of This Book".)

It was Alan also who first told me the real story behind the making of the *Braveheart* film – how it was really down to 'a bunch of lads in Glasgow' that the film had come out the way it did. When I heard this, it first seemed amazing – and then it seemed so obvious! For how *could* Wallace possibly have allowed a film about him to have emerged onto the world stage straight out of the glitter of *Hollywood*? - !

I imagine there are few, even today, who know this 'inside' story of the film – but it's all recorded anyway in an article which came out in *The Big Issue* of 1-14 Mar. '96. Those 'lads', who were of the Wallace Clan Trust in Glasgow, "caught the eye of a Hollywood scriptwriter who was wandering around Scotland in search of some authentic background for his film. The movie was called *Braveheart*, and the writer, whose original draft had all the integrity of a shortbread tin, was sent off with a flea in his ear. Cue transatlantic 'phone call. 'Hello, is that the Wallace Clan Trust? Mel Gibson here. It seems you have some problems with our script. I'm coming over to sort it out'."

Since the Clan" devote their energies to exploring the wild backwaters of history in search of the real Scotland", they were fortunately well able to "'show him how a real community operated in those dim and distant times. The film's gritty realism was down to us'." The Clan operated as Mel Gibson's unofficial bodyguard too, during his visit, shielding him from the press of fans and photographers – and it goes without saying are to be found playing their part in the crowd scenes in the film!

I am glad to include a reference to this 'inside story' here – for it seems to reveal something of the uniqueness of Wallace himself, as well as telling us something about the work of the Wallace Clan Trust.

I must now record a slightly earlier milestone on this journey. In December 1990 I went to stay with cousins in Edinburgh, and on the bookshelves in my bedroom found a book telling of the life of William Wallace. Having opened its pages, I could not put it down, and since it was but an overnight stay, so I read on through the night. The passages I quote here are exactly as I copied them down then, for though it was only a historical novel – (one of which I had never heard) – the contents concerning Wallace carried so stark a ring of truth about them that I could not think of leaving them behind:-

FROM: 'THE SCOTTISH CHIEFS', BY JANE PORTER
(A LIFE OF WILLIAM WALLACE)
Published by the Grand Coliseum Warehouse Co., Jamaica St., Glasgow
(Founded by Walter Wilson, 1869)

"... The issue showed that Bothwell was not mistaken. The majority of the Scottish nobles envied Wallace his glory, and hated him for that virtue which drew the eyes of the people to compare him with their selfish courses."

(p.443)

"... 'Dangerous to your crimes and ruinous to your ambition!' cried Kirkpatrick; 'for so help me God, as I believe, that an honester man than William Wallace lives not in Scotland! And that ye know; and his virtues overtopping your littleness, ye would uproot the greatness which ye cannot equal.'"

(p.450)

"(Wallace) looked on this range of his enemies with a fearless eye, and passing through the crowd ... spoke not, but with an unmoved countenance looked around upon the assembly."

(pp.455-456)

Seven years later, visiting the inspiring Wallace Exhibition (1997) organised by Elspeth King, Curator of the Stirling Smith Art Gallery and Museum in Stirling, to commemorate the 700th Anniversary of the Battle of Stirling Bridge, I was enormously interested to discover the sources of Jane Porter's book – and it was no wonder that its contents had so struck me, for it was far from being simply a historical novel. I took down the following information which was placed by a copy of the book on display there – which had been presented to William Thomas Tucker in 1886, and was now lent by Mrs. I. Tucker to the Exhibition.(With acknowledgements to the Stirling Smith Gallery):-

"Jane Porter (1776-1850) first published her Scottish Chiefs in Edinburgh in 1810. The subject is the life of Wallace, and the book was an immediate success. The author had heard the Wallace stories of Blind Harry re-told by Lucky Forbes, and her teacher. In the 19th Century, her book was the main vehicle for the Wallace story, as the film Braveheart is in the 20th Century.

"The Scottish Chiefs was translated into Russian, German and French, and inspired patriots everywhere. In 1844 the booksellers of New York presented the author with a splendid armchair, and in the twentieth century it was issued in a Classic Comics Edition in the U.S.A."[1]

Since this exhibition, Elspeth King has overseen the publication of a new edition of 'Blind Harry's Wallace by William Hamilton of Gilbertfield', and written an absorbing Introduction to it. (Published by the Luath Press, Edinburgh, 1998. Referred to in my letter to the Courier on Wallace)

It was this exhibition at the Stirling Smith Gallery, which properly brought home to me, for the first time, how widely the influence of Wallace had spread across the world, and how great has been his inspiration to freedom fighters in other lands. It was at this exhibition that I read for the first time the tribute to Wallace by Mazzini of Italy:-

---

[1] *Here I should relate that, in the summer of 1998, a surprise package arrived from my cousin in Edinburgh with a note tucked into it: 'Saw this book at the Christian Aid Book Sale in May and thought you might like to have your own copy.' A thrilling package! And so – in a Ward Lock & Co. Edition of 1911 – I now have my very own volume of The Scottish Chiefs.*

"Wallace stands forth from the dim twilight of the past as one of the high prophets of nationality to us all. Honour him. Worship his memory. Teach his name and deeds to your children."

Teach his name and deeds to your children! What is to be said of Scotland's *educational Establishment* now?

There was a further discovery from this exhibition, of the greatest interest. It concerns David Steuart Erskine, eleventh Earl of Buchan. No wonder that this eleventh Earl had written in his letter to George Washington, from Dryburgh Abbey in 1791 – (a letter I was already familiar with from DCM's Biographical Notes on Ogilvie): 'I have entrusted this sheet, enclosed in a box made of the oak that sheltered our great Sir William Wallace after the Battle of Falkirk …' (quoted in full in the Biog. Notes in this book). No wonder! For at the exhibition I learned that the eleventh Earl of Buchan was 'passionately interested in Scottish culture' and ' did much to popularise and pass on the story of Wallace', while Buchan's drawing of Wallace is 'the portrait on which most 18th and 19th Century portraits are based'. He also commissioned, in 1814, a statue of Wallace to stand on the family's land in the Borders.

It was this same Earl of Buchan who, of course, had warmly befriended William Ogilvie, and whom Burns so enjoyed visiting – all recounted in DCM's Biographical Notes. But this further information filled out the picture of the Earl, which those Notes presented. Such a champion of William Wallace clearly *could not but* have championed the later William Ogilvie's land reform proposals – for their central inspiration, 500 years on, was likewise the *freeing of the Scots.*

For – just as the celebrated 'freeing of the serfs' in Russia in the nineteenth century did nothing of the kind, in fact, since the serfs, *still without land*, had virtually to sell themselves back into serfdom again for a living;[2] so the freeing of the Scots, which Wallace fought and died for, can likewise never be accomplished by the mere attainment of *political* liberty, but awaits the breaking also of the *economic* servitude which land monopoly always ensures. For the economic power bestowed by land monopoly underlies and props up its political power – and it was the desire to hold onto that political power which motivated the treachery of the Scottish nobles towards Wallace. There is no need to ask whether Wallace understood the destructive power of land monopoly. Hence, the battle to rid Scotland of land monopoly – via *radical* land reform – may rightly be viewed as the continuation of Wallace's struggle.

There is, finally, an extraordinary irony attached to the life's work of the eleventh Earl of Buchan. As I learned from the Exhibition, he was not only 'passionately interested in Scottish culture', but was also 'instrumental in establishing the Society of Antiquaries'. Now what was the Society of Antiquaries – ? The forerunner of the *national museum of Scotland!* Thus – dare one imagine what this great champion of the greatest of our forebears would have made of the blundering *exclusion of any mention, by name or deed, of Wallace*, from the new National Museum of Scotland, opened in December 1998?

I would hazard that the vast majority of Scots would not have known what to make of it either – beyond our alien Establishment's ever familiar policy, *by now*, as touching William Wallace! A copy of the Lubeck letter (which only a public outcry managed to bring to light) is I presume now assured … now that it has come to light also (*Scotland on Sunday*, 6 Dec 98) that other documents are there, also only in copy form, already enjoying permanent space at the museum! But taking a broader look: if Scotland's history is such that it requires her to STRETCH the meaning of a museum a trifle, in order to incorporate it – then how about a caseful of those Pathfinder maps with the 83 Wallace place names on them? (For how many even of the Scots know how Wallace is imbedded in our landscape? I did not.) This would be a fine first STRETCH! - for since the geography of a country cannot be fitted into a museum, one or the other must give! Will our museum then be unique among national museums? If that be the measure of Wallace – so be it!

---

[2] *How different was the position in Scotland in the 18th Century? See the reference to the coalminers of the Central belt in 'Introducing William Wallace: the Life and Legacy of Scotland's Liberator', by Elspeth King. Today's on-going industrial slavery is disguised under such inventions as the 'Welfare State'.*

Innovation is entirely and always possible – even within the bounds of strictest *academia*! (Provided, of course, they manage that 'octave higher' in their thinking!) Since we have centuries of such neglect of Wallace to make up for, how about a special 'wing' where something of the interest, enjoyment *and education* on him achieved by the Stirling Smith exhibition may be extended and perpetuated?– (not to mention the contribution it would make to the coffers of the museum in these 'hard times'!)

Dear new 'National Museum of Scotland' – as of now, you have A HOLE IN YOUR HEART!

Times have not much changed in this respect from Wallace's time. As the Big Issue article said, referring to the Wallace Clan Trust, they appear to regard the last 500 years as 'one long English conspiracy to separate the noble Scot from his land and ancestry'.

I would alter one word only in the above. It is not, alas, as simple as being an 'English' conspiracy. It is unfortunately – (just as in Wallace's time) – one belonging to an Establishment *thickly populated also with Scots* (while many an honest Englishman, especially amongst those living in Scotland, no doubt deplores the situation as much as we do).

Let this latest farce of the new so-called 'National Museum of Scotland' be a sharp reminder to us, then, that we can never rid ourselves of the shame of this alien Establishment which at present presides over Scottish affairs, until we see the work of William Ogilvie set the full seal on Wallace's.

12 Feb. '99

*

And now let us take a look at some of our past history, in the following extracts from three little-known but absorbing studies of it that I have come across.

*

LEAVES FROM THE BOOK OF SCOTS

The following extracts are from *Leaves from the Book of Scots*, (already mentioned earlier in my Pt I), of sub-heading: *The Story of William Wallace, Robert the Bruce, Fletcher of Saltoun and Other Patriots*. Written by Morrison Davidson and published by the Scots Secretariat (no more in existence), undated, the contents indicate around 1910. It is held by the National Library of Scotland, through whose kind services I was able to purchase a photocopy (of clearer print than the one in my possession); and I assume that that same good service would be open to all.

Re-reading these Leaves after a long interval, and *since* my letter to the Courier, I see that Morrison Davidson writes, re the Battle of Falkirk (Leaf Five) that Wallace's plan, far from being a pitched battle at Falkirk, was 'to starve Edward into retreat', and that this plan 'nearly succeeded', *but for the betrayal to Edward, by two members of the Scottish nobility, of the position of Wallace's camp, near Falkirk,* (while the sources he quotes from are equally as damning of the Scots cavalry as admiring of Wallace's foot soldiers).

So far, then, from the Battle of Falkirk's signifying a defeat of Wallace, it seems that it was a simple *give-away* – down to Scotland's nobility! A gift to Edward from certain Scottish nobles! Not much can be added to that statement about those 'nobles'; but can one ever imagine the burden carried by Wallace from their ever-ready *treachery* – always waiting in the wings for him, to trick him, to trip him up, and to betray him–as finally at the end ? I was struck to learn from Elspeth King's Introduction to *Blind Harry's Wallace* that, in Randall Wallace's book *Braveheart*, the story 'follows the pattern of Jesus of Nazareth as told in the gospels'. Wallace trod a path of selfless service similarly marked by betrayal – and he too was put to death at the age of thirty-three.

It is surely time there was a reprint of this book, so full of interest on Scotland's early history. Meanwhile I am placing here the following extracts, which give, among other things, particularly penetrating glimpses of the advanced state of Scotland in those earlier times – far in advance, indeed, of her *neighbour* south of the Border!

*

LEAF ONE

"No! not yet the ancient spirit
Of our fathers hath not gone;
Take it to thee as a buckler,
Better far than steel or stone.
Oh, remember those that perished
For thy birthright at the time,
When to be a Scot was treason,
And to side with Wallace crime!'

Aytoun

Picts, Scots and Brythons

Two centuries after the legionaries of Rom had taken their departure, bag and baggage, *circa* 590 A.D., Caledonia north of Forth and Clyde (Argyll excepted) composed the kingdoms of Northern and Southern Pictavia, the latter embracing Perth, Fife, Forfar and Kincardine.

These redoubtable Picts have been an unspeakable worry to our learned historiographers, who, naturally enough, have never been able to ascertain what so suddenly became of them and their language – the fact being that the Picts never had any racial or linguistic existence (except territorially or tribally) distinct from that of other Goidelic Celts, like the Irish and Manx. Theirs was a mere name, or, peradventure, Roman bestowed nickname (*Picti* – 'tatooed'). Their descendants are the Scots of today.

Brythonic or Welsh Celts (more recently immigrated from the Continent than the Goidels) occupied the Kingdom of Strathclyde, extending from their capital, Alcluyd (Dumbarton) to the Derwent in Cumberland.

The 'Galloway Picts' held Kirkcudbright and Wigtown in the South Western corner; while in the South East lay Angle Bernicia, an extended arm of Northumbria, reaching to the Firth of Forth.
The Scots (Irish Gaels) had colonised Dalriada (Argyll) as early as 498 A.D.; but, though they ultimately came to give their name to Pictavia, it was not by reason of their numbers, or even their superiority in arms. It was their missionary monastic zeal and diplomatic arts that, in the main, earned them dominance...

When we consider how easily the 'Anglo Saxons' (the English) went down before the Danes and Normans, is it at all likely that those who fought under Wallace and Bruce 'were mainly of English blood?' The truth is, the Anglo Saxons were far 'owre saft' to maintain a life and death struggle of that kind. The Normans had more grit; but, then, they were only an insignificant part of the nation, and were not superior in energy to the Caledonians (Picts), Scots and Britons (Welsh) of Strathclyde ...

It is mainly to the valour of the Caledonians, Scots, and Britons, that, by the Grace of God, 'we owe the honour we possess of acknowledging no master but the Almighty, nor any happiness but what is consistent with Liberty'.

LEAF TWO

Freedom spake to the fierce old Scots,
When bid to bow the knee:
And their answer was Bruce and Bannockburn
And fighting from sea to sea!!
And still the name of Wallace wight,
And the death he died that day,
Breathe upon Scotland the sacred light
That never fades away.

Song of the 'Little Peoples'

Disputed Succession Troubles

These set in in earnest, in 1286, on the death of much lamented Alexander III, whose reign had been one of rare enlightenment and progress. Relatively, Scotland was then better governed, more 'civilised', than England, which had for generations been cruelly lacerated by royal and baronial brigandage. During the reigns of David I and Alexander III, the Burghs of Scotland had attained a large measure of wealth and importance. Berwick, in particular, was *negosiosa* – 'Alexandria of the North, whose wealth was the sea and the waves the walls thereof'. London even barely surpassed her as an emporium.
Moreover, and this is especially noteworthy, Mediaeval Scotland alone among the nations stood for Free Trade in Imports. Sapient King Jamie, 'the British Solomon', at last managed to infringe this policy, characteristically enough, 'for the entertaining of his princely port'; but the Convention of Royal Burghs rose to the occasion, condemning his innovation (of 1597) as 'ane new and intolerable custom'.* When Henry II, in an access of royal nescience and folly, drove all unprivileged foreigners out of England, the Scots received these industrious traders and mechanics with open arms, and verily they had their reward.

LEAF THREE

"I would relate
How, in tyrannic times, some high souled men,
Unnamed among the chronicles of Kings,
Suffered in silence for truth's sake; or tell
How Wallace fought for Scotland; left his name
Of 'Wallace' to be found, like a wild flower,
All over his dear country; left the deeds
Of Wallace, like a family of ghosts,
To people the steep rocks and river banks,
Her natural sanctuaries, with a local soul
Of independence and stern Liberty!"

– *Wordsworth*

"William Wallace sheds as bright a glory upon his valorous nation as ever was shed upon their country by the greatest men of Greece or Rome." – *Garibaldi*

* It is pathetic to see how the Scots have lost their earlier mental acuity on this major question. But free trade cannot flourish where land monopoly does. Henry George's excellent "Protection or Free Trade" shows us this - and so restores our mental acuity on free trade also. S-A.H.

... there have come down to us in the pages of Honest John of Fordun, earliest and best of Scottish Chroniclers, some precious words of self-revelation, almost certainly spoken by the knight of Ellerslie himself, with his back sorely to the wall. They afford a glimpse into the very soul of the hero:-

O DESOLATA SCOTIA!

When I was a lad in charge of my uncle, the Priest of Dunipace (Stirlingshire), one proverb more precious than all the riches of the world, he taught me, which has ever lived in my memory:-

Dico tibi verum; Libertas optima rerum.
Nunquam, servili sub nexu, vivito, fili!
(My son, I tell thee soothfastlie,
No gift is like to liberty,
Then, never live in slaverie!)

Therefore, in brief, I say that if the entire Scottish nation were to submit to the King of England, or if everyone else should abandon the cause of Freedom, I, and such Comrades as may incline to adhere to me, in this regard, will stand for the liberties of the country, and neither to the King of England, nor to his representatives, God being gracious, will we render obedience.

Here, in good sooth, we have a gospel far more comprehensive than National Independence. If that fail, why, does not Individual Freedom still remain intact to be fought for. *Omnia devicta praeter atrocem animum Catonis*. Wallace was, in fact, an Anarchist of the prime, as much opposed to majority rule – to 'the entire Scottish nation' itself gone astray – as to the odious One-Man Rule of an English Monarch. Verily, there have been Anarchists before strenuous Bakunin and sage Prince Kropotkin ...

England's Claim to Suzerainty

... That 'Hammer' Edward at first honestly intended to annex Scotland, not by Arms, but by Matrimony, there can be no reasonable doubt. The second string to the Norman bow was always the *marriage de convenance*, and its maleficent effects in Scotland visibly culminated when no fewer than thirteen competitors, professing to be 'sib.', greedily laid claim to the Royal 'Maid's' inheritance: thereby affording Edward some sort of moral pretext to assert his alleged suzerainty.

The Ragman Roll

Of the royal thirteen, eleven held estates in England as well as in Scotland, and were Englishmen first and Scotsmen a very long way after. Indeed, nearly all the greatest nobles or tenants of the Crown were of mixed Norman blood. They had not conquered Scotland as they had conquered England by the strong arm – far from it. They had come into possession by politic marriage and the most lavish gifts from Anglicising and feudalising native princes of Scotland. With large fiefs, but without a Fatherland, they formed a gang of unprincipled adventurers, unsurpassed in rapacity, treachery, and baseness in every form.

And behold, are not their sinister figures, limned in the nude, to be studied to execration in 'Our Noble Scottish Families'? Carlyle's corroboration is unforgettable: 'It is notable that the Nobles of the country (Scotland) have maintained a quite despicable behaviour from the days of Wallace downwards – a selfish, ferocious, famishing, unprincipled set of hyenas, from whom, at no time and in no way, has the country derived any benefit whatever.'

And the Bruces and the Baliols were about the worst of the lot. Hence the facility with which Edward was at first able to assert his claim to feudal superiority over the surprised and distracted country.

The Ragman Roll is a document of extraordinary infamy. It contains the names of nearly every man of consequence in Scotland - two thousand names or more - as formally assenting to the subjugation of the realm. But one name is not there - that of the Wallaces of Ellerslie, who, it may be very safely assumed, joined in the indignant protest of the Communitas - a most important document which Edward pronounced nihil efficax (not to the point) and almost succeeded in wholly suppressing.

Howbeit, the version of the "Great Roll of Scotland" in the Chronicles of St Alban's, contains a passage affecting a suspicious blank in the famous collection known as Rymer's "Foedera Anglicana", which is most important, inasmuch as it was in the name and by the authority of this "Communitas" that Wallace acted as Constitutional Chief of State.

The passage sets forth that, while the Bishops, Earls and Nobles sent in nothing at the Upsettlinton Conference (on Scottish soil) in reply to Edward's claim of suzerainty, the "Communitas" protested in writing, only to be told that its objections were frivolous. Nor was it again consulted. The reply of the "Communitas" was thus burked and treated as negligible.

But what of the "Communitas"? It consisted, it would seem, of Freeholders - of Probi Homines. How they met apart from the Magnates and framed their protest, we unfortunately do not know. But they were courageous Scottish patriots, that is clear, and one would give much to recover the precious terms of their lost memorial.

Yes, even in that hour of gloom there was unflinching patriotism among the commoners of Scotland, as there always has been and will be, however great be the odds against them.

LEAF FOUR

> He (Wallace) was the first man who fought, not to support a dynasty, but to free Scotland, and the first General who showed that Citizens could be an over-match for trained soldiers. No reproach of cruelty or self-seeking attaches to his term of Government, and the enemy of his country selected him as its first Martyr.
>
> - Charles H. Pearson: "History of England during the Early and Middle Ages."

Wallace's Humanity

Only four documents indited by Wallace have been preserved, and two of them are, I rejoice to say, instruments of Protection for the Persons and Property of Englishmen and in mitigation of the horrors of war.....

Wallace on Commerce

...(The name of) the lamented Andreas de Moravia who fell at Stirling Bridge...has first place in a document of singular interest - human, diplomatic and commercial - as devised by "Freebooter" Wallace, and fortunately unearthed some while ago by the learned Dr Lappenburg in the municipal archives of Hamburg:

> Andrew Moray and William Wallace, Commanders of the Army of Scotland and the Community of the same Kingdom: To the Prudent and Discreet Men and Well-beloved Friends, the Mayors and Commonwealths of Lubeck and Hamburg, Greeting and Perpetual Increase of sincere Friendship.
>
> To us it has been intimated by trustworthy Merchants of the said

Kingdom of Scotland that as a mark of your regard, you have been favourable to, couselling and assisting in all matters and transactions relating to us and said merchants, though such (good offices) may not have been preceeded by our deserts, and on that account we are more bound to tender you our thanks and a suitable return. This we have willingly engaged ourselves to (perform towards) you, requesting that, in so far as you cause your Merchants to be informed, they will now have safe access to all the parts of the Kingdom of Scotland with their Merchandise, as Scotland, thanks be to God, has by war been recovered from the power of the English.

Farewell. Given at Haddington, in Scotland, this 11th day of October, 1297.

Postscriptum. - We have, moreover, to request that you would condescend to forward the interests of our Merchants, John Burnet and John Frere, in their business in like manner as you may wish us to act towards your Merchants in their transactions.

Farewell. Dated as above.

"Honour him" (Wallace) enjoined Prophet Mazzini, "as one of the High Prophets of Nationality to us all. Worship his memory; teach his name and deeds to your children." In the thirteenth century, Wallace was to Scotland and to Europe what Mazzini, Garibaldi, aye, and Cavour were to the nineteenth century Italy. And yet his only reward was a cruel and shameful death; while another - Robert Bruce, who was not worthy to undo the hero's shoe-lace, greedily entered into his labours and reaped the harvest. And, alas, it has ever been so!

Truth for ever on the scaffold, Wrong for ever on the Throne;
Yet that scaffold sways the Future, while behind the dim unknown
Standeth God within the shadow, keeping watch above His own.

LEAF FIVE

If we except the Athenians and the Jews, no people so few in number have scored so deep a mark in the world's history as the Scots have done. No people have a juster right to be proud of their blood. - J.A. Froude

I have quoted two remarkable instruments under Wallace's hand, illustrating his wise and humane policy in peace and in war. But there is another, different in kind, which shows very clearly that he was no mere make-believe Custos Regni. It is a charter granted by him to Sir Alexander Scrimgeour..., as Standard-Bearer for Scotland, for faithful services in the field. It gives to Sir Alexander (whom he had knighted) certain Crown lands near Dundee, and bestows on him the lucrative office of Hereditary Constable of the town. It is dated "Torphichen, 12th May, 1298", and to it is affixed the Common Seal of the Realm. Nor was the validity of this instrument ever challenged by Bruce or his successors.

Wallace is now sole Chief of State, the rubric of the Scrimgeour parchment running: "Wilhelmes Walleys Knight, Guardian of Scotland, and Leader of her Armies, in the name of the illustrious Prince, Lord John (Balliol) by the consent of the Communitas - To all good men of the said Kingdom, wisheth Eternal Health in the Lord."

In other words, by the Consent of the Community, this extraordinary outlaw, not yet thirty, is virtual President of a Scottish Commonwealth, with "Our Noble Scottish Families" left hopelessly out in the cold! But the paralysed "nobles" were only biding their time, and, alas, it soon came.....

The Real Wallace

There is no substantial reason to doubt the tales of his extraordinary intrepidity of soul and strength of body. In that age no one but an invincible fighter could have tamed outlaws and terrorised feudal lords as he did. His assault on the garrison of Lanark, in which he killed the English Governor, Haselrig, whom he held responsible for the savage murder of his sweetheart or wife, Marion Braidfute, was a master-stroke of audacity.

His overpowering personality fascinated the minds of men, and the "Nobles" began to tremble at their rapid loss of authority over their own vassals. To their great alarm, Wallace burst the iron bonds of feudalism and called the latent democracy of Scotland into existence. Wholly disregarding the ties of vassalage he latterly ordered a conscription of all the able-bodied men of the realm, from 16 to 60. He even hanged (or threatened to hang) two leading burgesses (Nicol Jarvies, God ha'e mercy!) of Bonnie Aberdeen for unpatriotic remissness in the matter of recruiting. Even in the hostile pages of Hemingburgh we can see how it was:

> The whole followers (familia) of the nobility had attached themselves to him (Wallace); and though the persons of their lords were with the King of England, their hearts were with Wallace, who found his army reinforced by so immense a multitude of the Scots that the Community of the Land obeyed him as their Leader and Prince.

The "Cottonian M.S." is equally emphatic:

> So there crowded to Wallace all the Scots, of both sexes and of all ages, from the boy to the old man, so that in a brief space he had an army which, according to their own opinion, no Prince could possibly withstand...
>
> Whereupon a chief Earl of the nation invested the said William with the belt of Knighthood, thus transforming a robber into a knight, as a raven into a swan!

What, in these circumstances, were the noble signers of the Ragman Roll to do? There was nothing for it but break their oaths and turn patriots! The Steward of Scotland, Bishop Wishart of Glasgow, Sir Richard Lundin, Robert Bruce, and other "unprincipled hyenas", mustered accordingly a considerable force at Irvine, but on the approach of a well-appointed English host, they basely capitulated (9th July, 1297), again shamefully swearing allegiance to Edward. They could not fight for lack of cavalry! What wonder that Wallace should adopt as his motto the lofty words of rebuke: Patriae amantem armat Deus ("God armeth the patriot.")

It is not certain that Wallace and Bruce were in the same camp at Irvine, but the hero was undoubtedly in the neighbourhood, and at once called off his personal following, marching east through Selkirk Forest. In September he gave battle to Edward's Viceroy, Warrene, at Stirling Bridge, and utterly vanquished him, in spite of very great disparity in numbers and equipment. Wallace could muster only 180 horsemen all told. Warrene, evidently expecting another "Capitulation of Irvine", sent a couple of friars to Wallace to invite the Scots to sue for pardon. Whereupon, to quote Hemingburgh, "that robber (Wallace) replied: "Carry back to those that sent you this message, that we are not come here to sue for peace, but prepared for battle, to avenge our wrongs and liberate our country. Let them advance when they please; they will find us ready to meet them, even to their beards (etiam in barbas eorum.)" Wallace in person led the onset, charging at the head of his spearmen. Cressingham, Edward's hated Treasurer, was slain. Warrene fled across the Border, and Scotland was free...

The Fatal Fight at Falkirk

Presently Edward advanced into Scotland with a magnificent army - 90,000, say the Chroniclers, who are always most liberal with their ciphers. Wallace, with about a third or his numbers, fell back before him, laying waste the country in every direction. His object was to starve Edward into retreat, and then to harass him by surprises and night attacks. And the plan nearly succeeded. Edward had resolved on retreat when two of Carlyle's "unprincipled hyenas" (Earls Angus and March) betrayed to Edward the position of the Scottish camp, near Falkirk. Wallace, in consequence, had to fight, as rapid retreat was impossible in face of Edward's 10,000 mounted men. Knowing the peril of the situation, he grimly commented: "I have brought you to the ring, hop (dance) gif ye can!" His dispositions, however, were most masterly, and it was long before the English horse could make any impression on the four "schiltrons" of Scottish spearmen. These received the charging knights and squires of England in much the same formation as Wellington's foot received the French Cuirassiers at Waterloo. "As a castelle thei stode that was walled with stone", exclaims English Langtoft with honest admiration.

But he has a very different tale to tell of the Scots cavalry, 1000 strong. "Thei fled as fals cowardes." And Hemingburgh's testimony is about equally damning: "Immediately upon our men coming up, the Scottish cavalry fled, and without stroke of sword (absque ullo gladi ictu), a very few remaining, who proceeded to assist in arranging the ranks of the circles of infantry called "schiltrons".....but for the dastardly conduct of the Scots cavalry, Falkirk bade fair to be an earlier Bannockburn.

With superhuman effort, Wallace at last got his shattered "schiltrons" across the Carron into the shelter of the Torwood. On horseback he personally covered the retreat, slaying at the ford a renowned pursuer, Sir Brian de Jay, Grand Master of the Templars.

Besides the fugitive Comyn, only three of the greater nobles fought on the side of national independence - Sir John de Graham, of Dundaff, the bosom friend of Wallace and ancestor of "Our" Cunninghame Graham, the chivalrous and gifted; Macduff, uncle of the Earl of Fyfe; and Sir John Stewart of Bonkil. These three fought valiantly, and were slain at their posts. Stewart, in particular, displayed the greatest intrepidity, and along with him fell the whole splendid body of archers from Selkirk Forest, whom he commanded: "The Flowers of the Forest were a' wede awa'." Next day the English specially noted their stately forms lying in heaps around their chief.....

LEAF SIX

...And never again in the crash of the fight,
Shall a sword like to his be wielded for thee;
Or the spell of a name, so splendid and bright,
Be the theme and the fire of the songs of the free!
- Stewart Ross (Saladin).

The victory of Edward at Falkirk somehow profited the "Hammer of the Scots" (Malleus Scotorum) singularly little. Wallace speedily routed a detachment of his troops in a skirmish at Linlithgow; cut off any hope of local supplies by burning down Stirling and Perth; and compelled him, almost in a month's time, to retire to Carlisle.

But for Scotland's baronial "hyenas", the defeat was the very opportunity for which they had plotted. They recovered their lost seignorial influence so far as to embolden them to appoint a Committee of their own number (Comyn and Bruce among them!) Guardians of the Kingdom.

As for Wallace, all that is known is that he sailed from Dundee for the Continent, probably in the summer of 1299, attended by five faithful knights, for the purpose of soliciting for his country succour from abroad, secular and spiritual. While this fact rested on the unsupported evidence of Blind Harry, it was naturally distrusted, but later discoveries have placed it beyond all reasonable doubt.

A SPY'S EDIFYING LETTER

In a letter to Edward, a noble spy, De Hastings (National MSS.) reports ("Roxburgh, 20th August, 1299"):

> "David de Graham then demanded of the (Scottish) Council the lands and goods of Sir William Wallace, since he was gone out of the Kingdom without the leave of the Guardians (the noble Comyns and Bruces, forsooth!); and Sir Malcolm, brother of the said Sir William, replied that William's lands and goods could not be given, until it was found by a jury whether he went out of the Kingdom for the profit thereof or against it."

And this fraternal protest Sir Malcolm promptly backed by drawing his "knyff". A regular "scrap" or scrimmage thereupon followed among the "unprincipled hyenas" of the Council. Comyn seized Bruce by the throat, while his kinsman, Buchan, grappled with the Bishop of St. Andrews. Happily no fatal blow was struck, and Malcolm Wallace appears to have carried his amendment.

A document has been discovered in the Record Office of the Tower, which makes it almost certain that Wallace pleaded the cause of Scotland at Rome as well as at Paris. It is from Philip the Fair of France to his agents at Rome: "We command you to request the Supreme Pontiff to hold our beloved William, the Wallajs of Scotland, Knight (Militem), recommended to his favour in those things which with him he has to transact."

And what is more, Wallace's diplomacy seemed, at first, to prosper at both Courts. The Pope (Boniface VIII) issued a Bull strongly adverse to Edward's claim of suzerainty over Scotland. But "put not thy trust in Princes" or Priests. Edward and Philip mutually came to terms. Edward treacherously sacrificed his Flemish ally and Philip his Scottish. Thereupon his Holiness likewise promptly changed his tune. Edward suddenly becoming his "dearly beloved son in Christ", to oppose whom was "displeasing to the Divine Majesty, and to the inexpressible detriment of Scotland".

Wallace's Return to Scotland

For Wallace nothing now remained but to return to Scotland - to die. He resumed operations as a guerilla leader, and the "Wardrobe Account" of Edward I bears ample testimony to his renewed activity and daring.

In 1304, the noble "Guardians", Comyn at their head, capitulated, and only Wallace and Sir Simon Fraser kept the field. Presently Fraser also went under, and Wallace stood alone, at the end as at the beginning. All the oft forsworn nobles were received into the "King's peace" on more or less liberal terms; but as for "Sir William Le Walleys, the King means that he be received at his (Edward's) will, and subject to his disposal. Again, Edward writes (Kinghorn, 3rd March, 1304), to Sir Alexander Abernethy, in command at the Fords of the Forth: "Know this that it is not our pleasure, by any means, that either to Sir William Wallace or to any of his company, you hold out any word of peace, unless they place themselves absolutely, and in all things, at our will, without any exception whatever." And - tell it not in Glasgow, publish it not in the streets of Edinburgh! - there is a letter (same date) from Edward to Robert Bruce, warmly applauding Bruce's diligence in hunting down Scotland's Deliverer, and urging him, "as the cloak is well made so also make the hood!" Having once read that, I ceased to hold almost any stock in the Bruce of Bannockburn. Does any Scotsman who is not an "unprincipled hyena" wonder?

Capture and Execution of Wallace

At last the cruel hunt succeeded... Scotland's midnight hour had now come...

But Wallace's work was done, and it can never be undone. He inspired into Scotsmen a soul of freedom which has been of lasting service to mankind.

His military genius discovered the superiority of the peasant foot-soldier. As a General, Bruce merely copied his tactics in every detail. Stirling Bridge (1297) was followed by the Flemish Burghers' Courtrai (1302); Swiss Herdsmen's Mortgarten (1315); and Bannockburn (1314).

..."Nothing", says Goldwin Smith, "contributed more than the distinct national charactar (almost entirely the work of Wallace), and the distinct national religion of the Scots" - as a Democrat Knox had much in common with Wallace - "to save Britain being subjugated by the Absolutism of Strafford and the Anglicanism of a Laud."

This is high praise, but it seems to me not too high. I have eaten into the life and purpose of our national hero as faithfully as the perplexing data will permit, and I am satisfied that he was worthy of all - and more than all - the homage that Scotsmen have lavished on his memory. He had the very life of our Scottish Nation in his keeping, and he guarded it with a fidelity never surpassed in the history or even the legends of human heroism and endurance. He was faithful even unto death. There is not a blot upon his escutcheon, granting always, of course, that intolerable human wrongs may be legitimately redressed by the sword. Not one of "Plutarch's men" was his superior.

LEAF SEVEN

As I said in the last section, there is not a single discoverable blot on the unsullied escutcheon of the Knight of Ellerslie. He was faithful even unto death. Whoever might "break troth", Sir William broke none.

And his title to rule Scotland - what was that?

"By the Consent of the Communitas." In spirit and in letter, Wallace was the first Democratic Chief of State in Europe. How different was it with

THE VICTOR OF BANNOCKBURN!

Wallace and Bruce should really never be bracketed together as Scottish patriots. They stood, in fact, for internecine ends and principles. The one fought for a People, the other for a Crown, and, Bannockburn or no Bannockburn, divested of the glamour of the "bonnie fechter" - and he certainly was not a bonnier fighter than Wallace Wight - Bruce's personality was far from estimable. He was, in fact, a miracle of perfidy alike to Edward Longshanks and to William Wallace, on whose capture, as was seen, he was intent when forestalled...

The sacrilegious homicide of the Red Comyn at Dumfries (before the altar of a church - S-A.H.) was the turning point in his career. That deed of blood made him, for the first time in his life, a Scottish patriot willy-nilly. He had to assume the Wallace role and figure as the vindicator of Scottish nationhood. But for that he deserves no credit whatever. Wallace had in reality, during his brief term of Guardianship, burst the iron shackles of Feudalism by a most revolutionary ordinance decreeing national military conscription, regardless of the ties of Vassalage.

Wallace's military genius, moreover, revealed in his famous "Schiltron" formation the superiority of skilfully handled infantry over the superbest squadrons of cavalry. In a word, Wallace unquestionably taught the victor of Bannockburn the art of war. And yet in Barbour's "Brus" - Barbour was a courtier of Bruce's despicable son, David II - the very name of Wallace never once occurs. The royal and baronial gang thought in their wisdom to ignore his very existence, and certes, they were well advised; for his true life-story is the measure of their own limitless condemnation.....

Stands Scotland Where It Did?

Is Scotland still at heart the freedom-loving land of Wallace, Fletcher of

Saltoun, and Robert Burns? I am fain to hope that it is, and that the de-nationalising and demoralising cloud of Anglicisation, which has enveloped our nation so long, is about to pass away.

LEAF EIGHT

> "Scotland, we are told to weariness, never contained so much wealth as it does now. That is probably true. But it is no less true that never was Scotland's wealth so unequally distributed or sterilised in distribution. The gulf between Rich and Poor is wider than ever it was, because the Classes and the Masses have now no meeting ground or community of views, not even Religion. Both the old gaiety and the old earnestness of Scotland have disappeared. Whether they will reappear after a process of social transformation remains to be seen. At present Scotland is a dreary paradise of **bourgeois** prosperity and sectarianism, a country of 15 sects, 3000 churches, 300 bowling greens, 250 golf courses - and No Poet." - "National Review", August 1905.

Yes, that, I suspect, is pretty much the ugly outlook. Superficially at least, Scotland is distinctly decadent. She lives on her spiritual past, **plus** the Carnegie **shekels.** She is now neither an Aristocracy nor a Democracy, but a carefully-graded Plutocracy...

It is as if Sir William Wallace, John Knox, Fletcher of Saltoun, Napier of Merchiston, David Hume, Adam Smith, Robert Burns, Sir Walter Scott, James Watt, Thomas Carlyle, John Stuart Blackie, and scores of other gifted teachers had made no genuine impression whatever on the obdurate intellect and conscience of the nation.

But a process of social transformetion, I am satisfied, has undoubtedly begun, and it may very well be that the spirit of the stainless knight of Ellerslie will again manifest itself in the "land of the mountain and the flood", and direct its counsels...

And So Mote It Be!

Writing in 1703, just a century after the Union of the Crowns, and 389 years after Bannockburn...Fletcher of Saltoun thus gibbets the vile effects at that date of an Anglo-Scot Dual Monarchy:

> "It has been the misfortune of our country to have had our records twice destroyed by an English Usurpation, with a design to deprive us of all the glorious monuments of our Ancient Liberty, that we might the more easily be subjected as a Province of their Kingdom. But we did not suffer so much that way by Edward I and Oliver Cromwell - though in open war against us - as we have done through some of our own (Stuart) Princes, who, by the Union of the Crowns, became English Sovereigns.
>
> And as the collections of our laws before the Union of the Crowns are full of Acts to secure our Liberty, so those Laws that have been made since that time are directed chiefly to extend the (Royal) Prerogative. I must put the Representatives of the Scots in mind that no such (despotic) principles were known in this Kingdom before the Union of the Crowns, and that no Monarchy in Europe was more limited, nor any people more jealous of their Liberty than the Scots."

The Burglary of Scotland's National Archives by Edward and Cromwell, even though Fletcher could find worse tyrants amoung our native Stuart Rulers, struck at the nation's heart. They were most intelligently kept, and, had they been preserved, would have thrown a flood of light on much that is dark, or at best, conjectural, in Scotland's picturesque story.

...Cromwell, the Puritan "Man of Blood and Iron", unfortunately looted Scotland of something infinitely...precious... He ordered all the Scottish Records to be taken to London! After the Restoration they were sent back to Edinburgh; but, as the Lords of Session reported to the House of Lords in 1740, the frigate "Eagle" in which they had been placed for transport, was overtaken by a storm. From the "Eagle", "eighty-five hogsheads of papers" were transferred to another vessel which sank; and thus those priceless records perished irrevocably...

There is no reason why Federal Union - Home Rule All Round - should not have been set up in 1707 in place of abortive Incorporation, over two centuries ago. Fletcher and his friends, it is clear, understood its rationale perfectly well. In 1707 the Scottish Federalists were entirely on the right track... * Had a Federal Union been struck between Scotland and England in 1707, it is not too much to say that the example would have been followed by the Legislatures of England and Ireland in 1800, or earlier, and that there would be no everlasting Irish Home Rule trouble today.

The New Spirit.

But the gross selfishness of English Ministers and the rank habitual treason of the Scots "Nobles" (as in Wallace's day) were enough to ruin the most promising cause, nor did they fail to do so. Howbeit, methinks, Scotland is again awake, or awaking, and the grand old tide of her patriotic emotions has begun to flow in the old accustomed channels with something like pristine momentum.

The politics are base,
The letters do not cheer;
And 'tis far in the deeps of History,
The voice that speaketh clear.

But the voice of **Forward** is clear and resonant... The day of the "Little Peoples" is breaking fast...

LEAF NINE...

Disastrous Union of the Crowns

...it cannot be gainsaid that the immediate and direct effect of the Union of the Crowns (1603) on the liberties of Scotland was most disastrous. Every reactionary impulse in the national life was intensified. Before that event the Scots kings had to be on their good behaviour, and discerning Historian Buckle shall tell us the reason why:

> "There have been more rebellions in Scotland than in any other country, and the rebellions have been very sanguinary as well as very numerous. The Scots have made war on most of their Kings, and put to death many. To mention the treatment of a single dynasty. They murdered James I and James III; they rebelled against James II and James VII; they laid hold of James V and placed him in confinement; Mary they immured in a castle and afterwards deposed; her successor, James VI, they imprisoned; they led him captive about the country, and, on one occasion, attempted his life. Towards Charles I they showed the greatest animosity, and they were the first to restrain his mad career."

---

* Morrison Davidson includes in this LEAF a quotation from Fletcher of Saltoun - a passage strongly reminiscent of Thomas Jefferson's (see Part II ch.1 of this book) re decentralization; being woven through with exactly the same common sense as to the futility of placing extravagant powers and resources in the hands of a few overseers. How good to know that so sound a school of decentralism flourished in Scotland 300 years ago - and half a century before Jefferson was born.
– S-A.H.

It is a fact, peradventure, not generally known, that as early as the reign of James I, Scotland's Poet King, the famous words of Trajan, when he delivered the sword of office to the Governor of a Province: "Pro me; si merear, in me - For me; against me, if I deserve it" - were the motto on Scottish coins which were not called in till the crowning infamy of the Parliamentary Union with England in 1707...

The Quality of Scots Legislation.

As regards the quality of Scottish pre-Union (1707) legislation - the quantity was commendably small - Tory historian Sir Archibald Allison has written (and, need I say, **with knowledge**, of what he wrote), sixty years ago:

> "Such was the laudable brevity of those times that the whole Scottish Acts of Parliament, down to the Union, are contained in three duodecimo volumes. And yet, in these little volumes, we hesitate not to say, is to be found more of the spirit of real Freedom; more wise resolution and practically beneficial legislation; better provision for the liberty of the subject, and more equitable settlement of all the objects of the Popular Party at this time than is to be found in the whole thirty quarto volumes of the Statutes at Large, and all the efforts of English Freedom from Magna Charta to the Reform Bill (1832)."

Nor is this any idle vaunt; for Sir Archibald proceeds to demonstrate the superior attainments of Scottish legislative effort, along the whole legal gamut, with a wealth of illustration that is almost startling. Well may he conclude:

> "Whether these were important objects to have been gained by the Parliament of a remote, inconsiderable and distracted Kingdom, during the fifteenth, sixteenth and seventeenth centuries, I leave my readers to judge; but this I will affirm, that, if they were not, then is the whole Liberal Party of Great Britain at fault, and wandering in the dark at the present time; for almost the whole objects for the acquisition of which they profess such anxiety in England, in the middle of the Nineteenth Century, were secured for Scotland by her Native Parliament, before the end of the seventeenth.
>
> If the English legislators shall continue a course of wise and practical legal improvement, they will, perhaps, obtain, by the year 1900, most of the advantages which the Old Scottish Parliament secured for their country two centuries ago."

LOOK YE THERE! *

LEAF TEN...

The Treaty of Union (1707) by which the Predominant Partner's Parliament at Westminster swallowed up the Legislature of Scotland, was planned with unrivalled cunning.....the Treaty Commissioners, who sat in camera in London, pocketed £30,000 for their infamous breach of trust; while a further sum of £20,500, transmitted to the Scottish Treasury by Lord Godolphin, was assuredly distributed among thirty-two Members of Parliament, Peers and Commoners, in the name of "arrears of salary", to enable them to see their way to vote for the Treaty of Incorporating Union with their **"Auld Enemy"** - England...

How did they pass the Union?
  By perjury and fraud,
By slaves who sold their land for gold,
  As Judas sold his Lord!

---

* Whatever they **might have** secured, they have of course now handed over, along with their people, to a mega EURO-STATE! Alas that the Scots have lost 300 years to such folly! - S-A.H.

LEAF ELEVEN...

> "Everything in the last quarter of the 17th century points to a New Era in (Scotland's) history. Pathetic in other respects, the Union is tragic in this, that it for ever (?) closed the career of Scotland's Parliament, at the moment when, after long preparation, it was ready and able to play a fitting part in the nation's history." - Professor Terry. (Aberdeen); "Scottish Parliament (1603-1707)."

The Grand Betrayal

...The Estates of Scotland, as is well known, sat in One House, "so that the folks might not be bothered with the same blethers twice tauld". And, singularly enough, this House was never formally dissolved or closed. It was nominally "adjourned" till April 22. But the Records of Parliament contain no Minutes of Meetings later than March 25, 1707, when Lord Chancellor Seafield, who presided, perpretrated the heartless valedictory gibe which stung his countrymen like an adder: "There's the end of auld sang".

There was, of course, no General Election either before or after the Grand Betrayal. That ordeal the conspirators dared not face...

The "Auld Sang", and After

As it was, "the end of the auld sang" was duly reached at last, and Scotland's humiliating era of Suspended National Animation, or "Subordinate Patriotism" according to A.J. Balfour, with all its woes, set in in earnest. Incorporated Scotland became a rare corpus vile for experiments for insolent Southron administrators. *

...But cheer up, Professor Terry! ..."For ever" is a large order. Besides, as I have said, the Scots House only stands "adjourned" sine die... Scotland has "made history" before now, and, methinks, her opportunity is again fast maturing...

...And such (siste, viator!) is the Last Leaf (First Series) of

THE BOOK OF SCOTS.

*

---

* Yes! - right up to 1998's proposed vile lobotomy-without-consent experiment. S-A.H.

(Appx. to "Leaves from the Book of Scots".)

The Courier — 6th Jan. 1999

Sir,—I write on behalf of my own family, friends I met over the New Year holiday, and friends and relatives in England to express our disgust at BBC and ITV's Hogmanay programmes.

In the past, viewers could be sure of a good Scottish programme on Grampian, but now that control rests with STV it, too, is only interested, in cultural terms, in presentations of the lowest common denominator.

The show from Edinburgh, in particular, had all the glitzy shallowness of Lottery Live and, though it may have appealed to a few hundred thousand, there are millions in Scotland and England who expect Hogmanay to be a truly Scottish night.

Let us hope that at the end of 1999 we have an evening of all things Scottish including something akin to the White Heather Club which had a vast audience throughout Britain. To many Scots people, the last minutes of a year are the time when they remember the joys and sorrows of the year that has passed, and when their thoughts are with friends who have gone.

Let us hope that someone will see fit to reintroduce the few moments of reflection just before midnight thus finishing the year with dignity.

W. E. Scott.

Tomphubil Lodge,
Foss,
by Pitlochry.

There was a sentence in "Leaves from the Book of Scots" which I could not forget, from the first time ever that I read it - (it was quoted in the foregoing extract): "Both the old gaiety and the old seriousness of Scotland have disappeared".

It came back to me at once, vividly, when I read the letter above from Mr W.E. Scott, in the Courier, in the first days of 1999. For he draws attention at the end to an old Scottish custom - the few moments of silent reflection just before midnight at the turn of the year; a time when we used to "remember the joys and the sorrows of the year that has passed" and "friends who have gone".

This letter - (for which I would like to thank Mr Scott and the Courier) - brought back to me those words from "Leaves from the Book of Scots"; for what Mr Scott wrote seemed to me to epitomise so exactly both the "old seriousness" and the "old gaiety" we have lost in the losing of this old custom. For we may be sure that without the "seriousness" the "gaiety" can never be the same - (something his letter brings out too).

The de-culturising of the Scots has been going on for a long time, partly as a deliberate process but partly also as an inevitable one (under an alien domination), which many get caught up in unawares. Thus at the chiming in of the New Year on the radio once recently, I actually had to switch to Radio 2 in order to catch "Auld Lang Syne"! ...And how those very words of Scotland's traditional song for the bringing in of the New Year **invite** those moments of reflection! But trust Burns to combine so perfectly for us that "old gaiety and old seriousness" - and no wonder that it is sung across the world at that midnight hour.

Our New Year celebrations have only become vulgarised by the omission of those moments of silence, which allowed us to look back, and to gather up all that was dear to us in the passing year, before going forward again, into the new one.

We must resurrect our old customs - and what better time than when a new millennium awaits us also at the next turn of the year? Whether or not our media - still controlled from Westminster - will catch up in time, is really irrelevant. We are free to turn the media **off** for those few precious moments, and so follow our own - far better - way into the New Millennium.

A FEW WORDS

on George Buchanan

*

For these pages I am much indebted to Perth and Kinross public library (now A.K. Bell - formerly The Sandeman), who were able to provide me with a copy of George Buchanan's works, from which I took these pages in 1997.

D.C. MacDonald dedicated his volume on Ogilvie, ("Birthright in Land"), to "the memory of William Ogilvie, Robert Burns, John Locke, and, last but not least, George Buchanan". So here is an additional reason why it is good that something from George Buchanan should appear in this book.

I seem to recall that somewhere in his Biographical Notes on Ogilvie, D.C. MacDonald refers to George Buchanan as the "great-grandfather of British liberty" (or some such appellation - I quote from memory). Hence the reason why the Seven Wise Masters do not wish him in our history syllabuses - and another very good reason to include him here!

*

In confining myself, in these extracts, to just a few salient passages on Wallace's time, much of interest has naturally been omitted. But **unless** I so confine myself now... when will this book ever appear? - !

S-A.H, 16 Mar 99

THE

HISTORY

OF

SCOTLAND,

TRANSLATED FROM THE LATIN

OF

GEORGE BUCHANAN;

WITH

NOTES,

AND

A CONTINUATION TO THE UNION IN THE REIGN OF QUEEN ANNE.

BY JAMES AIKMAN, ESQ.

IN FOUR VOLUMES.

VOL. I.

GLASGOW:

PUBLISHED BY BLACKIE, FULLARTON & CO.
EAST CLYDE STREET;
AND ARCHIBALD FULLARTON & CO. BLAIR STREET,
EDINBURGH.
1827.

George Buchanan's History of Scotland

ADDRESS.

The fate of Scottish History has been peculiarly unfortunate; first the destruction of our most Ancient records by Edward I., and next, the political seizure of the remainder made under the Protectorate of Cromwell, when almost all our Authentic Documents were carried to England, and afterwards upon the restoration of Charles II., shipwrecked and lost on their return to their own country, have exposed the earlier period of our Monarchy to the jest of the wit, and the scepticism of the more judicious inquirer. In consequence, our original Historians, who wrote before the last and most destructive calamity that befell our literature, and who had access to documents which no longer exist, have been accused of credulity, and a love of fable; which modern investigation of the collateral proof afforded by cotemporary historians of other nations, tends in a great measure to remove.

. . . .

It were vain to expect for Scotland, what no other people on earth ever possessed,—a clear and succinct account of their transactions, during the ages in which they progressed from barbarism to civilization; but it would, indeed, have been strange if no memorial had existed of that period, in the history of a people who have ever been famed for their military genius, and spirit of enterprise. Buchanan, who had access to materials, the loss of which we must now deplore, embodied in his history all the information which the state papers of his country could afford; from his facilities as a Privy Counsellor, and as Tutor to the King, and as the first literary character, the *facile princeps* of his age, he possessed advantages which no subsequent writer could hope to possess; and his stern integrity, and undoubted veracity as a man, demand our assent to the truth of *that* which he vouches for, as an historian. The transcendent excellence of Buchanan's virtues, was the theme of unqualified praise to his cotemporary friends and admirers; while his private character reflected lustre on a genius which commanded reverence in an age of genius.

ADDRESS.

eloquence of our Historian is, indeed, extolled even higher by his enemies than his friends, perhaps as some atonement to his mighty shade for their attempts to detract from his moral worth; his history has not, however, yet appeared in a dress at all calculated to communicate to general readers, or to his countrymen, any idea of a work which excited the admiration of Europe upon its first appearance, and still is esteemed one of the finest monuments of modern literature. The present translator dares not avow how much he has come short of his own ideas of excellence, but he believes he may venture to affirm, that he presents to the public, the best English version of this work, ever yet laid before them. In the Notes which he has added, the Scottish Reader will probably not be less surprised than pleased, to find numerous facts and circumstances collected, as corroborative of some of the leading events in the reigns of some of the earliest of our monarchs, which prove, that by foreign historians, who lived near their time, they were not deemed fabulous personages.

. . . .

James Aikman

George Buchanan's History of Scotland

CONTENTS

OF

VOLUME FIRST.

CONTENTS.

xviii. But while the nobility, in general, appeared to have neither heart nor inclination for undertaking any great enterprise, William Wallace * arose. He was descended from an ancient and honourable family, but born and educated in rather indigent circumstances, and heir to only a very small paternal estate. He, however, performed exploits in this war, not only beyond expectation, but beyond belief. Endowed with great strength of body and boldness of mind, while quite a youth, he slew a young English nobleman, who haughtily insulted him. For this deed he was forced to become a fugitive and a wanderer, and passed many years in various lurking places. By this method of life, his body was hardened against all changes of fortune, and, by being often exposed to danger, his mind became strengthened for deeds of greater daring. At length, tired with his unsettled kind of life, he determined to attempt something nobler, however hazardous; and having collected a considerable body of men, attached to him by similarity of fortune, he not only attacked individuals, but often with small parties, engaged, and defeated, more numerous detachments, whom he occasionally surprised in convenient situations. He performed these actions with equal celerity and boldness, while he never allowed the enemy an opportunity of obtaining any advantage over him, so that in a short time his fame spread through both nations, and multitudes resorting to him from every quarter, either forced by the same causes, or excited by an equal love to their country, he speedily found himself at the head of no contemptible army. By this tumultuous assemblage, while the nobility, either through fear or slavish indolence, abstained from interfering in the management of public affairs, Wallace was proclaimed regent, and, as Baliol's lieutenant, governed the kingdom. He assumed this title, not from ambition, or the lust of ruling, but solely from compassion and love towards his countrymen. With this band, he first tried his strength in open combat at Lanark, where he slew the sheriff of the county, an English nobleman of rank; he then took and demolished many castles, which were either ill fortified, feebly garrisoned, or negligently kept; by which partial attempts, he so emboldened the spirits of his soldiers, that they shrunk from no danger under his direction, for his boldness was never either rash or unsuccessful.

xix. When the report of these transactions had spread abroad, increased and exaggerated according to the desires of the people, all who wished well to their country, or were afraid for their own safety, flocked to him, and he, eager to prosecute his good fortune, soon reduced, by the terror of his name, all the fortresses which the English held beyond the Forth, although sufficiently manned, and strongly fortified. He took and destroyed the castles of Dundee, Forfar, Brechin, and Montrose. By an unexpected assault he carried Dunnottar, which he garrisoned. The city of Aberdeen having been set on fire by the enemy, who were afraid of his coming, he entered it while yet in flames, and was prevented from taking the castle, only by the rumoured approach of the English army; for he had determined to oppose them at the Forth, being unwilling to risk a battle, except upon a field of his own choice.

* He was the younger son of Wallace of Ellerslie, near Paisley, in Renfrewshire, whose brother was Wallace of Riccarton. Lord Hailes, after exposing some of the errors of Blind Harry, says:—"The received opinion is, that he was outlawed for killing an Englishman;" and, after quoting Buchanan's account, adds:—"I *suspect*, however, that this is nothing more than an abridgment of Blind Harry in classical Latin." But with every respect for the acuteness, learning, and research, of Lord Hailes, I must observe, that this is a most unfair mode of animadverting upon a historian, it is raising a doubt where there is no ground for doubting; and after all, his lordship admits the fact of the outlawry, for which there is no more authority than for the specific offence.

George Buchanan's <u>History of Scotland</u>

(Following the events leading up to, and including, the Battle of Stirling Bridge):

XXI. The fields lying uncultivated, a famine followed this devastation, and a plague followed the famine, whence a greater number of deaths, it was feared, would arise than from the war. To alleviate as much as possible these calamities. Wallace ordered that all the young men, capable of military service, should meet him on a certain day, and he led them into England, thinking they would acquire health and strength by the exercise; and that by living in an enemy's country, during the winter, provisions at home would be spared, and his indigent soldiers, reap some of the fruits of war in an opulent country, which had so long enjoyed the blessings of peace. When he entered England, no one dared to oppose him, and having remained there from the 1st of November to the 1st of February,* when he had refreshed his men with the forage of the enemy, and enriched them with their spoils, he returned home surrounded with glory. This expedition, as it increased the renown and authority of Wallace among the people, so it excited against him the envy of the nobles; for his praises appeared to reproach the high and powerful chieftains, either with cowardice for not daring, or with treachery for being unwilling, to attempt what a gentleman in low circumstances, and destitute of every advantage of fortune, had not only bravely undertaken, but successfully accomplished.

(xxiii - Following the Battle of Falkirk):

After this unfortunate battle, when Wallace came to Perth, he disbanded his army, and yielded to that envy with which he found himself unequal to contend; neither did he ever afterward act as regent.* Yet, although he laid aside the title, he still, together with a few friends who constantly adhered to him, continued hostilities, and, whenever an opportunity presented itself of doing so with effect, pressed hard upon the English.

* Or general.

(Following Edward's renewed assault upon the Scots - after their victory at Roslin in 1302; with Wallace now practically alone continuing to harrass the victorious English forces...):

XXVI. The whole of Scotland being again reduced, an assembly of the estates was convoked by Edward, at St. Andrews, where all the principal men of the kingdom, terrified into compliance, took the oaths of allegiance, except Wallace alone; and he, dreading lest he should be given up to his most inveterate enemy, the king of England, by the nobility, who envied and hated him, retired, with a few followers, to his ancient lurking places. Edward having appointed governors and magistrates over all Scotland, returned into England. At his departure, he gave a remarkable proof of his hatred of the Scottish name. Not content with having removed all those who appeared likely to produce any revolution, he bent his soul, if possible, to abolish the very memory of the nation; he abrogated the ancient laws, altered the religious worship according to the English form, destroyed every history, treaty, and ancient monument, whether left by the Romans, or erected by the Scots, and carried off all the books and teachers of learning into England. He sent also to London, the rude marble stone with which the fate of the kingdom was commonly believed to be connected; nor did he leave any relic by which a generous mind might be roused at the remembrance of pristine greatness, or that might excite and encourage true magnanimity of soul; and thus, having not only broken the strength, but even, as he imagined, the spirits of the people, and reduced them to a state of servile humiliation, he promised himself perpetual peace from Scotland.

George Buchanan's <u>History of Scotland</u>

XXIX. About the same time, Wallace, betrayed by his own familiar friend, John Monteith, * who had been corrupted by English money, was taken in the county of Lanark, where he then lurked, and sent to London, where, by the infamous command of Edward, he was quartered, and his disjointed members hung up in the most remarkable places of England and Scotland, as a terror to others. Such was the end of a man, by far the most pre-eminent in the times in which he lived, who for greatness of soul in undertaking, and wisdom and fortitude in conducting perilous enterprises, may be compared with the most illustrious leaders of antiquity. In love to his country, inferior to none of the most eminent ancient patriots, amid the general slavery, HE stood alone unsubdued and free, and neither could rewards induce, nor terrors force him to desert the public cause, which he had once undertaken, and his death was the more grievous, because, unconquered by his enemies, he fell, betrayed by those from whom it was least to be expected.

*

- It was not "least to be expected" by Wallace, however.

At the Wallace Exhibition in 1997 at the Stirling Smith Gallery, already referred to, one of the unforgettable exhibits was a piece of sculpture showing a mass of snakes entwined. On the plaque placed beside it were the following words - (I may have abbreviated):-

> "The stone in front, stone of destiny, is full of snakes; symbols of danger and treachery. Not everyone will have the courage to sit upon the stone."

It was Wallace's destiny to do so, however. For he was not only Braveheart, but pure of heart as well.

*

From the Eve-of-battle Speech of the Caledonian Chieftain, Calgacus

During the Roman occupation of Britain, when Agricola was governor (78-85 A.D.), there was fought the Battle of Mons Graupius, which captured for the Romans the southern part of Caledonia – (a victory due mainly to Agricola's brilliance as a general, and fought with great courage by the people of Caledonia, whose weaponry on this occasion was considerably against them).

The inhabitants of Caledonia at that time consisted of a number of tribes. Pre-eminent among their chieftains by character and birth was one named Calgacus, who on the eve of that battle addressed their assembled forces, drawn from far and wide, in words which resonate with the same spirit of freedom as inspired Wallace.

> "As often as I survey the causes of this war and our present straits, my heart beats high that this very day and this unity of ours will be the beginning of liberty for all Britain. We are all of us untouched yet by slavery ... Former battles in which Rome was resisted left behind them hopes of help in us, because we, the noblest souls in all Britain, the dwellers in its inner shrine, had never seen the shores of slavery and had preserved our very eyes from the desecration and the contamination of tyranny: here at the world's end, on its last inch of liberty, we have lived unmolested to this day, in this sequestered nook of story; for the unknown is ever magnified.
>
> "But today the uttermost parts of Britain are laid bare; there are no other tribes to come; nothing but sea and cliffs and these more deadly Romans, whose arrogance you shun in vain by obedience and self-restraint. Harriers of the world ... they make a desolation and they call it peace.
>
> "Children and kin are by the law of nature

each man's dearest possessions; they are swept away from us by conscription to be slaves in other lands ... our goods and chattels go for tribute; our lands and harvests in requisitions of grain; life and limb themselves are used up in levelling marsh and forest to the accompaniment of gibes and blows ... so in this world-wide, age-old slave-gang, we, the new hands, worth least, are marked out to be made away with: we have no lands or mines or harbours for the working of which we might be set aside.

"Further, courage and high spirit in their subjects displease our masters: our very distance and seclusion, in proportion as they save us, make us more suspected: therefore abandon all hope of pardon, and even at this late hour take courage, whether safety or glory be most prized. Then let us fight as men untamed, men who have never fallen from freedom: let us show them at the very first encounter what manner of men Caledonia holds in reserve for her cause in her far places ..."

(From "Agricola", by Tacitus, translated by H. Mattingly, revised by S.A. Handford. Published by Penguin Books, 1948. Revised translation, 1970. With acknowledgements also to Alan Torrance, through whom this extract from Tacitus came to me.)

*

We walk the path of our ancestors.

For the past 250 years[1] we have been walking in shoes which are far too small for our feet and we are suffering for it. We no longer even realise it, because we are so inured to the pain.

It's time to take off our shoes and walk barefoot and feel the land of our ancestors beneath us again.

(Alan Torrance)

---

[1] *Act of Prohibition, 1746.*

"ON THE TRAIL OF WILLIAM WALLACE"

by David R. Ross

*

"Former guitarist David Ross is the author of "On the Trail of Wallace", a new book which offers a fresh and fascinating insight into the life of the revered Scots hero.

Here, he tells a Courier writer how he became interested in Wallace, and why the Scottish patriot is as relevant to Scotland and the Scots today as he has ever been."

(Extract from The Courier of 24 Feb 99 - all I have time for at this last moment - but I am so glad to include it.)

*

O Life that maketh all things new,
   The blooming earth, the thoughts of men;
Our pilgrim feet, wet with Thy dew,
   In gladness hither turn again.

From hand to hand the greeting flows,
   From eye to eye the signals run,
From heart to heart the bright hope glows,
   The seekers of the Light are one:

One in the freedom of the truth,
   One in the joy of paths untrod,
One in the heart's perennial youth,
   One in the larger thought of God; -

The freer step, the fuller breath,
   The wide horizon's grander view;
The sense of Life that knows no death, -
   The Life that maketh all things new.

Samuel Longfellow

*

Part II

by

Shirley-Anne Hardy

Signposts

. . . But God hath chosen the foolish things
of the world to confound the wise; and God hath chosen
the weak things of the world to confound the things
which are mighty;
And base things of the world, and things
which are despised, hath God chosen, yea and things which
are not, to bring to nought things that are.

I. Corinthians, ch. I

*

1. Community and Re-empowerment

2. Freedom's Full Price

3. For the Healing of Our Children.

The character and worth of individuals among the mass and the way they work themselves into membership of the whole body, receiving influences from it and giving others back, we can even today only partially and uncertainly understand.

One thing, however, is clear. Where the collective body works more strongly on the individual than the latter does upon it, the result is deterioration, because the noble element on which everything depends, viz., the spiritual and moral worthiness of the individual, is thereby necessarily constricted and hampered. Decay of the spiritual and moral life then sets in, which renders society incapable of understanding and solving the problems which it has to face. Therefore, sooner or later, it is involved in catastrophe.

(The Decay and the Restoration of Civilization, Albert Schweitzer, 1923)

*

Part II

*

Chapter I

Community and Re-Empowerment

It is in the shelter of each other that the people live

(*Celtic Traditional*)

*

"What meaning has the word 'Community' now?"

(*D.C. MacDonald*)

*

COMMUNITY AND RE-EMPOWERMENT

*

– A Message from the Mountains* –

The following passage is an extract from a letter written on 28 Oct 96 to the Convenor of *The Cairngorms Campaign* - an independent body with open membership - in response to a request to all members for their comments upon a certain Draft Management Strategy for the Cairngorms.

This Draft Management Strategy was the product of a government-sponsored body which had recently been set up, and had been named *The Cairngorms Partnership.*

Note: To make the extract fully intelligible, the opening section of the letter is placed here, within brackets - but may be skipped. (I should mention that no reply has yet been received to this letter, or to its follow-up dated 29 Jan 97.)

*

[Opening section of letter:

"I promised, in my letter to you of September 20th, that I would be sending you some comments, as requested, upon the Cairngorms Partnership Draft Management Policy. May I now write as follows?

As one who grew up in part in the Cairngorms - (indeed, in chief, if life influences are what count) - I owe to these mountains the *best* that I can give, in commenting upon the above devised 'Strategy'.

Where, then, does this 'Management Strategy' stand with me? Regrettably, this can be answered in one simple word: *NOWHERE.* Can one really be asked to take a document produced by this Partnership seriously, when clearly - (as your own report bears out only too well) - such a body is incapable of putting the interests of these Mountains above the interests of its own self-serving set-up? In short, I have to say that, to my regret, I find the 'Cairngorms Partnership' to be an imposture upon the Cairngorms, and an imposture, equally, upon the understanding of those attempting to preserve them.

Land tenure underlies use. It cannot do otherwise, since, under a structure of land monopoly, use will always tend to favour the *enhancement of the privately pocketable rental - including development - values of the land.* What is there, really, to surprise us in that 'industrially clad building' designed by the new owners of Glen Feshie, *favoured by government?* Or why should we be surprised at the hounding off, from a certain estate, of those unfortunate Duke of Edinburgh Award youngsters? Under a heartless regime, heartless measures easily become the order of the day.

Can we seriously expect government-approved or appointed bodies of *any* kind, rearing themselves up from the wretchedness and chaos of our falsely-structured society, to do aught but extend that chaos and wretchedness to whatever comes into their clutches? *Governments support the landed interest,* in any country where land monopoly - be it private or state - operates. They cannot do otherwise, according to the

---

* *The range of mountains known as the Cairngorms, in the Scottish highlands, constitutes a wilderness area unique in all of Europe - indeed, in the world scenario - and the running battle between conservers and developers goes back many years.*

elementary workings of things, whereby 'he who pays the piper calls the tune'. For economic monopoly builds up its own unerring power structure *right into government* - (see 'Professionalism and History' attached, along with 'Our Enemy the State' extract) - and the policy of this unnatural monopoly is PURE SELF-INTEREST. If it were not, monopoly would break itself up.

The *real* question we should be asking ourselves is: how is it we did not well understand all this - and set to work to right it - long ago? How is it that people have become so DISEMPOWERED IN THEIR THINKING that they can view such a 'partnership' seriously in the first place"]

*

Extract Proper

The process of DISEMPOWERMENT is easily traceable. Firstly, the landed interest, (via its own "laws" passed - by it - through parliament), succeeds in dispossessing the people of their land. Thus rendered economically unviable, a feeling of inadequacy gradually falls upon the dispossessed, at not being able to manage their own lives - not being able to stand upon their own feet. (*How*, if the ground under them has been removed?) Then a "benevolent State" - (monopoly interest wearing another hat) - steps in to "rescue" them: *not* in the only honest way, by ending land monopoly, but by doling them out, instead of justice, a meagre and ever-more-minimal living. *(On the dole.)* Thus is economic take-over bolstered by political takeover. I.e., the *people cease to believe in themselves.* They believe, instead, in "the State" - tragically mistaking the State for people-power, the real thing.

In this way, first belittled in their own eyes, next - befuddled as to the real origins of their situation, there comes about the worst of all disempowerments - the DISEMPOWERMENT OF THEIR OWN THINKING. The people can now only follow-my-leader on the disastrous downward pathway always taken by land monopoly - while piteously still clinging to their belief in "the benevolence of the State": a belief which of course transfers itself to belief in the "honest intentions" of any government-appointed body - (which body has - for sure! - been given, by the government, *ultimate power of decision in any matters to be discussed!* - including matters to be decided by the "voluntary principle" - !!!!! - unless this ultimate power is retained, *even more* securely, by the government itself).

And what of THE LAND in all this? How can we see those wise and all-comprehending Mountains, that regard us, viewing this matter? To what, or to whom, do *they* look? The land looks naturally to its only true guardians and preservers. That is to say - it looks to THE PEOPLE THEMSELVES. The land knows well that it can only be preserved as *all ordinary people have a stake in its preservation* - a situation that can only manifest when that day comes, that land monopoly, with all of its cruelly disempowering mechanisms, is done away with forever. For the land knows well that it can only be saved, in its every part, by those who actually walk upon it, know it, and love it at first hand, being familiar with it as part of their *own home ground.*

The idea that a "Secretary of State for Scotland", in some prestigious building in Edinburgh - a solitary individual, *and*, immured in his office, lacking proper knowledge of any area at first hand - should be thought to be capable of taking a sane decision about any part of Scotland, (including the area of the Cairngorms): the idea that he should be expected to - that we should *look to him to do this!* is surely an example of the ultimate idiocy of our decision-making structure, revealing the pitiable spectacle of a people who have *lost their way* - lost touch with themselves because they have lost touch with their land. Truly we are a society of the dispossessed, and as the saying goes: divorce a people from their land, and they will gradually become capable of any insanity.

What hope, then, is there, either for the Cairngorms, or for ourselves?

We must look to the ROOTS of our situation. We must EXAMINE THE STRUCTURE OF LAND TENURE.

It is *this* that the Cairngorms are asking of us – not a shameful co-operation with a fatally-flawed body – fatally flawed from the start, in such a way as to be incapable of true commitment to aught but its own aggrandisement.

Let us note the following words, uttered by one of the dukes of Fife:-

> "My ancestors purchased all the lands I possess, with the exception of some commons, such as Cairngorm or Benmacdhui, acquired merely as their share of the spoil when the other landlords were having a general scramble for all the hills and glens of Scotland." (From the Biographical Notes on William Ogilvie, of D.C. McDonald, in his publication "Birthright in Land", Kegan Paul, 1891.)*

– And we think that our efforts for the Cairngorms can build upon an edifice of THIS foundation – !!!!!

Finally, I must tell you that, contrary to expectations, I am prevented from attending the Annual General Meeting of the Cairngorms Campaign, at Fishers Hotel, in Pitlochry, on November 2nd. I trust, however, that what I have written here will make its own contribution to the work of the Campaign, for

THE PRESERVATION OF THE CAIRNGORMS.

Yours sincerely,
(sgd.) Shirley-Anne Hardy
(Founder Member of the Cairngorms Campaign.)

Note: My statement above is made without prejudice to the individuals making up the body called the Cairngorms Partnership. It is the *structure of our society* - (both primarily, in its land tenure, and secondarily, in the various bodies which this form of land tenure gives rise to) - that are focused upon here; *not* the individuals, (none of whom are known to me), who make up the Cairngorms Partnership - or any other government-sponsored body; among whom there may even be those who find themselves responding positively to what I have written, and willing to help bring about the necessary radical changes in our society, for the sake both of the people and of the land, and (most especially in our context) of the CAIRNGORM MOUNTAINS themselves. S-A.H.

> ". . . the only way to find the solution to our problems is [for] those who can see the mistakes of the past. . . to expose for all [their] worth the attitudes which have been responsible for our present predicament. A new attitude about what is important should then begin to pervade the majority of the people, so that the will of the people will enforce a change that can never be reversed." (Victor Schauberger, in "Living Water", Gateway Books, 1990, with successive reprints. See further Part II, ch. 2.)

---

* ***Note:*** *the re-publication of D.C. McDonald's book by the Scottish Ogilvie Society, expected that autumn, was here referred to. But see ch. "The Making of This Book".*

"The ownership of land is the great fundamental fact which ultimately determines the social, the political, and consequently the intellectual and moral condition of a people." (Henry George, in "Progress and Poverty". The Henry George Foundation, London. Continuous reprints.)

(END OF EXTRACT)

Note: The above-quoted extract, slightly abbreviated, was published in the July-August 1997 issue of *The Science of Thought Review,* (Bosham, Chichester, Sussex), preceded by a note from the Editor: "This is an extract of an article/letter one of our readers sent, in response to the Draft Management Strategy of the newly set-up government-sponsored *Cairngorms Partnership.* She raises issues that are of paramount importance today, addressing the relationship of the land to the common people."

*

The disempowerment most anguishingly close to us, and affecting by far the greatest number, is of course – the absence of any real possibility of having a bit of land, a home-place of our own *not* mortgaged for life to its land values; a place where an occupation at least of some elementary kind could be carried on in today's job-precarious scene – a workshop constructed, enterprise and initiative given place where they should be, *at root* – healthy food grown, children found safe space to play. . The dream has so many faces. . .

Landowners – (*despite* their lobby's recent efforts at restrictive legislation!) – like to boast that we are more or less free, still, to roam "their" land. But that is – so long as we keep walking, of course! We can pause long enough to admire the view, or to picnic – but not long enough to put down roots – not to build ourselves houses or plant ourselves orchards or vegetable plots.

The "community" that exists is in reality the community of landowners; and in rural areas one of the myths propping this community up is the myth that we look to it for the preservation of the countryside for us all!

It is entirely through the disempowerment of our thinking – due largely to a false educational system itself propped up by land monopoly – that there continues apace this incredible maze of myths and disempowerments we live among. So it is that the ability to retrieve our own thinking – the power to think things through afresh for ourselves – is, at the deepest level, what this reform is about.

Now there is an aspect of this land reform that particularly requires us to view it with a fresh thought, for it is an aspect that uniquely empowers the idea of community – the real thing. Consider for a moment the implications of the fact that – LAND IS LOCAL! In a nutshell - land business is our business! Not just in the general sense we have been looking at, (i.e. that it is our one true social fund), but in a quite specific way, a way that has immediate bearing upon those local services we so powerlessly watch being stripped away from us, as local councillors, for necessary funding, go cap-in-hand to central government. . .and get neatly "capped" for their pains! For not only is land rent our true social fund, but land – the land which carries those rental values – being *local*, presents that social fund to us as something which it makes sense to collect locally too. Indeed – which in all logic *requires to be* collected locally – and hence, locally disbursed as well.

Here's a turning-topsy-turvy of the economic and political scene in one! Here's local re-empowerment at one stride!

And lest anyone think this idea is too far-fetched – by no means! It's been about for quite a while. It's just that it too, naturally, gets missed out of our educational syllabuses.

Here is one crack in the curtaining , from the pages of A.J. Nock in *Our Enemy the State* – (the entire fun of whose pages makes a political education perhaps without parallel, perfectly partnering the economic one from Henry George). The context of the quotation is Nock's examination of the essentially *anti*-social nature of the State, and it is the famous American president who is quoted in the following:-

> "One mind, indeed, came within reaching distance of the fundamentals of the matter, not by employing the historical method, but by a homespun kind of reasoning, aided by a sound and sensitive instinct. . . Mr Jefferson. .believed that the ultimate political unit, the repository and source of political authority and initiative, should be the smallest unit; not the federal unit, state unit, or county unit, but a township, or, as he called it, the "ward". The township, and the township only, should determine the delegation of power upwards to the county, the state, and the federal units. His system of extreme decentralization is interesting and perhaps worth a moment's examination, because if the idea of *the State* is ever displaced by the idea of *government*, it seems probable that the practical expression of this idea would come out very nearly in that form. . . .it is interesting to remind ourselves that more than a hundred and fifty years ago, one American succeeded in getting below the surface of things, and that he probably to some degree anticipated the judgement of an immeasurably distant future. (Chapter IV)

One can but hope that Scotland saves it from being *immeasurably* distant!

We need to turn, here, to Nock's footnote on Jefferson's proposal, to find the idea in its completion – in view of the fact that political power always, of course, *follows on* **economic**. ("He who pays the piper calls the tune".) But a word, first, upon Jefferson's use of the term "township" or "ward"; and further, upon Nock's distinction between the idea of the State, and that of government – something which is fundamental to his whole book.

"Townships", in the America of Jefferson's time – comparatively recently populated as it was, and still a mainly agricultural society – cannot be thought of as anything like the towns, (let alone cities), that exist in the Britain, or even Scotland, of today. To arrive at a working equivalent, we shall need to think of our towns as divided into something more comparable to village areas, (more consonant with the term "ward") – an idea we shall return to.

On the distinction between *government* and the *State*: in an earlier chapter of his book, Nock comments on the view of government outlined by Thomas Paine – famous eighteenth century author of *The Rights of Man* – as expressed in another of his works, *Common Sense.* (Good title!) Nock sums up with approval Paine's view of the matter as follows. "It would seem that in Paine's view the code of government should be that of the legendary King Pausole, who prescribed but two laws for his subjects, the first being, 'Hurt no man', and the second, 'Then do as you please'; and that the whole business of government should be the purely negative one of seeing that this code is carried out." (From Nock's ch.II. Today's scene confronts us of course with the further warning from the Bible, in Revelations - Hurt not the earth.) On the following page,

Nock points out how well actualized this idea of *government* has in fact been by various peoples, including the Virginian Indians of Jefferson's own time.

The State, by contrast, is the term Nock applies to that highly centralized body of bureaucratic power we know so well today, which directly opposes, and to a vast (and ever increasing) degree *usurps* the functions of *social* power - that is, the functions which should belong to ordinary people, or, what we are discussing as the *community*. As Nock points out: contrary to our frequent confusions of the idea of "the State" with the idea of something of "social" intent, *social* (or community) power and *State* power are as opposed to one another in principle as in operation they unfailingly prove.

So we see Nock adding to Jefferson's view the yet further strength of his own – from our day and age,and far greater experience of the State: that not the centralization, but the *de*-centralization of power, is the pathway to the future.

To Nock, then, let us turn for the completion of Jefferson's proposal, as mentioned above. It is found in a footnote to the proposal, in that same ch. IV of his book:-

> "In fact, the only modification of (Jefferson's proposal) that one can foresee as necessary is that the smallest unit should reserve the taxing- power strictly to itself. The larger units should have no power whatever of direct or indirect taxation, but should present their requirements to the townships, to be met by quote. This would tend to reduce the organizations of the larger units to skeleton form, and would operate strongly against their assuming any functions but those assigned them. . ."

(Here we must take "taxing-power" in its general meaning of "revenue-raising", for Nock was of course a strictly and one hundred per cent land rent man.)

Jefferson was far from alone in thinking as he did, even at that time. In *Forerunners of Henry George* already referred to, we read that Turgot and others of the Physiocratic School - an early "Georgist" movement, active in France just prior to the revolution - were possible influencers of Jefferson. Joseph Dana Miller - who, like Nock, regarded the Physiocrats' proposal of "home rule" (as he refers to it), as something to which our civilization has not yet advanced - writes in *Forerunners of Henry George*:-

> "This was a theory which Physiocrats urged. Turgot, in his 'Essay on Municipalities', advocated home rule minutely, beginning with village communities which should rule in strictly village matters, sending delegates to county assemblies, ruling county affairs; they, in turn, sending delegates to provincial assemblies; these last sending delegates to a national assembly. . . We find as minute a subdivision suggested by Jefferson, probably learned from du Pont (*Works*, Ford's ed., 1:113). . .How benighted we are compared with the Physiocrats, may be realized from the fact that as long ago as 1750 Mirabeau pleaded for decentralization – home rule (Higgs' Physiocrats, p.20)."

Home rule, as a Physiocratic term, had its base, we note, resting firmly at *village* level. And how particularly interesting this is for us, who are considering the matter in relation to land rent reform, since the Physiocrats were – as already stated – an *early Georgist movement*!

How far we have turned the clock *back* in the succeeding interval, in our childish march towards ever more centralized, *ever less people-responsible*, power! "Benighted" is Joseph Dana Miller's word for our infantile predilection for raising up a "Nanny" to take charge of our affairs. And can we deny his description of us, as we continue to defeat ourselves all along the line, never-ending being our complaints – whether from community councils against the decisions of local councils, local councils against central government rulings – or ordinary citizens against the whole gamut of power-wielders of every shape and kind! To tolerate such wastage of energies is infantile in itself. Is it not obvious that, as man matures, he must spread his wings and leave the nest and Nanny – or turn her out, bag and baggage? "When I was a child, I spake as a child, I understood as a child, I thought as a child: but when I became a man, I put away childish things." (Sound political lesson owing to Paul! 1 Cor.13.)

It is worth returning to Jefferson to ponder the psychological insights he brings also to bear upon this scene. These insights are so impossible to dismiss – so instantly recognizable to each and every one of us – that there is no way our present crazy pathway could have maintained itself, except by a most thorough *disorienting* of our thinking, at its most elementary level. The following is further from Nock's ch. IV:–

> "In February, 1816, Mr Jefferson wrote a letter to Joseph C, Cabell, in which he expounded the philosophy behind his system of political organization. What is it, he asks, that has 'destroyed liberty and the rights of man in every government which has ever existed under the sun? The generalizing and concentrating all cares and powers into one body, no matter whether of the autocrats of Russia or France or of the aristocrats of a Venetian senate'. . . The secret of freedom will be the individual 'making himself the depository of the powers respecting himself, so far as he is competent to them, and delegating only what is beyond his competence, by a synthetical process, to higher and higher orders of functionaries, so as to trust fewer and fewer powers in proportion as the trustees become more and more oligarchical'. . .
>
> "This idea rests on accurate observation, for we are all aware that not only the wisdom of the ordinary man, but also his interest and sentiment, have a very short radius of operation; they can not be stretched over an area of much more than township-size; and it is the acme of absurdity to suppose that any man or any body of men can arbitrarily exercise their wisdom, interest and sentiment over a state-wide or nation-wide area with any kind of success."

So – the "acme of absurdity"! There we have it! We mark the picture Scotland presents of herself today! But what words are left to describe our *Euro*-folly? Even Jefferson could not have been expected to foresee the construction of such a *super*-absurdity.

By contrast, here are some glimpses from Jefferson's pen of a people who know properly how to manage their affairs. They take the precaution of "placing under everyone what his own eye may superintend", knowing well that the "surest safeguard" for a society exists where "every man is a sharer in the direction of his ward-republic, or of some of the higher ones, and feels that he is participator in the government of affairs, not merely at an election one day in the year, but every day".

As one may say – (borrowing Paine's good title) – *Common Sense!*

Before leaving this matter of *true* devolution – (devolution requiring full independence in the first place, need we say) – let us draw upon the reflections of a certain European – one whom we might indeed call a *true* European, and we might just ponder that, too, as we consider what he has to say.

Carlo Levi – like his namesake Primo Levi, (who makes interesting mention of him) - was an Italian Jew. He was half a generation senior to Primo, and falling under the eye of Mussolini for his adamant opposition to fascism, was presently banished to the wilds of Lucania – one of those "lost" peasant regions of the south of Italy which was simply *beyond the ken* of Italians in general. It was here that he underwent an experience of the profoundest political education, and it is the account of how he gained it – gradually, unconsciously at first, simply by observing, listening to, and sharing in, as he could, the lives of these oppressed and impoverished southern peasants – which forms the fascinating content of his book, *Christ Stopped at Eboli*, a book which some thirty years ago was on everyone's lips – and understandably.

In that desolate region of Italy – consisting entirely of denuded or swampy land, and suffering such over-all impoverishment that even the landed power was minimalized – it was the political aspect of life, the long arm of the State reaching out from Rome to direct affairs it knew nothing about, which drove the peasants to their deepest despairs. *

Thus Carlo Levi – the doctor and artist who moved among them, and whom they came to love - was driven himself in turn to understand what the peasants understood with their whole being: that is, in what direction alone salvation lay. And his profound political insights speak equally to our own condition – to our own absurd, disempowered, quango-ridden, State-ridden state.

As the train he is travelling on moves out of Rome one night, carrying him back to Lucania from a rare permitted visit to his family in the north, Carlo Levi finds himself unable to sleep, turning over in his mind the peasants' situation - their blunted, despairing lives – and equally, the complete failure of his friends in the city to comprehend the problems of the south, which they knew only from a distance, and not at first hand, and which they placed their entire faith upon "the State" to sort out.

At bottom, as Carlo Levi now perceived, his friends were all "unconscious worshippers of the state". All of them adhered to the view that the state "should do something about it" – (i.e., about the peasant problem) – and were shocked when he told them that the State, as they conceived it, was "the greatest obstacle to the accomplishment of anything". As Carlo Levi tried to get through to them, the State could not "solve the problem of the south", because "the problem which we call by this name is none other than the problem of the state itself".

These words might have come straight from the mouth of A.J. Nock,** and one may note, in fact, the contemporanity of their two writings, *Our Enemy the State* having appeared in the very year, 1935, which saw Carlo Levi's banishment under Mussolini – (at the start of Italy's Abyssinian War). Nock, having pondered the matter for a longer period, had reached the point of writing the word "State" thus, with a capital "S", so distinguishing it from the more general noun, (and – outside of Carlo Levi's text – I have kept to this rule).

---

* *But of course the State is reared upon that* ***overall*** *pattern of land monopoly – holding an entire country in its grip. (See especially extract from A. J. Nock in Part III.)*

** *Interestingly,* ***Our Enemy the State*** *does bear, in its course, stout witness to the struggle of the only comparable class in America to those Lucanian peasants: that is, the small farmers and artisans of America, who, at the time of the shaping of the Articles of Confederation (the 1780s), found themselves likewise* ***up*** *against the immoral arm of the landed and moneyed classes, who were busily engrossing, to their own advantage, precisely the* ***power of the State*** *. . . and so successfully that – (a piece of history usefully leaked to us from Nock) – the* ***original*** *Articles of Confederation were*

What was it that Carlo Levi, from his sojourn among them, perceived so clearly to be the sole solution for this disempowered people of Lucania?

If we turn to Thomas Jefferson's words again, we will find ourselves looking at exactly what Carlo Levi saw - and not just as political theory, but out of direct, first-hand political experience. That is - he saw, precisely, that "their own eye" must be able to "superintend" their own business, and that they must have power over their affairs "every day" of the year.

Carlo Levi recognised that what was required was no small matter. He saw that it meant we must "mak(e) ourselves capable of inventing a new form of government", no less. The challenge, as he saw, was to replace the concept of the *State* with that of the *individual*, which we must make the basis of government. He saw that there was only one way forward out of the vicious circle of political antagonisms, which he realized were incapable of solving the people's problems. (And do we not, by now, all know it?)

Autonomy was the name of the way forward which was brought home so clearly to Carlo Levi out of this experience. "The state can only be a group of autonomies, an organic federation." In short, the only type of organization through which the people of Lucania could fittingly partake in the complex life of the nation must be "the autonomous or self-governing rural community". It was fully plain to Carlo Levi that "the problem of the south" would disappear of itself, once the peasants had ceased to be booted about by Rome – (forced to slaughter goats crucial to their economy, and given "bonanza" horses they could not feed) – and once they had freed themselves also from the various local mismanagers of their affairs, who flourished under the "Rome" system.

** *simply torn up and "tossed into the waste paper basket"! How many Americans know* ***that*** *missing little piece of their history?*

As to the Articles of Confederation that took their place – as Nock shows, exactly the same words may be applied to them as may be applied to today's United Nations Charter of Human Rights. (See further on.) No wonder that the famous "Give me you poor, you tired . . . ", etc., of the Statue of Liberty – overlooking New York harbour where the great mass of immigrants arrived – now has nowhere to put them but on the streets!

Interestingly, Nock – (who kept his private life strictly private) – must also, it seems, have had deep community links, for he served for ten years as an episcopal minister. So his political insights may well have sprung from the same source – a deep personal involvement with the people he lived among. The only difference is, that we surmise this about Nock. About Carlo Levi, we know it.

It must by now be clear that A.J. Nock has been a major influence on my life. Indeed he has. So perhaps I may place here my personal tribute to Carlo Levi.

I feel I owe it to Carlo Levi's gift as a writer – and also to my enjoyment of his book – to state that the effect of reading ***Christ Stopped at Eboli*** *is somewhat as of watching a myriad of tiny tricklets of water lost on some upper mountain-slope – watching them gradually assert themselves, begin to gather strength as visible streams, and finally unite into a great and powerful current of water, fraught with eddies, whirlpools and undertows – now rapidly commanding a powerful respect.*

Something such – and precisely the more, on account of the meandering and apparently inconsequential beginnings of the history related in the book – is the effect upon the reader of the powerful current of its emergent thought.

But this is not all. Inevitably, Carlo Levi found a fuller logic unfolding gradually out of his initial ponderings. He realized that "the autonomy or self-government of the community cannot exist without the autonomy of the factory, the school, and the city", indeed – "of every form of social life".

Carlo Levi does not – (not in *Christ Stopped at Eboli*, that is to say) – proceed further, as do Jefferson *et al.*, to make mention of the higher federated structures by which the smaller units would achieve their natural linkages. But he makes the essential discovery. He arrives at the one and only possible basis of the whole – the *small self-governing community*.

What is so especially valuable about Carlo Levi's work on this matter, (for work it was – the relentlessly searching, dedicated work of his period in exile), is that he was neither a politician nor a social economist. He was primarily an artist; a painter –(he managed to paint quite a bit in Lucania), and a writer; with just a smattering of medical skills – but enough for the poor peasants of Lucania to turn constantly to him. Hence, the reason that he came to wrestle with this question of political power was – the simplest and best of all reasons: because he came to love the people he was so unexpectedly thrown among – and so, to feel for their sufferings as for his own. Tolstoy once said that we cannot really know what people need unless we love them –(a truth self-evident, once spoken). Hence, I think we have to concede that Carlo Levi, in what he thought and wrote upon this matter, possessed a *unique* knowledge – a knowledge that therefore awaits our recognition today. And how good a thing it is to be able to set these insights on grass-roots empowerment – the insights of a true European – against our present mad "Euro" scene! Indeed, can we possibly imagine how Carlo Levi would have viewed the mad carousel that it is?

Carlo Levi had small chance of course, in Mussolini's Italy, of making acquaintance with the Law of Rent. But with his powers of discernment, it is unlikely he would have failed to recognize, in that law, a fully natural partner, and essential economic base, for the system of grass-roots empowerment he envisaged.

It is much to be hoped that Carlo Levi's work will come to the fore again – in a Europe that was never more in need of his sanity than it is today; and that he will in time be recognized as not merely an artist – in paint *and* in words – but as one of those *forerunners* – makers of the truer society that shall be.

Let us now look again at Nock's footnote on Jefferson's proposal - and partner it here with the paragraph which follows it in his book:-

> "In fact, the only modification of it that one can foresee as necessary is that the smallest unit should reserve the taxing-power strictly to itself. The larger units should have no power whatever of direct or indirect taxation, but should present their requirements to the townships, to be met by quota. This would tend to reduce the organizations of the larger units to skeleton form, and would operate strongly against their assuming any functions but those assigned them, which under a strictly governmental regime would be very few - for the federal unit, indeed, extremely few.
>
> "It is interesting to imagine the suppression of every bureaucratic activity in Washington today that has to do with the maintenance and administration of the political means, and see how little would be left. If the State were superseded by government, probably every federal activity could be housed in the Senate Office Building - quite possibly with room to spare." (Footnote 23 to ch. IV, *Our Enemy the State.*)

Birthright. . .and. . .Scotland Today

– To which, at this very day, we might add rejoinder: whatever are the Scots embarking upon that *multi-million* parliament building in Edinburgh for?

And let us relish for a moment this picture of a future St Andrews House coming, for its requirements, cap in hand to the local townships!

Here we have, then, a fitting blue-print for Scotland's way forward - one that is lacking in neither the economic, the political, *nor the psychological* elements of that most necessary wisdom for the forward way.

Community re-empowerment is the name of it.

*

Let us now examine the scene in a little more depth.

We have already mentioned in a footnote the united Nations Charter on Human Rights. Alas that the Charter, which we think of as filled with righteous statements, has been a major instrument of our *mis*-education and hence of our *dis*-empowerment – spreading its influence through society as it has, and indeed across the globe.

I came upon a reminder of the disempowering "rights" built into it, recently, in the publication of a generally excellent "ethical investment" initiative, in which a speaker from a well-known overseas aid programme is quoted. Referring to the Article in the charter which states that "everyone has a right to an adequate standard of living. . including. . .adequate housing", the speaker goes on to comment that the right to a home is "one of the most Basic rights of all", and one which people all over the world "have every right to expect to be met".

What the foregoing overlooks is a very basic and important matter: if the peoples of the world have *the right* to such things – (and the full list ranges on to the right to employment, to social protection, to rest and leisure – and even to periodic holidays with pay!) – then, by what strange means are *some* amongst us empowered to be the golden providers of these things?

As Frank Dupuis states in his excellent critique of this Charter, entitled *On Human Rights*:-

> "(These) are all statements of claims for things which everybody has the alleged right to compel everybody to provide. If A has the right to be well-paid employment with paid holidays, B must necessarily provide it; but if B has the same right, then A must also provide B with the same. This is not a statement of universal human rights in the enjoyment of which all might freely provide for themselves; it is a code of regulations for a dependent world."

As Dupuis goes on to point out, it is a code which might well have been drawn up by a committee of well-meaning persons who, *taking slavery for granted*, "were concerned to ensure that the slaves were well-treated", while a further page of his article goes to the heart of the matter: it is a document which "the most selfish landowner or trade monopolist" would find it simple to sign.

Let Scotland include no such nonsenses in any declaration of human rights *she* draws up! – but make good use of Frank Dupuis' powerful critique of this spineless charter – (included here in full in Part III).

Unfortunately, our own Welfare State was founded on just the same kind of false beneficence. "We want to look after them from the cradle to the grave" was, as I have read, the concept of its founders. But who is this "we" that proposes so lordly a looking after of "them"? – when it is "them" who in fact look after the State!. . .which, having no money of its own, has nothing to pay its beneficiaries out of, of course, except the productive work of those who toil. (With the breaking down of the Welfare State, we now read that Labour likes to think of itself as "guardian of the people's money".* Ah – AH!)

"Welfare-to-work" has become the cry – now that we see the earlier "welfare" idea doesn't quite work! But we know just what land monopoly makes of *that!* Pure Alice-in-Wonderland!

This theme of the *State* looking after the *people* exacts, unfortunately, a heavy toll from its implanting in our psyche. Those looked after "from the cradle to the grave" are not intended to grow up – and may well find difficulty in doing so. It becomes too familiar a habit to run to "Nanny". Let the State do this! - let the State look after that! Let us take a good lesson from the Children of Israel who nurtured a similarly infantile outlook – *Give us a king to reign over us!* – and note the astute reply of the Lord to *that* one! – (I Samuel, ch. 8). More or less straight out of the mouth of Henry George!

No wonder if it is those who have largely missed out on the "right" to the kind of education envisaged in the United Nations Charter - or who have chosen to supplement it with some independent studies and a goodly dollop of "My Universities"** besides – who are best making their way forward today to a real future for themselves. As evidence of this, one could hardly find more inspirational reading than in the pages of the book, *Living with the Land: Communities Restoring the Earth.****

Even a quick look through the book is enough to reassure one that the poor and dispossessed of this world have a grasp of their own situation infinitely beyond the drawers-up of that Charter! – (as also beyond most of those who, with whatever good intentions, are seeking to aid from *above*). One after another the pages unfold the quite remarkable initiatives that are springing up, in both First and Third worlds, whereby communities of the dispossessed - (even those up against false land rights *all* of the time, and well aware that this is the root of their troubles) are beginning to solve, or make solid inroads into, the multitude of problems besetting them. They could not more clearly state the case for grass-roots people empowerment as *the* solution to society's – and to the planet's – ills. Just indeed as Turgot, Jefferson, Carlo Levi, Nock and others have already foreseen. In short, this book makes a powerful tonic for any Reds – or Greens – stricken with the blues.

But then, as David Korten reminds us: "Contrary to what some would have us believe, the poor are among the most resourceful of people. If there is a way to meet their needs, they will generally find it. . . It is helpful to recall that throughout history most of the world's housing has been constructed by the people who need it, often with the voluntary help of their immediate neighbours. Furthermore, to this day a substantial

---

* *Report in Scotland on Sunday, 29 March 1998.*

** *So the Russian writer Gorky entitled his book on his own education – out in the world.*

*** *Published in the New Catalyst Bioregional Series, U.S.A. Available in Britain from Jon Carpenter Publishing.*

portion of new housing, especially in low income countries, is still being produced on a self-help basis." *

So what about that stream of homeless and housing-list applicants which, in Scotland alone, Shelter tells us, now stretches to an *111-mile long queue?*

In response to that – how good to see a no less burgeoning awareness in this country that "Nanny" is never going to make it for us - and indeed, that we would rather do-it-ourselves in any case. Right at the top must surely come the 1990s movement started by George Monbiot - (one whose "education" is woven of *every* brilliant strand!) – and fittingly launched under the name, *The Land Is Ours*.** The cream of their numerous occupations of unused and derelict land - (always impeccably organised and including a courteous invitation to the local police to visit the site) – must surely be their "squat", cleverly named *Pure Genius*, on an area owned by Guinness in the heart of London, and seven years left lying derelict. (See report in Part III.)

Then, too, one need only glance at a directory of community-powered projects around Britain such as that published by Groundswell, (c/o CHAR, 5-15, Cromer St, London W.C. 1), to realize that such grass-roots initiatives are gradually becoming a major force for change – such that the more imaginative strands in officialdom are here and there beginning to link up with them. (This no doubt reflects the fact that, in any official body, there will always be a certain number both wise and humble enough never to have lost sight of the fact that they are, themselves, first and foremost, but *members of that very community*, and that only secondarily do they hold official position within it. Thus there is no need for anyone, in any official body, to feel excluded. It is simply up to them to reckon their situation aright. The simple fact of the matter is that *community empowerment is for everyone.*)

Guiness, of course, was only sitting tight on all that idle land – which sprouted so suddenly under their eyes into homes, gardens, food-producing areas and community open space! – as speculators on the most propitious moment to capture those developmental values bestowed on "their" land by *that very dispossessed community*! Land rent for revenue is the lynch-pin of the matter which has yet to come fully to light – (it is in fact part of the policy of The Land Is Ours) – to bring the incredible cheat of our incredible "house of cards" to its own unaided collapse, just as Tolstoy said.

The scandal of the unused and derelict land right in our midst, and the sheer dimension of it, is one few are awake to as yet. Our present "shortage of land" is something artificially created. It is not so much a shortage of land, as an over-plus of land artificially locked up – precisely for purposes of *speculation in its rental values*, (or those same rental values converted into capital ones). The annual hundred-per-cent collection of these rental values would open our eyes wide. Meanwhile all today's mouthings of care and concern about the poor and homeless, from whatever political party, are just so much dandelion fluff. Self-empowering communities are the other arm of a pincer movement which will require *both* to crush the land monopoly between them.

---

* *Article "Property Rights v. Living Rights", (**The Mercury**, Spring 97, published by the Henry George School of N. California. Editor: Mary-Rose Kaczorowski.) I cannot forbear to mention here also the account – saga, more fittingly –recorded in the book by the Egyptian architect, Hassan Fathy, **Architecture for the Poor: an Experiment in Rural Egypt**. Even a brief dip in fills one with marvelling – laughter – disbelief – and again marvelling. One day I have promised myself the enjoyment of reading it from end to end. (Chicago Press, U.S.A., but obtainable from the Royal Institute of British Architecture, London.)*

** *P.O. Box E, 111 Magdalen Road, Oxford OX4 1RQ.*

*

There are crude ways of disempowering people - and there are also subtle ways.

Of cruder ways, a good example is given in *Living with the Land*, in the concluding words of the chapter describing a Honduran initiative. Here the Indian peasants, or *campesinos*, through the re-discovery of their own knowledge and traditions stretching back to Mayan times, are at last beginning to hold their heads up proudly again, after five hundred years of – Oh, you're just ignorant Indian campesinos!

As to more subtle methods, the technique is a very simple one. Remove from the people their power of decision-making, *without their realizing* that you are removing it. In time, their practice of decision-making will gradually wither away. The history of America-in-the-making as disclosed by A.J. Nock, and a review of our own history – not to mention the more recent "European" chapter of it – shows the subtle method to have been the one favoured by the First World establishments when dealing with their peoples – and to have been strikingly successfully used.

To understand how far democracy in Britain has now become de-*mock*-racy, we can turn to an article which appeared in *The Economist* of 14 Oct 95, entitled *Britain's Constitution: the Case for Reform*. This researched and informative article by David Manasian charts carefully the stepping-stones of the pathway by which we have arrived at where we now are – which, it makes clear, is practically at an "elective dictatorship", (as Lord Hailsham complained in the 1970s - when the Tories were *out of* power!).

Such is the real nature of our vaunted democracy which has been held up to us as so splendid a pattern – influencing the growth of democracies in other parts of the world *and* as being all the more credit to us for having needed no bill of rights to achieve it. (I can remember how our class was impressed with this, when taught it at school in the middle 40s! Hopefully it can't quite be got away with today. . .)

In fact, the lack of any bill of rights, or written constitution, has been our very undoing. It has handed to our politicians virtually "carte blanche" to bring in fundamental change, unchecked and unchallenged; stealth taking over as the simplest means – and great temptation – to this end. ("British governments run by both main parties have been among the most secretive of all the western democracies. . ." Ibid.) The upshot of this is that the reality of the choice now left to the British people is, in practical terms, that of choosing between one of two small committees, (or *cabinets*), every four or five years, to run matters as they see fit, "constrained only by what they think is politically possible, and with almost no legal or institutional checks on what they can do". (So *of course* it was found "politically possible" by New Labour to keep – with some pretence "democratizing" – Scotland's Tory-imposed Water Quangos – and to toss their election promise into the dust!)

How, precisely, did things go so wrong? The key concept pioneered by Britain – a concept which so greatly influenced the building of democracies elsewhere – was, as *The Economist* article points out – "the separation of the executive, legislative and judicial branches of government", so as to provide the necessary checks and balances, and the guarantee of "fundamental rights protected from the encroachments of an overmighty government". These concepts, however – born, as the article points out , of Parliament's battle to restrain the monarch in the seventeenth and eighteenth centuries – were *"never firmly established in Britain"*. (Emphasis added.) A contemporary jurist of renown gave sound warning of the likely trend ahead:–

> "In 1765 Sir William Blackstone, the leading English legal authority at the time, wrote that the total union of the executive and legislative branches of government

> 'would be productive of tyranny'. Over the next century such a union is precisely what Britain achieved. The cabinet in effect assumed the executive role of the monarch. With the extension of the voting franchise to the middle and working classes and the rise of mass parties, the cabinet (and more particularly the prime minister) could stay in office only by exerting an iron discipline on its party supporters in the Commons, further concentrating power in its hands. By 1867 Walter Bagehot was praising the cabinet's control of nearly all government affairs, its 'near complete fusion of the executive and legislative powers', as the efficient secret' of the constitution." (Ibid.)

What is so interesting is, precisely, those starkly opposed views of William, in 1765, and Walter exactly a hundred years later. That what was so clearly foreseen by William as a highway to "tyranny" – that this should actually have been *praised* by the later Walter as the "efficient secret" of Britain's (unwritten) constitution, is in itself the starkest evidence of – and comment upon – the demise of democracy which had been accomplished in Britain over that period. (Superfluous to add that the name of *Bagehot* comes back to me, powerfully praisefully, from those early education syllabuses – whereas that of Blackstone I can recall no mention of at all.) As is pointed out by the writer of this article, it is not to the democrat, *but to the autocrat*, that "the smooth exercise of silent power" appears as the ideal.

How did the judicial power come to be successfully merged with the other two?

> "*With no bill of rights to constrain them*, both Labour and Tory governments have extended police powers, restricted press freedom, and sometimes suspended the ordinary workings of the criminal law. Those moves, touching the basic freedoms of all citizens, *have been impossible to challenge in British courts*." (Ibid. Emphasis added at both places.)

As an example given of the political overruling of a fundamental right – which Britain's judiciary could only stand by and witness – there was the "severe restricting", by the government, in 1994, of the right to silence in criminal trials, "allowing judges and juries to draw adverse inferences from a defendant's refusal to testify". Thus was eliminated, "at a stroke", a right which had "for centuries been thought of as a pillar of Britain's judicial system".

Perhaps it is since the writing of this Economist article that steps were also taken to disallow a "not proven" verdict in a trial? – (a particular feature of Scottish law). I certainly remember coming across, in recent years, a paper in stout defence of that latter right, by a body of those within Scotland's legal profession representative of its more radical members. It is to be hoped that Scotland's legal system has not yet, in these matters, quite 'gone the way of Westminster'.

Now, more than two years on from the time of the Economist article, and with New (?) Labour running our "elective dictatorship", the press, at the end of Jan 98, carries a report of yet another incursion into the sphere of civil rights – indeed, into the sphere of *basic human* rights this time. Stemming straight from the Scottish Office – (for in the "best" of traditions it was to be tried out first on the Scots) – news came of a proposal of a barbaric nature – to permit *radical brain surgery* to be carried out on those suffering from "obsessive compulsive behaviour"; to be carried out at the word merely of a sheriff, and even *against the wishes of the family involved.*

Oh – it was to be "cleared", of course, by a (State-oriented?) medic. (The B.M.A. have *never raised a whisper* against that other imposition, fluoridation – medical students learning of it as a "health" measure, and commending it thoroughly in turn.)

This piece of barbarity the Scottish Office apparently considered "politically feasible", or – something that could be "got away with", in Nock's more down-to-earth terms . . . But then – perhaps it could *not* be "got away with" after all? "Confusion over surgery plans", we read in a sprint of a follow-on – the Scottish Office "distance(ing) itself . . . late last night . . . from its earlier statement"!* The vociferous, instant response from the public was just too much? *Watch it!* – those Seven Wise Masters have a long arm, *and a voluminous sleeve to go with it!* Somewhere, tucked up there, could the present state of "confusion" at the Scottish Office perhaps be *biding its time*. . .?

*

> "Quangos – the curse of Scotland? *Unelected and unaccountable.* One Russian tells us that he thought he was back in Old Moscow when he realised how much power has been taken away from the electorate in Scotland."

This lively report from the Loch Ness Free Press** of 8 Jan 98 makes an extremely interesting parallel with Old Russia. The difference is, however, that the people of that country were not left in any doubt about the loss of their political power. By contrast, I believe that the great majority of Scots have yet to wake up to it. Our difficulty is that the proliferation of these new bodies appearing on the scene *do not announce themselves as quangos*, and therefore do not raise suspicions. We just do not realize the number of quangos that are abroad today. But let me make clear here that, as always, my observations make no personal reflection upon those serving within such bodies, many of whom are deeply dedicated individuals, and may indeed regret the existence of quangos themselves. It is simply that these institutions are *totally unacceptable to a democracy.*

Quangos are "always in the interest of Ministers and civil servants. . .the whole argument of Quangos bringing power closer to the people is bogus": The Observer of 4 July 93, reporting the words of Sir Philip Holland, a former Tory M.P. and "legendary quango hunter of the Seventies"! – when there were already plenty to hunt, as the Tories apparently created thousands of them.

So that was it! The idea was to "sell" them to us as *decentralizing of power!* Coming on these words of Sir Philip's recently, from the early 90s, has at last explained a conundrum – how it is that Labour is still propaganding us that they are the party of *de-centralization*. They've got stuck in the gramophone grooves of that old quango-tango! – (invented by the Tories!) – ever hopeful that a naive Scotland can be persuaded to tangle with it too!

Of course Labour is "the party of de-centralization"! – the game of "devolution" is safely played in a country so quango-ized!

*

It is easy to regale ourselves with the half-hilarious report in the Loch Ness Free Press of the terrier-like tussle that took place between the Highland Council, allied with practically the whole of the local population, and the duo of quangos who had their teeth well sunk into Urquhart Castle and its environs for their pet development plan! It is perhaps less easy to take on board *what we must be prepared to shoulder*, if we would bring such absurdities to an end.

---

* *Quotations from the Dundee Courier of that time.*

** *Editor: Mike Takala, 3 Balbeg of Benloit, Drumnadrochit, Inverness-shire.*

> "Let us hope and pray that this new Scottish Parliament makes it a priority to rid this country of the myriad quangos that soak up the taxpayers' money and distribute it around their own pet projects through their fellow unelected colleagues." (Loch Ness Free Press.)

Splendid sentiments, but – the new Scottish Parliament? As at present envisaged, under our party political system – we must have serious doubts about that. One need only observe how skilfully New Labour, the *promoters* of the Scottish Parliament, continue to dance their notorious Water Qu-*wangle.*

But what about Scotland's National Party? Suppose they emerge as the leaders in the new Parliament?

Political leadership, however idealistic in its aspirations, when tied to so corrupt, entirely *State* – not people – oriented a political system, may find it difficult not to become compromised itself. I believe I have reason to say this.

About twenty years ago – shortly after the first referendum on independence, and not long after I had returned to Scotland – I wrote to a leading member of the Scottish National Party concerning the fundamental reform, land rent for revenue, having found nothing of this reform in their land policy paper. I was much interested to learn from this individual's reply, in a letter written in their own hand, that upon first coming into politics some years earlier they had learned all about the work of Henry George – (our string of Scottish predecessors were not, of course, known in Scotland at that time . . . or so I thought . . .) – and that they fully agreed that the failure to put in hand what Henry George had proposed, (i.e., what *Scotland's own thinkers and writers* had proposed, as it transpired), would be a disaster. (I had not at that time yet written *The Land Question*, or received *Forerunners of Henry George* from across the Atlantic and so was not yet aware that there was an actual lineage of Scottish writers on this subject.)

As I had heard no mention of this matter by the Scottish National Party at the time of the referendum in 1976, the information received in this letter had remained in my mind as something of a curiosity – a matter deeply interesting, but perplexing; an isolated bit of information with nothing to hang it on. That is, until a quite unexpected happening recently, some twenty years later.

It began in the summer of 1996 – when I was already engaged in the journey of this book – when I was reading, (kindly obtained by the public library), an out-of-print book, an anthology of essays on economics under the main title *Why the – German Republic Fell.** Published in 1941, and edited by A.W. Madsen – (the widely respected head of the Georgist London office at that time) – it contained a chapter, written by Madsen himself, on Patrick Edward Dove, and it was in the closing sentence of this chapter that I read: "In his (Dove's) case, says Morrison Davidson (*Four Precursors of Henry George*), 'the adage "jack of all trades and master of none" was strikingly falsified'."

I was thunderstruck! Here was Morrison Davidson, whom I had known of only as the author of that remarkable volume *Leaves from the Book of Scots* (see Part I),** now

* *See Part I.*

** *Morrison Davidson's book* ***Four Precursors of Henry George*** *is in fact referred to in Forerunners of Henry George; but no connection with Scotland being made there, his name had not imprinted itself on my mind.*

discovered to be a *Georgist* – and clearly one of the line of Scottish Georgist thinkers on this matter. There flashed instantly upon my thought the capital "L" and "Q" with which Morrison Davidson had referred to the land question in *Leaves from the Book of Scots* – for it had struck me at the time that it would be unusual for anyone but a Georgist land reformer to do this. *Leaves from the Book of Scots* was of course published from The Scots Secretariat in Carlops. So here now appeared to be stunning evidence, via Madsen writing in London – (it seems to be either from across the Atlantic or from across the Border that Scots have to find out their history!) – that there had been an ardent Georgist land reformer pursuing the land question from Jess Cottage, Carlops (in Peeblesshire) in the early part of this century, and keeping alive, for the Scots, a knowledge of *their own* thinkers and writers on this subject. I immediately wanted to know more – both about Morrison Davidson and about the mysterious Scots Secretariat.

However, a year's interval intervened, while the journey of this book took up my time, so it was not until the later part of 1997 that I was able to take up this matter again. Various searches kindly then made for me – (including at the Henry George Foundation in London and through the public library) – for a copy of *Four Precursors of Henry George*, all drew a blank. By now it seemed to me that the only hope of finding a copy might be in the environs of Jess Cottage, (if the cottage still existed), or tucked away in an unexpected corner of a Scottish bookshelf somewhere; and short of time by now for further searches myself, I had decided to enquire through the pages of this book – when quite unexpectedly the name of Jesse Cottage (now with this spelling) sprang to me out of the pages of the *Scottish Organic Gardener!* I at once contacted the present occupiers, and their most helpful searches locally, although bringing no copy of the *Four Precursors*, brought to light so much other material published by the Scots Secretariat that I felt our own National Library must assuredly know something about that publishing body.

Thus it was that, towards the end of 1997, I wrote to the National Library of Scotland – and a most rewarding contact it turned out. Not only did they hold a copy of *Four Precursors of Henry George*, (which from a quick look-through seems an excellent little volume – see Reading-List); but from letters dated 12th and 13th January from the Reference Services and the Manuscripts Division of the Library, I learned that The Scots Seretariat was an organization "established and funded in the 1930s by the businessman and doyen of the Scottish Nationalist Movement, Roland E. Muirhead (1868-1964)", and that it "functioned mainly as an education, information and propaganda vehicle for the national movement", publishing also "a range of books, pamphlets and leaflets".

So! – The Scots Secretariat had been, amongst other things, an educational organ or the Scottish Nationalist Movement! I further learned that Dr. Archie Lamont, a geologist and keen Scottish Nationalist, was the one who had actually set up the Scots Secretariat printing press "as a vehicle for nationalist publishing", material from the press being published "during the 1970/80's". Archie Lamont was "closely associated with Muirhead in the work of the Secretariat", and it seems he "continued its publication activities after the death of (Muirhead), publishing latterly from his home at Jess Cottage, Carlops". Finally, it was from Jess Cottage that the Manuscripts Division of the Library "collected the Lamont Papers in 1986" – (most of the Archives of The Secretariat having already been acquired by them in the 1960s); at which time they learned that the cottage was to be sold.

Birthright. . .and. . .Scotland Today

Thus it was not, as I had believed, Morrison Davidson who had lived at Jess Cottage, but Dr. Archie Lamont. Thus was explained the six-digit postcode on my edition of *Leaves from the Book of Scots* – a work clearly written in the *early* part of this century. *Four Precursors of Henry George* reveals that Morrison Davidson studied law at Aberdeen, but he apparently made his career in London, for printed under the author's name in that book are the words "(of the Middle Temple), Barrister-at-Law".

It would be interesting to know if J. Morrison Davidson (to give him his full name) ever returned to Scotland? – and even more interesting to know whether those who ran The Scots Secretariat shared Morrison Davidson's acute grasp of the land question ...? Certainly, *Four Precursors of Henry George* appears *not* – (from the listings of Scots Secretariat publications that appear on the back of their pamphlets) – ever to have been re-published by The Scots Secretariat; which seems somewhat curious. Even more curious: *nowhere* in those listings does the name Morrison Davidson *ever* appear by his volume, *Leaves from the Book of Scots,* (in the numerous pamphlets from The Scots Secretariat that have come my way), although the book is frequently listed in these, and although *other* authors' names appear by *their* works. This seems very curious indeed. Could there have been some wish on the part of The Scots Secretariat not to have itself associated with J. Morrison Davidson's radical views on the land question?

It is only in actually setting down these matters for this book – as I work on late this February evening – that this puzzling situation has emerged to capture my attention; and in seeking what answers can be gained from the material to hand, I have just, at this point, made an amazing discovery – which I shall recount just as it happened.

The work of William H. Marwick – published by The Scots Secretariat – had already caught my attention, on account of his excellent *Scotland and the Common Market*, so pertinent to our times, (see Part III). From the National Library of Scotland I had learned that Marwick had been a "Senior Lecturer in Economic and Social History at Edinburgh University" and had "passed away some years ago". Now, on opening another of Marwick's articles – (appearing in the *Scottish Journal of Science* of June 72 – also published by The Scots Secretariat) – I find in the "Abstract" written at the top of it that "Scotland requires both Socialism and Self-government". *Socialism*! So!

I now went and fetched again my – precious albeit very poor – photo-copy of Morrison Davidson's *Leaves from the Book of Scots*, to see whether this later printing of it – (the six-digit postcode one – the only one I had, and clearly, it seemed to me, after Morrison Davidson's time) – might yield any clues I had missed. . . . It was now I noticed for the first time that this was not merely a re-print, but a *new edition.* With my curiosity really aroused, I turned back the top sheet of the photo-copy – and now noticed, for the first time, that on the left-hand side of the next duo of pages, (i.e., as what had appeared inside the front cover), there was a very dark page – the original cover having been a dark green. The page before me was actually *black* – but it showed two brief paragraphs at the top, which were clearly an introduction to the new edition. How unbelievably frustrating, then, that while MORRISON DAVIDSON (in heavy capitals) could be made out as the first two words, and "a Scot" was just discernible to follow . . . that then should come a longer word, also beginning with a capital S, followed by "from Aberdeen", *but the first word quite indecipherable* – with the rest remaining also firmly "silence"!

Twisting the black page this way and that – in my *resolve* to resolve the enigma! – I suddenly thought of holding it up against the direct glare of a light bulb . . . when lo and behold, the words appeared! *And what were the words?*

> "MORRISON DAVIDSON, a Scots Socialist from Aberdeen, was the outstanding advocate of Scottish Self-Government in the years between the Crofters' Revolt and the First Great War."

Morrison Davidson – a *Scots Socialist*? He who was a *radical land rent* economic-and-social reformer? No wonder this was a "new" edition! More accurately, a *post-Morrison-Davidson* one! That puny "Socialist" was enough to have turned him in his grave! I could not but be struck by the fact that the black sheet had so blackened out the execrable word – as though he himself had willed it so.

Many questions were raised in my mind by this discovery – but more particularly: what was the original edition of *Leaves from the Book of Scots*, and was it possible that it contained any clue which might help to identify Morrison Davidson as a Georgist – an Ogilvist – a Doveist? – more simply, as a *truest of true Scots?* My thought turned again at once to our helpful National Library. Upon enquiry, I discovered that they did indeed possess an original edition, dated 1914, and were able to supply me with a copy. This first edition was published by the Civic Press Ltd., 164 Howard Street, Glasgow, and on the front cover is the verse:–

> "Oh, remember those that perished
> For thy birthright at the time
> When to be a Scot was treason,
> And to side with Wallace crime."
> – Aytoun.

(Reprinted from "FORWARD".)

Inside is a printed dedication, "To Roland E. Muirhead (Bridge of Weir), with the esteem of J.M.D. Common Room, Middle Temple, London. 3/7/14." There appears no other clue in it as to J.M.D.'s radical stance – (although it is impossible for me to check through every page at this time) – and so it seems he preferred to leave that one hint unadorned. At least, however, this original edition is free of the miscreant "execrable word"!

. . . Now as I type out the final draft of this chapter in the last days of March 1998, my attention is caught by my February reference to *two* "brief paragraphs" at the top of that inside-front-cover page. I seem not to have paused to investigate the second one, that February night – ("And at my back I always hear Time's winged chariot hurrying near" – haunts me as I work on this book!) So I have now made a second sally to fetch again that later edition of *Leaves from the Book of Scots*, intrigued to know what I may have missed in the *second* introductory paragraph on that page.

I am not disappointed! Another revelation!

> "The SCOTTISH SECRETARIAT hopes to reprint other pamphlets of this period by Tories like the Third Marquis of Bute and Professor John Stuart Blackie and by Liberals like Charles Waddie who was for many years Secretary of the Scottish Home Rule Association."

Well I never! Coming under the first paragraph there, which describes Morrison Davidson as "the outstanding advocate of Scottish Self-Government in the time between the Crofters' Revolt and the First Great War", "this period" in the second paragraph can only refer to the time when Morrison Davidson himself was active. So how come that a Tory, some Liberals and a professor were to be published on Home Rule, and *nothing* from the "outstanding advocate" of it at that time? Morrison Davidson could not have been the "outstanding advocate" of it (as the first paragraph there had stated) unless he had *spoken*. So where are his words? Were they possibly just too rough-and-tumble for such company? Could he perchance have leaked, alongside, that, for instance, that fighting body, the Highland Land League, had come into being *due to the inspiration of Henry George?* Not by any means irrelevant to the needs for a good fighting body at *that* time – as in ours. So what *about* his words? – and are they still hidden away somewhere? We can do with the words of the "outstanding advocate of Scottish Self-Government" at that time – at *this* time!

There is too much we do not know about J. Morrison Davidson – and about his time, just as with D.C. MacDonald. For instance, what lies behind the second part of this intriguing passage, near the opening of *Four Precursors of Henry George?* –

> "(Ogilvie's) Essay was published anonymously, and the author's identity, in his own day, was a well-kept secret, except to a small circle of intimate friends. The 'George Campaign' in Scotland, however, led to its disinterment in the Granite City, and ultimate republication in 1891 . . . by D.C. MacDonald."

The "George Campaign", and "its disinterment"? Who were those Scots who were the keepers of Ogilvie's work all this time, and so were able to bring it to the light? . . . about whom MacDonald, a canny lawyer like Morrison Davidson, no doubt hesitated to say too much even then – and Morrison Davidson's time was not long after. Did their lives intersect at all, one wonders?

We know quite a bit about Henry George's visit to Scotland – how the whole Georgist movement in Britain started with those he inspired first *north* of the Border. But just to think of those earlier hives of radical thinking on the land question – stemming all, it would seem, from the work of Ogilvie – that must have existed scattered about in Scotland through the continuing dark age on this matter – perhaps adding to their thought from others, like Paine and Spence and Dove – tending the precious candle for the time ahead . . . and what Henry George's bursting upon the scene must have meant to them – the huge interest and excitement of finding a living link with Ogilvie . . . and we know nothing about it at all! Is it possible that we *shall* know – some day, some time?

It is not only our economic and social life – our cultural life has been hugely diminished too by the centuries-long hide-up of Scotland's tradition of Radicalism in economic thinking. I remember taking up *A Drunken Man Looks at a Thistle*, (McDiarmid's best-known poem), feeling I must acquaint myself with this work, and – whatever of good poetry it may have contained – turning away at the end sickened by the confusion of its sentiments; while in reading Lewis Grassick Gibbons' *A Scots Quair,* for *all* its splendid writing, I could not but ache for the chapters missing from it – for the great adventure missed and the huge interest it would have added – seeing how intent was the search of that young man for a truly radical pathway . . . and only dull old Socialism to be found! By contrast, I turn now to a passage from Patrick Edward Dove – one that Morrison Davidson chooses to introduce his *Four Precursors* – and find that, although written in prose, it is in places, sheerly from the contained *but rising* passion of it, transmuted almost into poetry:–

> "Gradually but surely has the separation been taking place between the privileged Landowner and the unprivileged Labourer.

> And the time will come at last when there shall be but two parties looking each other in the face, and knowing that the destruction of the one is an event of necessary consequence. That event *must* come. Nor is it in man to stay in or produce it. It will come as the result of the laws that govern nature and govern man.
>
> Of the two parties one must give way, one must sink to rise no more; one must disappear from the earth. Their continued existence is incompatible. Nature cannot support both.
>
> (Patrick E. Dove: Theory of Progression, 1850.)*

I repeat: alas for the diminution of our cultural life by the hide-up on this matter.

One bit of history of a more personal nature Morrison Davidson does reveal to us, – and it is impossible to leave him without sharing something so startling:–

> "The very first day the 'Prophet of San Francisco' set foot in London, in the fall of 1881, I had the good fortune to encounter him in Fleet Street, and in the famous 'Old Cheshire Cheese' we dined together, and before we parted I was in full possession of whatever is of abiding value in 'Progress and Poverty'."

Well! Some opening passage to the *Four Precursors*! It seems Providence had firmly singled out Morrison Davidson to be a link in the chain! And no wonder if he found George's *Progress and Poverty* not quite up to that stunning first introduction to it! – while it is possible too that, as a lawyer, he found himself more in tune with Ogilvie's "Euclidean" phrasing.

No doubt Morrison Davidson's times still called for considerable canniness, for as to how he learned of Ogilvie's work – following that historic meeting – we hear no word either. As always – too much is silence in Scotland's history. It seems that, over and over again, the teaching of true fundamental economics – our very own teaching – has surfaced in Scotland – or nearly so . . . only to be cast down again . . . Like an object carried on the tide, over and over again, which over and over again nearly makes it to the shore . . .

Next time! . . . THIS TIME!

*

We have travelled a bit from our look at the political scene – but return the richer, I think, for our travels. For it has surely revealed to us the unwisdom of trusting fully to any political party. The one political party that held fully within its ken the knowledge not only of the pathway of economic liberation via land rent reform, but the knowledge also that this was a *part of Scotland's genius to have made direct discovery*

---

* *Preceding the passage from Dove – with both placed under the heading FOREWORDS – is inscribed a six-line verse, which, being without signature, is possibly by Morrison Davidson himself. It is worthily penned, but I do not quote it here, not only because it refers to rocks as "cold" – (whereas I am persuaded that Scotland's rocks have much fire in them!) – but also because I find in Dove's prose lines actually finer poetry.*

I should like, however, to include here Morrison Davidson's fine dedication of his book, as follows – (the helots were the serfs of ancient Sparta): "To the disinherited landless helots of town and country, at home and abroad, this small but precious compendium of IMPERISHABLE TRUTHS on THE LAND PROBLEM is with the deepest sympathy inscribed by J.D.M., Common Room, Middle Temple, London, Nov. 10, 1899." How good that the Common Room of the Middle Temple should witness that historic dedication – just as the later one also of 1914! One cannot but wonder whether any other human sympathiser was present on either occasion, or whether an otherwise human solitude witnessed both . . . ***Not for ever****!*

of . . . have not only never uttered it from their political platform, but in their educational undertakings also have allowed this treasury of knowledge to remain locked away from us. I remain convinced that that political party missed its flagship – that had they trusted to the all-important **land question**, and to the people of Scotland, we would have had independence long ere this.

We cannot, however, altogether blame the individuals who act within a political party. We must remember that our political system is now drastically coded in to the centralization of power. Jefferson, casting an eye upon it in his day – (America's political system equally now, of course) – observed that it was not in fact a two-party system, but a single party one – of *bi*-partisanship. Because all could not "cuddle into . . the nest of office" at once, they were divided into two parties, the Ins and the Outs." There is one matter in particular that in recent history vividly evidences this. Ever since the ugly fluoridation proposal raised its masked head in this country, at the end of the 1950s, neither the Conservatives nor Labour – Old or "New" – have once wavered in their unstinting support for, and propaganding of, this nefarious scheme. Cuddlesome nest indeed! – (or perhaps cuddlesome Costa Fluor-ida now? See part III. Article by Griffiths and Bryson.)) One must also observe that neither the Soc.-Lib. Dems. nor the Scottish National Party have failed to contribute their part in providing top ranking political protagonists for this top-ranking *political machination*.

Against the above background, let us consider a Bill of Rights for Scotland. There are certain measures that are obviously of primary and fundamental importance. For example:–

(1) The inviolability of the individual's person and hence right to refuse medical treatment of any kind, whether directly administered, or indirectly – as, for example, via the public water supply.

Considering the political history of Britain in its full round, can we really trust ourselves to *any* political party – (in particular, a party toying with the idea of *legalizing brain surgery without consent*) – for the inclusion in Scotland's Bill of Rights of such a clause? Let us not be too politically naive.

Here is another clause we may term fundamental and primary:–

(2) The equal right of access to land, for all, to be established by the collecting of the rental value of the land a hundred per cent annually from every occupation, in lieu of all taxation: the assessing, collecting and disbursing of this rental fund to be carried out at local community level.*

Do we really believe that we can trust ourselves to any political party, for the bringing in of a measure so radical as this? Again – our political system is geared to the centralization of power both political *and* economic. This is the system that will be inherited by whichever party leads, in the new Scottish parliament. Practically all the levers of power work *from the centre – out*. Directly after independence – it is still this machinery that will be in operation. So, once again, let us be realistic.

Even regarding the matter with the fullest sympathy: to look to those who will be operating that power-ship to proceed forthwith to dismantle it – is it not much like asking those who are sitting on the branch of a tree to proceed to saw it off right under

---

* *We have yet to discuss the precise meaning of this last term. It should be added that, in the above, (1) necessarily precedes (2), since how can we safeguard our right to the land if we are so doctored that we cannot think straight?*

them? Suppose there is the political will to dismantle the quangos? But the quangos are simply the latest phase of centralization, in a system unhealthily centralized even before . . . unhealthily centralized since ever we lost our truly local councils – the village, parish and small burgh ones.

Supposing, then, there existed the political will of those in parliament to reverse *that* stage of centralization as well – to restore to us our former truly grass-roots local government? Even then, it is not just a return to these we seek either – part of an *economic* system, as they were, that never solved the gap between rich and poor. It is the decentralization of *economic* power we seek as well – the returning of the land rent to the community to end the enslaving power of land rent monopoly; and its *collection* at community level as well.

Can we really expect any of our political parties, not one of whom has yet even murmured the phrase "land rent", not only to propose that this be now the source of Scotland's revenue, but *also* to propose the *equally* vital matter of its collection by those smallest local government units? **

Power is heady stuff – which is exactly why Jefferson spoke his wise warning on the matter. It is frankly hard to imagine any ruling party in parliament, even in an independent Scotland, going so far as to disempower itself entirely in that manner – going so far, that is, as to empty itself of *all* its both political and economic power. Hence elementary wisdom dictates that, while we may *hope* that it may, we, the people of Scotland – (which so happily includes *every one of those sitting in that parliament* if they can but see it) – must begin to make our way forward in our own way; and ourselves take responsibility for that necessary bill of rights.

But while those grass-roots local councils do not yet exist let alone have the land rent revenue to run themselves, how do we bring them into being? How do we take off on this matter – find our first steps?

The first steps of the new dance are already awaiting us – of that real dance which is a reel-dance indeed! Those who are at the humblest, grass-roots level of society will find they can do a powerful thing. They can start making their own land rent maps. As Mr. J. Pot of Holland recently proposed this sound and excellent idea:–

> "Everybody should do it NOW. Take a sheet of paper. Draw by hand a map of the properties around your home. Compare the rental values with that of your own site. Show it to everyone you meet. Ask them to do the same."

The great point is that, by undertaking this practical piece of work, we find a fully practical way to launch ourselves into the new scene. For not only do we begin to acquaint ourselves at first hand with the rental values in our area,* but we thus – working each in our own area – begin the creation of a *network* – that network so necessary as the basis from which to work for the time of transition ahead – and as the framework for our own self-governance to follow.

No one, then, need fear the sawing off of that branch – the dismantling of that power-ship. For, unlike at "the top", at grass-roots level all can find a place – for their place was always there waiting for them. And this place will be one of far greater reward than is offered at present by the falsely-inflated positions of today's power systems. If true greatness is found in service – (and it surely is) – then that greatness is

---

* *We have at present, of course, no record of the value of the land separate from that of its improvements – but this is a point we shall come to.*

** Labour has since made a (muted) mention of "land value taxation" in its policy papers on land reform. But see S-A.H's letters to the Scottish Office on this in Part III.

certainly signposted by the new direction we shall be taking; for in the demands it will make on all of us, service will mark its way from the start. But it is a service that will bring happiness to us, for being bound up with our own home-ground it will involve our hearts as well as our heads.

*

. . . Having stepped into the arena of map-making, I paused here in typing out the draft of this chapter to go and fetch a book on bioregionalism – one which I had long meant to acquire and which had now arrived – having dipped into its inspiring opening paragraph about the magic of *maps!*

. . . It was a long pause – and an amazing discovery! For I had not realized that the bioregionalists – (whose concept I had adopted immediately on hearing of it as being of the simplest common sense) – were into the actual down-to-earth business of *map-making* themselves! Indeed, there is a point in the book where it says – almost in the words of Mr. J. Pot – just go out and DO it! . . . Yes, as you can see, I could not put the book down, but read it from start to finish, making notes as I went.

The book is entitled *Boundaries of Home*, with subtitle *Mapping for Local Empowerment* – (mark that!). It is a collection of writings on the subject edited – and part-written too – by Doug Aberley, who it seems is a Scot now working in British Columbia, for completing the acknowledgements at the front are the inspiring words: "This volume is dedicated to the future of Caledonia – old and new". (Perhaps Doug is back in Scotland now, for under his name, there, is written "Edinburgh, Alba".) What a volume to have come into my hands at what a moment! For I find that everything I had envisioned in this chapter about grass-roots local empowerment – in town as well as in country – and the part that it must play in society, is, in this book, *underlined* – *supported* – and indeed, carried into a yet wider field of grass-roots action. In short, the bioregional movement is a perfect natural partner for Georgism; while, (as became transparently clear to me in the reading), the Georgist movement would in turn lend a power to the bioregional movement which yet awaits the discovery of bioregionalists.

What *is* bioregionalism? In brief, the concept means *allowing the land to delineate its own boundaries to us* – (as a friend, at once equally enthused, summed it up on the spot! – when on a chance meeting I spoke to her of this inspiring book). These boundaries are formed of its natural geographical features – primarily, watersheds and river-basins. Then in addition there are its natural geological features – rock, soil, hills and valleys; then too, its vegetation – its tree cover, and the habitats of flora and fauna, with what is indigenous particularly to be noted. Finally it incorporates the areas of human occupation and activity. Here is particularly noted, how the original habitations had formed themselves, since these give insight into the original self-sustainability of an area; something we shall need to re-discover and – planet-wide – live within, if we are to continue on this planet.

The great and laudable purpose of the bioregional movement is – besides the preservation of our planet – to rescue its inhabitants from the terrible sense of *powerlessness* we suffer from, in seeing the huge conglomerates of today virtually rape the earth of its resources, destroy the fertility of our fields – and equally in the cities, backed by un-enlightened planning policies, destroy those things which we most treasure and would have preserved. Georgists would enrich this catalogue by extending its scope to take in the powerlessness people feel, under our economic system, in increasing measure, in the sphere of homes, jobs, the getting of daily bread –

and indeed health-care, education and a whole lot more: a powerlessness bred of fundamental *economic robbery*.

How does map-making – *our own* map-making – start to give back to us power over our own lives? Here I will shift to what I had already seen simply from following out Mr. Pot's proposal of mapping the land's rental values. As I saw it, the great excellence of this proposal – beyond its practical use – was that it would attune us, in a direct and powerful manner, to a fact only too well masked from us by the present system: that is, we would come to see vividly that the values we are dealing with are indeed our very own values, created by ourselves – by the entire community. This in turn would act as a powerful tool in breaking down present barriers between the possessors and the dispossessed, as we come to realize, in a real and three-dimensional way, that we *all* stand on an equal footing with one another, since we all – by our very presence and need for land – contribute to the values that we are mapping.

Here I would like to introduce a most excellent term from the bioregionalists' vocabulary. They speak of *re-inhabiting* the land. And I find that this word most exactly describes the feeling that took hold of me as I was first drafting the above paragraph and envisioning the actual process of mapping the land rents. I had felt, indeed, just that! – that in undertaking this mapping of our environs we would come to feel we inhabited our home-ground *anew*, in a different and far more meaningful way. And here I am reminded of the very title of a book written by the American, Kirkpatrick Sale – a beautiful title, *Dwellers in the Land.* This was, I believe, the *original* book on bioregionalism. It certainly remains very much top-of-the-list, and is obviously one to study.

Returning to those words I had written above, about how land rent mapping would attune us to a reality "so well masked from us by the present system", I was struck by Doug Aberley's words towards the end of the book, that "to build that (bioregional) utopia will require the dismantling of a system whose strength partially depends on its mystery". But really to uncover that "mystery" most certainly requires the *unmasking* of our land tenure system, and hence of what has been falsely extracted from society by way of its land rental values; and this is indeed the one example of "extraction" pointedly absent from an otherwise excellent examination, in the book, of other exploitative extracts that have been made from the land, such as in commercial fishing, mining and forestry.

Concluding his paragraph here, Doug Aberley writes: "By understanding how major parts of the existing economy of your bioregion are structured, you will be empowered to begin their transformation". One can but offer the bioregional movement, from Mr. Pot of Holland, the added land rent layer to their maps! It is excellent to read, a little earlier in that same chapter (*How to Map Your Bioregion*) that: "The bioregional alternative is as much concerned with achieving social justice as it is with stewarding life within ecological carrying capacities". Yes – but in the understanding of social justice issues, it is the land rent map rather than the "study of census information" that is the dynamic first step needed.

We have already touched, earlier in this book, on the new permaculture movement, and permaculture principles form a natural part of the bioregional approach. How indeed could it be otherwise, since permaculture too is about sustainability and learning to live within the capacities of the land that carries us. But the bioregionalists have yet to discover what a powerful tool radical land reform would be in bringing forward the permaculture – as the bioregional – ideal. If the rent of the land is acknowledged to be our true social fund, then it is important that land is valued according to its *best* potential (sustainable) use, otherwise society may be missing out on social revenue rightly owing to it.

There is yet another excellence to this project. For, as a friend with whom I was discussing it keenly emphasised, the valuations must take into account the best *permaculture* use of land. Land which from its present usage appears unpromising and of poor return, may well find an enhanced value when considered in permaculture terms. A foremost permaculture principle is that of marrying the needs of the human population with the needs of the land itself, in order to ensure a sustainable, non-exploitative type of usage; a principle widely disregarded by the type of land-use officially encouraged – *and grant-aided* – today. A further principle is that of studying a piece of land with sufficient care and imagination to be able to see, instead of its problems and difficulties, the opportunities and solutions that may be lying there – simply undetected as yet, awaiting our notice. These principles can find imaginative applications in urban areas too, where problems of poor land use similarly abound. The main destroyer of our cities' patterns, however, is neglect of collecting the land rental values for society. Land rental values amassing on land year after year, uncollected by society, allow the build-up of a capital value . . . which it is then too tempting for local councils not to reap gain from by selling off – be it "buildings" (in reality the land values lying under them) or derelict land – for a development project which may well be quite adverse to that locality's real needs. Thus in their mapping for the improvement of the environment, the bioregionalists have so far missed an ace card.

On this matter of the presently unrecognized potential of so much of our land, one may mention the successful Loch Garry Tree Planting Project in highland Perthshire, initiated in the 1980s by Ron Greer. As a result of this pioneering work, a plantation of young trees is now growing and flourishing in an area previously desolate and *which was almost universally held to be incapable of supporting tree growth.* Until we take back our land, we shall never begin to discover the appalling wastage of it that Scotland has endured, not just over decades, but over centuries.

The Loch Garry project won an award in a nationwide competition, for its achievement. Where trees can grow, as Ron points out, people can live. Part of the background rationale for the maintenance of our huge sporting estates is to instill into us the belief that "they would not support a human population anyway". Now just what impact does such an unbethought of plantation of flourishing young trees – amidst a uniformly bleak surrounding landscape – have on the project of mapping an area's *land rental values?* – !

For the mapping of the land's rental values to be carried out locally – by those who actually indwell an area – makes sense in every way. If we are setting on foot a new system, it is as well to do it in a way that exemplifies wisdom from the start – and the wisdom of this way is well instilled into us by a book already referred to, *Living with the Land.* As peasant communities there found, it is not enough to know about landscapes in general. It is *this* river, *this* tree that we must know about – and teach our children about too. "Experts" brought in to a rural area in India found their knowledge of the local soils – (upon which their advice would have been founded) – completely confuted by that of the local population who *knew and worked their land at first hand.* In short, before true valuations of land can be made, there must be true maps backed by a true knowledge of what they are depicting; and for this, first-hand local knowledge is clearly indispensable.

While this may be true of the countryside, what of city areas? If we stand back for a moment and take a larger look through bioregional spectacles, we shall find that in fact it is *just the same* there.

Doug Aberley's book has a chapter in it, *Mapping the Wild Onion Bioregion*, by Beatrice Briggs. (How delightful to find that the nodding wild onion, *Allium cernuum*, is believed to have inspired the name "che-cau-gou", or "place of strong smells", which the Potowatami Indians originally gave to what is now heavily urbanized Chicago!) The bioregional group in Chicago, in attempting to map their area, found themselves with a problem. Their bioregion lay within a watershed and catchment area extending for a very great distance beyond it – so how were they to solve the problem of mapping their bioregion "without either expanding its boundaries beyond what felt to be 'right' or ignoring the very real connection between 'our' rivers and the others which join them in the journey to the Gulf of Mexico/". They turned for help to a local cartographer* who "suggested showing the entire watershed of the Upper Illinois Valley, and then identifying the Wild Onion Bioregion within that context." Once we saw the map drawn in this way, we were dismayed that we had not seen this elegant, truthful solution before. All we needed was a good map to teach us some important lessons about the place we call home".

Now just how important is it to see one's home town or city set within its larger bioregional area? A specific example can mightily illumine a general proposition – and we have one right now, right here. For at this very time the fair city of Perth is engaged in implementing Scotland's "biggest flood prevention scheme" – given the go-ahead with £20 million of taxpayers' money approved by the Scottish Office.** No bioregional mapping has, of course, taken place to provide a proper overview of flood prevention management. What would we have seen – and how much wiser would we have been – if it had? A well-known countryman who speaks on a regular Radio Scotland programme, in a winter 1997-98 edition of it referred to this flood prevention scheme – corroborating various statements on the matter I had already heard from elsewhere – with the words, *they shouldn't push the rivers*.

The meaning of those words was, of course, that those living and farming, or forestry-ing, on the upper reaches of the river Tay had been working their land in ways which had added huge volumes of water to those upper stretches – water which had then been inexorably carried downstream finally to dump itself on the flatter terrain around Perth. Following the disastrous floods of a few years ago, Perth is now involved in building the inevitable *embankments* (blocking many cherished views of the river), against the possibility of yet further flood damage . . . from waters which never should be arriving there in the first place. But to have dealt with those added volumes of water where they arose would have meant tackling a host of landowners involved in ownership of those upper reaches of the river. The Establishment finds it easier to authorize a £20 million pay-out from the tax-payer! But they only get away with this misuse of public funds in the absence of a bioregional viewpoint, and in the presence of a disempowered, kept-in-ignorance citizenry. If proper bioregional management of such flood schemes is to prevail it means, of course, allowing the land to delineate its own boundaries for us in a bioregional map, and then – (as the Wild Onion Bioregion found) – allowing our map, similarly, to "teach us some important lessons about the place we call home". Finally it means all the communities along that river basin – re-empowered at local level, as Jefferson, Carlo Levi and others have

* *Tom Willcockson of the Newberry Library, a "private research facility" in Chicago.*

** *Possiby including some E.U. taxpayers' money in it.*

shown so clearly is the way ahead – coming together for the joint management of a major and treasured river, whose flow affects *all* dwelling in its vicinity.*

This example of both the impoverishment of a city and the misuse of public funds – (the latter with nationwide bearing under a centralized funding system) – is but one instance of the kind of errant policies that may be brought to light through the adoption of a wider, bioregional view of our cities – a view which clearly must have our first attention in mapping the land rentals of our urban areas. If we think about it, this wider view in fact falls well within the Georgist perspective, since all that it is really doing is setting an unfamiliarly broad background to the fully familiar Georgist concept of valuing for the *best potential use of the land.* To share with you, however, just how far this "best potential use", for a bioregionalist, outstrips what Georgists as present – (or anyone else for that matter) – are accustomed to thinking in terms of, let me take you to the chapter in Doug Aberley's book – *Wild at the Heart: Planning from the Wild Center Out*, by George Tukel.

George Tukel's proposal stems from an idea called Biosphere Reserves, which originated apparently from within the United Nations. It takes its inspiration from the anciently charted territories of wild regionalism – (there is an excellent chapter on this earlier in the book) – made by the peoples who indwelt them, before the white men came to America and before our industrial and technological age. The concept of Biosphere Reserves turns the current view of our dwellership of earth inside out – it sees our cities as out-posts of our bioregions, and says "goodbye to the city as the center of the world". I shall not enlarge upon the excellent and innovative idea of "cores" and "corridors", beyond explaining that these are the terms used by George Tukel to propose how we work with today's cities and industralized areas – now drastically human-dominated – to preserve what oases of wilderness they may yet contain ("cores"), and to link these back ("corridors") to the wild heartland, beyond, of *biodiversity.* The point is that, without these "corridors" of vital linkage, the small "core" areas, left in isolation, will lose that biodiversity which is an essential feature of a healthy bioregion. Yet, upon the nurturing of biodiversity on this planet the human race depends; and the cities and industrialized areas must play their part.

In the renewal of these urban areas, (just as of others), bioregionalism and Georgism form, it seems to me, a natural partnership. Land monopoly has been the invisible force behind the destruction of our urban environments, both in encouraging, for speculative purposes, the lying idle of useful land, so leading to urban sprawl, and – (through land monopoly's build-up of capital monopoly in turn) – by placing the role of "developer" in the hands of huge and heartless conglomerates which step in, from outside, to areas they have no real link with, nor any feelings for. With land monopoly gone, the collection of the land rent as our social revenue will undoubtedly bring onto the scene much land-space we did not know we possessed. "Five per cent of the urban area of Britain is derelict – London alone has an area of vacant land the size of the borough of Westminster." (*The Land is Ours.*) We simply do not realize how much there is.

There is where the marriage of the bioregional view with the Georgist one can be of special value. In two ways, indeed. Firstly, in the assessing of the "best potential use" of such precious spaces – small or large – in the midst of industralized or city areas. For if it was felt that they were best developed as cores or corridors, to be a part

---

* *G.I.S. (Geog. Inf. Sys) mapping etc. can help here, but basically such mapping must still be in the hands of local people.*

of the biodiversity network of the region, then when it came to valuing such land it could be given zero rating. (As, indeed, could any land that it was decided to turn back to such use.)

There is another aspect of this marriage, however, and an equally important one, already briefly noted, which applies overall. Let us give attention, for a moment, to what Gene Marshall says in his chapter on *Mapping the Biosphere* in order to exchange the political demarcations of our space, (which define largely the power to exploit), for boundaries of federated life-regions instead:-

> "The way we conceive our geography expresses who we are and defines how we are assuming responsibility for all that surrounds us. This deeply personal level of mapping has primary importance. We cannot turn our mapping task to some professional geographer. Maps which are superimposed upon us from 'higher authorities' or 'scientific theorists' mean nothing to us personally unless data from such sources resonate with our personally-felt senses of place."

Thus the bioregional movement, which is dedicated to aligning the human world with the natural, places the vital task of re-creating society as fairly and squarely into the arena of *local empowerment*, as does Georgism – informed in its turn by the *political* wisdom of (among others) Turgot, Jefferson and Carlo Levi.

*

Of what size shall those communities be which must now undertake this twofold task – of restoring its ecological balance to the planet, and social justice to its inhabitants? Jefferson drew the line at the "wardship" of small town size; and indeed it seems that our earlier communities – delineated in village, parish and small burgh – would have served us very well, had their activities not been impossibly geared to the corrupt workings of land monopoly.

Certainly, the larger units that have since been forced have placed us in painful conflict with our more natural bioregions. Gene Marshall, in his chapter referred to earlier, speaks of the chaos of human-delineated districts that U.S. citizens now live among – state, county, city, congressional, judicial, water control, and postal-and-telephone coded. As he says, most of these are personally meaningless to us, while "some are gerry-mandered and re-gerrymandered into ridiculous patterns". It is no different here. "Communities torn apart by gerrymandering" runs a headline in the Dundee Courier of early March 1998, with reference to some recently re-drawn electoral boundaries.

As local communities start to create their bioregional maps it would not be surprising if it were found that, even now, those earlier parishes and small burghs – (perhaps some subdividing now required) – still from our natural "Neighbourhoods" areas. This is the smallest of the bioregions that Gene Marshall proposes, proceeding thence to Community, Local Bioregion, Sub-Biome, Continent and Planet. ("Neighbourhood" seems the equivalent roughly of our "Parish – a word which may just never have crossed the Atlantic. See further on, the reference to the work of *Common Ground* in England.) How about the process of delineating the smallest units, where a conflict arises over boundaries? Doug Aberley describes the working out of these miniest boundary-lines as a process of friendly "jiggling" between the parties concerned.

What of our cities and our larger towns? This is what I had already earlier written, before opening Doug Aberley's book: the larger centres of population are similarly best regarded as an *assembly of villages* – each having its own distinct character, its own deeply-felt needs. How happy, then, I was to read in Doug Aberley's opening chapter, of "cities envisioned as clusters of villages where the impacts of human concentration are offset by maximizing self-reliance and proper respect for supporting rural ecosystems". I had already been struck by the achievements of *The Land Is Ours* (see Part III) in their 1996 occupation of that Wandsworth Guinness site. It was impressive to see the immense talents and stream of innovative ideas that sprang so quickly into bloom there, to create human habitations and a nurturing environment with an absolute minimum of financial expenditure – completely giving the lie to the repeated bleats today for "massive injections of capital from the top"! The real down-to-earth of what is needed is a massive setting-free of the locked-up and frustrated energies of countless dispossessed who, being shut off from the land, have simply no way of exercising their multitudinous skills.

Today's artificially concocted "job-training schemes" are all barking up the wrong tree. There are *huge reserves of unutilized skills* lying out there, rotting, in our society, on account of the iniquitous locking up of the land under land monopoly – a feature of our society we carefully avert our gaze from as we run about "job-training", "skill-training", and all the rest of it. (Whatever happened to our *sound apprentice system*, incidentally?) Let people back onto the land – and then watch their skills come into operation. Presently rental value will arise too, for society to collect – a double saving of funds.

There may be planners who would throw up their hands at this idea – at the idea of make-shift dwellings springing up in our towns. But the people living in them were *happy*, and those visiting the site from the surrounding area were happy too. What such planners need to ask themselves is, what would be *my* choice? Live in my own self-built bit of shelter – or sleep on the streets? *Just as* importantly: people engaged in creating their own areas of living-space are discovering something more satisfying than the drugs that many take to. Are we serious about today's drugs problem? – which continues to escalate and about which nobody has an effective answer . . . of course not, because we are not *looking at the root*.

Furthermore, where people create their own ideas of living-space there are *gardens* too. Not only for enjoyment, but elementary £-S-D-household-economy . . . in today's society of ever-rising (Euro-blessed) food prices. And is not the State scraping the bottom of the barrel to find those *family benefits*? Families best know how to "benefit" themselves, and at Wandsworth not only self-built shelters arose, but lovingly-constructed borders of vegetables, herbs, flowers and shrubs – feeding people with the extra boon of *un-pesticided* food, as well as helping clean up air pollution for the whole of the area, as every form of greenery helps to do.

Whatever are we waiting for? The exuberant, life-bestowed energies of countless extraordinary-ordinary people must one day soon in any case burst the dam of false land rights locking them up, and make something of a more fundamental claim upon society than their pittance of "benefit" . . . that is, if they are not first destroyed *and society along with them* via the drugs menace, with the crime and violence that soar alongside. Meanwhile "New" Labour – blissfully unaware of the clock ticking us to our doom – is busy shedding crocodile tears over the plight of the "socially excluded"! Yes – *The Land Is Ours* has certainly done a wonderful job in making such a thorough exposure of the roots of that "social exclusion"!

Henry George pointed to the wastage of the talents and gifts of the dispossessed –

(a wastage indicated by Ogilvie in his Essay too) – as the most appalling of all wastages of our unjustly-founded society. Short shrift *they* would have made of today's drugs scene that has us wringing our hands in impotence. Can't we raise our imaginations for a moment to their level and take a leaf from their thinking? Fortunately, bioregional/land rent mapping will find no difficulty in taking the scene on board *whole* and moving things forward in a more positive way. "Social exclusion" is a non-starter in this approach, the unique value of each individual being fundamental to it. Sellers of *The Big Issue* – all who sleep on the streets – will be natural partakers in the mapping of their "village" areas, speaking for themselves of what is important or meaningless to them about their environment, and expressing their own vision of change; while in the more country parts it is the travelling people who may well prove to have the greatest knowledge of – and insights into – our natural bioregions.

"If only we could still darn in Dundee!" Such is the heading of a gem of an article by Jim Crumley (Dundee Courier, 3 Feb. 98) on the ruin of that city under centralized planning – (developments spurred, of course, by the thought of reaping those speculative gains from *community-created* land values hugely enhanced by planning permissions centrally bestowed). Where, indeed, is the "village" any longer to be found in the "curved mall of shops with 107,000 square feet of Debenhams at one end and parking for 1100 cars at the other"? I quote from Jim Crumley's article. I cannot do better, I think, than quote again, from its closing passage:-

> "In Old Town Edinburgh, I used to listen to architects (one or two of them who were human enough – and, yes, romantic enough – to think small and acknowledge tradition as a force with a future) talk about 'patchwork darning in the fabric of the Old Town'.
>
> But darning is something else which has gone out of fashion, another lost skill. You just chuck away the old sock and buy a new pair. Probably in Debenhams."

Well, the "patchwork darning", of human scale, can only be expected from thinking that is human scale too, of course. And that, (with all due acknowledgement to our few exceptional architects and planners), can only be relied upon as coming from the people themselves – just as we saw at Wandsworth; From communities empowered, then, via land rent reform, (with the rent collected *at local level*), to take back charge and responsibility over *their own* economic resources, which have been so vastly (in every sense) misused in other hands; and with bioregional mapping able so powerfully to enhance that process now, too.

As to the "107,000 square feet of shopping mall" at one end and "parking for 1100 cars" at the other, let us remind ourselves that, wherever such false idols have been set up in our midst, they can be *deported away* again! And replaced. Maybe, I had thought – (and especially as food supplies give way under planet mismanagement) – with community-organised open space of trees and gardens, orchards and vegetable plots. (See the inspiring example of such use of a derelict inner city area in Vancouver, Canada, in *Living with the Land*.) The politicians and planners are so out-of-touch, they have little idea how deeply felt is this need among just ordinary city-dwellers today – people who probably never enter a health food store. As one elderly woman living in the heart of Glasgow, whom I met quite casually last year, said to me: "What is the use of *them* telling us to eat more fruit and vegetables, when we know it's all poisoned with pesticides anyway?" We still have not caught up with the book *Human Ecology*, by George Stapledon, (Faber and Faber 1964), in its inspired thinking along these lines more than thirty years ago.

Birthright. . .and. . .Scotland Today

I said above that *maybe* – and I had *thought* . . . But it must be confessed that, since reading the book on *bioregionalism*, one is might tempted to see that invitingly extensive and curved shopping mall as a bountiful "corridor" (or "swathe" as it is also described) of valuable inner-city *biodiversity*, with the 1100-cars parking space at one end of it as an equally valuable inner-city "core"! Maybe some vegetable patches and fruit-trees could be tucked in too, of course . . . ? But maybe a re-construction of some also valuable human-scale housing, to resurrect the old Overgate as people remember it, would be the first choice of the . . . *bordering* "village" areas. (What village can be found in a mall and a parking lot? – !) For myself, I know Dundee very little – and I now understand better why. A meeting with an acquaintance to discuss the threat of fluoridation at that time, first took me to Dundee on my return to Scotland in the late 1970s. My first acquaintanceship also with Dundee, it alas left me with no real wish to return, and in the decades since I have contented myself thankfully with Perth . . . (now alas to lose its river view . . .).

Equally outraged confrontations take place in the countryside over destructive acts by "them". "Furious row over removal of golf course trees", ran a headline in the *Dundee Courier* of 11 Feb 98 – the committee concerned being brought into direct conflict with an angry body of members, over the destruction of a plantation of forty trees standing around a green. The committee's action apparently had the support of "experts" brought in, and was "purely for the good of the course". But this is just the trouble, of course. "Purely for the good of the course" is not good enough, since golf courses do not exist in a vacuum, but only as used and enjoyed by people. Doug Aberley's words on the spiritual aspect of our environment are relevant here too – on the need to preserve "places which somehow link humans to a spiritual connection with nature"; for golf (uniquely among ball games) is frequently enjoyed, in our age of stress, more for the spiritual refreshment gained from time spent in contact with nature, than for the actual game itself. Can one imagine the kind of wound that the sudden destruction of a plantation of as many as forty trees must have inflicted on many of those club members?

Again, the practice, in a neighbourhood, of bioregional mapping, would have avoided this painful type of confrontation with the huge drain on emotional energies involved. Here is the opening paragraph of an excellent chapter contributed to the book by Angela King,* who has helped found a bioregional group in Britain under the name of *Common Ground*:–

> "*Common Ground's* Parish Maps Project starts with the simple question, "What do you value in your place?" This puts everyone in the role of expert. It was launched in 1985 with the purpose of encouraging people to share information about their localities and to record aspects they cared about. At a time of such rapid change, both in town and country, it is important that the feelings of local people about the places where they live are taken into consideration. Too often, valued features and places are lost by default."

Yes! "This puts everyone in the role of expert". Precisely! So there is no way that, against a bioregionally inspired local viewpoint, any outside "expert" purely on golf courses *in general*, could have been allowed to overrule this far wider range of

---

* *"Angela King, a habitat and species conservationist, is a founding director and co-ordinator, with Sue Clifford, of Common Ground, 41 Sheldon Street, London, U.K. WC2H 9HJ." For the equivalent of $2.50 you can buy a copy of Parish Maps, a 19-page booklet describing how to make your own local map.*

local expertise, which a full round-table conference would quickly have brought to light. (For instance, for their course to rank as top-champion may not have been top-of-the-list with this membership.) The widening of our thinking to acknowledge that we all live, in the first place, on a shared planet, is something much talked about. Bioregional mapping's gift of *good strong teeth* to this talk – such that we are not left "reacting on the sidelines to decisions made afar off" (Gene Marshall again) – or even near at hand – is its especial gift to us. For all our sakes, such mapping cannot start too soon. (Meanwhile, perhaps some re-planting of trees can take place on that golf course – this time safely bioregionally mapped.)

On this very question of lost features: where, I wonder, is Pitlochry's old well – the construction round it, that is, that used to stand on the main street, and round which I believe the cattle used to have to weave their way . . . until cars of course had to weave their way round it too? Had a bioregional movement existed in those days, it would surely never have been allowed to be dismembered and rudely scattered. Perhaps it is still possible for the parts of this historic well to be located and re-assembled, to stand as a still cherished feature of the town . . . perhaps in the garden area nearby? Now *there* would be a "tourist attraction", if you want one!

*

The knowledge of neighbourhood (or parish) boundaries of old can be used "to show where new urban village governments could be constituted". (Doug Aberley.) Our study of the words of sound decentralists such as Jefferson, Carlo Levi, and others mentioned in *Our Enemy the State*, have already pointed us in this direction. But what tremendous added empowerment is given their words by this burgeoning new movement of bioregionalism, which surely belongs to our new millenium! These "village" bodies – of country or town – are clearly the ones, then, that will carry the responsibility for the collecting of our local land rents too.

The importance of this local collecting, and handling, of our social revenue can scarcely be overstated, in view of the truism that "political power follows upon economic". Plainly, no real decentralization of *political* power can be achieved without the economic power being decentralized in the first place. And this decentralization of economic power is a matter, as we have seen, not limited simply to preventing the unjust build-up of that power in certain hands via land monopoly. It concerns also the matter of the disbursing of that land rent fund, once it is collected for society.

Nock puts his finger on it where, in emphasising that power over disbursing the social fund works best from bottom up, he points out that this method will "operate strongly against their (i.e. the higher echelons of power) assuming any factors but those assigned to them". And how necessary it is that society at grass-roots is the strict assigner of those functions! – which means in the first place, of course, of the funds that pay for their functioning. For where the State holds the purse-strings, there are no end to lunatic goings-on.

Merely as one example, (but with far-reaching implications for health – both ours and that of our children), we can have business companies, under pseudo agricultural names, coming into Scotland and sowing her fields down to *genetically-modified* crops – whose cross-pollination with growth in the surrounding areas (and even far-distant) will have effects that no one – *but on one* – can at present reckon, but which are likely to prove the proverbial Pandora-box, adversely affecting our environment – hence food – hence health, with the legacy of all that passed on inexorably to our children in turn.

And all because a government "advisory" committee has the power to mouth soothing, meaningless words – faithfully intoned in turn by the "agro" company. The risk is "negligible"! Behold our State "Nanny" – the keeper of the nation's health and the nation's fields! – (which carry many other health risks too, we now know).*

---

* *Since writing the above, I have come upon the following report:–*

UNPREDICTABLE ECOLOGICAL DAMAGE

1. Scientists have bred oilseed rape which is resistant to the herbicide Roundup. This oilseed rape has crossbred with the weed, wild raddish, so now there is Roundup resistent wild radish! There are an increasing number of transgenic crops and little understanding of the ultimate dangers of genetically engineered crops crossing with weeds to create 'superweeds'.

2. Scientists have bred aphid resistant potatoes and this caused, directly or indirectly, ladybirds in the vicinity to become sterile![1]

3. Genetically engineered bacteria bred to decompose 2,4D (a herbicide which persists in the environment). The result has been that the 2,4D was converted into an even more toxic substance which, amongst other things, has led to the death of soil fungi which is fundamental to soil health.

4. One type of genetically engineered soya bean has been found to cause dangerous allergic reactions. Another genetically engineered product containing a bacteria used to produce large quantities of the food supplement – the amino acid tryptophan – has been found to produce toxic contaminants which have killed 37 people and permanently disabled 1,500 others in the U.S.A.[2]

---

1 Source: Farming Today, BBC Radio 4, 17 November 1997.

2. Source: Greenpeace, London.

Gratefully acknowledged to: Permaculture Magazine, No. 17.

Some "negligible"!

Some *Nanny!*

How plain it is that, as long as government departments – and their quannie-nanny offshoots – are left with control over the use of our land, through being gifted by a naive people with the purse-strings to empower them in that, the people themselves will never obtain the freedom of their land *despite* whatever achievement in collecting the land's rental values. For – as surely as "he that pays the piper calls the tune" – we shall only have got rid of *one* set of masters; the other set will remain entrenched as before. But why should we be surprised if those Seven Wise Ones prove equally masters of *both* fields? It is both these spheres of operation, then, that we must take back into our own hands – the political sphere as firmly and surely as the economic one – if we would truly regain the freedom of our land.

There is another aspect of this folly of centralized house-keeping that is worth touching upon here – (I quote from the Dundee Courier of 17 Sept. 97):–

> "An immediate Government inquiry was launched last night to investigate why £65 million of taxpayers' money earmarked for humanitarian aid in India was misused . . .
>
> Ms. Short last night compared the scandal to the case of the Pergau Dam in Malaysia, where it was ruled that £234 million of aid was misused."

Some house-keeping! The State in the role of "keeper" of the nation's money! Can't we understand the elementary? – The huge agglomerations of money like this are just asking for such "misuse"! – and on it goes . . . One day a full-scale government department – the next, a quango one (including an unfortunate number of "health" quangos, it must be said) – while anon a local council becomes involved . . . Can't we get the elementary message? Human beings are just not suited to handling huge sums like this – sums which represent *economic power* – any more than they are suited to handling that power in any quantity politically, either. Jefferson's words are so plain! However much of an effort it may be for us to grow up, we, at grass-roots – parish – level, must start to take charge of our own affairs.

As this is so "revolutionary" a concept, however – or rather, *e*volutionary, to name it by its truer name, it will not be out of place, I think, to look at Nock's passage about this in his book, in its fuller wording, again:–

> "In fact, the only modification of (Jefferson's proposal) that one can foresee as necessary is that the smallest unit should reserve the taxing-power strictly to itself. The larger units should have no power whatever of direct or indirect taxation, but should present their requirements to the townships, to be met by quota. This would tend to reduce the organizations of the larger units to skeleton form, and would operate strongly against their assuming any functions but those assigned them . . ."

(We have already dealt with the meaning, here, of "taxing-power" and of "townships".)

In view of the strength of these words by Nock – carrying with them so thoroughly the spirit of that whole decentralist school – it will be as well to look at a certain challenge which has recently risen, to this concept, within a certain sphere of the Georgist movement.

The challenge has arisen in the context of countries having federal as well as state governments – such as Australia and America; but (as it was stated) would equally apply *within* a state. The concept holds that cross-border economic activity – (i.e. people going to work, or investing *into* an area, from outside) – if identifying areas that are especially rich in natural resources, indicates the following: that the land rentals in those areas, being enhanced by energies and investment flowing *in* from outside, belong to the federal community as a whole, and not to the state one. (Or then, within a state, would belong in chief part to the entire state community, and not to the locality where it arose.) Hence this concept proposes that it is possibly only a small part of the land rent which originates within such a locality and should remain there.

If the above proposition be true – that, for this reason, most (or a large part – a difficult thing to compute?) of the land rent fund belongs to the citizenry in general from the beginning; then the natural corollary is that the whole of the land rent should be collected from the start by the overall state (or federal) authority – and assigned by that authority *downwards* – (after deciding quite arbitrarily what *it* wished to keep) – in exactly the opposite way from that set out by Nock.

This would bring us right back, of course, to square one – to the hugely centralized political system that we live (*groan!)* under today. As we have already seen, it will not be enough just to undo the centralization of *economic* power which arises under land monopoly. Unless we dismantle the equally corrupt *political* system which has grown up with it – (and would gladly handle that economic power to its own ends!) – the freedom which we seek will escape us still. (Over and over again Nock emphasises in his book how State power is *antipathetic to social (people) power* in its very idea and essence – and how it so invariably proves in its workings.) It is important, therefore, that we examine the above proposition carefully, to discover if there is any truth in it.

If a community finds that people coming in from outside enhance the land rents there, then – to whom should their land rents go?

Still to that local community. For two reasons.

Firstly, where great numbers of people congregate, greater infrastructure of public services is inevitably required. The larger rental collection will therefore be needed in considerable measure, in the first place, to offset that.

Secondly, and more importantly: are we to suppose that areas drawing to themselves less economic activity are not rich in other ways? They may enjoy many other advantages. For instance, beauty of landscape can considerably enhance quality of life in ways that money cannot buy. There may be close access to sea or to hills providing – not necessarily the rewards of economic activity, but those of adventure and spiritual nourishment – equally vital for the human creature. One need only think of that haunting verse of the highlander torn from a homeland where existence, *in economic terms*, was only too bare and harsh:–

"From the lone shieling of the misty island,
Mountains divide us and the waste of seas –
Yet still the blood is strong, the heart is Highland,
And we in dreams behold the Hebrides!"
(Canadian Boat Song.)

. . . While the refrain at the end of each verse intones the bitterness of that exiled state. But let us remember, in any case, just why existence in that land had been so bare and harsh. No word, I think, need be added to what D.C. MacDonald recounts in this volume – and Ogilvie himself. The true riches of a country are its land and its people. We have not, as yet, seen what quality of life these can provide for the Scots *in any part of* their land; and shall not, until the removal of economic monopoly – *and* of *political* monopoly along with it.

So what does this all amount to? There are riches that are quantifiable in material terms – and riches that are not so quantifiable (or at least much less so) but that are riches none the less. If, according to the above proposition, we start trying to transfer those that are quantifiable, we are seeing only half of the picture, a dangerous and tunnel-invisioned way to go about things. Looked at all-in-all, it seems to me, in fact, that the proposition we have been discussing reflects a very materialistic view of life – a view of life natural in a society where just to get a living is so great a struggle for the great mass of people. However, to a people living in freedom, this more materialist view of life is not necessarily natural.

Of course, it may well prove that – under the economic liberation of land rent reform – those same areas of riches that are at present less quantifiable in material terms *do* come to produce higher rental values, as people choose to spread out more over the land. If so – well and good. But if not – let us remember the second half of that undeniable equation – that the true riches of a country are its land and its people – and what this signifies.

What does it signify?

Human beings are infinite in their variety. Some simply *do not wish* material riches in the same degree as others. How rich is that society which possesses members who eschew the more material idea of wealth and deliberately choose values of another kind! – And how rich is that society which is able to appreciate the worth of such variations amongst its membership!

Let us not, then, exert ourselves falsely in attempting to bring all the members of a society down to one identical *materialist* common denominator. That society in which certain members deliberately choose a different standard of values from the purely materialistic, will be a far happier society *for all* – and a far more interesting society for others to visit.

*

For these reasons, therefore, I remain with the view of Nock and others on this matter. And this – not only because I find that the proposition put does not, when examined, stand up to scrutiny; but also because it is plain that, even were there anything to be said for it, it is clear enough from our own study that an incalculably greater good for society would be lost, by adopting it, than is to be gained by its refusal.

. . . Hold on a minute, though! Isn't it all there in Nock's statement anyway? Look again at the middle sentence of his paragraph quoted above – the end part of it. "The larger units should have no power whatever of direct or indirect taxation, but should present their requirements to the townships, to be met by quota." *To be met by quota!* This of course means that the smaller "cells" in the social structure each give *in proportion to their revenue* towards society's few more general undertakings. Or *pro rata*, as is the neat and familiar Latin term. Hence, those localities richer in social revenue will, in any case, under decentralist government, be providing larger sums to the overall community for precisely those more overall undertakings – (rail networks, defence, etc.) We can note that there would be no need for any complex computations to be involved in this exercise, either; while we can further note that the ones that give more will, by their concensus in this, be acknowledging the *equal worth* of the ones that give less.*

So we in fact arrive at the same end, regarding the overall undertakings that a society requires; but not by a bureaucratic removal of social revenue, by the State, from the smaller localities where it arises, but simply by the natural workings of the decentralist form of government, which distributes the economic power from the bottom up. The great difference is that, distributed thus from the bottom up, it would not just be a small part of their land rent that would remain to the local community – (as that proposition would have had it . . . even if more were intended to "trickle down", a song we are somehow familiar with!) No – it would be by far the larger part.

---

* *All could not give the same, it stands to reason, or the funds of the poorer localities might be completely wiped out. Proportional giving would be the* ***only*** *way.*

For few would be the tasks required to be undertaken by the higher echelons – because the lower echelons would make quite sure they were few! – nearly all the social input needed in the smaller areas being organized and undertaken by those localities on the spot.

Can we begin to imagine the savings of our extraordinary wastages that would come about – and not least in the array of official salaries involved in first *collecting* large revenues *in*, from the bottom to the top . . . and then distributing them all the way back down again – (what does get back down)? We will assuredly come to look back on such systems as crazydom! So obviously crackers that no wonder the cracks in the present one widen yearly and it is a wonder it is standing at all.

Here's another thought: in view of the enormous social revenue that many believe would come to hand under land rent reform, can we not just imagine the extra-celebratory gallops of the State given *that* charge! Expanded tango-bands – fox-trottings on the sly – "Anniversary Waltzes" ad lib., and all . . . For Scotland, at any rate, enough! ENOUGH!

*

We arrive, now, at the question – the all-important question – of the tiding-over period. The "quannies" cannot all be dismantled in a day. And a people so long disempowered cannot learn it all in a day, either.

How shall we find our way forward?

Here, Jefferson's words seem to me to hold useful guidance for us. I quote again from Nock, in his fourth chapter:–

> "The secret of freedom will be the individual making himself the depository of the powers respecting himself, so far as he is competent to them, and delegating only what is beyond his competence, by the synthetical process, to higher and higher orders of funtionaries, so as to trust fewer and fewer powers in proportion as the trustees become more and more oligarchical."

The key phrases for us here – at this interim time – are those concerning what we are "competent to", and what as yet lies "beyond our competence. These phrases, it seems to me, are of direct guidance in a time of transition, since what we are "competent to", in our local area, will clearly be something of an evolving matter. Let us look at it this way. No one will want to be *without* their local schools, hospitals, police-force, etc. Thus the ordinary intelligence of ordinary people at work on such matters will surely qualify them to delegate what is "beyond their competence" in each sphere. In the early days, many social tasks will indeed need to be delegated upwards – to outsiders at present more competent for them. So be it. We can be learning all the time towards taking them over ourselves. But one can hardly see any of these necessary public services *collapsing* because the local people have the deciding power in the disbursement – (horizontally and vertically) – of their local revenue! Undoubtedly we would see a few *quangos* collapsing however! How about, for a start, those tangling with the £12 million of taxpayers' money being rushed forward for that extremely questionable Cairngorms funicular – a sum that will "create", we are assured, 100 jobs. Yes – at £10,000 a-piece? I think our village communities could have done better! So much for the quango Cairngorms Partnership's part in all this.

We already had a people's body, of course – the *Cairngorms Campaign*. But the government didn't like its advice. So – "I know! We'll create *another* body, of our *own*. We've got the cash. – And call it . . . 'The Cairngorms Partnership' – a real 'people' sound! Then we take the 'advice' of the body *we* have created – and ignore the people's one!" This tango-variation is called side-stepping – fox-trotting, maybe . . (The *Seven Wise Masters* know them all.) Another fox-trot is – you "consult" the people, but decide *ahead* that you ignore the result anyway. Thus came into being the S.E.P.A. quango: ". . . we learn that SEPA (Scottish Environmental Protection Agency) could be operational by 1996, although its creation has been opposed by forty local authorities and six of the seven river purification boards . . . SEPA does not seem to be what we want . . ." So reported *The Fletcher Forum* of April 1993, under the heading "What Price Democracy?"* There's another one coming up yet – more of a "Surprise Polka" perhaps? A Scottish Office minister "told councils they should be less hands-on and instead play a more strategic role in service delivery" (???) Furthermore, he "would support the introduction of full-time councillors who are paid a salary commensurate with the job". (But *who will be the paymaster?* – And who knows the end of *that* journey . . .?) "His remarks sparked fears that councils would be dramatically reduced in size and left running a rump of services, with the rest being given to private and voluntary sectors." (*Dundee Courier*, 23 Jan 98.) Time for our village councils to step forward, methinks – *hands-on* and all!

This brief digression in considering the transition period in taking up our grass-root reins has not been without profit. Pausing on this unending "march towards reorganization and centralization" over the past two decades when our local government has been reorganized to bits, a particularly crazy-gang aspect of it all has struck me forcibly. Had Health and Water – (to name just the two most obvious) – remained in the hands-on-hands of local bodies, (even if not yet quite at village level), we would not at this point be so hard put to it in taking back the managing of our own business. As the most glaring instance – from the days of local council control over water, we now have a mere *three* Quango Water Boards** covering the whole of Scotland. Quangos are not only a most disreputably undemocratic concept, they are also a most cunning pathway to people disempowerment. For not only do they un-accustom local people from looking after their own affairs, but, along with this, they remove also from that area the *knowledge of how to do so.*

---

* ***The Fletcher Forum*** *further reported on this that "the new body will not be given powers to co-ordinate flood control or powers to prosecute polluters".*

** *A chairman designate of one of these three Boards wrote in the press in March 98 that the Secretary of state for Scotland, in his Dec 97 review of the "water industry", had decided to increase the representation of elected members on these boards "to 50%".*

"50%"? No such thing! I have before me a copy of that very Review, and it tells us that the Secretary of State has upped the number of elected local councillors on these Boards to ***16 out of 33****. So what? Are we all meant to be dunces? – too deficient in mental arithmetic to be able to work that one out!*

De-centralize is the "in" word,
(So from our good scouts we have heard).
Then trumpet it! But – sweet surprise! –
In fact instead ***we'll centralize!***

Funny, isn't it, how a slightly more elevated position gives ~~a~~ one slightly new qu-ANGLE on affairs!

It is hard to know how much this may have been a deliberate part of quango-ising from the start; but with the distinct possibility of planetary upheavals ahead following from our human misbehaviours, it is a foolish community that will move forward into the new millenium not knowing how to operate its own social support system – *not to mention its life-support systems.* Such as its water supply? Without doubt local communities will have to take back charge of their water supplies again – working out whatever steps may be necessary to do so.

The interim period (following full independence – but we can prepare for it now) in establishing government from grass-roots up, is obviously going to be a difficult one and extremely challenging. It will be no easy way forward – out of the MESS that we have arrived at, following three hundred years of dancing to that "scrap of paper".* I remain convinced that it will be best to set certain matters on foot right from the start. Thus – there is at present no machinery in existence either for valuing the land rentals or for collecting them. I am convinced that, in creating this necessary twofold machinery, we should do it *at local level from the beginning.* We have to make a beginning in re-learning how to manage our own affairs, so here is an ideal starting-point – for it is the marrying-point of the decentralization of both economic and political power. Were we to allow that machinery to be set up as a *central* institution, I believe that it would be extremely difficult to get that pattern altered. We have, precisely, to BREAK the pattern of centralized control over our lives. If we have the determination to do this at all – then here is a critical place upon which to stamp our determination from the start. To show that *what we say, we mean.*

In any case, bioregional mapping – which is essentially a parish affair and cannot be carried out in any other way since this is the very essence of it – provides the ideal starting-point also for land rent mapping; which mapping must obviously underpin the land rent valuing process. So here is a direct and powerful reason to set the matter on foot at parish level.

Consider too: the new Scottish parliament is going to have an initial five-year run during which its financial terms will be strictly restricted to that game of three-pence-pieces. There is, therefor, *no possibility* of its having any remit to set up a land rent valuing procedure itself. Hence – a five-year head-start is given us in this matter. A gift indeed! *See we make use of it!*

There are two more points to deal with of a specific nature. Firstly – how do we elect our "village" bodies, in each parish, or neighbourhood (equally bioregional terms) – or small burgh, indeed? It may be worth mentioning a method that I believe was once used in Switzerland, when the names of all those in the community were put into a "hat" – and the names of those to serve for the next period were drawn from it. These would receive payment, during their term of office, from the land rent fund. I put forward this suggestion, simply in case it is felt that a somewhat determined break needs to be made with the present hierarchical structure of society, which would not be so well achievable in any other way. However, it is very likely that, in plunging into this very new scene, there will be some wish to include – and some wisdom in including – a few at least of those local or community councillors, or officers, who we feel have served us faithfully in the past, and have some experience to bring to bear on the new scene.

---

* *The 1707* ***Treaty of Union*** *with England, which signed away Scotland's power of self-government* ***without*** *the consent of the people and indeed contrary to their wishes. (See* ***Leaves from the Book of Scots*** *in Reading List.)*

As part of this new and truly grass-roots form of government – (a unique offering from Scotland to the planet today?) – there must obviously be regular sessions when those who are elected gather together with *all* of the people of that parish or neighbourhood, to report to them, and to receive their instructions as need be; hopefully by consensus but where necessary by vote. So perhaps, in setting on foot this truer concept of democracy, we could allow our seating to reflect it too, avoiding raised platforms or any pattern that sets the elected apart from their electors (*whom they serve*). I believe it was the way with the Indians of North America to seat themselves in a circular manner for such conferrings, so that none would be placed in a position of superiority, nor any led to feel inferior or less able to contribute.

These are my few thoughts upon the matter that I humbly offer at this stage.

Finally there is the practical question of the actual mapping itself for land rent – Mr. J. Pot of Holland's excellent idea; for which we do not at present, of course, have the necessary separation of the values of the land rent from those of the improvements occupying the ground – (part of the long hide-up!) However, even under today's land tenure system there is plenty of knowledge of the separate values of land from improvements – (as I think I have said before even from the point of view of valuing the improvements for insurance purposes) – both in city areas and in the countryside, and the valuing expertise of estate agents is usually fairly locally available. There is no reason why those engaged in such work, under the present system, should not welcome a change to a different future for Scotland as well as any of us. (There have been one or two useful studies made of land valuing for rental collection, and I hope to place something on this in the Reading-List.)

In general, in setting out on this way, we will need experiment and trial on the widest front as to how to proceed at each stage. Here neighbouring communities can be of help to one another, sharing what they have learned and trialled, or decided to test. Angela King's offering from *Common Ground*, (mentioned in an earlier footnote in this chapter), seems an obviously helpful starting-point.

The initial steps on this journey will undoubtedly be ones of adventure and challenge. But who ever said that freedom was not worth a struggle? Besides, when you set out determinedly enough to reach a certain goal, it very often happens that that goal starts coming towards you. – And right here, from a new and unexpected quarter, a marvellous piece of encouragement indeed comes to us!

*

Science has recently made a new discovery. Yet, in reviewing it, it could scarcely be a more natural or obvious one. Quite simply, it is the discovery in another sphere, existent and flourishing, of that grass-roots empowerment which Carlo Levi and others have been talking about!

Yes! For it seems that the living structures of the universe, from the tiniest atoms to the most complex life forms, are held together – not by any outer controlling force, as had previously been thought), but by their *own internal mechanisms and intelligence.*

Just let us think what this means for a fully natural order of society. Such a society will not be governed by external controls imposed from without, but by its *own inner* intelligence and structures.

In an absorbing article published in *The Scientific American* of January 1998 and called "The Architecture of Life", Donald E. Ingber writes of this newly discovered principle named *tensegrity*: that is, the way that living systems, at every stage of their development, have evolved their own ways of stabilizing themselves – and linking up with one another. It stems from an internal pattern of "tensional and compressive forces",* which are "distributed and balanced" *within* the structure. Hence their capacity to self-stabilize. Now let us think of our *de*-stabilized society, falling apart in every direction, with drugs and crime burgeoning against a background of collapsing jobs. That cannot be in a tensegrity structure – for there is no member of a tensegrity structure that is jobless! It is ruled out from the very beauty of the design, since a "critical feature" of all tensegrity structures is that tension is "continuously transmitted across all structural members . . . an increase in tension in one of the members results in increased tension in members throughout the structure – even ones on the opposite side".

One cannot but marvel at such a description of a *real* community, where the needs of the different members – their pains, griefs and anxieties – are sensed by all. Nor is this just a static affair, for "essentially, all the interconnected structural elements of a tensegrity model re-arrange themselves in response to a local stress". Endless are the parallels that unfold . . . but how could it be otherwise? For if atoms, molecules, cells, tissues, and organs, up to living creatures, all choose to structure themselves in this way – each ascending step arising naturally as the result of the free association of units of the previous (less complex) order: then is not the equally free association of *living creatures* – (effected by their own volition) – just the natural further step forward, to create the true and living structures of a *society* in this most natural order of things?

Apparently, even as late as the 1970s, however, biologists still viewed the cell "as a viscous fluid or gel surrounded by a membrane, much like a balloon filled with molasses". One cannot help a smile in reviewing the awful blunder of the State's parallel concept of society: as a "viscous fluid or gel", to be surrounded by a "membrane" – the State's own arbitrary, superimposed network of *controls* over the live "molasses", ever hopeful of keeping it contained!

So! – the way these living structures organize themselves harmoniously to build from atom to cell and so on to living creature, is not from the top down but *from the bottom up* – just as we have been studying in those radical political thinkers!

Of course, we well know that we cannot organize the life of our cells and molecules. So let us just remember the tale of the millipede, who, on being asked how it could possibly organize all those legs, promptly came to a full-stop and fell over into a ditch! That's just about where our society has landed now! Our society is like a disfunctional millipede, its own naturally burgeoning inner forces and energies in a state of pitiful paralysis from the mistaken belief that its functions require organizing from above. No wonder if employment, housing, community care, and a myriad other aspects of our social life are in the doldrums or almost seized up! En route to this brain seizure is the belief that businesses cannot function now without P.R.s and a host of other professionals to back them up – and piles and piles of paperwork besides; as if the making and exchanging of goods and services was not the most entirely natural activity of human beings on this earth, for as long as ever they have inhabited this planet. No wonder if a penchant for early retirement grows lustily amidst this decay!

---

* *Re "tensional" and "compressive": "The principles of tensegrity apply at essentially every detectable size scale in the body . . . in the complex tensegrity structure inside every one of us, bones are the compression struts, and muscles, tendons and ligaments are the tension-bearing members."*

The process of disfuntioning the millipede can take a wide variety of forms. A "surfeit of consultative documents" from the Scottish Office nearly bowled out the business of a local council committee recently! – much to the exasperation of its councillors. (Dundee Courier, 23 Jan and 14 Feb 98.) By contrast, the dance of tensegrity accepts no "consultative documents" from above, weaving as it does its own plays of self-assembly and holding all its blue-prints safely within. Could there be a more beautiful patterning forth of that prophetic vision of Carlo Levi's – of the society of "autonomous self-governing" communities, where "the State can only be a group of autonomies, an organic federation"? Carlo Levi's words are a perfect mirror-writing of the tensegrity principle. So one European was able to foresee the unfolding form of the true society ahead, and pluck this blossoming of understanding of it from an experience or derogation and exile! Your vision, Carlo Levi, is even now bringing the great Euro-trumpetings of today to nought.

As for who shall most readily take it up – for the sake of the whole planet how fortunate it is that the Scots, the very people now poised to take a leap forward into freedom again, are a nation so exceptionally attuned to that vision – to the political and economic dance of tensegrity. For the Scots, in the days of their freedom, ruled their kings with a rod of iron!* In that dance of tensegrity the dance of devolution is quite gobbled up! But why weep for that? Three hundred years of it have surely seen us fed to satiety with the bread of our disaster!

There is another aspect of the tensegrity principle that would swiftly warn us freedom must be grasped *now*. It was observed that, when a living structure such as a cell linked up with another living structure, the natural and flexible interplay between the two allowed a harmonious adjustment of the stresses and tensions between them . . (reminding one of that happy term "jiggling" in bioregionalism – and what a tensegrity movement *that* is!) But what happened when a cell was *artificially* constrained by being forcibly fastened to an *in*flexible structure . . . (our "Nannies" ruling us with a rod of iron?) . . . what happened then?

The cell, robbed of its purpose and vitality, the structure pulled all one way – (by those apron-strings?) – unable to fulfil its function properly, is diverted from its true genetic programme. A Health article in the Radio Times of 28 Feb 98 reiterates it: cells which are "poorly differentiated and functionally useless" tend to be *cancer cells*.

How clearly we see reflected in this the present destruction of society! But this is not all. It was noted, of cells "artificially constrained" and *prevented from spreading* – (...our *land monopoly*?) – that they activated, in due course, "a death program known as apoptosis".

Let us take a look at this. There has been quite a bit of press coverage given lately (early months of 1998) to the conundrum of the *declining population of the Scots* . . . and what the reason for this might be.

This conundrum has mostly been examined through the same tunnel-visioned kinds of spectacles that regard with curiosity animals artificially constrained – in the delusion that something useful can be learned thereby.

Particularly with the Scots – this will not do. For the Scots have always been a people peculiarly hefted to their land. Artificially constrained in cities, the land filched from them – what, through our peering spectacles, can we possibly hope to learn from

---

* ***Leaves from the Book of Scots***. *See Reading-List.*

them *there*? . . . gazing, as it were, upon some phenomenon of plant growth without taking thought to glance at its **roots** . . .

Without good soil at the roots, the most burgeoning plant growth will come to nought. Animals, *caged*, have been known to lie down and die.

We have boasted about the flowering of the Scots across the world – but how much have we really cared about it – beyond our boast?

The eventual chosen *apoptosis* of those falsely constrained tensegrity structures may well provide the clue to the declining population of the Scots . . .

Time for the people of Scotland to take back their LIVES!

*

For myself – (could this be a part of my inheritance as a Scot – a natural attunement to tensegrity structures?) – the only surprising thing I find about the tensegrity principle is that it has taken so long for it to come to light. Surely it is the life-force flowing through all forms of life that sustains them, and surely it would be bound to manifest itself in some palpable way?

I find it significant that Donald Ingber, who played so large a part in its discovery, in his student days at Yale University was studying sculpture alongside biology. Understandably this cross-fertilization of ideas between science and art gave him an extra broad perspective when studying life's forms. We would have a far higher type of science today, were all its students required to study a branch of the arts at the same time – *and* to write a paper on the light which the study of each threw on the other! We might then find ourselves throwing out many more of our tunnel-visioned ways!

Interestingly, heading the reading-list given with the article is the work of a Scot – of more than half a century ago, so well ahead of his time too, it seems. "On Growth and Form" was written by the zoologist and mathematician, D'Arcy Thompson. – A good cross-fertilization of branches of science, anyway, but he may well have been musical also. For the name D'Arcy Thompson is not easily forgotten, and I remember from childhood his daughter, Ruth, (herself an impressive woman) – a musician who taught music appreciation in schools around Edinburgh. It was common knowledge that she had "a very brilliant father". His book, originally published by the Cambridge University Press, has recently been reprinted.

The principle of tensegrity can hardly be studied too deeply, or its lessons taken too much to heart. My eye has just fallen on an earlier note I had made – which, come upon again, conjures up vividly the collapse of those East European states in recent times – with all the chaos and suffering that always follow on such events. As I had noted: "It is solely on account of the self-organized structures of their tinier component parts, that the overall organ has any stability". *Stability!* And I had further noted: "It is only out of their (these tinier components') bonding together, on the same tensegrity principle, that the larger organ can have any security". Stability! Security! In our society *as at present*? – ! The State we bow down to is doomed!

Returning to Nock's *Our Enemy the State* after reading *The Architecture of Life* – to Nock's review of the inevitable collapse, throughout history, of these mammoth institutions once they have too far demolished social (people) power – it is interesting to become aware of Nock's natural tensegrity vocabulary. One thinks of those flattened tensegrity organisms – depicting so well the ruination of people power – as he writes of the inevitable follow-on: "the shock of some irruption which the social structure was too far weakened to resist, and from which it was left too disorganized to recover; and then the end".

Time to jump ship, methinks! And time for those who man the present system to grasp – at last – that they are not in charge either. Rather – they themselves are victims of a process far beyond their control. How many of today's State servants, for instance, are aware that the main function of Britain's heavy Official Secrets Act is for *supra-national business to rule the State?* *

Time for the State's servants to jump ship too, methinks!

*

I have always loved the story of the prince of India who gave his name to *serendipity*. Lo, you go in search of one thing – and you find something else!

So it was with me, one evening in early February 1998. Looking for something in a file, "something else" fell out. It was the first issue of The Fletcher Forum, of date April 1993 – (already referred to in this chapter); the only issue I have, and I gather it is now out-of-publication. This paper – needless to say – was named in honour of Scotland's great patriot, Fletcher of Saltoun. Of incorruptible character, he had opposed the 1707 union with England to the bitter end. (See further in Part I – a chapter I have not yet put together, but am determined to include.) Remembering this was the only issue of the Forum I had, I decided to give it a quick read-through. It proved a fortunate read – a fortunate find! – as, with attention riveted, I found myself absorbing the following, on its second page:-

> "The late Lord Cooper, Lord President of the Court of Session, declared: 'The principle of the sovereignty of Parliament is a distinctly English principle which has no counterpart in Scottish constitutional law!' In Scotland the people are still sovereign."
> (Article PUBLIC WATER AND PRIVATE PROFITS, by Ian Hamilton, Q.C.)

I was astonished. To see the matter stated so unequivocally – so clearly – and yet never to have heard even an inkling of it before . . . Was there *any end* to the cover-ups? I decided to address myself to a top Scottish legal body on the matter, and as their office was in Edinburgh, to deliver the letter there by hand . . . and did so on Friday, February 13th. (Having grown up in "Edinburgh 13", as its simple coding was in the old days, "13" is a number I am quite at home with, even on a Friday!)

A month passed – five weeks. Still no reply. On 20th March I found myself once more in Edinburgh, and left a reminder at the same reception desk – *enclosing a copy of the original* and stating it had been delivered by hand, and writing "Delivered by Hand" on the reminder.

Meanwhile I had decided to try the question out on a top political body – (s.a.e. for reply being enclosed in both cases). With this latter, a variant on silence was played in a variant upon serendipity; you ask one question – and a *different* question comes back answered!

---

* *From a letter headed "The Secret Sell-Out of Democracy", dated 17 Mar 1977. Written by an M.P. linked with a parliamentary committee at that time studying the matter, it was addressed to the editor of a county newspaper and later published by an anti-fluoridation organization. (Need we wonder that Scotland has now been made the dumping-ground of the entire U.K's nuclear arsenal? "They" need Scotland alright!)*

Tonight as I type this, (already into April), a reply has finally arrived from the legal body. My letter of February 13th "cannot be traced" in their office". (!) Further, I am advised that the questions I had asked "are not properly questions" which that legal body can answer, and I am advised to try two other parties – which are *both* political ones, (one being that which had already sent me the serendipity-variation reply!) However, if it is a question involving "Scottish constitutional law", it seems to me that a *political* body is not one fully competent to deal with it.

I shall progress with this matter alongside working on this book; but it is fairly plain, by now, that here we have stumbled on the "unanswerable" – (a second "Midlothian" question, as we in Scotland might say!)

My question had concerned why our local councils are having their future "spelt out" to them (Dundee Courier, 23 Jan 98) via merely Parliamentary-based authority, since surely the local councils should be consulting the (sovereign) people *direct*, as to their own wishes on this matter?

Certainly it is as plain as daylight, from the words of Lord Cooper, that an extraordinary vital peice of *political knowledge* has been kept locked up from us . . . concerning a political fact (arising from Scotland's constitutional law) we were clearly never meant to re-discover!

The political *significance* of this fact – (while having repercussions in every direction, including that of dismantling the Water Quangos) – certainly means that no obstacle stands in the way of the people of Scotland settling the matter of their future for themselves.

At the last resort, therefore, should their given Parliament fail them, then their own grass-roots networks (named as they choose), linking up progressively in "Sub-Biome" and "Biome" groupings, (or by whatever other name chosen – see Doug Aberley's book), can move forward with confidence, upon Scotland's own ultimately authoritative basis of *sovereignty of the people*, and – *retaining the supreme power always at grass-roots level* – arrive at the setting up of their very own Parliament themselves.

*

Something else fell out of that serendipity file. With joy I pounced on a faded cutting about the Italian "street" actor, Dario Fo – a performer once seen, never forgotten! "Unique in world theatre, playwright, actor, clown, teacher and philosopher . . . and great hero of the Italian Left" – (Radio Times of 25 Feb 83).

Fo revived the *Comedia dell' Arte* of Italy of the Middle Ages – that street theatre which had in it a strongly satirical element; its purpose being – in that age of something-less-than-free speech – to allow the ordinary people, labouring under the cruelties of a land feudalism that held all of Europe in its thrall, (the real cause of the Peasant Wars), in this safe "comedy" way to denounce those social structures under which they felt and knew themselves *trapped.*

When I say that Dario Fo revived this old *Comedia dell' Arte*, in fact it was still very much alive and flourishing in the Lucania of Carlo Levi's exile; and his account of it there, in his book – with the people's mysterious borrowing of his doctor's accoutrements for their performance! – is one of its most unforgettable passages . . . as we share in how brilliantly-bitterly through their acting the inside story of their lives is revealed.

We can do with some street theatre right here in Scotland – right now. The Scots can do it as well as anyone. – I could hardly tear myself away from the performance I stumbled on, so deliciously unexpectedly, on leaving Glasgow's Garden Festival one evening in 1988. I know little about the Scots' equivalent of the *Comedia dell' Arte*, for I confess I have never seen *The Three Estates*. But the old Morality Plays had their Seven Deadly Sins, did they not? – which no doubt might approximate to the Seven Wise Masters!

Or why not turn the spotlight on ourselves? We must have been asleep a long time to have remained so "trapped" until now. So what about another Seven? What were their names?

HAPPY: Just happy getting on with their own life, because it's a life worth getting on with.

GRUMPY: Best at complaining!

SLEEPY: Not quite "with it"!

SNEEZY: Focussed on personal aggravations.

BASHFUL: Hanging back from gearing up!

DOPEY: Distracted by addictions . . .

DOC: Still bent on doctoring the undoctorable!

Snowhite needed a big heart! We can have one too. . .

But – TIME TO WAKE UP! Time to go walk-about and map the land!

Shirley-Anne Hardy
~ Easter 1998 ~

PART II

*

Chapter 2

FREEDOM'S FULL PRICE

"How else should it be done then?"
was always the immediate question.
The answer is simple: "Exactly
in the opposite way that it is done today".
(Viktor Schauberger, 1885-1958.)

*

Even in a time of dark confusion,
the true way is readily discernible by
those able to see with their own eyes.
*(S-A.H., 30 July 98.)**

*

---

* *The original words are from Goethe's **Faust**, which I first came upon many years ago, in the opening pages of F. McEachran's book, **Freedom – the Only End**, (see Part III), and was greatly struck by. I have given them here a looser translation, reflecting my own thoughts at this time:–*

"Ein guter Mensch in seinen dunklen Drange,
Ist sich des rechten Weges wohl bewusst."

FREEDOM'S FULL PRICE

THE WORK OF VIKTOR SCHAUBERGER

At the portals of the New Millennium that we would enter stands one – of that line whose vision reaches far ahead of their time. Of this great soul few yet have heard. His name is Viktor Schauberger.

I said above, not "that we are about to enter". For as to whether we truly enter into that New Millennium, or continue on our present path to an inevitable doom, much will depend upon our willingness to hearken to the voice of Viktor Schauberger. Moreover, as we shall see, his work is profoundly linked with the reforms discussed in this book.

Born towards the end of the last century into the family of an Austrian forester, of a long line of foresters, Schauberger grew up amidst forests which, in the Austria of that time, existed still in a pristine, almost primeval state. Here – as his forefathers had done – he learned to listen, to look, to observe; and possessing also an exceptionally keen mind, he was gradually drawn into a profound relationship with, and understanding of, that marvellous natural world surrounding him – a world virtually lost to us today. For not only is a major part of our natural environment now destroyed, but what remains of it is, as Viktor Schauberger unequivocally shows us, following from our blundering ways, in an advanced state of disease and decay; and no proper understanding of *health* can be gained from studying a *diseased body* – (something that practitioners of natural healing have always well understood).

It is therefore not too much to say that, if we would leave this planet a place still able to support our children, then we must cling to Viktor Schauberger for that very life which we would leave them. That is to say, we must take up his work and – allowing it to develop our own insights – raise our awareness in turn so that we are able truly to "Kapieren und Kopieren", or *comprehend and copy Nature*, as one of his great sayings was.

Before the end of his life, Viktor Schauberger had unlocked the secrets of a technology that was able to function without the heat and violence which characterizes ours – a technology able to supply the human race with limitless energy as virtually no cost; and we shall return to this. But in order to bring home, right at the start, the immediacy of Schauberger's work to each and every one of us, let us begin with what was his over-riding passion and interest all through his life – that whose inner workings he observed in those forests lost to us now, and which also underlay the discoveries of his echotechnology: WATER.

First, it should be emphasised that those who develop the ability to see into the natural world with the eye of a master invariable possess one quality before all others: that is – reverence and humility. To them, there is nought strange in viewing the universe as vibrantly alive. Nothing is inert. Everything vibrates at its own level of existence. For those who doubt – turn to the words of one of today's top physicists, Fritjof Capra, in Part III. Here, then, is a significant and fundamental statement by Viktor Schauberger regarding water:–

"The upholder of the cycles which supports the whole of Life,
is WATER. In every drop of water dwells a Deity, whom we all serve;
there also dwells Life, the soul of the 'First' substance."

(From *Our Senseless Toil*, shortly to be published by Gateway Books.)

Compare this with the chemical formula for water of a mechanistic age: an apparently inert substance, having the properties of H_2O. No wonder there is a gap between our understanding of our situation and Viktor Schauberger's! Here is what Schauberger is trying to show us – nearly half a century ago, and just think of the progress since!) – if I were to attempt to put it in my own words.

> Through our ignorance and misarrangements, we have allowed to become diseased the bloodstream of the Earth – which are its water-courses; and so our own water-courses, which are the blood-streams of our bodies, are diseased in turn.
>
> There is no 'cure' that any laboratory can produce to arrest the scourge of cancer and proliferation of other diseases which we have brought upon ourselves, because they are bred of our entire, so-called 'natural' surroundings, whose *un*naturalness we do not recognize on account of the degradation of our sensibilities (precisely through their diseased state), and also on account of our blinding by false science which Viktor Schauberger found opposing him all his life).
>
> What is involved in a restoration of our health is therefore a restoration, in the first place, of the health of the planet. This cannot be accomplished without a proper reverence for, and understanding of, the true nature and workings of WATER; something that our present practice of hydraulic engineering – *including* the piping of supplies for human consumption – is at variance with, and in profound betrayal of.

Before examining the nature of Water more closely through Schauberger's eyes, it should be emphasised that his pronouncements upon Water, (as upon all else), were fully borne out by his works. Even in his early days as a forester, his log flumes –(channels artificially constructed to transport timber) – became legendary. Following his innovative design for a particularly problematical timber-flotation – (when a whole company of people, *including* professional water engineers, was left gasping who thought they had gathered to see him make a fool of himself) – his help had frequently to be sought for the solution of problems by other water engineers who, to their chagrin, despite (because of?) their university education, were quite unable to emulate his skills. There is a delicious account of the log-flume episode in *Living Water*, by Olaf Alexandersson* – a book which also makes an excellent introduction to Schauberger's work.

Before our closer examination of water – a word about the scope of this work. Here, a debt almost beyond calculation is owed to Callum Coats, an architect who became profoundly interested in Viktor Schauberger and has dedicated twenty years to researching his discoveries, working with Schauberger's son, Walter, during the latter period of Walter's life. It is chiefly Callum Coats who has salvaged Viktor's work for us – (a work spanning the realms of higher physics), presenting it in a masterly succession of volumes,** and he also

---

* *Published by Gateway Books. See also Reading List. We are indebted to Alick Bartholomew of this publishing company, whose interest in Viktor Schauberger was initially so sparked by this Swedish work that he arranged for an English translation of it to be made, and so first brought Schauberger before an English speaking public – although I understand that Men of the Trees, (now The Tree Society International), in earlier decades also published extracts from Schauberger's work in their journal,* ***Trees.***

** ***Living Energies****, by Callum Coats – surely the definitive work on Schauberger for a long period to come, if not for all time – was published in autumn 1996;* ***The Water Wizard****, spring 1998 – the first of a four-part production, by Callum Coats, of Schauberger's own writings. The second,* ***Nature as Teacher****, has just appeared (autumn 98), and the further two are to follow presently. All are similarly published by Gateway Books, with Alick Bartholomew contributing much, on the production side, to Callum Coats's work.*

who has reconstructed for us, as far as was possible, some of Viktor's amazing machines. For – in what may perhaps most simply be described as *the best tradition of the Seven Wise Masters* – some key parts of the designs of these machines were 'highjacked' and lost to us, in the closing somewhat tragic chapter of Schauberger's life.

In speaking of Viktor Schauberger's work, I find difficulty in referring to his "ideas" – as though these were somewhere up in his head. All that he came to see, to understand – and to prove by practical works – was the fruit of a unique and intensive labour in which his whole being was engaged. The forest was his university – that forest in which flowed Water pulsating with a life-force virtually lost to it – and us – today. It was here, in this ancient, living environment, that he spent his time – outside the duties of a forest warden – observing, reflecting, and testing out what he had come to understand. It was here that were developed his insights into the nature of Water, of energy, of trees, and of the living Earth. For he would not follow his brother to university, seeing what it had done to his thinking.

"Despite" having gone to no university but the forest, Schauberger refuted, by his practical work, both the Second Law of Thermodynamics and also the conventional understanding of electrolysis, (both of which are still taught unchanged in our universities today!) Further, the work he did with energy, in the machines that he built, can only be explained by his having converted energy back into an original "4th or 5th dimensional state" – a process that is now beginning to be understood in terms of "layered space".* Whence did Viktor possess this flow of *inner* knowledge that directed all his work? His answer – given in response to some interested questioners when he was busy transforming "stinking sewage solution into clear spring water"** – is a testimony to the appalling degeneracy of our whole culture today.

Having been deeply impressed by the immensity of Schauberger's work – its scope, its insights, and also the brief, arresting 'commentaries' on our economic and political plight which punctuate his work – and realizing also his vital connection with the message of this book – during the early weeks of this summer (1998), I set aside all other work on my own book and devoted my energies instead to a deeper study of Schauberger; reading through for a second time both Living Water and Living Energies, and for the first time *The Water Wizard* (which had just recently come out). This study proved an infinitely rewarding and inspiring task, deepening my appreciation of Schauberger at every page.

Interestingly, too, I emerged from it with a strengthened feeling that Schauberger must have known something of the work of Henry George. Schauberger did meet Rudolf Steiner – (another remarkable Austrian of that time, founder of the Anthroposophical movement and of the Biodynamic movement in agriculture today) – and I have seen a brief reference by Steiner to the work of Henry George. Any discussion between two such figures, in the Austria of that time, must undoubtedly have ranged wide and deep, and have covered the connection between the destruction of agriculture – something so vivid to them both – and the political and economic regimes that agriculture suffered under. However, although having read – and appreciated – a certain amount of Steiner's writings, I cannot say that they suggest a grasp of the message of Henry George in the way that Schauberger's do.

---

* *See ch. "Implosion" in **Living Energies**.*

** *See ch. "Schauberger's Heritage" in **Living Water**.*

It is, then, from the many pages of notes made during that study in the early part of the summer that the following survey has been taken of Schauberger's insights into our present pathway – which he saw had reached such a state of degeneracy that we do not even see the danger we are in.

What does Schauberger see as lying at the root of this degeneracy? He saw that we are a society *cut off from Nature*. Students of the land question know the beginnings of *that*, of course – and I suspect that Schauberger understood it equally well. Losing touch with out life-support systems – now organized for us by people who dwell in cities and work in laboratories – we have naturally lost our understanding of the true nature of those life-support systems, the soil, water, trees, etc., *on which we absolutely depend*; and so, also, our understanding of how to maintain their health. (Once we must have known that, without major tree-cover, there will come a time when there is no water – and "without water – no bread, no bread – no life".) Hence the degenerate state into which these systems, lacking the first-hand care of their users, have inevitably lapsed, is in turn now profoundly affecting ourselves – physically, mentally and spiritually.

A key mechanism of this dangerous and degenerate science, which now controls all of our life-systems, Schauberger saw to be the 'compart-mentality' outlook it fosters – and inflicts upon society.

The real sickness of this 'compart-mentality' outlook is that it inhibits our natural inclination to see things whole – "to see things as they really are"; and its key controlling device is an educational system ruled by what we might well term the Seven Wise Masters – the same who saw to the removal of the people from the land in the first place.

Seeing things whole and "as they really are". ...Familiar territory? We have certainly discovered where this leads in economics! To the Seven Wise Masters it holds always, of course, the danger that we might set ourselves free, and we have seen how simple this becomes in economics – (by collecting the rental value of the land!) What is the particular freedom Viktor Schauberger holds out to us that was so threatening to those "Masters", whom he found himself up against all his life?

As already mentioned, Schauberger had discovered a way whereby man could provide himself with unlimited, non-polluted energy, almost cost-free – a discovery that had grown out of his study of Water; and he answers our question from that point of view himself, most interestingly, as follows:–

> "Far back in history, there is evidence that men who have attempted to solve the riddle of water have been bitterly attacked. Every attempt to explain the nature of water in old books has been demolished in later editions. In any case, maintaining the sense of mystery about water ensures the prosperity of the capital intensive economy, for financial interest thrives only on a defective economy . . . Maintaining the mystery of water, therefore, maintains the value of capital, so every effort to come nearer to an explanation is attacked." (*Living Water*, ch. 3.)

(...And do not tell me that Schauberger did not know very well the foundation on which that "capital intensive economy" and "financial interest" rested.)

The above passage shows us how remarkably deeply and widely read Schauberger became, as a result of his years spent in the forest university. Beyond this explanation that he gives himself, however, regarding the Establishment's fear of his discoveries about Water, I have come to feel – reading at times between the lines of his writing – that Schauberger realized the threat he posed lay beyond even the dismantling of society's economic structure; and that the *Seven Wise Masters* sensed this as well.

Certainly, for myself, it is very clear that the only hope for a *reversal* of the terrible self-destruction in which Schauberger shows us we are all now enmeshed, is for the people themselves to take back, not just their rental values, but the *full governance* of their fields, their hills and their water supplies. That is, economic *and political* decentralization must go hand-in-hand, with no power over land *use* remaining outside of local control, any more than the land rent itself. Schauberger reveals quite enough through his writings to afford us a similar view of affairs as his own. Hence this book may hopefully provide a useful context in which to consider Schauberger's work as *coming alive*.

*

ON SEEING THINGS WHOLE. INDEPENDENCE – THE REAL TEST

While the practical importance to us of Schauberger's insights is very great – they include a fundamental look at the reason for the spread of cancer and for the increasing proliferation of health-destroying bacteria and pathogens today – let us start with that essential matter of *seeing things whole*. In what ways did the ability to do this function so exceptionally in this man?

There could hardly be a better illustration of this than Schauberger's comment about Newton, (who first propounded the Law of Gravity). Instead, said Viktor Schauberger, of asking why the apple fell to the ground, he should have asked how it got up there in the first place!

Our reaction is, of course, to smile at so enjoyably simple an upside-down view of things. But the point is – Viktor proved that this view was, scientifically and practically, the *right way up*! It is the very question we should *all* have been asking ourselves! (And who knows how many of us, at a yet unspoilt age, in a now forgotten moment of childhood, once did indeed look up in wonder and ask ourselves that very thing?)

For Viktor, free to look at things as they really are, in those far-off, unsought forests he roamed, so far from the universities – free to give himself to long periods of observation of the movements of Water, of the movements of trout in Water, of stones and of logs similarly, and of the way those amazing mosses grew . . . out of these long sessions in the forest university, there came to him gradually the discovery of an unsuspected law at work in Nature, a law which is contrary to that of gravity – the *Law of Levitation*.

It was, then, out of his original passion for Water that Schauberger came to discern the operations of this unsuspected law – came to work out how to utilise the *energy of levitation*, and to build his machines which demonstrated it. Now Callum Coats has done a tremendous work for us in re-building a whole array of these machines – despite the great technical difficulties he describes, from their incomplete and sometimes chronologically confusing data, (no doubt due largely to the loss of so much of Schauberger's work in that painful closing chapter of his life already mentioned). These machines, with meticulous diagrams and descriptions, are presented by Callum for our own use and development, in the chapter "Implosion" in *Living Energies*. How much we are indebted to him!

In addition, in an earlier chapter of that book, Callum Coats describes fully – in order that it may never be patented but will remain free for implementation by any and all – a method, set out by Schauberger, whereby practically limitless energy can be gained from the sea. All this, from Schauberger's dedicated study of the nature of Water – whose *inner* character, and hence whose potential, is quite unsuspected by orthodox science today.

Scotland is surrounded by water! How great it would be to have this idea pioneered in our own country, In a new era of economic and political liberty!

In the early 1920's (by a device which he patented in 1930), Viktor had already successfully provided lighting for the house of one of his forest wardens (which was too remote to be connected to the grid), simply by using water according to the laws he had discovered, with no other input of energy; and on a visit to Austria in the 1980's, Callum met a group of Schauberger enthusiasts living around the township of Schladening, who were working on a similar device. (Recounted in *Living Energies*.)

Let me quote at this point a most relevant passage from the second chapter of *Living Energies*:–

> "The pursuit of profit and power for its own sake [by science and politics], coupled with the necessary systems of control, have relegated the mass of humanity to a state of almost total dependency for everything it needs in the way of food, energy, health and all other necessities of life ... Independence . . . is the last thing . . . mega-businesses wish to bestow on humanity, because their ultimate dominance would thereby be lost. Independent people are free people and not answerable to control ... At the forefront of this battle is the control over the systems of energy."

*

THE LAW OF LEVITATION. 'A' AND 'B' TYPE ENERGIES

The Law of Levitation which Viktor Schauberger discovered is something we are in fact perfectly familiar with – but we notice it without noticing, as it were. It is active in those springs of highest quality water which arise high up on hill or mountainside – well above the level where rainfall could account for them. (There is a special chapter on springs in *Living Energies*.) We glimpse it too in the child jumping for joy that jumps higher and higher . . . (and as I write these words, I realize that it must have been that very same power that was operating when William Ogilvie drew me up into his dance!) More generally, it is at work in every living plant – which otherwise, as Schauberger points out, would spread out as a green, amorphous heap on the ground. (Yes – we certainly did miss the real questions about the apple!)

Interestingly Rudolf Steiner, with his similar ability to see into the heart of things – (and who 'diagnosed' BSE in the 1920s – see Part III), observed that the growing plant uses a *spiral* form of movement to ascend. Schauberger points out that this spiral motion is a movement that conforms with planetary motion, which forms a cycloid, spiral space-curve. So this spiral motion – (as opposed to our civilization's preferred form of motion, using straight lines) – this *planet-patterned* motion, is the *original* motion of *life*. Being so, how natural that it should hold the key for us to the law of levitation – not gravity! (I am reminded here how my mother, on occasional trips up to Perth from Edinburgh on the old winding roads that followed more the contours of the land, remarked when the straightened and far speedier A9 was built that the joy of the journey was lost since you arrived before you knew it. A feeling of being let down – gravity in another form as opposed to levitation! But of course business – our dispossessed-from-the-land type of business – requires straight lines and speed at all costs. It is interesting to ponder for a moment the hints in the ancient wisdom teachings about discovering the journey itself to be the goal . . .)

How exactly does this energy of levitation function? We see it at work in its most dramatic form in the tornado. At the centre of the spiralling motion of a tornado there is an *updraught*; and this levitational energy is simultaneously present as a force secretly at play in the free-flowing forest-cooled waters of a healthy mountain stream. It was this same levitational energy that Schauberger saw directed *upwards* the growing tips of the mosses, submerged in the down-rushing mountain stream – in silent witness to the health and vitality of those bubbling, forest-cooled waters; a phenomenon scarcely to be found in our degraded environment now.

It is empowered by this same energy – as well as by the intricate dance of the waters along their aquatic forms – that trout and salmon make their swift darts upstream against the strongly-rushing current, and their tremendous, apparently effortless upward leaps. Asking a professor once – (who had become genuinely interested in his work and was observing this phenomenon with him in the forest) – why it was that the trout always darted *up*stream, to escape even the shadow of a stick, Schauberger could not resist the humorous response to his bewilderment: "Well, Professor, it is because it never had any academic training. Were you in this gushing stream, you would be swept away!" The fascinating movements of the water involved in the upstream dart of the trout are described in detail in ch.11 of *Living Energies*, but it is the levitational energy at the core of the mountain stream which is the essential background against which it all happens. For the energy of healthily-flowing water invariably forms a central vortice that moves downstream in a planetary 'cycloid spiral space-curve' form of motion, and these longitudinal vortices release at their core a *reverse* energy-current of rising and expanding cold, (supremely utilized in the acrobatics of the fish).* This was the energy that Viktor utilized in his machines.

It seems strange to us to envisage an energy of *rising and expanding cold*, when we have been educated to think only in terms of rising and expanding *heat*. Upon this latter we have based all our technology. Yet it is the other form of energy that is primarily at work in the cosmos. "Viewed from space, a high-energy state of risen and expanded cold, we can see that a condition of falling and concentrating heat gradually evolves as we approach the Earth's surface . . ." (*Living Energies*, ch.7.)

So there exists this 'contrary' form of temperature/density relationship, (that is – rising and expanding cold accompanied by falling and concentrating heat, as opposed to rising and expanding heat accompanied by falling and concentrating cold). Remarkably, this 'contrary' form, involving rising and expanding cold, which Callum Coats helpfully designates Type A, has as yet "neither been recognised nor investigated by science, although according to Viktor Schauberger it is the predominant form and the one that makes life possible". (Ibid.**)

Yet – another example of our 'noticing without noticing' – we actually encounter the Type A temperature continuously in the round both of our day and of our year. We are quite familiar with the 'frost pockets' of winter when cold air congregates low down, and this is the pattern of night-time also, during both of which periods the

---

* *"Longitudinal . . . are those vessels which create and enhance the counterflow of levitational energy, the immaterial psyche of a waterway." (**Living Energies**, ch. 13, "They Dynamics of Flow".)*

** *Shortened form of a useful Latin term meaning 'the same' – so here refers again to **Living Energies**, ch. 7.*

warmer air rises and expands: Type B temperature. In reversal of this, Type A temperature operates by day and in summertime – when we are again familiar with how heat falls and concentrates in the valleys while the cold air rises and expands. This last, Type A, is the type we have ignored – but considering it is the one that accompanies the *growing* hours and seasons of our year, we should surely have been giving it our special attention!

It is important to observe that *both* types of temperature – Type A and Type B – are necessary for the maintenance of life on earth, since life on earth is sustained by a balancing of opposites, as Viktor Schauberger points out – but he stresses that it is the life-enhancing one of any pair of opposites that must predominate, if life is to prevail.

It is worth having paused a moment to consider these two different types of temperature, for it is not only the way that we power our machines that it at stake here, but the way that we power ourselves. Viktor Schauberger's discoveries about water led him to develop a new kind of energy – but, as he points out, that water in the first place powers *us*. Water is the 'blood of the earth', and our blood is up to 90% composed of water – plants have a rough equivalent). So it may truly be said – "sap, blood and water are synonymous". (*Living Energies*, ch. 8.)

In the Introduction to Living Water, Olaf Alexandersson points out that "Viktor Schauberger's central theme was 'Prevailing technology uses the wrong forms of motion'." But we have so degraded our water (in ways we shall come to see) that *it* now moves with the wrong forms of motion too. Consider in this light Viktor Schauberger's further words: "Our machines and processes channel such agents as air, water and other liquids and gases into the type of motion which Nature uses only to decompose and dissolve matter. Nature uses another form of motion for rebuilding. When our technology only uses the decomposing motion, it becomes a dead technology, a destructive one, dangerously affecting all of Nature".

Such – by our 'seeding into it' wrong forms of motion – have we made of our water: a carrier now of "decomposing" forces, "dangerously affecting all of Nature" indeed, and – with our boasted modern water-supply technology boosting that very process – our own bodies right in the front line.

In reviewing this whole matter of our water's degradation, we come to find that, besides the way we have destroyed its health through our direct mismanagements of its motion – (by altering of natural water courses, by hydro-electric works, and by the way we pipe our supplies, all of which we shall come to) – there is something else we have done which, acting in an *in*direct way and in the very first place, has made ruin of our water's health.

What is at the heart of this "decomposing motion" Schauberger speaks of with regard to our technology? It is, of course, the A type energy we have gone for – a technology based on rising and expanding heat. This kind of energy – being *ex*plosive (therefore inherently violent) – moves of course with *centrifugal* force, (outward from the centre). This is in direct contrast to the *im*plosive energies of Viktor's machines, *and also* to the energies of those longitudinal river vortices, whose cycloid spiral space-curve motion is inward-turning (*centripetal**), manifesting the Type A energy: essentially non-violent and upward-building – in short, the motion of *life*.

Our technology manifests, (as we had already observed), the Type B energy of rising and expanding heat, as opposed to the Type A energy of rising and expanding cold. But we stumble upon something very particular here, with regard to Water – something bound up with that 'rising and expanding cold' of the life-enhancing Type A energy.

Because in our crassness we have never bothered to explore the true character of Water, but have considered it simply in terms of an inert chemical formula – H_2O, there

---

* See following page for this footnote.

is something important that we have failed to note. Down the core of these forest-shaded mountain streams that Schauberger observed, the centripetally-turning longitudinal vortices nurturing the levitational energies carried the *coldest* water of the flow. This was the inner secret of their high energy content; and it is this question of the *temperature of water*, even in its minutest variations – a factor totally ignored by water engineers to this day, as also by our physicians – that is profoundly bound up with the question of its – and of our – health.

At this point we should note that the natural flow of a river produces transverse vortices as well as longitudinal ones – (indeed, a large part of the enjoyment of watching water flow is precisely seeing the interplay of the oppositional ripples created by these vortices, as they move in different directions on the surface). Viktor Schauberger discovered also . . . (what did he not discover about Water?) . . . that the vital part played by these transverse vortices was to allow a river to *control its own energies from within*, the transverse vortices forming a natural break to the flow in its descent, preventing the river from running amok – the whole healthful and joyous play dependent upon the interactions of the *minute variations in temperature* of the water's different 'layers'.

However, the transverse vortices carry *water of warmer temperature*, the longitudinal ones, as we have seen, transporting always the coldest flow. Now, while the overall pattern of these opposing vortices, so long as held within *Nature's* balance, is a life-enhancing one – (the necessary one of the pair always uppermost where *life* and *health* are her aim) – this fortunate situation does not necessarily continue to prevail under clumsy human interference with her patternings. And so we come to the following passage in *Living Energies*, in the chapter "The Dynamics of Flow"–

> "Since longitudinal vortices are associated with natural, self-cooling flows, the energies they release are cold-sourced, through processes Viktor called 'cold fermentation' and their effect is therefore beneficial ... With transverse vortices however, and vertically aligned transverse vortices in particular which form because the water has become over-warmed by over-exposure to the Sun, or through unnatural regulation, the energies emitted are *heat-sourced* and debilitating ... Here we are concerned with warm fermentation, which gives rise to the propagation of pathogenic bacteria."

So – now we see what we have done by *cutting down the trees* – destroying our forests. For the devastation of the forests has not only triggered climate-change (on a scale we have yet to discover through Schauberger), it has also involved *devastation of our health* – by a chain of events that had never occurred to us, caught up with or chain-saws as we were, rather than with Nature. In short – (without going into the precise meaning of cold and warm 'fermentation') – we see, from the contrasted terms 'cold-sourced' and 'heat-sourced', that what we have done is allow our vital waterways to become contaminated with that same Type B energy of *rising and expanding heat* that is utilized by our degenerate form of technology. As this form of energy is the one we saw Nature uses "only to decompose matter", do we then wonder that the earth's blood-stream – which is in turn *our* blood-stream, should begin to proliferate "pathogenic bacteria"?

---

* *While 'centrifugal' is self-explantory (from our word 'fugitive'), 'centripetal seems more difficult – until we remember our verb 'to petition', meaning 'to seek . And so – 'seeking the centre'. (Both from the Latin.)*

At this point there comes to mind a particularly lovely passage by Callum Coats in *Living Energies*, in the chapter "The Nature of Water". It begins, "Conceived in the cool dark cradle of the virgin forest", and there is an image of almost heartbreaking happiness in the description that follows, of the as yet undespoiled energies of the bubbling, descending mountain stream. By just such a stream Viktor Schauberger must often have sat, as he learned from it how to let his mind 'travel where the eye cannot reach', and so – how to read the secrets of Water. (This technique Viktor describes to us in his own words – see *Living Energies*, ch. 1 – a technique it is open to any of us to follow who is able.)

Doubtless, it was through this technique that Schauberger came to discern, in Water, its higher energy forms (allied with those 4th and 5th dimensional states already mentioned, with which science is only just beginning now to catch up) – energy forms to which he gave the name 'ethericities'. These 'ethericities', which are released into the environment as certain points in a river's flow, act upon that environment as 'up-building' and 'life-enhancing' energies of a high order. But where the health of Water has been despoiled, the opposite occurs, and these higher energies are in turn rendered dangerously detrimental to all higher life-forms of that environment.

We should pause a moment on this aspect of Schauberger's work – for may it not perhaps have some bearing upon the question of the lethal, food-infecting bacteria E Coli 0157, of which Scotland is at present experiencing a "worrying increase"?

Consider that our tree-divested environment now nurtures rivers whose over-warmed waters "give rise to the propagation of pathogenic bacteria". Consider that these bacteria must infect the surrounding environment – and consider that cattle and sheep frequently graze by waterways and that infections travel easily. Is it possible that among these bacteria might be the deadly form of E Coli: 0157?

Yet another factor is involved. These higher ethericities we have just spoken of, acting upon *diseased* Water, broadcast "lethal horizontally propagated radiation . . . harmful to the surroundings, functioning in a manner similar to Wilhelm Reich's 'deadly orgone radiation' (DOR), whose insidious effect is to *upset the metabolism of all organic life*". (*Living Energies*, ch. "The Dynamics of Flow". Emphasis added.)* So it is clear that from our degraded rivers we are now seeding into our environment detrimental forces of an ever more dangerous kind. For *higher* forms of energy (such as these ethericities) carry a correspondingly higher potency – either *for* life or *against* it.

Even were the E Coli bacteria not to be directly involved, then, the health of these animals and their stamina to withstand infection is something we are engaged in severely depleting. But – "research by government scientists shows that just over 15% of cows and 2% of sheep sent for slaughter are infected with E Coli 0157". (*Scotland on Sunday*, 23 Aug. 98.) Whatever, then, may be the findings re the hygiene in butchers' shops, it seems that these animals were *already* infected from the environments they inhabited and grazed, before ever they reached the butchers'.

The "chairman of the Chartered Institute of Environmental Health Officers' food committee accused butchers of playing 'Russian roulette' with the health of the public".

---

* *This contrasts with the release into the environment at certain points, from a healthy river's flow, of its "up-building or immaterial energies or ethericities . . . which, as a form of energy, are akin to the life-endowing, animalistic 'orgone' energies of Wilhelm Reich". (Ibid.)*

(Ibid.) Butchers are clearly a very useful scapegoat. The problem of E Coli with its deadly form 0157 cannot, however, be considered divorced from the *whole* sphere of the politics that have governed the management of our waterways, our agriculture and our forestry – in short, the *entire catastrophic mismanagement* that we have condoned, of our environment. This directs our attention back to where Schauberger was always directing it, the false science that we have allowed to rule us – false in its very foundations. That is: this attempt to solve the problem of E Coli 0157 in isolation from these other spheres of our damage, is simply a most damning example of that carefully-cultivated-and-educated-into-us (by the *Seven Wise Masters*) '*compart-mentality*' which Schauberger so repeatedly denounced: the inability to see things 'whole' and 'as they really are'.

Nor is it only in the physical sphere that enormous danger now confronts us. These higher etheric forms that Viktor Schauberger discerned in Water – its ethericities, allied with 4th and 5th dimensional states – he discerned also as playing a primary role in the up-building of the *mental and spiritual attributes of a people*; and he repeatedly warned that only widespread degeneracy can follow from the degrading of these higher energies. As we look around our crumbling society and its crumbling values, with its escalating drugs, crime and abuse of every kind – his words add light to the scene. He urged that we think "an octave higher", which means of course that we *care* an octave higher. And we see now that we must do this – for our very life's sake.

This means: a fully practical caring for these higher energies where they exist in our environment right at the beginning – *in Water*. For – "the upholder of the cycles which supports the whole of life, is WATER". And we understand better now Schauberger's view of Water as holding for us "the Soul of the 'First' substance" – for he describes it as the *ur-source** of what we call *consciousness*. How can we have a healthy society in any sense of the word, unless we have *health-filled, sparkling, life-enhancing* WATER?

*

THE HYDROLOGICAL CYCLE

Before examining more closely the ruin we have made of our piped supplies – (and how this may be righted) – we must stand back a moment for a wider look at the water cycle of the Earth in its completeness. For while we can certainly do a great deal to right our piped supplies, yet, without the ultimate righting of the whole Water cycle, we shall never have the water to drink that we should have – either ourselves or the Earth. This wider look involved once again the vital question of temperature, Viktor Schauberger's discoveries about which lie at the heart of his understanding of Water. For this question of temperature affects not only the health of Water; it affects also the way that it is able to more in fulfilling, *or otherwise*, the Earth's needs – which are our needs in turn: that is, the question of the *Full Hydrological Cycle*.

We live on this Earth today blissfully unaware – (such is the competence of our "science") – that we are drastically losing Water, both below ground and above – unaware that the Earth is gradually dying of thirst, as Viktor points out. Hence –

---

* *"Ur" is, briefly, an older and more emphatic term for original. (German.) Callum Coats has a full and interesting footnote on it, in* ***Living Energies****, ch.1.*

millions on earth are now dying of thirst too, as both they and their crops suffer horrendous drought; whilst torrential rains and floods – the reverse side of this bad coin – destroy the lives of other millions in turn.*

It is vital we understand how all this is happening, and Viktor Schauberger's work carries the examination to new depths.

For the Earth's water-supply to be maintained, the rain falling from the clouds must be able to penetrate the Earth deeply enough to replenish the groundwater table in the Earth's interior. These groundwater basins hold the water reserves for us all, and their level is now sinking dangerously. For, as Viktor Schauberger came to see, water can only infiltrate deep into the earth under a *positive* temperature gradient – that is, when the Earth is cooler than the falling rain. It is easy to remember which way round this is, for as Callum Coats says:–

> "We have all seen how cold water sizzles and skitters rapidly sideways when it falls on a hot-plate. A hot, dry ground-surface produces the same effects, making it impossible for the rainwater to infiltrate and in many hot countries,

---

* *News of the vast areas under flood in China (Aug. 98) raises its own train of thought. China – the land which inspired F.H. King's classic* ***Farmers of Forty Centuries****. China – where dwelt a people who, over that long span of time, had so ably preserved their soil's fertility – the loss of which brought the collapse of various other civilizations during that same period; a loss preceded always by the destruction of the indigenous peasants, who are, in every civilization, uniquely the guardians of its soil. Alas, it has not taken China long, following the adoption of "advanced" Western technology, to set herself on that same ruinous pathway, with its inevitable tragedies. Alas for the destruction of the ways of that ancient Chinese peasantry, whose understanding of the ways of the soil was so far superior! Strategies against flooding must have been woven into their practices.*

The disastrous floods of Bangladesh (Sept. 98) seem to be of a slightly different order – a scream for the organization of human society along bioregional lines:–

> *"Many Bangladeshis are blaming the Indians. Barrages and dams build by India enable the Indians to control the flow of water not only in the lean period but also in the monsoons. The lower reaches which make up Bangladesh thus remain at the mercy of the upper reaches in India.*
>
> *During the last lean period, India did not give Bangladesh enough water, even though it had signed a 30-year water-sharing treaty. Sudden rains in some parts of India caused a quick rise in water in the Padma. India opened the gates of the Farraka and other barrages and swelled the Ganges to save itself from flooding. This water then flowed down into Bangladesh which simply cannot take such a volume. A total of 57 rivers originate outside Bangladesh. A back flow tide from the Bay of Bengal, coinciding with the rivers peaking, creates the ultimate horrifying turn, as has happened this year . . .*
>
> *Relief agencies simply do not know how to* confront *such a vast, ongoing disaster ..." (Article in* ***Scotland on Sunday****, 13 Sept. 98.)*

No – but the peasant peoples of the world would, given that political boundaries were exchanged for bioregional ones. There is plenty more reading in Dr. Vandana Shiva's ***The Violence of the Green Revolution*** *showing the disaster of water management when conducted by centralized officialdom, and not by the peasants at ground level themselves. However, back of all this lies the usual forest devastation, in countries lying far above Bangladesh. (See The Water Wizard, footnote p. 157.) Another scream for bioregionalism."*

denuded of vegetation, dry valleys and creeks are suddenly engulfed by a wall of water as terrifying flash-floods sweep away everything in their path." (Living Energies, ch. "The Hydrological Cycle".)

For the water cycle to fulfil itself – (the Full Hydrological Cycle) – the *Earth must be cooler than the falling rain.* It is in this quite special way too, then, that trees are the supreme guardians of Earth's water supplies. By cooling the ground, they keep the temperature gradient *positive*, so allowing the falling rain to infiltrate deep into the Earth to reach and replenish the groundwater table; while in turn, by transpiring moisture through their leaves, they help to maintain in a stable condition the Earth's atmosphere.

"Once the forest has been removed, the exposed ground heats up rapidly, all the more so if dry, and to much higher temperatures. A *negative* temperature gradient now prevails because the ground temperature in general is hotter than the incident rain."

With no groundwater recharge, the groundwater table sinks until, in Callum's vivid words:–

"(it) is virtually lost forever, vanished into the bowels of the Earth from whence it originally came . . . Although all the evidence is there in the way of deserts, it seems that mankind has never learned that to take away the trees is to take away the water." (Ibid.)

We have now lost the Full Hydrological Cycle and are into the Half one. Furthermore: where, under a *negative* temperature gradient, water cannot infiltrate the ground as it should, but spreads *over* the ground instead, what should have gone deep into the earth now rises up quickly again in evaporation. Thus the atmosphere soon becomes overloaded with water vapour, and in this way the process takes on a horrifying repetition – as the vapour descents again as rain and flood gives rise to flood. Alternatively, the water vapour may be transported to other parts, leaving in its wake a dried-out earth and drought. The only solution against both drought and flood is to restore the Earth's forest-cover – and here we may take a lesson right at home:–

"Heavy rain caused a massive landslide blocking one of the main roads to the Kintyre peninsula. Hundreds of tons of rubble were brought down by the bad weather on Sunday night onto the A83 . . ." (Dundee Courier, 21 July, 98.)*

By the "bad weather"? Time we rid ourselves of that accursed *compart-mentality!*

The year 1998 has been a year whose widespread extremes of weather right across the world have raised a new awareness that we have entered some kind of a climate-shift. General opinion still appears to back the worn-out old race-horse of global warming, but it seems that a rather different scenario in fact awaits our recognition. For the sinking of the groundwater table – reducing the vital Full Hydrological Cycle to a Half one (now almost world-wide) – is only a part of the picture: "not only is water lost in the depths, but it also begins to be lost at great heights". As Callum Coats explains, Viktor Schauberger discerned the process whereby the water vapour of the *Half* Hydrological Cycle is pushed to higher than normal altitudes, where conditions act to separate the oxygen from the hydrogen in the water-molecule. The lighter hydrogen then rises into the higher stratosphere, while the

* *There was a similar incident on 29 Oct. 98, causing considerable train delays – (as I well know, since I was caught up in them!)*

oxygen sinks. Thus the Earth suffers an on-going "leakage" of water upwards, from her ecology, as well as downwards.

Further, as it is the water-vapour in the atmosphere that helps to keep the Earth warm, so:–

> "In the long-term all of these effects act to reduce the general ambient temperatures and the presence of atmospheric water, and while initially the temperature in parts of the Earth will rise, in the end it will inevitably cool off dramatically as the precursor to a new ice-age." (Living energies, ch. "The Earth's Atmospheric Envelope".

As Callum Coats goes on to point out, all this was seen by Viktor Schauberger as long ago as 1933 – long before the idea of global warming was around, or of a new ice-age as some are now speaking of – and he described it in detail in his book, *Our Senseless Toil – the Source of the World Crisis.**

We are not likely to hear, of course, of global *cooling* from our politicians. What on earth have *they* to offer us in that alarming scenaria? Nor are the *Seven Wise Masters* likely to occupy themselves with the workings of the *hydrological* cycle – they have far other cycles in mind! How rightly Callum Coats emphasises that, if the Full Hydrological Cycle is to be restored, the difference between the Full and the Half Cycle is something that the public at large must grasp and make themselves fully familiar with.

Moreover, this is a matter of the first priority, for while it takes a long span of time for the earth to emerge from an ice-age, the entering upon one is a far abrupter affair. Indeed, scientists have discovered from the study of pollens that the final stage may take no longer than twenty years – and some say that we are already well on the way towards that last stride. So this is a matter that affects us both intimately and critically – if not our very selves, then very possibly the children we have brought into this world, and for whom we wished to leave a bright future.

This grasping of the matter of the Earth's Hydrological Cycle, and what it means for Earth's children, is something that awaits urgently a people set free from economic slavery through radical land reform, and at the same time bound together by those 'bonds of freedom' epitomized in the bioregional concept. For a restructuring of society on the bioregional principle will at last bind us as we would be bound – through a common love for our Earthly Mother, and in ways that will allow us full expression for that love – full freedom to act upon it. But if the Earth needs the restoration of the Full Hydrological Cycle, we, her children, need it yet more. For the Earth will survive her ice-age. For us, the choice is a more drastic one.

*

ICE-AGE ... SOIL RE-MINERALIZATION

There is a further feature of the Hydrological Cycle – and an important one:–

> ". . . under a half hydrological cycle the nutrients present in the upper zones of the groundwater table, which are normally raised up by the trees to a level accessible to other lesser plants, are left below and sink with the sinking groundwater. It subsides to levels far beyond the reach of even deep-rooted trees, taking all soil moisture and trace-elements down with it." (*Living Energies*, ch. "The Hydrological Cycle".)

---

* *Currently being prepared by Callum Coats for publication, similarly by Gateway Books.*

It is only tree-roots that reach deep enough into the earth to tap these nutrients – which, with the generous scattering of their leaves at leaf-fall are re-cycled on, further nourishing the Earth – and ourselves in turn.

No wonder, then, that Viktor Schauberger tells us the Earth is not only dying of thirst, it is dying of slow starvation too. Not to mention that we then force-feed her with massive amounts of falsely-devised, man-concocted 'fertilizers' – with the addition of barrages of pesticides against the pests with which our false ways full suitably reward us. Thus we destroy Earth's riches and her energies – upon which all living things depend.

Does Schauberger's point about the depletion of minerals from the Earth's food supply have a familiar ring? Small wonder that today we are besieged by a market offering us mineral supplements of every kind! The loss of the Full Hydrological Cycle has repercussions on our lives that go far and deep . . .

> "The farmer of today treats Mother Earth in a worse manner than a whore. Moreover, he prays to a god, whom he believes is up above but in reality is under his feet. . He strips yearly the skin of the earth and applies poison as artificial manure . . . Infested water and poisoned nutrients cannot produce healthy blood . . ." (*Living Water*, ch. 9.)

In speaking of "poisoned nutrients", Viktor Schauberger was not even talking about pesticides – just our artificial fetilizers, (the pesticide market not yet being in full swing at that time). What *would* he say of today's scene?

The demineralization of the Earth's soil became the focal concern of another of this century's pioneers – one, John Hamaker, an American, an engineer and agriculturist, who passed away only in 1994, and whose work is also mentioned by Callum Coats. John Hamaker – whose book, *The Survival of Civilization*, written in collaboration with Don Weaver, was published about twenty years ago – arrived independently at the same conclusion as Viktor Schauberger: that what we face is not global warming (which is only, he realized like Schauberger, an interim phenomenon), but in fact an impending ice-age. With his background in engineering, he reached his conclusions from another direction: from pondering the huge excess of carbon gas in our atmosphere, resulting from our fossil-fuel-based industry – (producing Schauberger's B Type energy, of course) – and from our desecration of the vital tree-cover of the earth. (In a marvellous interweaving of their life with man's, trees breathe *out* the oxygen that we need, and breathe *in* the carbon we exhale.)

Hamaker saw that the earth is now burdened by a huge surplus of carbon gas in her atmosphere – and at the same time drastic demineralization of her precious soils through man's depletion of her tree-cover, (whose fallen leaves feed back their nutrients into the soil). He held the view that, in such a situation, the Earth will fall back on her own ways of safe-guarding her life-processes – whist in addition checking man's foolish ways; and he saw that her process of ridding herself of this surplus carbon, while starting with volatile weather patterns, *must* ultimately bring upon us Earth's free-fall into cold – i.e., *glaciation*.

Hamaker saw, however, that the purpose of the ice-age was not merely negative – not merely an end result – but that it was the start of something new. He saw it as the start of Earth's process of *self-remineralization*. For, as the glaciers begin to melt and move – (when an ice-age has run its roughly 10,000-year course) – they grind up the rocks in their path, allowing Earth's top-soil, thus, a rich replenishment of minerals. This is the *loess dust*, which then blows about the denuded world. We are now living off the last remnants of the fertility bequeathed to us by the last ice-age. For the top-soil of the planet – then enriched for us (re-mineralized) to a depth of $7^1/_2$ feet – is now down to its frightening last few inches . . . which we are busy mistreating as though there were no tomorrow indeed.*

Is it any wonder that the health of both people and planet is cracking up? "What we are experiencing today is no crisis. it is the dying of the Whole." (Viktor Schauberger – and that was already several decades ago.) **

The work of John Hamaker has born fine fruitage in the growth of a world-wide movement for soil remineralization,***a movement which has now won the interest even of America's department of agriculture. This – on account of the quite phenomenal effect on plant life, both as to quality and size, when it is grown in remineralized soils – (and those who have used rock dust, of whom I am one, can certainly vouch for this). John saw a major remineralization or Earth's soils as the only hope of arresting an otherwise inevitable ice-age. (A new edition of his book is to be published soon.****)

It is always of especial interest when a pioneering train of thought is found arising in two individuals, quite independently of one another. Here it points to the same phenomenon as we have already observed in the sphere of land reform – namely, the discernment of the working of a natural law.

A natural law is not like a human law – something we can alter as we please. When I think of a natural law, it always conjures up that image portrayed in the Bible (Luke, ch. 20): "Whosoever shall fall upon that stone shall be broken; but on whomsoever it shall fall, it will grind him to powder" – (imagery of a certain aptness, it must be said, in reviewing the rock dust scene!)

Not all, of course, are enlightened enough to see it that way! I remember in the early 80s, when the first papers connected with John Hamaker's work were circulating around the globe, that there was an account, in one, of a top-class political conference held somewhere in America where journalists were told: "Now, you make it global warming! We don't want to hear any word about an ice-age. Mind – no word of any ice-age in your reports!"

But of that same stone we are told: "The stone which the builders rejected, the same is become the head of the corner."

We had better watch out!

---

* *I am indebted for some of the above information to the article,* ***Soil Remineralization & Its Feasible Role in Stabilising the Climate Shift****, by Cameron Thomson, the* ***Conclusion*** *from which, with its brilliant analogy of "Gaia's fertility cycles", will be found in Part III. Cameron and Moira Thomson run the SEER (Sustainable Ecological Earth Remineralization) Centre in Scotland, which is open annually to the public and very much worth visiting. For further information, see under that item.*

** *In view of the avalanche tragedies of winter 98-99, Viktor warns in his writings – (with explanation as to why: basically our devastation of the Water cycle) – of* ***increasing*** *avalanches, also where never experienced before.*

*** ***Remineralize the Earth*** *is published roughly three times a year. Editor: Joanna Campe, 152 South Street, Northampton, MA 01060-4021, USA.*

**** *Hamaker-Weaver Publishers, P.O. Box 1961, Burlingame, CA 94010, USA.*

---

*

WATER CYCLE – KEY TO EARTH'S NATURAL RE-MINERALIZATION

It was Viktor Schauberger's particular genius that he discerned not only the workings of Earth's Hydrological Cycle, but – (as we have seen) – that a full remineralizaton cycle was included as an *inbuilt part of it.* Indeed, where the Full Hydrological Cycle is reduced to a Half one, Schauberger precisely describes the drastic loss of nutrients accompanying it as a *biological short-circuit.* (As we may call it – the Half Hydrological Cycle's other face.)

We can see now that the powerful up-drawing, by trees, of the Earth's mineral nutrients, under the Full Hydrological Cycle, is a clear part of Earth's own chosen way of maintaining her fertility. For soils that are rich in a full range of nutrients are an essential, for maintenance of more highly evolved life-forms. It is a commonplace with us that trees replenish the soil with mineral nutrients, obtained from deep below-ground, via the autumn bounty of their fallen leaves – (providing good humus, or vegetable-matter, at the same time). The hitherto unrecognized feature of this process that Schauberger has brought to light for us, is that *access to* these mineral nutrients, by the trees' roots, is entirely dependent upon the healthy (i.e., *continuously replenished*) state of the Earth's groundwater table. Should that sink – with it go the minerals also. In short, Schauberger's achievement here was to crack the more secret code of Earth's natural self-remineralizing process – ie., *the essential pre-condition of it*, which is the *Full Hydrological Cycle* of the Earth.

With this urgent message from two of Earth's children, who both devoted great passion and energies to trying to awaken us to our grim plight, the least we can do, for their sakes as well as our own, is to LISTEN, and then – bringing all our forces to bear, for our children's sake if not for ours – to forge our way forward, faithful to life, not death. Then Earth might never need to draw that cold mantle round her shoulders again . . .

*

WATER SUPPLY

Our look at the Hydrological Cycle provides a useful introduction to the question of our water supplies.

Consider that: if Water is intended, in its earthly visitations, to make the journey of the Full Hydrological Cycle, then, if we deprive it of this, reducing its journey to a Half one, shall we not in turn suffer for this? – not only because of our minerally depleted soils (from that "biological short-circuit") but from minerally depleted water too? Water falling from the skies needs to make its full hydrological cycle, in order fully to restore its character and energies again. It has need of a return to that "cool dark cradle" far beneath the forest floor, in the deep womb of the Earth, there to be allowed to develop in its own time. Just as someone deprived of sleep and food cannot give of their best – so, how should we expect Water to either? Just as we need our hours of sleep at night to refresh us, does not Water need its time of rest as well? But we send it under the cruel yoke of the Half Hydrological Cycle, robbing it of its repose as well as of its nutrients.

Depriving Water of its full re-vivifying cycle, how badly we treat – how badly we *cheat* – ourselves! For there is water . . . and water. There is Water of such a quality that, if one kilogram of it is drunk, it will add only 800 grams to a person's bodyweight.

What has happened to the missing 200 grams? They were converted straight into energy! Such energy is not simply the energy of life – it is the energy of *health* – that is, of life as it should be. In our increasingly disease-ridden society, how much we are in need of such energy – *such Water* – today!

It is hardly surprising that this was the only water which Viktor Schauberger considered fit to drink. No need to ask any real countryman where such water is to be found. We have already mentioned it – those springs, (true springs as opposed to seepage ones), which come from deep down in the earth and contain *levitational energies*. Cut off from those levitational energies, is it any wonder that many people feel so generally "pulled down" today?

What is the secret of those levitational energies – which cannot lie surely just in the trace elements and minerals collected from the Full Hydrological Cycle? Indeed, no! We are linked back here with the question of how Water in its natural state moves – linked back to those forest-shaded mountain streams emerging from deep under the earth, whose central core, carrying the coldest water of the flow, moves (with its levitational energies) in *unity with the "dance of the spheres"* – (those centripetally-turning longitudinal vortices).

But – how do we know that that same dance of the "centripetally-turning longitudinal vortices" describes the form in which water chooses to travel, not just laterally in rivers, but also *upwards*, to the surface of the Earth? In his chapter "The Formation of Springs" in *Living Energies*, Callum Coats points out that we can see this from looking at glaciers, "where meltwater plunges down crevasses in the ice". It does not fall in straight lines, but *dances* down, and in the "twisting, convoluted shapes" made by the falling water, we find evidence of "the way in which water likes to move naturally". As Callum continues, if we then see these crevasses as upside-down, we "get some idea of the shape of the shafts in which spring water comes to the surface".

So the high energy of Water, so necessary for our health, is dependent upon its preferred form of *dance* – (the free dance of the mountain-stream); and as this dance is one of a cosmic nature, the linking with it of high energy cannot be a surprise. The point is that we *destroy* the energy we would drink of, when we thoughtlessly entrap Water in the kinds of pipes we use to supply us today.

There is something else special about water that rises to the surface of the Earth in the form of springs, from deep below ground. Schauberger describes how it is forced upwards by complex movements of waters of differing temperature/density relationship in the ground-table below; and how, then, it is transported upwards, too, by its (temperature-and-motion related) levitational energies. But there is something else. The upward-rising spiral of Water is now richly endowed with the minerals and trace elements of its full biological (Hydrological) Cycle; and Schauberger coined a special term, translated into English as 'carbones', to signify this whole range of Earth's elements – everything, that is, except Oxygen and Hydrogen. These 'carbones' he speaks of as having a *feminine* nature, in contrast with the *masculine* nature of oxygen.* The uprising spring-water is therefore carbone-rich (from all the minerals and trace-elements gathered on its

* *". . . in Victor Schauberger's view the Earth is a female entity and . . . all the energies and elements she secretes within her body, principally the carbones, are also of feminite nature. The Sun and Oxygen on the other hand are male and fertilising."* **(L.E.,** *Ch. 10.) "Hydrogen, however, is in a category of its own, for Viktor viewed it as the carrier substance of both oxygen and carbone . . . If we look at the world from space this concept is quite factual, because we can see that our planet, composed as it is of carbones and fertilized by oxygen, is floating in the carrier ocean of the hydrogen that fills all space."* **(L.E.,** *Ch.5.)*

sojourn deep below ground) – but it is also "virtually totally deficient in oxygen", (having lost the dissolved oxygen it was carrying on its downward journey, to tree-roots and other organisms, on the way down.). The uprising of spring-water is therefore further energised by the hunger of the female carbones for the male (or "fertilising") oxygen waiting above-ground, the higher energy forms (ethericities) in the Water playing their part in this. Hence why spring-water should not be drunk straight at its mouth, before its own overriding hunger for oxygen has been saturated – since otherwise the carbones will attack the human lungs in their oxygen-hunger, bringing on the excruciating pains of what has been called 'galloping consumption'. However, it requires only about ten yards from its source for the carbone-oxygen balance to be fully restored. (This phenomenon of the attraction of the carbones and oxygen for one another is the *real* reason why fish brought up out of the sea, from great ocean depths, burst open, poor creatures! This is just another of the fascinating things one learns from Schauberger's work.)

There is another feature of Water concerned with *temperature*, involved in the matter of its quality – and a most significant one in view of drinking water supplies. We have already seen how it is the coldest water in a natural flow that carries the highest energy, this matter – of energy and of cold – being linked with its form of motion. But what is the precise temperature at which the energies of Water – (those *levitational* energies) – are at their highest?

Unlike any other liquid, Water is at its densest at +4°C. (Hence why ice floats: ice is water in a less dense state than the cold waters surrounding it.)* Water that is at its *densest* – (and at +4°C it is virtually incompressible) – is water also in its *highest energy* state. Because Water is unique as a liquid in being densest at *above* freezing, so this +4°C temperature of Water, registering its highest density, is called the 'anomaly point' of Water – ('anomaly' meaning – an exception to the law). What a marvellous thing for us it is that Water is not like other liquids, at their densest when frozen – or it would not be possible for us to drink it in its highest energy state! Students of science will know all about the anomaly point of Water – but it is only Viktor Schauberger who brings to our attention the fact with such bearing on our health, namely, that Water at this temperature is also at its *highest energetic*. This is a matter very much bound up with the conveyance of our piped water supplies.

It is not simply a question, however, of putting water, (even good quality water), into the fridge and drinking it at that temperature. For as we have seen, Water's energies are bound up also with the question of its *flow*. In Schauberger's eyes – (and we can hardly afford to ignore his views!) – Water is a living, moving being, and unless we accord it our full respect as such, cannot bestow on us its full gifts. Callum Coats has a most interesting section of the storage of Water, in his chapter in *Living Energies*, "Drinking Water Supply". From it we discover the far superior understanding of Water possessed by the ancient Egyptians and Greeks, as evidenced in their Water storage techniques.

Finally, in our look at the movement of Water, we come again upon the terms *positive* and *negative temperature gradients* – (which we have already met earlier

---

* *Hence also the, reaching far back in Viktor's family, to float logs by night – and especially by tradition moonlight. Not being conversant with the question of the Water's density, they described it well in their own way – that Water, when the sun is out, grows "lazy", and "curls up and sleeps", (In that state of more risen temperature, it is of course, as Viktor has shown us, less dense.)*

regarding rainfall: positive when it meets a cooler Earth, negative when it meets warmer terrain). These terms have a further, and useful, role in describing for us the *internal* state of Water, as it moves. Here it is perhaps easy to guess that, in describing the state of Water's actual flow, the *positive* (beneficial) temperature gradient operates where the temperature of Water, moving in unimpeded longitudinal vortices, is consistently approaching that densest, highest energetic point of +4°C; while the *negative* one operates where the temperature of Water is moving *away* from that +4°C 'anomaly point' – whether upwards or downwards.*

So now we have further insight into what is involved in the piping of our water supplies. We see what a vital matter for our health is not only the temperature of Water at any given point, but the *ruling temperature gradient* (positive or negative) *under which it moves*. For, Water moving in a wholly unvarying environment – as in our water-pipes – if it is not moving under a positive temperature gradient (the healthful type), but instead under a negative one, will not only be in a poor state but will be *continually deteriorating in quality as it moves*. So – Water's health-nurturing energies (which flourish in the naturally-moving forest-cooled river) will have no chance to operate upon water so conveyed. We shall return to this matter of the pipes in which our water is channelled – and to Viktor Schauberger's very different ideas for these.

*

DIFFERENT QUALITIES OF WATER

We have come to understand, through Schauberger, some of the secrets of spring-water. I know people –(and small wonder) – who make what may almost be described as a pilgrimage to drink from these sources, such is the re-vivifying power of the Water, such its sheer deliciousness. The term 'dynagens' seems fitted indeed to describe those immaterial forces, in such Water, that are converted straight to energy.**

In sharp contrast: which of us has heard of 'juvenile water'? And here we could not move more dramatically from the sphere of *giving* to that of *taking*! Juvenile water is water which, having "no developed character and qualities" of its own –

> ". . . grasps like a baby at everything within reach. It absorbs the characteristics and properties of whatever it comes into contact with or has attracted to itself in order to grow to maturity. This 'everything' – the 'impurities' – takes the form of trace elements, minerals, salts and even smells! Were we to drink pure H_2O constantly, it would quickly leach out all our store of minerals and trace elements,

---

* *Here we should remind ourselves that in all living processes on this Earth, opposite forces are invariably at work. The essential matter for life and health is that the* ***life-promoting one*** *should be* ***dominant****.*

> *"For example, if the positive temperature gradient is very powerful, then the effect of the reciprocally weaker negative temperature gradient is beneficial" – (acting but to qualify or modify the positive one in certain respects). "The positive temperature gradient, however, like temperature Type A . . . must play the principal role if evolution is to unfold creatively." (****L.E.****, Ch.8 "The Nature of Water".)*

** *Schauberger considered the ethericities to be threefold, and named them qualigens, fructigens and dynagens – terms fairly well self-explanatory.*

debilitating and ultimately killing us . . . Were water merely the sterile, distilled H_2O as presently described by science, it would be poisonous to all living things."

Such, then, is distilled water – the 'purest of the pure'! I cannot resist quoting Callum Coats's further words on it: "Having no characteristics other than total purity, it has a pre-programmed will to unite with or acquire, to extract or attract to itself all the substances it needs to become mature . . . When distilled water (*aqua distillata*) is drunk it acts as a purgative, stripping the body of trace minerals and elements." For this very reason, it has been used therapeutically "in the so-called 'Kneipp Cure', where it acts to purge the body of excessive deposits of various materials." Be sure, then, that you're in need of the Kneipp Cure, before you drink distilled water!

It is interesting to recall a radio phone-in on the subject of drinking water, in early 1998. The question of peaty water was raised by a caller in the north of Scotland – (peaty water can be slightly discoloured by peat) – and it sparked two opposing views. One caller was in favour of the peaty water – which must have been natural, untreated water, for she "liked its taste". The other expressed the fear that, if there was peat in it – "what else might not be in it too?" This is just the point, of course – only not as the speaker intended, but in an entirely positive sense, as we have just seen. This reminds me of how our mother used to say, as the school holidays approached, that she could not wait to get up to Boat-of-Garten again,* to drink the peaty water once more and taste the iron in it. (No chlorine was added to water in country places pre-war.) That most people today can only think of *bad* things being in water shows the state of our ignorance – and the state of our water too.

The chapter "The Nature of Water" in *Living Energies* briefly surveys the different types of water – from Distilled Water, up through meteoric or Rainwater, Juvenile Water (as occurring in nature), Surface Water – (dams, reservoirs, etc. – generally despoiled by heating from the sun, and by over-oxygenation) – to Groundwater (which includes Seepage Springs), and so to the true Springwater at the top. Well-water "would probably lie between groundwater and seepage-springs . . . it depends on how deep the well is, and what stratum of water is tapped".

There is certainly some good well-water in Scotland. I know of one place where an official was sent from the council's water board, many years ago, (when the post-war frenzy for chlorination had got under way), to close down the local well, while setting on foot the chlorination of the town's supply. But the residents stood round the well and would not permit it. They said that friends and relations in hospital asked for the water, and that it made them better . . . (and we now know what wisdom those country-folk had – far beyond that of their water board).**

---

* *In the area of the Cairngorm mountains, where our Aunts had a house and we enjoyed unforgettable childhood holidays.*

** *The fuller account of this is, I think, worth relating. Following his retirement, the same water board official admitted that the residents of the town had been perfectly justified in their vociferous objections to the chlorination of their water, for although official-speak had proclaimed it necessary for health's sake, their water had in fact been without fault and of excellent quality. More recently, a plumber now in senior years who remembers well the history of water supply in that earlier post-war time, related how the real push for chlorination had come from the growth of tourism – (or rather, our "tourist industry", since everything has to be an* ***industry*** *now!) . . . since visitors to Scotland were being knocked back by our too vibrant, healthy water. So much for the sacred cow of tourism! As we shall see – infinitely preferable would have been to have* ***extolled*** *our super-quality water, while offering free chlorine tablets – (such as are distributed to troops serving overseas) – to those for whom it proved too strong: i.e., those poor unfortunates already so debilitated by drinking chlorinated water that they could not cope with the real thing. As we shall come to see, whoever set this move on foot did not know what they were doing – and nor did the officialdom which backed it either.*

That must have been a well of excellent quality – and fortunate indeed the residents of that small country town! Let us hope that Scotland's wells are as stoutly defended today – we shall soon see even better reason why. ...Come to think of it – we might have rcognized the shadowy figure-behind-the-scenes in all this. The Seven Wise Masters were well into the business of the shutting down of wells. . .something that, as William Ogilvie said of another of their ploys, *should be resisted to the utmost*. (Just as he himself resisted the shutting down of the well in his own confrontation with them.) Fortunately, with some unusually dry summers striking in the mid-70s, a cetain turning of the tide has subsequently taken place in this shutting-down-of-the-wells policy. . . . .

To return to the question of the different types of water: regarding rainwater, which is of course a form of *juvenile* water – (we need, for drinking, not what falls from above, but what comes up from below) – Callum Coats cautions on the need to supplement the poor mineral quality of such water by suspension in the tank of "an artificial fibre sack (rot-proof) containing the dust of crushed basalt or other igneous rock used for road-building (commonly known as 'crusher dust' . . .)" (*L.E.*, chapter "Drinking Water Supply", with further reference to ch. 19.) Other juvenile water occurring in Nature is water from underground, but which has not gone through the necessary processes of maturation. It sometimes emerges in the form of a geyser.

*

PIPED WATER SUPPLY

Viktor Schauberger was not only a great thinker and visionary – he had brilliant practical powers to match. He was also a philanthropist of the highest order, and was forever trying to help humankind, knowing keenly as he did – (who better?) – the pathway of suffering they were on. Appalled at the rising incidence of cancer in Vienna following extension of the original water-mains (of wood – a natural material) with others of man's devising (whose hazards he perceived only too well), and instructed by his insights into the true nature of water, he set himself the task of constructing an apparatus that would produce high-quality water; and succeeded both in this and in having it patented.

By means of this apparatus, out of lower-grade (**but not chlorinated**) water, he was able to produce high-grade, spring-quality drinking water, such that – as Olaf Alexanderson recounts in *Living Water* – "sent to laboratories for analysis . . .(it) could not be differentiated from spa water" . . . "Rumour soon spread that Viktor Schauberger could make 'living water' and people streamed to his home to try it. The general opinion was that the water was very refreshing; the sick felt better, fevers abated and recovery quickened.*

Schauberger had "already been nicknamed 'water magician' when building his timber chutes, and now he was really thought to be one". However, as Callum Coats takes up the tale, the fact that he was able, with this water, to help "many people stricken with cancer" that he was able to "achieve remission in quite a large measure", resulted – (as the reader has doubtless guessed) – in bringing him up against the "established authorities, who accused him of charlatanism and lack of qualifications to

---

* *Not surprisingly, Schauberger stated of such water that, if sipped slowly, it could restore a man's potency.*

treat cancer, since he was merely a forester with no medical training or background. Ultimately they forced him to quit, confiscated his machine and destroyed it."

The *Seven Wise Masters* are, as ever, vigilant as to any trespass on their grounds – (and to such a pass have they brought us today that it is practically forbidden for any claim to be made, on behalf of any 'unorthodox' therapy, that cancer can be successfully treated by it). Viktor's work with this healing water brings into focus again the figure of William Ogilvie, since we can now see, from what we have learnt from Schauberger, that the well he defended must have been of "excellent quality" indeed, (just as he averred), its constant presence in summer when others were apt to fail indicating that it came from a very deep source. How much these warrior-souls would have had in common, with their brilliant minds and ractical powers and similarly philanthropic outlooks – and how readily we can picture William Ogilvie leaning over Viktor's apparatus, absorbed in its workings, and doubtless offering some comments on it himself, from time to time . . .

It is impossible not to imagine Ogilvie's equal interest in the remarkable water pipes which Schauberger also devised and patented. These pipes were for conveying water to the point of use, such that it would arrive in a state of top health, with *no* artificial treatments used in the process. Let us look together at these pipes, which are of such direct interest to us.

Firstly, there was the material chosen for the pipes – which would have been that used in Ogilvie's own time. Water, as a living entity, needs to be able to interact with its environment. Viktor Schauberger's pipes were therefore constructed of wood – which _breathes. The extension to the water mains in Vienna had been of cast iron or steel, lined with a bituminous material against rust, all of which created many problems. Today we have pipes of man-made materials (strictly non-breathing and unfortunately having that slight tendency t*o warm*th which is so undesirable for ter. Wood and natural stone were the two materials used for the construction of water pipes in earlier times. I quote here Viktor Schauberger's words from *The Water Wizard*:–

> "As things now stand if water warms up on its long journey through pipes, which unfortunately are today made mainly of good thermal conductors, then both carbones and oxygen in the water becomes more aggressive . . . if such carbon-deficient and oxygen-rich water succeeds in entering the body, (under) suitable temperatures it will . . . inaugurate transformation processes in the body's prescribed substances. These are not body-building processes, but manifestations of decay. Under these circumstances the consumption of such water will become one of the major causes of the scourge of the twentieth century – cancer." (Ch. "Water Supply and the Mechanical Production of Drinking Water".)

The replacement of the present system of water-supply pipes will be a huge task – but is surely not one that the people themselves, taking back the reins of power, would balk at. Rather, it is one that power returned to grass-roots level would be likely to place high on the agenda. *Community* land rents, or *community* ground rents, (as we may now call them), applied as revenue to the real needs of the people at ground level, would surely include a ready apportionment for the provision of a healthful water supply. This quest, along with the construction of houses – both requiring plenty of hands on the task – would undoubtedly be high on the agendas of communities set seriously to tackle at last the problems of health and homelessness *which they alone can solve* – while the "problem of unemployment" recedes fast into the mists where it ever belonged.

Birthright. . .and. . .Scotland Today

We read repeatedly in the press today that a major reason given by the young for betaking themselves to both drugs and drink is – *boredom!* What more damning indictment of a society by its youth! It just shows how far we have alienated the young from all real contact with life – from that need to meet our basic requirements which gives to tasks a meaning and a purpose. The high-running physical energies of youth are something older people *dangerously forget*. Can we not understand what it is we are looking at?

Once a society travels the road of artificial living, for that society to be in the hands of an artificially attuned set of elders who think they can achieve an artificial directing of the energies of the young – is to make a fatal mistake. The sight of young people stacking supermarket shelves with "food" (most of it rubbish), to the frustrating of their bounding physical energies – (and if not frustrated it just shows the depleted state of our health) – well illustrates the extent to which we have become blind, and have cheated even those that are in jobs, or real work. We have tossed the proverbial "sop to the plebs". No wonder they are bored and run off to drugs and drink! Time that we took stock of ourselves. Time that we *stopped, looked* – and radically altered course.

Does the change to grass-roots people-power from land-monopoly-based privilege-power seem an overwhelming step? Just think what overnight re-direction of forces and energies (*and* of finance) is accomplished in time of war! What brings this about? A *recognition of emergency* – plus the will to accomplish the needed change. But surely the emergency is staring us hard enough in the face by now? – with both drink and drugs reaching our primary schools. ("Seven-year-olds with drink problem" – front-page headline in The Courier, 2 Nov. 98.) Can we really sink much deeper and have *any* tomorrow left? And what of will? A political establishment sprung of land monopoly is *essentially emasculated*. It possesses no real will at all. Only techniques of bullying. That necessary will awaits its re-awakening where only it ever *can* re-awaken. That is – in the hearts of the people. *By the re-awakening of the people themselves.*

Here is the moment to pause on those trenchant words of Viktor Schauberger's, where he gives answer to the question: How is it to be done? – with: *Exactly in the opposite way that it is done today.* (See opening to this chapter.) What exactly does he mean by these words? In making this forceful and somewhat enigmatic pronouncement, there is no doubt in my mind at all that Viktor was reviewing the *full spectrum* of the human scene that lay before him.

Why do I say this?

Because, through the unremitting frustrations of his scientific work by endless "authorities" which he encountered in his career, Viktor Schauberger saw not only that the scientific and politico-economic establishments of our time act *as one* – he also saw which one wielded the more fundamental power. Here is how he once put it: "The whole of science and all its hangers-on are nothing but a band of thieves, who are suspended like marionettes and must dance to whatever tune their well-camouflaged slave-masters deem necessary".

Strong words, but not too strong, surely, for an *official* science which to this day, (as so crudely in Viktor's experience), subtly subverts the offering of alternative treatments for cancer – would impose upon whole populations the fraudulent *and dangerous* programme of water fluoridation . . . (our sacred Water) – and which builds itself upon the unspeakable cruelty and immorality (*and* unscientific procedures*) of

---

* *See **Vivisection Unveiled**, by Dr. Tony Page.*

vivisection. And incidentally, in those last words of his just quoted – what a description Schauberger encapsulates of that famous *Seven!*

Thus Schauberger saw as clearly as did William Ogilvie – and just as Henry George and so many others have seen – that "exactly in the opposite way" applies *first*, not even to the matter of a healthful water supply, (which Viktor saw to be so essential), but to the politico-economic scenario, which must first undergo a most necessary and radical change namely, the removal of that too-long-held stamping-ground from under the *Seven Wise Masters'* feet, and the restoring of it, as *sacred* ground, to the people, to whom it in the first place belongs.

All this therefore awaits us in Schauberger's powerful (and after all not so enigmatic) statement, regarding *exactly in the opposite way*. But let it return us, now, to his more precise meaning of these words, as they concern our water supplies.

*

In considering piped water supplies, we come face to face again with the effects upon health of the *temperature* of Water, which we have already looked at as affecting the health of flowing rivers. We now however gain further insight into the matter for our piped supplies, from our later look at the positive and negative temperature gradients present in moving Water – (*positive* as *approaching*, and *negative* as *deviating from*, Water's highest energetic – 'anomaly' – point of +4°C).

The question of *piped* Water presents a very particular problem, (as we have briefly observed), since in its totally enclosed environment, even flowing through "breathable" pipes made of wood or natural stone, it will have lost the impetus which is present in the freedom of an open flow, to form those essential *longitudinal vortices*, with their positive, *cooling* effect upon the Water's health; and lacking these, the further it flows in enclosed pipes, the more damaged the Water will be. We now see, from the chapter "The Nature of Water" in Callum Coats's *Living Energies*, the fuller significance of this:-

> "As it flows, water acts completely differently according to whichever temperature gradient is in force. In its concentrative, cooling, energising function the +4°C-approaching, positive temperature gradient has a formative effect. It is a process whereunder living systems can be built up, since in water it draws the ionized substances together into intimate and productive contact, for here the contained oxygen becomes passive and is easily bound by the cool carbons, thereby contributing beneficially to healthy growth and development. The +4°C-deviating, negative temperature gradient, on the other hand, has a disintergrative, debilitative function, for with increasing warming the structure of a given body becomes more loosely knit with a commensurate loss in cohering energy. In this case, due to the rising temperatures, the oxygen becomes increasingly aggressive and *reverses its role as co-creator and benefactor, turning into a destroyer and fosterer of diseases and pathogens.* (Emphasis added.)*

The profound effect upon the health of Water, of the role played by the oxygen in it, is one especially to note. For when the oxygen in Water is in passive form – (i.e., when it is "bound by the cool carbons") – it is beneficial to us. However when, in reverse, the oxygen

* *"The gases absorbed in a good mountain spring consist of 96% carbon matter." (**Living Water**, ch. 3.) Here are included all of Schauberger's 'carbons'. Hence why the bubbliness of spring water is so healthful for us.*

takes on an *aggressive* role, and instead binds the carbons, the result is unfortunately disease-producing, and this has its further repercussions upon the body's chemistry:-

> "(The) dreadful scourge (of cancer) which, despite all the efforts and skills of our medical research institutes, can neither be accurately recognised for what it is nor effectively controlled, and whose spread affects more and more victims, is primarily in an after-effect of unhealthy of badly-conducted water. This not only contributes to the chemical make-up of our food and the constitution of our blood, but also determines the quality of the composition of the atmosphere directly surrounding the organisms inside the body. Relevant statistical data clearly reveal that cancer is more prevalent in those districts where no good, high-quality springwater is available. Even in those places where the springwater is still good and healthy, it will deteriorate as a result of being transported in pipelines sometimes hundreds of kilometres long. The emerging pattern of the spread of cancer can be measured against the length of the pipes in which domestic and drinking water flows to its point of use." (Viktor Schauberger, in *The Water Wizard*, ch. "The Quantitative and Qualitative Deterioration of Water!)

How can I fail to observe, as this point, that in the very area where I live a hugely-heralded new water scheme has just been set on foot, whereby a highly-centralized supply-point now undertakes the conduction of water on miles-long journeys, to reach numerous small localities which were *previously* served by a directly local supply. We now see the dire health implications of this huge expenditure of public money. Whilst we have heard nothing from public figures in the area but panegyrics of praise over this great new supply, it is interesting that many local people – largely out of intuition – have privately been expressing serious doubts as to the wisdom of it all – a sterling example of the intrinsically superior wisdom of ordinary people above that of the "experts". The need for the control of water supply at grass-roots level could not cry much louder. (Meanwhile, I am glad I did at least deliver to one of our water boards a copy of Viktor Schauberger's *Living Water*, urging its study, two years ago – in the autumn of 1996 – nil though the fruitage of that act appears to be.)*

As Schauberger continues:-

> "This assertion will be immediately countered by the statement that the water has undergone all conceivable tests and its day-to-day content of dissolved and absorbed matter is accurately monitored. If we continue to drink sterilised water only, we must also accept the ensuing consequences. If we do not wish to suffer a slow death in mind and body, we must search and strive for other ways to cast the Devil out of today's drinking water, but not with the Devil himself!"

Viktor Schauberger found such a way; and it is time now to look at the simple yet brilliant manner in which he designed for us a *health*-delivering water-supply pipe.

In this pipe of Viktor's design, the movement of the water is guided as he had first discovered how to guide it in the making of his triumphant log-flume . . . (inspired by that last-moment, providential intervention of the water-snake – a truly breathtaking saga!) That is, he designed it with 'guide-vanes' or 'rifling' attached to the interior of the walls of the pipe, at intervals.

---

* *There are, of course, settling tanks en route, on this long piped journey, but unless these are designed to allow for the re-vivifying processes needed, as explained by Viktor Schauberger, they will not restore the natural energies, hence health, of the water on its way, which will but suffer a further decline.*

Callum Coats has done a wonderfully detailed drawing of this pipe, showing the complex movements of the "toroidal vortices" which the internal formation of the pipe induced, and it can be studied in the chapter "Water Supply" in *Living Energies*.* I will quote here but the last sentence describing it – which fully illustrates, I think, how brilliant in its simplicity the design is: "These toroidal vortices act to transfer oxygen, bacteria and other impurities to the periphery of the pipe, where, due to the accumulation of excessive oxygen, the inferior, pathogenic bacteria are destroyed and the water rendered bacteria-free" – (while the higher quality micro-organisms, non-harmful or beneficial to health, remain largely unscathed).

The fuller description of the workings of this pipe are truly fascinating, both as given in this chapter of *Living Energies*, on the following page, and also in *The Water Wizard*, chapter "The Conduction of the Earth's Blood" – where Viktor Schauberger explains how the result of Water's flowing in this manner is the "*qualitative uplifting of its physical, material, energetic and immaterial attributes*" – (top-grade water indeed) – with the further result that the pores of a wooden pipe are, via all these interactions, *sealed*, thus making it "*more durable than iron*". (Emphases – V.S.)

Just think of the interest to young people – indeed, to those of all ages – of making all these discoveries about water, testing them out for themselves – and so learning how to induce a *healthful* flow of water to supply to their own communities!

This type of pipe which he designed, was described by Viktor as a "double-spiral-flow pipe". (Same chapter in *The Water Wizard.*)

No chlorine was used in the production of this disease-free and high quality Water.

*

CHLORINE

What was Schauberger's view of chlorine?

It was the use of chlorine in Vienna, in addition to the question of the inferior material used for the extended pipes, that drove Viktor to devise his apparatus for producing spring water, and also to design a pipe that would preserve water's healthful qualities in transport.

We have already encountered Viktor's warnings against the drinking of sterilised water. Here, now, are his own words concerning chlorine, as well as other water purifiers he saw in use, from his *Our Senseless Toil*, (quoted in *The Water Wizard*).

> "There is hardly a city where water is not disinfected or sterilised through the addition of chlorine, compounds of silver, or irradiation with quartz lamps. In all these processes oxygen *in statu nascendi*, or an allotropic from of common oxygen, is produced which will kill off all living organisms. If water thus treated is drunk continually then the very same processes that we wish to achieve through water sterilisation must also take place in our bodies. Frightful consequences can ensue from the constant consumption of such water. When sterilisation only is taken into account, there arise the various forms of the disease we collectively call cancer." (Ch. "The Quantitative and Qualitative Deterioration of Water", in *The Water Wizard.*)

Of the disease-causing function of chlorine, Callum Coats records, (ch. "Drinking Water Supply" in *Living Energies*): "a recent study found that in water purification it" (chlorine) "produces by-products that cause 18% of rectal cancers and 9% of bladder

---

* *The design bears Callum Coats's name, with the date July 1992.*

cancers". (The following reference is given for this information: *American Journal of Health*, as reported in *The Australian* newspaper of 2 July 92.)

Causes of cancer have of course proliferated since Schauberger's time. But the restoring to us of top-quality water would not only remove what is *against* health in it for us. It would also bring us Water's extra-ordinary gifts *for* health and for our healing from disease. As the supreme "*Giver of Life*" (V. Sch.) – such as Water "always was and always must be" (*The Water Wizard*, p. 105) – Water must ever receive the highest reverence from human life on this earth, and the keenest safe-guarding of its energies from source to supply.

I further quote from Callum Coats (in the same chapter) the following passage on this matter, so vital that *we ourselves* understand, because our water engineers – indeed, the whole of our official scientific establishment, and equally our political – totally ignore it, (while most are probably totally ignorant of it themselves*):-

> ". . . the broad mass of the population blithely continues to bask in the luxury of apparently disease-free water in complete ignorance of the perils arising from its constant consumption, for what is never stated in official explanations is the cumulative effect this treatment of water has on the organisms forced to drink it . . .
>
> In its function as water steriliser or disinfectant, chlorine eradicates all type of bacteria, beneficial and harmful alike, so that what arrives at the tap or faucet, while indeed free of every possible organism, is water that has been sterilised to death; in other words, a water-corpse. More importantly and more alarmingly, however, it also disinfects the blood (up to 90% water) or sap (ditto) and in doing so kills off or seriously weakens many of the immunity-enhancing micro-organisms. . . This eventually impairs their immune systems to such a degree that they are no longer able to eject viruses, germs and cancer cells, to which the respective host bodies ultimately fall victim . . . Even the appearance of other lethal afflictions such as AIDS would have come as no surprise to Viktor Schauberger, for . . . as early as 1933 he foresaw all these unwholesome developments as the legitimate and inevitable consequence of the mistreatment and artificial pollution of water with chemical additives."

(Whereby re-sounds a further death-knell to *fluoridation* too!)

In *The Water Wizard* (ibid.), Schauberger explains more specifically how cancer results, indirectly, from "incorrect metabolic interactions", taking place within the body which consumes unhealthy water. He delineates the process involved. Further, by taking in *good* food, *good* air and "healthy *mature* water", we aid the development in our bodies of highly complex bacteria which are friendly to us, and consume the low-grade life-forms. But if we ingest *inferior* food, or *carbone-deficient* water, the high-quality bacteria cannot evolve. The way is then left open for the lower life-forms that develop, to consume the body, which was "originally brought to life and uplifted by high-grade bacteria".

How vividly this shows us how little we knew what we were doing – (and how little tourism knew, if it did play such a part) – in setting on foot our crude water chlorination policies!

Our task in setting to rights our water sources and supply is urgent. Viktor warns us that not only are we now having to rely on "worn out, stale and consequently diseased water", but through our dreadful mistreatments of the Earth, arising from our polluting industrial and agricultural policies – all of which lead to the "decomposition of the Earth's blood" – we are now in addition beginning to witness the *dying of the soil that feeds us.*

---

* *Copies of both Living Water and Living Energies were delivered by me also to the Scottish Office (Autumn 97), but this attempt to draw attention to Viktor Schauberger's work and findings at top level has clearly borne little fruit.*

Regarding the extracting of coal and oil from underground, in our dangerous ignorance we are also dangerously taking from what water needs in order to reconstitute itself properly on its journey back to us, and Viktor warns that it will lead eventually to the *disappearance of water*. He also warns that the qualitative deterioration of increasingly scarce residual sources of water will in due course render "not just drinking water but even domestic water directly harmful to health". (*The Water Wizard*, chapter "The conduction of the Earth's Blood".)

As I hear fresh rumblings on the news of ecological disasters here and there across the globe, on this evening of early September 98 that I write, I find myself staring at the words of Viktor Schauberger, where *The Water Wizard* lies open on my table:-

> ". . . and now our own head is finally on the chopping-block. This had to happen in order to bring humanity to its senses and to the understanding that nothing in this world goes unpunished. Ultimately every foolish interference with Life's wondrous workings – Nature – must exact its vengeance on humanity itself."

Just as A.J. Nock said – *Nature abhors disorder.*

Time to get to our feet – to *our own* feet. Through radical economic and political reform. "To wait until the ponderous scientific establishment has laboriously adapted itself to new guidelines is out of the question." (Viktor Schauberger – *The Water Wizard*.)

*

TEMPERATURE ... DANGERS

There is a final feature regarding the temperature of water that we must note – and its practical importance for us is surely a matter or wonder and praise.

Of all liquids, Water possesses the quality of having the *highest specific heat*. This means that it has the strongest resistance of any liquid to a rise or fall in temperature. Since our blood – (and sap likewise) – consists of up to 90% of water, this means that water's especial resistance to changes in temperature marvellously bolsters us against external changes in temperature too. What this tells us is that we have evolved averse to any great changes in our body's temperature, (and as Callum Coats points out, we begin to feel unwell if our body temperature rises by as little as .5°C).

Hence, on the question of even the most minimal changes in temperature, Viktor Schauberger has this warning for us:-

> "In Nature all life is a question of the minutest, but extremely precisely graduated differences in the particular thermal motion within every single body . . . The slightest disturbance of this harmony can lead to the most disastrous consequences for the major life forms . . . it is vital that the *characteristic* ***inner*** *temperature* of each of the millions of micro-organisms contained in the macro-organisms be maintained."

As Callum Coats points out in the same chapter, our society's chosen life-style causes the dissipation into the atmosphere of "large amounts of unnatural, technical heat, noise, noxious fumes and vapour . . . while soil and water are subjected poisonous materials". A propos of these "massive doses of poisonous materials", Schauberger tells us that *stress* is a factor in the raising of temperature – (hardly surprisingly!) – and hence in the onset of disease. The poisons with which we have, in our folly, so widely affected both soil and water today, will undoubtedly be a major cause of STRESS to the energies and life-forces of the soil and plantlife involved. We now fittingly therefore, reap the fruits of this, in being compelled, (nearly all of us) to eat not only poisoned and chemicalized, but also what is obviously now also *disease-prone* food. Perhaps a little pondering on this factor of *stress*, and on the way things in life can unexpectedly BOOMERANG, will help us – should we ever be tempted to use biocides of any kind on the land – to stop in our tracks and think just what we are doing . . . *to ourselves*, if we can't get to thinking beyond that.

The monoculture of trees and crops – of plantlife of any kind – is another cause of stress. Here it is brought about by the quite abnormal – (there is no monoculture in Nature) – competition for nutrients by the plantlife all foraging at the one root level. So here too, (as is explained in later chapters on trees, etc., in *Living Energies*), the resultant stress causes a rise in temperature, which in turn disturbs the health and vitality of the plantlife. Let us remind ourselves from Viktor's words above how very *slight* this disturbance need be – and of the "millions of micro-organisms" involved . . . Thus inevitably that plantlife is laid open to attack by fungus or parasite. No wonder that Schauberger called these latter 'Nature's Health Police', whose job it is precisely to weed out unhealthy organisms. But we instead in our stupidity treat them as enemies, and add to the damage we have already done by applying biocides.

Natural forests of *mixed* species, instead of our mono-plantations, and *perma*culture instead of monocultural field-crops – these are the ways forward for the future. As for other traditionally monocultural scenarios such as golf courses, with the drastically stressful kind of environment they create – (which was not of course how golf began) – golfers need to realize that broad-leaved plants scattered through the course are a positive mercy – and a small price to be paid for reducing the awful stress of such spreads of wickedly *monocultural* growing besides bringing back some of the sport into the game – (but see footnote). ...While one of the first articles on permaculture I read was a delicious one by its founder, Bill Mollison, on growing an edible lawn! And what rewards!

As Callum Coats continues in the same chapter, the "misguided practices" of our lifestyle – (the technical heat, noise, fumes, etc. of today's society) – all tend to "raise the general level of temperature above the naturally normal, thus bringing about subtle and sometimes lethal changes in cellular function". Further:-

> "The fact that temperature plays a role in the development of cancer . . . has now at least been recognized in the sphere of mammography. According to a recent report ...the degree of cancer risk is determined by temperature! ...Using a Chanobra scanning device, the daily changes in breast temperature are measured at 1 minute intervals. It was determined that there was a different rhythm for high-risk breasts and that their overall temperature was higher than healthy ones."

For the full quotation here, see chapter "Temperature" in *Living Energies*. (This

---

Footnote: *To her great credit, Scotland's golf courses have now zoomed ahead in this sphere – (there is nothing similar south of the Border) – by getting going the Scottish Golf Courses Wildlife Initiative, dedicated to restoring such areas of land to a more natural state; hence drastically reducing biocide use,* ***and*** *encouraging wildlife at the same time. No less than 140 of Scotland's golf courses have now joined in this excellent more – which is backed by the Royal and Ancient Golf Club itself. Enough of pampered golf which has lost all its sport! The golfer that cannot tackle a daisy or dandelion should not be carrying a bag of clubs! But it is frequently not the gofers, but our-of-touch course managements, that remain fast asleep in outmoded ways.* ***Shake them awake!*** *(Scottish Golf Courses Wildlife Initiative, c/o the Scottish Greenbelt Co. Ltd. – about to move from Glasgow to an address in the Leith area of Edinburgh. Adviser: Jonathan Smith.)*

information referenced 'Beyond 2000', channel 7 television, Australia, 25 June 91.) As Callum Coats concludes: "Now what did Viktor Schauberger just say?"

The kinds of stress that raise our bodies' temperatures have proliferated since Schauberger's time. Stresses multiply in a society that has taken the wrong turning – and our information-technology society is running high on them. From televisions and computers to mobile phones and power-lines – to say nothing of micro-wave cookers – we now live in a sea of electro-magnetic emissions dangerously out of kilter with our bodies' bio-rhythms. *Stress in-built!*

Moreover, info-technology quickly runs to inf-obesity – businesses are now finding the sheer quantity of information technology to be a stressful factor in itself. (Letter in The Times, summer 1997). It would not be surprising if a contributor to Alzheimer's Disease turned out to be "mere" television, for we were certainly not created to sit for hours with such rays boring through our heads. We are knocking ourselves out with our clevernesses – our obsession with info-technology a royal highway to No-Man's Land indeed, for there'll be no one left to inhabit it! Yet on we drive! – our universities now working "closely with industry" towards the "design of exciting new generations of super-fast, highly flexible computers and information systems".* ("Oh where is the wisdom we have lost in . . . information?") Talk about the prostitution of places of learning! . . . and knocking the human psyche ever harder on the head, or more precisely – punching it in the solar plexus! But when the day finally comes that we are without food because we have forgotten the soil – we will wake up to our Faustian deal.

"In the beginning, man could hear the grass grow. He sang with the music of the Universe".** There are those on the planet today who have never left this pathway, and who speak to us of "a world where our inner technology is just as fantastic as your outer technology".***

Can we have missed a signpost somewhere?

19 Nov. 98.

*

RIVER REGULATION ... FLOODS ... HYDRO-ELECTRICITY

There is another sphere of Water management which powerfully affects the lives of us all – including the matter of our health. This is the *primary* sphere of its management: river regulation.

Let me start by quoting one or two passages which sum up Viktor Schauberger's entirely revolutionary approach to this – (here identifying the books simply by their initials):-

---

* *Article in **Scotland on Sunday**, 13 Sept. 98.*

** *From **The Occult**, by Colin Wilson, Granada Publ. Co., 1975. (Hodder and Stoughton, 1971.) I only had the book in my hands for a few moments this summer, but could not miss this from it.*

*** *El Edul, of the Pachakamac Ecomovment, 24th April 1996. Quoted in an article by Hanne Jahr in the Science of Thought Review, entitled "A Message from Bolivia".*

"Properly managed water . . . cannot attack riverbanks." (W.W., p. 145.)

"A water course . . . should never be regulated from its banks, but instead from within the flowing content itself." (L.W., p. 41.)

and finally:-

". . . humanity constantly does the most idiotic thing imaginable by trying to regulate these waterways by means of their banks – by influencing the flow mechanically, instead of taking into account that water is itself a living entity." (W.W., p. 16.)

What is the significance of this for river management – that water is "a living entity? The significance of it is something we are already familiar with – the matter of its *temperature*.

"The number one enemy of water is excessive heat or over-exposure to the Sun's rays . . . When water becomes over-heated, due principally to the increasing widespread clear-felling of the forest, the health-maintaining pattern of longitudinal vortices changes into transverse ones. These not only undermine and gouge into the river-bank and embankment works, eventually bursting them, but also create pot-holes in the riverbed itself, bringing even greater disorder to an already chaotic channel-profile." (W.W., "Introduction".)

In short, water as "a living entity" has a particular "body temperature" vital for *its* health, just as we have for ours. (Indeed – just as has every living thing.) In the sphere of river management, (as elsewhere with water), we ignore this at our peril – and at huge cost to the public purse.

In thinking how to convey, as swiftly and simply as possible, Schauberger's revolutionary ideas on river management – and all that is at stake in our having followed a false direction – and seeing that I must push on hard with this book now, I have decided to do it through a series of direct quotations from these three remarkable books which have formed my study of Schauberger, once again expressing my acknowledgement to Callum Coats for placing Viktor Schauberger's work before us as he has done!* (Source and page number will be placed by each, and the quotations from *The Water Wizard* are all Viktor Schauberger's words, unless otherwise stated.) The care of our rivers is something that is vital we *all* understand; for our rivers will never be saved from their present disastrous decline, (which includes a decline in fish stocks, a decline in the fertility of our soils – and a most dangerous decline in health all round), unless the people themselves become guardians of their own water-courses, as of their land, in ways already discussed.

In view of the major floodings now reported world-wide. . . But here, as I type out this text, let me pause a moment, both out of respect for the people of Central America who have just (early Nov. 98) suffered such catastrophe, and also that we may *all* pause a moment on the solemnity of the thought that the colossal devastation in Central America is now openly recognized to have originated from broad-scale de-forestation of the land. Let this drive home to us how we, like children, are playing about with the terrain of this planet, knowing not what we do – which goes also for the millions of tons of biocides launched annually on our earthly Mother. *Our every folly will overturn us in the end.*

To resume: in view of the disastrous flooding now reported world-wide –

---

* *See also chapter, "The Making of this Book".*

following from the Planet's major loss of its Full Hydrological Cycle through forest devastations – there must be countless flood prevention schemes being put in hand across the globe. As earlier noted, Scotland is now embarked upon her own scheme for Perth and its environs, costing £20 million plus – a scheme which, without doubt, would have come under Schauberger's heading of *Our Senseless Toil.* Another scheme of flood prevention, for the Clyde area, is only just beginning to be discussed (according to the radio news of early Sept. 98). Let us hope that it, at any rate – and others across the world – can do better for the Planet's rivers, (and equally for public funds), by incorporating a full study of this fascinating and powerful section of Schauberger's work. To plunge in, then:-

> "It is possible to regulate watercourses over any given distance without embankment works." (*L.E.*, p. 108).

> ". . . attention should be drawn to a very important factor hitherto ignored in all hydraulic engineering practices: *the temperature of water in relation to šoil and aid temperature*" – (i.e., the question of the Full, or Half, Hydrological Cycle, which we have already covered) – *"as well as the internal variations in temperature* (temperature gradients) *in flowing or standing water.*" (*W.W.*, p. 94.)

> **". . . The forward velocity of every particle of water is associated with a specific temperature"** . . . (*L.E.*, p. 142.)

> ". . . (and the) *particular velocity . . . corresponds to its specific weight* (as it moves) *down a given gradient* . . . (When the) specific weight is modified by *outside* influences, such as by solar radiation (or) by the gradient . . . the water is unable to adjust itself readily to the new velocity without a transitional phase . . . (It) *breaks*, or in more common parlance *becomes turbulent*" – (i.e., from the longitudinal vortices erupt transverse ones) – "which is the *activation* of a hitherto-unrecognized *precision brake* in moving water . . ." (*W.W.*, p. 92.)*

> In addition – "this turbidity plays an important role, because it protects the deeper water-strata from the heating-effect of the sun. Being in a denser state, the colder bottom-strata retain the power to shift sediment of larger grain-size (pebbles, gravel, etc.) from the centre of the watercourse. In this way the danger of flooding is reduced to a minimum." (*W.W.*, p. 6.)

> "However, due to the senseless malpractice of the clear-felling of forests . . . the water warms up prematurely to such an extent that it is warmed right down to the channel-bed. No cool , dense water-strata remain and the sediment is left lying on the bottom. This blocks the flow, dislocates the channel and results in the inevitable, often catastrophic floods. Yet we still have the effrontery to call these awesome events 'natural disasters', as if Nature herself were responsible." (*W.W.*, pp. 7-8)

> "*The natural regulators of the drainage of water are forests and lakes.* By cooling the ground in their immediate vicinity, forests create a permanent positive temperature gradient" – (hence Full Hydrological Cycle).

> "The reason why water has been generally mistreated is because the importance of the temperature gradient for the movement of water according to inner law has been unknown until now.

---

* *The parts in brackets here, **within** the quotation-marks, are where I have paraphrased Schauberger's words, for a more helpful abbreviation of the text.*

"When forests have been felled and natural lakes are absent, it is necessary to create a substitute an artificial impoundment of water which must be correctly built and properly operated . . . impounded lakes are often built to enable the orderly management of water resources. However, these have not always proved satisfactory and have often achieved the opposite of what was desired . . . the generation of half-cycles, with their well-known detrimental effect in the spawning of floods and the resulting damage.

"River engineering carried out without consideration of the temperature gradient, and concerned exclusively with draining of the watermasses down the riverbed-gradient, ultimately leads to disturbance of the proper sequence of temperature gradients, or to development of a one-sided temperature gradient – and hence to catastrophes and inundations . . .

"The . . . artificial re-establishment where necessary of temperature gradients that under normal circumstances come into existence naturally – is the only correct solution to the problem of bringing about natural draining of water or its retention in the ground . . . Only in this way will it . . . be possible to avert the devastation of floods." (*W.W.*, pp. 102-105.)

"The duration of the positive temperature gradient can be extended, or it can be re-created where necessary in four principal ways:

1. By shading the river through the re-planting of trees.*
2. By the construction of appropriately designed dams in which the temperature of the discharge can be suited to the prevailing air temperatures and the water temperatures of the downstream flow regime.
3. By installing flow-deflecting guides which direct the flow of the water at the bends towards the centre of the river and simultaneously cause the creation of cooling longitudinal vortices.
4. By the implanting of 'energy-bodies' in the river-bed, which re-energise the water by inducing the formation of longitudinal vortices." (*L.E.*, p. 159.)

In the chapter from which this last quotation was taken, "The Dynamics of Flow", Callum Coats explains how, regarding (1), trees planted along riversides – particularly certain species of trees, and at particular points in the river – act "like refrigerators". (Explained in detail in his text.)

Regarding (2) and (3), Callum reports: "Viktor Schauberger built fourteen of these dams. Their efficacy was confirmed in a paper given by Professor Forchheimer" – (a hydrologist or world renown) – "on April 15th, 1930, in which he stated:

'Finally it may be said that Herr Schauberger has already built a number of dams which have proved successful. Some of his structures I myself have inspected, and I can confirm that these new concepts of Schauberger's have completely fulfilled the purpose for which they were designed.'"**

---

* *In Perth, huge old trees have been cut down – (not all, I believe, under absolute necessity). The new trees will all be much smaller – (and is the type chosen capable* ***ever*** *of reaching the same size?)*

** *Viktor Schauberger re-discovered, in his designing of these dams, the secret of the ancient Egyptians, whose structures contain "poreless stones that have remained unchanged for thousands of years, for there too all water and therefore every possibility for movement in the wall have been eliminated".* ***(W.W.,*** *p. 127.) What would we not give to build such structures ourselves? Schauberger's work and discoveries – through the good bringing to light of them by Callum Coats – are ours to emulate.*

Viktor Schauberger patented the dam design that is illustrated in this chapter. Further, Professor Forchheimer gave as his "expert opinion" that Schauberger's rifling device "produces a sharp increase in the flow-velocity". These 'rifling devices' we have already met: as the equivalent of the 'flow-deflecting guides' mentioned in (3) above, they are applied in Schauberger's water-pipes. The effect of both is to induce to flow, in the *central* channel, the cold, dense, *heaviest* (as well as swiftest-flowing) waters of the longitudinal vortices. The effect of these, in rivers, is naturally to *deepen their own channel* – i.e., scour our the centre of the river-bed; so that it is not water that washes up on the banks to flood over in due course, but *sediment* – to create a barrier *against* that flooding "Water-masses which flow under a positive temperature gradient build up the riverbank." (*W.W.*, p. 18.)

Regarding (4) above – that is, the use of specially designed 'energy-bodies': on one occasion Viktor Schauberger "secretly installed these in a sediment-choked stream during the night. By morning it had all been carried away, the channel-bed deepened considerably and the natural flow of water restored. All this to the amazement of the engineers in charge of the stream's regulation, whose gross mismanagement coupled with the equally serious misdemeanours of the forestry department had brought about the constriction of the channel in the first place." (*L.E.*, p. 163.) Schauberger himself writes of it as follows: "When I *secretly* installed these energising bodies in the Steyrling stream about fourteen years ago, within the space of one night the river was washed out to such a degree that hundreds of cubic metres of sand and gravel were thrown up in great heaps into the so-called sand-trap. The stream sank right down to the bedrock overnight."

Place *this* picture over the one of flooded Perth of a few years ago! It's in the waters of the Tay themselves, not on its banks, (except for the planting of trees, of the kind and in the way explained by Callum) – and in those waters long before they reach Perth too – that the real flood prevention works should have been done. Moreover – at a fraction of the cost. In addition, of course, is the question of adverse land use practices affecting the course of the waters in the upper reaches of the Tay, already referred to earlier – something that would here come under scrutiny as a matter of course, in a society sane enough to be constituted on bioregional lines.

I have made the extracts here from Schauberger's writings for a particular purpose also.

More than a year ago – (and thus a year before the work on the flood prevention scheme in Perth began) – on 13 Oct. 97 I wrote to the Scottish Office a letter headed:-

"Tay River Flood Prevention Scheme: URGENT.
Also: Programme for Dismantling Scotland's Water Quangos."

I extract here the section referring to the flood prevention scheme:-

> "I heard, in recent days, on the radio, the news that the new scheme for prevention of the flooding of the Tay River, has just been given the go-ahead by the Scottish Office – at an estimated cost of £20 million.
>
> There must still be time, then, to consider weaving in to that scheme techniques which would help accomplish the desired end, both in sounder and in far less costly ways.
>
> I wonder if you have heard of the work of Viktor Schauberger? – the very advanced work of this Austrian, in the sphere of river management – as in so many other spheres – which has only recently been brought fully to light? As

you may not yet have come across it, I write now to bring it to your attention, and tell you something about it.

Scotland has produced an abundance of world-class engineers, and, in this land of 'the mountain and the flood', the sphere of water-management should be particularly hers. A combination of far-sightedness, with an in-depth study of Viktor Schauberger's work, could mean Scotland succeeding in a very advanced approach to river-management, which might then be explored, and emulated, by others coming from other countries to see it, in turn.

The essence of Schauberger's approach, in the sphere of river management, was that the *energies of the river itself be utilized* to manage its own course – to deepen its own bed, throwing only the *silt* up on the *banks*. Thus, an inbuilt self-prevention flood mechanism lies at the core of his techniques.

Last autumn, I delivered a copy of the introductory work on Schauberger – ('Living Water', the smaller book here enclosed) – to" (one of our Water Boards). . . . "Since then, however, I have acquired a copy of the advanced work on Schauberger, 'Living Energies', published just last year – having come across a notice of it last autumn. it is the second book here enclosed, and is a brilliant work, written by an architect who subsequently spent twenty years studying Viktor's work – much of it with Viktor's son, Walter.

While much of the content of this 'master-work' on Schauberger will only be comprehensible to those of advanced knowledge in various scientific fields – (as will be seen from a glance at the book, where such areas are helpfully put into special 'boxes') – even to the ordinary layman what Viktor Schauberger is showing us is perfectly plain: namely, as earlier stated, that the *energies themselves of the river* need to be brought into *positive* play, if the river is to run its course safely and without flooding – and without, too, incurring those stupendous costs that today's flood-prevention schemes always incur, the present one, it seems, being no exception.

I hope to place these two precious volumes in your hands myself, for I shall be in Edinburgh tomorrow." (they were duly delivered.) ..."I should appreciate hearing from you in interim acknowledgement of them; and then, later, your more considered reply, after an interval of full consultation with those who are Scotland's *top water-engineers* – whether or not they have been engaged in the present Tay Flood Prevention Scheme: along with those who have been so engaged. For I *cannot think* that the genius of the Scots will allow them to place the work of someone of the stature of Viktor Schauberger – (so obviously a trail-blazer for our entire planet, whose work on energy will be recognized and put into practice, in due course, planet-wide) ...aside on a shelf merely to gather dust."

Since that effort of a year ago was clearly made in vain, so far as the flood prevention scheme for Perth is concerned,* I am thinking now of the river Clyde. And

---

* *The books were returned to me three weeks later, and I finally responded – (letter of 31 Dec. 97):-*

> *"Concerning the work of Viktor Schauberger sent you (two books), your reply was quite inadequate. As you know, they were sent to you for the specific purpose of letting Scotland's top water engineers review their contents. . . . . The books were certainly not sent just for someone in the Scottish Office to have 'a view of'."*

In fact, Scotland's top water engineers may well, in any case, be selling the Big Issue on the streets of our cities at present, or even 'doing time' in other ways. Such is our society's scorn of its children...

in thinking of the Clyde, my hope must lie – not in our juggernaut of a power structure (ripe for collapse as it is), which is clearly incapable of bringing to bear either the necessary intelligence or flexibility of approach.* My hope must lie rather in the people of the Clyde area taking up this matter themselves. In setting out here, however briefly, Schauberger's quite specific teachings on flood prevention, (which can be fully studied in the books quoted from), the people of that area may then know for themselves what are the features of *a tr*ue flood prevention scheme, and so hopefully will be able to ensure the preservation of the Clyde in its full beauty and character, without thobliterations being set on foot elsewhere – and some bioregional mapping would be an excellent starting-point. Let us have a flood prevention scheme for the Clyde, at least, that will draw people from across the world to examine and admire.

How vividly all this brings to mind the warning words of Jacob Bronowski – that knowledge must be not only up in the seats of power – it must "sit in the homes and heads" of ordinary people. It would be hard to imagine a more glaring instance and evidence of the truth of those words. Not only does the present power structure betray the people, all along the way and over and over again. It also (as Henry George points out somewhere) involves a huge and dreadful waste of the ideas ready to be contributed to society by the people themselves.

For all the buzz about "community involvement" today – (for the juggernaut has somehow to try to mount that precarious band-wagon!) – I have observed plentifully, in the years since returning to Scotland, that under a land-monopoly-based power structure, the *reality* of such involvement must remain a pipe-dream. It is not only knowledge that must sit "in the homes and heads" of the people. The economic and political power must sit there too.

Here is perhaps the place to observe that, under radical reform as discussed in the chapters of this book, today's "politics" would virtually die a natural (merciful!) death. For what is it that today's politics is essentially about? Why – the ever-crying matter of the *rich and the poor*, and how to deal with. . .what is undealable-with so long as the economic slavery of land monopoly persists.

To return to the matter of flood prevention: there are other stretches of the Tay in the environs of Perth which hopefully may yet fare better**, but as for Perth, for the time

---

* *An approach to the local bodies involved in the flood scheme was not omited, in my attempts re this matter. But under the present power structure, independence of thought in the lower rankings was clearly not something encouraged, the picture conjured up being more or less that of lesser 'cogs' in the great 'machine'.*

** *The Courier of 5 Nov. 98 carried a report on flood prevention work being undertaken on the River Ruchill in Perthshire. The following is extracted from it:-*

> *"In the autumn of 1997 Perth and Kinross Council undertook £18,000 worth of flood alleviation work on the river following a series of local floods and pressure from local residents. In January this year the work was criticised by the Scottish Wildlife Trust and the World Wide Fund for Nature, who claimed that no environmental or hydrological assessments had been carried out into landscape, wildlife and environmental impacts of the work. They also believed that the work had caused damage to the wildlife habitat and would not actually prevent flooding in the long term.*
>
> *Yesterday's meeting marks the start of a new approach to flood management, with the three groups looking again at flood prevention works on the Water of Ruchill, but this time doing it together. . . Steven Bell, from WWF'S wild rivers demonstration and advisory project (said), 'Flood management schemes which are designed to work with the river rather than against it are those which are sustainable and a good investment in the future for both people and wildlife'. ...the SWT's river valleys project aims to bring together a wide variety of groups, organisations and individuals with an interest in river management and river-area land use." (SWT's river valleys officer is Peter Pollard.)*

being at any rate – we have lost it. The works are under way. I have read of cafes and such things, to be staged along its banks in compensation for the general loss of view. No doubt a positive effort – for those having time to sit. But it will also bring noise and chatter, which will only seem to vulgarize the memory of the original beauty and gift to us of the Tay at Perth: the uncluttered magic of its moving waters, and the chance to link with that magic under the great trees which lined its banks. When we consider that it was through just such times of contemplation that Schauberger discovered how to let the 'mind travel where eye cannot see', and discover the inner secrets of water and of life – I cannot but feel keenly all that is being torn from us, in this ruin of Perth's greatest gift. As Viktor warns us too – it may still not meet the Tay's real needs, (and it must be said that some of Perth's residents express a similar view)...Who knows, then, if at some future day, Perth may not again reclaim her river-view?...

But to return: the last-quoted passage above from Schauberger – about the Steyrling – occurs in *The Water Wizard*, in the chapter "The Rhine and the Danube". What had Viktor Schauberger to say about the Rhine?

> "If nothing is done (the effects of dredging* only *accelerate* the havoc) then one day the Rhine must break out and create a new bed, because in its old sick-bed" – (much of the Rhine had been artificially channelled) – "it can no longer *move*. Perhaps you now understand the jittery anxiety of today's engineers and what they are liable for, once people experience the extent of the mistakes that have been made. There can only be *one* choice for courageous, upstanding men to own up to their mistakes honestly (for to err is human) and to assist personally in the work of rectification and reconstruction."

We know, of course, that those river engineers did nothing of the kind, but departed this earth leaving their bad work behind them – and that Viktor Schauberger's

---

* *"The lowering of the bed of the Rhine by 4-6m (13-20 ft) is simply a question of the* ***status of the tractive force****. This can only be solved by regulating water* ***temperature*** *and costs only a small fraction of what conventional systems of river regulation usually devour.*

*"****Dredging*** *is an absolutely absurd procedure. One flood suffices to fill the dredged holes up again. Indeed it should be remembered that the amount of sediment brought down into the valley by the Rhine annually is estimated at about 100,000m^3 (3,531,000 cu ft)! Every increase in the height of levées, however, only increases the danger of a breach, which is* ***inevitable*** *should a* ***warm*** *flood one day eventuate.*

"They should commission me! Minimal expenditure will suffice to banish the danger forever. The successful regulation will be guaranteed. ***The regulatory works will need only be paid for once the bed of the Rhine has sunk by about 2m (6ft 6in)."*** *(W.W. p. 179.)*

Imagine the river authorities refusing such an offer! Betrayers not only of the river but of the public purse as well. It is not likely that the villagers, townsmen, farmers, etc., living along the Rhine would have hesitated in accepting it! Here we observe, quite simply, the fatal partnership of science with politico-economic monopoly – which keeps the people down. How familiar its face! There is a footnote on this page (p. 180) which I see belongs to the account of the Steyrling but is as suitably quoted here: ***"If water is additionally stimulated through the introduction of metallic bodies, an increase in the tractive force ensues with the result that stones and ores float like softwood."*** *(V.S. in a letter to Dr. Dagmar Sarkar, 1949.) Another intriguing Viktor Schauberger revelation!*

Had but the ***villagers along the Rhine****, at that crucial time, held – under bioregional mapping – the political and economic power!...*

Birthright. . .and. . .Scotland Today

dire prophecy was only too fully realized fifty years on, with the record floodings of the Rhine in 1993 and 1995. Everyone knows of those extensive floodings – but scarce a soul will think but that it was another of those "natural" disasters. Good that we learn more and more how *un*natural most of our "natural" disasters are, and how man-made. Good, too, that we begin to glimpse something of the stature of the man, Viktor Schauberger – as of that forest university wherein he did his learning.

The Rhine floods brought incalculable human misery in their wake; but it was the incalculable folly – the incalculable pride and arrogance – of the officialdom of his day, which brought Schauberger's valiant efforts to save both Rhine and Danube to nought. it is instructive to read Callum Coats's graphic account of what took place, those hopeless institutions being the real 'thorn', of course – (in *society's* side as well as Viktor's):-

> "Always a thorn in the side of scientific and government institutions, Viktor's long battle to save both the Rhine and the Danube from total ruin was ultimately lost through their rejection of his practical suggestions. In early 1932 he wrote a paper about the rehabilitation of the Danube detailing the measures that needed to be taken in order to reinstate it as the magnificent river it had been in days of yore. This paper was included in a separate chapter in "The Danube", a study undertaken by the International Danube Commission and consisting of submissions from the Danube's various contiguous countries.
>
> When officialdom discovered with horror that Viktor's contribution had been incorporated into this major work, the whole edition was recalled, destroyed and republished in Oct 32 omitting the offending article, disregarding the publishing costs of the original edition which amounted to over 100,000 schillings – a very large sum at the time. All this happened largely due to the actions of Viktor Schauberger's implacable antagonist Dr. Ehrenberger, who hounded him wherever he went. . ." (L.E., ch. "Who was Viktor Schauberger?")

In surveying the awful betrayals, in these sagas of the Rhine and the Danube – both of Viktor Schauberger's work and of sheer common sense – the warning left us by Simone Weil comes vividly alive: that *bureaucracy always betrays*. As strong an argument as any for the *reclaiming of people-power*. I will leave the reader to discover the further dramatic events that coloured Viktor Schauberger's life in the 1930s – of which Callum so truly writes that "Viktor's guardian angels must have been very alert"; and of how "now hardened to setbacks" he nevertheless "with indomitable courage" continued to work on . . .

Of course the Seven Wise Masters could not even spot a good well when they saw one, so how could we expect them to be bothered about rivers? But they would heartily approve of *bottling and selling* the stuff today!

It will surely have occurred to the reader by now that, as we have so deeply affected for the worse the health of the waters in our rivers, so too we will have undermined the health of the creatures that indwell them; and most obviously, that of the fish.

> "It is a well-known fact that oxygen is present in all processes of organic growth and decay. Whether its energies are harnessed for either one or the other is to a very great extent, if not wholly, dependent on the temperature of the water as itself or in the form of blood or sap. As long as the water-temperature is below +9°C (+48.2°F), its oxygen content remains passive. Under such conditions the

oxygen assists in the build-up of beneficial, high-grade micro-organisms and other organic life. However if the water temperature rises above this level, then the oxygen becomes increasingly active and aggressive. This aggressiveness increases as the temperature rises, promoting the propagation of pathogenic bacteria, which, when drunk with the water, infest the organism of the drinker." (V.S., W.W., p. 7.)

How not, then, the fish?

"Small causes, too commonplace to be noticed, produce large effects." (V.S., (*W.W.* p. 9.) The declining stocks of fish in Scotland's rivers have for some time been a cause of much concern. Viktor Schauberger's work throws light on this, and inevitably the whole scene involves all present-day hydro-electric installations. The chapter "The Dynamics of Flow" (*L.E.*) describes the disastrous effect of these upon the water: how, after being "thrust down cylindrical pipes with enormous pressure", it is then "hurled against steel turbine blades where it is smashed to smithereens. The physical structure of the water is literally demolished and all the dissolved oxygen, and even some of the oxygen in the water molecules itself, is centrifuged out of the water."

"What emerges as the end-product of this physical and energetic disintegration, while certainly a liquid, is merely the skeleton of what was once healthy water. When this fragmented and largely oxygen-deficient water is finally ejected into the river, it has a disastrous effect on the fish and other aquatic life. It has long been known that certain species of fish disappear once these power statins are commissioned, and other forms of life have great difficulty in surviving below them . . . Generally speaking, it is only the more inferior species of fish that do manage to exist."*

Callum Coats describes how fish below these installations may be killed by a phenomenon akin to the 'bends' suffered by deep-sea divers, and cites an instance of this in Tasmania. But the fish arc in jeopardy on another count too. for this destroyed water, now 'ravenous' for oxygen and other high quality substances of which it has been bereft, seeks out and attacks aquatic organisms which can supply its needs. Fish are "especially prone to attack" by this oxygen-hungry water, "as it is drawn in through their very delicate gill systems. But fish-life is not the only victim, the soil bordering on the river is also leached of its nutrients as the water searches to recover these for itself. The result: a large drop in soil fertility and productivity." However:- ,

"This extraordinarily destructive power-generating process. . .is totally unnecessary, because there is another way of generating hydro-electric power which does not harm the water. Not only that, but this method, devised by Viktor Schauberger in the early 1920s and eventually patented in 1930, can produce 90% more electicity with a given volume of water, i.e. his invention uses 10% of the volume of water presently used to generate the same amount of power. . ." (We have already referred to the device by which Schauberger lighted his forest warden's house in a remote location.) ". . .The design shown in fig. 13.24 is very simple, reflecting his statement that what is natural is silent, simple and cheap." (*L.E.*, ch. "The Dynamics of Flow".)

Cheap? and ninety per cent *more efficient?* How many Scots would not like to

* *Anyone can observe for themselves how, in the vicinity of such an installation, the river-water is clearly n a state of stress, running hither and thither like a flock of disoriented sheep.*

see their electricity bills reduced by that amount! – not to mention living more lightly on this Planet. Considering the inventiveness of the Scots in the field of science, there must be a huge number of us – or potentially so (even if currently crushed under impossible social deprivations) – who would take to Viktor Schauberger's way of thinking like the proverbial 'duck to water', and happily work all this (and yet more) out for themselves. The bleakly tunnel-visioned scienc we suffer from, hitched up to our hopelessly tunnel visioned juggernaut of centralized power: these are simply the natural offspring of *underlying economic monopoly*, the juggernaut now carryng with it the destruction of our river-fish as well. . .

Time, methinks, for the Scots to take back the care of their rivers – under radical bioregional and land rent reform!

*

PATH OF DESOLATIONS

It is impossible to celebrate here the full scope of Schauberger's work, which stretches on through forestry into agriculture – that practice of *true* soil husbandry which Ogilvie held as the nearest thing to wisdom. But from the following passage we glimpse once more the breadth of knowledge of one who all his life chose his own "universities" – while glimpsing something at the same time of the paradise we have lost:-

> ". . .optimum conditions, resembling Paradise, must have existed during periods when humanity was unable to interfere. Only thus can we explain how extraordinarily fertile soil once existed in a large part of the north coast of Africa, where today wilderness and barren wastes are on the increase. According to the testimony of ancient scribes, in Carthage one could wander all day long i n the shade of olive, pomegranate and almond trees. The Carthaginians were delighted to see their vines heavy with grape twice a year and their crops produce more than a 200-fold yield. In contrast to this legendary fertility, reports of the downfall of whole nations through colossal downpours and whirlwinds have also been handed down to us. Paradise and deluge are therefore not to be depreciated as mere fable. These catastrophes and upheavals were initiated by humanity alone, and we are still causing them today." (*W.W.*, p. 140.)*

How painful it must have been for viktor Schauberger, seeing so clearly what those causes were, to survey the ruin man has since made of his habitat! In the following passasge he seeks to convey to us what he so vividly saw – through the shuddering image of the disoriented mother devouring her offspring. . .on to that devourer-offspring itself which, in turn, we are now so hideously arming against ourselves:-

---

* *Elsewhere he writes tellingly, concerning the fall of Carthage, how – we* ***see their water installations****. (i.e., They came to ruin their water, just as we are also doing.)*

Note also: *"The ancient Greeks have provided us with information about the practices of long-vanished peoples, whose knowledge must have been considerably more advanced than theirs. Thus in his opus* ***Timaeus and Critias****, Plato relates that the inhabitants of erstwhile Atlantis regulated their waterways with the aid of* ***cold*** *and* ***warm*** *water." (W.W., p. 136.)*

[It's interesting as showing that Viktor's discoveries re the ***temperature*** *of water were indeed the re-discovery of an ancient knowledge. It also shows us again how well-and-deeply read he was.]*

"The more extensive regulatory works become, destroying water's naturally-ordained inner functions, the greater the ensuing danger to the riverbanks and the surrounding area. Now *characterless*, the water breaks its bonds. Having become unstable, it seeks to regain its soul with one last supreme effort. The water-masses abandon their proper course and countless water-borne energy-bodies are dropped by the exhausted water. Disoriented, it now turns on these organisms and robs them of their life-force. Deprived of their souls, their sources of energy, they begin to rot. Bacteria develop and the Earth's arteries are suffused with cancerous decay.

Sinking into the ground, this diseased water now contaminates groundwater. As it rises through the capillaries of the soil and vegetation, this very Blood of the Earth carries the embryo of this fearful disease with it up into the widest variety of plants. This leads to the qualitative degeneration of vegetation, principally in the internal decay of forest trees. As a further consequence, it leads to a regression in the quality of everything in which water circulates. Ultimately in accordance with a law which operates with awesome constancy, it will slowly but surely come around to our turn. The spreading of the most terrible of all diseases – cancer – is the inevitable consequence of these unnatural systems of regulation. It goes without saying that specialists in other fields also have a hand in this work of destruction." (*W.W.*, p. 19.)

Our turn, it seems, has indeed "come around", with cancer now targetting one in two men and one in three women, and 25% of us doomed to die that way – (to quote just some of the figures one reads). But are we *ever* going to come out of our artificial laboratories and into the laboratory of real life? Are we *ever* going to interest ourselves in discovering and removing the causes – rather than remaining under our present fatal fascination with the *effects?* – which can never thus be dealt with aright.

What are these other "fields" Viktor refers to, as being responsible, besides water management? Prime among them – forestry and agriculture. Forestry, with its denudations of the land's foresat-cover, causing the fundamentally dangerous over-heating of the earth's blood-stream; and agriculture, whch already in Schauberger's time, post World War II, was in full swing (though not as full a swing as in ours) with the corrupting of that bloodstream with *artificial food*, which is what artificial fertilisers are to our Earth Mother. Viktor spoke out strongly against this, as against every other false practice. What would he have had to say of our catastrophic further descent down this degenerative slope – today's targetting of our Earthly Mother with *biocidal poisons*, which of course enter into her bloodstream, and in turn into ours? What are any of us to think of it, supposing that we do actually give ourselves to think about it, from time to time?

"All things are connected like the blood which unites one family. All things are connected." So speaks the wisdom of a more *connected* people – (Chief Seattle, see Pt. III.) For those who have lost all their connections, including with reality, there remain the words of Ralph Waldo Emerson:-

"If the red slayer think he slays
Or if the slain think he is slain,
They know now well the subtle ways
I keep, and pass, and turn again . . ."

Birthright. . .and. . .Scotland Today

*

ALL THINGS ARE CONNECTED

On taking our leave of Schauberger, let us keep close to us the memory of those diseased rivers. For there is something else they are trying to tell us.

Schauberger writes of the "malpractice" of human interference with the banks of a river, in attempts to control its course:-

> "If its natural flow is brutally constrained by the riverbank, then what was originally 'good-natured' water will become increasingly diseased, malicious and dangerous until it dies and seems to disappear. It then returns with punitive vengeance to confound those who robbed it of its health, and who denied its very existence." (*W.W.*, p. 44.)

And who denied its very existence! Could anything be plainer? Our very mirror-image! So *we* "brutally constrain" the energies of those we have shut out from the land. So *we* "deny their very existence". And so our "malpractice" is similarly finding *us* out, as the lost energies of a people too long wickedly dumbed down return at last with "punitive vengeance" indeed, to "confound" us with such social malaise as Scotland is now near cracking under.

"Diseased, malicious, dangerous". . .?

If this describes the originally healthy energies of a river under false constraints – then what of the healthy, and subsequently falsely constrained, energies of *a people*. . .?

So what if the Scots do have the highest percentage of prison population in Europe (as we are told)? Perhaps the Scots are just not quite so easily palmed off –? And what if the Scots have the highest record of domestic violence? – and if a town like Edinburgh is fast becoming one of the drug capitals of the world?

"All things are connected, all things are connected."

And if the Scots have the highest incidence of heart disease too? Heart – blood – blood-stream – rivers – LAND. H-E-A-R-T-L-A-N-D. "All things are connected". . .

*

PRISONS ... GOSABA ... EDUCATION ... RACISM

> "The spring that bubbles out of the ground in a healthy forest under the shelter of healthily-grown and undisturbed mother trees has important tasks to perform on its way down into the valley." (*W.W.*, p. 141.)

Yes! the spring has *work to do!* And just how could it *not?* How could anything alive on this incredible planet not have its appointed place and contribution to make? "As it flows down, this water transplants nutrients" – for both the plant-life and the animal-life it meets on its way. A healthy river's energies cannot *not* be engaged in work. Cannot *not* be helping to sustain and nurture the other life-forms it moves among. As Schauberger makes so clear, a river that is not at work is a river that is diseased – unhealthy – morbid.

"I'm just a piece of s. . ." It's the same language as the rivers. A young Scots girl is speaking in the language of the rivers. A young Scots girl is *educating* us. Just a lass who had set her heart on a job in caring – nurturing those "other life-forms" that she moves among. But she didn't get it – and there wasn't another, it seems. (No place for that caring heart in a society desperate for carers.) Being young and intelligent, and seeing the need for carers, naturally all she could make of it was – "I'm just a piece of s. . ." And all her parents can make of it is: there-must-be-something-we've-done-wrong – what-is-it? – because the child has been in trouble ever since. (What have *they* done. . .?)

The parents, with their loving hearts, speak of the money they have spent on presents for their daughter – apparently to no avail. But the child – (for she's hardly more than a child) – knows better. She knows that she doesn't want to *be given*. SHE WANTS TO GIVE. She can't express it in human language – so she speaks with the voice of the rivers, in the language of the heart. The adult world no longer understands the language or hears the voice. And so the pantomime goes on, for many a month. . . The legal fraternity, prison officers and social workers scratch their heads and wrack their brains. Still the stalwart young lass stubbornly refuses to be fooled.

> "The political workers of Europe and America occupy themselves with all sorts of things for the welfare of their peoples: tariffs. . .income tax. . . socialistic assemblies, unions and syndicates. . ." – (and we could add a whole host of other 'welfare' projects today!) – "anything except the one thing without which there cannot be any true improvement in the people's condition – *the re-establishment of the infringed right of all men to use the land.*" (Tolstoy, in *A Great Iniquity*. Emphasis added.)

Tolstoy – the great champion of Henry George! And a hndred years on we still live in the same sham world!

We had better take care! We had better arouse ourselves from that fatal addiction of ours – the addiction of *not looking – not wanting* to look – *not wanting to know*. It's we who are the original 'drug addicts', and we had better take care, for:-

> ". . .even in this terrible straitjacket in which the water is confined, it still strives to dance and to waltz. . .to adopt its natural energetic flow-pattern in order to regain its former vitality. . ."

Now, having lost all inner controls, having –

> "no automatic brake to restrain its forward movement, when the opportunity arises the water smashes into all in its path as it tries with its sheer weight and momentum to destroy the very structures that have robbed it of its psyche and to free itself of its bonds." (*L.E.*, pp. 174-6.)

. . .So it comes about that the human sufferers, of energies equally "brutally constrained" – end up facing us in the dock. *Who is it that really stands in the dock? The whole of that society – that has not wanted to know.* Not wanted to know because it has itself forgotten whence it came, and what its own energies were given it for!. . . Ultimately the docks will be overturned and society smashed to pieces. . .

Of course, the real culprit that stands in the dock is an Establishment – (of both Left and Right) – which has made very sure that we *shall* forget, through a careful lifelong process of 'education'! It is therefore scarcely surprising to read in the press lately that "education for the Scots 'from the cradle to the grave' is identified as Labour's top priority". (Well! – we didn't really expect the *Seven Wise Masters* to change their stripes!)

We have to go back to the rivers for our *real* education – back to Nature's school-room. When the river is alive and healthy, it is a "carrier, mediator, accumulator and transformer of life-energies". Then what does it mean for *us* to be "carriers, mediators, accumulators and transformers of life-energies"? What else but to be creatively at work, of course – like the rivers. Unfortunately, for most people today their work would be unrecognisable in such terms. For most people, work has become a deadening, soul-destroying business – in fact, an *abuser* of creative energies. In such a society, many people would as soon be on the dole as at work – which should show us somethng about the state of depravity into which the world of work has fallen, rather than the supposed 'depravity' of the individual who turns his back on that world.

How can anyone who is cheated of the opportunity of joyous, creative work possibly be "healthily alive"? The great mass of people today endure such circumstances as reach only to T.S. Eliot's "living and partly living" – or "the end of living and the beginning of survival" (Chief Seattle). How could it be otherwise? From dispossession follows poverty, and from poverty follows impoverishment of every kind. Neither health nor creative energy can possibly flourish except in a state of *freedom*, and that freedom means equal opportunity of access to land, which all need both to live and to work upon – and access to which denied makes of men slaves.

Slaves can revolt, however – and that makes it difficult for a society that tries to hide its slavery up. As the rivers have shown us, constrained energies can not only run amok, they can start to *self-destruct*. What is so surprising about our spate of prison suicides? – and especially, one must say, among the Scots, from whom Wallace sprang. . .

We had better stop building those prisons. We had better come to our senses before it is too late, and try to understand the havoc we have caused in countless young lives – and not so young – by turning a blind eye on those cruelly pent-up energies – denied their creative scope by being *falsely shut out from the land.*

Where we sow havoc, we surely reap havoc in return – and society is showing us just that. The drug culture is escalating, we hear. But the drug culture is fundamentally a *culture of despair*. . .

If we will only pause and look for long enough – *and long for long enough* – then perhaps, from beyond and through the so familiar scene, somethng else may finally at last emerge, to dawn upon us.

> ...The teacher of music had sat for some time looking at the familiar view in the green countryside, feeling at a very low ebb, when suddenly – "it seemed as if the world had been turned inside out. The grass, trees and sky took on a new intensity of light and colour as if the whole vista represented a glittering crystal in the process of formation. It came to him that all his life he had been looking at the wrong side of a work of art and that he was seeing the right side of the canvas and the true picture for the first time; that by means of this shimmering scene he was being offered an explanation of all things and a hidden meaning, just beyond his human power to grasp. . ."*

And so it is with us – exactly so! We too have been looking at "the wrong side" of the canvas and the *un*true picture – (the drugs, the violence, the prisons) – and we have been looking at these things for so long that we have become fixated upon them,

---

* *The quotation is from the article "Garden Thoughts", by Michael Donnelly, published in the Science of Thought Review, (a 1997 issue).*

so that it has become impossible for us to believe that a "right side" and a *different* picture can possibly exist. But exist it does. And it is here, right before our eyes, in the account of Gosaba. ("Gosaba – a Modern Miracle". See Pt. III.) Gosaba is – (perhaps was, for who knows if it has been able to survive on-going processes of centralization in India as elsewhere) – Gosaba was until quite recently, at any rate, a flourishing settlement in India, in the area of Bengal. And the creation of this marvellous and exemplary community will be of particular interest to the Scots, for it was a Scottish partnership – a husband and wife team – that conceived it and was at the heart of its achievement.

"Conceived it"! Now what does that mean? A Scottish couple possessed, quite simply, enough vision to look *beyond*. . . Enough vision to conjure up the "true picture" and "the right side of the canvas" out of the *false* picture and the *wrong* side which was so vividly and so persistently held up to their gaze. Of course this settlement was founded on the *land rent* concept, or it could hardly have been what it was – and this makes it not only the more interesting but also the less surprising that two Scots were at the heart of it, since we now know that the Scots have an almost intuitive grasp of the law of land rent.

The achievement of Gosaba (which had its first beginnings in 1903) was manifold. Firstly – it was the building of a community which enjoyed a high state of health, both among its individual members *and* as a society. Its population rose to 22,000 people – yet there was never a prison or a policeman on Gosaba – ("on", because it was a threesome of islands in the delta of the Ganges; while its system of law, which carried no administrative costs, was as simple as it was successful.* Whilst it was open to any to take their case to the formal courts of Bengal, none ever did so. Most strikingly also: when the surrounding regions were struck by the severe famine of 1943, there was *no* famine on Gosaba, which on the contrary was able to supply the government of India with its own surplus harvests during that crisis – (which tells us a good deal about 'famine').

Upon the wise foundations of Gosaba, further wisdom flourished. The children of Gosaba grew up trained from early years in soil-productive work, tending the plots of land that were attached to every school, and doing *all* the work on them except for the ploughing. Thus they grew not only vegetables and flowers, but also rice. So the children of Gosaba reached adulthood not only knowing where their food came from, but proficient themselves in producing it – proficient, every one of them, in soil husbandry. Remembering once more Ogilvie's words about soil-work being "almost of blood relationship with wisdom", we would do well to pause on this foundational feature of Gosaba's *virtually crimeless society.* Contact with soil *earths you.* By contrast, our children grow up – feet off the ground (except kicking a football) and heads over-stuffed. It is hopeless to think of *wisdom* or *character-building* flourishing under such a regime – and we reap the consequences. (Labour's latest brain-wave for children is to give each child an e-mail address!)

For our children's sake as well as for our own, we need to earth ourselves on the only true – the only *intelligent* foundation for any child's schooling. And since I have never found this better expressed than in the teachings of Gandhi, I did not hesitate to

---

* *It just strikes me as I write this that the Scots may well, in earlier times – (perhaps in Pictish times?) – have had, themselves, a system more approximating to the Indian* ***panchayats.***

ask permission again to reproduce the extract from del Vasto's *Return to the Source*. (See Pt. III. Included in my earlier *The Land Question*.)

Perhaps an independent Scotland will at last make the break with the dishonest, unbalanced, bookish and energy-destructive type of education we have so long endured . . . a system that runs in crystal-clear harmony with a land monopoly regime. The State has no actual business being involved in education at all. . .(which it has used unscrupulously to teach such things as the 'beauties' of fluoridation). It is 'there' in education, just as it is 'there' in health, housing, agriculture, industry, and practically the whole gamut of fields of human endeavour – simply, on the one hand, to pay for the dispossessed and impoverished, (who have been robbed of the means to pay for themselves); and on the other, to support the hidden agenda of a landed establishment, plus that of its monopoly-capitalist offspring. Usually (as in education) it is *both*. Education is simply a matter for parents and teachers in their own localities to get together on, with a bountiful ingredient of Gandhian common sense; and there should be as wide a field of experimentation in it as possible, with plentiful exchanges of ideas between the different localities – bringing in the children right from the start.

There is something further about Gosaba we would do well to ponder. Could one really imagine racial or religious strife in such a community? Impossible! For the simple reason that Gosaba offered to all of its inhabitants far more interesting and rewarding occupations and opportunities in life – (and we do at least know that there were Christians in that community alongside the Hindus, while it seems very possible there were Moslems too, considering the wide cross section of society that made up the first settlers). We could learn a great deal about such things as "race relations" and "religious warfare" by quietly mentally observing the kind of society which grew up on Gosaba. As the article points out, the secret of Gosaba was its "creation of conditions under which human beings can rise from the depths of misery to a state of happy contentment". Who – in a society for whom the way is open to *all* to achieve, by their own energies and efforts, a state of "happy contentment" – is going to engage in anything so narrow, mean and inward-looking as racial or religious strife?

The racism in our society (which considerably exercises the Scots at the moment) – the racism both on our streets and in our schools – all roots back to the *primary* question: that great question of the getting of a just living on this planet. With all such intransigent problems – no matter what the goodwill expressed by some, or by many, within the given framework – until the crooked nature of that framework itself is addressed, we wrestle with them in vain.

The article on Gosaba ends as follows: "Time has shown that the conception of Gosaba was not Utopian. It works. . . The happiness of the people of Gosaba is, now, an example of how successful government of the people, for the people, by the people *must* be, if and when it is given a real chance".

If given a real chance – government *of* the people, *for* the people, *by* the people...? H'mm. Early one day in September, (hardly able to believe it), I heard these words twice repeated on a news bulletin *with the final, most vital three missing!* WATCH IT!

*

GOSABA AND THE HAMILTONS

The article on Gosaba rightly points out – speaking of Sir (as he later became) Daniel and Lady Hamilton – that "their mere presence alone could not be the whole secret of Gosaba's success. It was only a contribution. The real secret lies elsewhere" – (i.e., in the justice of its foundation, the land rent concept enshrined in it from the start).

Yet they must have been an exceptional couple to have laid Gosaba on such a foundation, and it is not so surprising to read that the scheme did not really take off until they made a practice of spending regular periods on the island themselves. One pictures them "going down from Calcutta by launch" for their long weekends there, while Sir Daniel was still active in the shipping business. What did those manning the launch make of it all, one wonders? Did they realize what was going on right under their noses? And what of his own steamship company, Mackinnon Mackenzie and Co. . .? What of the government, thus supplied with goodly quantities of *local* rice amidst that grim and widespread famine of 1943? Did *they* take any note? Did one spark of interest ever erupt from *their* hearts? Alas, the 'British Raj' was clearly beyond redemption long e'er it reached India!

Reading of how Gosaba only really grew once the Hamiltons took to staying there, I could not help a smile remembering the experience of the Menabonis! – (Americans, both great bird-lovers, and he an outstanding painter of birds). On visits to their house while it was under construction in a wild and wooded part of America, the Menabonis used to puzzle over the scarcity of birds there. ...That is, until the day that they moved in!

For the last thirty years of Sir Daniel's life, the couple lived on Gosaba – latterly spending their summers in Scotland. What, one wonders, did their contemporary Scots come to know of these amazing goings-on in far-off India? Did any of the press of that time in Scotland carry articles on it? Who in the first place wrote the article *here?** And in the *very* first place – where did Sir Daniel, or his wife, come upon the land rent teaching back at the turn of the century? Is it possible that either of them heard Henry George speak on his visit to Scotland? Or could the Hamiltons have learned of it at first hand from their contemporary, Dr. G.T. Wrench. . .(already mentioned in Pt. I of this book, and see also Pt. III). . .one of that remarkable British 'school' in India, who occupied various posts in agriculture under the British Raj, and had the intelligence to betake themselves to learning about health and nutrition from the indigenous Indians,

---

* *My only researches to date (Mar. 99) via the India Office in London and the Nat. Library of Scotland, have proved unfruitful despite kind searches made – (but the Nat. Library will seek further, and an address in India has been given to me too). Other Scots besides myself will surely also be curious regarding this article, and the interesting further questions that pose themselves? There must be those still with us – in their eighties? – who have a memory of these things. . .or don't tell me that this is* ***another*** *Scottish archive that has 'slipped through our grasp' – !*

of such splendid physique, who dwelt in the Himalayan foothills.* ...Or was it simply a part of their own 'race' memory?

There is more than a touch of William Ogilvie about Sir Daniel, in his remarkable versatility – (we do not know, of course, how much was also owed to his wife). For here was a man fully engaged in the world of business, who yet knew enough about the land to set about a truly remarkable feat of land reclamation, (as recounted in the article); someone who was also clearly conversant with the history of older India, and so in time was able to establish, from both Indian and Scottish roots, sound and flourishing structures on Gosaba of justice, of agriculture and health, of education and of law. Like the best of the Scots – (and more than a touch of William Ogilvie indeed).

How immensely interesting it would be to read a life-story of the Hamiltons! In particular – to know something of the influences that helped nurture, in two such souls, that tremendous power of *vision*. We do know that Lady Hamilton was "a daughter of the Manse", and before her marriage a missionary in Calcutta, which certainly shows a spirit of inner adventure, (although the church is not, alas, known for its interest in *the land question.*) Since Sir Daniel passed away only in 1939, surely there must be a few living memories of this remarkable couple amongst us yet? Another bit of missing Scottish archive. . . There must be almost enough to make up a library, and we should start searching it out without more delay, not only in records (which can have a way of disappearing), but capturing where possible the still living memories. . .

---

* *Besides Dr. Wrench, there was Sir Robert McCarrison – (the inspirer of the present-day McCarrison Society) – and Sir Albert Howard, who brought back to Britain from India the Indore method of composting. The knighthoods of both followed from their work in India – but since that time the* ***Seven Wise Masters*** *have taken rather more care to purge official agriculture of these wayward influences!*
The books written by all three of the above are inspiring and highly educational as to the roots of that health that we have so destroyed today: the health of people, plant and animal, and the essential foundation of all – the health of the **soil**. *Although long out of print – (the very mark of our degenerate society) – some may yet be obtained through the public library or at second hand. I will just mention one here:* ***The Wheel of Health: a study of a very healthy people****, by Dr. G.T. Wrench, published by The C.W. Daniel Co. Ltd. in 1938, with later reprints. For information on the Scottish McCarrison Society, send s.a.e. to: Ingrid Burger, 70 Hay Street, Perth PH1 5HP.*

*

"THE WHEEL OF HEALTH" ... AGRICULTURE: TRUE AND FALSE

Gosaba – "a modern miracle". But Gosaba is not unique. Gosaba is not alone. Only there is a dearth of reportage on such communities. A particularly shining example of the same unity as ruled on Gosaba is afforded us by the people of Hunza, and they figure largely in Dr. Wrench's book, *The Wheel of Health*. These people have interested me deeply since I came upon Renee Taylor's book, *Hunza Health Secrets*, and I already mentioned them briefly in *Ecologists and the Land*, (1975. See Part III.)

"Where India meets Afghanistan and the Chinese Empire and is closest to the Soviet Republics, there, amidst a congress of great mountains, is the Native State of Hunza". So runs the opening paragraph of the opening chapter of Dr. Wrench's book – (the names according to the political map of the 1930s). In this mountainous area in the region of the Himalayas, the people of Hunza – descended, it would seem, from a remnant of the army of Alexander the Great – remained almost inaccessible to the outside world until the building of the Korakoram Highway in the 1980s. This finally opened their society up to the influences of our corrupt Western culture with its fatal surface glitter – with the usual unfortunate consequences for a highly cultured but more innocent people.

Under a just system of land-holding well suited to their simpler form of society, they lived free of our primitive exploitation of man's need for land; and the same happy combination of physical and social health was enjoyed by them as by the inhabitants of Gosaba. Renee Taylor's fascinating book (hopefully still in print) tells us how, living on a sparse but nutritious diet, they suffered no sickness of any kind, and only their skilled bone-setter had occasionally to be called upon. They lived far beyond a hundred years of age, enjoying their favourite sport of basketball energetically to the end. What is of especial interest, in view of the new and world-wide movement for soil remineralization, is that the terraces on which they grew their food, cut into the mountainside, were irrigated by waters from the glaciers above – waters rich in the minerals and trace-elements gathered on their rocky descent. Can one not imagine how Schauberger's "ethericities", particularly the *dynagens*, would be bubbling in them too? As already indicated – just as on Gosaba, the people lived without prisons and without crime.

Considering how we are bankrupting ourselves in attempts to keep up with ever escalating sicknesses, both physical and social, it is worth pausing on three significant features of these societies – societies of which there are many other examples, as we shall see. Or rather, were, until very recent times, for our decadent culture now reaches to almost every corner of the world.

Firstly, they were free of our society's primitive exploitation of the human need for land – a huge feature of our society and deserving of that word 'primitive' in its lowest sense. (What indeed do we have to offer the more 'primitive' peoples of this world, when we fail at the very first testing as being the lowest form of 'primitive' ourselves?) Secondly, they were all small societies governing their own affairs. I.e., in our terms, they were radically *decentralist* in form. We have already discussed the decentralization of both economic and political power as essential to the flourishing of a free society. We come now to a third, and important, feature, which follows naturally from the two previous ones.

We have observed – (and will further discover) – how in all such societies a high state of physical health of their people is an integral part of the whole. There is good reason why this should be so – and why, indeed, it is perhaps even an inalienable part of any free (i.e., unexploited and self-governing) society.

Power of overlordship by the few over the many (where not conducted on the basis of actual shackle slavery) begins with power over land. but power over the land includes *power over the soil* – that soil from which we feed. Thus there is a very special equation written into the land monopoly business. With power over the land goes not only power over our labour, but *power over our health*.

Soil-holding is a unique aspect of land-holding, because it is in their soil that a people's health is vested.

In vain do we build more hospitals. In vain – invent more drugs. In vain do we profligate body-parts, or sacrifice animals on the altars of our hideous laboratories. The path of health runs on the simplest and most elemental tracks of our lives: those of the food with which we sustain ourselves – and of the soil which sustains that food. Quite simply: healthy food to eat, healthy water to drink, and healthy air to breathe: these are the foundations of health. So it was on the tropical island of Gosaba, and in the high, cold mountains of the Hunza people; and in numerous other communities we shall briefly review, the same law holds. Take good care of the soil, and it will take care of you. Look to the health of the soil – and it will look to yours.

A people enslaved by land dispossession by the same stroke lose power over their soil – and this places them in a most dangerous pass. The more so when the elite of such a society, replete with the spoils of concentrated capital gleaned from land monopoly, retreat more and more from the real world in their infatuation with the business of *invention*. For inventions can spill over into the soil – where they have no business to be.

The soil has no truck with our inventions. Its secrets lie far beyond the range of our clevernesses; and unless we learn its secrets – as also the secrets of its rivers, which are our blood-streams – we shall never be able to pluck from it the health that we need. Our business with the soil is the business of *learning* – of learning at first hand: of looking, of listening – of handling, smelling, sensing – of sensing what it needs us to give to it, in order that it may be able to give back to us. . .to give back to us our health.

Invention is natural, is excellent – indeed is a survival trait. But the trouble with invention linked to inordinate power (as in a land-monopoly-based culture) is that, cut off from reality – i.e., from the checks and balances instilled in us through the needful getting of a livelihood – it can all too rapidly turn to exploitation. Under this heading comes our use of artificial fertilizers and abominable biocides. They have nothing to do with food production, nor with soil husbandry, nor with environmental care of any kind. They are to do precisely with *exploitation* – as replacing nurturing; with improvements to the *pump* rather than to the well – as we have already quoted Aldo Leopold.

Let us remind ourselves of the real picture concerning food production. In 1965, the government switched the goal-posts. Henceforward the measure of productivity became – not production *per acre*, but production *per man unit*. Thus was set on foot in a most weaselly manner the hidden agenda of monopoly capitalism, with the neat replacement of the land-worker by machines; the purpose being to create a huge new demand for monopoly capitalism's machinery, and at the same time – hey presto! – to '*up*' productivity!

Since then, real soil productivity, needless to say, has dramatically declined. An apparent increase has been sustained only through the false stimulation of the soil, by its artificial boosting with artificial fertilizers – (which cheat in feeding the plant direct – by-passing the essential contribution, for both the plant and ourselves, of the *soil*); and in addition by the use of dangerous (so-called "safe-level"!) pesticides of all kinds. The result of all this is an on-going deterioration of the life of the soil, as to both its health *and* its structure – something we shall dearly pay for. . . and indeed, are already paying dearly for in the on-going deterioration of our health.

Now that I have actually taken Dr. Wrench's *The Wheel of Health* into my hands again – (for I have never yet managed more than a dip into this treasured volume) – I have turned up a thing or two ripe for sharing at this time.

Firstly, I had always wondered, at a vaguely subconscious level – (perhaps the reader has too?) – why it was that this remarkable school of natural agriculture arose in

India, and not in England where its exponents originated from. Certainly, there were those native peoples of India of superb physique to inspire it, but was this the *whole* story? It was not! – as I have just now discovered. Here is the more inside bit:–

> "Soon after McCarrison was made Surgeon to the Gilgit Agency, Howard was sent out to India as the Imperial Economic Botanist to the Government of India. He held the post for twenty years, 1905-1924. He then became Director of the Institute of Plant Industry, Indore, 1924-31.
>
> He had had, of course, a very thorough training in England before being given such an important post. He had already been a research worker in agriculture for six years, but though he had had a laboratory he had never had a farm of his own. In India, at Pusa, he was allotted one of seventy-five acres, "on which I could grow crops in my own way and study their reaction to insect and fungous pests and other things. My real education in agriculture then began."

Well! So Albert Howard, in England, had had a laboratory – but *no farm!* Some revelation! No wonder he found his "real education in agriculture" had to await that India posting! As for the British establishment: for sheer hypocrisy – for the attempt to build the health of soil and of people as castles-in-the-air – it would be hard to beat.

Howard wasted no time in his new situation:-

> "Pusa was to Howard what Coonoor later became to McCarrison, a place where he had the opportunity and authority of freedom "to try out an idea, namely, to observe what happened when insect and fungous diseases were left alone and allowed to develop unchecked, and where indirect methods only, such as improved cultivation, were employed to prevent attacks'.
>
> . . .As an early part of the story which concerns us here, it was in Quetta that Howard was given an extra experimental station, 1910-18, and Quetta belongs to the Vivilov area of north-western India. . . So it was in quetta that Howard observed perfect health in fruit trees and their fruits, provided their cultivators carried out the terraced agriculture with thoroughness. As in the case of McCarrison, so also in that of Howard, it was in north-western India that western observation and eastern tradition met. . ."

In short – it is doubtful if Imperial Britain quite understood what she was letting loose in India in the person of Albert Howard! – or McCarrison.

Putting assiduously into practice all that he observed, Howard raised crops and animals that were *impervious to disease.* Such was his confidence that right soil feeding – learned from this people of north-western India – had overcome all dangers of disease, that he offered to import the "various cotton boll-worms and boll-weevils" from America, which were wreaking (and continue to wreak) such havoc in that country, to try out on his crops, assured that they would have found his cotton cultures "very indifferent nourishment". He wrote of his seven years at Indore that, during the whole of the time he was there – "I cannot recall a single case of insect or fungus attack".

Anyone who has looked through the Friends of the Earth publication *Your drinking water is being polluted*, to the pollution contribution of the various biocides (pesticides, fungicides and herbicides) that our agriculture makes use of – by government policy – can now recognize the realm of total delusion that these official policies operate in. So, yes – we pour biocides onto the land, they pollute the soil, the water, our food and our health. . .and then we wail that our National Health Service –

(more properly National Sickness Service) – is *underfunded*! Our society carries on in a totally infantile way. (Let us note, too, just the measure of intelligence operating in an Establishment now eager to 'treat' us to fluoridation. Those who preside over a National Sickness Service are the last people fit to be trusted – and *no compulsory medication* under any circumstances!)

The immunity of the plant-life was naturally passed on to the animals that fed from it – and this, equally, at Indore in central India, well away from that top-health north-west frontier. And so: the same with humans, of course. The same virtual immunity from disease is possible for us:-

> " 'For twenty-one years (1910-1931),' Howard writes, in 'The Role of Insects and Fungi in Agriculture' (The Empire Cotton Growing review, vol. xiii), 'I was able to study the reaction of well-fed animals to epidemic diseases, such as rinderpest, foot-and-mouth disease, septicaemia, and so forth, which frequently devastated the countryside. None of my animals was segregated; none was inoculated; the frequently came in contact with diseased stock. No case of infectious disease occurred. The reward of well-nourished protoplasm was a very high degree of disease resistance, which might even be described as immunity.'* It will be noted by experts that the resistance covered diseases caused by filter-passing viruses, as well as those due to microbes." (Quoted from *The Wheel of Health*, Ch. X.)

As Wrench sums it up at the start of this paragraph, the animals which were ("fed on the healthy plant-life seemed to take upon themselves the character of the plants". But we note Howard's animals were fed on *plant*-life, which is the natural food of such animals – not on the *un*natural food of *animal* derivation such as was fed to our wretched BSE herds. So whether the BSE arose directly out of that false feeding – or whether, (as is now being investigated**) – it arose from what are at last beginning to be recognized as the extremely dangerous group of OP (organo-phospate) pesticides, in this case used against warble-fly – once again it is clear that the huge uproar and tragedy of BSE was a tragedy of our own making. And it is all the more shameful in that the records of Howard's work in India must be among the government's own records. BURIED AND IGNORED.

How on earth can we now be talking about setting up yet another body to monitor "food safety"? We are miles out at sea beyond that port. Are we never going to wake up to the fact that the system which governs under monopoly capitalism – born out of land monopoly – is corrupt in its entirety? Irretrievably – from start to finish, bottom to top and inside to out.

Dr. Wrench makes the following summary of Howard's work – using the latter's own words:–

> "Howard's two principal conclusions in this paper are so important that I have presumed to interpolate some italics. The two conclusions are:

---

* *Let us take note –we who live now under collapsing imme systems! It is* ***our own doing*** *– and now our own* ***un****doing, as it was bound to be.*

** *One must mention, regarding this, the valiant pioneering work done by organic farmer, Mark Purdey.*

'1. Insects and fungi are not the real cause of plant diseases, and only attack unsuitable varieties or crops improperly grown. *Their true role in agriculture is that of censors for pointing out the crops which are imperfectly nourished. Disease resistance seems to be the natural reward of healthy and well-nourished protoplasm. The first step is to make the soil live by seeing that the supply of humus is maintained.*

2. The policy of protecting crops from pests by means of sprays, powders and so forth is thoroughly unscientific and radically unsound; even when successful, this procedure merely preserves material hardly worth saving. The annihilation or avoidance of a pest involves the destruction of the real problem; such methods constitute no scientific solution of the trouble but are mere evasions.' "

"Material hardly worth saving". And that's what we are feeding ourselves on, in the stuff that comes into the shops! Is it any wonder that our health is failing us on all sides? Moreover, this is what we are feeding *to our children* – those children whose health must be our prime concern, since they form the coming generation. If the taking over of that responsibility, ourselves, from those who have so shamelessly betrayed it is a part of 'freedom's full price', then we must be willing to pay that full price – for our children's sake if not for our own – by equipping ourselves with the knowledge of what constitutes *fit food* and the willingness to produce it ourselves in our new freedom. . .taking that knowledge into "our own heads and homes" – and not leaving it up to a corrupt Establishment, where the *Seven Wise Masters* are seated firmly upon its closed files.

To return to Howard's summary above – his use of the word "destruction" towards the end may seem slightly misleading here, but what is obviously meant is that these violent assaults upon so-called 'pests', via pesticides etc., completely *obliterate* the possibility of our learning why the plant or animal has succumbed to such an attack in the first place. (By "avoidance" of a pest would be meant the concept of preventative spraying against its possible assault – all too freely engaged in by our irresponsible agriculture.)

Howard's description of the use of pesticides etc., supposedly to 'protect' crops, as "thoroughly unscientific" shows how fully as an agriculturist he shared Viktor Schauberger's view of today's science. It is enlightening to discover that the same profound knowledge of *true* soil scients was apparently followed in very ancient Rome – (not, of course, the merely 'ancient' Rome we are taught about in our history lessons!). For Dr. Wrench refers also in his book to a real "golden age" – "such an age as the elder Pliny thought upon when he said that for six centuries the men of Rome had needed no physicians". Stumbline along with our bankrupt 'health' service nearly breaking our backs, we could do with some of that more 'ancient' knowledge. We could do with it in our schools and colleges as well.

I make no apology for quoting at length from this fine book by Dr. Wrench, in order to set this long-BURIED material before the public again. My gratitude goes to The C.W. Daniel Co. Ltd., (still at the forefront of publishing today), who over the years have published so many volumes of great worth* – (while I must acknowledge too the task of this book that has led me unexpectedly to delve again into Dr. Wrench's work!)

---

* *And for the adventurous, let me mention here* ***The Water of Life****, by J.W.Armstrong.*

Howard speaks of our false solutions as "mere evasions". Well, we know what 'evasions' are: those things what we think we have managed to escape (or tried not to notice), but that rise up out of the unexpected somewhere ahead to confront us again.

A huge sphere of our 'evasion' is the real cost to us – the real cost to our *soil* – which has followed from the inordinate export to our big cities of its most valuable properties, in the form of food. . .(those cities that aare themselves the unnatural offspring of land monopoly and dispossession). Since one continues to hear wails from the farming community today that we need sheep on the hills because there is nothing else that can be done with the land, I think it worth giving the fuller picture of what this commercial rearing of sheep has meant. . .(also from *The Wheel of Health*); for Scotland is cited as an example in the midst of it.

Dr. Wrench is quoting here from "Sir John Orr's excellent treatise on *Minerals in Pasture*" – and no wonder that it cites Scotland, for Sir John Boyd Orr was, in the 1930s, head of our own Rowett Research Institute in Aberdeen, so that he knew the Scottish hill-farming scene at first-hand. I must say that it was especially interesting to me to come upon Sir John Boyd Orr's words – for he was a household name in the days of the war when I grew up. Later, he became head of the international FAO (Food and Agricultural Organization). Further, in 1935 he was "commissioned by the government . . .to investigate the quality of the national diet", while he was also "commissioned by the Agriculture and the Health Ministries of England, Scotland, Wales and Northern Ireland" to write his book, *Food Income and Health.** So there is a wealth of his wisdom also buried away quietly somewhere in those 'lost' archives. Here, then, is the passage from his *Minerals in Pasture*, as quoted in Wrench's book:-

> " 'Munro reports that in the Falkland Islands sheep have been reared and exported for forty years without any return to the soil to replace the minerals removed. During the last twenty years it has become increasingly difficult to rear lambs. The other animals are also deteriorating.' The sheep are exported to the United Kingdom, and with them goes the mineral food of the soil which they represent.
>
> This is a typical instance of what is a widespread loss due to the same causes. 'The process of depletion', Orr writes, 'and the resulting deterioration which shows itelsf in decreased rate of growth and production, and in extreme cases by the appearance of disease, is proceeding on all pastures from which milk, carcases or other animal products are taken off without a correspnding replacement being made. Accompanying the visible movement of milk and beef, there is a slow invisible flow of fertility. Every cargo of beef or milk products, every shipload of bones, leaves the exporting country somuch the poorer. In many of the grazing grounds of the world this depletion has become a serious economic problem.
>
> 'In Scotland, for example, generation after generation of sheep have been taken off the hills with little compensatory returns. Accompanying the resulting deterioraton of the pasture, the stock tend to be reduced in the rough hill grazings...this process of depletion of the Scottish hills has been going on with

---

* *For this further information, I am indebted to the book* ***The Politics of Food****, by Geoffrey Cannon – a superb book, published in 1987, now unfortunately out of print. I am indebted too to the kind friend who brought it to my attention and lent me a copy.*

increasing rapidity since the time when the produce of the animals, instead of being consumed on the land and therefore returned to the soil, began to be driven off to be consumed in the industrial areas. There are now districts in the Highlands which could not support populations which once lived there, even though the people were willing to accept the standard of living of their ancestors...this process of depletion has been going on for many years, especially in hill pastures, and it is probable that the recognized decrease in the value of hill pastures in certain areas, owing to the increase in the diseases and mortality of sheep, is associated with the gradual process of the impoverishment of the pasture and its soil.' "

Interestingly, I recall a passage in Henry George's writings, which records his very same observation, as to how the wealth of the countryside was thus increasingly being sucked away into America's fast-growing cities.

Where does all this wealth end up but in the seas, of course – (out of our sewers); and quoting from other sources Wrench reckons this (*already* over half a century ago), to have amounted – annually, per million of population – to: 5,974,000 – 12,000,000 pounds of nitrogen; 1,881,900 – 4,151,000 pounts of potassium; and 777,200 to 3,057,600 pounds of phosphorus.

What must it amount to today? – while we pay for *artifical* fertilizers – artificial nitrogen, artificial potassium and artificial phosphorus – to ruin our soil *yet further*. Is this crazydom, or what?

So this additional huge destuction of our soil is added to the destruction of human lives that lies at the door of land monopoly! How much has it to answer for? And how much longer can this go on? Not much – as we shall see.

(Wrench again.) "This waste shows some of the impoverishment of the soil. . . We hear in these days. . .of poverty in the midst of plenty. . . Meanwhile a greater and more radical poverty continually steals upon us and is accepted."

Why "greater" and "more radical" – when it seems nothing could be more so than the economic poverty woven into our society?

A more fundamental picture of the cost to us of the 'evading' of this responsibility for our soil, may be gleaned from other sources closer to home.

Those whose business takes them around Scotland – and for whom a farming background allows something of an insider view – have some weird tales to tell.

In the mud-ridden autumn of this year of 1998 – one individual said they could show me, in a fertile area of Scotland, a good 500 acres where tatties* have been left to rot because rain has made the fields impassible for heavy machinery. Human hands could have done it, of course – but gone is the 'tattie-houking' I remember from my own school-days. Of course, the machinery just *may* get in yet – but whether or no, no hand-picking. But where would one find hand-pickers, in any case, today?

Another comment: "Twenty to twenty-six tons of tatties per acre. Incredible tonnage – ripping the ground to smithereens." (All down to *artificials*, of course.)

Then – a design was drawn for me of how a tattie-field is nowadays prepared. Extra deep furrows are made in the overall ridge-and-furrow pattern, into which the

---

* *For overseas readers – the Scots don't bother with the word 'potato'!*

stones – taken up by a machine and 'winnowed' of their soil – are buried, *below* the tattie-planting depth, so that the machines coming into the field won't be bothered with them at harvest-time. Forget that the stones provide the soil with some essential *structure* against compaction and water-logging – (water-logging, did we say?) – by helping to keep open the air-ducts, the breathing 'capillaries' of the soil. Forget, too, that stones left among plant-roots provide valuable, slow, long-term *soil-re-mineralization*, through the interaction with their surfaces of the microscopic inhabitants of the soil. . . .But we can more or less forget this invaluable microscopic soil-life anyway, because it doesn't like artificials biocides. Artificials themselves silt up the air passages of the soil. . .

Then – what of tatties, or any root-crop, planted alongside a *river*? On a meadow flood-plain in the old days, a farmer would only ever grow grain – which leaves a root-stubble over winter to hold the soil against flood. *Now*, once the root-crop is lifted, should the river flood,huge quantities of soil are carried away by the river. . . .And what about the added impetus to flooding down-stream, with the additional load of silt the river now carries? – and no Schauberger river technology to ensure its throwing *out* of the river's channel? What, also, about the carrying into the river of these artificial fertilizers, plus the pesticides, fungicides and herbicides used to grow the crop? Yes – what about the carrying of all *that* burden into the river along with the soil that is carried off in the flood? And this in addition, of course, to the general seepage throughout the year, be there a flood or no? What part might *that* not play in the decline of our declining fish-stock?. . .(not to mention the whole wider field of destructiveness involved, as revealed by Schauberger). And yet we have a *combined* Ministry of *Agriculture and Fisheries*.....!

. . .So we lose precious soil down our rivers (and augment down-stream flooding). But that is not all. Come spring and strong winds and the structureless – bodiless – soil is now blown over our roads. "There were snow-ploughs out in the north-east of Scotland this spring (1998) clearing the roads of *soil*".

. . .Such is the state of the land of Scotland under our official agriculture! "If you ever had a week to spare, I could drive you around and show you some horrific examples of land mis-use." (With farming being so subsidy-oriented today, the Scots are not only over-seeing the ruin of their soil, they are paying heavily to see it too.) "Some of these guys are so hyped up into cuckoo-land, it's incredible." (This – of the overseers.)

Yes – it's incredible! Not the individual farmers, who are governed by the system – but *the system itself* that is incredible. But it is time the farmers woke up too – of whose judgement false education has made such a ruin. We must *all* of us awaken – awaken from our political naiveté – tear up the last shreds of that mistaken belief of ours that "they" know better, and recognize what is going on for what it is – simply, one colossal fraud. Time to take the responsibility for the soil *back into our own hands*.

For the reality otherwise is grim. As we have already quoted: "Historical periods of culture and civilization come and go, but the soil, the producer of life, is lasting. It continues, while they wax and wane. And, if a civilization is such that it degrades the soil, then it is the civilization, and not the soil, that comes to an end." (Dr. G.T. Wrench.) Or – to paraphrase Schauberger's succinct wording of it: "No soil – no bread; no bread – no life".

Birthright. . .and. . .Scotland Today

Do we really want it to be as in the days of Noah? – when they were eating and drinking and marrying and giving in marriage until suddenly the flood came and took them? For if it goes on that 'the rains come and winds blow', it'll be enough for us that the floods and the winds come and take our soil. That'll do for us too – just as well!

*

INVENTIONS ... OR THE LABOURS OF LOVE?

We return to the matter of *invention* we were discussing – in particular, inventions foisted on the soil.

This kind of invention has many faces. I came upon a new one late this summer – or rather, a further stage of an old and familiar one. It was a forecast about Scotland's future, and the manner of her food production, and it ran something like this. Our food production is going to be in the hands of fewer and fewer 'experts', and most of Scotland's land will be down to rough grazing. . .(which-if-all-that-it-is-fit-for-anyway, being the plain message as to *that*!)

What *is* one to reply to so multi-faceted a gem of an invention! – ?

When we get back the land, we get back the soil. And we – not the 'experts', but the people of Scotland – will be feeding ourselves!

Yes – and in those "rough grazings" too, because now we know the lie about those. As our own John Boyd Orr brought to light (but his light got extinguished somehow), people back living on them is the *very thing they need!* And here's another very simple equation built into this whole matter. The planet can't afford all this meat-eating involved in stock-rearing. It makes too heavy a demand on land, where trees are needed. A vegetarian, it is estimated, can life off .6 of an acre – just over a half. A meat-eater requires nearly three times that amount, in order to pasture animals.

It will take time to get the land back into heart – but, as I have read, the *highest* art of soil husbandry practiced on this planet has not been that on its lush plains, but where human hands, in high mountain country, have *created* such terrains through their own skills and dedicated care. We can read about some of these in *The Wheel of Health*.

. . .How painfully we have lost the labours of love – and taken on the labours of unemployment and drugs and crime instead. . .

*

THE FUTURE OF SCOTLAND'S SOIL

The State power which has so persistently betrayed both our soil and our people – (and then betrayed the work of such as would have exposed those betrayals) – can never be trusted in the matter either of our people or our soil. How is it we have failed to understand that, whichever party is in office, it is the same *Seven Wise Masters* who are waving the flag? Fortunately radical land reform will in any case remove that usurpive power.

A weaselly attempt is currently being made by the *Seven* to 'promote' organic agriculture. As one organic farmer shrewdly observed of this – they are going to have to 're-invent the wheel'! The fundamental of organic cultivation is the care of the soil *by human hands* – people back on the land.

Fortunately, the entire impetus of the organic movement has been, from the start, a grass-roots, people-based one, the movement arising directly out of strongly felt opposition to State chemical agricultural policies; and the people are therefore fully fitted to carry the movement forward themselves. – *Who else? – !* Already there are wide net-workings of organic groups of all kinds,* some of them offering training as well. The only requirement for a wider burst of this flourishing – (right now experiencing a tremendous boost on account of the newly-erupting GMO scene** – of government blessing!) – is the restoring of that full people-power which will come with the ending of economic monopoly, and the ending of that chemical agriculture which it operates – in our names.

Already, too – as some indication of the scale of what awaits our reclamation: far up in the western highlands of Scotland – following the fencing off of a two-acre area of land – a ten-year trial has been set on foot "to study the regeneration of indigenous oakwood", (*Scotland on Sunday*, 7th June 98). So! – *oakwoods* once flourished there! ...where current land-use is reduced to "sport and conservation", with one sheep-farm thrown in! One must commend this imaginative step – set on foot largely by the clearly 'benevolent' (in today's terms) foreign owner of the land. But this is an estate consisting of the best part of *100,000 acres*! (87,000 to be precise). Granted that quite an area is clearly mountainous country above the habitation line, and decidedly most precious to us as the wilderness it is – yet this huge estate apparently, (from the information in the report), employs scarcely a dozen people, and *costs* £100,000 to run! We have clearly been robbed not only of our land, but of our senses.

Oakwoods. . .and the restoring of life to impoverished soils that trees so exceptionally bring about: stabilizing the water cycles, bringing up nutrients through their deep-rooting systems and scattering this enrichment on the land at leaf-fall. . .this in turn helping to supply the essential humus from rotted vegetation, etc., that must marry with soil remineralization for the latter to do *its* tremendous soil regeneration work ... And what about those human wastes that (*knowledgeably composted*) can add *their* precious quotients to the soil – so much more readily in the country than in the towns? What with all this – and especially the huge extra help of soil remineralization today – our "rough grazings" are fully open to us to restore, and without waiting an age either.***

There is just *so much* open to us – so much awaiting us. As Ron Greer of the Loch Garry Tree Planting Project said: where trees can flourish, the land can be

---

* *Scottish Organic Gardeners (SOG), Flat 2FL, 54 East Claremont Street, Edinburgh EH7 4JR.*
Henry Doubleday Research Assoc. (HDRA), Ryton-on-Dunsmore, Coventry CV8 3LG.
Permaculture (Britain), P.O. Box 1, Buckfastleigh, Devon TQ11 0LH.
Reference has already been made to the SEER Centre in Scotland, for soil remineralization. See also Part III.
The above are just the ones that spring immediately to mind.

** *Genetically Modified Organisms.*

*** *There would, of course, be no community ground rent due until the land was above marginal, and capable of yielding rent".*

reclaimed and people can flourish too.* The land needs people on it, to nurture and care for it. People in their turn need the land – to nurture and care for themselves. They also *need* it to fulfil that deep need which is in all of us to care for our Earthly Mother – no matter how long it has been buried away. So – the land is waiting for the people. The people are waiting for the land.

What else is there left for us but to confront the fact, at last, that our greatest and foolishest 'evasion' of all has been – *the evasion of the land question?*

Well, as we have already paused to ponder – our evasions are all paid for in the end. And this can add up to a heavy price.

. . . Not to mention the GMOs,
Crazier than we may yet suppose!

– and we will come to that too.

But first, time to turn to Weston Price – who is aptly named for telling us something more fully of the price that we pay.

*

For the remark-
able healing powers of –
Ragwort –
See Part IV –
"The Natural World"

---

* *How welcome to read of the Woodland Trust's plan for Glen Finglas, as part of a major tree-planting scheme – "to bring back to Scotland the concept of wooded pasture – sheep and cattle grazing, not in open fields, but in an area of well spread out trees." (The Scotsman, 3 Dec. 98). Definitely a step in a good direction – and we note, bring* ***back***.

THE WORK OF DR. WESTON PRICE.

Nutrition and Physical Degeneration, by Weston A. Price, D.D.S. – which I was so fortunate as to come upon through the chance remark of a friend in the summer of 1996* – is a remarkable book. So remarkable that at first I wondered how it could possibly still be in print. (Written in 1939, it seems that it was first published just after the war.) It would certainly be highly unlikely to be included in the syllabuses of any of our places of education today, for it is far too big a give-away of what we have done *and are doing* to ourselves. I found the answer to my puzzle in the front of this "50th Anniversary Edition"; for it is published by the Price-Pottinger Nutrition Foundation, which was established after Dr. Weston Price's death by his widow, in order that his valuable work might not be lost to us; and the Foundation now hold the responsibility "for continued publication of his classic book".

It must also be the generosity of the Price-Pottinger Foundation which has kept the price so moderate for a work of this nature. (After looking at a copy obtained through the kind services of the public library, I realized it was one that I must get.) At £15-odd, it is a full-sized, thick (running to over 500 pages) hardback. Its crowning feature is the inclusion of a wealth of photographs from across the world: pictures of faces, people mouths – (Dr. Weston Price was a dentist) – all of which adds a further invaluable dimension of instruction to its remarkable text.

Working in the same tradition – and at the same time – as that school in India of Albert Howard *et al.*, (although it seems neither knew of the other), Dr. Weston Price was another of those thinkers and workers far ahead of his time – as still of ours. "As shocking and relevant in its implications today as when it was first written" – a citation from Dr. Melvyn R. Werbach, M.D. on the back cover of this "50th" edition. Today, the links between poor nutrition and poor health can no longer be completely hidden up. They have finally broken through to the surface – just as every repressed truth must finally do. Even certain 'unsocial traits', such as hyperactivity in children – or "hyperactivity attention deficit disorder" to give it its full name – (how carefully we phrase things in our guilt) – are now well documented as being attributable to our highly chemicalized diet; and in more adventurous trials concerning 'criminal behaviour', an American study has shown a 40% drop in violence in their prisons after offering more fruit and vegetables. There is evidence that a low-vitamin diet "can affect the chemistry of the brain".**

Dr. Weston Price's work delves far deeper than this, however. He shows that our depleted diet is indeed affecting our internal chemistry, including that of the brain. But this – not only in a direct and immediate way. In a much deeper way as well. Weston

* *In fact, he was a speaker at the 1996 Open Day at the SEER Centre (already mentioned), which was given a great launching at that event by David Bellamy. After a certain other speaker at the event, had finished and sat down, he asked if there was something he might add. I happened to be chairing the Speakers' Session, and of course said – Yes. . .and have rarely said a better Yes in my life!*

** *Prison Phoenix Trust Newsletter, Autumn 1997. An excellent initiative, P.O. Box 328, Oxford OX1 1PJ. Send* s.a.e. for inquiry, but I have no doubt a small donation would also be welcome to this excellent voluntary body.
WDDTY (What Doctors Don't Tell You), Oct. 98. Another publication doing sterling work: 4 Wallace Rd, London N1 2PG. Send s.a.e. for inquiry.
In addition, see Part III, "The Criminal-Mineral Link".

Price showed that – in the formation of the dental arch is involved the growth and functioning of the *vital pituitary gland*, and that this may have direct repercussions upon the functioning of the brain itself. Moreover, he shows that all this starts a long way back, with the health (i.e., *the diet*) of the parents – right from the child's conception; and that our present ignorance of these deeper implications of our diet have unfortunate repercussions for us *as a society*, as well as for the individuals concerned.

We cannot afford to overlook Weston Price's important findings. And the less can we afford to, since they so beautifully *and so finally* give the lie to that ugly so-called 'science of eugenics': that is, the pretence of one race's superiority over another, or equally, of certain superior strains as existing within a race – with the false and dangerous pathway that follows from it, of attempting to breed a superior kind of human being. For this false science shows signs of trying to resurrect itself today, as scientists turn to the inventions of genetic engineering.

There is, furthermore, a growing tendency to be noticed in the press of late – the sloppy attribution of certain diseases to 'heredity' or to 'genetics', (usefully now taking the place of the rather outworn 'virus' theory!). In this new scenario, it is interesting that the Scots seem to have been particularly singled out, (as we shall later observe).

In this connection, one is inevitably led to ponder a certain parallel singling out of Scotland that is, both as the dumping-ground (*and* arsenal) of Britain, nuclearwise, and in addition (through inferior 'Scotland' legislation) as the recipients – as we now know from the recent Greengairs scandal – of toxic landfill which it is illegal to dump south of the Border. (Or *was*. Under the glare of this uncomfortable spotlight, a promise of amendment was hastily rushed forward!) Furthermore, the taking of a *Scottish* island for that obscene anthrax experiment. . .

Whilst the scientists themselves will be innocently engaged in the 'excitement' of the new genetic scene, it is impossible not to ponder connections, when part of a society set on so aberrant a course as ours. And so – it is impossible *not* to see that, where one part of a country has been especially marked to the assigning of such notorious materials, a special assigning of some genetic shortfall to its people would at least fit comfortably with the same scene. . . (a kind of gentle 'educating' in inferiority!)

To those who would throw up their hands at the outrageousness of any such suggestion, one must point out that the latter assigning seems scarcely more insulting than the former. (If a country is a dump, what are its people?) They would therefore do better to ponder fully – as they clearly have not done to date – just how insulting to the Scots those former assignings have been.

To this whole scene, Weston Price's work comes as a breath of sanity. Not heredity, but the *way we care for ourselves*, through our diet – which is in the first place the *way we care for our soil* (emphasised in the later chapters of his book): it is this, *this* that lies at the root of our diseased, or otherwise, condition. Of course the school in India of Howard *et al.* demonstrated this too. But Weston Price carries the matter a stage further. This is because, as a dentist, he was led to the study, in particular, of the face: its structure, and the effect of this upon the brain, especially the all-important *fore-brain*. His great importance to us is that, in revealing this deeper dimension of the damage done to us by a deficiency diet, he destroys, *at a yet deeper level*, the accusing finger now being pointed at us, regarding our supposed inherited 'genetic deficiencies'. Illustrating how sound diet can reverse even in a single generation many so-called 'genetic' or 'hereditary' defects, he coined a new and powerful phrase – *intercepted heredity*. It is a phrase we would do well to arm ourselves with, and make a part of our understanding and vocabulary.

Before plunging into Weston Price's work, a word about the more intractable 'inherited' conditions, such as haemophilia. As we shall see, in accompanying Weston Price in his investigations, such conditions are typical of a civilization that has lost touch with its soil, and therefore with its health.* Think of those very ancient Romans who needed no physician throughout six centuries! A condition that has persisted already through several generations may well take more than one generation to reverse. But if the children of such a family are fed *consistently and exclusively* on a top-quality nutritional diet, produced from equally soundly nourished soil, its reversal will assuredly in due course come about. Who amongst those suffering from more prolonged *intercepted heredity* today – (which is what such conditions represent) – lives on such a diet? Similarly, one may inherit a *susceptibility to* certain afflictions, by the same pathway, but *not* – and this is the great difference – through any inherent *genetic* defect. (Therefore, where such susceptibilities are inherited, it becomes our task to undertake our own programme for *reversing* such a trend, to the best of our ability.)

A particularly beautiful aspect of the above concept of intercepted heredity, is that it fulfils so perfectly the concept of redemption. That we can, and should, *resurrect ourselves*, by following his example – (not overlooking the part played by grace) – was the essential teaching of Jesus and other similarly great souls. Are we supposed to be a Christian society? Then why do we not blazon its tenets through our philosophy of health instead of taking refuge in that Old Testament view of eternal damnation? – with our only salvation *human engineering*!

To turn to Weston Price's book, then – and plunge in at the heart of the matter: to help us to understand all that we have got caught up in. . .(so unawares, while the new 'lords of the soil' have held our health in their hands). . .he proposes we think of the face in a new way, as being the *floor* of the anterior (i.e., the front part) of the brain:-

> "The pituitary body is situated on the underside of the brain just back of the eyes. It is the governing body for the activity of growth, and largely controls the functioning of several of the other glands of internal secretion. It is, as it were, the master of the ship." (Ch., "Physical and Mental Deterioration".)

What role does the pituitary gland play in the functioning of the brain?

As we consider this question, let us bear in mind that, for its *own* proper functioning, the pituitary gland is heavily dependent upon vitamin E, and that – (to quote from the same chapter) – "one of the best sources of vitamin E is wheat germ, most of which is removed from white flour, usually along with four-fifths of the mineral". Thus we see clearly "one cause of the tragedy that is overwhelming so many individuals in our modern civilization" – and that it is entirely of our own making.

---

* *What about those millions of peasant peoples who have not lost touch with their soil, struggling to survive still as peasants today? Living under the cruel system of land monopoly as virtual slaves, compelled to grow crops for export to survive – and usually with the whole arsenal of artificial agriculture – their in-touchness with the soil has, equally, been drastically and decisively intercepted – to use Weston Price's sound term. I recall one of the most interesting chapters in the book earlier referred to, Living with the Land, as being precisely about a peasant people (in Central America, I think), reclaiming their health, by recovering their older knowledge and practices of healing, as a vital part of the reclaiming of their lives.*

What tragedy, precisely? We must examine the role that the pituitary plays in the functioning of the brain.

This same chapter, ("Physical and Mental deterioration"), contains a riveting account of a young patient who came into Dr. Weston Price's hands. A lad of sixteen, he suffered from Down's Syndrome – (the term used is "Mongol", the one current at the time*) – and could only play on the floor with blocks and rattles like a child. His upper jaw was so much smaller than his lower that it went inside it, making it difficult for him to eat, and Dr. Weston Price – who, as a dental surgeon, was practised in orthodontics – decided with the agreement of his mother to widen the upper arch "by moving the maxillary bones apart about one-half inch", this being accomplished gradually over the space of thirty days.

The results were dramatic. He immediately started to grow a moustache, added three inches to his height over four months, and in the space of three months had developed all the sexual attributes of a man:-

> "His mental change was even more marked. . . In a few weeks' time he passed through stages that usually take several years. At first, he got behind the door to frighten us; later, he put bent pins on chairs to see us jump when we sat down, and finally be became the cause of a policeman's coming to the office from where he was conducting traffic on the corner below to find who it was squirting water on him when his back was turned. He developed a great fondness for calling people over the telephone, wanted to borrow my automobile to take his mother for a drive, and with his arm caressingly about the shoulders of one of the secretaries, invited her to go with him to a dance."

This young man (as we must now call him) lived in another city. On returning to his home, he was now able to go to the grocery store for his mother and bring back the groceries with the change – and also to tell if the change was correct. He was then able "to come alone to me ninety miles by railroad and make two changes of trains and the various transfers on the street cars of the city with accuracy and safety." During this time he also learned to read children's stories and newspaper headings, and "spent much time doing to".

How is the amazing development of this lad to be explained – which saw him in the space of three months change from being a child playing with bricks on the floor, to a youth able to lead a reasonably enjoyable life and to take reasonable care of himself? As we read on, let us pause for a moment on the solemn thought of the growing army of *carers* our society is becoming dependent upon, and so gain some initial insights into the appalling harvest we are reaping for ourselves, from so much *ignorant destruction of our health.*

The space between the maxillary bones had been widened by about a half-inch in roughly thirty days. This lateral pressure on the maxillary bones was accomplished by "rigid attachments to the teeth of the two sides of the upper arch", and the half-inch opening in the upper arch was filled "by supplying two teeth on a restoration".

---

* *The following note is placed at the front of the book: "Since this invaluable book was published 50 years ago, mores and social attitudes have changed to such an extent that some readers may be offended by references to "savages" and other out-of-date nomenclatures, as well as by some of the research studies that are no longer timely. However, in the interest of authenticity and completeness, the publisher feels an obligation to reprint the book exactly as Dr. Price wrote it in 1939." And I think we can respect that decision.*

As Dr. Weston Price explains, the outward movement of the maxillary bones (forming the roof of the mouth and sides of the nose) now, through pressure on the temporal bones, created a "*tension downwards*" against the floor of the anterior part of the brain, this in turn "*stimulating the pituitary gland in the base of the brain*". (Emphases added.) The involvement of the pituitary gland in this astonishing transformation of the boy was doubly verified in that, the appliance becoming dislodged once, and the maxillary bones settling together again, "immediately, in a day or two", he "lapsed into his old condition of lethargy", until "with the readaption of the separating appliance and the reconstruction of the retaining appliance", the dramatic improvement was restored. Incidentally, the six photographs accompanying this part of the text form an absorbing addition to it, as the sadly vacant stare of the first picture gives place, in the last, to the smile of a handsome young man.

Let us think back again to what we have just learned of the pituitary gland's heavy dependence upon Vitamin E, *and what we are doing to ourselves* – AND TO OUR CHILDREN – even in just this one matter of eating the travesty of bread that we now eat. Even though the effects may not be the dramatic effects of the above case, EFFECTS THERE ALWAYS ARE. Is it not a sad reflection on dentistry today that not a whisper has reached us over the intervening more-than-half-century of the great work of Dr. Weston Price – not only regarding teeth and such transformations, but about health in general (as we shall see): whilst instead official dentistry runs after such follies as *fluoridation*!

On this very matter of fluoridation, it is worth quoting here the sound and intelligent observation of Dr. Weston Price, since it is a sound exposé of the *un*intelligence, incompetence *and gross cover-up* – affecting nearly the entire body of dentists in this country through the B.D.A. – which is evidenced in our successive government' ridiculous obsession with fluoridating the water supply, over precisely the same half-century-plus:-

> "Tooth decay is not only unnecessary, but an indication of our divergence from Nature's fundamental laws of life and health. It is very important that in the consideration of the dental caries problem it shall be kept in mind continually, that it is only one of a large group of symptoms of modern physical degeneration and when teeth are decaying other things are going wrong in the body. Fluorine treatment, like dental extractions, cannot be a panacea for dental caries. . . *Adding it to the food or water for general use is beyond the practice of dentistry.*" (Chs. 21 and 24. Emphasis added.)

Forget fluoridation, British Dental Association – and take a good glassful of WESTON PRICE COMMON SENSE!

*

THE PITUITARY GLAND ... VITAMINE 'E' ... OUR DEPLETED BREAD

The discoveries made by Dr. Weston Price regarding the vital link between the healthful functioning of the pituitary gland and the structure of the face and dental arch, did not stand alone. They were endorsed by a number of his contemporaries, in particular by Dr. Hector Mortimer and his associates at McGill University, Montreal, of whom Weston Price records: "Dr Mortimer's excellent investigations seem to indicate clearly that facial and dental arch form are directly related to and controlled by the functioning of the pituitary body in the base of the brain".

Dr. Weston Price's work adds, however, a new dimension to our understanding of this connection. for he brings to light that the effect of this may extend to the brain's functioning. Nor did he leave it there. His work with the Down's Syndrome child shows us plainly that, when the pituitary gland, on account of poor nutrition, has been unable to function as it should – (to form the necessary facial structure to allow the proper development of the brain – it may be possible to *reverse* this damaging situation, at least to a considerable extent; and to bring about the needed stimulation of the brain through the pituitary gland, by the altering of an ill-formed dental arch to a more nearly normal form. Thus he establishes himself in the world of health, dentistry and nutrition not only as a discoverer, but as something of yet greater worth – as a healer too. Dr. Weston Price would of course, at the same time, have been supervising the boy's nutrition (and particularly in respect of vitamin E), since a sound nutritional programme for every patient was and integral part of his dental practice.

The pituitary gland's requirement of a good supply of vitamin E – ("since this vitamin plays so major a role in the nutrition of the pituitary body") – relates of course, in the first place, to the health of the parents, and particularly of the mother, who carries the child. The majority of children born with Down's Syndrome are born to mothers of over forty years of age. Dr. Weston Price does not discount the age factor – but the physical depletion of the mother of slightly older years he sees as itself related to the question of nutrition. (We need only to think of the people of Hunza. . .)

In this whole scene, we need to remind ourselves that the case of the Down's Syndrome child was simply an extreme one, and that a diet depleted of vitamin E (as is almost everyone's diet today) *must have a deleterious effect*, at the very least in lowering physical health, whether we are aware of it or not. That we should, then, allow the *vital germ of the wheat*, with its high vitamin E content, to be *removed* (by 'all-beneficent' government sanction) from the flour with which our bread is made – (simply to give the bread a longer shelf-life, since the flour from which white bread is made is 'dead') – shows us the extent of the crime being committed against the health of the nation. . .by that State power which at the same time pretends to be running the nation's 'Health' Service.

The 'food safety' body which is currently being pressed for by the public – (and the government is so 'shy' of setting up) – is *right to hand*. It consists of that body of perfectly ordinary concerned individuals which exists in every community, and awaits but decentralised grass-roots re-empowerment, under radical land reform, to assert itself again, in the most natural way. It will then be the most natural thing in the world to see local bakeries springing up once more, in response to demand, to provide whole bread *locally*, *daily* – where shelf-life is as much a thing of the past as is State interference in any shape or form with either our food or our health.

But let us for a moment suppose that, under our present regime of State power, the wheat-germ *were* retained. Does not that wheat-germ *in any case* (except for the rare amount organically grown) harbour a plethora of unseen dangers for the unborn child? According to one press report, during its growing season a wheat crop is sprayed "once with insecticides, twice with herbicides, twice with fungicides and once with a growth-regulating chemical". . .(Incidentally, just think of all that going into the rivers too, especially in river-margin fields. How *could* fish-stocks *not* be adversely affected?...) But can we even begin to imagine the effect of all this on the extremely delicate embryo of the child in the womb? – with its as yet only embryonic immune system too?

Birthright. . .and. . .Scotland Today

In short – how swiftly in surveying this scene, in the now added light of Dr. Weston Price's work, we are returned to that 'special equation' built into land monopoly: to the question of *control over our soil* as the starting-point of *control over our health.*

*

TRAVELS OF EXPLORATION

In 1930, Weston Price decided to abandon a brilliant career in dentistry, (which had included "teaching and the publication of many scientific articles and several professional dental textbooks"), in order to devote himself to wider-ranging research into the subject of nutrition – like Schauberger, out in the *real* laboratory, the open laboratory of the living world. From 1930 until the start of World War II in 1939, he travelled extensively. Along with his wife, who shared his own deep interest in this field,* he covered in all more than 100,000 miles, travelling to all corners of the globe, and searching out and recording his discoveries concerning health and nutrition in text, in photograph and on film. These were gathered from encounters, fascinatingly described, with peoples as diverse as the Eskimos of the north and the equatorial Africans, to the peoples of the South Pacific and the New Zealand Maoris.

The findings of these travels, so fully documented in his work are of twofold interest. Firstly, at that period, seventy years ago, he was able to study the different societies he visited when they were only just at the start of 'contamination' with Western culture, or yet free of it. Contact with the West invariably brought with it a change from a diet of wholefood nutriment – (gathered, in addition, from an *unpolluted environment*) – to the deficiency-type diet which is practically universal in the West today, depleted of its goodness and laced with pollution of every kind. The evidence of the disastrous effects upon the health of these original peoples, even within one generation, of this fundamental alteration to their dietary, presents us with incontrovertible evidence of what we have done to ourselves. It places beyond question the origin of those degenerative diseases of our society – diseases to which the West has no answer, and which we have, in our ignorance, come to take for granted as an inevitable part of 'life'. It takes us straight back to Viktor Schauberger, and to his similar warnings (from a yet wider panorama) of the calamitous pathway we are on.

The second finding of Weston Price's travels is no less significant. In these more 'primitive' communities, (in reality, simply more *original* – and decidedly more noble), which he visited, we are back once more with the peoples of Hunza and of Gosaba. Their social health mirrored the physical.

Without exception, Weston Price found these more original peoples open, friendly, generous, noble of character, totally to be depended upon and trustworthy in every respect. The picture he draws of them is all the more poignant to read, in view of the 'other' journey he made (also recorded in his book) – a journey through the various institutions in America for the 'less adequate' members of society, including a State Penitentiary, or Prison. In what he writes of those far-off communities he visited,

---

* *The following tribute to his wife appears at the start of the book: "To the memory of that kindred soul, my wife, Florence, who assisted me so greatly on these difficult expeditions, this book is lovingly dedicated". After she died, he later married Monica, who set up the Price-Pottenger Nutrition Foundation, as earlier mentioned, and to whom, as his widow, the Heritage Edition of the book is dedicated.*

before their contamination by Western culture, we are brought face-to-face with our own self-destructions in a peculiarly vivid way. His sharp eye as a social observer is part of the interest of the book, and unobtrusively as such material is woven in, it is particularly rich – as we shall see – when it comes to his visit to "the Gaelics", the people of our own western isles! But let us plunge in in more distant fields.

Under one typical illustration, in Dr. Weston Price's book, of four fine faces displaying sets of immaculate and gleaming teeth, we read: "Since the discovery of New Zealand, the primitive natives, the Maoris, have had the reputation of having the finest teeth and finest bodies of any race in the world. These faces are typical. Only about one tooth per thousand teeth had been attacked by tooth decay before they came under the influence of the white man". (Incidentally, the rows of perfect teeth portrayed in the book from this broad survey of original peoples, owed nothing to hygiene, for they were as untouched by a tooth-brush as they were by tooth decay. Of course, where *rotten* foods are concerned, better clean them out of your mouth as fast as possible. But let's get back to sound nutrition – sound dentition – and throw our tooth-brushes away too!

A couple of pages further on, under a very different picture, we read: "In striking contrast with the beautiful faces of the primitive Maori, those born since the adoption of deficient modernized foods are grossly deformed. . ." – and in the accompanying text, referring to the white peoples of Australia and New Zealand amongst whom tooth decay was "severe", Weston Price notes the "striking. . .similarity between the deformities of the dental arches which occur in the Maori people who were born after their parents adopted the modern foods, and those of the whites".

Nearby, another picture catches my eye with the words: "Whereas the original primitive had reportedly the finest teeth in the world, the whites now in New Zealand are claimed to have the poorest in the world. . . An analysis of the two types of food reveals the reason". But not to New Zealand's dental-dom, of course! – who, instead of siezing the opportunity for some sound investigating on 'Weston Price' lines, followed by some sound education in nutrition to improve the health of New Zealand's population as a whole, beyond just their teeth, went for the predictable folly of a *countrywide fluoridation programme*! Dental-*dumb* – more to the point, methinks! However, one of New Zealand's originally strongest proponents of fluoridation, high up in the dental world, has since, very commendably, travelled across the world, helping to expose the fraud that it is.

There is a particularly telling caption under another picture in the book. The photograph is of four young Seminole Indians, of America. . . But let us first turn to the previous page. Here are four Seminole Indians of the primitive type, showing strong and well-developed faces, all displaying rows of perfect teeth: "The Seminole Indians living today in southern Florida largely beyond contact with the white civilization still produce magnificent teeth and dental arches of which these are typical. They live in the Everglade forest and still obtain the native foods." (Any more, one wonders?) Now we turn back to the other picture, and here is the caption to it: "Seminole Indians. Note the change in facial and dental arch form in the children of this modernized group. . . Their faces are stamped with the blight which so many often think of as normal because it is so common with us."

Which so many think of as normal because it is so common with us. I was transported back to the New Zealand scene, and the blindness of those dentists.

Although the reason for the deteriorated state of both modern Maori and white was obvious enough – (let us say, something that a McCarrison would not have missed any more than a Weston Price) – to those dentists it was truly invisible. Suddenly, there it was, right before my eyes like a shaft of light – the warning of Viktor Schauberger: that we have become so degenerate we *cannot actually see* how degenerate we are. The shaft of light switched and spread over the fluoridation scene: that degeneracy is a decay at a deeper level than teeth – nor can our teeth ever be restored to us while it operates.

What is it that makes the difference between those blind dentists and one of Weston Price's stature? Weston Price was clearly marked by that same visionary capacity which possessed the founders of Gosaba – but I enjoy the rather special light shed on it by something else I came across in this book. It is part of a tribute to Weston Price which appears in the Foreward to the book, written by Earnest A. Hooton, of Harvard University:-

> "Since we have known for a long time that savages have excellent teeth and that civilized men have terrible teeth, it seems to me that we have been extraordinary stupid in concentrating all of our attention upon the task of finding our why our teeth are so poor, without ever bothering to learn why savage teeth are so good. Dr. Weston Price seems to be the only person who possesses the scientific horse sense to supplement his knowledge of the probable causes of dental disease with a study of the dietary regimens which are associated with dental health. In other words, Dr. Price has accomplished one of those epochal pieces of research which make every other investigator desirous of kicking himself because he never thought of doing the same thing. This is an exemplification of the fact that really gifted scientists are those who can appreciate the obvious."

This is indeed an excellent statement of the matter – that what is at work here is a fine example of *common sense*! And I could not help an extra smile on remembering Viktor Schauberger's – "he should have asked how it got up there in the first place"!

But supposing such common sense *did* prevail, what on earth would happen to our Department of Agriculture and Fisheries? – of Health? – of Education. . .?

I suddenly remember a rather delicious saying I once came upon:-

> If all of modern medicines were at the bottom
> of the sea, it would be very much the better for
> mankind – and very much the worse for the fishes!

*

THE FOREBRAIN

On the 24th of February, 1998, an article appeared in the Dundee Courier which was headed "The Real Price of Ecstasy" – and it caught my attention. It first stated that tests had shown Ecstasy's users to have considerably poorer memories that non-users. Then it went on to report something else. Research (in Wales, Edinburgh and the United States) revealed Ecstasy users as showing "more impulsivity – a 'classic phenomenon' of damage to the frontal lobes of the brain". "More impulsivity" sounds harmless enough – but maybe not if we delve a little further.

It so happens that Dr. Weston Price's book carries a Supplement – material added later, as he saw the 'increasing perils' that faced our civilization on its present path. The reference in the Courier article to the "frontal lobes of the brain" brought to mind sharply some additional information regarding the forebrain, carried in that Supplement and contained in the chapter "How Mother Nature Made Us".

Weston Price writes, in this chapter, of the forebrain as that part of the brain which, through "nutritionally produced growth", increases its functions to become capable of "super-mentality, exalted personality, noble music, arts, social reforms and altruism". Conversely, he points out, where there are "parental nutritional injuries of foetus with defects of forebrain", the outcome is the opposite, with "loss or lowering of inhibitions (for sex urge and appetite) with character change, delinquency patterns and mentally retarded". Pausing over the content of this latter quotation, we may perhaps better appreciate the significance of that "more impulsivity" and *all* that may be contained in it.

What indeed have we done to ourselves – and what indeed to our children? What aberrant pathways have we not sent them forth upon, by bringing them *ill-equipped* into the world – ill-equipped, because we did not understand that "all our qualities, physical, mental *and moral* are primarily determined by the adequacy of our nutrition"? (Preface to Supplement. Emphasis added.)

As Dr. Weston Price makes the point in this fine book: society punishes the culprit – but *who is the real culprit*? Is it the individual – *or is it society*?

"Mother Nature", at any rate, seems to have no doubt where the real fault lies. How very interesting that she should have situated the forebrain in so nutritionally vulnerable a part of the human body! How clearly we can now see woven into her design for us, from the very outset, the irreversible decree that *no society shall be allowed to flourish on this earth* which does not honour her laws.

. . .How little we realized that in the shaping of our destiny, so literally, the shaping of our faces is involved. . .all starting with *our food and the soil it is grown from*. . .and all this carrying back to the nutrition of our parents and the soil their food was grown from – well before the time of our conception. How solemnizing it is to read in the Preface to the Supplement, where Weston Price quotes the words of "distinguished anatomist and anthropologist" Dr. M.F. Ashley-Montagu:-

> "In spite of our enormous technological advances we spiritually and as human beings are not the equal of the average Aboriginal or the average Eskimo – we are very definitely their inferiors. . .Theirs are the only true democracies where every individual finds his happiness in catering to the happiness of the group and where anyone who in any way threatens the welfare of the group is dealt with as an abnormality." (Article "The Socio-Biology of Man", published in *Scientific Monthly*, June 1940.)

. . .*Where every individual finds his happiness in catering to the happiness of the group* – and any *opposite* orientation is considered an abnormality. . . Can *we* possibly imagine *ourselves* living in such a manner – we who continue to spiral helplessly downhill on our drugs-wagon – a drugs-wagon we can now see, from these added insights from Dr. Price, is indeed destroying *the very fabric of our society*?

> "The complacency with which the masses of the people as well as the politicians view our trend is not unlike the drifting of a merry party in the rapids

above a great cataract. There seems to be no appropriate sense of impending doom." (Ch. 20.)

Dr. Price's words could scarcely paint in more powerful terms the tragedy that awaits us – a tragedy originating from the loss of our connection with the soil – that is, from the loss of our land. Fortunately, the families of drug victims, particularly the mothers, are fast breaking through that "complacency" now. How soon will they see that the *last* word lies with Henry George? –

> "The ownership of land is the great fundamental fact which ultimately determines the social, the political, and consequently the intellectual and moral condition of a people."

How soon will they see that there is no way forward for us, in any direction, except we take upon ourselves the full task of the undoing of that *initial* loss – the twofold loss of our connection with our soil and our land?

*

THE EXTENT OF OUR SELF-DESTRUCTIONS

The account of Weston Price's other, sadder 'journey', on home ground, through the various State institutions for the retarded, the delinquent and the criminal, may be read in his chapter "Physical and Mental Deterioration". Over and over again he noted the huge proportion of those suffering from "disturbances of facial form and the shape of the dental arches". Again – "I did not see one with a typically normal facial development".

Dr. Weston Price is at pains to point out that these (strictly abnormal) facial structures are scattered freely throughout the population today – and among people contributing shiningly to society in every field. To us – they are normal. To us – *we* are normal! Nor indeed would we have *a single feature* altered, of those we know or meet. Each is precious to us. And this is understandable; for the light of the soul within illumines the outer, making every feature its own. This need not, however, prevent us from observing, as Dr. Weston Price teaches us to observe, from the outer, the direction in which we are moving – especially considering how many generations down this pathway we already are:-

> "Recent intergenerational research in animals and people has shown that, on a uniformly poor diet, the offspring of each generation deteriorates more and more, and in rats this continues up to eight generations. We do not know what the final stage will be in human deterioration. I suspect that many of the people with psychiatric disorders today, the addicts, the high degree of violence, the tremendous number of depressions and tension states, and the great number of physical degenerations. . .are the modern manifestations of this continuing degeneration. I have seen no experiments, however, which show what happens when the diet continues to get worse with time. I shudder to think of the final outcome." (Abram Hoffer, M.D., Ph.D. Among the New Introductions in this *50th Anniversary Edition*.)

. . .When the diet continues to get worse with time – ? Where are we now? Refined foods, tinned foods, processed foods, pasteurized milk, artificial fertilizers, pesticides of every kind, chemical additives to food, nuclear fallout-contamination, pollution from every source – including now ubiquitous electro-magnetic networks, the whole gamut of water treatments, threatened fluoridation, food irradiation, onto GMOs... Is it not *yet* enough?

Here is what Sir Arbuthnot Lane had to say, speaking as a "world renowned authority on "the disturbances of the intestinal tract of the modernized whites as compared with the more normal functioning of primitive races", in his Preface to *Maori Symbolism*. And this – already half-a-century ago:-

> "Long surgical experience has proved to me conclusively that there is something radically and fundamentally wrong with the civilized mode of life, and I believe that unless the present dietetic and health customs of the White Nations are reorganized, social decay and race deterioration are inevitable." (Ch. 26.)

The decay and deterioration are moreover – (as we now know from Schauberger, Weston Price and others – by no means limited to the physical. *The mental and moral follow suit* – and here is a good comment on the latter aspects from the well-known writer, Ernest Thomson Seton, in *The Gospel of the Red Man*, (quoted in ch. 26):-

> "The culture and civilization of the White man are essentially material; his measure of success is 'How much property have I acquired for myself?' ¯ The culture of the Red man is fundamentally spiritual; his measure of success is, 'How much service have I rendered to my people?'

Is it any wonder that he concludes:-

> "The civilization of the white man is a failure; it is visibly crumbling around us. It has failed at every crucial test. No one who measures things by results can question this fundamental statement."

. . . . . Time to REVERSE DIRECTION!

*

ADOLESCENTS

Special mention deserves to be made of the light which Dr. Weston Price's work throws on the problems of adolescence, for these problems tragically afflict, especially, *already damaged* children. The experience of his practice revealed to him at first hand that when children reach the age of adolescence, their "supplies of minerals and vitamins are inadequate to meet Nature's demands and the system borrows minerals from the skeleton to maintain vital processes", (i.e., those involved in reaching sexual maturity). In the clearest proof of this, their susceptibility to dental caries increases significantly at this time, while according to tests made at a school attended by disadvantaged children in America, the "intelligence quotient" of the children also declined as they approached that stage in their life; that is – just when they stand at the brink of manhood and womanhood and need *every* finest human attribute to cope at this crucial time, including with the looming world of work just ahead of them.

It is scarcely surprising, therefore, to find the following comment recorded in Weston Price's book, in a report written by one who was making a study of problems associated with degeneration: "It is almost as though crime were some contagious disease, to which the constitutionally susceptible were suddenly exposed at puberty, or to which puberty left them peculiarly prone". Well – so it does, of course, in a society which so wickedly deprives its young of that nutrition so especially needful to them at this time. What they are in reality, of course, "suddenly exposed to" at puberty, is the full force of the physical – *and mental* – experience of drastic, long-term *nutritional deficiency*; a deficiency inflicted upon them by an ignorant, *itself deficient and defective*, society.

Could anything shout louder at us – "Who are the real culprits here?" "Who is it that should *really* be standing in the dock?" These are our *damaged adolescents*.

One wants to ask: have no other dentists ever noticed the particular features of tooth decay at puberty? – or ever wondered about them? But of course, as has just been pointed out to us, the worth of 'common sense' Weston Price possessed is rare in science today. These children's bodies – *our* children's, *Scotland's* children – are simply crying out to us for proper sustenance. And what do they get? A Scottish doctor who has worked in refugee camps among the displaced of the world, apparently referred to a certain inner city area that she visited back home as – just another huge refugee camp. What "nutrition"– of body, mind *and* soul – for tomorrow's parents! *Of course* they are refugee camps – displaced masses live here too. Those displaced from the land and still waiting to get back. Meanwhile consuming chips and coke. . .the parents of tomorrow's children! If we can't summon up some good, healthy fear on our own behalves, surely the contemplation of this scene must run us scared for what we are leaving to our children.

"What is the alternative, then?"

"We must learn entirely anew. With hands empty and ready to receive, we must climb up into the mountains towards the dawn." (Werner Zimmerman, quoted in *The Water Wizard*.) Viktor Schauberger – like Weston Price and the founders of Gosaba – inspired others to look *up*, amidst all the surrounding decay, to where the answers are waiting for us. Answers a-plenty as we have seen. No wonder Schauberger was wont to observe that we – "think an octave too low"!

*

"ARTIFICIAL MEN AND WOMEN"

We should complete Dr. Weston Price's sound teaching on this question of the body's borrowings, by referring to the more general scene. It is this same borrowing syndrome which, as he points out, is the root of the syndrome of hip fractures of the elderly, which are such a feature of our time and were already observable in Dr. Weston Price's day. (Incidentally – aggravated by the fluoridation of water supplies, as varies scientific studies have shown.*)

Meanwhile, in the usual way, we are led to look upon hip fractures as *normal*! – a "normal" part of "normal" life! Ditto, pyorrhoea of the gums! While we may be sure that osteoporosis – (that painful disease of *general* bone depletion now so much on the increase, and linked with the hip fractures, of course) – receives no mention in Weston Price's text simply because, sixty years ago, we had not yet quite reached this still steeper stage in our decline. . .

No wonder Dr. Abram Hoffer shuddered to think of "the final outcome", as our increasingly deficient foodstuffs continue to take their increasing toll, while we continue happily and unswervingly on destroying ourselves – in the surest proof of how far we are already destroyed!

I am reminded of a splendid summing-up of the matter by Albert Howard, in his book *An Agricultural Testament*, published by the Oxford University Press in 1943. Fifty years ago we were not yet fully launched into the pesticide scene, but even just writing about artificial manures (fertilizers), he says it well enough for the whole:-

---

* *See Part III: "Fluoride, Teeth and the Atomic Bomb", by Joel Griffiths and Chris Bryson.*

"Artificial manures lead inevitably to artificial nutrition, artificial food, artificial animals, and finally to artificial men and women."

So – there we have it! Artificial men and women! The artificial food we so proudly harvest, thinking we can cheat nature, has the last laugh on us by *remaking us in its own image*!

Viktor Schauberger has added another dimension to the scene, of course – *artificial water*!

No wonder such a society, faced with a growing array of problems that are all too *real*, can only come up with ARTIFICIAL SOLUTIONS!

Incidentally, Albert Howard coined an incomparable term for those artificial fertilizers: *devil's dust*! A term long overdue for resurrection, methinks – and even more applicable to today's pesticides. As to these latter in their commoner, liquid form – we surely need no prompting to recognize them as *the devil's drams*!

*

MODERN "EUGENICS"

There is one solid thread of gold woven through Weston Price's discoveries of the destruction we have made of ourselves. As already mentioned, his work dispenses entirely with the modern science of eugenics.

I say here "modern", because my 1951 Concise Oxford Dictionary tells me that the meaning of *eugenics* is simply: "the science of the production of fine offspring" – which is, of course, exactly what Dr. Weston Price's work is about. However, an article in The Herald of 26 Aug. 97 cites a dictionary definition of the word which is clearly more recent, and it has five words added to it which introduce the sinister note associated with eugenics today: "the science of the production of fine offspring by control of inherited qualities". That "control", in our society, by no means refers to *obeying Nature's laws*.

"Secret Pursuit of a Pure Species" was the heading of that Herald article – and it reveals that the "search for the master race" was not confined to Hitler's Third Reich: "in Sweden, Denmark and Norway between the mid 1920s and the mid 1970s, more than 100,000 people, 90% of them women, were sterilized because their race, lifestyle or mental capacities were deemed undesirable". More recently, the Swedish government denounced the policy as having been "barbaric and a national disgrace". Nevertheless, continuing into the 1970s, Swedish housing workers had been "asked to report tenants who they believed should not procreate".

Thus was corrupted the science of eugenics. Thus was it converted from its original, innocent and laudable beginnings into a ready-to-hand instrument for political agendas of the most debased kind. The essential failure was the failure of society to recognize the vital third influence in our development, pinpointed by Dr. Weston Price. That is: besides the two factors of true heredity, and environment, the third and powerful one of *intercepted heredity*. This is the heredity which stares back at us when we have contravened Nature's laws, and in just punishment for this we are affected mentally as well as physically. Thus Britain's Eugenics Education Society, "concerned by the growing problem presented by the 'feeble-minded' " in our midst, could not see that it was their own feeble minds that were in the first place staring back at them!

*

FALSE AND MISCREANT POWER

The obedience to Nature's laws, and reverence for them, that allows true heredity to operate, requires self-discipline: *power over oneself.* It is interesting that, as we follow in Dr. Weston Price's footsteps in his encounters with these more 'primitive' communities he visited, we find that, in respect of *power*, this seems to be as far as a people living in obedience to Nature were ever intended to go – (save for power of that type held by the elders in such societies, arising solely out of their generally acknowledged superior *wisdom* – such as we saw served the free society of Gosaba so well). The power games of our society were completely absent from those communities – (which, as communities, retained the necessary fundamental power over their soil and their land, of course).

If we should do unto others – and *be* unto others – as we would have them do, and be, unto us – (an aphorism of all Earth's great teachers): then power over ourself is clearly the only right wielding of power in our social relationships.

We can see, then, that where that proper field of power-wielding is drastically interfered with – as in a society where land monopoly pursues its enslaving course – the 'dark twin' of that true and bright original must inevitably come into play.

Power over others, and the lust for it, grows apace – the virtually uncontrollable *substitute urge* for the real thing; the shadowing forth, in this dark way – (with all its terrible repercussions on other lives) – of the unconscious longing, in all of us, for the wielding of that true power whose field of play is our self.

In standing against that 'dark twin' of power wielded over others – (which involves so terrible a prostitution of its wielder's own nature) – we therefore make a stand not only for ourselves, but for that other (the wielder of it) too.

To survey the larger picture: when a people lose the groundwork of their being (their land and their soil), they become an *on-going* casualty of the false power which instituted the robbery – a power of a most dangerous because *intrinsically run-away* kind. Those engaged in wielding that false power, unable to discover the true field of its play (the self), in their mad, unconscious searching for it run riot through every department of human life. Thus our Western civilization now presents an arena of 'power politics' of the purest self-abandonment (corruption), intent only on pursuing ever further its own mad career. It is easy to see that the sphere of false eugenics – especially given new impetus by the new *genetic engineering* – offers such power politics an almost irresistible field of play.

In this connection, the opposers of the fluoridation of public water supplies have always been standing also against a threat beyond just the immediately apparent. Valium was once recommended by certain scientists in America for addition to the water supplies as a general tranquillizer. (No doubt there are those who would well wish to 'tranquillize' the fiery Scots! – and indeed papers have been written concerning the addition of fluoride to water supplies for that very purpose...) The possibility of universal birth-control via the tap is also of course well within today's drug pharmacy. . .from which further vistas easily open up. . .

That 'dark twin' which runs riot through our science and our politics today awaits the healing which can reach it through *one* avenue only: that of the re-empowerment of the people themselves at grass-roots level, who, taking up the reins of power over *their own* affairs will remove fundamentally and forever, from that miscreant power, its field of play.

Meanwhile, until the people inaugurate that bright and regenerative step for society – (pray heaven, soon) – we have to confront the new world of genetic engineering which is now fully upon us. How fortunate for us, then, that whether it occupies itself with trying to chase up that *genetic defect* which is the supposed 'cause' of our various afflictions, or whether it should attempt to 'improve on' our genes in search of that elusive *master-race*, we have, in the work of that school in India, as in the work of Dr. Weston Price, a fully sufficient exposé of the falsity, *the frivolity*, of all such pursuits. Sir Albert Howard's work in India shows us plainly – (just as do the travels of Dr. Weston Price) – that heredity is not to blame for the diseases, either physical or mental, which we wrestle with today. As Dr. Wrench sums it up in *The Wheel of Health*: "The genes of heredity are sound and eternally faithful to healthy life" – (and we note the significance of those last two words). "Any question of 'heredity' is now generally discredited" – a statement recorded in ch. VIII, where we may find the fuller background to it.

However, as we see, under the wing of the new genetics the false doctrine of heredity is putting forth its face again, in these closing years of the twentieth century. We therefore owe a large debt of gratitude to all these pioneers of the true science of health. But to Dr. Weston Price we own it in special measure, for through his work he bequeaths to us, in that powerful term *intercepted heredity*, a weapon with which we are able to put to flight every onslaught of today's false eugenics – while it also bequeaths to us the conclusive evidence, from his far-reaching investigations, that it is Mother Nature, and Mother Nature alone, who, *through our obedience to her laws*, possesses the ability to fashion that long aspired-to 'master race'. (As for the GMOs – we shall come to those.)

. . .And how that term 'master race' conjures up in one's mind again, from the pages of Dr. Weston Price's book, the pictures of the Maoris – of the superb Masai warriors – of the Eskimos, the Indians, and – yes, too! – of "the Gaelics" as he calls them: the people of the remote islands of Scotland, as they were at that time. Let us travel to the islands of the Hebrides!

*

THE "GAELICS"

To dip into the pages of Weston Price's chapter on the "Isolated and Modern Gaelics" is an incredible adventure – a whole chapter of Scottish history retrieved from oblivion! Of no people in all his book did he speak with more admiration than of these Gaels. It is not too much to say that Weston Price has preserved for the Scots, in the pages devoted to this chapter, one of our lost historical archives, particularly as he gives us so vivid a picture not only of their health and hardiness, but of their *mental acuity* as well!

First let me quote some of his own words direct about the "isolated Gaelics" that he met – (ie., those who still lived on their indigenous island diet of mostly oat products and fish):-

> "It was a. . .happy (surprise) to find such high types of manhood and womanhood as exist among the occupants of these rustic thatched-roof homes, usually located in an expanse of heather-covered treeless plains. . .the people of early Scottish descent. . .possess a physique that rivals that found in almost any place in the world. . .

It would be difficult to find examples of womanhood combining a higher degree of physical perfection and more exalted ideals than these weather-beaten toilers. . .One marvels at their gentleness, refinement and sweetness of character... One wonders if the bleak winds which thrash the north Atlantic from our Labrador and Greenland coasts have not tempered the souls of these people and created in them higher levels of nobility and exalted human expression. These people are the outposts of the western fringe of the European continent."*

Weston Price travelled about the islands as far as transport allowed him; and he undertook a particularly interesting study of "the growing boys and girls at a place called Scalpay in the Isle of Harris". Here he found – "only one tooth out of every hundred examined had ever been attacked by tooth decay", while the "general physical development of these children was excellent". In stark contrast was the examination he made of the children of the Harris shipping port of Tarbert. Here there were 32.4 carious teeth out of every hundred examined. Although the distance between the two places was only ten miles – and both, being on the coast, had equal access to sea foods – need it be said that only at Tarbert was there to be found a "white bread bakery store with modern jams, marmalade, and other kinds of canned foods"; and a young man, about to have all his teeth extracted, told him that it was the common experience of the adult people that they lost all their teeth. Praise be – thinking of the bridge linking Scalpay with Harris, opened with such fanfare this summer – that it did not exist in Weston Price's time! That would have been "a bridge too far" indeed!

Exactly the same difference was to be found, on the island of Lewis, between the population of the more isolated interior and that of Stornoway, the sea-port town: "In Stornoway one could purchase angel food cake, white bread, as snow white as that to be found in any country in the world, many other white-flour products; also, canned marmalades, canned vegetables, sweetened fruit juices, jams, confections of every type filled the store windows and counters... The difference in physical appearance of the child life of Stornoway from that of the interior of the Isle of Lewis was striking." Unfortunately, such a distinction will have been well ironed out today, with deficiency foods the diet of all.

Similar were Weston Price's findings on the Isle of Skye, where the department of dental inspection for north Scotland told him that, a few years previously, one school of thirty-six children had shown not a single case of dental caries. On visiting this community, he found that they had since been connected to the outside world by daily steamboat. . .with the inevitable sprouting up of the same white bread bakery. "The district was just in the process of being modernized", he explains to us and one senses the wry smile hovering over that last word!

So here, too, there was a population showing the inevitable disparities between those living on "primitive" and those living on "modern" foods. It is cheering to read that on Skye, among the elderly firmly wedded to their sound diet, there was great concern at the "rapid decline in health" of the young people of the district. They saw a generation growing up that "had not the health of former generations" – their words a

* *I cherish here a personal recollection of a particularly wonderful childhood holiday spent up in Sutherland, at Bettyhill – (during just the time, I now realize, that Weston Price was making his historic journeys). It left me with many lasting memories – the call of the corncrakes, the huge black rocks, the exciting crabs – and our mother's half-knitted socks inherited by the mermaids! But I particularly remember our mother exclaiming at the health and vigour of the grandfather of the croft where we stayed _ well on in his eighties. Her words must have engraved themselves at once on my memory – "leaping over the rocks like a young boy!" . . .Nor have I ever tasted such porridge since. . .*

telling testimony to the fact that tooth decay is never an isolated phenomenon, but a warning to us that the *health of the body in general* is impaired. But we are besotted with our 'compart-mentality' of course!

Returning to mainland Scotland, Weston Price sought information from government officials relevant to this whole matter of declining health. He learned that in the last fifty years the average height of the Scots had in some districts decreased by as much as four inches, and that this had been "coincident with" the general increase in tooth decay. Studying the local market places, Weston Price was able to see that a large part of the people's nutrition, instead of being found locally, was in fact "shipped in. . .in the form of refined flours and canned goods and sugar". When Weston Price had enquired of the older folk on Skye the reason for the decline they were witnessing, they had "pointed to two stone grinding mills which they said had ground the oats for oatcakes and porridge for their families and preceding families for hundreds of years". But trust those bureaucrats, with the damning statistics at their finger-tips, to leave their cosy offices and do a little *field studying* – (such as their diligent questioner had crossed the Atlantic and gone round the world to do) – ! Trust them even to do a little intelligent putting of two and two together! Weston Price's archive contains a good deal of interesting history *all round*!

In his effort to meet "primitive Gaelic people" in the high country of Wales – (an effort without success) – he was advised to visit the island of Bardsay off the north Wales coast. Here he found mainly newly-imported colonists, the previous islanders having largely died out due to tuberculosis. Here too, then, the usual history. With most foodstuffs imported – and of the usual kind – it was only the older generation with their more indigenous lifestyle who were untouched by tooth decay. "From a conference with the director of public health. . .I learned that tuberculosis constituted a very great problem, not only for the people on this island, but for those of many districts of northern Wales." It was ascribed to the "lowered defence of the people due to causes unknown". . .albeit it was also noted that "individuals with rampant tooth decay" were more susceptible to tuberculosis. Weston Price adds no comment in his text to this inept communication – but somehow it follows, in invisible ink!

Less surprising was the response of the islanders, newly "imported" as they were, when questioned on the reason for the widespread tooth decay. They said that they "were familiar with the cause and that it was due to close contact with the salt water and salt air" – ! When Weston Price pointed to the excellent teeth of the old people who had lived close to the sea all their lives, all they could respond was that "this. . .was the reason they had been given in answer to their inquiries". So! – the public health official consulted, while innocently declaring to Weston Price that it was all "causes unknown", was at the same time heavily involved in the cunning disseminations of complete falsities on the matter, among the affected populace! Of course he knew such falsities would never pass with Weston Price – but that did not prevent him, at their interview, from shedding his crocodile tears over the "sad story" of how this new population on Bardsay was breaking down from tuberculosis as fast as the old!

The annals of Weston Price on his visit to the Outer Hebrides contain a particularly illuminating section. It concerns the question of the "black-houses" in which the people lived. First, of interest is the view of the people themselves, which Weston Price records "They resent, and I think justly so, the critical and uncomplimentary references made to their houses in attaching to them the name 'black-houses'. Several that we visited were artistically decorated with clean wallpaper and improvised hangings." Then follows the heart of the matter:-

> "The thatch of the roof plays a very important role. It is replaced each October, and the old thatch is believed by the natives to have great value as a special fertilizer for their soil because of its impregnation with chemicals that have been obtained from the peat smoke which may be seen seeping through all parts of the roof at all seasons of the year. Peat fires are kept burning for this explicit purpose even when the heat is not needed. . . Some of the houses have no chimney because it is desirable that the smoke leaves the building through the thatched roof."

Well! Never have I seen *this* information attached to any description of these black-houses today. But more, of much interest, follows.

At the time Weston Price visited the Isle of Lewis, tuberculosis was spreading rapidly among the younger generation – of the "modernized part" of the island, of course. The superintendent of the hospital which had been specially built for its sufferers spoke with "deep concern" of "the rapidity with which this menace is growing". What was the official view of the reason for this? The dramatic change of diet had, as usual, passed officialdom by. Instead, "much blame had been placed upon the housing conditions, it being thought that the thatched-roof house with its smoke-laden air was an important contributing factor". So much for the customary official ineptness! However, the people of Lewis, not being an "imported" population as on Bardsay but staunch and deep-rooted islanders, were not deceived. Not only had former generations lived in these same thatched cottages, or 'black-houses', quite free of the disease, but the islanders also told Weston Price that "the incidence of tuberculosis was frequently the same in the modern houses as it was in the thatched-roof houses" – !

So – officialdom neatly puts its *second* blind eye to the telescope Let us just remember that it is *this same officialdom* that is governing our health agendas today. No wonder that we have ever-increasing disease – backed up by idiot schemes such as fluoridation!. . . (*fully* the equal of that 'black-houses' fiasco!)

Weston Price's researches in his travels were not focused solely upon the physical, of course – and this matter of the contest over the 'black-houses', observed during his stay amongst these resourceful island people, afforded him some exceptionally interesting psychological insights! "It was of special interest to observe the mental attitude of the native with regard to the thatched-roof house. Again and again, we saw the new house built beside the old one, and the people apparently living in the new one, but still keeping the smoke smudging through the thatch of the old thatched-roof house." Enquiring about this, he was told, (as in the passage already quoted), that something from the smoke in the thatch doubled the growth of plants and the yield of their grain, while "with keen interest. . .one of the clear-thinking residents" showed him some patches of growing grain, which indeed visibly proved the point.

It is our considerable gain that this display of indigenous know-how, in the face of such official obtuseness, so intrigued our investigative traveller that he determined to carry the matter to its full conclusion. As he relates towards the end of this chapter:-

"Since a fundamental part of this study involves an examination of the accumulated wisdom of the primitive racial stocks, it is important that we look further into the matter of the smoked thatch. I was advised by the old residents that a serious conflict existed between them and the health officials who came from outside their island. The latter blamed the smoke for the sudden development of tuberculosis in acute form, and they insisted that the old procedure be entirely discontinued. For this purpose the government gave very substantial assistance in the building of new and model homes. The experienced natives contended that the oat crop would not mature in that severe climate without being fertilized with the smoked thatch. While they were willing to move into the new house, they were not willing to give up the smoking of the oatstraw used for the thatch to prepare it for fertilizing the ground."

Weston Price obtained some of the smoked thatch and brought it back with him to America. There he devised a set of pot tests, in which oat seeds were planted with varying amounts of the thatch. There is a clear illustration of the six pots planted up, and their results – to immortalize for all time this supreme and hilarious example of the folly of *un-earthed officialdom*, and the wisdom of the 'uneducated' people of the soil with their hands right in the stuff!

"In Fig. 8 will be seen the result. The pot to the right shows the result of planting the oats in a sandy soil almost like that of the Islands of the Outer Hebrides. The oats only grew to the fuzzy limited condition shown. As increasing amounts of this thatch were added to the soil, there was an increase in the ruggedness of the plants so that in the last pot to the left tall stalks were developed heavily loaded with grain which ripened by the time the growth shown in the other pots had occurred."

As Weston Price points out, the results of the chemical analysis – (which showed a quantity of fixed nitrogen as well as other chemicals to be present in the smoked thatch) – fully vindicated the insistence of "the hardy old natives" that they be permitted to continue smoking their thatches, even if not "permitted" (by that imbecilic bureaucracy) to continue living in the thatched house.

There must presumably be a museum on Lewis dedicated to preserving some account of the old ways of the islanders – but one wonders if it contains the *authentic* history of the final chapter of these black-houses? ...One does not even need to wonder if the educational syllabuses studied on Lewis (drawn up by that same officialdom) make any reference to it! It would be nice to think that any such museum might – (with due request made to the Price-Pottenger Foundation) – come to include a fully-blown-up reproduction of Dr. Weston Price's pages – giving so informative an account of his visit to the "Gaelics" of our western isles. And especially an enlarged reproduction of the all-important picture of the six pots of oats, so clearly shown in Figure 8. Such steps would make a serious contribution to the reclaiming of our lost culture – which has not been so much lost as *assiduously blanked out*.

Moreover, if the school-children of Lewis were to embark upon an exact replica sowing and harvesting of thatch-smoke-fertilized oats, they would learn something valuable not only about their island roots, but about real nutrition, and real social history as well ...which their own first-hand experience would never let them forget.

While it would be nice to think that the *Seven Wise Masters* behind these crazy "modernization" schemes were now proved to be just *Seven Simpletons*, we must concede the contrary is the case. They knew what they were doing alright. It was clearly impossible for them to reorient by *direct* means this strongly soil-bound people. For that soil husbandry which Ogilvie marked as so akin to wisdom carries extraordinary resoluteness with it. It would have been interesting to have witnessed some of the battles that took place between the two sides on this matter! – for confronted by those stalwart islanders the *Seven* clearly did not *dare* disallow the continued use of their smoked thatches!

Ultimately, however, they knew that none of this really mattered. Give another generation, and besides the popularizing of artificial foods, there was artificial education being brought forward in artificial schools – and of course the enticing new grants for the new artificial agriculture. Naturally the next generation was caught on this well-pronged fork – and most probably the children in our schools today are being taught how the government *saved* the people from the awful TB that was afflicting them from living in those awful black-houses!

Alas for the consequences of all this artificial progress! As told me recently by someone married to an islander from Lewis, by about twenty years on from the time of Weston Price's travels, the islanders were so completely involved with those "artificial manures", that their wretched cows were afflicted with painfully bloating 'green-belly' – so called from the over-lush (equals *unhealthily rapidly grown*) grass which was now stimulated with their *grant-aided artificials*.

One cannot help remembering Viktor Schauberger's observation, which captures the scene so well: "Externally everything seems to ripen and thrive, but it is only a facade". Alas, by that time the islanders had apparently quite lost touch with that original 'soil wisdom' so enjoyably described by Schauberger concerning the earlier farmers of his own Austria:-

> "The supposedly simple farmers, who include the high forest farmers of Mühlviertel. . .grew, for about forty years, the best potatoes and the heaviest oats. If you asked a farmer how this was achieved he would, with an artful smile, promptly reply that you must always remain true to the very ancient beliefs of the land and avoid any kind of instruction, if you want to be fortunate in agriculture" – !

*

FAULTY *GENES* - ? ... GENETIC *STRENGTHS* – AND BIOLOGICAL THINKING

Dr. Weston Price's account of his time spent among the people of the Hebrides is instructive not only in itself. It has considerable bearing upon the trend, already mentioned, to substitute for the 'virus' theory that of 'heredity' or *faulty genes*, and particularly (as also already mentioned) to fasten these things on the Scots. In reviewing what follows, we would do well to keep in mind Weston Price's portrait, drawn from life, of those more original Scots, who can show us a more *original* portrait of our *genes* in turn.

"The Curse of the Celts." Such is the startling sub-heading to be found in a chapter on "Vitamins and Minerals", in Geoffrey Cannon's book already mentioned, *The Politics of Food*. Such was the stigma placed upon the Scots, (along with the Welsh and Northern Irelanders), in the 1970s, concerning "babies born with deformities of the central nervous system: in particular spina bifida (damaged spinal column) or anencephaly (no brain)".

Geoffrey Cannon makes a thorough investigation of the circumstances surrounding this stigma, and although his book (published in 1987) is now out of print, hopefully it is still obtainable through the public library. It is worth briefly tracing his findings:-

> "Spina bifida is sometimes called 'the curse of the Celts', because rates of spina bifida in Scotland, Wales and Ireland have been by far the highest recorded anywhere in the world. In the mid-1970s, one in every three hundred babies born in England and Wales was damaged by spina bifida: a higher rate than elsewhere in Europe. But in Scotland, Wales, N. Ireland and the Republic of Ireland, the rate was up to one in every hundred in some hospitals. It was officially suggested that 'the capacity to produce offspring with central nervous system malfunctions may be associated with the Celtic race'."

Some association! ANENCEPHALY! – *NO BRAIN!*

However, a growing number of experts in child health presently began to point the finger at environmental causes – specifically, "the food mothers eat". Now the battle is launched, with one professor at a London hospital declaring: "It is quite bizarre that this country has one of the highest frequencies of NTD (neural tube defects) in the world – but are we most likely to be malnourished? This is quite clearly not so" – (! How about those old islanders on Skye who pointed Weston Price to their old oat-grinding mill knowing far more about the matter than this professor? But that's what you get when people shut themselves away in artificial laboratories pretending to research into the field of *life*, instead of going out into that field and researching it at first hand for themselves as Weston Price did.)

However, the work of other professors (at Leeds University and the Welsh National School of Medicine) came strongly down on the side of "bad food" as being "the key cause of NTDs" – so the South Wales Echo of 13 Feb. 84 appears with the banner-line: "SOUTH WALES PROJECT TO PREVENT TRAGIC ILLNESS. POP, CHIPS BLAMED FOR SPINA BIFIDA"; catching up on a professor at Oxford who had already declared in late 1982 that NTDs now have "the status of a deficiency disease". (Sanity staring us in the face.) But can one calculate the suffering of thousands of young mothers who had damaged babies born to them during those years – and no doubt in addition were made to feel it was a curse they had brought on themselves?

> "There appears to be a 40-year rule in medicine. Major discoveries have required over 40 years before becoming generally accepted. Thus the English navy added citrus fruits to the navy diet 40 years after Sir James Lind proved they were curative for scurvy. During those 40 years, an estimated 100,000 English seamen died from scurvy – the high price of delay." (Dr. Abram Hoffer, in Weston Price's book.)

Is it not obvious from this account of scurvy, added to that of spina bifida and other equally unnecessary sufferings, that we have a health system hopelessly cut off from reality? But how could it be otherwise in a society which is *cut off from the roots?* And it is the thousands upon thousands of ordinary people who have, over and over again, paid the "high price" of that *centralized insanity.*

We must leave there the further details of the spina bifida fray, except to record that up to the time of publication of Geoffrey Cannon's book, the Medical Research Council was still sticking to its (opposite) guns. . .while there is a final fascinating revelation from Geoffrey Cannon's investigations into this matter, when he picks up a *re*-issue of a certain DHSS* report on the subject, and writes of it under the *double-entendre* heading of "The Disappearing (Spinal) column" – ! (Well. . .such official antics have been *not unknown* in the battle against fluoridation!) So much for the trumped-up 'Curse of the Celts'! So much for attempting to scapegoat the Scots – to lay at the door of Scottish genes the *misdemeanours of the Seven Wise Masters!*

Even as an armchair traveller with Dr. Weston Price on his wonderful voyages, anyone who can add to his account their own practical experiences of health-building at first hand – along the same fundamental lines, with all the efforts and rewards involved in this – is well able to recognize for themselves the true essentials of *genetic tendency.* That is, that –

> The human race is *genetically predisposed* to flourish on a diet of unpolluted and untampered-with wholefoods.

Not all your geneticists' researching in all the laboratories of the world can throw *that* up _ but it takes those who follow in the footsteps of the Weston Prices – the Schaubergers – the Henry Georges of this world, to see the 'obvious'.

There has been a sound, increasing awareness of the part played in health by nutrition, in the decade since Geoffrey Cannon's book appeared – and no doubt his book played a considerable part in this. As a result the Scots are now well off the hook regarding spina bifida. However, other such scapegoatings have presented themselves in the press more recently.

"Researchers investigate gene link to strokes" – ran a heading in the Dundee Courier in July 98. "The answer to one of the country's major killers could lie in our genes, new research has revealed. . .Scotland still has one of the poorest stroke records in Europe. Now. . .Glasgow scientist claims the success of a patient's recovery could depend on their genetic make-up."** Amazingly, the reason given for pressing on with this gene research is that "it is very difficult to change behaviour – and prevent people from smoking, drinking and eating unhealthily!" – ! Well, at that rate we're also hanging on, of course, to – diabetes – arthritis – ME – MS – heart disease – cancer. . .

---

* *Department of Health and Social Security. – (Possibly more recently under a new name, but of course – the same face.)*

** *Incidentally, I have seen proven before my eyes, in a member of my own family, that the success of a patient's recovery from stroke is vitally linked to the simple matter of REST. Doubtless no doctor would dispute this – but how many would concede that a vital part of RESTING is FASTING? (We just do not realize the amount of energy that must be drawn upon by the body to process the food that we eat.) Hence – a strict abstinence from food for a least the first ten days, and a limiting of intake to healthful drinks, along with complete rest, is the recipe for best freeing the body's energies for the essential work of healing.*

*(**Note:** I do not write as a health practitioner and take no responsibility whatsoever for anyone else attempting to follow this pathway. I simply recount what I have witnessed in a remarkable healing. Those who wish to consider such a pathway should equip themselves by studying the considerable literature that exists on the subject of natural health* ***including*** *fasting; and should avail themselves of the guidance of a qualified health practitioner.)*

Virtually: you-name-it. Any one of the multitudinous 'degenerative diseases of modern civilization'. . .to which, we should note, new forms and names are relentlessly being added; further varieties of strange and previously unheard-of afflictions, many of these involving small children – denoting a further steep descent down that dangerous slope of degeneration. So why not get down and mend the very roots of the situation? Why not take to heart the grim warning of Dr. Weston Price in the closing sentence of his chapter "Isolated and Modern 'Gaelics" – to which I will take the liberty of adding a few further words outside the quotation marks:-

> "A seriously degenerated stock followed the displacement of. . .(the indigenous) diet with a typical modern diet consisting of white bread, sugar, jams, syrup, chocolate, coffee, some fish without livers, canned vegetables and eggs"... all of which inevitably followed from the *prior* displacing of the people from a proper presiding over of their own land, their own soil and their own health.

Dr. Weston Price uses the term, *seriously degenerated stock.* Grim warning indeed! The "gen" in that word is of the same origin as that in "genetic". But degenerated *stock* is the whole thing, and can never be mended by chasing isolate genes around in a laboratory – even supposing there had been some particular Scottish link.

So – what other failings are laid at our door? An article on multiple sclerosis appeared in the Courier of 16 June 98 under the dramatic heading, "Study claims that Macs more likely to have MS". Well! A sharp increase in MS north of the Border was apparently – (according to researchers south of the Border) – "difficult to explain in terms of environmental factors and suggested a genetic difference". Fortunately the view of the Multiple Sclerosis Society is given in the closing paragraph: "Although this study indicates an increased susceptibility to MS in southern Scotland, there is no single gene involved. MS is not, it is believed, caused without the intervention of an, as yet unknown, environmental factor." Soundly spoken!

There is unfortunately no one to conclude with equal sanity an article (Scotland on Sunday, 16 Aug. 98) on oral Crohn's Disease. Now afflicting a large number, especially of young people, in the West of Scotland, a 'genetic predisposition' to the allergy was here suggested also: "An in-depth study has been conducted into the epidemic and experts now say that people living in the West of Scotland have a genetic predisposition to developing the allergic reaction which leads to oral Crohn's Disease." The condition is reported in the article as being linked (unsurprisingly) with "fizzy drinks and preservatives" – (fizzy drinks are a feast of chemicals themselves, if you read the labels); and in addition "bacteria linked to Crohn's Disease had been found in one fifth of pasteurised milk supplies"... (sending the Ministry of Agriculture scurrying forward with "an investigation into the alarming levels of bacteria in pasteurized and unpasteurized milk" – !!)

While there are "only 40 cases of oral Crohn's Disease in the whole of the USA", "500 Scots, mainly youngsters, have Crohn's Disease of the mouth and 440 of them live on the West coast. That figure is considered by scientists to be phenomenal. . ." It is – but it seems very obvious that some environmental factor is here at work – perhaps one that *reacts* especially *badly* with the bacteria and chemicals involved? We're running into deep waters here, of course – that of the *cocktail of poisons* we all carry within us now, and whose reactions to one another (including to any particularly persistent environmental one?) are completely beyond our ken. But how *could* our officialdom acknowledge *that*? It would open a Pandora's box on every front! Best to encourage the idea of "genetic disposition" – (and keep the Scots from researching into how far their environment has been polluted. . .) Against which background many a good-hearted scientist works on, hugely in the dark.

Returning to the multiple sclerosis article, I was struck by an interesting point. These MS findings were also felt to explain the prevalence of the disease "in countries to which large numbers of Scots had emigrated, such as New Zealand". This took my thought back to the revealing pictures of the white immigrants to New Zealand, in the section of Weston Price's book we have just been looking at, and the recognition that these would indeed very likely have been Scots. I pondered again how amongst the fourteen groups chronicled in Dr. Weston Price's pages as showing an earlier, and finer, type, the English do not find a place. They could not. How could any remnant have been found today among the English, whose (equally disastrous) 'clearances' – (the enclosure of their commons forcibly 'modernizing' them into the industrial cities from then on) – reached its summit several centuries ago?

The inclusion in Weston Price's pages of this remnant among the Scots (whose Clearances were of such recent times) then came to me as having a peculiar additional significance that had not struck me before: that of the peculiar vulnerability which belongs to all more 'primitive' peoples who are brought into sudden contact with modern 'civilization'. In Weston Price's chapter on "the Gaelics", there occurs the following sentence concerning the population of the island of Bardsay (which as we know had recently had to be entirely replaced). I have emphasised the significant words. "The director of public health of. . .Bardsay Island told me the story of the decline and *almost complete extinction* of the" (original) "population due to tuberculosis." I suddenly saw that the experience of the people of Bardsay was no different from that of the Indians and Eskimos which Weston Price relates a few pages further on: "Like the Indian, the Eskimo thrived as long as he was not blighted by the touch of modern civilization, but with it, like all primitives, he *withers and dies*." He withers and dies. . . "Almost complete extinction". . . The original *Celtic* people of Bardsay.

Suddenly a significant further part of the picture struck me – the gift the Scots have of 'second sight', a gift still found among them today. For this is a gift belonging to a people who have decidedly preserved their more 'primitive', i.e., *intuitive*, faculties. But the intuitive faculty is *not unlinked with vulnerability*. Weston Price's work brings to light the *physical* vulnerability involved. but I am thinking here of vulnerability not just in the physical sense, but in the profounder *soul* sense, which is involved too – and which in its turn will unquestionably have profound effect upon the physical.

I am thinking here of a passage I read earlier this year from *Rob Roy MacGregor* by W.H. Murray,* describing the way of life of the Highlanders:-

> "Many days and nights together had to be spent on the hills hunting and tracking, which meant careful, close observation of all wildlife, weather, land forms, sun and stars, the continuous, constant use of eyes, ears and nose, and the

* *I am indebted for this passage to Jim Crumley's article, "No place for faint hearts", which appeared in the Courier of 6 Jan. 98, and in which he refers to W.H. Murray as "one of the most eloquent of all Scotland's mountaineers". (An article by Jim Crumley will be found in Part III.)*

sense of touch in response to wind shifts, until the senses remained alert all day long without conscious effort, recording, warning, informing, guiding, in ways now lost to man in the Highlands, where by comparison he is now only half alive . . . This fact of their life rewarded them with a deeper love of their Highland ground than Lowlanders could appreciate, or be expected to understand. They did not understand, or example, that to deprive such men of such land was to uproot them as a tree is up-rooted. They might exist, but no longer feel alive."

But no longer feel alive. What does this have to say to us about that profounder *soul* vulnerability? And just what effect might this not have upon a people at a deep level, upon their *immune systems* so much involved in today's diseases? Surely such links as this are no longer quite beyond our grasp – in this day when we are at last (re)-awakening to the effect of the emotional body upon the physical? How not then of the *soul* body also? For it is a memory of the deep *psyche* that is here involved, since in the psyche of the Highlander the memories of his uprooting are recent still. I am convinced there is more to the apparent 'vulnerability' of the Scots to the diseases of modern civilization than has ever yet dawned on us.

I looked back to the article on multiple sclerosis. The survey of the Scots which supposed them to have a 'genetic tendency' to multiple sclerosis was made in "the Lothian and Border regions". It involved there "a total of 589" people who had Scottish surnames beginning with one of the Highland prefixed, Mc or Mac, which was a figure "significantly higher than the 476 expected, based on the general frequency of Scottish names in the regions". The frequency, in the Border regions, of the Highland prefix, shows precisely how well mixed through Lowland blood that Highland blood now is; and as the Highlander may so well carry, from the psychic memory of his profound *violation*, this *vulnerability* of the immune system, we can readily see how its outward patterning might appear in the Borders today as well as anywhere else, among the Scots.

In the light of the above, we can now view such "outward patternings", (via whatever modern disease involving the immune system – and most do), for what they really are: that is, the tragic expression in today's terms of an original *genetic strength*. . . .A reverberation from deep within the psyche of the Scots, of that ancient, powerful and irrepressible insistence upon our *birthright in land* – the land with all of its sights, sounds, textures, tastes and smells, yes – and its original, *untampered-with, Mother-breasted food*, as well.

In short, if a 'genetic tendency' among the Scots there be, it is that which cries out for a return to the land, and will not be denied. It is but typical of the degeneracy of our times that we fail to recognize it for what it is. – And who dare assess the cost to us of our blindness now, which carries with it the whole of today's drugs scene?

Regarding the "unknown environmental factors" cited at the end of the press article on Multiple Sclerosis, and involving today's diseases of degeneration, it is of course impossible that such factors should *not* be a part of the whole scene. We need only consider the huge extra burden that the poisoning of our environment – (hence of practically all food and water) – places upon our bodies, in *addition to* all that Weston Price records we have done to ourselves by eating deficient and artificial foods. The real onslaught of poisons upon our environment started, of course, only after Weston Price's day, being the result – as Rachel Carson points out in *Silent Spring* – of our society's 'need' to find a new market for its wartime chemicals. Agriculture was the answer.

Birthright. . .and. . .Scotland Today

In pausing to take a further look at this more recent scene, we find ourselves at a point where damage to the genes of the human race is indeed a most decided possibility. For the "synthetic compounds" which issue from today's laboratories, in the form of pesticides, herbicides, and the whole host of other pollutants (both industrial and agricultural), are *"completely foreign to the experience of man's biological make-up"*. (I quote again from Granville Knight, at the start of Weston Price's book. Emphasis added.) We can therefore usefully note also, regarding such genetic damage, that any disruption to the human genes arising from the labours of those pseudo-scientists will occur in the population *indiscriminately*, and will have nothing whatsoever to do with any racial type, Scots or otherwise.

If we now take a fuller look at this scene, and at Dr. Granville Knight's warning as to the dangers we are exposed to by it, my term above, "pseudo-scientists", will be seen to be fully justified, since the word "scientist" comes from the Latin verb "scire", to know. Just how do these myriads of different poisons now spewed into our environment react with it – and us? –

> ". . .human beings are increasingly exposed to thousands of chemicals in air, food and water. They are also dosing themselves – or being dosed – with a multitude of drugs... Many of these are...completely foreign to the experience of man's biochemical make-up...
>
> ...Most drugs and chemicals act by slowing down or accelerating one or more of the *estimated 5,000 enzyme systems in each body cell.* Since many of these may act synergistically, only time will tell the possible cumulative effects on human beings of minute amounts of many different chemicals. They could be disastrous." (Dr. Granville F. Knight, M.D., in a Foreword to Weston Price's book. Emphasis added.)

Now just what does anyone know – just what *could* anyone *possibly* know – about how even just *one* of these 5,000 enzyme systems, in even just *one* of our body's (millions of) cells, operates, as affected by the *countless* factors in the environment in any *one* area...multiplied again by the countless factors that operate *individually* in the lives of all of those even living in one common environment? Are we crazy? "Pseudo-scientists" alright!

There is only ONE answer. NO ONE CAN POSSIBLY KNOW! No wonder that, in speaking of the need for a rapid phasing out of pesticides and herbicides, Dr. Granville Knight proposes that we ban the sale of these from all household use immediately, instead seeking "control of insect pests and weeds through other means. Well-nourished plants are more resistant to insects and fungi than deficient ones." Meanwhile *Land Health*, and *The Purpose of Disease*, and indeed *A G.P.'s Debt to Nature Cure* – (all in Part III of this book) – all emphasise again, just as did Albert Howard's work, that it is typical of today's science, with its foolishly fragmented outlook, to regard these things as *pests*, which are in fact our best friends and invaluable *scouts for our health*!

It is a great mystery to great numbers of ordinary people, (for ordinary people in general retain a more holistic view of things – as witness the spontaneous grass-roots opposition to GMOs), how today's science can possibly remain so blind to the dangers of our situation. Here Viktor Schauberger's work again throws helpful light on the matter, in the insights it adds to Weston Price's. It concerns the damage we have done to the actual structure of our brains, and I shall quote here from Callum Coats in *Living*

Energies, who describes it so well – for it becomes even more pertinent in the light of Weston Price's findings:-

> "Viktor saw the proper physical formation of the brain as being crucial to what it was able to produce in the way of concepts, ideas and behaviour, ethical and otherwise; the lower the quality of the physical structure, the more inferior the morals and ethics. In the same way that the narrowly spaced annual rings of trees produced high-quality, resonant timber, the production of good thoughts in harmony with Nature, and in consequence good character traits, was only possible with a well and healthily-grown and developed brain with close-knit windings.
>
> "Unwholesome food, poor water and the resultant slight overheating, in his view, gave rise to the formation of coarse convolutions in the brain's overall structure, creating a brain that was incapable of either functioning intuitively or of comprehending the subtleties of Nature's processes. It degenerated into an organ able only to think logically, but never biologically, never with a living logic aware of natural energetic interrelations and interdependencies." (Ch. "Drinking Water Supply".)

How aptly these words speak for our scene today! To the biologically aware, the intricate interweavings of the natural world are so obvious that Viktor Schauberger's words seem the only possible explanation regarding those who are today insensible to them: that is – their thinking processes have degenerated to the realm of the *purely logical.*

So what of the official assurances of safety, so oft repeated re these biocides? Are they *even logical*? No! Because the only logic that applies in the natural world is *bio*logic. Need it be said that our *biologic* Mother has no time for mere human *logicality* in her domain – and presently will have no place for it either.

Rachel Carson, in contemplating the same problem – those who could not see the damage being done to the natural world – saw one of our great handicaps as being that we *lack instruments fine enough to detect injury before symptoms appear.* As I was pondering these words one day, it suddenly struck me that the *primary* instrument we make use of is – our thinking! So Rachel Carson's words themselves lead us back to Viktor Schauberger's, reinforcing them yet further. We can now see the terrifying plight we are in: that the destruction of the natural world taking place today is being orchestrated and overseen by those whose capacity for biological thinking has been *totally eclipsed.*

If we place Weston Price's and Viktor Schauberger's findings side by side , we see that Weston Price showed us how, through the unsuspected fruitage of an appallingly deficient dietary, our society is unwittingly nurturing and profligating in its midst tendencies of a *socially* criminally kind. Schauberger, taking the scene further and speaking for the latter half of the twentieth century, extends Weston Price's view to encompass the *ecological* criminality which we are now also dealing in.

But how could it *not* have progressed to this? Or do we suppose that the manner of our patterning, in the growth of our brains, is somehow superior to that of the trees?

Birthright. . .and. . .Scotland Today

– and that it somehow manages to proceed outside of the laws of Nature's governance?*

Contemporary forestry is apparently still ignorant of the real significance of these spacings of a tree's annual rings, which reflect its growth. (L.E., ch. 17.) Stradivarius made his famous violins from trees that had grown in natural conditions, and which therefore had the *close-knot* windings which produce high-grade timber of a *fine and resonant quality*. Poorer quality timber has widely-spaced rings – indicating an over-exposure to light, and therefore to *heat*. (As Callum Coats points out, only today's crude forestry, intent on quantity at all costs, regards the inferior growth of over-heated timber, with its wider spaced rings, as *desirable*).

If we, as a society, wished to nurture the kind of thinking that would resonate on this Planet with the quality of a Stradivarius violin – thinking that is of a *biological* orientation – we have taken a decidedly wrong turning somewhere!

Looking around at our Planet today, being destroyed in ruthless and reckless ways, we see that "miscreant power" we earlier spoke of – now running riot through our environment with its latest "GMO" toys.

So what did we expect? Ruthless and reckless is that pathway our society was set on right from its original ruthless and reckless filching from the people of their land. And right there and then, in that initial act of unlimited violence, our capacity for "biological thinking", as a society, received a most fatal blow. For is not biological thinking about interrelatedness and interconnectedness? And is not the very first sphere of relations and connections that of a people with their land?

Here we can see how other, and less material, energies come into the picture also, to contribute to that unhealthy "overheating" of the system to which biological thinking succumbs. And just as steam is more powerful than water, so those less material energies are more powerful in their destructiveness for being less material too.

Callum Coats writes tellingly in *Living Energies*, ch. 4, of the *acquisitive gravitational impulse* – (that is, an impulse inherently devoid of respect for relationships). And he contrasts it with its opposite: the *levitational energy* which

---

* *That the structuring of our brains discerned by Schauberger was another of his remarkable insights – (whether alterations occur at the physical, or at a higher etheric, level) – seems fully borne out by the account of just such a phenomenon given in **A Forerunner of the New Race** by Tara Mata, 1900-71, (published by the Self-Realization Fellowship, U.S.A.)-*

> *"**Physiological Changes**. He was aware, during this first period of illumination and during the weeks which followed, of a number of physiological changes within himself. The most striking was what seemed a rearrangement of molecular structure in his brain, or the opening up of new cell-territory there. Ceaselessly, day and night, he was conscious of this work going on. It seemed as though a kind of electrical drill was boring out new cellular thought-channels. This phenomenon is strong proof of Bucke's theory that cosmic consciousness is a natural faculty of man, for it gives evidence that the brain cells which are connected with this faculty are already present in man, although inactive or non-functioning in the majority of human beings at the present time."*

*I recall a similar account in one of the cases included in Dr. Richard Maurice Bucke's book, **Cosmic Consciousness**, (recently re-published by Arkana Books, 1991).*

induces "radial expansion" towards "unconditional love". (We remember, from our earlier look at water, how levitational energies are always associated with *cooling*, and *health*; whilst gravitational energies – with *heating*, leading to a loosening of structure, debilitation and disease.)

Surveying our society, we may well ask ourselves just what greater impetus could that *acquisitive gravitational energy* possibly have received, to run riot through our land now with its GMOs, than it received from its original act of seizing that land itself from under our feet? No wonder, then, if the wielders of that "miscreant power" have lost altogether their biological orientation! – (whilst we can appreciate now, too, from Schauberger's work, the destructive "overheating" of the finer, *inner* energies of those involved in such miscreant acts, by which such a process must be marked).

There is only one way that biological thinking can flourish in a society, and that is – as the people themselves act as its guardians. And there is only one way that the people can act as its guardians: that is, as they are the guardians of that land itself whereon they dwell.

For the guardians of the land are the guardians of the soil. And it is only through our direct relationship with the soil that our biological thinking – our awareness of connections – can truly flourish; since the soil, (whether we know it or not), lies at the foundations of all those connections and relationships – even the human ones.

Schauberger writes very simply of this. He is speaking in the context of the farmer – but we can fitly put it in more general terms: "(We) pray to a god who (we) believe is up above, but in reality is under our feet".

How fitting that, to touch the soil, we need to stoop down! – an act of worship in itself.

That humility which is engendered in us by soil contact, and soil nurturing, is the foundational quality upon which biological thinking rests. Moreover, in as much as this direct contact with the soil, in humility, brings us in touch with Nature's cooling, levitational energies, imperceptibly slowly it also nurtures in us the understanding of unconditional love.

*

A FULLER LOOK AT SCOTLAND'S WATER

The question of the high incidence of stroke among the Scots brings us unexpectedly face to face again with an old friend – *Chlorine*! Yes! In his booklet entitled *Coronaries, Cholesterol, Chlorine,** Dr. Joseph Price, M.D., seems to have made a straightforward and fairly irrefutable case for the last named's being the real culprit in today's high incidence of both heart disease *and* stroke – while at the same time de-bunking the long overworked cholesterol theory. (Those healthy Esquimaux "may eat several pounds of blubber at a sitting". . ."about as saturated a fat as exists". So our medical indoctrination's suffer another de-railment!)

More and more warnings are turning up of late, in fact, in a variety of health publications, about the dangers of Chlorine – and for a wide range of troubles too. All that Viktor Schauberger has warned about it is now being verified. However, as Dr. Joseph Price says, the use of chlorine for purifying drinking water is one of the 'sacred cows' of today's science, so that such warnings are unlikely to reach us through orthodox channels. (No wonder that Westminster desires to keep control of Scotland's media – but we haven't heard the end of *that* yet!)

---

* Available from C. Owens, Banhadlog Hall, Tylwch, Llanidloes, Powys, Wales SY18 6JR. £2.50 per copy, incl. p.&p. ISBN 0 946924 015.

To me there is something poignant about the special susceptibility, (if such it be), of the Scots to chlorinated water. Whilst centralized power speaks sternly to the Scots today about the poor quality of our water, it is *that same centralized power that has made it so.* For can we imagine the people of Scotland themselves, under a system of land justice – as guardians and trustees of their very own land – ever having despoiled themselves of those sources of life-giving energy? – waters which were, until recent times, among the best and purest in the world. But as we know, the *Seven Wise Masters* didn't even notice good water when it was under their feet. As the Cree Indian saying has it – only when the last tree has died, the last fish been caught, and the *last river been poisoned*, "will we realize we cannot eat money". And here perhaps the dunce's cap may finally be placed on the head of *Seven Simpletons*.

Yes – to me there is a special poignancy about the ruin of Scotland's water. We need only think of the Highlander depicted by W.H. Murray in his *Rob Roy*, and of what those pure mountain streams must have meant to such a people, to feel unsurprised should a certain *genetic vulnerability* to chlorinated water be present in the Scots today. . .simply another aspect of their genetic yearning.

Meanwhile we could cite some instances of a decided over-enthusiasm in the administration of this ubiquitous 'purifier' today. There seems to be a rising number of 'ladies' retiring rooms' of late where you have to go in holding your breath and run out again as fast as you can if you don't want your lungs positively scrubbed down by the stuff – remembering the effective *immune-system-destroyer* it is; while there are other public places where it is a real trial to have to sit, the 'purified' air being almost unbreathable. Even more alarming – most people are so drugged by these 'treatments', it seems they no longer even notice that the air they are breathing is *not fit to breathe.* Trains are frequently similarly afflicted. The chemical companies are making fortunes out of damage to our lungs.

"Your seeds aren't sprouting? No, no, it won't be the peat – that's fine. It'll be the *chlorine*." But the nice water official at the other end of the line seems to have no inkling that what's no good for seeds is *no good for us either*!

"The drinking water in. . .became impossible to drink and we had to buy bottled water. The water tasted strongly of detergent and often smelled like bleach" – !

I don't know about bleach or detergent, but you can boil chlorine off. Only – "the major sources of exposure to chloroform – a gas that. . .can cause cancer in animals subject to high concentrations – are showers. . .clothes washers. . .and boiling water".* ("High concentrations". . .Yes, but all those tiny doses *add up.*) Meanwhile some doctors in chlorinated areas are having to send patients off to buy bottled water, the chlorinated tap water apparently now linked to their symptoms of ill-health.

"In 1993 North West Water" (in England) "increased the chlorine levels in their water from .03 mg/litre to .103 mg/litre, presumably to protect against contamination from minute organisms. Some residents began to experience symptoms of tiredness, headaches, indigestion, nausea, fluid retention, vertigo, tinnitus, muscle weakness and shaking – all early symptoms of chlorine poisoning. Long-term effects can include

---

* *Article in* ***The Scientific American****, Feb. 1998. I should have included in the above quotation, for perfect clarity: "It (chloroform) forms from the chlorine used to treat water supplies".*

colo-rectal cancer, damage to the immune and nervous systems, and heart attacks and strokes." (*Environment and Health News*, Summer 97.)

There are certainly those in Scotland whose chronic tiredness has turned out in the end to be *chlorine* tiredness – and vanished when they stopped drinking chlorinated water. But on the parallel of the 'super-bugs' now beginning to beat every antibiotic*, it would not be surprising if 'super-micro-organisms in our water had also developed a super-resistance to chlorine. Hence the up-ing of the chlorine dosages that are now beating the population down as well as the bugs. . .so creating another vicious circle for us. Meanwhile, one of Scotland's newest water supply systems, whilst apparently having rid itself of chlorine, leaves kettles that regularly boil it in so pristine-clean a state, (devoid of any furring), that some of its users are wisely resorting to drinking water from more natural sources. "Wisely", in view of Viktor Schauberger's serious warnings, already noted, about the long-term effects of drinking such drastically 'pure' water. *Later:* Since writing the above I have found that this boasted new water-supply system has by no means rid itself of chlorine – which still comes gushing from the tap at intervals, sometimes with a positive *stench*.

A now retired country plumber told me once how, in the days of his apprenticeship, they were taught that water tumbling over six rocks in succession was naturally purified. Man-made pollutants are a different matter, however, and the only answer to these is to *cease the manufacturing and dispersing of them*. But this will never come about until the people themselves, under bioregional and land rent reform, re-assume charge of their own water supplies.

For what is officialdom's attitude today? "Warning issued over toxic blue-green algae. . .Waters which have been polluted by agricultural, domestic or industrial discharges are prone to develop blue-green algae." (The Courier, 16 Apr. 98, reporting on a certain Scottish loch.) "Swallowing affected water or algae scum can cause vomiting, diarrhoea and pains in muscles and joints. . .animals which come into contact. . .can also fall ill. . .there have been cases of dogs dying. . .(due to) affected lochs. Research is in progress." But *action*? ". . .if the monitoring reveals traces of blooms, warning notices will be posted." And *this is our Mother's blood-stream*! – ours in turn. *This is the land of Scotland!* What guardians are these?

"the Ultimate food – Blue-green Algae. . .Llamath Lake Blue-Green Algae is one of nature's most amazing sources of nourishment. In this unique ecologically balanced environment. . .in Oregon. . .blue-green algae flourishes. . ."** But Scotland's now degraded ecology is capable only of producing the scum kind.

Yet in the notes at the end of Olaf Alexandersson's *Living Water*, we read that: "In Värle Och Vetande, No. 1, 1966, J. Westbury describes similar occurrences on Scottish lochs to those on the Ödemark lakes" – that is, water in Scotland's lochs that

---

* *Fortunately "nature's antibiotic", Colloidal Silver, is now making a comeback. (Send s.a.e. for information to ECHO UK, Woodside, Melmerby, Ripon, N. Yorks. EH4 5EZ.) Also: "Studies have shown that garlic (Allium sativum) is not only an anti-viral agent, but also has an effective antibiotic effect against staphylococcus, streptococcus and mycobacterium, and does not disturb your friendly bowel flora. (Ind. J. Exp. Biol., 1977; 15: 466-8.)" Quoted from* ***What Doctors Don't Tell You****, Feb. 98.*

** *Nature's Gold, 783a Fulham Road, London SW6 5HD. Quoted from one of their leaflets.*

was of a power and purity capable of "*develop(ing) a higher form of life*". (Ibid., ch 3. Emphasis added.)

Who can measure the loss that Scotland has suffered in the ruin of her waters now? And no wonder that the Highlanders of old were the people that they were! No wonder their gifts of second sight!

The Scots will never be the race that they once were – (*and can be again*) – until the people in each locality, under radical land rent and bioregional reform, resume control over their own water resources – their rivers, lochs and water supplies; exploring Viktor Schauberger's teachings on water to the full, and linking up with those today across the world who are engaged in demonstrating these – dedicated to carrying them further. (See closing section of *Living Water*.) Let us find out which Scottish lochs J. Westbury was referring to in that so interesting passage quoted – and let us see we restore *all* of our lochs and rivers to their earlier state of highest potency: that potency with which the gods originally blessed Scotland – rich in Schauberger's ethericities.

*

GENETICALLY MODIFIED ORGANISMS

As we prepare ourselves for the radical unmaking *at source* of that "miscreant power" we have referred to, we find ourselves looking forth upon its latest prodigy – the Genetically Modified Organisms. And as we look, we are aghast. *Yet we are not aghast enough.* But this lack in us is inevitable, for in a society so uprooted from its soil there are holes in the biological thinking even of those of us who think biologically.

The opening paragraph to an article in the New Scientist of 31 Oct. 98 – suitably given a supra-heading in the single word "SHOCK", and listing a variety of Genetically Modified 'treats' yet in store for us – rounds off with: "They are the remote part that exists only in the labs and the imaginations of scientists. GM food is different. It's already left the labs."

It's already left the labs. And who bats an eyelid at that? – save for the horror that's now abroad.

We should be asking ourselves: What was it doing in the labs in the first place?

A society which had remained rooted to its soil would never have embarked upon such craziness. It could not, for it would never have let such a crazy travesty of Nature's laboratory assume the master role in its life.

Here is a warning from one who brought to our *primary* laboratory the best gifts of his mind and soul. That Schauberger was "always paying attention to the apparently insignificant" is very *significant* in itself – both as to his extraordinary insights, and as to our lack of them:-

> "Nature works uncommonly slowly. For this reason it is also impossible to observe the exalted processes taking place in Nature by way of laboratory experiments, since the proper relationships and preconditions are missing. . . Observations over several decades are essential in order to understand the infinitely subtle, constantly-increasing potential in the interplay of forces, which even then is only perceptible through its. . .effects. The causes. . .remain mostly unnoticed and overlooked. . . this explains why. . .we have only ever seen and striven to control the effects themselves." (W.W., p. 141.)

While the latter part of the quotation refers to river engineering, the whole clearly has far wider reference. We keep dealing with effects only, not causes, since the causes themselves are very subtle and result from the ***overall** interplay of forces in the natural world.* In short, the effects are part of a far wider scene which cannot enter into the artificial laboratory, but exist only in the realm of Nature itself. (This is also the realm of the holistic medicine of the alternative health movement.) But today's compartmentality science, instead of acknowledging this, insists on trying to control *effects* without understanding their causes. Viktor warns that this will only result in an aggravation of both cause and effect, and in the end will *provoke catastrophe.*

There have been catastrophes already in the GMO scene – such as when "a genetically engineered batch of L-Tryptophan was implicated in an incident which killed 36 people in the U.S. and left 1,500 others with serious blood disorders".* But the potential for catastrophes that lies ahead of us boggles the imagination. This is because genetic engineering sets a scene – as we have seen – *cut off* from reality; while some of the arguments used to justify it are so familiar from the fluoridation battle that it is almost funny. ("It's a natural process." Nature does not, of course, cross donkeys with carrots! "It's perfectly safe." The L-Tryptophan incident? And so on.)

Dr. Wrench – (unknowingly, sixty years ago) – as sternly as Viktor Schauberger, warns us against this unnatural meddling with genes. He writes in *The Wheel of Health* (ch. IX) of the great danger to plant life of man's manipulations of it, particularly in view of the *slowness of the instincts* in plant and animal life to respond to change: "plants subjected to conditions that are unfamiliar, in which, therefore, their instincts have been out-stripped". As he continues: in such circumstances, the likelihood is that "nature hits back, and she hits back with disease". What scale, when "in the next ten years, the major companies hope to introduce thousands of gene-spliced organisms over millions of acres of land and even into the water"?** Well, they will get into the water anyway, of course. That is obvious. But somehow I sense the shadow of Schauberger fallen already darkly over that scene. . .

When scientists study water in a laboratory, they study only a water *corpse*, we are warned by Viktor Schauberger. The same must be said of plant life, therefore – that, in the labs, the scientists hold it too in their hands as *a corpse*. There is a kind of macabre and hollow ring, then, to the statement of a molecular biologist that "for the first time in all time, a living creature understands its origin and can undertake to design its future" – !!

As Dr. Wrench puts it (ibid. ch. VI) – so finely fragmented is the field of knowledge of the experts that, as "in a Sudanese dust-storm. . .one loses sight of the real world" – !

It is impossible to write of genetic engineering and not speak of Dr. Mae-Wan Ho's quite outstanding book: *Genetic Engineering: Dream or Nightmare*? – with sub-heading, the *Brave New World of Bad Science and Big Business.* (Gateway Books, 1998.) Written for the layman, its purpose is to bring home to us all the dangerous realities of the unfolding scene:-

---

* ***World News**, Sept 98. (Published by Out of This World.)*

** *Article by Jeremy Rifkin in the same issue of the **New Scientist**.*

"To understand why genetic engineering biotechnology is so inherently hazardous, we have to appreciate the prodigious power of microbes to proliferate and the protean promiscuity of the genes they carry, with their ability to jump, to spread, to mutate and recombine." (Ch. 10.)

In ch. 3, "The Science that Fails the Reality Test", among the reasons she explains for this is that:-

> "Genes and genomes are inherently fluid and dynamic. It is the failure of reductionist science to recognize that *genetic stability* is a property, not of the gene transferred, *but of the ecological whole in which the organism is entangled.*" (Emphasis added.)

This reminds me of her superb summary of the matter, which I think I read in her interview with Friends of the Earth (Scotland): that while reductionist science (Schauberger's "compart-mentality") is very good at solving problems in isolation, "it has no ecological foresight whatsoever". How those six words conjure up the scale of the folly we are embarked on!

Dr. Mae-Wan Ho makes some interesting references to the E Coli 0157 bacterium, which caused so many deaths in Scotland recently; and in warning of new routes for cancer development, of powerful new viruses and virulent new pathogens, she writes (Ch. 10): "We are already experiencing a prelude to the nightmare scenario of uncontrollable, cross-species epidemics that are invulnerable to treatment".

She also delivers a very strong warning against the danger of the growing tendency (we have already noted) to impute diseases to *genes*, at the expense of considering the vital field of environmental factors that is always involved.

Impressively and encouragingly, Dr. Mae-Wan Ho writes in the introduction to ch. 14:-

> "It is clear that we need a deep and sustained change in direction *in all spheres of life* before the dreams of solving all the problems facing the world today by genetic engineering biotechnology turn into nightmares." (Emphasis added.)

Let Scotland take the good lead, then, that now lies open to her – to bring about that *essential* "change in direction" which can *no longer be delayed.*

It is impossible to write of the genetic engineering scene and not to mention also *The Ecologist*, whose Sept. 98 issue is wholly – and under heroic circumstances – devoted to this scenario. There is a quotation on the front cover, so powerful and so appropriate, that I should like to quote it right here. It sounds almost Biblical but, no attribution being given for it, I suspect it was in fact written by the Editors! Buy it and enjoy it for yourselves! – along with its full contents.*

As we have recognized, for biological thinking to be allowed to shape a society that society must allow itself to be shaped by its people's *direct* relationship with the soil. The utter folly of allowing a society to build itself *without* this basis is highlighted for us by certain yet wilder dreams of the geneticists.

> "It's 2020. You're lying on a lemon-scented lawn. The roses are blue." (Another article in the same New Scientist.)

---

* *The Ecologist, c/o Cissbury House, Furze View, Five Oaks Road, Slinfold, West Sussex RH13 7RH. (Annual sub. £24. Single copies available at £4.)*

But then – the lawn might be blue too, it turns out – or even red. Ornamental flowers could have kaleidoscopes of colour – "leaves and stems awash with floral pigments". And the blue roses might have pink leaves. As for trees, "technicoloured timber" is quite on the cards. There's "nothing about the biology of the plant pigments that means grass has to be green or wood has to be a yellowy brown". Let us look more closely at this.

An interesting section in *Living Energies*, (ch. "Trees and Light") describes in some detail the chlorophyll molecule. "Photosynthesis" – (which, let us note, is at the heart of the production of carbohydrates in plants, *and hence – of the food cycles of this Planet*) – "photosynthesis, as a process, is closely associated with the production of chlorophyll."

Studying, then, the molecular structure of chlorophyll, the molecule principally responsible for the *green colour in vegetation*, we find that at the very centre of the ring of 137 atoms comprising it, is one atom of magnesium. "The magnesium atom is king of the chlorophyll molecule." (Just as iron is at the centre of the molecular structure of human blood.) Moreover, "137 is a prime number, i.e., a number devisable only by itself or by 1. Chlorophyll – (responsible for the *green in vegetation*, and largely responsible for *photosynthesis* which is at the heart of *food production*) – chlorophyll "is thus a very stable molecule, securely rooted as it is in the indivisibility of a prime number, and rightly so, since, as a fundamental building block of vegetation, it is one of the essential bases for life on this planet".

So the pigment genes the geneticists would be playing about with turns out to involve, in the case of green, "a fundamental building block of vegetation. . .one of the essential bases for life on this planet"? What kind of a scenario is this? Gene transfers "have invariably led to 'unexpected changes in the recipient organism' – 'unexpected' only because reductionists fail to take account of complexity and interconnectedness". (Dr. Mae-Wan Ho, in ch. 3.) As one biotechnologist has admitted in another area of genetic work: "we might have underestimated. . .the complexity of the pathways we are trying to manipulate" (*New Scientist*.)

Well! They are never guilty of *understatement*, are they? – ! And so, in fooling around with our colour-scapes, like the proverbial child with the box of matches, they are unwittingly, gaily, chancing on bringing the whole thing to ruin? For that building-block into which Nature was so careful to build *super-stability*, on account of its being one of the *essential bases of life on this Planet*: just supposing that the colour green, of the chlorophyll, should prove to have held *a hidden key* to that stability? – and that the 'how' and 'why' of it were just some of those "complexities of the pathways" that turn out not to have been quite foreseen. . .? Not that the new plaything out in the environment can ever be *recalled* of course – for here we're into the realm of "jumping genes" and "escaper genes", just to add to all the fun and games. – Just some more of those 'unforeseen complexities'. . .?

If anything could illustrate the utterly childish mentality of the society we inhabit, this is it. We are content to let loose a handful of the most irresponsible of our children – those pseudo-scientists *devoid of biological thinking* – with *carte blanche* to re-design our entire world as they please. . .and the usurpers who presently hold the reins of power in their hands are happy to applaud them on their way! Surely we have reached here one of those milestones Schauberger warns us of, when "the conditions for all life will begin to disappear". (*W.W.*, p. 158.) Perhaps we can now see clearly the fundamental madness we have nurtured – a race of Earth's children who have built themselves a society fundamentally crazy from being CUT OFF FROM THE SOIL.

Birthright. . .and. . .Scotland Today

There are some children of the Earth who have long felt that our occupation of this Planet – our huge cities and 99.9% of the work we are engaged upon – that these things are *incompatible with* the life of the Planet. Long have some of us felt that every Earth-child should know something direct about soil husbandry – and that it is useless for anyone to argue they are not interested in the soil, since it is from that soil that we live. But instead of honouring the wide natural laboratory given to us, we betook ourselves to building artificial ones for our delight – and so have ended up with an *artificial view of life*.

We can now see it with our own eyes – the utter futility of our ways. *Without the foundations of a soil that is treasured by each and every one of us* – we price ourselves out of existence without even noticing what we are doing. The "day the flood came" may well turn out this time, simply – a flood of genetic blue or genetic red.

The geneticists have got hold of Pandora's box alright – but the box of tricks turned out to be a box of trip-wires. We think we can operate upon our environment? We shall find ourselves operated upon – *and direly* – by our own works.

How do we imagine the *trees* of the Planet will respond to all these tamperings? We are in trouble from the very beginning. For trees are not just timber. As Schauberger teaches us, each tree is also a column of water, *and a power-house for the surrounding area*. We therefore do ill to meddle with the subtle energies of a tree. but handled in the geneticists' laboratories, they are at once subjected to the whole network of electro-magnetic emissions that all such places now contain – emissions that are already damaging to trees in the outdoor environment, as is well documented. Nor does it necessarily require a gross assault to cause profound damage, as we know – (now that the tenets of homeopathy have been fully vindicated*) Merely to consider this one aspect of the tree, then – that the grown tree is an *energy-centre to the whole surrounding area*, an energy-centre we relate to: consider what damage to our own energy-centres we are sowing in all this. . .**

But the genetic engineering scene raves on. The intention is to sow the world with plant-based vaccines, plant-based plastics ("biodegradable", of course), plant-based wall-papers. . . There's no end. You-name-it!. . . "They will re-seed the planet with a second genesis."*** All in our own diseased image, naturally – for we have developed our very own special 'Midas' touch!

But supposing that that plant-life has an inbuilt *will* not so to be enslaved. . .by our enslaving culture? Suppose that Schauberger's *ethericities* win out in the end? Suppose that that dangerously slow-working *instinct* should surface finally with the last word – ? The long suppression of the fundamental instincts of a human being can prove a wrecker. "If you shut up the truth and bury it under the ground, it will but grow and gather to itself such explosive power that the day it bursts through it will blow up everything in its way." (Zola.) So the planned "second genesis" turns out to be instead an *un*planned series of catastrophic *Revelations*. . .?

And what of the *aura* which all of us carry with us? Just how is *it* supposed to survive

---

* *See **The Memory of Water**, by Michael Schiff, on the work of Jacques Benveniste.*

** *See **Living Energies**; also Water, Electricity and Health, by Alan Hall, and other books on electro-magnetic stress.*

*** *Same issue of the **New Scientist**.*

in this new scene? – the aura whose colours reflect the colours of the universe as it was made. . .the aura which subtly interconnects also with the colours of the chakras (our energy-centres) – and hence with our *health*, including our *mental health*. . . Just another of those unbethought of "complexities" of the scene? But safe in their "Sudanese duststorm", what *would* the geneticists know of the light of the aura – ?

If the geneticists were to start re-colouring the Earth we dwell in, the likelihood is that we would gradually all go stark, staring mad. There is of course that very saying, "whom the gods would destroy, they first drive mad", which has been handed down to us by the ancient Greeks – but then, in our 'compart-mentality' society, there are not likely to be any *classical scholars* among our geneticists!

The quotation from the front of *The Ecologist* fittingly returns to me at this moment – a fitting epitaph on the whole *genetic* outrage. Fitting epitaph. . .for that society which fails to embark forthwith upon the "deep and sustained change in direction" now demanded of us in "*all*" spheres of our life indeed.

Let the GMO scene spell it out for us with a new intensity. The people themselves must take back *the full* jurisdiction over their land. I.e., not only is radical economic reform required – (land rent reform, to remove economic slavery); but radical political reform, as already discussed – (that is, the *full grass-roots power over* those rental values) – is absolutely required equally. It is required in order to ensure that *no utilization* takes place, of the *people's* funds, to fund *centrally*-instituted bodies to lay down conditions regarding land-use. . .such as, decrees for novel types of "set-asides" – to be set aside for GMO experimental crops. . .?

Urgent? "Every government" – (Britain's no exception) – "says it is regulating scientifically the introduction of genetically engineered organisms into the environment. but all the players know that there is absolutely *no risk-assessment science by which to do it*." (Jeremy Rifkin, in the New Scientist. Emphasis added.) And just as though the betrayal weren't deep *enough*: "It has emerged that a key Government report initiated by ministers, into the effect on the environment of growing genetically-modified crops, has been suppressed within Whitehall, owing to its controversial findings, and its authors warned not to discuss it!" (Extract from a letter by Derek S. Paton, in the Courier of 23 Dec. 98.)

Why not say it? We know it so well of old! This country is not governed by a government, but by that *Seven-Strong-Gang*!. . .with their puppet government. . .* 'Tis under their aegis that a new tribe of gnomes is now running wild in the garden. G-Monster ones! GMOmes!

*

And a fitting footnote to the above, methinks!

A recent Scottish Office circular to Community Councils has "stressed the importance of Community Councils positively acting to obtain opinion from the local community on matters of general interest". The Scottish Office booklet makes the point that "the opinions of Community Councillors did not always represent those of the community in general". (From a report in *Newsround North*, Dec. 98.)

* *And this puppet government presumes to speak of having vision in its dealings with the land question! (See Part III.) Vision comes not form the puppet-hearted! Best leave that to the people of Scotland!*

My pen was poised to indite a commentary on the above – when the following was suddenly spun out of me as if on a waiting reel:

Dear Scottish Office, why not take
A glass of your own physic?
You seem a trifle out-of-touch –
Not want to face the music?

Your fluoridation schemes are daft,
Your GMOs are dafter –
And now this unctuous C.C. circ
Puts us in fits of laughter.

You are so twisted up in knots
There's only one solution:
We will exchange our crazy roles
And end all this confusion!

C.C.s are folding here and there –
But do not be deceived!
'Tis to re-surge – and with those teeth
Of which YOU'LL be bereaved!

S-A.H. 16 Dec. 98
('Dragon's Teeth'! – *and not Jason's*!**)

*

DR. A. TOMATIS – "EINSTEIN OF THE EAR"

The deep and indestructible genetic yearning of all peoples for their soil receives fresh insights form the work of a remarkable healer of our time – work which adds its own strongest warning against any GMO tampering with this Earth.

When I refer to Dr. Tomatis as a healer, it is in fact his own insistence that he does not heal people – he awakens them. Yet what a profound description of healing that **is**!**

Dr. Alfred A. Tomatis began his work as an ear, nose and throat specialist and surgeon, and he has now, through the discoveries he has made in his fifty years of consecrated work, earned for himself the title of 'Einstein of the ear'! Tomatis's study of the ear led him to "look beneath the surface";*** and this, for him, meant studying the ear literally *in utero* – in the womb: that is, the ear of the unborn child.

---

* *The allusion is to a Greek myth.*

** *Suddenly I find myself thinking again of those tall blocks of flats I saw in Moscow in 1964 – their hideousness so poignantly transformed by the greenery which hung in curtains from every balcony, speaking of the streaming green wounds of a people not long wrenched from their soil and still clinging to those last shreds of contact with her. Alas, two generations on, how far will that memory have faded? How much "awakening" would be needed now?*

**** *This, and the further quotations, are from an absorbing article on Tomatis's work that appeared in* ***Caduceus****, issue no. 28, (38, Russell Terrace, Leamington Spa, Warwickshire CV31 1HE):* ***A Sympathetic Vibration****, by Joshua Leeds. Dr. Tomatis's book is entitled* ***The Conscious Ear: My Life of Transformation through Listening****.*

Hearing is said to be the last of the senses to leave us when we leave this earth. It is also the first of the senses that we develop, and is already operating four-and-a-half months before we are born. What has Dr. Tomatis discovered to be the role of the ear during this – the earliest stage of its existence? To help us *grow the brain*. The "psychological input of the mother's voice is as important as the physiological necessity of the umbilical cord".* To the infant in the womb, sound is *nutrient*, profoundly affecting the brain's development. "Sound waves, 'digested' by the ear, provide electrical impulses that charge the brain", and the higher frequencies of the mother's voice "literally nourish the foetus", while sound continues to act as the same vital nourishment to us after we are born. Upon the early experience, therefore, of our listening, and upon the quality of it, much depends. It becomes a decisive factor in the development, through childhood, of our communication skills, our learning ability and our social adjustment, involving even states such as autism.**

What tragedy for the child, then – and giving rise to what problems in later life – should it arrive on earth with its vital listening ability already impaired! Yet how hard for it to be otherwise for the child helplessly trapped in the situation of its parents, should that be one of *social deprivation*. A father who arrived 'home' with his wife and first-born child to a homeless person's unit, was so filled with shame that this was all he could provide for his son that he sat down and wept. To take responsible care for one's family is a wholly natural role for a man. Social deprivation – even just being compelled to live on State hand-outs – debases and perverts the fine qualities of true manhood. Their intolerable situation of cramped hopelessness drove the father presently to shouting at both mother and child, in a situation that spiralled on down. The emotional trauma suffered we can easily understand. But Dr. Tomatis's work reveals a whole new dimension of the damage done to such children, focusing upon the extremely sensitive area of the actual *development of the brain*, as a distinctive part of such damaging.

Can we not see – even if we are incapable of taking into account the human suffering – that, even from the point of view of social costs, the ever-escalating social deprivation that is built into land monopoly is bringing us to social and economic *ruin*? For there is no way that a society can continue to fund a pathway of ever deepening

---

* *I would like to testify to Dr. Tomatis's work myself, in its unexpected explanation of a feature of my own childhood. The voice of my Mother affected me extraordinarily deeply in my childhood; and even as an older child, standing beside her in church, I would be overcome at the sound of her singing, and unable to join in.*

It was only a few years ago that my elder sister told me of her memories of Durban (Africa) – of how, while she was paddling in the sea, our mother would be sitting on the sands absorbed in thoughts of her infant daughter lying in the hospital there. No wonder the doctors could do nothing for my amoebic dysentery! My yearning for the healing of my Primal Mother must have been deeply compounded with the longing for my human mother's voice – a memory which, it seems, haunted me on through childhood.

** *What is the consequence of this to the hearing impaired? We are not dependent solely upon the ear for the absorption of sound. "Dr. Tomatis believes skin perceives sound waves, that we can sing with our bones! It is the middle ear that translates this potential to the brain, and it may arrive through many routes." The remarkable contemporary Scottish musician, Evelyn Glennie, certainly bears testimony to this.*

disaster. Is it not obvious that there is no other answer to our situation but to END the underlying land monopoly in which all such social deprivation – that is, SOCIAL EXCLUSION – is rooted?

Intolerable circumstances of life, springing directly from such social exclusion, are a main cause of partnership breakdowns, breakdowns in which thousands of children must be involved every year. Before the point of breakdown comes, how much simply of verbal abuse will the child not have suffered – or been a trapped and terrified witness to – quite apart from emotional or physical abuse endured?

If the role of the ear at this vital, formative stage is to *grow the brain*, let us ask ourselves just what must be the effect upon the brain of an ear that *shrinks from hearing* – that shrinks from hearing what it cannot bear to hear? For it seems that that word "shrinks" must describe, in a simultaneous reflex action, an actual *stunting* of the receptor organ – the brain.

Significantly, I recently read that two-thirds of the American prison population has learning disabilities. Can the situation be so different in Britain? In Scotland? Once more – just as through the work of Viktor Schauberger and Weston Price – so now, through the work of Dr. Tomatis too, we are brought face-to-face with the fruits of our own folly. For in sending people to prison, in the vast majority of cases – and even perhaps in all, if we reflect for a moment upon Gosaba and other truly free communities such as Weston Price describes – society is busy meting out punishment to already damaged souls. . .already damaged from tragic earlier chapters of their lives. – Victimizing anew those who are already victims. Yet still the Seven Wise Masters are building prisons in our land. . .

Even thinking of random acts of brutality and violence that seem unaccountable, we cannot escape, even here, society's responsibility. For is not the society such souls grew up in the bearer and inculcator of an *inherently violent ethos*? Then why should we expect its children to escape contamination by it? Even such acts, then, cannot be considered outside of the context of a society that is itself founded on brutality and violence – the fundamental brutality and violence of LAND DISPOSSESSION. For so long as that fundamental remains unreversed, it will continue to carry its subtle and ill-boding reverberations, affecting every avenue and activity of our lives.

But there are further implications of Dr. Tomatis's work which are impossible to miss. For beyond, beneath, above and around the person of our human mother is that yet greater presence of the one who is the Primary Mother of us all. To consider just the most immediate and obvious elements of this scene: what if – bereft of her embrace – *her* voice cannot reach us in the womb, or through the formative years of our childhood?

> "There is no quiet place in the white man's cities. No place to hear the unfurling of leaves in spring, or the rustle of an insect's wing. . . The clatter only seems to insult the ears." (Chief Seattle.)

So – if our children are insulted in the most sensitive areas of their being by the environment they are nurtured amidst and born into, is it any wonder if they then hurl those insults back at us? – or take refuge in a fantasy world of drugs? Our children are truly the barometers of the environment we have created for them – just as much as each is the barometer of their personal one.

Nor is the sensory deprivation of our cities confined to the sense of hearing:-

> "The air is precious to the red man. . .the smell of wind. . . scented with piñon pine. . .The perfumed flowers are our sisters. . .The white man does not seem to notice the air he breathes. Like a man dying for many days, he is numb to the stench." (Ibid.)

What do we do bringing our children into an environment which starves them of their sense of smell? For the sense of smell has *its* nutrients for us too Perhaps an "Einstein of the nose" will one day tell us just what damage we inflict upon our children in depriving them of the nutrients of the nose.* For the smells of the city no less "insult" the nose. Nor are our eyes spared, denied the infinite loveliness and diversity of forms of the Earthly Mother – assaulted as we are, in our cities, by a man-made environment and man-made objects on every side. As for the sense of touch – rarely in city streets do we find the joy of contact with *Her*. Our cities are places of severe sensory deprivation all round – something that may well form part of the subtler background to abuse. Nor is this situation radically contradicted in the countryside, if contact with that Primal Mother is circumscribed by the condition of *slavery* – that is, held only upon another's terms.

Yet what do we do when we put people into prisons? We deprive them of the sensory experience of that Primal Mother practically altogether. Artificial "solutions" from those who can only think artificially themselves! No wonder that drugs are running rife and ever rifer in our prisons today!

In the article in Caduceus, Joshua Leeds writes: "According to Tomatis, when a baby is separated from its mother, the vital sound connection between them is severed. While outer nutrition can be supplied elsewhere, this sonic lifeline is a critical biological connection. Sometimes aural transference to another mother can take place, often it doesn't."** But for our Earthly Mother – the Primary Mother of us all – there is no substitute. No other "transference" is possible for us.

What of the situation, then, of the human mother, marooned amidst a city environment? What of her ability to feed to her child those happy sounds of our Primal

---

* *Interestingly, since writing the above* - (first hand-written draft) - *in Oct. 98, an article has appeared* ***(Scotland on Sunday**, 13 Dec. 98) confirming exactly what I state. Headed "Scent of a woman: mummy's smell helps cure the blues", it tells of the discovery of a 'mummy odour' – a "smell which resembles sandalwood", discovered from "taking. . .swabs from the armpits of young women". It is planned to market it as a* ***medicine for stress and anxiety****. "Young babies are instantly attracted to the mummy odour. It is prevalent in all women. . .and immediately attractive to all humans. . . It is curious that sandalwood has been burned in Buddhist temples in the Far East for thousands of years to aid relaxation."*

As we know from Dr. Tomatis's work, the 'mummy smell' is far from being the ***only*** *reason that "babies bond so closely with their mothers" – but it powerfully afirms the extent of the damage inflicted on a people by their clearance from the land. What about the "medicine for stress and anxiety" provided by the* ***Earthly Mother*** *herself? Strangely enough, I have always held that no scent of any flower, however sweet, is to be compared simply with the smell of* ***grass****. No wonder, for it also is the smell of our Mother's* ***skin****! This, in turn, underlines a peculiar wickedness in the submerging of society in today's cocktails of chemicals, which enter also by the nose. It would appear to be a major factor in the widespread loss, today, of the sense of* ***smell****. . .*

** *A vital matter to take into account, where small children are involved in the break-up of families.*

Mother that it must also yearn for – sounds that will make the ear *want* to grow the brain, to be able to feed more fully on them – sounds that will soothe the human mother too? Viktor Schauberger's mother used to say to him: "If occasionally life is really hard, and you don't know where to turn, go to a stream and listen to its music. Then everything will be alright again." In the city the sound of the stream is the sound of the stream of traffic. It is impossible not to see that the damage Dr. Tomatis is dealing with has a far further dimension – a damage that reaches far back too, beyond the needs of the immediate human mother, through generations of the dispossessed. The primal and primitive need for our Primary Mother runs through us all at the deepest core. The market in 'sounds of Nature' tapes today is a poignant witness to it. But the most deeply deprived do not know Her even to look for. . .

Dr. Tomatis's treatment for his patients uses "filtered sound" – (including that of the Mother's voice where possible) – to resemble most closely the sounds that the ear would receive in the womb. Sound works through vibration; and it seems to me not impossible that, as the healing process takes place, the actual structure of the brain may undergo some transformation as a part of that healing, (since "the ear grows the brain"); perhaps rediscovering, something of those "finer windings" that Viktor Schauberger speaks of, even if manifesting only at the invisible or energy ("etheric") level. Here, at any rate, is what Joshua Leeds writes of the experience of Tomatis's patients – who include also women that have suffered childhood abuse and experienced profound release from their sufferings:-

> "Most spoke of letting the sonic water cleanse and soothe, quietly and gently. . . The use of vibration, which is frequency, which is sound, to restore original innocence, and the perfection of awareness that goes with it, is a masterstroke of awareness. All physical matter resonates. Therefore, using sound to reharmonize our systems is at the same time logical and magical."

This remarkable passage carries one's thought back to our prison scenes today, and to Tomatis's words: "I do not *treat* the children who are brought to me – I *awaken* them". How many in our prisons are not crying out to be similarly "awakened" – to a part of themselves too long painfully locked away, a part they have never dared let themselves discover?

But so long as the present structure of society remains unchanged, even with Dr. Tomatis's remarkable healing work we would *still* only be sending such souls back out again into that greater prison-yard – the continuing prison-yard of '*land monopoly* . . .where they are either denied the nurturing voice of their Earthly Mother altogether, or where it can only reach them via *another's* permissions, on *another's* terms. But that will not meet the needs of the child, for the child needs the full freedom of the mother's body.

Unless, therefore, we are able to apply to this *greater* scenario the profound lesson of Dr. Tomatis's work, we shall miss its most vital message for us – a message unconsciously cried out for by countless deeply damaged souls in our midst today.

Are we going to continue to allow these wounded souls – with or without Dr. Tomatis's healing – simply to return to that greater prison-yard out of which they came?

Or shall we give them back – by taking it back for ourselves, for all of us – the chance to be nurtured again by the voice and touch of our great Primal Mother?. . .She to whom unseverable umbilical cords hold us fast and forever, whether we know it or not.

*

Birthright. . .and. . .Scotland Today

SUICIDES

We come now to a matter which has deep links with the foregoing section.

In mid-December 98 by attention was caught by a television programme. It was on the tragic matter of why so many young men commit suicide today – (and the rate has doubled in the last twenty years). The thing that struck me so forcibly on watching the programme was how little the adult world understands the plight of the young today. And in particular, how little it understands the *real* plight of its *male* young – of the youth that finally emerges fully onto the stage of life. . .in an uprooted society. Much more, it seems to me, it understood – and spoken and written – about women.

There are many layers to this failure. My concern is with the deepest and hidden one, which alone to me fully addresses the problem. But – to take a quick look at the more visible layers first.

Most of these young men were suffering from the dreadful 'unemployment' scenario. We know now what a cover-front this is – (and not surprisingly it covers the "hidden layer"). But to look at it more simply first: what more treacherous blow to the sense of self-worth at that vulnerable age – (indeed at any age) – than to discover that your gifts are not wanted by society, although if you're lucky you might get some crumbs of charity tossed to you. Cruel contrast indeed with the early post-war years of my experience, when the world was literally swimming with jobs and there was no difficulty in flying the nest and striking out on your own – even if your job was meaningless and survival a struggle (and even more so when the landlady put up your rent by two-and-sixpence a week for the electricity, because she said you read all through the night). For the youth of today *not* to be able to take that natural step and leave the nest, as every young bird does, is itself a cruel psychological situation in which to be held.

For myself, at any rate, I knew it was an essential first step to any real discovery of who I was or what life was about. In addition, it provides of course some incomparable early training in building that *character* whereby one learns to cope with life standing on one's own feet. That this is a step becoming ever more impossible for the young of today is a serious matter. For it is a situation not only damaging to the young, but one that rebounds damagingly on society too, since such young people will not impossibly become society's casualties if bereft of their early, natural testing-grounds. Even, simply – casualties of *despair* through being unable to spread their wings. It is, of course, locked-up *land* that locks up affordable living-space. But does our society *care*? Does it have the smallest understanding, even of what is at stake here? Good heavens, no! The young should stay firmly at home with their parents, even into their twenties, is the advice Nanny gives out – (Nanny, the *concierge* who carries the keys, of course!)

There's nothing like locked-up land for compounding the problems a society builds for itself. I can speak with first-hand knowledge of certain young people who have had to spend spells *in mental institutions*, whose basic problem was simply that they were compelled to continue living in home surroundings that had become – RIGHTLY – intolerable to them, so bringing on what may well be called a 'crisis of identity'. It is not impossible that such an experience, long enough drawn out, induces a suicidal tendency. What unspeakable mental cruelty is inflicted on the young by us, in our blindness.

There is also the experience, for many just entering adult life, of a sense of deep alienation from the society into which they are emerging. This did not come explicitly into the picture presented, of these young men; but although unexpressed, I sensed it as a thread forming part of their experiences too, (a part of the same "hidden layer" surfacing, that we shall come to). I remember in my own case it ran so deep that I used to think of the Newhaven fishwives back at home – (I was alone and in London): the stalwart, cheery women who tramped the outskirts of Edinburgh, then, with their creels on their backs. I used to think – if only I had been born a Newhaven fishwife, I could feel I had some real place in this alien society. (The words "green" and "ecology" were not yet any part of our vocabulary in the 1940s, of course, so how could I understand what it was I was really searching for – and in the city could not find – ?) I remember too the convent which beckoned as an escape-route, which I passed every day on my way to work. . .

But none of this addresses the deepest problem which, it seems to me, confronted these young men. To address this, I must speak from insights gained at a later stage in my life. So I must speak first of these.

In the early 1970s – (when it finally became clear that the doors to liberal studies lecturing were firmly closed against one who was infecting young students with an enthusiasm for Henry George!) – I spoke to my husband, who was then retired, and suggested we should leave the city scene, which I felt becoming increasingly precarious in any case. Perhaps I could get a job teaching Russian in the country somewhere, and at least we could invest some serious energies in organic growing.

It was a suggestion my husband welcomed. So he began taking me on trips to various parts of England which he knew and loved (being English himself). We visited many pleasant places – but to my astonishment, and my concern, I was left completely 'cold' by all of them.

I could not understand it. My husband remained unperturbed – but it was disturbing to me. It seemed to me that I had some deep streak of ingratitude or discontent in me, if this was all the response I could manage. This was all I could make of it – there must be something wrong with me. But I could not explain it to anyone. How could I, when I could not explain it to myself? For my rejection of those places had not been a light thing, but something that came up from my whole being. So the problem was clearly an internal one – no one else could help. I must sort it out for myself – so I *kept silent*.

. . .And as I am writing these last words, I am thinking, of course, of these young men – who also "kept silent". The programme was called, *Boys Don't Cry*. But to me there was something involved far, far deeper than this. The outcome of my own experience tells me so. My experience has no other parallels with theirs, and by comparison its circumstances were trivial. But in this one way – which proved to be so significant as to the resolving of my own problem – the parallel is a striking one, and indeed cries and screams out to us.

How did the resolution of my own situation come about? I made one of my regular trips to Wholefoods in Baker Street -- but this time chanced to pick up an alternative magazine as I left. Upon opening its pages, I found myself reading an article by a woman who told how, after having spent many years south of the Border, she had *returned back to her roots in Scotland.*

In a flash I realized that there was nothing wrong with me whatsoever. In fact, I was entirely right-side-up. It was the *whole of the surrounding scene* that was 'wrong'. I lived in a society so devoid of any proper identity itself – (apart from its mass-culture)

– that it practically forbade anyone living in it from discovering their real identity either. I knew at once, and for the first time in my life, that I was Scottish not just as a matter of fact, but in the guts and marrow of me – and that my roots were calling me home.

It was a strange thing for me to find my world suddenly right way up and know that there was nothing wrong with *me*. . .(and it speaks deeply to me of the tragedies of these young men). I was also astonished since, once I saw the thing, it was so obvious I wondered how it could possibly have escaped me for so long. Then I remembered the saying – "the third generation is just in time to get back to the land", and felt I now understood that saying *from the inside*. If you are not even aware that there is something waiting to be recognized – waiting for *you* recognize *it* – if you're convinced it's just you who are peculiar, that there's something amiss with you – (or, in grimmer scenarios, just you who have an *empty hole inside you* that nobody else seems to have?) – then of course there is nothing to go out and search for. Nothing to go out and fight for. And nothing to say about it either. *Nothing to say to anyone*.

You haven't even got anything to cry for. It's more a numbness. *Boys Don't Cry* may describe well enough the situation for some, who would confide if they could in some sympathetic ear. But there are others, I am convinced, (and the most deeply wounded of all), for whom these words are quite inadequate to describe the experience they could no longer cope with – which they could not live with any more.

How, then, are we to understand their trouble? Was there some deep and hidden problem of identity affecting them similarly? – an identity which our society had forbidden them, too, even to recognize. . .and which their life was left so meaningless – MEANINGLESS – without?

Let us turn now to the pages of an animal welfare publication, which came my way recently. It describes what may happen when a cat is caged up, in one of our institutions for *animal experimentation*. . . .And how aptly those last words ring out, as I write them! For what our society is perpetuating is indeed a vast, on-going experiment, of an appallingly cruel nature, upon its young males.

But let me return to the cat – in its *sterile, unnatural* environment. It is a she-cat, and she produces kittens. What does she then do? The article relates that in some cases the mother cat will *bite* and *even devour* her kittens born in such circumstances.

For the cat knows better than the laboratory worker. But suddenly, with these words too, I see all those ranged up there in their seats of political power in that very same guise. – As *laboratory-workers*, similarly, conducting their cold, detached experiments upon the young male population held under their scrutiny. . .with all their careful *reports* on them, *statistics, white papers* – and on and on forever.

They say that women are coping well in a man's world today. Let's put it in its more down-to earth, brutal terms. They are coping well in a world of *wage-slavery*.

But *that's not a man's world either*. It's a travesty of a man's world – and part of a route that may well lead to suicide.

Let us remember the instincts Dr. Wrench speaks so warningly about, and the dangers of *outstripping* those instincts.

What are the basic instincts for a man – which his identity is so closely bound up with – ? We know that the two most basic human instincts are those for survival and reproduction. But in what terms do these find their necessary expression for the male born onto this Earth?

Birthright. . .and. . .Scotland Today

This brings me to think of Scott Nearing, an American intellectual and radical who, in his middle years, left the academic world and, with his wife Helen, pioneered the back-to-the-land, homesteading movement in America; together building, growing – still travelling and lecturing in the winters – and writing their inspiring books.* Together they built several houses, and Scot lived to be a hundred years of age, active to the last. It was out of this later stage of his life, and from his own first-hand experience, that Scott came to speak of it as a *basic instinct* for a man to want to build his own house – and indeed to want to build it with his own hands. These were not the findings of someone born to that life at all, since Scott had been an academic. They were a *direct discovery* from this later stage of his life, when they were living in the kind of freedom which, quite simply, allowed the instincts to find a *natural surfacing*.

If we consider the matter, the instinct to reproduce must, in the human being, be supported by some instinct having regard to the nurturing of offspring, since the human young need care for a considerable span of their early lives. This places Scott's good 'discovery' in the light of the obvious. It *must* be an elementary instinct in the male to provide himself with his own home, a home in which to raise a family – or engage in whatever other creative work he came to Earth to do.

But of course a *home* means *land*. . .

So how does the State cope with this most 'uncomfortable' of *basic instincts*?

By maximally reducing its ground of play – and erasing as far as possible even the memory of it. Thus it comes about that – not a home but a *job* is held up as the great object of attainment! Scott Nearing never lacked for a *job*! His and Helen's days were filled to overflowing with a huge range of fascinating undertakings, involving many and varied testings of their skills and ingenuity too. As they had no mortgage and were practically self-sufficient in food, they managed to make enough from their various other undertakings based on their home, including their writing, never to have to think of a pension either. Of course, their top health – nurtured by their whole life-style as well as their *home-grown produce* – induced no sense of retirement, and they were both happily active for all of their days.

But as to that *job* – a 'job' under land monopoly is something that hugely depends on the whim of the system, of course. If times are lucky, and you are lucky, you may get one. A man's basic instinct tells him that he is not born to be dependent upon the whim of a system, but to make his own way in life – to make his own way and provide himself with his own home.

So we should not take lightly the words that Scott Nearing spoke – nor take lightly the fact that the human *instinct* has in this matter been so drastically *outstripped*. Viktor Schauberger warned us of reaching a state presently when we are "stripped of all human feeling". And that human feeling is fundamentally bound up with *instinct*. It may be refined at higher levels, but our instincts remain at its source and we *dangerously ignore them*. For they *will* speak, even if in terms that are indecipherable to us, (just as I experienced it in the homing instinct). But should they be indecipherable to us and in a *sufficiently basic scenario*, then their pressures upon us may acquire *explosive force*.

Let us remind ourselves of Zola's words once more, for they have great

---

* *"Living the Good Life", "Continuing the Good Life", etc.*
Contact: Forest Farm, Harborside, ME 04642, U.S.A.

application in this scene – this scene of *intolerable pressures*: "If you shut up the truth" – (or a basic instinct?) – "and bury it under the ground" – (attempt to obliterate it from consciousness?) – "it will but grow and gather to itself such explosive power that the day it bursts through it will blow up everything in its way." Viktor Schauberger warns exactly similarly – speaking of falsely constrained water as bent on "destroying the very structures that have robbed it of its psyche" as it seeks in vain to *regain its lost soul.*

The "lost soul". . . "Robbed of its psyche". . . "Blowing up everything in its way". . . So what of such a victim – (in a society which has no place for such 'crazy' outbursts) – uncomprehendingly doing his best to hold *back* that "explosive force" – and so becoming, himself, that which is tragically, fatally, *standing in its way* – ? Had we not better come to understand the brutal forces of *destruction* our society now wields, before the suicide figures double again? Destruction of the basic instincts, and so of the basic *identity*, of the male?

In other scenes, you read in the papers of a man coming home from the pub one night and breaking the house up – wrecking all the furniture. Wife and children are terrified. "Drunken lout" is the verdict. (For our society has well schooled us to skim lightly over the surface of such matters.)

"Drunken lout" is no doubt the verdict of the man himself, when he comes round. When he comes 'to himself'. But *is* it himself? Or is it a ghost of himself – with a hole in the heart that he tries not to think about because he cannot cope with it – but only go out and 'drown' it from time to time?

Yes, it's hard for the women. *But it's also hard for the men.*

Others betake themselves to violence against wife and child. Women and children are battered – and animals too. . .in that sterile, unnatural environment we have created for ourselves, in which terrible deeds can erupt.* But if we want to understand and not just expostulate, we must betake ourselves to a decidedly deeper look at the scene. We must remember what the mother cat, in that same sterile environment, betook herself to. . .

---

* *The link between the battering of animals and the battering of children is now well established. But how could they not be linked? – the battering of the helpless. . . The entire ghastly live export trade is a part of the same scene. (For contact: C.I.W.F. – Compassion in World Farming – 20, Lavant Street, Petersfield, Hants, GU32 3EW.)*

Again, how many meat-eaters are acquainted at first hand with what takes place in the abattoir?

*Further, now that Christmas is behind us again, let us look at the turkeys: "Most turkeys are kept in intensive units, with 20,000 to 25,000 confined in large windowless buildings, similar to broiler chicken houses. . .Infectious disease, heart attacks, lung congestion, heat stress and starvation. . .are amongst the principal causes (of high mortality rates). . .violent handling by the catching teams is widespread. . .The slaughter process is equally gruesome. . .hung upside-down on a conveyor-belt. . .turkeys can be left to hang for as long as 6 minutes before they reach the knife. . .stunning methods are widely acknowledged to be inefficient. . .Most birds are killed by an automatic knife. This method too is far from foolproof and some turkeys pass through the equipment and into the scalding tank injured but still alive." **(Outrage**, Aut-Wtr, 98.) The scalding tank is to loosen feathers and make plucking easier. Enjoy your turkey! But what do we think this kind of work does to the human beings involved in it? We wish to live in a 'caring' society? We cannot have it both ways.*

The dispossession of a people from their land means a fundamental *emasculation of the male*. It involves a *perversion* of the most fundamental of his instincts. And yet, in other directions too, we dare to wonder at the 'perverted' behaviour that is bred from this? – at 'random and inexplicable' acts of violence that erupt. Energies that are denied a natural scope of play are already perverted – abused – by being turned in upon themselves. Are not such perverted energies bound to take their revenge? So why wonder if, in turn, they betake themselves to perversions – to pornography, paedophile rings, abuses of all kinds?

Even the rich in far from 'sterile' environments may become contaminated from living within such a framework. For if they enjoy different circumstances simply by privilege and not as of right – are they not too living in an overall *sterile* environment? – and are they not too *emasculated*, despite whatever contrary outward show?

We do not recognize how energies are turned in upon themselves in our *un*natural society, because we have no pattern to go by of a *natural* one – a society where people live in a truly normal state with full scope for their energies to turn *out*wards. But it was a pattern typified by the societies visited by Weston Price, and indeed by Gosaba – which offered no scope for perversion or for crime. No possible scope for any 'crises of identity' – or for energies to frustrate and run wild.

The dispossession of a people from their land causes a fundamental dislocation in the life of the people in every sphere and is the *great and fundamental DIVORCE* – the destruction of the most fundamental of all marriages: that of a people to their land. Yet now we have the spectacle of a government which presides over, maintains, sanctions and blesses that great and fundamental DIVORCE – now proposing the setting up of 'advisory bodies' to 'advise' the people on how to *prevent* divorce and retrieve partnership break-ups – ! Could farce be carried further?

More! The government is setting up a Scottish Partnership on Domestic Violence, to "draw up policy ideas on tackling violence against women and children"! (The Courier, 9 Nov. 98.) Here's your vital, fundamental *policy plank* on *that*: START WITH THE MEN! – Which means: START WITH THE LAND!

The fundamental disempowerment of the role of the male in our society, through the locking up of the land, subverts the most fundamental of his instincts and challenges the matter of his identity to the roots. No wonder if it is tearing our youth apart.

Men are the natural providers for the family, but our wage-slave society has flung that role on the dust-heap. . .and flung the male on the dust-heap with it. Why should we be surprised if, as a result, "all hell breaks loose" in our midst?

Women are the chief nurturers of children within the home – but what happens when the provider of the home is not there, and women must take on the nurturing of the children and the provision of the home as well? Or simply – women must provide themselves with a home, in a society where it is even harder for a woman than for a man? Then it is doubly hard for the woman indeed, and no doubt women's suicide rates also show appalling figures.

Is it not time that we came to our senses? Is it not time at last to look full in the face what is being done to our youth? – to our older men? – and to our women young and old, and to our children? Is it not time to get ourselves *out of* this laboratory of cruel experimentation on the living, and back onto the living land before the suicide rate goes any higher?

The endless cry goes up: with people dying of cold in Scotland, *the government* must do something about it.

Just who is living in an unreal world? There are some in Scotland dying of cold...while others are working off frustrated energies in destruction and tragedy. Including the drug-pushers.

Just who is living in an unreal world?

Time to get *out of* this dreadful laboratory and take charge of our own affairs.

And while we are about it, see we shut down those laboratories of cruel animal experimentation too, that positively inculcate callousness in all who work in them.

It's all one.

..."Stripped of all human feeling"...

*

OTHER FORMS OF SUICIDE

Domestic violence takes many forms. One may say – suicide takes many forms also:-

> "Today everyone has eaten so much pesticide-laden food that their systems are markedly more toxic. And that, my dear, is the sad reason why we are seeing so many young people getting cancer – people in their 40s, ever more children. Older people who grew up in the 30s and 40s started out with a better diet, and that has stood them in good stead. But children are in danger now." (Charlotte Gerson.*)

We are doing all this *to ourselves*. So are we not quite simply committing suicide? But this cannot be said of the children on whom our modern agriculture inflicts its ills – they are entirely its victims.

It is no surprise that "the rise in the incidence of cancer in the population from a pre-war figure of 1 in 14" is now "approaching 1 in 2", (*New Leaves*, July 98.**) If this apparently unstoppable drive continues, it is not obvious it will soon be the fate of all? How much do parents care about the fate of their children? The above scenario exactly correlates with the chemical industries' transfer of their attentions from the fields of war to the *fields of food* – to *our* food, *our* agriculture – following the end of W.W.II. And it has all naturally been carried out, supported and maintained, with official sanction and official blessing – and paid for by the people themselves. Twice over. As tax-payers; and as sufferers – they and their families – from the effects of this assault. Meanwhile, successive governments sit on evidence of harm, and continue so to sit – until some scandal finally blows up in their faces:-

> ". . .a 31 year old farmer's son, James Penny. . .recently committed suicide. . .a consultant psychologist. . .had decided that James was an ME sufferer, despite James's protestations that he had been involved in dipping sheep with his father since he was a small boy. . .The inquest is to be held on 3/3/98. We must not forget all those OP victims who have died as a result of ignorance, secrecy and dishonesty of government

---

* *From an article in **You**, 27 Sept. 98. Charlotte Gerson is the daughter of Dr. Max Gerson, who founded his famous clinic to treat cancer by unorthodox means. "His 1958 book, **A Cancer Therapy**, details the cures of 50 patients and is still in print. Albert Schweitzer, his most famous patient, whom he treated for diabetes, wrote of him: 'I see in Dr. Gerson one of the most eminent geniuses in medical history.'"*

** *A valuable publication on the vegan way of life. (47, Highlands Road, Letherhead, Surrey KT22 8NQ. Send s.a.e. for inquiry.)*

officials and their scientific advisers. OPIN has accused these people publicly of committing a crime against the farming community of our country."*

James had been put on a drug that was particularly dangerous to OP sufferers – (i.e., one suffering from poisoning by an *o*rgano-*p*hosphorous insecticide – such as, be it noted, it was until recently *mandatory, by government order*, to dip sheep with). But the above "crime" clearly extends well beyond the farming community, involving gardeners, golfers, indeed the population in general via residues in food, and particularly – innocent and helpless cats and dogs, imprisoned in the horror of OP-impregnated flea-collars; while incredibly, OPs are actually permitted to be used even *inside food-selling establishments.***

But these betrayals of the public interest by officialdom are simply *built into* the system! – the crazy system of 'remote control' which is the crazy offspring of crazy land monopoly, its remote control reaching from top to bottom of society, and through every avenue of life. Remote control – the flourishing of *facelessness*. Irresponsible, uncaring, the antithesis of life and of health. Time we rid ourselves of *remote control*!

Time for grass-roots re-empowerment on a bioregional basis! And incidentally, in our taking back of the land of Scotland from its destructive sheep-culture as well – (and many other monocultures too) – it is interesting to note that Dr. Wrench, in *The Wheel of Health*, tells how the people of Hunza, as also of China, Japan, ancient Peru and Dutch Java,*** all looked upon their agriculture as a kind of "gardening" – indicating that in their vital work of life-supporting cultivation, the land was nurtured in human-sized ways. Let us remember that these were the peoples who created the highest types of agriculture known to the world.

The concept of a diversity of small areas, each having its own micro-climate, is very much that of the permaculture movement of today. Moreover, by creating raised beds (of maximum 4 ft. width) and mulching them deeply, minimal-work food-growing can be achieved. Planting can be far closer on untrodden, richly built-up beds. The mulch retains the moisture beneath it, suppresses weeds, and provides the soil with an on-going supply of nutrients.**** Quinoa, (used by the ancient Peruvians and rich in

---

* *Quoted from OP News, Mar. 98. The OP Inf. Network (OPIN) was established by Elizabeth Sigmund, of Heathfield, Callington, Cornwall PL17, whose valiant work has successfully spearheaded the move to expose the OP scandal. Send s.a.e. for inquiry. There must be plenty of sheep-farmers in Scotland who would be glad to receive it. No wonder that suicides among farmers have shows a worrying trend in recent years.*

** *An informative small booklet issued by Green Network 9 Clairmont Road, Lexden, Colchester, Essex CO3. Annual sub. £12. Concerned golfers should apply to the Scottish Golf Courses Wildlife Initiative, already mentioned, for advice on moving out of this shameful scene. Time a sister organization was started south of the Border!*

*** *I hope to include in Part III an account of a fascinating and little-known chapter in the history of Java: "Sir Stamford Raffles in Indonesia".*

**** *Mulch is best applied in three layers – phonetically, 3 Cs! Carpets, Quilts and Canopies.* ***Carpets****: of fine material, such as grass clippings. (Must be applied* ***thickly****, since it shrinks considerably on drying.)* ***Quilts****: rougher leafage, such as nettles, comfrey, sweet cicely, etc.* ***Canopies****: to protect seedlings against excessive heat from the sun. . .(perhaps Scotland will have a summer in 1999!) Fine twigs or branches – birch is ideal. As the plants grow on, they shade the whole bed themselves. Once the system is set up, it needs little attention, apart from the annual mulching. But above all -- MAKE YOUR OWN EXPERIMENTS! Rock dust, in our minerally depleted soils, decidedly enhances growth.*

amino-acids) can be experimented with as a substitute for cereals. *Plants for a Future*, a fascinating and absorbing book by Ken Fern,* opens yet further horizons. In short, a whole world of exploration and growing awaits us when we regain our land – an exploration in which we shall assuredly discover how much we have missed out on for how long, *including* the building of our own vibrant health and that of our children.

An important aspect of this is the *freshness* of our food. The food that lines our supermarket shelves – quite apart from its pesticide residues and other contaminations – cannot give us vitality, since it has lost its own in travelling hundreds – perhaps thousands – of 'food miles', these contributing hugely to pollution as well. The centralization of something as vital as our food supplies is a *top priority* of that 'remote control' – both of people and of resources – that is exercised over us. Naturally, since people cannot live without food!

Let us therefore in the interests of self-preservation – both of our sanity and of our health – rescue our food from the barbarics of remote control! Let us become gardeners in our own land – and *cease to slay ourselves*!

*

OUR 'CARING' SOCIETY

Meanwhile the destruction of our chidren's health proceeds apace by an ever-widening variety of routes.

Irritable bowel syndrome (IBS or Crohn's disease) – another of those 'diseases of modern civilization', of "cause unknown" and apparently incurable by orthodox means – "is increasing world-wide each year, especially among children". (Leading article in *What Doctors Don't Tell You*, Dec. 1977.) And while we are looking at these things: osteoporosis and Alzheimer's disease are also increasing "alarmingly" – (radio news report of 5 Dec. 97); whilst mere obesity – which can lead to diabetes, cancer, high blood pressure, heart disease and stroke, we are told – has become "a global epidemic". (The Courier, 8 Aug. 97.) *It's a global nightmare*. Nor does this touch on the growing number one reads about, of previously unheard of diseases and afflictions that small children are suffering from today.

It does not touch, either, on the question of mental illness. A quarter of a million under-16 year olds have serious mental health problems, and this rises to two million up to 25 year olds. (Radio Scotland news report, late 97.) I thought Scotland's population was only six million, so what *are* we looking at? (Indeed, someone recently corrected me: five million – on account of its late 'mysterious' (?) decline.) It seems that this 'caring' society of ours is more than a trifle care*less*.

But *would we know it*? Of course not! We're so blazingly cheerful about living in our 'caring' society, that we simply haven't noticed the number of those requiring care will soon outnumber the carers. Once more: "The complacency with which the masses of the people as well as the politicians view our trend is not unlike the drifting of a merry party in the rapids above a great cataract. There seems to be no appropriate sense of impending doom." (Dr. Weston Price.)

But as we well know now, the picture *could not have been otherwise* under our

---

* *Ken Fern, P.F.A.F., The Field, Penpol, Lostwhithiel, Cornwall PL22 0NG. (Send s.a.e. with your enquiry.)*

system of centralized power. So our progressively destroyed soil – that soil which is the very foundation of our health – waits. . .and waits. . .for the hands and hearts which alone can minister to it what it is crying out for – that is, for the touch of those same hearts and hands – (ministering to themselves as well as to the soïl) – reclaiming that soil along with their land:-

> "Burying our hands in the earth and turning the turf. . .was an amazing experience. . . As Barry Lopez put it: 'I know of no restorative of heart, body and soul more effective against hopelessness than the restoration of the Earth. Like childbirth, like the giving and receiving of gifts, like the passion and gesture of the various forms of human love, it is holy.' " (*Voices from Earth First*. See where earlier quoted, in Part I.)

And when we read that word "hopelessness", let us think of the hopelessness of those who commit suicide.

Meanwhile, so mesmerized are we by the trappings of centralized power – to such an extent has it paralysed our thinking processes – that farmers can actually be found saying of certain agricultural practices: "If the regulatory authorities thought it wasn't safe then they wouldn't allow us to use it" – ! (Spokesman for the N.F.U., The Courier, 5 Feb. 98.) That very State whose various, *but unvarying*, vandalisms of the soil – as of its products – are now paraded before us in the awful deficits of the nation's health! That same State, moreover, whose crime against *those very same farmers* is now also paraded before us, in the matter of the sheep-dip!

A 'caring' society must clearly take *first* care of its thinking. We must reclaim our thinking from the false shackles which have for too long subjugated it, and learn to think again for ourselves. There is only *one* way to embark upon this: that is, to free the land, whose original shackling it is that has *shackled both us and our thinking*, in turn:-

> "A free people can only grow out of a free earth. Any people that violates Mother-Earth has no right to a homeland, because in soils destroyed by speculation, high-quality races can find no abode, i.e. they are physical masses divorced of all connection with the Earth. Masses without roots perish. They have to travel the terrible road of decay until, like unsuitable fertilizers, they lose their stubborn wills and only when they have reached this condition, and starting again from the very beginning, will they be allowed to enter the mighty course of evolution." (Viktor Schauberger. *Living Energies*, ch. 20.)

And let none say now that Vikor Schauberger was not fully conversant with the meaning of radical land reform.

*

THE 'WORK' CHARADE

In reading through Dr. Mae-Wan Ho's excellent book on genetic engineering, already referred to, it was interesting to stumble on a classic presentation of the condition of *enslavement*, which in our society passes for 'work':-

> "I was recently involved in a debate on genetic engineering biotechnology organized by the Society of Chemical Industry at Cambridge University. At dinner afterwards, I found myself sitting next to the CEO (Chief Executive Officer) of a biotech company. In an unguarded moment, he confessed that he personally didn't feel happy about his company's involvement with biotechnology, but what could he do? It was the system, and mortgages had to be paid. He was coping, he

said, by practising Transcendental Meditation, unlike his colleagues, most of whom were on Prozac." (Ch. 3, "The Science that Fails the Reality Test".)

There are many variations on the theme of stress – but not perhaps so many *fundamental chords*. Mort-gage. Mort-engagement – (it roots back to the same word). Dancing with death – dicing with death. But it's the Planet ultimately that's being diced with, of course – *mort-gaged*. And the breaking of the 'system' the CEO refers to – the system of *centralized power* sprung of land monopoly – is the only way to end this dance-of-death. For we know where all those mort-gages come from.

Meanwhile the dreadful dance goes on. Just how many mort-gages must have been involved in that massed protest in a certain part of Scotland last October (98), when banners were held aloft and cries went up loud and strong to *that same* centralized-power-set-up to "do something" about jobs, (some large overseas investors having suddenly pulled out of the area, leaving thousands 'without work'). This grim mort-engagement can only be broken as we ourselves determine to get back to basics – tear the veils from our own eyes, *reclaim our thinking*, and so denounce the whole cruel charade.

> "At one time, a certain set of terms regarding man's place in nature gave organized Christianity the power largely to control mens consciences and direct their conduct; and this power has dwindled to the point of disappearance for no other reason than that men generally stopped thinking in those terms.
>
> The persistence of our unstable and iniquitous economic system is not due to the power of accumulated capital, the force of propaganda, or to any force or combination of forces commonly alleged as its cause. It is due solely to a certain set of terms in which men think of the opportunity to work; they regard this opportunity as something to be *given*. Nowhere is there any other idea about it than that the opportunity to apply labour and capital to natural resources for the production of wealth is not in any sense a right, but a concession. This is all that keeps our system alive." (From ch. V of A.J. Nock's *Our Enemy the State*.)

This blind belief – (which Nock so rightly points out is all that it is) – that work is something to be "given", has sprouted a new offspring in our time. Jobs can be 'created' too! What a marvellous dazzle the phrase has – conjuring up the sparkles from a magician's wand! But –

> ". . .no wonder" (Hyundai creates several thousand jobs) "when they get £120,000 per employee. . . the truth is that foreign companies don't come here for a great work-force, they're here because of huge subsidies given them by unelected quangos."*

It's extraordinary the lengths that are gone to, to keep the Scots off their land! And it's extraordinary the amount the Scots can be got to pay our to keep *themselves* off the land too!. . .via such 'co-operative (taxpayer-government) deals'. The land of Scotland must be very valuable to someone! But *just how cheap is it being sold*?

"Wheresoever the carcase is, there will the eagles be gathered together." (Matthew, ch. 24.) Or – the *Seven Wise Masters*? Just so Nock warns us of the fatal outcome of *the progressive absorption of social power by the State*. (Same ch. V.) . . . But no! – with banners waving and renewed energies we *still* throw ourselves upon its hands!

---

* *Extract from a letter by Richard Sim, Isle of Arran, published in Scotland on Sunday, 15 Sept. 97.*

Hasn't the dream turned nightmare enough *yet* to make us want to wake up? Hyundai Via Systems – National Semi-Conductors – Seagate's Micro-Electronics Company. . . One by one these godlike powers – our far-flung 'saviour-investors' – *ditch us*. But no! "LOCATE IN SCOTLAND!" – the well-grooved record continues to send forth its familiar bleats!

Now what did Viktor Schauberger say about being "totally stripped of human feeling"? We're clearly well on the way there, for we've lost our sense of humour for a start! Just think what derision the plea to *locate in Scotland* would have received at the hands of the old Highlanders! But never a single joke have I seen or heard today on this truly *risible* title!

Locate in Scotland? Why, the Scots are queuing up for it! Yet they're *advertising* for people too come and *do* it!

Locate-In-Scotland more! L.I.S.-more – *Lismore*! Perhaps we could raise another fun-piece like the one on our Scottish islands* – built on these irrepressibly infantile fantasisings of ours! S.E.P.A.: Scots – Ever Present Aspirants! S.S.S.I.: Scots Step Straight In! L.E.C.: Locate! – Every Caledonian!**

L.I.S. – Let In the Scots!

And let's have some *real* "Scottish Enterprise" at last – *provided by the Scots themselves*!

So! – we've got no jobs? What we thought these great capital conglomerates from overseas were *putting in* to Scotland they are now *pulling out* again. . .? Because rather than have the sense to go for *land* and *people*, (which can't get "pulled out"), we went for *capital* instead! But those huge capital conglomerates are in any case hugely compounded of stolen goods – *land rents* – the miseries of other people. So now they have ended in compounding *our* miseries in turn! Well, we've fairly earned it! Just how could they *ever* have blessed us? Yet still we go running after them. Has our shame not even yet reached its nadir? Shamelessly for years having hugged to ourselves the title "Silicon Glen", Scotland is now being touted as the *call-centre* capital of Europe. Rightly named – and *some prostitution it is*!

As for "Silicon Glen": "according to disturbing new evidence. . .toxic chemicals used by the silicon industry have caused an alarming number of miscarriages among its workers", including many Scots. (The Courier, 17 Feb. 98.) In general, many workers began to suffer "health problems, particularly severe migraine, nausea and vomiting". But who cares? "Silicon Glen will soon rival Silicon Valley in California", boasted a radio announcement of 28 Apr. 98 – on news of a new jobs boost for "Silicon Glen"!

"Jobs in call centres, leisure and tourism" are growing. (An illuminating article by Rob Stokes in *Scotland on Sunday*, 5 July 98). In fact, "tourism is the world's largest industry employing 127 million world-wide" – (Perth College Newsletter, 1998 issue.) Somewhere I read a definition of tourism as the "embalming fluid of culture". Maybe of more than culture, too. What happens to those "tourists" when the bread runs out?. . .

---

* *See Part III.*

** *S.E.P.A. stands (at present!) for Scottish Environmental Protection Agency; S.S.S.I. – for Site of Special Scientific Interest; and L.E.C. – for Local Enterprise Company.*

or we're all dying of cancer anyway?. . .or so riddled with Alzheimer's our society can't operate any more?

"Employment in the shopping-trolley workplace overtook manufacturing. . .and pulled ahead dramatically last year." Well, what *about* those shopping trolleys? In the summer of 1998 I came upon a small book of great excellence. Let me quote from it:-

> "Since becoming more self-sufficient I've begun to believe that our position on this planet is becoming rapidly untenable, even if the queue at Tesco *et al* seven days a week seem to the happy living in a completely parallel universe. . .why don't all those sad trolley-pushers realise, the main reason we consume food is to live; we are what we eat, so why settle for consuming such crap?
>
> Living here where they produce some of the supermarket glop. . .I've been lucky enough to see first-hand how it's all done. Abandon those trolleys whilst you still have the use of what you were born with. At best what most of us eat does us no good at all, at worst, well don't even think about it.
>
> Believe me, farmers no longer take any responsibility for the quality of what they grow. They can't, they don't understand any longer what they're doing. In the days gone by there was regional expertise, farmers growing crops suited to the soil and climate of the area. Today it's just an ingredient in a 'product'. . .and the 'industry' will provide the necessary to make it grow anywhere. . . Nobody really knows or cares whether our food is safe." (From *My Kind of Self-Sufficiency*, by Phil Rooksby.*)

Yes – so much for having handed over our soil along with our land! We're dying of cancer because hardly anyone knows any more how to produce real food – outside of the valiant organic movement. No wonder that the initiative of the *organic boxed vegetables* scheme has grown so dramatically in recent months.

On this very point, let me fittingly testify concerning close friends of my own. The husband had been attending the local hospital for several weeks for cancer of the prostate, when they decided to subscribe to such a local scheme, and each week received a delicious box of organically grown vegetables-and-fruit-in-season. A few weeks later, the husband was told that he should return no more to the hospital since his trouble had departed.

Such evidence – (of what must be the origins of so much cancer today) – is usually downgraded by being described as 'merely anectotal'. From our discussions in this book, however, we are now able to turn that judgement on its head. Such evidence stems, in fact, from a *laboratory* itself! – the laboratory which, as we have seen, is the primary laboratory: that of real life. Naturally it cannot produce the kind of proof demanded by the reductionist (compart-mentality) science of our *artificial* laboratories. But in the laboratory of real life that kind of reductionist proof is of very limited value in any case, for it is quite incapable of embracing the *whole* scene as the 'anectotal' one does – that is, the scene of real life, which is the same scene in which our loved ones sicken and suffer. . .so often so 'suddenly' and so 'mysteriously' too. But these things have been *a long time building up*, only we are not conversant with their beginnings, having lost touch with our bodies' subtler vibrations – through having lost our living touch with the soil.

Those of us who have at present no opportunity to grow our own organic food

---

* *To obtain a copy, send £5 direct to the Author, at Midsummer Cottage, Sessay, N. Yorks, YO7 3NL. It is also available from certain of the larger branches of Waterstone's bookshops.*

would therefore do well to obtain organic produce for ourselves and our families, as one of the solidest insurances against too much tragedy waiting-in-the-wings in a society such as ours, whose orthodox professionals – bar some grand and shining exceptions – have nothing of guidance to offer us whatsoever in today's *real-life* scene. And this is the tragedy of those extensive hospital waiting-lists also: that our hospitals could be hugely emptied were our successive governments but *students of William Ogilvie*! – (*soil* nurturer as well as land reformer, that he was) – instead of being tied to the *Seven Wise Masters'* apron-strings.*

To return to Phil Rooksby's inspiring book – (which incidentally carries a beautiful home-crafted and designed cover too): Phil and Maureen Rooksby had just taken on an additional mortgage, for a piece of derelict orchard – when "the sky fell in". He lost his job. "Overnight we were one income less and the very new and naive owners of one acre of prime wilderness. At 35 and with 'the c.v. from hell' it wasn't going to be easy finding work. Even temping. I sat down with the bank statement, did some sums, and everything indeed was doomed". . .

> "The first weeks were a little bit crazy – a 'twister' of moods – anger, fear, guilt and uncertainty accentuated by my virtual imprisonment at home, six miles from the nearest shop or town without transport. . .
>
> I started out by just wanting to have some dignity, and work to maintain the fabric of the mortgaged roof over our heads. Working with what I could find around me or scrounge I progressed on to making furniture. Recreating objects we would once have bought, and that brought me back into contact with the 'making' feeling. I'd finally discovered how to switch the 'light' on. In fact, everything I do here feels like that, it's connected with that age-old thing of 'providing' (food/shelter/fire and water). There's an energy to be had from being so in touch with the basics of life. I feel so much more alive and interested in things now, in fact there's just not enough time to do everything.
>
> You learn that. . .shopping. . .is not the answer. It's a short-term gratification that blunts the imagination, devalues craft, and has no respect for the environment – consuming the world at an alarming rate. . .I can see all around me what the last hundred years of 'shopping' have achieved – a cataract, masquerading as 'progress'. It has blurred our vision, so we no longer see the beauty and vividness of an artisan-based way of life. If we really want to enjoy life then we need to get back and 'earth' ourselves with some practical tasks and skills.
>
> . . .we grow virtually all our own vegetables now, and with each year I get more ambitious at the choice gets a bit wider. . . We get all our fruit juice, and a good proportion of fresh soft and tree fruit – everything organically produced of course – from the garden. . . In the autumn we press all the apples and pears. . . The garden has become so very important to me. I can't imagine living without one now. . .
>
> Having to make ends meet, or self-sufficiency as I now know it, gave me a

---

* *For information on organic boxed vegetable schemes in your area, send s.a.e. to:*

Let us also note the following: Dr. Ann Wigmore states: "The most thrilling experience I can recall was to see cancer cells taken from a human body and thriving on cooked food, but unable to survive on the same food when it was uncooked". (Be Your Own Doctor.)

fresh chance to deviate from the work-hard play-hard community and strike out. Freedom from the drudgery of work makes you think about whether you really want to be part of a society that makes life so miserable. I see now the popular crusade for 'jobs' at any cost for what it is and cringe. . . I feel betrayed. Everything I was taught to be/see/believe in as 'good' is probably supported by an economic imperative rather than a valid ethical one."

. . .Which (last sentence) just about sums up the entire shaping of our society under fundamental NON-ETHICAL land monopoly!

For so many reasons, Phil Rooksby's book was a joyful discovery. So how about those would-be defenders of the status quo, who try to insist – "Oh, the people in the cities don't want to get back onto the land" – ! Those in a position to know at first hand know well that there are masses of people in the cities who would do anything to get out. And now Phil Rooksby answers those hopeful defenders of the status quo from his own experience at first hand: "There's an energy to be had from being so in touch with the basics of life. . .there's just not enough time to do everything. . .If you really want to enjoy life. . ." Who doesn't? Phil and Maureen had come out of the city themselves – a place they now describe rather aptly as "a giant concrete zoo with just one species on display" – ! I think Helen and Scott Nearing would have enjoyed that description! – as so much else in Phil's book too.

"As the land in the city becomes more valuable, more and more goes to rent. The bigger the city, the deeper the poverty; the bigger the city, the more degradation. . . It is better for the men who own the earth to have big cities – but for no one else." (Clarence Darrow, in *Progress*, May-June 98.)

And so, once more – L.I.S.! *L*et *I*n the *S*cots! *Unlock the land*! But that is something the Scots are now well set, methinks, to do for themselves!

(See footnote ~ p402.)

MORE 'WORK' SCENARIOS

Stand back a little further from the scene, and further vistas open. How is it possible, except in a society of *wage slaves*, that people could be found putting themselves forward to be part of a work force producing deadly chemicals?

'Death Probe into DIY Best Seller' ran the heading to a news item in The Observer of 13th November, 1988, where a worker in his mid forties had suddenly died and getting on for half the small work force was sick. But – "if you tell 'the bosses', they just say, 'get along with you, you're not sick'." Few workers took days off sick. "If you do, you lose your monthly bonus, or a percentage of it. People need the money, so you don't go sick, even when you need to." Wage slavery with a vengeance! Probably in this case not to keep up with a mortgage, but just to have enough to be able to cope with the weekly rent – *(rent)*. The toxicologist appealed to had advised on 'dozens of cases' of a similar kind, involving other chemical companies.

A friend wrote me recently from somewhere in Fife – I extract as follows:-

> "Here in ... we are surrounded by all manner of pollutants. Rosyth Dockyard with its many hidden horrors, Mossmorran Petro-Chemical Plant ... Grangemouth Oil Refinery and Longannet Power Station ... Day and night great clouds of noxious smoke are emitted from these establishments, and the smell is so nauseating that it is impossible to open the windows without inhaling huge draughts of these potentially lethal concoctions.
>
> "I have noticed a fall in the amount of wildlife in the area since I moved here some two decades ago. For example, I recall seeing a great many bats on summer evenings, but have not seen one for several years. I feel sure that they are being poisoned, just as surely as is the human population of the area. My windows are always smeared with a sticky, grey substance, which is almost impossible to remove. It is little wonder that there is a very high incidence of leukaemia in this area. Local councillors appear completely apathetic. It is quite terrifying that we are about to enter a new millennium without having taken heed of the dreadful lessons of this one."

The view from 'X' cannot be unique in Scotland. It is as well we reckon the price being paid by thousands of Scots for all these wonderful *jobs* and *industries* that we 'cannot live without'. The words of Jesus as powerfully oppose the hells-on-earth we have built since his time: "Whosoever shall offend one of these little ones ... it is better for him that a millstone were hanged about his neck and he were cast into the sea".

But to those bewitched by today's Work Wizard – (bewitched just as surely as we were those of earlier times by the false 'magicians' of Christianity) – to those so *bewitched* little children are expendable.

It is not necessary to create such hell holes in order that we may live on this Planet. As Edward Goldsmith said (in another remarkable issue of *The Ecologist*[1], the time has come when we must simply *stop producing* materials that are proving lethal to us; while Viktor Schauberger has shown us the ruin we are causing to all forms of life on Earth in pursuing present heat-based power technology, and explains exactly why coal and oil must be left *in the ground* – as providing the essential nutrients of the Earth's blood stream, which forms *our* blood streams in turn. It is time we looked in

---

[1] *Mar-Apr '98 Issue. Devoted entirely to cancer, including good news of alternative treatments*

the face that the present industrial scene – reared upon land monopoly – is one of monumental ruination. Instead of arguing feebly that we cannot live without the products of our industrial society, why not recognise the far more obvious fact that we cannot live *with* them? We shall discover it sooner or later anyway, as we inexorably price ourselves out of existence on our present path.

There is a further reason why. The disposal of the toxic wastes of our industrial society is now such an escalating problem that, as landfill sites (a horror story in themselves) begin to run out, increasingly irresponsible solutions are being resorted to. Toxic wastes are now being re-cycled as fuel to industry (and so – dispersed over the land again). They are incorporated in building materials, added to sludge, and even added to 'the artificial fertiliser' that is spread out over our agricultural land (some Government scientists even having the gall to assure us that this actually improves the soil'. (*The Ecologist*) So – we eat the stuff whether we like it or not! And our 'health' advisers tell us to eat more fruit and vegetables, and never think to add the word 'organic'. The more down-to-earth words are left to an OP sufferer: "Even though our children may be eating their recommended daily intake of fruit and vegetables, they may also be absorbing high doses of pesticides" (*The Countess of Mar, in her Lecture to the British Housewives League, House of Commons, April '98*)[2]

Even more incredible, we now have – as Edward Goldsmith points out – a new *directive* from the European Commission that 'legalises the incorporation of radioactive waste in consumer products'. Already 'British Nuclear Fuels are making available the radioactive remnants of a dismantled nuclear reactor for the manufacture of pots and pans'. 'Making available' – a fine generosity! So – with the sanction and blessing of the E.U., you could be gently setting your child 'a-glow' just by cooking him a homely meal. For those 'minute' amounts all add up, and safety levels in *every* sphere have time and again proved the fantasy they always were. But as they say, a leopard does not change its spots, and we already had a good look at these particular spots back in the 1970's. As Edward Goldsmith sums the situation up: "We shall thus be living in an increasingly chemicalised and radioactive environment in which the cancer rate can only escalate further until it eventually becomes generalised in the human population." And all they can think about is those hospital waiting lists ... while the leak in the boat smiles ever wider.

Those hospital waiting lists are our own creation. And further on the matter of toxicity: I recently learned that the previous Forth River Purification Board was not permitted to monitor the emissions from Rosyth Dockyard. *Not permitted!* As we already knew, of course – SCOTLAND CAN TAKE IT! (The ultimate in 'safe' toxic waste disposal!) One can imagine the outrage this must have been to one of those former independent minded water bodies —self-constituted, as they were, as independent boards. But – *too* independent by a long chalk! And so, against the expressed wish of our local representative bodies, they were simply closed down by central government and the network of SEPA's set up in their place.[3] SEPAS – safely tied to Scottish Office apron strings from the start. A Scottish Office brain child! (ScOff's – Environmental Protection Agency, according to many a report!)

---

[2] *Quoted from Green Network (already referred to).*

[3] *'The march towards reorganisation and centralisation, regardless of what is needed or wanted, continues, and we learn that SEPA (Scottish Environmental Protection Agency) could be operational by 1996, although its creation has been opposed by forty local authorities and six of the seven river purification boards. The new body will not be given powers to co-ordinate flood control or powers to prosecute polluters.' (The Fletcher Forum, April 1993).*

But we have by no means yet plumbed the depths of our situation. For underlying the whole dreadful edifice of wage slavery we find a yet more terrible ranking of slave labourers. These ones do not receive wages, for they are strictly 'commodities', and as such – to be utilised and discarded. It is interesting that Dr. Mae-Wan Ho, in the introduction to Ch.7 of her book, speaks of how genes are looked upon, by a society such as ours, as 'commodities'. But this is only a yet further descent down the slope of our degradation:-

> "Latest government figures reveal that during 1997, 2,635,969 'procedures' were carried out on living animals ...
>
> "As well as being poisoned to death, they are subjected to psychological stress ... thermal injury ... 'physical trauma' ... they are irradiated ... injected into the brain ... forced to inhale noxious substances ... or undergo 'aversive training'..."[4]

The government prefers the word 'procedures'. 'Experiments' is too near the brutal truth – and too great a give away of our own cowardice. Merely cancer research – (any human volunteers?) – 'involved 300,938 experiments'. Those who give to medical research little understand the horrors they are in nearly every case subscribing to. In addition, pharmaceuticals involved 890,492 'procedures'; pollution testing – 27,571; and the testing for safety – *('safety'!)* – of pesticides, herbicides, industrial chemicals and consumer products – 140,814. Things are done to animals in these places that the ordinary citizen would be prosecuted for doing – but in the name of 'science' anything goes. 'Dogs are employed for poison tests with rarely any pain relief. These tests can last for months.' Let those who indulge in the use of such things as pesticides and herbicides now look full in the face just what kind of business they are supporting.

We may be sure that no society can flourish which carries so dreadful a cargo in its midst. As for what is done in the name of 'medicine': if we cannot climb to heaven on the backs of tormented creatures, we certainly cannot climb to health that way either.[5] The acceptance of vivisection by our society constitutes a 'hole' in our biological thinking of some magnitude.

No wonder that the appeal of more traditional healing therapies, such as herbalism, continues to grow – (while we vote that modern drug medicine sometimes tries to adopt that word 'traditional' into its own vocabulary!)

From the treating of people as *virtual* commodities through land monopoly, to the treating of animals as *outright* commodities was simply – a natural progression. The animal rights campaigners need to take a look from further back in the scene, if they would do their best work. They need to understand the *original* slavery that underpins it all – 'man shall sell his Earthly Mother into slavery'[6] – and lend their strength, or at least their voice, to the undoing of that, if they would set the creatures free.

Beyond the endless scenarios of industrial horror – ('darkroom disease' and 'white finger' just two recent additions to the count) – I once read of a girl who 'ran

---

[4] *Outrage, Aut-Wtr. '98. Published by Animal Aid, The Old Chapel, Bradford St., Tonbridge, Kent, TN9. (Send s.a.e. for inquiry).*

[5] *Vivisection Unveiled, by Dr. Tony Page – an illuminating read – reveals how our obsession with animal experimentation has repaid us in fact by holding back true medical advance. Humane research – using human tissue – is a far superior method and points the way ahead. (Humane Research Trust, 29 Bramhall Lane South, Bramhall, Stockport, Cheshire, SK7 2DN. Send s.a.e. for inquiry)*

[6] *See The Gospel of the Essences, Part III.*

screaming from an egg packing station'. But why do I say *beyond* the *industrial* horror? Farming *is* an industry today – self-confessed; and battery farming is an hideous an industry as any. "I see now the popular crusade for 'jobs' at any cost for what it is and cringe." *(Phil Rooksby)* That screaming lass is a living evocation of Phil's words – more vociferously, in that live scene, taking to her heels.

It is a question, how much of today's work place would vanish in a society that was self-respecting —that is, a society that did not exploit the Earth, the animals or men. We must take those good steps we have discussed, and discover. Let us take a lesson from Viktor Schauberger, and recognise the parallels from his words:-

> "The world is not subject to random accident but is governed according to inner laws ... Left to herself, Nature would have supplanted the earlier vegetation with newer forms, and not only would have transformed the world into a blossoming garden of immense fertility and stable temperature, but in addition would have renewed herself in cycles ..." (W.W., p.139)

The society that places itself in obedience to those 'inner' laws – (that is – *natural* laws, such as the *Law of Rent*) – will find those inner laws operative in its midst in the social scene, just as in the ecological. We too, planted in freedom, would by now have evolved those 'newer forms' of creative living and working, transforming human society into a veritable 'blossoming garden' likewise.

Edward Goldsmith understandably argues that 'a huge popular campaign is required' to end the production of toxic, cancer-producing materials. But a better and swifter way lies open to us – and to end more than that. It lies open to the Scots, at any rate. For us: at this unique time in our history, it lies open to us once and for all to DE-FROCK those Seven Wise Masters – the *usurpers* in our midst who preside over, and hold down, today's whole monstrous *slave establishment.*

*

MORE 'LOWER DEPTHS'[7]

On the 27th December, 1998, two horror headlines for Scotland were carried by *Scotland on Sunday.*

One was the banner headline of the front page, which announced the hundredth death from drugs this year in Scotland, on Christmas morning. As one spokesman commented, when is the government going to take this matter seriously? But since we know now what 'taking the matter seriously' must involve, it may safely be said that the only people capable of taking it seriously ENOUGH are the people of Scotland themselves, and above all those directly involved in these tragedies. We shall return to the drug scene presently.

The other horror headline appears at the foot of an inside page: "Cancer, blindness and early death: Is the chip industry to blame?"

Since I have long held deep reservations about Scotland's chip industry – but only ever seen one news item (referred to earlier), and that a recent one, carrying any report of suspected hazards, I could not pass this headline by. 'Semiconductor manufacturing staff are suing employers, writes Ross Davidson in San Francisco', was the sub-heading, and the report was worth reading, not only for the hazards revealed,

---

[7] *A phrase immortalised by the Russian writer, Gorky.*

but also as showing just what guinea pigs have been made of the Scots. Scotland has been a major base for the U.K. chip industry, and no wonder the government was happy to plant a 'Silicon Glen' north of the Border. All those flattering words about Scotland's skilled work force can now be seen early for what they were – a necessary 'gimmick' for selling the grisly business to us.

To pick out a few highlights from this interesting report: firstly, the usual "growing chorus of scientists and occupational health experts" who are "now saying that chip plants can be dangerous". *Now!* That's right! Make sure you get your decade or two of trial guinea pigs and profits first! Then – the term 'clean room' finally comes into the light of day as having meant 'clean' for the *chips*. 'They protect the silicon wafers from the people, not the people from the chemicals.' How weird can you be?

Surprise, surprise – the 'mix of chemicals could cause unanticipated health problems'. Surely not *unanticipated?* Didn't Rachel Carson write her book half-a-century ago?[8]

'You could have 50 different chemicals and high total fumes, but each of these chemicals could be below the' (legal) 'limit'. I think the best comment on that comes out of the article itself: 'The engineers in this business are superb but the biologists are still in the 14th Century'. In fact, I would consider that an insult to the 14th Century, considering the school of Alchemists. What does it *really* mean? It means that engineers – of that blighting 'B' technology of Schauberger's stern warnings to us – are running the Earth, that the biologists are as devoid as are the engineers of *biological thinking* – and that we are pricing ourselves out of existence with a vengeance we won't wake up to till we are gone.

There were miscarriages suffered by some of the Scotswomen working for the chip industry. One is tempted to say that it may have been as well for some that they *were* miscarriages. "Zachary Ruffing was born blind and with severe multiple birth defects. Aged 13 and now living in Kentucky, he is active and intelligent but has to breathe through a tube in his neck and has had at least 20 operations on his head and face." His parents had both worked in 'clean rooms' at a silicon chip plant in America. I am reminded of Callum Coat's words in *Living Energies* (p.197) about the dangers, in imbibing unfit water, of passing on 'a terrible genetic legacy to our children'. The most terrible genetic legacies must be those which take more than one generation to show up. We simply do not know what the full fruitage of the silicon chip industry may yet be.

Amidst the chorus of 'All hails' being poured out on Silicon Glen in the early 70's – without exception – my own private comment at the time, tucked away in a file, came to light again the other day:-

A silly con called silicon! Goodbye, Mr. Chips!

As it turns out, we might have been better blessed with that goodbye. 'Don't cry for me, Caledonia!' ...

---

[8] *'Between the major groups of insecticides, and between them and other chemicals, there are interactions that have serious potentials. Whether released into soil or water or a man's blood, these unrelated chemicals do not remain segregated; there are mysterious and unseen changes by which one alters the power of another for harm.' (Silent Spring)*
Rachel Carson was writing primarily of the environmental scene. Her words will apply no less to the industrial.

The catalogue of industrial injuries is of course almost endless, peaking in many another horror story such as the infamous asbestos one. But how many of us know of the deformities among children in the environs of Dounreay? A misplaced eye ... no fingers on one hand ... This was told me by a young woman who had spent some time recently among the children in that area, and saw these things for herself. But there are 'lower depths' also in the upper heights, so to speak.

Those who can get hold of a copy of *The Secret War and the Fluoride Conspiracy*, by Dr. Geoffrey E. Smith,[9] will learn something of interest about the scarcely ever mentioned but exceptionally toxic air pollutant, *hydrogen fluoride* – (and of its links with the whole fluoridation story, need one say, i.e., popularise fluoridation, at all costs!) This "dangerous but relatively unknown" air pollutant, hydrogen fluoride, is produced by some of the most powerful industries, Dr. Geoffrey Smith tells us, including such things as steel and iron works, plastics manufacturers, agro-chemical factories, petro-chemical refineries, coal-burning power stations and nuclear processing plants, and apparently if air pollution standards were to be set for it that were harmless, certain key industries of our society would 'almost grind to a halt'. (One cannot help wondering if there is a link here with that embargo placed upon the former Forth River Purification Board) The fall-out from this exceptionally toxic hidden-up air pollutant is obviously at huge, *hidden* costs to our health as well. Those hospital waiting lists look more skewed than ever.

I have only just been able to glance briefly at the book, but having referred earlier in this text to the matter, I was interested to note confirmed in the opening paragraph of its Introduction that fluoride is indeed a 'mind dulling' drug, and that it was used as such to treat drinking water, both in the Nazi concentration camps and in the Soviet gulags.

As already said – there are no doubt those who would just love to render more docile the fiery Scots! But, martialled – manoeuvred – manipulated, as in today's *jobs* scene, that fieriness is already put to a considerable test. Gandhi, writing on work and leisure, well summarises the essential nature of factory work-

> 'The worker enslaved in a serial production ... fritters himself away. He is selling what a freeman does not sell: his life. He is a slave.' (See further in Part III)

Slavery once established at the base of society (as in land monopoly), and once accepted as a normal part of it, can only progress and deepen, infecting every 'advance' that society makes. We see now where slavery inevitably leads – to the flourishing of 'lower depths' on all sides, and the enslaving in turn of every order of creation. Simply on the matter of health, why do we not acknowledge that we are on an unstoppably break-down track, because we insist on living in a way that on all sides – technological, industrial, agricultural, environmental – is making us sicker and sicker? The birth of damaged children – one of the most terrible experiences for any parent – is something that can only increase.

Slavery is a slippery slope. Better understand NOW just how slippery that slope is, and resolve to end the vile business – vile in every sense – forthwith; by the necessary radical re-structuring of society, from bottom up. As Jesus warned, not one iota of the law shall be changed, but it *shall all* be changed, i.e., it is no good tinkering

---

[9] *Epeius Publishing Associates, 2 Edna St., Frankston, Victoria, Australia 3199.*

on the surface. But these and other radical teachings of his naturally do not appear in the *State-subsumed* texts of the Bible!

*

**THE 'LEISURE' CHARADE –
AND STRUCTURED PLAY**

Somewhere I once read that one of the tragedies of humankind is that we mistakenly separate work from leisure, while the angels draw the two together and make of them a third – 'like music'.

Certainly, to read (as in the *Courier* of 31 July '98) of two planning applications being submitted for Perth, together representing 'a £12 million leisure project' – applications now approved by the local council – somehow signals, as little else can, the awful barrenness of our lives! No wonder if, in such a society, the reason some young people give for betaking themselves to drugs, drink or vandalism is – sheer boredom!

Structured play! Such is the concept that we inflict upon our young also. An article in *The New Scientist* of 29 Aug. '98, "Game for anything", examines the vital need that children have to create their own play and games; and it so happens that a young father had just been telling me how – in watching the local children in their usual pre-structured play space – he had noticed how they tended not to use it in the way that the adults had planned it for them, but to adapt it to *different* ideas of *their own*. As he said – not all our human artifice can offer them what a piece of wild land does, where they can develop their own forms of play, their imaginations given a free run; and that what children need more than anything to play in is a piece of wilderness. Yet today children's play areas are positively advertised as 'structured'! One begins to perceive how deeply the blight of the *structured* system we live under has eaten into our very thinking!

This is no light matter. The *New Scientist* article, essentially reviewing the book *Animal Play* (edited by Bekoff & Byres), opens as follows:-

> "Thirty years ago an engineering student at the University of Texas climbed the Austin campus tower with a rifle. He killed 17 people and wounded 31 before the police gunned him down. What compelled this young man with a 'Mr. Clean' public image to become a mass murderer? Psychologist Stuart Brown, one of the contributors to *Animal Play*, led the task force set up to find the answer. Signs of a brain tumour or serious drug addiction were expected ... Yet in the end the experts blamed an abusive father and a childhood devoid of play.
>
> "Brown went on to study dozens of young murderers, only to find that 'normal play behaviour was virtually absent throughout their lives'. He now believes that play enables children to develop empathy, social altruism and the means to handle stress, humiliation and powerlessness, and that play-starved children become adults at risk of social and personal breakdown."

The above all seems so obvious – the kind of thing, I am wont to say, that Juliet's nurse could have told us (down to earth, unforgettable character in Shakespeare's *Romeo & Juliet*) – that it seems a pity we had not understood it better in the thirty years since that Austin episode ...

However, just how much scope is there, anyway, for us to observe how children learn to handle 'stress, humiliation and powerlessness', for example – and hence for us to grasp how important it is for them to do so, at that early stage in their life – when their interactions are confined to *structured* areas of play? Where playtime is spent largely interacting with furniture – slides, swings, etc. – scope for interaction with one another, as in the old games of their playtimes – must necessarily be greatly reduced. *Structured* play indicates *stunted* play – and this may well have a subtly stunting effect upon the development of character in turn. And so, these children grow up to be adults ... and whether they have been able to develop the character necessary to deal with the difficult conditions of our unnatural adult society ... may end up affecting that society in turn ...

What children need most of all is – as my friend said – a piece of wild space. Here they can also discover nature, and develop their creativity, instead of just using manmade toys. But a request for wild space is immediately a request for *land* space – a kind of taboo demand in our land monopoly structured society! And where is any *wild* space to be found in our manmade cities?

Now we are making the same mistake regarding our adult populations. We persistently lavish tax payers' money on *structured* play spaces also for them – what we call 'leisure complexes' (and it does seen to indicate a kind of hidden 'complex' in us that we so eagerly do so!) It would have been better for the people who live in the area of these million-pound leisure-complexes to take that land instead, for themselves, for their own creative uses of whatever kind; whether as individual gardens, allotments, or as some kind of communal space – but as decided by the individuals of the locality themselves; a use of space created *by* them, and not *for* them – such usage as, under bio-regionalism, would evolve naturally. (It would save a lot of public money too).

Somewhere Viktor Schauberger writes tellingly of flowing water – how we would be wise to 'let the river do its physical jerks', i.e., play in freedom without our trying to structure that play, since then, he says, the whole surrounding environment will flourish. ... There are lessons to be taken from Schauberger for nearly every sphere of our life.

Meanwhile, all these structured play spaces ... for producing structured adults! But that's what the Seven Wise Masters *want*, of course!

A woman now living in the city, bereft of a garden, speaks of what a great resource the garden had been, which they had previously had in the city – a resource for the whole family. In particular, it was a place that had created a strong bond between herself and her father, simply through spending time quietly there together, working away on the various projects that a garden inspires. (A place, then, where influence can quietly pass from parent to child too. What comparable opportunity is offered by the indoor world? – especially with ubiquitous television today). The garden gone – those links had been cut; and she looked back in sadness from that break. There was also the lost feeling of connectedness with the land that the garden had given her.

The feeling of connectedness with the land that a garden bestows, underlying all its more visible gifts, is its supreme gift to us. Remove the possibility of having a garden from people for long enough – and they don't even know that they lack a fundamental dimension to their lives any more ... (just as I did not know that it was Scottish soil I was seeking for my roots). But the feeling of connectedness with the land is the supreme gift of the garden that the Seven Wise Masters have wished above all to rob us of.

More has been destroyed than we realise through the depriving us of proper garden space in our towns and cities – nor can all those million dollar leisure complexes ever outbid that deprivation, or compensate for it.

The solving of the 'problem' of leisure goes hand-in-hand with the solving of the 'problem' of work.

Thus it may be that, one day not too far off, in a Scotland of unlocked land – where we have once more managed to make a marriage of our work and our leisure as it should be – we shall find again that lost 'third' state, and the music of the angels. And in that day we shall take back all those leisure-complexes too!

*

DRUGS

Yes, our structured society has much to answer for. Apart from its intrinsic boredom, it has given rise to that falsely structured thinking already noted – incapable of solving society's problems because its main problem is itself!

There is a permaculture principle which is as good as a perennial philosophy: if you can, turn a problem around – and see it transform itself into a solution. A solution of a *broader* kind.

Scotland is burdened with an appalling drugs problem; on a late date in October '98 reported finally to have reached primary school level, with a packet of heroin in the possession of an eleven-year-old.

Scotland's drug problem worsens, and there seems no way of turning it back. Let us put the permaculture principle to work, and see if we can turn it around.

If we will only see it – it is *we ourselves*, the people of Scotland as a whole, who suffer from addiction – are locked into so consuming an overall addiction that, so long as we remain thus locked, we cannot possibly hope to solve the drug addiction in our midst. Those who are deep in addiction cannot help the addicted.

Yes – we ourselves are the ones on drugs! For do we not similarly keep looking to an endless succession of shots in the arm – those *injections* (of capital from outside), to provide us with work, instead of looking to ourselves, to our people and our land? So long as we keep looking to those false injections, the drug users in our midst may wait until doomsday, but we cannot rescue them. *Our society is itself totally drugged.*

Our solutions (like those of the drug users), lie actually *within.* For they lie in the land and in the people of Scotland. But there is this difference. Our scenario is the broader one – and it is therefore our first task to right *it.* For this broader scenario encompasses *the land.* And in encompassing the land, it encompasses what those drug users have need of before there can be any real release of the riches that lie within them – waiting to play their powerful and necessary part in their process of rehabilitation.

And what *are* these riches? What is in all young people? Energy, enthusiasm – the eagerness and aspirations of youth. Dreams, longings, powers of resolve and dedication, which all reach a peak at this time. *Just the qualities our society so desperately needs.* But all must remain hopelessly locked up inside them – inaccessible to us as to them – so long as that land lies hopelessly *locked up and inaccessible*, wherein alone those forces can find true play.

We have ignored the land of Scotland – and it is the worse for the drug users just as it is the worse for us all.

Birthright ... and ... Scotland Today

In his description of how he managed to achieve 'resistance-less' motion in his machines, Viktor Schauberger wrote of it as 'a motion ... we have for so long not understood, because we ourselves are the resistance, which under the most difficult circumstances has to move itself in order to evolve'.

What an illuminating statement upon this very scene! – and what an interesting way Viktor Schauberger has of saying things! So *we* have 'not understood' that we ourselves form the 'resistance' to the solution of the drugs scene. And that 'resistance' which we embody has to move itself under the 'most difficult circumstances' indeed. For it is the embodiment of so long a tradition of structured, *dispossession-based* thinking, that – (as with the drug users) – it is scarcely able to imagine any other conditions for itself than that endured. Yet – move itself it must, if it would 'evolve', as Viktor Schauberger points out.

If we can only understand that *this* is what the drugs scene in Scotland is really asking of us – if we can but understand that the drug users wait upon *us* to overcome our own, yet greater addiction than theirs – our own yet greater resistance than theirs, to change: then at last we shall 'evolve' ... to that necessary truer understanding of the drugs scene and of its radical solution; setting the drug users free at last – *and ourselves no less* – to discard old and outmoded ways.

We should ponder well those words of Viktor Schauberger's, that pinpoint so well our own resistance to *necessary change*.

Are we serious in our desire to resolve the drugs problem in our midst?

Then we know what to do. And those in our midst, the drug users, are waiting for us to do it.

*

NEW WORLD ORDER

We would do well to rid ourselves of our addiction to these huge capital conglomerates in any case – *now*, before the economic scene unfolds any further.

'Could this be the new world order?' Such was the heading of an article in *The Big Issue* of Mar. '98 which looked at this unfolding scene, with opening sentence: 'A frightening change is taking place in the world's economy'. (See Part III)

A Multilateral Agreement on Investment, or MAI, powered by big trans-national corporations under the "auspices" of the (weaselly so-called) "Organisation for Economic Co-operation and Development" (OECD), is being foisted on the world. It will give these multi-nationals "rights that extend far beyond those available to governments or individuals", and will allow them "to sue governments – in an unaccountable international tribunal – over any policy or law that discriminates against them". How might this work out? At the date of publication of the article (Mar. '98), in Mexico "local authorities are being sued for refusing U.S. companies permission to set up toxic waste dumps". Should that refusal stand, the U.S. companies of course *pull out* their "foreign investment" in Mexico. Such is the picture.

The MAI will be *binding on the new Scottish Parliament.* "Policies to direct incoming investment, support local businesses, create jobs, provide training and protect the environment could all breach the treaty. This could potentially lead to multi-nationals suing the Scottish state." So, what price freedom for the Scots, indeed? – did Scotland not have her own trump card up her sleeve.

Governments "may be forced to consider abandoning their commitments to education, health, social services and environmental protection in the scramble to attract investment". Yes – and the very people of a country may feel "forced to ... abandon" such commitments too. For an article in *The Guardian* of 31 July '98 reported how "Switzerland recently had a referendum on the future of biotechnology" – (involving those genetically modified organisms we have had a look at and that ordinary people around the world are revolting against). What was the result? Biotechnology in Switzerland 'was approved but only after massive lobbying by the Swiss-based drug and chemical companies *who threatened to leave*." (Emphasis added) The shape of things to come, as nations who have run themselves into a position of dependence on such corporations sell their very souls.

Let us return to that news item about Mexico for a moment. I am reminded of what a friend once wrote me – that "the military mindless moguls see Scotland as a vast military establishment ... 'If Scotland did not exist, NATO would have to invent it'." The need today is not only for places to store military stuff *(Trident)* but for places to store toxic stuff – including of course nuclear dumping grounds. Multi-corporations always have their plans laid well ahead. In view of her present situation already referred to, it would not be in the least surprising if Scotland was already singled out to be one of the worlds major *toxic dumping sites* – along with Mexico and a few other 'backwaters' of the world with their 'backward' (? - !) peoples. These trans-corporations are deep in toxic producing businesses – and are undoubtedly looking for dumping grounds to serve their needs.[10]

'Scotland could find herself on the losing side as the battle rages for control of the planet.' Scotland has thankfully, however – as William Ogilvie has reminded us, and others who followed him – *her own trump card.* She can decide to *rid* herself of that terrible universal addiction – the addiction which persuaded the Swiss to sell their souls even in a people's referendum. Scotland can resolve to look to her *own internal* resources – to her land and her people (the only ever stable resources of any economy); and from this she can build up her own capital – her own *true* capital – as required.

This – (as we saw in Part I) – "will be capital of a very different kind from that which parades as capital today". For it will not be paper capital – not capital of that corrupt, rent-robbery-based, blow-away-in-the-wind, pull-out-the-plug kind. It will, instead, be the real products of her own growing, manufacturing and making, traded and exchanged on those terms *alone* that have her free consent. For her own people, empowered at last through radical economic reform to buy the things they themselves produce, will be the first purchasers in her markets, in any case. Thus she will not be looking for 'overseas aid' of any kind.

Do we balk at the idea of 'going it alone' in this manner? Balk at opting for *sanity*? - !

If we cannot emulate the spirit of adventure of our grandest forebears, we deserve *nothing.*

> "Do not follow where the path may lead. Go, instead, where there is no path, and leave a trail." (Origin unknown)

---

[10] *'Lorries rattle in from England. WHY? What is Glasgow taking that England isn't? That question needs to be asked all over Scotland. Why do we have as many as 467 toxic dumps? In Wales, every site is being investigated following worries over birth defects.' (Dorothy-Grace Elder, in* *Scotland on Sunday, 20 Dec. '98)*

Heaven preserve us from going where *yonder* pathway is leading! Better far that we blaze our own trail – in today's **miasm** of darkness. And blazon SANITY!

**Note*: The Jan. '99 issue of "The Ecologist" reports that this attempted MAI has failed. But as they rightly point out, it is unlikely to be the end of the matter. 'They' will be back in another form.

*

TECHNO-FIX

How is it we have not yet understood that our chip-based technology is driving us like a drug-fix? The repeatedly stronger doses come as ever upgradings into ever-newer models, each one suctioning more of the human being into the machine – creating still higher levels of stress.

Just as surely as monopoly-based capitalism could only strip the resources of the natural world, so the monopoly-based technology sprung of it can only strip the resources of the human psyche.

The resources of both Earth and psyche are potentially infinite; for the Earth, and the psyche in all of us, are female. But our monopolistic culture, over-geared to left-brain masculinity – (which is a part of all of us too) – knows only to CONTROL THE ETERNAL WOMEN, as Schauberger put it so well! All that escalates is a devouring STRESS – to the psyche as to the Earth.

Only a people drastically cut off from the Original Female, the EARTH MOTHER, could so have failed to recognise the excess of masculine (left-brain) energy driving today's technology.

Viktor Schauberger's words powerfully address our situation. Let us hear it again: 'it is ... vital ... to create a close to Nature land culture before the whole of mankind is *totally stripped of human feeling*. (*L.W.*, p.106 – emphasis added) Let us remember the message of the Bolivian Indians. Technology has other ways of flowering – from more feminine roots. But we shall not discover these until we are ourselves re-rooted – plugged back into the original energy circuits, which are the energy circuits of the Earth – the Great Female, our Earthly Mother.

Just as A.J. Nock (from his Georgist background), brings so clearly home to us that the Industrial Revolution, in the hideous form in which it came about, was but the violent offspring of inherently violent *land monopoly*, so that it can only proceed to destroy what it takes hold of ...finally fingering the world as a piece of genetic engineering ... so it is time we recognised that today's technology is the offspring of that same fatal VIOLENCE. Its suffocation of the (female) psyche is as inbuilt a part of its progression. Only sickness can ensue, and the price will ultimately be paid.

"Crashing the barriers" (*New Scientist*, 7 Nov. '98), on exploring the world of the ever-vanishing chip, conjures up a world of techno-scientists whose backs are so firmly turned on reality, that the greater likelihood is – what we shall presently find crashing is the familiar world ... about our ears.

"The development of any culture is directly related to the understanding of its environment – both water and vegetation." (*W.W.*, p.137)

Here is the culture of SANITY – a 'new world order' indeed! And – under radical and bio-regional land reform – waiting wide open for Scotland to explore.

*

GENE-FIX

I have just been reading of a new science called "genomics". It is described as being "the potentially lucrative new science of deciphering DNA sequences in genes to understand and manipulate their functions." (*The Courier*, 18 Jan. '99)

Well! I'm glad the GeOrgists got in with geOnomics first! For if *genomics* is geared to 'understanding and manipulating' the laws (Greek *nomos*) of the gene, it must both be said that *geOnomics* has a decidedly more wholesome dedication: namely – to understanding *and respecting* the laws of the Earth (geo)!

It is interesting how hard it is to imagine thinkers of the calibre of an Ogilvie, a Henry George, or a Schauberger utilising that term 'to manipulate' at all. It does not sit easily with those who are dedicated to a respect for law – (speaking of law here as in Nature's, not man's, dominions; natural, not man-made, law).

Schauberger has well stated our necessary position as being to 'comprehend *and copy* Nature'; while Weston Price summed it up – 'Life in its fullness is *Mother Nature obeyed*'. (Emphases added.)

Similarly, what place could the term "rogue gene" possibly have in the vocabulary of those cognisant that – "the genes of heredity are sound and eternally faithful to healthy life. It is not they who are the givers of disease ... it is outer causes" - ? (I quote from *The Wheel of Health* by Dr. G.T. Wrench, already cited) So who are the *original rogues*? - !

But – *rogue genes* are a formidable constituent of the new gene research: 'A new cancer gene has been discovered ... The rogue gene, labelled Bcl10, was originally thought to be implicated only in a rare cancer ... but researchers have now established that it is also linked to many other cancers ...' (*The Courier*, 5 Jan. '99)

Let us place once more beside the above the sanely broader view of Dr. Wrench's, just quoted: "it is not they (the genes) who are the givers of disease. It is outer causes". Is it not obvious that while we continue – through our industrial, agricultural, technological and environmental malpractices – to pour poisons and pollutants into our systems, cancer along with a whole host of other modern degenerative diseases *can only* proliferate, as also, more and more damage to children in the womb? The new gene technology – even supposing that it were on a sound track – can *never* catch up.

Never? Never mind! The chief behind-the-scenes motivation of the research in which these ardent bio-technologists have got caught up is not necessarily healing. "The search for new genes is the biotechnology equivalent of a gold rush which is just beginning to get under way" (*The Courier*, 8 Jan. '99) – while "shares in leading European drug companies rise again" (*Scotland on Sunday*, 17 Jan. '99) ... the whole abomination tied up also, of course, with the hidden chambers of vivisection.

Meanwhile – "the gene Bcl10 is thought to be abnormal in at least 50% of cancers ... It is hoped the mutated Bcl10 gene might provide a target for new anti-cancer drugs." (*The Courier*, 8 Jan. '99) How can one fail to recognise, here, the very same mindset now gearing itself up anew to *bulleting* the 'rogue' plants, insects, etc., of our environment – neatly converted into the essential 'rogue' vocabulary of 'weeds' and 'pests'? The same finger on the trigger, just as with all those spray guns ... The same military mindset as operates the world of nukes ... The same infantile logical thinking – bereft of its *bio*logical dimension – disporting itself in the *bio*logical world, and ever busy out-patterning in that biological world the violence of its land monopoly progenitor.

Similarly we were treated to a New Year '99 Bulletin that – scientists have now pinpointed a gene involved in leukaemia. So there's another 'rogue' for you! But how about those *Seven Roguesters* themselves – now so gleefully engaged in wise-ing the situation up? "An end to all that 'leukaemia cluster' talk! It's YOU, PARENTS that are the guilty ones!"

It is hoped that the discovery of this 'rogue' version of the gene Bc110 will ultimately help in finding a cure for "the 'big' cancers, which threaten the lives of so many people". (*The Courier*, 8 Jan. '99) But *the* big 'cancer' – the real 'rogue' one which "threatens the lives of" us all – is the *cancer of (land) monopoly capitalism* which holds both us and the Earth in its jaws. It is *this* that we must rid ourselves of, and all its misbegotten progeny, if we would turn the tide against cancer at last – and yet further horrors on the horizon. For we read of the possible development now of 'lethal viruses capable of infecting only genes carried by people of particular ethnic groups'. (*Sunday Times*, 17 Jan. '99) Yet further dimensions of horror – and further enticing 'targets' for those 'guns' ...

Is it not time we grasped finally now, at last – in the unfolding of this now more than 'rogue', this villainous, gene scene – what Viktor Schauberger tried so hard to drive home to us: that we are dealing here solely with *effects* – not with causes; that the causes are anterior – hidden in the environment, beyond the reach of our degraded logical thinking; and that if we continue to pursue our *mania* for *manipulating* mere EFFECTS of whose real causes we are IGNORANT – we will end only in **PROVOKING CATASTROPHE**.

By what route might it come? Beware the 'memory of water'![11] The blood and lymph which pervade our bodies are chiefly water. Hence, what price the following? –

> "Specialist research teams 'will search for key ways to unlock the secrets of genes ...'
>
> "A key aim will be to provide British researchers with technology to screen vast numbers of genes quickly and efficiently. These include the micro-assay, a type of microchip carrying thousands of pieces of DNA that enable it to record instantly whether or not a particular gene is operating in a cell at any given time." (The Courier, 18 Jan. '99)"

Whether or not ... is operating ...? Beware the MEMORY of water!

We are already 'way, 'way out of our depth ...

So! – the children think they can invade the body of the Great Mother herself, and control and re-design her inner workings?

How that ridiculously solemn statement echoes back – that "for the first time in all time a living creature understands its origin and can undertake to design its future" -! In response, I hear only a peal of maniacal laughter.

The only attitude that logic-confined brains can conceive of when confronted by the gene is – *control the eternal woman!* (V. Sch.)

But I am afraid the discovery awaits – that in the Primal Mother they more than have met their match.

---

[11] *The Memory of Water, by Michel Schiff (already referred to).*

*

SEEDING THE WORLD WITH 'GENTLE GIANTS'

Let us linger a moment with the culture of sanity we were looking at earlier – the one really true culture, which – as Viktor Schauberger has shown us – is rooted in the understanding of its environment.

> "Tongues in trees, books in the running brooks,
> Sermons in stones ..."

There is no need for me to search back the pages of my Shakespeare for these words, for they have been 'rooted' in me since ever I first came upon them. The great laboratory of Nature is indeed waiting to communicate with us on every hand – there are tongues on all sides for our deciphering. We need but to *look* and to *listen* ...

When I came on the work of the American 'horse whisperer', Monty Roberts – who has single handedly transformed the often cruel business of horse-breaking into an art of gentleness, with repercussions now spreading across the globe – I searched out his autobiography[12] in my interest to learn more fully how he had come to understand the 'lingus equus', as he calls it, in the way that he did. (Although not a horse-rider, I had gone to see Monty Roberts demonstrate his remarkable skills at Gleneagles, when he visited Scotland a few years ago). His description, in his autobiography, of the time he had spent out in the wilds *looking* and *listening*, observing the wild horses in their natural habitat and so gradually gaining his insights into their language – was the gem of the book to me. And afterwards I could not help smiling, to think how exactly similarly Schauberger had gone about learning the 'lingus aquus' in the wild forestlands of Austria!

The essential discovery of both Monty Roberts and Viktor Schauberger has its fruitful application in other spheres of our life. Monty Roberts discovered that horses really only *want* to co-operate with us – if we will but learn, with sufficient patience, their language, so that we may come to know how to invite that co-operation. Similarly, Viktor Schauberger writes of how we have so foolishly made the flowing water of our rivers 'a defiant rebel ... when all it actually desires to be, and could be, is our friend'. (*W.W.*, p.104.) Just so, our society is weighed down today with its 'intransigeant problems' – all self-created, as we seek to impose our ignorant and impatient wills upon both the natural world and upon those human beings unfortunate enough – in our falsely structured society – to come under our dominion. So we arrive at the most hideous accounts of bullying in work places of every rank – even in high up offices of State. This ugly morale of our society naturally invades the class room in turn, affecting the children – while the unfortunate teachers come across it in both directions, feeling they are being 'dictated to' over the Higher Still issue "by a coterie of civil servants",[13] (or "bureaucratic pen pushers" as it was aptly put elsewhere). And of course, yet further down this same bullying road flourishes a signpost – '*thou shalt drink fluoridated water!*'

Thus we come face to face yet again with the ill fruits of our falsely structured society, whose ethos is built up amidst the crowded and high tempo environments of city living, far cut off from the natural world where life unfolds *slowly* – (far too slowly, as Viktor stressed, to be observed in a laboratory); that natural world where, if we wish to work with success, prolonged *looking* and *listening* are the inescapable

---

[12] *The Man who Listens to Horses, (publd. c. 1997 – my copy is currently on loan).*
[13] *Article in Scotland on Sunday, 15 Nov. '98.*

law.[14] On top of this, we are beset today with all the paraphernalia of computer technology which allows time only to *see* and to *hear* – (the more passive receptor functions, as compared with the active, contributory functions of looking and listening). Thus we more and more lack the insights which are so naturally born of the practice of long and patient listening and looking ... out of which co-operative dealings with one another must fruit as naturally as bullying – from classroom to top government departments – fruits in our society today.

We were not meant to live as we do, in our world of over-crammed human and technological vibrations – vibrations far too tightly packed for us, not to mention the deadening effect of concrete and manmade surroundings. Such an environment is unbalanced and unhealthy in its very essence. "By the end of the day I'm completely exhausted. It's such a stressful place." (From article, 'The New Dark Satanic Mills', on the growth of call centres, by Mark Williams, *Scotland on Sunday,* 22 Nov. '98.) But what other direction *could* our left-brain-dominated culture – bereft of any remnant of its biological thinking – possibly have taken?

And so – the world of TVs – computers – information technology, and further 'treats' no doubt in store for us – thinks it is taking over? - ! Part of the great attraction of 'the Web' on this land-monopolised Planet of ours, is undoubtedly that it offers a world of unlimited space – a space equally open for all comers to explore, and none in danger of being accounted 'trespassers'! A world of unlimited space ... but *virtual* only, of course ...

Where does all this lead? As we slide deeper and deeper into this world of *viewers,* not *doers,* we will gradually cease to notice that the soil is slipping through our fingers, and the Planet itself retreating ever deeper into our world of virtual reality as its rivers dry up and its vegetation dies ... while we, its children, are busy disporting ourselves, dancing on the Web instead of in the wild woods ...

We'll become virtual people ourselves, presently! But that's what the *Seven Wise Masters* want, of course!

... Until, at some point in all this insanity, a dispossessed people somewhere gathers its strength again and *wrests back* the land from its dispossessors. The interest of doing and listening will then come into their own once more – to lift away bullying and cruelty – and we will find a whole race of those 'gentle giants' springing up among us, to bless the Earth again.

*

CYBERSPACE

I am looking at an article headed "Gatekeepers Cash in on Cyberspace", (*Land and Liberty,* Summer 1998). It draws our attention to a certain bit of overlooking in the rental resource field – cyberspace! "Electronic shopping, accessing the wired catalogue of the 21st century, will reduce the demand for high street retail outlets." This will "increase the rental value of cyberspace ... The implications for government tax revenue are hardly perceived today. The loss of revenue will cause a crisis as nation states discover that much of their traditional tax base has been shifted into outer space and channelled into the bank accounts of elusive, multi-national corporations."

---

[14] *I am reminded here of the sub-title of Dr. Tomatis's book: "My Life of Transformation through Listening"*

That's true enough, indeed, as a picture of things for a society that lingers in the unreal world of consumerdom – of rotten foods and throw away goods; for a society structured on dispossession and land monopoly, with monopoly capitalism as a crown to its follies. For an inescapable feature of such a society, as we have already noted, is on the one hand a soil despised and betrayed – and on the other, those dispossessed and duped *trolley-pushers* of whose plight Phil Rooksby so eloquently speaks.

But what of those who have made the great shift from land dispossession to land justice? What of those whose soil, with all its potential, has come into their hands again, and who – freed from wage-slavery – have a chance to nurture real health from it for their families, and to re-discover the enjoyment of being in touch with "the basics of life"? Such an idea of living had previously sounded too 'primitive' to attract us – but we had missed to point. *Independent people are a free people and not answerable to control.* (*L.E.*, p.31.) Freedom is not a 'primitive' concept – nor is it a sophisticated one. It is quite simply a *primary* concept, without which no society can build happiness - or indeed, build itself at all.

It seems to me more than possible that a society of people who have rediscovered, as Phil Rooksby did, something of that freedom and independence which is the real joy of life – who similarly find that "there's just not enough time to do everything" – will come to regard that cyberspace shopping-mall from a somewhat different angle: As Phil Rooksby summed up such shopping-malls – as "a cataract, masquerading as 'progress'". For a people who have found freedom, it seems to me that it will come to it that cyberspace is – most damning of all accolades! – BORING!

Certain it is that we can't fill our stomachs from cyberspace – any more than, as soil people once more, we would dream of feeding off its multimops' trolleys! ... And so, the day will undoubtedly arrive when all those high-flying cyberspace values will *collapse* – when the world can't find its bread any more.

> "If a civilisation is such that it degrades the soil, then it is the civilisation, and not the soil, that comes to and end." (Dr. G.T. Wrench.)

The day will come when the health of a society – its social health as well as its physical – will be measured by the solid rental values accruing to it from its soil.

Therefore – sing on, Cyberspace, and have your fling! – for it seems your dancing days are numbered! – And the dancing days of all who waltz with you ... when they find that their bread has danced away with them into outer space as well!

*

SERENDIPITIES!

Some of us will doubtless know the legend of the Prince of India who journeyed forth from home in search of a certain object on which his heart was set. He failed to find it, but found something else, quite unexpectedly, instead. His name was Serendipity.

It often seems to me that there are all manner of good things our society is seeking which can never be found by a direct search for them – but which we will quite easily stumble upon as 'serendipities', on another route.

*

- Cars and Motorways

For instance: Where will be the need for all those vehicles and motorways, when the people themselves are fanned out over the countryside 'doing their own thing' – crazy commuterdom laid to rest? Yet how we torment ourselves today with our confrontations over motorway building, and the pollution of our cities from traffic fumes! Of course, in all this we're unfortunately deep into Schauberger's B type energy too. As to those traffic fumes, and the ever reducing availability of oxygen on this planet: In one of those vivid vignettes he has bequeathed us, Viktor Schauberger speaks of our present situation as much like that of a fish swimming about in a bucket of drastically reducing water – blissfully unaware of the fact that it is well on the way to being *without,* altogether!

"Pollution is everywhere. As toxins contaminate the air they replace oxygen. The earth's air used to be 40% oxygen, now it's 20% and in some places, like Japan, it's 12%!" (*Essential Energies Ltd.)*[15] So: What is our generation thinking of leaving to its children? - as we ignorantly go bashing on with our poison sprays, etc.? Time we got to fanning ourselves out over the land again! ... Travelling-people will enjoy a new-found freedom too.

*

- The 'Problem' of Wastes

'Given enough information and education to help people understand what happens to waste that is flushed away ...' - !

We will surely come to look back in disbelief on the dark ages we once lived in when what happened to our wastes was something we actually needed "information and education" about! With local grass roots re-empowerment, and bioregional mapping in our hands, our biological thinking will take off in a resurgence entirely natural; and the idea of once *not* having known what happened to such things – or of having our wastes and rubbish flushed away, or carried off, to create problems of dumping elsewhere – will be well recognised for the crayzdom it always was.

On the question of sewage, there do of course exist ways of recycling it perfectly safely to use on the land – as witness a front page picture, in *The Scotsman* of 5 Sept. '98, of the environmental scientist for Southern Water standing "among the company's bumper crop of 100,000 sunflowers,[16] which were grown using organic fertiliser made from recycled sewage"; this "natural fertiliser" being "a pale grey powdery substance which is odour free", and "the result of improved sewage treatment methods". Well – it's good to know it's happening elsewhere, even if Scotland's soil has only been deemed good enough for barrages of the *un*treated stuff (with what hazards of E coli and all indeed!) But – 'Scotland can take it!' is ever the official code of practice ... until a local grass-roots campaign finally carries the matter *beyond* incompetent officialdom.

There is a willow-and-reed-bed system for treating sewage – (articles on it have appeared in various Permaculture publications) – which provides a simple and safe method for such treatment, and which any local community could set up and operate for itself. Indeed – any individual household; and many are in operation around the land. When such schemes are operated locally, self-sustainability takes root as the

---

[15] *1A Leicester Mews, Leicester Road, East Finchley, London, N2 9DV.*

[16] *Or is it only 10,000? It was printed as 10,0000 – hopefully a printing error and we have not reached quite such an abyss of numeral illiteracy yet!*

local soil is enriched through the endless re-cycling of its own products; and *superior nutrition* is the product of such soil. Most importantly, the ridiculous 'problem' cited above, of having to 'inform' and 'educate' the public on the disposal of their own wastes ... is non-existent. The local community can take a natural and knowledgeable pride in its simple willow-and-reed-bed operations – which will be a worthy feature of the locality, and involve other uses for the willows as they grow on, too. And just think of the interest for the local children in learning what the *full cycle* in sound nutrition means!

> "Howard transferred the health of the soil to that of the vegetable, and that of the vegetable to that of the animal, and those of the vegetable and animal back again to the soil.
>
> "Transference, transference, transference, - three transferences, that is the secret of health. These three transferences – soil to vegetable, vegetable to animal, animal and vegetable back to the soil – form the eternal wheel of health." (The Wheel of Health, by Dr. G.T.Wrench, already cited.)

The recently published *The Humanure Handbook,* by J.C. Jenkins – rich in both knowledge and humour! – is clearly another splendid manual on this all-important subject, (although I have only managed a very brief dip in so far). One thing is certain – *all human wastes must be returned to the soil.* Sound nutrition absolutely requires it. We have already earlier quoted the tonnages of this truest of fertilisers which we at present annually toss away so that we can buy in false – a farce indeed, which only the *Seven Wise Masters* could have devised.

The same principle applies to wastes of every kind. When society is based on *local community* power – (instead of organised in weaselly ways by centralists, as now) – *which* local community will be willing to provide the 'landfill sites' for unwanted wastes from other ones? And just how many 'landfill sites' will a community be willing to set aside in its own area, for *itself?* In a society organised on such a basis, is it not obvious that most of what demands 'landfill' space today simply *would not be produced?*[17]

It is not so much 'information and education' our society needs as *local empowerment* – with its concomitant *local responsibility.* Then we will all be fully 'informed and educated' through the natural processes of our own decision-making.

Present waste 'problems' belong in reality to a quite different order of problem – the problem of a falsely constructed, and hence *intrinsically irresponsible* society.

What about our cities? *Weeds* will grow up in the large empty spaces that will succeed the e-migration of people back to the land – (just as also on many a motorway). Willow-and-reed-beds will find their natural habitats.

The Chinese have a saying – 'A journey of a thousand miles begins with the first step'.

That saying has taken to translating itself spontaneously in my mind into – 'With the first step, a journey of a thousand miles is *already under way*'.

Perhaps that will prove one of our serendipitous findings, too!

---

[17] *They would not have been produced, and we would not have the rampaging sicknesses and degenerate diseases that are with us today. See the Jan.-Feb. '99 Issue of The Ecologist for a fine update on that! Those hospital waiting lists can only extend and extend. The latest 'solution' proposed is 7 more incinerators for Scotland – resuscitating shades of the unlaid Rechem ghost ...*

*

- Cut-Throat Markets

"It is important that firms use multimedia as part of an overall strategy, which is consistent with their business goals ... Scottish companies have been slow to recognise the opportunities available. They are scared of computers and are very conservative. There is a lot of 'we have managed before without it' ... Scottish companies have been slow, to the point of timidity, to inquire how new media can help them achieve their business goals." (Article in *Scotland on Sunday*, 8 Nov. '98)

So what *are* these business goals? Ah!

> "It's a deal: Scottish companies are finally waking up to the persuasive powers of multimedia technology and expert design in their effort to win new business in cut throat markets." (*Ibid.*)

There we have it – out of the bag! CUT THROAT MARKETS!

Well, perhaps those Scottish companies were not quite such slow-coaches after all! Perhaps the Scots are simply people who like to take a bit more of a *deliberate look at things* ... For instance: 'Nature is founded far more on co-operation than on competition ... the whole concept of the primacy of competition needs to be re-examined.' (*L.E.*, ch.16) Do the 'canny Scots' have some truer inklings, perhaps?

So, yes – what *about* those 'cut throat markets'? The same creation, of course (and by quite the same hand) as are those dispossessed, impoverished masses of the Scots who cannot-buy-the-goods-they-have-themselves-produced-at-home-because-their-economic-clout-has-been-stolen-from-them, along with their land. Stolen by quite those same powers-behind-the-scenes that are now busy-busy-devising the ultimate, multi-mate 'media approaches' for still further hoodwinking and hooking up the innocents to that great charade of the CUT-THROAT MARKETS! – and getting them to pay over yet more of their earnings to that multi-media technology of ever new matings, ever new updatings ...

For we mustn't let them catch their breaths for an *instant* – especially those laggard Scots!

But supposing those 'laggard' Scots are just a naturally SERENDIPITOUS people!

*

- A Word More on Education

'You can't make a scholar in a school' No truer maxim! But they're doing their best at it, of course.

I have a note on my desk from sometime around the end of 1998: 'Dunce's' – (can that have been his name?) – 'report on language teaching in Scottish schools. Stern measures are to be taken to improve results, on account of the global markets.'

But – just suppose that Scotland's children have some *inbuilt resistance* to being educated for those (cut-throat) 'global markets'? Just suppose they have some uncanny inner grasp of that brave 'new world order' we're being geared up for? Or perhaps, when it comes to languages, it's simply that they prefer – the lingus equus, the lingus aquus, the lingus arborus ... the lingus *humanurus*!

Never mind! – there's always the two pronged approach. Global markets require the literacy of multi-mediacy, so – what about that load of old cobbled computers?

Late Dec. '98 news bulletin: the government's education wing is welcoming the generous gift from businesses of their old or outdated computers, so that every school child can become 'computer competent'. ... Never mind the state of their competence on fit food, water or air – or even in the use of their own language![18]

The use of their own language? But the computers are getting that sorted out too. For instance, with the latest models (which will be landing on the children's laps tomorrow at the present rate of turnover): if you're bold enough to write 'colour', and turn on the spell-check, it will rap you on the knuckles. It's 'color' – the American way.

"The best way to control people is to tell them what to do *and how to speak.*" (Alan Torrance.) And Burns would underwrite that!

Beware, then! For machines that can convert themselves from servant into master – as today's tend to do – when dealing with language, tend to *control our thinking.*

But that's what the Seven Wise Masters always did intend, of course!

... And how about dumbing down the children's life energies at the same time – not to mention the teachers' - ?

> "The TV and the computer are very complex and powerful machines which generate a spectrum of fields and vibrations which are not in harmony with the life forces of the human being. These disturbances all arise as a by-product of the electrical and mechanical design, and are quite arbitrary as far as human physiology and consciousness are concerned ... This sort of complex pollution of our environment acts on us in many ways ... The vibrating fields inhibit the flow of our life energy ...' (From ch.8 of Water, Electricity and Health, by Alan Hall, Hawthorn Press, 1997)

Inhibit the flow of our life energy! The sooner we wrest our bairns from Nanny's clutches, the better – for health's sake as well as education.

Fortunately – 'you can't make a scholar in a school'.

An even truer saying today, it seems!

And no more serendipitous discovery for the children!

*

- Population: the 'Pop Panic'

"Order imposed from without breeds disorder." Just how piercingly these words penetrate to the heart of our situation on every side! I have these words recorded under the name of Krishnamurti; and it is possible Krishnamurti intended them as a general statement on the matter – no doubt referring to the life of the individual as well as of society.

There is a particular context, however, in which they are of a most particular relevance, and it would be well to take note of it. It is the sphere of what I have long regarded as the *pop panic*: that is, our society's somewhat clouded view of the matter of the increasing population of this Earth ... and of course, of how it is to be *catered*

---

[18] *According to the 'primitives' Weston Price got to know, for whom child bearing was a natural and simple event: girls should in any case lead a mostly outdoor life up to the age of puberty, since the development of the pelvic girdle is as important for them as the dental arch.*

for, since 'the people' are never competent to *cater for themselves*! So the whole thing becomes, itself, a prime caterer for our familiar friend – *centralised control* ... of land, and of course of that *soil* that goes with it! Our warfare-type agriculture – with the GMO stunters the latest to join in the 'we will feed this world' dementia!

Let us look at various more peripheral aspects of this matter, before we approach the heart of it:-

> "Every single person in the world could have an acre of land in an area smaller than the continent of North America, at an average density of 640 people per square mile – less dense than Japan today ... Enough arable land exists in India to give each person in the country approximately half an acre – that's not just raw land, remember, but arable land ... Around the world, deforestation and desertification result from peasants pushing into sub-marginal land while high quality farmland is held out of use." (Extracts from *Over Population? No such thing*, by Lindy Davies, *The Georgist Journal*, Winter 1997)

> "FACT. A U.N. study of 83 countries showed that less than 5% of rural landowners control three-quarters of the land ... 'a mere 2.5% of landowners with more than 100 hectares control nearly three quarters of all the land in the world'." (Susan George, *How the Other Half Dies*. The whole quoted from *Financing Planet Management*, by Alanna Hartzok, published by the Robert Schalkenbach Foundation, U.S.A.)

So – land hoarding, drastic under-use, or simply altogether *non-use* of *huge* areas of potentially food-producing land ... with further vast acreages (especially in South America) used purely as cattle ranches to satisfy the appetite for meat (which in the Third World is exclusively the food of the *rich*): such are the unvarying and familiar first-fruits of *land monopoly*.

"Give our men land – give our men land. Then we shall not be sold into prostitution". The unforgettable heart-cry of a young girl in India, as reported a few years ago in an Anti-Slavery International Publication. More fully mapped out, it reads: "Give our men land – then we shall not be brought-into-this-world-to-be sold into prostitution." Another hefty factor in the growth of world population. So also Dr. Vandana Shiva – (the remarkable Indian physicist turned campaigner and author[19]) – put the peasants' side in a radio interview I once heard: the landowner can buy a tractor – the peasants can only have more children. The second fruits, as one might say, of crushingly monopolistic land tenure. The whole of the hideous 'debt bondage' plight of people in Third World countries is similarly due simply to *landlessness* – the capture of the land by the few from the many who need to live from that land no less. Why not be honest and acknowledge that we in Britain support – nay, champion – this very same *landless* policy ourselves? For upon *landlessness*, just the same, our own society is structured. First World mournings at the plight of the landless in the Third World – are crocodile tears. We want to cancel Third World debt? Institute radical land reform – and cancel it for all time to come.

Finally – there is the gigantic, untapped potential of the Earth itself, husbanded intimately, and under free conditions, by loving hands in traditional peasant ways, which have always achieved a far higher output per acre than modern mechanistic

---

[19] *See her book, The Violence of the Green Revolution: Ecological Degradation and Political Conflict in Punjab, a masterly expose of the familiar earlier 'we will feed the world' deception – and of much else besides. Published by the Author in 1989.*

industrial agriculture has done. "Since the early 1990's, a number of non-governmental organisations have joined forces to form the Latin American Consortium on Agroecology and Development to promote agroecological techniques which are sensitive to the complexities of local farming methods. Yields have tripled or quadrupled within a year. Large-scale implementation of biodynamic farming and sustainable agriculture is succeeding in the Philippines."[20] SACRED AFRICA is another such initiative on that continent, founded in Kenya.[21] So as far as soil productivity goes, there is clearly still vast untapped potential on this Earth – as some of us have been aware for a long time. In *The Wheel of Health*, Dr. Wrench records the view, concerning Britain, of Prince Kropotkin (the Russian revolutionary who had to escape from Russia, and lived in Britain 1886-1921): "that great authority, Prince Kropotkin, calculated that she (Britain) could produce sufficient food for a hundred million people". Which gives one to think! – of what we have destroyed ...

In addition to all of the above, however, there is a fundamental *psychological* factor which the pop panicers have completely failed to take into account; and it is all embracing.

How can those whose self-respect is destroyed under a system of slavery be expected to express a true respect for the Planet? If the population of the Earth is burgeoning – if people have 'lost control' over themselves: is it not obvious that it is because they have lost control over their *living* ... because they have lost control over their *land*? Even in affluent America (affluent for some) Weston Price records how, once families had lived on State relief for over a year, *the birth rate went up by 60%.* But surely this was an entirely forecastable outcome. If Nanny is now the one in charge of the family, what need for the family to be *self*-responsible? It is tellingly put in the words of Henry George:-

> "Make (a man's) condition such that it cannot be much worse, while there is little hope that anything he can do will make it much better, and he will cease to look beyond the day." (Progress and Poverty)

By contrast, amongst those 'primitive' peoples that Weston Price moved among and made a close study of – where, that is, a people was found living in circumstances of sufficient control over their own lives and environment – the need to limit their population to what that environment could sustain, was something woven into the very fundaments of their life. Again – is it not obvious that it must be so? Primitives limited their families in various ways, particularly by the number of years between children. "One of the most important lessons we should learn from the primitive races is that of the need for maintaining a balance between soil productivity, plant growth and human babies. Even in a country with so low a fertility as obtains in the greater part of Australia, the Aborigines for a very long period were able to maintain this balance. Their system of birth control was very efficient and exacting." (Ch. "Application of Primitive Wisdom" in his book)[22]

---

[20] *Quoted from article, 'The Inevitable Return to a Sane Agriculture', by Dr. Mae-Wan Ho, in The Ecologist, Sep.–Oct. '98.*

[21] *P.O. Box 2275, Bungoma, Kenya. Dr. Eusebius J. Mukhwana.*

[22] *Dr. Weston Price documented, and rightly extolled, the diets of the 'primitives' he visited. Most were considerably, and many were heavily, dependent upon animal foods. However, life on this Planet evolves on the inner planes as well as the outer. So it was that Rose Elliot (already a vegetarian) renounced dairy food on the spot, on having it explained to her by the stationmaster, that the calves so piteously lowing for their mothers were going off to the slaughterhouse so that she could have milk for*

The "need for maintaining a balance between soil productivity, plant growth and human babies", so well understood by the Australian Aborigines (as also other primitive peoples), describes the true situation of Earth's children. Today – when we have so hugely and selfishly destroyed the habitats of our many fellow-dwellers on this Planet – we might well extend the above words to read, "... a balance between soil productivity, plant growth and the sustaining of all Earth's populations" (not forgetting the oceans, either). However, this is an aspect of wisdom entirely lacking in our culture. (Just catch the Seven Wise Masters allowing dangerous stuff like that to creep into our education syllabuses!) No – we rely instead on lying propaganda – (chemical agriculture, the 'green revolution' and now the GMO's) – and on the ignorance of a dispossessed people to lap it all heartily up. For soil productivity, the real thing, can only be understood – as it can only be nurtured – by a people who are Earth-bonded, plugged into the living circuits of the Earth's energies themselves; just as those peoples in the Third World are showing us today. Meanwhile, the *Seven Wise Masters* are so ignorant of the fact that the soil is *alive* that they are overseeing the application to the soil, in Britain, of 70,000 tons every year of a *soil sterilant*, as I have recently read! A kind of soil *chlorination programme* – just to do a proper job all round!

All in all – from the general survey of our situation that this book has allowed us – it seems plain enough that anxieties about feeding 'the extra 5-6 billion people who will live in the world in the next 40 years' (a farming article in the *Courier*, 2 Oct. '98) are a trifle misplaced! But there – biological thinking is thin on the ground in our times! The multiplication of our follies on every hand can leave little doubt – in a quiet contemplation of the scene – that upon our present pathway the Earth will have disposed of a large part of her population well before then. Indeed, the male sperm count is in such serious decline – (with "environmental factors clearly to blame", as if we needed to be told!) – that it is evident that the Planet is already launched on the simplest of all ways of achieving the necessary clear-out of its system.

We should cease to wring our hands, then, in despair over 'uncontrolled population growth'. In any case, it is a pathway we have chosen for ourselves. But if our concern on the matter is genuine, we know full well what is asked of us to do. We must embark on *radical economic reform*, which is *radical land reform*, thus going to the heart of the matter by *restoring to people power over their own lives* – (while solving a host of other problems at the same time).

Finally, before leaving this scene, let us stand back from it for a few moments, holding a small candle of hope in our hearts – and consider how a society fully restored to our Primary Mother, and hence to the full range of responsibilities that it carries on

---

her tea. Veganism was not then on the map, and she did not even know if one could live without dairy food – but she lived on to become a flourishing pioneer of the movement (and wrote her excellent 'Not Just a Load of Old Lentils' and other books).

A study of Viktor Schauberger's work on soil and plant growth in the later chapters of 'Living Energies', and other absorbing books such as Tompkins' and Bird's 'Secrets of the Soil' and 'Plants for a Future' by Ken Fern – the article from 'Acres' included in Part III here, the growing soil remineralisation movement, the special qualities of raw and sprouting food – (see among other books, 'The Gospel of Peace of Christ Jesus', published by the C.W. Daniel Co. Ltd.), and in addition the development of deep rooting tree crops instead of so much monoculture of grain – (the practice of agroforestry and alley-cropping is increasing): all these show new ways of enhancing our life and energies through the soil and plant world, such that we need prey no more on the animal kingdom. It is a path that seems in keeping with a new age of responsibility towards both the Planet and our co-habitants here. 'I do not eat my friends', as George Bernard Shaw so simply said.

this Earth – let us consider how such a society might then look back upon the saying of Krishnamurti's quoted at the start of this section.

For a full all-round perspective on that *pop panic* which our society so likes to indulge itself in – (while indulging of course with equal heartiness in *land monopoly* and all its fruits at the same time!) – it could surely scarcely be bettered:-

Order imposed from without BREEDS DISORDER!

There you have it – in a nutshell! And for the all-round richness of that saying, one might truly add – a *princely* bit of serendipitous finding too!

*

- Peace on Earth[23]

It has been said that if those who profited from wars paid for them, there would be precious few wars fought on this earth.

A friend recently observed to me that there was one really good development he saw since the last war: young people today would not be willing to fight wars like that any more, since they realised they would be fighting mainly just to prop up an establishment of wealth and privilege.

Sharpen the focus of that perspective a little. Consider the part played, in the structuring of that wealth and privilege, by *stolen rental values* – those values created by 'everyman' – and we realise that in war, just as no less in peace, it is the poor who support the rich, and the rich who live off the poor all the way.

> "General Monk, originally a Royal Office who deserted to Parliament, was the main instrument of the Restoration. He became a duke with a state pension of £7,000 per annum and large estates. The yeomen who won Naseby and Marston Moor were not so fortunate. At the remarkable army discussions in 1647, Edward Sexby, speaking for the private soldiers, declared: 'We have ventured our lives to recover our birthrights and privileges as Englishmen. But it seems now that except a man hath a fixed estate he hath no right on this kingdom. I wonder we were so deceived'." (Frank Dupuis[24]).

Three hundred years later, in Scotland, the Seven Men of Knoydart decided to un-deceive ... both themselves and the Establishment on this matter. Returned to their homeland from W.W.II, they firmly staked out their claim to land on their own soil of Knoydart. Of course the instigators of the original 'sasines' (*siezings*) could not contemplate the idea of such *re*-siezings – and by the mere proletariat! ... But our

[23] *It is right to express my indebtedness here to Jim Crumley for his article on this subject, which appeared in the Courier of 5 Jan. '99. It was a timely reminder to me of a serious omission in my own book – for which I have since written this section.*

[24] *This extract is from an article by Frank entitled 'Professionalism and History', earlier mentioned in this book – an article I have long treasured. It was published in* Land and Liberty *– some decades ago now. My sheet is undated.*

In case I did not state it earlier – (no time to check back now) – I would like to record the pleasure and privilege it was to meet Frank Dupuis at the International Georgist Conference in Hanover in 1959 – when I was still new to the movement. An earlier article of his on the very different political situation between the Rhodesias and Nyasaland, hence opposing their federation – (he had been in the colonial service) – Nyasaland's far 'humaner' rule stemming from its stronger links with the Church of Scotland rather than the Colonial Office – apart from its keen interest to me being about Nyasaland, was extremely enlightening on British colonial rule

Seven Men of Knoydart will take the crown of wisdom from off those *Seven Whizz Kids* yet!

'Order imposed from without breeds disorder.' Not one of those nations which today attempts to act as peace-broker in our troubled world, or is partaker in a peace keeping exercise, has any example to offer of living in a state free from that *dis*order themselves. Not one can show an example of a state of order *at home*, sprung from the *elimination of land rent injustice*. No amount of peace-keeping words can have the effect of even *one* visible example of a nation living truly at peace within itself, flourishing on the just foundation of the land rent code. "Order imposed from without breeds disorder" – and even more must this be so when those seeking to impose it are living in a state of disorder themselves.

But there is more than one area in the world today where the divisions between different peoples sharing one territory – or claiming one territory – (through previous falsely imposed 'solutions') – run deeper even than the divisions between the rich and the poor within them. Where can such a bitterness of strife find its practical solution?

"The Earth does not belong to us – we belong to the Earth." This saying has become woven into our growing ecological awareness – and become a saying whose truth we all recognise. But it has remained to date a purely *ecological* recognition, having no political teeth.

Bioregionalism – is a movement waiting to give it those political teeth. Bioregionalism recognises the above ecological statement, but sees it not merely as ecological – sees it as a fundamental principle of social living as well. Thus bioregionalism stands ready to enter the *political* fields. But not, of course, in the orthodox political way.

In our age of ecological awakenings, bioregionalism emerges as the natural partner, and guardian, of *radical land rent reform* – waiting to 'flesh out' the land rent justice principle in its necessary new *ecological* garb.

Bioregionalism is a force able to 'broker' the more difficult agreements between Earth's aversive tribes. For that is how the Earth sees us – simply as 'tribes', as *her* children ... despite our claims to be the children of mostly false and arrogantly constructed human States. What is true and original of nationhood – rooting back to Earth-defined origins – will never be lost through bioregionalism, but will be enhanced by it.

Bioregionalism places the land rent principle in its true and dynamic context – a context both old and new: the context of – not Earth's *children* first, but EARTH first herself ... as clearly we must live if we are to have any future. Earth's natural folds and pleats – where her mountains and rivers run – outline for her children their natural neighbourhoods. Here, on the grounds of that *first* caring – for the Earth, which bioregionalism instills – we can live, under the included patterning of land rent justice, *sharing* the Earth with one another, instead of glaring at one another across artificial State boundaries. Ethnic and racial groupings will find themselves at home, and free of quarrels of competing 'Statehoods' – for the Earth Mother swallows these up. Hers is a seamless garment.

It may seem difficult at present to envisage the coming together of the various peoples on Earth today who at present confront one another in their various stark, bitter and violent oppositions; and it is not likely that it is in these regions of the Earth that bioregionalism will first flourish. Once more (and just as with the land rent principle), it is a living example that is needed, above all else, of the bioregional way – an example from a part of the Planet that is less plagued by strife today.

On this very point, I recently had a letter from a friend in Cheshire. She wrote me:-

> "Re 'the land question', there are some of us in N.W. England very interested in what is happening in Scotland. As you can probably imagine, most of us are of mixed Irish, Scots, Welsh and English ancestry and we are not really happy about being ruled by 'them in London'. I think we are a bit envious about developments in Wales and Scotland and quite regularly now you will hear us bleating 'What about us? Where does all this leave us?'"

'Of mixed Irish, Scots, Welsh and English ancestry.' What a grand, rich mixture! – just crying out for a *bioregional embrace*!

And is not just as rich a tapestry awaiting weaving – as yet off-stage – of ethnic Albanians, Croats, Serbs, and others in similar divided situations? A penetrating observation of Karl Jung's comes to mind as I survey these scenes: A problem is never solved at its own level. How well this sums up the overwhelming need of this whole panorama to move from *State structure* to *bioregionalism* – and discover just the wisdom of those words! And isn't this the very same wisdom that Schauberger was gently trying to drum into us, when he spoke of our need to think an octave higher? But we humans will need to exert our biological thinking if we wish to do this, and so help forward peace on Earth. For here is something else that becomes plain in this scenario: our State-structured political world is hopelessly attuned to those impoverished levels of *logical* thinking Schauberger also warned us of. It is the *biological* thinking we have spoken of which belongs to the realm of bioregionalism – and which bioregionalism is calling upon us to develop, for the sake of peace as well as for the Earth's sake.

Returning to the letter from my friend in Cheshire: while there are other areas of Britain today that similarly feel estranged from 'them in London', it is undoubtedly Scotland which, at this moment in history, stands readiest to embark upon the sane adventure of the bioregional way. The areas of the Tweed and the Solway Firth – at present constituting the *State*-structured boundary with England – would naturally need to await the 'infecting' of our southern neighbours with our bioregional example, to enjoy full bioregionalism; but that same situation will affect every lingering State boundary of every country in the world at first. Scotland is fortunate in having fewer than most. Needless to say, bioregionalism stands apart from all such State-structured bodies as the E.U.

The declaration of Scotland as a *bioregion of the Earth* will, it seems to me, be greatly strengthened, and made more visible, by the re-christening of our land with a bioregional name Whether – Caledonia, or some name recognising the Pictish ancestry of ours which seems to have been so Earth oriented ... others will have more knowledge of these things than I.[25]

In the writing of this section, a certain memory has returned vividly to my mind. It is the memory of a young Israeli girl who passed by here, many summers ago now, with a companion. We got talking, and they came and had tea in the garden. She spoke to me openly of how she had no quarrel with the Arabs —that she felt no

[25] *Later: Having just re-read "Leaves from the Book of Scots", I see that the word "Caledonia" is in fact associated with the Picts*

animosity towards them whatsoever. She spoke of how she wished to live side by side with them, and live in peace. Moreover – and I remember still how particularly joyfully this struck me – there were masses of other young people in Israel, she said, who felt exactly the same.

Thinking of the area of what was former Yugoslavia – (an artificially created State), I am reminded now too of the truly inspiring accounts I have come across – (mainly in the quarterly publication, *Caduceus* and other 'alternative' sources) of similar stands taken by small groups of individuals in that warring region, with women particularly to the fore – who have steadfastly refused to become infected by the hatreds at present tearing that area apart, maintaining their stance, even through great sufferings. I have read moving accounts of this.

It is significant that it is only through these 'byways' of information that such news reaches us. We scarcely read of such happenings in the national press. If we go by the official news media, we must believe that the violence and hatreds so endlessly reported from such areas have everyone in their grip. But then – how *could* this scattered and heroic evidence to the contrary be expected to receive reportage through orthodox channels? The shadowy *Seven Strong Mafia* are a controlling influence here.

This brings me to a third memory – this time concerning Ireland. Many years ago – perhaps as many as twenty – a passing Irishman (from Southern Ireland, Eire) spoke to me of that island's beleaguered state. His words were forthright. While at the start of the troubles there had been political ideals, which ran high, of more recent times, he said, Ireland – both north and south – had fallen to the hands of behind-the-scenes *gunrunners*. Political idealism, he told me, had become the victim of those intent on prolonging the strife to make money out of guns – and loath to let up.

It is scarcely to be doubted that a similar behind-the-scenes fuelling of violence forms a part of the picture in all such trouble spots in the world today, where the conflict appears to be an unresolvable one arising out of race, religion, etc. This points as little else can – (except for such equal horrors as *drug-running*) – to the absolute necessity of the bringing in, as partner to bioregionalism, of *radical land rent reform*; since the inducement to profit from violence and destruction – (such things as guns and drugs) – *must* flourish where there exists not the opportunity to make a just living on this Earth. And that opportunity *cannot* exist under the dispossession of land rent robbery.

The glimpses I have been given of many courageous souls standing for peace today amidst turmoil and terror – (such glimpses as have doubtless been vouchsafed to many other besides) – bring back to me those words earlier quoted in Part I:-

"All things
by immortal power,
near or far,
hiddenly
to each other
linked are ...

In whatever steps Scotland now takes, let us recognise that she does not – she *cannot*, by the very nature of things – take them for herself alone. "All things ... hiddenly to each other linked are ..." The reverberations of our decisions and actions *will bear fruit* in far and war-torn regions that are not before our eyes, and possibly not even before our thought. *Let us think of them, then.*

Much as I dislike alluding to it, it must be said that, regarding the present 'jockeying for position' going on on all sides within the political parties of Scotland for power places in the devolution game – (the people themselves compelled to bow to the political choices of the 'masters') – all of which is a cause of acute embarrassment, I feel, to the majority of Scots: it is a perfect display of the state of *infancy* in which State-spawned political structures have us locked. Until we allow the EARTH orientation of bioregionalism to balance out the overwhelmingly left-brain logic of our State-structuring, and re-direct our ways – there exists little hope of our outgrowing this present truly infantile state.

It is time to throw off our swaddling clothes – time to resuscitate our powers of biological thinking – time to set forth upon the pathway of linked bioregionalism and land rent reform.

Who knows – it may even find us stumbling, en route, upon the true meaning of "serendipity" – seren ... serene ... at peace ... ?

Perhaps, hidden within the word, this was the *real* message for us from the Indian tale –

\- PEACE ON EARTH -

*

WHERE THE DANGER IS . . .

'Where the danger is, there the saving grace is growing alongside.' (The German Post, Hölderlin. Translation as I remember it)

Viewed at sufficient depth, the spectacle or our collapsing society signals to us in reality a *ray of hope*. For it signals – without FREEDOM, no living thing can flourish.

As we have seen, it is a question of turning the picture the right way up. If all were flourishing in a society constructed as ours is – then indeed might we despair of our destiny. Yet even in this time of "dark confusion", most still see well enough "with their own eyes", and not the eyes of their slave masters.

The dark scenes of drugs, violence, suicide, etc., signal a *refusal to adjust to* what is false. Perhaps we can understand now why – from behind the visible – from deep down in the *in*visible – there is a cry that MUST go up, and that must intrude upon our physical world in just such guises. A cry from the world of "beauty and completeness"[26] that *can* only reach us as discord – as terrible discord – via the impoverished 'instruments' of our own creating.

In pondering the true account of the Pied Piper of Hamelin (included here in Part III), the more terrible origins speak to us of that saying 'he who pays the piper calls the tune' – a saying which trips so easily off our tongues. Have the mothers of this world not had *enough* of losing their children to the bastions of privilege? Surely the mother of every drug victim would say so.

In Ch.15 of *Living Energies*, Callum Coats speaks of our need for a body of 'unintimidatable' individuals to bring about needed change. I have long felt that it is the mothers of this world who best fit that role.

---

[26] *The article "Golden Thoughts", by Michael Donnelly, earlier referred to.*

"The future of the world lies in its villages." These words are placed in quotation marks because – whether or not exact – they are Gandhi's thought and express one of his most passionate convictions. His dream of a village-based India came to nought, as we know, in the face of imposed Western centralisation both economic and political – *and* educational (the same triad of ruin marking Britain's involvement in Africa and every other 'outpost' of her 'Empire').

Nevertheless, Gandhi's vision and words are surely prophetic. They harmonise entirely with the bioregional concept – for Gandhi's insistence was that the villages should be autonomous and self-supporting fully as far as it was practicable for them to be so.[27] It is a vision with which both Schauberger's work and Georgist principles are equally at home. In addition, the village is the arena in which the influence of the mothers has its fullest play, and the most durable fabric of the community is therefore woven: that is, from the fundamental links made between the families of the area through the mothers' self-organised play groups for their little ones, allowing the mothers to get to know each other at first hand, and so giving rise to other activities of shared interest in turn. So a community becomes soundly cemented together through fundamental links between the families.

Do we fear times of chaos ahead, such as may punctuate the road to freedom? Let us fortify ourselves with a reminder first of those words of Krishnamurti's, about how order imposed from without – (which is all we have now) – is in any case a breeder of *dis*order ... whose fruits we shall clearly finally reap. Let us remember also that very same warning of Nock's (which we looked at in Part I) about the disaster of 'order' superimposed on us by the State. The **good** news is that the concept of chaos has, on the other hand, a positive side – and Callum Coats tells us something about this in his book, *Living Energies*. For chaos is of *two* kinds. While the one signals the break up and dissolution of what is no longer fit for life – (and we earlier saw Schauberger's stern warning to us about this) – we may take heart from the knowledge that the other is part of an entirely *positive* and *creative* process.

In ch.19 of *Living Energies*, Callum describes the Japanese Art of sword making. To create the finest possible instrument, the metal must be alternatively heated to incandescence, and then beaten out, or 'structured', with a hammer as it cools. This process is repeated over and over again – until finally the article formed has reached perfection, the blade fine and true, and at the same time flexible ... (Some may recognise here certain stages of their own inner journey through life)

I found Callum's description of this process deeply interesting; nor is it perhaps without a special meaning for a country which bore, in her past, a swordsman of the stature of Wallace. Callum speaks similarly of how, in the creating of a natural soil fertiliser by the biodynamic method, the same process must take place. Here, too, the successive stages are involved of *apparent* chaos, which again are an essential part of the "gradual building up and structuring" of certain *higher, internal* energies. Schauberger's account of the "clay singing" of the old Austrian farmer describes a similar process; and interestingly, from a note written in the summer of 1998, I see I came across something comparable in Tompkins' and Bird's fascinating *Secrets of the Soil*: i.e., about how order emerges out of chaos only where there is an *open* plan. I

[27] *I once read of an experiment – somewhere in America I think it was – where the local community decided that any offenders against the community should not be sent away from it, but should be dealt with within that community itself, where they were known to all; dealt with in a manner positive and constructive. The experiment was an entire success – and once having read about it, it seemed the most natural thing in the world that this should be how offenders against the community are dealt with.*

seem not to have marked the page, but it clearly describes the same thing - the exact antithesis of the 'order' of a State-structured society under the *Seven Wise Masters'* rule.

Now what might this process of *creative* chaos – involving the "gradual building up and structuring" of certain "higher internal" energies – *refer to*, in a society that finds itself suddenly re-empowered at its grass roots?

One can imagine the possible upheavals, as new talent and ideas burgeon up from below: the flowering of the 'higher inner' energies, indeed, of those many - too long smothered by the present stultifying structure of society - impatiently challenging the established ways of doing things which are all that the new grass-roots-empowered communities will be inheriting, to work with, at the start. Through just such healthy upheavals we shall no doubt discover the incipient Ogilvies, Schaubergers, etc., in our midst. Henry George always maintained that the greatest waste to society under our stultifying land monopoly structure, was the *waste of human talent* – and no doubt we shall discover just how great that waste has been.

If we wish to survey a scene of potential *real* chaos – of the (falsely imposed) order-breeds-disorder kind – we need to look at a rather different scenario, which confronts us right now on our horizon – and which we have far from taken full reck of yet.

It seems that the Millennium Bug may be the least of our worries, concerning today's technology. A television programme towards the end of 1998 focused a useful spotlight on our digital world. Firstly – there were a few statements made of the kind that are by now familiar, but we foolishly refuse to consider seriously: "If the computers go wrong, the technology which we all depend on fails ... Destroy the internet, and you could practically destroy the world."[28], etc.

What was exceptionally interesting about this programme, however, was that those who were speaking on it – top 'intelligensia' of the computer world – spoke with a fully serious intent. They wished to shake us out of our state of arrant heedlessness and complacency, as we waltz so innocently on, on this dangerous path. And so the speakers gradually brought us to the heart of the matter: "You understand the potential devastation, if someone should decide to focus on a nation's ability to function ... Power lies not with the nation today, but with the individual ... The vulnerabilities for nations today are profound, and they are very scary ... A terminal allows you to tunnel through ... without anyone knowing who is doing it ... Our vulnerability on account of these systems is something we have never thought through."

Something we have never thought through! But on we waltz!

There were two further telling statements. "Manipulating information and controlling people will be more important than blitzing cities." (That's right! – and be sure you get the weans hooked up to the web at the earliest opportunity! I remember my small nephew saying to me, already back in the 1960's, in a serious voice: "This is the age of information, Auntie Shirley-Anne!" ... "*Whose information*, Jock?" - !) Finally – and most interesting of all: "Our technology is built around a notion of *alienation from each other*. People don't sit around in their porches and talk any more." Whether they do not still do so now and then in more country places, the

[28] *I have used quotation marks for clarity of presentation here, and in what follows, but these are not exact quotes – they are from my scribbled notes at the time.*

central point remains that this technology is built around that notion. In this sense, it surely merits the name – the devil's technology.

This is the pivotal point of the madness that our digital world is flourishing on. In alienating us more and more from one another, and ruling us more and more by buttons, it is a policy fully at home with increasing distrust between us as individuals. But it is *that technology itself* our distrust should be focused upon.

"Where the danger is, there the saving grace is growing alongside." To quote Dan Sullivan aptly: "Villagers of the world untie! You have nothing to lose but your strings!" ... and the villagers of our cities very much included.[29]

To loosen ourselves of Nanny's apron strings – 'tis time long past indeed! Time to take the road that leads to a *true* 'new world order' – and away from chaos of a kind too appalling to contemplate. For the beauty of village communities, of both country and city, is that alienation is replaced by *direct* intercourse and computer buttons give place to human hands. Moreover, we will eat the food that we ourselves grow – while making sure also that our water supply is health-*giving* and not health-*subtracting*. It is such communities that will be best fitted, in every way, to withstand the times of chaos that are more likely to come upon us from the collapsing of the rotten structures of our society – including the digital one.

Schauberger's warning to us could not be more timely: a true culture is founded on the *understanding of its environment* – both water and vegetation. The digital world knows nothing of such things. Yet certain it is that a society which ignores that warning will pass away.

The signposts are plain, then, which we must follow: Equal rights of all to land – and to the touch and breath of our Earthly Mother!

So Ogilvie taught us. And Wallace has left us his great example. It is for us to make that beginning *now* – here in Scotland.

For out of just such small beginnings, it will grow. Societies of beauty and of worth – gardens of Gosaba across the world.

As Schauberger was wont to say – we think an octave too low. We just need to lift up our gaze a bit. It's all there.

S-A.H.
(End of Jan. '99)

*

[29] *Georgist Dan Sullivan's clever variation – (especially with 'untie' an anagram of 'unite'!) – of the more familiar Marxist slogan: 'Eggheads of the world unite! You have nothing to lose but your yolks!"*

TRIBUTE
TO
VIKTOR SCHAUBERGER
(1885 - 1958)

*

TRIBUTE TO VIKTOR SCHAUBERGER

"The day will come when Schauberger's ideas
will change the whole world."
(Professor Philipp Forchheimer.)

*

Were I to be asked what statement of Viktor Schauberger's in my view most clearly reflects the grandeur of his mind, and gives insight into the force of his ideas and thinking, it would be the following that would come to me:-

> "The majority believe that everything hard to comprehend must be very profound. This is incorrect. What is hard to understand is what is immature, unclear and often false. The highest wisdom is simple, and passes through the brain directly into the heart."

The cultivation of such wisdom inevitably requires long periods spent apart, in stillness, silence and solitude. Pondering this once, my thought came to rest on the family motto of the Schaubergers, "Fidus in silvis silentibus". . .and a fruitful voyage of discovery then followed.

I recollect having seen this motto translated either as "faith in the silent forests", or as "faithful in the silent forests". The Latin word for "faith" is however "fides", the adjective being "fidelis", or (as here) "fidus"; and while "fidelis" can sometimes be used as a noun (to signify "a faithful person"), there is no indication in my dictionary that "fidus" can be used as a noun at all. I make no pretence to being a Latin scholar – but it appears that the motto must read "faithful in the silent forests". This translation, however, has never fully satisfied me, since treating the forests simply as a location did not seem to me to say anything of significance at all.

One afternoon late last summer, I finally took up my Latin dictionary again – (an old one, but Oxford University Press) – and looked up in it the Latin word "in" with its various meanings when used with the ablative case. I presently came upon a use of it which signified "in the style of" – and for the first time sensed some real light thrown upon the situation: "faithful in the style of – or, in the manner of – the silent forests". Here for the first time the motto, it seemed to me, revealed its true significance.

However, my translation was decidedly too wordy for a motto. So I moved on to "faithful as are the silent forests" – and then finally came to rest on, "as the silent forests – faithful". Simplest of all; and also focusing our thought primarily where I believe Viktor would have wished it focused – on the forests themselves.

I believe that, with this translation, the motto then becomes fully worthy of Viktor Schauberger – who gave his whole strength, as well as his life, to the cause of Life. Just as the forests do.

FIDUS IN SILVIS SILENTIBUS

*

Birthright. . .and. . .Scotland Today

Part II

*

Chapter 3

For the Healing of Our Children

*

Where there is no vision,
the people perish.
(*Proverbs, ch.29*)

1) Gosaba – A Modern Miracle
(*Source unknown*)

2) These Green Things,
by Catherine Sneed

3) The Earth's Healing Powers,
by Professor Lindsay Robb

*

The kiss of the sun for pardon,
    The song of the birds for mirth -
You are nearer God's heart in a garden
    Than anywhere else on earth.

(Source unknown.)

*

GOSABA - A MODERN MIRACLE

In Gosaba there is no poverty. Everybody is well fed, well housed, well schooled. Hindus, Mahommedans, Christians live side by side so amicably that there is not a single policeman among the 22,000 population. There is an air of happiness and well being about that makes a striking contrast to the misery and tension so evident elsewhere in Bengal.

How has such a transformation been achieved? To find the answer it is necessary to go back to 1903. Then Mr. Daniel Hamilton, and his wife, later Sir Daniel and Lady Hamilton, conceived the idea of doing something to improve the terrible conditions under which the villagers of Bengal lived. Both were Scots. Sir Daniel was a partner in the well known shipping firm, Mackinnon Mackenzie & Co., Calcutta. Before her marriage Lady Hamilton, a daughter of the Manse, as Miss Wilkie Brown was a Missionary in Calcutta.

After considerable study of the possibilities and obstacles to be surmounted, Sir Daniel became convinced life in the village could be transformed, from misery to happiness, from poverty to plenty, from ill health to joyous strength. He realised the obstacles would be tremendous but he never doubted it would be possible to demonstrate all obstacles could be overcome. And he succeeded.

The first step was to find a suitable location for the experiment. Gosaba, an island in the Sunderbans was selected, and a lease of it for forty years obtained from the Government of Bengal. The settlement now includes two other neighbouring islands also, but to simplify matters the word Gosaba is used in this article to mean the group of three islands. Up to 1903 there was no settled human life on the island. Occasional wood cutters came to cut wood, collectors of wild honey came in the honey season, a few shikaris came to conduct tiger hunts from time to time. The permanent inhabitants were tigers, crocodiles, boars and numerous other wild jungle animals. The island was densely covered with scrub jungle, short stocky trees, shrubs, creepers, grass, all adapted through the centuries to growing in the particularly saline soil of that area. At spring tides, twice monthly, salt water seeped in from the sea and inundated all but the highest points on the island. Sir Daniel realised that the first step toward making the island inhabitable would have to be the building of bundhs to keep back the sea. He got imported, hired labour from other parts of Bengal to build the first bundhs round an area of about a hundred acres or so. Understandably, when the then state of the island is remembered, workers of the right type were very reluctant to go., Destitutes from Calcutta were tried, ex-jail birds, victims of famine from Midnapore and from East Bengal. In fact a cross section of what most people would consider the worst elements in society. Apart from the human element, and the fear of attack by wild animals, an indication of the natural obstacles to be overcome was the fact that no drinking water could be found on the island. Until a distilling plant was installed all drinking water had to be brought from outside.

When the first small area had been successfully protected from the sea, the thick scrub jungle in the enclosed area was cut down and the land prepared for cultivation. Then it was found the frequent inundations by seawater had made the land too saline to grow paddy (rice) or other suitable grain. Nothing daunted, Sir Daniel directed tanks should be excavated to catch rain from the next monsoon. Then, when the tanks were full, a system of sluices were installed and the monsoon (sweet) water flushed on the ground to extract sufficient of the excessive salinity in the top few inches to make cultivation possible. This system, it may be mentioned, is in line with the ancient Indian irrigation practice. It is still successfully used at Gosaba and provides an interesting demonstration of the value of irrigation in an area with a heavy monsoon rainfall. Now there are upwards of 150 miles of protecting bundhs at Gosaba, enclosing nearly 66,000 bighas (22,000) acres of land all under intensive cultivation, where forty years ago tigers reigned supreme.

From the time of commencing work on the island until the harvesting of the first crop demonstrated that it was possible to establish conditions suitable for cultivation was about five years. In that time there were many apparent failures, particularly of the human element. At one stage the London Missionary Society were in charge of operations, at another the Salvation Army. Neither of those bodies made the desired amount of progress and Gosaba did not make the hoped for advance until Sir Daniel and Lady Hamilton decided to live as much as possible on the island themselves, so that they could direct operations on the spot. Before Sir Daniel's retirement from business, in 1910, they visited the island for long weekends, going down from Calcutta by launch. After his retirement they lived on Gosaba more or less permanently until 1919. From that time until his death in 1939 they resided at Gosaba during the winter, in Scotland during the summer, except when ill health prevented him going to Gosaba on a few occasions. There is no doubt the presence of Sir Daniel and Lady Hamilton contributed a great deal to the happy state of affairs that exists today. But their mere presence alone could not be the whole secret. It was only a contribution. The real secret lies elsewhere. It lies in the creation of conditions under which human beings can rise from the depths of misery to a state of happy contentment. Conditions under which nobody got any material benefit for nothing. Everything received had to be consciously earned. No one was allowed to be a parasite. Everybody in course of time was expected to contribute in some way to the general good; thereby an increasing sense of responsibility was inculcated. With excellent results.

When he had established conditions suitable for cultivation over a few hundred acres Sir Daniel invited cultivators from various parts of Bengal to become his tenants and settle on Gosaba permanently. Very wisely he made it a principle from the very beginning that there was to be no suggestion of charity in his scheme. His aim being to make cultivators independent they were required to pay for the land they settled on. [See further – they paid *rent (SAH)*]. Nobody on Gosaba at any time has got anything for nothing. A careful record was kept of all expenditure on bundh-making, jungle clearing, etc., and the equivalent recovered from proceeds of crops in later years. Similarly famine victims and other cultivators having no ready money who came to settle in Gosaba (and where in Bengal, except now at Gosaba, has any cultivator ready money?), had to undertake to settle their liability to the estate from their harvests.

At first the response was very poor. A few of the labourers who had worked at bundh-making or jungle clearing elected to settle permanently. Also a few cultivators who were influenced by the missionary organisations who knew of Sir Daniel's scheme. But in 1910, that is seven years after taking a lease of the land, the population amounted to less than 900, the majority of these being paid labourers, not cultivator settlers. By that time approximately 10,000 bighas (about 3,300 acres) had been reclaimed. A series of crop failures in Midnapore and East Bengal about that time provided an impetus and from 1911 onwards there was a steady increase in the number of cultivators seeking to become settlers. In keeping with his desire not to enrich a few but to help many, Sir Daniel made it a condition of settlement that no one person could have more than 25 bighas of land.[1] That he considered sufficient for an able bodied

[1] *Gosaba, as so tiny an enclave of justice in Bengal – indeed, in all of India (an India we had now ruined with the introduction of our land-capitalisation economy) – may well have been wisely safeguarded in*

man to attempt to cultivate. If properly cultivated that area will provide amply for an average family. A full rent has always been charged for every holding, but after paying land revenue to the Government, the tribute exacted by the Hamilton Estate from the cultivators is returned to the area in the form of medical services, schools, research work on seeds, cattle, etc.[2]

Following the success of the co-operative idea in finance, co-operation was extended to other aspects of the cultivator's life. A co-operative agency was established for the selling of paddy, then a co-operative rice mill was built where members' paddy is milled. The resultant rice in pre-war times was sold in Calcutta, and essentials such as cloth, mustard oil, kerosene, etc., brought back from Calcutta in the boats used to transport the rice. Those essentials in their turn were sold to members through a Co-operative store. All these activities flourished and provided living tributes to what can be done by and through co-operative effort when properly directed. Since the imposition of war time controls the Government procurement agency takes over surplus supplies of rice from the mill, and it is a striking fact that Gosaba supplied considerable quantities of grain to the Government during the terrible famine of 1943 when the people in most other places in the district had to get supplies from Government stocks, or die. In the district many once thickly populated villages became mausoleums, villages of the dead. Villages where five hundred had lived before the famine had fifty at the end and those fifty gaunt, haggard bundles of bones with lifeless eyes looking but seeing not. On Gosaba there was no famine.

Schools at Gosaba are based on a combination of the ancient Indian conception of sitting at the feet of the master and the old Scotch system of village education. They are controlled by locally elected boards of management, and like the co-operative banks, provide a shining example of progressive success among Bengal's record of educational failures. An interesting development is the growing of paddy, vegetables and flowers in school plots attached to every school. Apart from the annual ploughing, which is done by parents, all work on the plots is done by the children. Prizes are given annually for the best results, results which are, in many cases, astonishingly good.

The health of the community is cared for by three fully qualified doctors and a maternity and child welfare scheme. Being in a position to retain for family consumption practically all the results of their labour the community is well fed and the incidence of disease is very slight. Each doctor has under his control a well-stocked dispensary from which medicines are issued free to the sick. The medicines, the doctors' remuneration and other expenses of maintaining health services are provided by the Hamilton estate out of the sums paid by cultivators as rent. So are the cost of running the schools, plant research station, agricultural institute, maintaining roads and bundhs.

By far the most interesting experiment at Gosaba, and probably the most successful, is a reversion to the ancient Indian system of self-government by panchayat, a system of submitting problems to five wise men. In ancient days such panchayata had legal sanction and there have been in recent years, in some parts of India, a few halfhearted attempts to revive the system. But only for the settlement of minor

---

this way. It could scarcely have jeopardised the land rent principle (which is based on land rental values, not size), since in the exceptionally primitive circumstances of Gosaba, all the land must have been roughly of the same value. (Had it been otherwise, there would undoubtedly have arisen complaints)

[2] *Thus the Hamiltons simply acted as the local administrators of the local land rent fund – or, the community ground rent.*

disputes. At Gosaba an all-out attempt was made to settle all matters by the panchayat system. And it succeeded. There being no legal authority to set up formal panchayat courts, it was decided to refer disputes, of any and every nature, to a panchayat selected from the committee of management of the co-operative society of the village concerned. For many years now, all disputes of whatever nature have in fact been so referred. The panchayat listens to both parties to the dispute and gives a decision. If one party to any dispute still feels aggrieved after the decision of the first panchayat, the dispute is referred to a panchayat composed of nominees from two other co-operative societies. Should that panchayats' decision not be acceptable to both disputants then the dispute is considered by the panchayat composed of nominees from the Central Co-operative Society, the co-ordinating Society of all the 25 societies at Gosaba. If any party did not accept the decision of that panchayat he could take recourse to the ordinary courts of Bengal. He could also, of course, take that recourse without going before any of the Gosaba panchayats. So far nobody from Gosaba has done so. The settlement of disputes by reference to panchayats has proved over the years to be completely satisfactory. The system is speedy and costs nothing to public revenue for administrative costs. Proceedings are held in public, spectators, when necessary, intervene to correct witnesses who appear to be inclined to give tainted evidence. There are no rules of evidence but the ready acceptance of panchayat decisions proves that the truth is generally established. As a direct result of having such an excellent system, Gosaba is in the unique position of being able to dispense with policemen. There are none on the island.

Time has shown that the conception of Gosaba was not Utopian. It works. Today it provides twenty two thousand happy, healthy human beings as evidence of the soundness and practicability of the conception. The happiness of the people is the test by which the Government (or Governments), of India of the future, as all Governments, will be judged by history. The happiness of the people at Gosaba is, now, an example of how successful Government of the people, for the people, by the people *must* be, if and when it is given a real chance.

*

THESE GREEN THINGS

CATHERINE SNEED AND THE SAN FRANCISCO GARDEN PROJECT

These quotations are from an article that originally appeared in
Orion 195 Main Street, Great Barrington, MA 01230, U.S.A.
Gratefully acknowledged.

Her boss, the sheriff of San Francisco says, "Cathy has a magical ability to change people's lives." Cathrine Sneed has trained in the law and agroecology, studied biodynamic gardening at Emerson in England and completed the Agroecology Programme at the University of California. Currently director of The Garden Project, Sneed is the founder of the horticultural Programme for the San Francisco County Jail where, in an eight-acre garden, prisoners grow produce using the biodynamic French intensive method. Weekly, the garden's organic produce is delivered to projects that supply food to seniors, homeless people, and AIDS victims. Above all, this organic, chemical-free garden is a living metaphor for the healthy lives the jail gardeners are trying to create.

After being released, many of the former prisoners choose to continue working with plants in The Garden Project, a series of Programmes that helps released prisoners re-enter their communities as good citizens. They begin at the Carroll Street training garden, a half-acre organic garden where they grow tender vegetables for sale to local restaurants, notably the legendary Chez Panisse run by the legendary Alice Waters. After training, students can join The Tree Corps, which plants and maintains trees in low-income areas of San Francisco. In addition to these Programmes, The Garden Project is establishing organic urban gardens that offer long-term jobs for Programme graduates. This model 'ladder' towards employment and participation in the community is a wise, effective alternative to the more typical scenario for former prisoners. Often lacking skills, resources and support, up to eighty percent of prisoners released from county jails return within three months. Financially draining to society, the pattern is also morally unacceptable – one gauge of the cycle of racism, injustice, poverty, and crime that has wounded the national soul.

In addition to her attention to the jail garden and its offshoots, Cathrine Sneed is co-chair of the San Francisco Tree Advisory and a board member of Elmwood Institute. She has received many awards; most recently she was named a 'Hero of the Earth' by the Eddie Bauer Corporation, and was honoured by The Foundation for the Improvement of Justice. Looking on her works, it is easy to understand why Alice Waters has said of Cathrine Sneed: "I would do anything she asks me to do. Anything. When I look at her, I feel real hope for the world." About her transformative powers, Sneed herself will only say, "It is embarrassing to me when people say all of the different things they say about me because I don't really figure in the equation. It is the garden that changes people's lives. It is working with these green things."

This is the story of the San Francisco County Jail Garden and The Garden Project, told in the words of their founder and guiding spirit, based on talks she gave at the Aspen Design Conference and at Harvard College.

*

Catherine Sneed Speaks about her Work with Prisoners and Gardens

Hello. I always love to talk to people about what we're doing in San Francisco because hearing about it gives people ideas about what can happen in places other than San Francisco.

I have spent a lot of time in jail myself – as a counsellor to women serving time there. It was my job to try to help these women find ways to do something with their lives other than what they had been doing. Most of them were in jail for drug use, drug possession, and drug sales. Most of them had been and were prostitutes, and most of them had children. These women *wanted* to believe me when I told them there was something else they could do with their lives, but the reality was that they didn't have any education. In San Francisco, we test everyone that comes in our jail. The median reading level is fourth grade, fifth grade, and sixth grade. Most of the people in our jail have never had jobs. And so as much as these women wanted to say, "Yeah, Cathy, we believe what you're saying, we *can* do something else with our lives," the reality was grim.

After several years working closely with these women, and despairing about their situation, I learned that I had gotten a serious kidney disease. I was twenty-eight and I had two little kids, and it was a shock when the doctor said, "Well, it doesn't look good. You're not responding to drugs and you can either stay here in hospital and die or you can go home and die." Just before my doctor came up with that statement, a good friend of mine had given me *The Grapes of Wrath.* I read it, and what struck me was this – Steinbeck is saying that to be really alive, these people felt that they must be connected with the soil, with the earth. I grew up in Newark, New Jersey and I had not had much connection with the earth. Now, lying in the hospital, it occurred to me that since San Francisco's jail stands right on what was, in the 1930s, a 145-acre farm, it made good sense to bring prisoners outside of the jail buildings, onto the land, and try to grow things again.

I was fortunate, because I was supposed to kick the bucket any minute, and when my dear friend, Michael Hennessey, our sheriff, visited me in the hospital he said, "Yeah, Cathy, if you want to take them outside and garden, fine. Why don't you do that?" He said this thinking that I was going to kick the bucket, but that in the mean time I would feel good. Well, I didn't die, and when I got out of the hospital, I set out with four prisoners onto the old farm. I wish you could have seen their faces when they said, "We're going to do *what* here?" I said, "Well, first of all, we have to start by cleaning up this mess."

And so we started cleaning up. For twenty years, the sheriff's department had used the old farm as a storage area and it took us three years to clean up the mess. We did it without tools, without wheelbarrows. The jail gardeners literally tore down old buildings with their hands. They didn't have jackets or raingear. They had their T-shirts and their thin jail clothes and little thin shoes to clip-clop around in. What began to touch me was that I started to see these people care about something for the first time. I started to see them *care* that we were slowly cleaning up this mess, and *care* that I was so excited about it. And then I saw *them* get excited. From that point on we began to grow things.

One of the first people who came out into the garden with me was a man I'll never forget. His name is Forrest. Forrest was about forty-five then, with a criminal history that spanned three decades. He had ten arrests for assault with a deadly weapon, probably fifteen arrests for drunk driving, and related things. Not a nice guy. And yet Forrest came out with me, busted his butt to clean up this old dump, this old farm. Soon, a wonderful horticulture therapist named Arlene Hamilton joined us. We started to grow herbs. We started slowly, with only $300 from the sheriff and his friends to buy a few things, and maybe ten gardeners in 1984. Today, 160 prisoners go out every day to an eight-acre garden. It is fenced for the deer, because we have lots of deer. We have tools now and we grow an amazing amount of food that we give to the soup kitchens, and to projects that feed seniors, the homeless, and people too sick with AIDS to feed themselves. A lot of people ask me, "Why do you *give* the food away?" We give the food away because it is important for the prisoners to have an opportunity to feel good about themselves.

People ask me, "What is it about gardening – getting your hands in the earth – that makes the connection with these people. Why couldn't it be getting them on a computer? What do you think is so good about the gardening?" Well, in fact it is important to say that gardening isn't for everyone, but growing things does give many people a sense of power. They made it happen with their hands! And also it is the experience of living things, green things, beauty, Mother Nature. This reminds me of something Wendell Berry said in *The Unsettling of America.* He talks about how, in America, anything done with your hands is looked down on. I look at the community I'm working with, and I think, "What's missing is nature and beauty, the beauty that can be made with our hands." I say to these guys, "Look, you guys, let's weed the baby lettuces, and then let's watch what happens. They're going to grow more, they'll be better. And people will pay top organic dollar for them." Growing things is a metaphor, I also say to them, "if we don't put chemicals on this stuff that we're growing, people are going to pay more for it. It's the same for you. If you don't put heroin into your arm, you are going to be better off. Your family will be better off." The experience of growing works in terms of healing, of my counselling. I can *show* them what I'm talking about. Many, many people here in the jail are substance dependent. One thing the garden shows them is how much better life is without chemicals. You can take chemicals and put them in the garden, and get fast results, but look what it does to the soil.

My concern with farm Programme in the jail is – well, I'm sure you all saw that movie with Paul Newman, *Cool Hand Luke* – in which prisoners were *forced* to do agricultural labour in chain gangs. I mean, there have been jail farms forever, and it is very, very important that our jail people have a *choice.* Either you can work in the farm and grow food for the soup kitchen, *or* you can go to computer class, *or* the literacy class. There has to be a choice. It's very, very important that you give people who have hurt people, who have killed people, an opportunity to be able to look in the mirror and say, "God, I can do something good."

People in our country do want solutions, and I have seen many, many people like Forrest go from all those long convictions to being a kick-ass radish grower. Now he is the first person to come up to you in the garden. At first, it is kind of menacing, because he looks king of menacing. He's got tattoos everywhere, but what he wants to do is give you a bouquet of flowers, because he is very proud of the flowers. That is transformation. This Programme makes people who have no hope have hope, which is a tremendously powerful thing. It is working with these green things that gives them a sense of life. And most of them have never had it from anywhere else. Another prisoner, named Danny, said to me, "I'd like to go work on a farm for somebody. And I want to be dedicated to the farm like I am here. I was like a dead tree when I first came here. And I've seen what watering does: if you water the tree and feed it nice, it grows up and it has fruit. I don't want to go back to the streets and just hang around, and waste, and die." And these women – who are almost all in here for prostitution – are *strong* women. Do you know how hard it is to stand on a street corner every night for hours, in the cold, with practically no clothes on? *Strong women*, only on the wrong path.

I want to tell you something, because not many people like you get an opportunity to visit a jail – jails are bleak places. Our jail is so bleak, despite our beautiful garden, that I always wonder – *How can we keep people in this horrible situation in horrible cages, and then expect then to come back and be normal nice people, living with everyone?* That's not going to happen. The people I work with are the kind of people who, when you see them, you cross the street because they are scary people. But this garden Programme helps people understand that they aren't just scary, they are part of a community. They leave our jails all over the country and they come back and live in our communities, they ride the bus with us.

For many years I felt it was wonderful that we had this garden, that we were feeding people, that people's lives were changing. But it is frustrating to realise that for most of the people in our jail, being in the garden Programme is better than their lives at home – *better* than living on the street, than living in hotels for homeless, than living in projects. It was devastating for me to realise that for many of these people, the garden Programme was the best experience of their adult lives, of their whole lives. At the end of their sentence, may people came up to me and said, "Cathy, I don't want to go, I want to stay here." In fact, some of them ended up back in jail just because they wanted to be back in our garden. But most of them returned to selling their bodies and drugs because no one would hire them to do anything else. So I realised we needed another Programme to help them continue the experiences they had in our garden, but outside the jail.

I often bring people from the community to the jail to see what we are doing. One day, a local business person came, a man named Elliot Hoffman who has a large bakery named Just Deserts. He looked around and he said, "You know, I need so many strawberries. You could grow strawberries and I could buy them from you." Personally, I was hoping that this man would say, "Hey, I'll give you a check. You can buy tools." But he kept saying, "No, no, I would really like to buy strawberries from you." So he invited me out to his bakery in Hunter's Point. Behind his bakery was this old garbage dump, about a half an acre. And he said, "You could bring the people here and you could grow a lot of strawberries." I kept looking at this garbage dump and thinking to myself, "You know, I have enough to do here at the *jail*, I would really just like a check from this person."

Fortunately for us all, Elliot persisted and finally after a couple of hours when it became clear to me that he wasn't going to give me a check we decided to start a post-release Programme for people leaving the jail. Today, people can leave our jail Programme and come to this half-acre garden and continue to grow food that we sell to Chez Panisse, which is a very fancy, wonderful restaurant in Berkeley run by Alice Waters. We also sell a lot of fruit to Just Desserts and we are involving other businesses. We're talking with The Body Shop, We're talking with Esprit. We're talking with any business that will listen about spreading this idea. We call this place in Hunter's Point "The Garden Project." After a while, Elliot got to know our people and hired some of them. Of course, that first guy Elliot hired disappeared with the Just Desserts Truck. He had just gone to cruise his neighbourhood and he didn't think anything about it because he had never had a job before. Elliot didn't get scared by that, and he has hired more people from our programme for his bakery.

When we first started The Garden Project the land belonged to a certain huge corporation. I said to them. "Well look, you guys, you have a garbage dump in this poor neighbourhood. Let us help you clean it up; we'll grow things on it, and your property won't be a wreck anymore." The huge corporation said to me, "Look, lady, we're not a charity. Give us $500,000 for the land." It seemed to me there was no way I was going to give them a dime. And so we climbed over their fence and made a garden. Now, this is felony trespassing, and remember on my little business card it says, "Special Assistant to the Sheriff." So I said to the sheriff, I said, "Michael, this huge corporation says I need $500,000 and what I'd like to do is clean up their dump and start a garden. "Michael said, "Do it. And don't forget that not only are they going to have to put *you* in jail, They're going to have to put *me* in jail." I always encourage people to say *no* to anybody who says it can't be done.

What we have throughout this country is poor people and vacant land. I grew up in Newark, New Jersey, and when I left, twenty years ago, there were acres and acres of land where buildings were burnt in the riots after Martin Luther King died. Now, instead of having people standing out on the corner, they could instead be growing fruit that Ben & Jerry's says they'll buy. They could do that in Newark; they could do that in Denver. What we're doing is finding ways to connect nature and people.

I go from feeling very hopeful to feeling extremely sad in my work. I feel very sad when I go to our jail and see so many African-American men, so many Spanish-speaking men and women who do not have any hope. And, it's discouraging when I hear cops say, "Well, that's all they want," or when I hear people say, "They can make more money selling crack." That's so false. The people out there selling drugs for the most part are making barely enough to buy the crack they are using. They are on a path that is destructive – for all of us. Crime affects all of us, every day, and it's important that we start looking at what's happening in our country. We are producing millions of people who have no hope, who have nothing to lose, and if you have nothing to lose, you're a dangerous, dangerous person. What happened in Los Angeles is what happens when many, many people feel that they don't matter, that they don't count. The sadness that I feel about these human situations, and I'm sure all of us feel in some way numbs us. It makes us feel that it might be easier to protect the spotted owl or to protect land. With land, you know, you can buy it up and make sure that no one builds on it. But to help people to change, it doesn't take a year. It takes many years, many other people.

When I was asked to speak here [at the Aspen Design Conference] I thought, oh, what am I going to say to these people? They cannot know what I'm doing. But then I realised that you are the people who are *designing* our communities. And I feel very hopeful that you want to hear about this. I feel very hopeful that with your understanding and all your expertise, you can start designing an America that *includes* the men and women that I work with, the men and women who fill our jails. You know, California spends many millions of dollars building jails, and fewer millions of dollars educating children. It costs $25,000 a year to keep a person in a cage. They could go to Harvard! They could go a lot of places. What I see in our project is what happens when government, business, and community people join together. I'm asking you to help to redesign a new world. When I tell my students, "I went to Aspen and to Harvard and told those people what we're doing here in the garden, and they listened and they *cared*," my students know that it means that they *count*, that there's hope. They hold their heads up a little, and they think "God, we matter. We count."

When I told the San Francisco Unified School District that Alice Waters at Chez Panisse wants to buy all the vegetables we can grow, they said, "Well, we have land all over and we're spending to clear the weeds, so why don't you do something with it?" That's good, that's good. We can grow a lot of radishes for Alice on what used to be school district land. The Department of Forestry is also spending a lot of money trying to safeguard our forests. Now, the Angeles Forest is not so far from South-Central Los Angeles, so I said to them, "Let's pay the people that are standing around the streets in South-Central Los Angeles to plant trees. Let's pay them to maintain the trees." What we are talking about is putting people and the environment together. It starts with us saying, "We can do better," because we *can* do better. Last Friday, I spoke at the funeral of Donell, a man who was in my garden Programme four years ago. He had just turned eighteen. This man could not tell time. He could not read. So I asked Smith & Hawken, which is a fancy tool company, to hire this young man when he left our programme in the jail, and they did. But after two months of him coming to work late, and a few times of him stealing clothes that they were trying to sell, they said, "Cathy, we really want to help your project, but, you know, this guy isn't working." I understood when they let him go. But when they did, he went back to the Sunnydale projects, back to selling drugs. He was killed by a young man with whom he had had an argument. The young man came back after the argument and blew his head off. This happens every day.

Donnell was one of those young men who did not want to leave our jail, the garden. He said, "Cathy, I don't want to go back our there. Can I stay here?" I said, "Donnell, you *cannot* stay in jail. It's, it's illegal!" Donnell said to me "Cathy, you know a lot of people. You can pull some strings. The sheriff's your friend. Please ask the sheriff to let me stay here." I asked Sheriff Hennessy, who's a wonderful, wonderful man, "Michael, can we let Donnell stay? He's afraid to go back." Michael said, "Cathy, it *is* illegal, and our jail is over crowded. People are sleeping on the floor. We can't keep Donnell in the jail." When I was talking at his funeral, I was aware that most of the people attending were young men, and most of the young men knew who I was, and it was not because they heard me on National Public Radio or read about me in *The New York Times*. Anywhere I go in San Francisco people come up to me and say, "Oh, I know you." If they're African-American, I know they know me from the jail. Something's very wrong.

People say, "You seen so passionate about this. It seems like more than a job to you. What keeps you going?" What keeps me going is that the young men and young women in our jail look very much like the young men and young women who live in my house – my children, my nieces and nephews. If you look at statistics, I know that my daughter and my son don't have a future. We are talking about reconstruction, redirecting, rebuilding. We are talking about hope and solutions. I look at these lupines and trees on the stage with us today, and I think – We could be paying somebody to be watering these plants. The somebodies could be people like the people in my programme. When I see vacant lots and garbage dumps, I know who would love to have the opportunity to clean them up. We need to see that, despite the enormous obstacles these young women and men face, they are remaking their lives.

The people, who have said, "This makes sense" come from all over. I got a letter not so long ago from California's attorney general. I have to say I was afraid to open the envelope; I thought maybe I was being indicted. The attorney general wrote to me to say "Cathy, what you're doing is a model for law enforcement, throughout this state. It is an inspiration to law enforcement and I'm sending information about it to all the attorney general's offices in the state, and I am going to *make* them come visit you." And so many people hear of our programme and we are getting more support and requests to help begin similar programmes.

Last summer, we got a contract to plant trees for San Francisco. Since then we've planted over 2,000 trees in the city. The people planting trees are called The Tree Corps and are getting eight dollars an hour to plant trees. They used to be crack sellers. They used to sell crack to pregnant mothers, to their own mothers. Now they're selling hope because when they're out there planting trees in Hunter's Point and in The Mission, people look at them and say, "Wait a minute. I don't have to sell crack. I can do something else 'cause if my uncle and my cousin and my brother can plant trees, *I* can plant trees." I have a *waiting* list of people who want to plant trees, and wherever we go, people follow us. This one young man came, and he said, "Cathy, I'm sorry to come to you like this." He had an Uzi under his little jacket and crack in the pockets. He said, "I'm sorry to come to you like this, but I don't want to do this. I want to plant trees." I want to be able to give him an opportunity to plant trees because we need trees. You *have* heard of global warming?

Planting trees is super work and, for me, the most powerful thing is when you consider that the person doing it used to be selling drugs, hurting other people, and is now trying to figure out whether the tree pit is deep enough. When you give people an alternative to throwing their lives away most people choose that. And I will never forget my first day when The Tree Corps and I began working with John, the Department of Public Works employee who was first assigned to work with us. His co-workers were teasing him, but John just puffed out his chest and said, "Wait a minute, these people are just like you. They are going to learn a skill." And then John proceeded to teach our students as much as he knew – and he has been a tree trimmer and planter for twenty years. But what he really taught our students is that people care. And that you can learn Latin names if you want to. It was a powerful relationship. John has since been transferred and we are doing it on our own. Now that The Tree Corps reflects the people in the neighbourhood, people know that this tree in the ground means that their uncle, or brother, or sister has a job and so theyprotect the tree, whereas before they often cut it down. It is not weird, but quite wonderful.

One of our planters is Rumaldo. He is about fifty-three years old and he has been to jail six times. Rumaldo had four grown children and now he brings his children around and says, "I planted that tree," and then he tells them the Latin name for the tree and what the tree needs and he puffs out his chest and he doesn't hurt people anymore. Because he is too tired – he is out planting trees. But it is a long, constant struggle. I got a message the other day from a man named Burl who was with us for about six months. When he started working with The Tree Corps he had just overcome his crack addiction. He came to work every day but he had nowhere to live and was living in his car, and he got back on the street and re-addicted. I got a message the other day that he was asking whether or not I was too mad at him to consider allowing him to rejoin the Programme. And of course I am not too mad at him.

*

What some of those involved in the garden project have said about the way it helped change their lives

"The Programme helped me to want to do things the right way. When I do leave I will think of The Garden project as my family. Hopefully I can take the garden with me in my heart and remember that this was the first thing that got me on my feet. It's time for me to get up and go on in my life. I'm going to be okay."

*

"It's a good Programme – it changed my life quickly. It made me see that there is a good side to life. It made me feel like a human being again. There is a chance to change and I think I can do it right here."

*

"Flowers have a special way of expressing the love feeling, very warm, healthy feeling. Each individual – we're going to die sooner than we should. And if we take care of ourselves, our bodies, we have a chance of living a little bit longer. I never thought I'd be the person that I am right now at this point."

*

People should not have to go to jail to get reconnected with the earth! Every day I get calls from schools to make gardens. A garden can produce revenue, and for kids who have no way of getting money to buy sneakers or something they want, selling carrots beats the hell out of selling crack.

Cathy Sneed

*

THE EARTH'S HEALING POWERS

by Professor Lindsay Robb

After the long trek up the western desert with the 8th Army which ended the Libyan campaign, Colonel Lindsay Robb, as he then was, was appointed Director of Agriculture under the British Administration. This involved the rehabilitation of war-ravaged land and people and generally restoring order from chaos in agriculture. In the course of this work he had an experience of the healing powers of the earth which we asked him to describe for us.

*

While I was Director of Agriculture I met a psychiatrist who was in charge of the medical section for the treatment of nerve shattered soldiers from the different British and Allied units. Frequent meetings followed as my psychiatrist friend was fond of riding and I had a considerable stud of Arab horses. In our many discussions I stressed the affinity between medicine and agriculture, and my belief that they were natural partners and should work in close co-operation within a single Ministry of Health and Land Use.

Impressed by my interest and beliefs about medicine and agriculture, the psychiatrist persuaded me to pay him a visit and see his soldier patients. Rarely in my life have I received such a shock. There was not a single tree, bush, flower, piece of grass, cereal, root crop or live animal. The temperature was in the nineties and the ground was barren sand – and this was the headquarters of the nerve shattered soldiers. After I had accompanied my psychiatrist friend on his professional round of his soldier patients, I was invited to express my views about response to treatment. I had to admit frankly that I could see no signs of recovery – no response to the questions put to them – only despair and hopelessness on their faces. Since I myself would have had to struggle to keep fit under such conditions, I could see no hope for complete recovery of nerve shattered soldiers in this environment of misery and discomfort. So I offered the fullest help that agriculture could give.

A few days after the visit, I received an urgent call to the headquarters of the G.O.C. but no information about why I should go. In additions to the G.O.C. and his Staff, the O.C. Military Administration and the psychiatrist were also present at the meeting. Without any preliminaries, the General turned to me and said "Robb, I hear you *think* you could cure the nerve shattered soldiers". I resented the emphasis he put on the work 'think' and replied "I don't have to think, Sir, I know". "Indeed", was the General's response. As this was not a very propitious opening to our discussion, I said "Perhaps I ought to explain, Sir, that we men of the land have known for centuries of the healing power of the earth and that I would apply this healing power to those sick men". He became intensely interested and after a short discussion about details and requirements for this new course of treatment, he gave an order that I was to have everything required to put it into operation as soon as possible.

Forty-eight hours later we had all the soldier patients moved into our agricultural headquarters at Sidi Mesri, an experimental farm a few miles from Tripoli, which had been established by the Turks several centuries ago, and more recently developed by the Italians. It was one of the most beautiful headquarters in Libya during the Desert Campaign and an ideal centre for sick men to regain health. In addition to spacious artistic buildings to line in, irrigation tanks to swim in, trees for shade, grass and gardens full of flowers and fruit, we had the experimental farm with a large dairy herd, a variety of cultivated crops and a stud of Arab horses.

The course included bringing the patients into daily contact with the soil, plants and animals, and how they function. We had accommodation for 50. The effect of moving the men out of their military headquarters of barren sand into their new agricultural environment of beauty, peace and tranquillity, was electric. They were literally bewildered by the sudden change. Was this a dream from which they would wake up again in the desert sand? It was too good to be true! So I was told later by several of the patients in describing their first reactions to this almost unbelievable change.

This change in surroundings was a basic part of what we in agriculture regard as essential in the treatment of these nerve shattered men. They were sick physically, mentally and spiritually, and positive human health means complete physical, mental and spiritual harmony between man and his total environment.

Our agricultural approach to the problem of restoring these soldiers to health was entirely ecological. The problem had to be seen in its entirety as an inter-relationship with health as a whole, and man as a whole within a particular environment. The first step towards recovery was to remove the cause of the shattered nerves which resulted from excessive strain under battle conditions. This was achieved by moving the men from an environment of lifeless barren sand into one of living soil, teaming with life in a setting of beauty and peace.

With the removal of the cause of their illness the process of recovery began. Army rations were supplemented by additions of fresh fruit, vegetables and dairy products from the farm to improve nutrition and physical health. Daily exposure to, and contact with, the healing power of the earth through participation in the normal tasks associated with the cultivation and harvesting of crops and management of livestock produced an immediate response. On a busy farm, life flows on without interruption, but not without constant changes in tasks according to the stages in crop production and varying needs of growing and productive animals.

The response of animals to the care and love of humans is well known and it engenders among humans a love for all forms of life and it helps to develop within man himself a better balance between the material and non-material forces. The therapeutic effect of all this on our soldier patients was very striking, though it is doubtful whether any of them were aware of the hidden healing forces which were contributing so rapidly and effectively to their total physical, mental and spiritual health and harmony.

Birthright ... and ... Scotland Today

An important feature inherent in the management of the farm which contributed so much to our agricultural effort was the fact that practically all the farm workers were Italians, and Italians are by nature happy and exceptionally musical. They sing at their work because they are happy. And happiness is infectious, no less than some diseases. Before they had been long in residence, one could hear snatches of song coming from a group of soldier patients if one happened to pass within range.

One day early in the programme, an Army padre friend called at our headquarters, and being naturally interested and deeply concerned with the welfare of sick soldiers, offered his help in what he regarded as the ideal manner of our approach to heal the sick – to treat man in his entire physical, mental and spiritual entity. Our soldier patients accepted at once an invitation to join us in a short service which they so much enjoyed that they asked for it to be a weekly affair. This was a simple open-air service, with everyone sitting around a fountain in the shade of an old fig tree. The hymns were chosen by the men and the padre gave a very short talk on the relationship between simple healing methods to restore health and that greater all-embracing power of the Master Healer available to all.

The average period of recovery to fitness for rejoining their regiments was one month, but the speed and completeness with which health was restored could not, in my opinion, be explained entirely by our physical contributions. There was another dimension – a life force of high intensity – which in this case may be referred to as the 'healing power of the earth' – and which is sometimes called Factor X.

*

Yea, I have loved thee
with an everlasting love:
therefore with loving kindness
have I drawn thee.

(Jeremiah, ch.31)

*

Part III

KALEIDOSCOPE

*

When I was a little girl, my Aunts gave me, one Christmas, a kaleidoscope, which became the source of much enjoyment to me. For on shaking it, and looking through the top, I found that a succession of beautiful coloured images was formed from the original 'mosaic', through the reflecting glasses surrounding and extending it.

My hope is that this section - in something of a different sphere! - may provide to readers the same kind of enjoyment.

*

Part III

KALEIDOSCOPE

*

1) THREE FUNDAMENTALS
2) SOCIO-POLITICO-ECONOMIC
3) BROADER PERSPECTIVES
4) THE NATURAL WORLD
5) A FEW FANDANGOS ... AND FLUORIDATION!
6) ASPECTS OF THE TASK!
7) THE GIFT OF THE GAFFE
8) SOME FAVOURITE PIECES AND SPECIAL LOVES
9) WHO ARE THEY?
10) PHOTOGRAPHS
11) GLIMPSES
12) AND - A FEW WORDS IN FAREWELL!

*

Part III

KALEIDOSCOPE

*

*

"THIS EARTH.....

In 1854, the "Great White Chief" in Washington made an offer for a large area of Indian land, and promised a 'reservation' for the Indian

*

How can you buy or sell the sky, the warmth of the land? The idea is strange to us
If we do not own the freshness of the air and the sparkle of the water, how can you buy them?

ALL SACRED

Every part of this earth is sacred to my people.

Every shining pine needle, every sandy shore, every mist in the dark woods, every clearing and humming insect is holy in the memory and experience of my people. The sap which courses through the trees carries the memories of the red man.

The white man's dead forget the country of their birth when they go to walk among the stars. Our dead never forget this beautiful earth, for it is the mother of the red man.

We are part of the earth and it is part of us.

The perfumed flowers are our sisters; the deer, the horse, the great eagle, these are our brothers.

The rocky crests, the juices in the meadows, the body heat of the pony, and man — all belong to the same family

NOT EASY

So, when the Great Chief in Washington sends word that he wishes to buy our land, he asks much of us. The Great Chief sends word he will reserve us a place so that we can live comfortably to ourselves.

He will be our father and we will be his children. So we will consider your offer to buy our land.

But it will not be easy. For this land is sacred to us.

This shining water that moves in the streams and rivers is not just water but the blood of our ancestors.

If we sell you land, you must remember that it is sacred, and you must teach your children that it is sacred and that each ghostly reflection in the clear water of the lakes tells of events and memories in the life of my people.

The water's murmur is the voice of my father's father.

KINDNESS

The rivers are our brothers, they quench our thirst. The rivers carry our canoes, and feed our children. If we sell you our land, you must remember, and teach your children, that the rivers are our brothers, and yours, and you must henceforth give the rivers the kindness you would give any brother.

We know that the white man does not understand our ways. One portion of land is the same to him as the next, for he is a stranger who comes in the night and takes from the land whatever he needs.

The earth is not his brother, but his enemy, and when he has conquered it, he moves on.

He leaves his father's graves behind, and he does not care. He kidnaps the earth from his children, and he does not care.

His father's grave, and his children's birthright, are forgotten. He treats his mother, the earth, and his brother, the sky, as things to be bought, plundered, sold like sheep or bright beads.

His appetite will devour the earth and leave behind only a desert.

I do not know. Our ways are different from your ways.

The sight of your cities pains the eyes of the red man. But perhaps it is because the red man is a savage and does not understand

There is no quiet place in the white man's cities. No place to hear the unfurling of leaves in spring, or the rustle of an insect's wings.

But perhaps it is because I am a savage and do not understand.

The clatter only seems to insult the ears. And what is there to life if a man cannot hear the lonely cry of the whippoorwill or the arguments of the frogs around a pond at night? I am a red man and do not understand.

The Indian prefers the soft sound of the wind darting over the face of a pond, and the smell of the wind itself, cleaned by a midday rain, or scented with the pinon pine.

. . . . . IS PRECIOUS"

people. Chief Seattle's reply, published here in full, has been described as the most beautiful and profound statement on the environment ever made.

*

PRECIOUS

The air is precious to the red man, for all things share the same breath — the beast, the tree, the man, they all share the same breath.

The white man does not seem to notice the air he breathes. Like a man dying for many days, he is numb to the stench.

But if we sell you our land, you must remember that the air is precious to us, that the air shares its spirit with all the life it supports. The wind that gave our grandfather his first breath also receives his last sigh.

And if we sell you our land, you must keep it apart and sacred, as a place where even the white man can go to taste the wind that is sweetened by the meadow's flowers.

ONE CONDITION

So we will consider your offer to buy our land. If we decide to accept, I will make one condition: the white man must treat the beasts of this land as his brothers.

I am a savage and I do not understand any other way.

I have seen a thousand rotting buffaloes on the prairie, left by the white man who shot them from a passing train.

I am a savage and I do not understand how the smoking iron horse can be more important than the buffalo that we kill only to stay alive.

What is man without the beasts? If all the beasts were gone, man would die from a great loneliness of spirit.

For whatever happens to the beasts, soon happens to man. All things are connected.

THE ASHES

You must teach your children that the ground beneath their feet is the ashes of your grandfathers. So that they will respect the land, tell your children that the earth is rich with the lives of our kin.

Teach your children what we have taught our children, that the earth is our mother.

Whatever befalls the earth befalls the sons of the earth. If men spit upon the ground, they spit upon themselves.

This we know: the earth does not belong to man; man belongs to the earth. This we know.

All things are connected like the blood which unites one family. All things are connected.

Whatever befalls the earth befalls the sons of the earth. Man did not weave the web of life: he is merely a strand in it. Whatever he does to the web, he does to himself.

Even the white man, whose God walks and talks with him as friend to friend, cannot be exempt from the common destiny.

We may be brothers after all.

We shall see.

One thing we know, which the white man may one day discover — our God is the same God.

You may think now that you own Him as you wish to own our land; but you cannot. He is the God of man, and His compassion is equal for the red man and the white.

This earth is precious to Him, and to harm the earth is to heap contempt on its Creator.

The whites too shall pass; perhaps sooner than all other tribes. Contaminate your bed, and you will one night suffocate in your own waste.

But in your perishing you will shine brightly, fired by the strength of the God who brought you to this land and for some special purpose gave you dominion over this land and over the red man.

That destiny is a mystery to us, for we do not understand when the buffalo are all slaughtered, the wild horses are tamed, the secret corners of the forest heavy with scent of many men, and the view of the ripe hills blotted by talking wires.

Where is the thicket? Gone.

Where is the eagle? Gone.

The end of living and the beginning of survival.

THE ESSENE GOSPEL OF PEACE

BOOK FOUR

THE TEACHINGS OF THE ELECT

The Original Hebrew and Aramaic Texts translated and edited by

EDMOND BORDEAUX SZEKELY

MCMLXXXI
INTERNATIONAL BIOGENIC SOCIETY

I.B.S. INTERNATIONAL
P.O. BOX 849,
NELSON, B.C. V1L 6A5
CANADA.

*

"I tell you truly, you are one with the Earthly Mother; she is in you, and you in her. Of her were you born, in her do you live, and to her shall you return again. It is the blood of our Earthly Mother which falls from the clouds and flows in the rivers; it is the breath of our Earthly Mother which whispers in the leaves of the forest and blows with a mighty wind from the mountains; sweet and firm is the flesh of our Earthly Mother in the fruits of the trees; strong and unflinching are the bones of our Earthly Mother in the giant rocks and stones which stand as sentinels of the lost times; truly, we are one with our Earthly Mother, and he who clings to the laws of his Mother, to him shall his Mother cling also.

"But there will come a day when the Son of Man will turn his face from his Earthly Mother, and betray her, even denying his Mother and his birthright. Then shall he sell her into slavery, and her flesh shall be ravaged, her blood polluted, and her breath smothered; he will bring the fire of death into all the parts of her kingdom, and his hunger will devour all her gifts and leave in their place only a desert.

"All these things will he do out of ignorance of the Law, and as a man dying slowly cannot smell his own stench, so will the Son of Man be blind to the truth; that as he plunders and ravages and destroys his Earthly Mother, so does he plunder and ravage and destroy himself. For he was born of his Earthly Mother, and he is one with her, and all that he does to his Mother, even so does he do to himself.

"Long ago, before the Great Flood, the Great Ones walked the earth, and the giant trees, even those which now are no more than legend, were their home and their kingdom. They lived many score of generations, for they ate from the table of the Earthly Mother, and slept in the arms of the Heavenly Father, and they knew not diseases, old age, or death. To the Sons of Men did they bequeath all the glory of their kingdoms, even the hidden knowledge of the Tree of Life, which stood in the middle of the Eternal Sea. But the eyes of the Sons of men were blinded by the visions of Satan, and by promises of power, even that power which conquers by might and blood. And then did the Son of Man sever the golden threads that bound him to his Earthly Mother and his Heavenly Father; he stepped from the Holy Stream of Life where his body, his thoughts, and his feelings were one with the Law, and began to use only his own deeds, making hundreds of laws, where before there was only One.

"And so did the Sons of Men exile themselves from their home, and ever since have they huddled behind their stone walls, hearing not the sighing of the wind in the tall trees of the forests beyond their towns.

"I tell you truly, the Book of Nature is a Holy Scroll, and if you would have the Sons of Men save themselves and find everlasting life, teach them how once again to read from the living pages of the Earthly Mother. For in everything that is life, is the law written. It is written in the grass, in the trees, in rivers, mountains, birds of the sky and fishes of the sea; and most of all within the Son of Man. Only when he returns to the bosom of his Earthly Mother will he find everlasting life and the Stream of Life which leads to his heavenly Father; only thus may the dark vision of the future come not to pass.

*

IMPRISONED IDEAS

by

W.J. Brown, M.P.

Reproduced by kind permission of *The Spectator*, in which it appeared on 19th September 1947

There are many classifications into which men and women may be divided – as upper, middle or lower class; rich, well-to-do and poor; religious, sceptical and atheist; Conservative, Liberal, Labour; Catholic, Protestant; master and man; and so forth and so on, *ad infinitum*. But, as I think, the only categorisation, which really matters, is that which divides men as between the Servants of the Spirit and the Prisoners of the Organisation. That classification, which cuts right across all other classifications, is indeed the fundamental one. The idea, the inspiration, originates in the internal world, the world of the spirit. But, just as the human spirit must incarnate in a body, so must the idea incarnate in an organisation. Whether the organisation be political, religious or social is immaterial to my present argument. The point is that, the idea having embodied itself in organisation, the organisation then proceeds gradually to slay the idea which gave it birth.

We may see this process at work in many fields. Let us take one or two by way of illustration. In the field of religion a prophet, an inspired man, will see a vision of truth. He expresses that vision as best he may in words. He will not say all he saw. For every expression of truth is a limitation of it. But he will, so to speak, express the sense of his vision. What he says is only partly understood by those who hear him; and when they repeat what they understand him to have meant, there will already be a considerable departure from the original vision of the prophet. Upon what his disciples understand of the prophet's message, an organisation, a Church will be built. The half-understood message will crystallise into a creed. Before long the principal concern of the Church will be to sustain itself as an organisation. To this end any departure from the creed must be controverted and if necessary suppressed as heresy. In a few score or a few hundred years what was conceived, as a vehicle of a new and higher truth has become a prison for the souls of men. And men are murdering each other for the love of God. The thing has become its opposite.

In the field of politics the dispossessed dream of a social order, which shall be based on righteousness, a system in which men shall not exploit their fellowmen, in which each shall contribute according to his capacity and each shall receive according to his need. Upon this conception a political party is built. It gives battles, over the years, to the existing order of things. As with the Church, it is not long before the primary concern of the party is to sustain itself. Here, again, any departure from the political creed must be repressed. The 'party line' must be kept straight and dissent kept under. In the course of time the party achieves power. By this time it is led no longer by starry eyed idealists, but by extremely tough guys – who then proceed to use their newly acquired power to establish a stronger despotism than the one they overthrew, and to sew up all the holes in it that they themselves discovered in the old. What emerges is not freedom and social justice, but a more comprehensive and totalitarian control, used to maintain a new privileged class, which, because of the earlier experience of its members, is still more ruthless than the old.

Similar illustrations could be drawn from all fields of life. But these two will suffice to demonstrate the truth with which I am here concerned. It is that, the idea having given birth to the organisation, the organisation develops a self-interest, which has no connection with, and becomes inimical to, the idea with which it began. Now the thing which permits this process of diversion to take place, so that the organisation comes to stand for the opposite of the idea which originally inspired it, is the tendency in men and women to become Prisoners of the Organisation, instead of being Servants of the Spirit. In this tendency there are many elements. There is a sense in which you cannot run an organisation without becoming its prisoner. Organisation has its own necessities, in the interests of which the original idea has to be somewhat qualified. As soon as the idea passes from the unmanifested and embodies itself in the actual, it begins to be invaded by what the poet called 'the world's slow stain'. In this there need be no conscious infidelity on the part of the leaders. Better, they may well argue that the great idea should be only partly manifested than that it should remain merely an idea in vacuo. Better half the ideal loaf than no bread at all.

Next, the wider the area to which the idea is introduced, the larger the circle of men and women to whom it is propagated through the organisation, the more it must be 'stepped down' for propaganda purposes. The idea which gives birth to a party which wants to establish the co-operative commonwealth must be translated into practical proposals, such as the eight hour day, the five day week and what not, if it is to attract a mass backing. And so the organisation becomes less the vehicle of the idea than a channel through which particular interests must be served. The service of such particular interests attracts the backing of other organised bodies more interested in the limited objectives, which the organisation has now adopted than in the great idea itself. And the pressure of such bodies is felt by the organisation, with the result that the idea tends to retreat into the background in favour of less ambitious objectives. In this world the Devil walks, and it is necessary sometimes to hold a candle to the Devil.

Another element is this. Prophets always stand a good chance of being bumped off. This chance is increased if they come down from the hills into the market place, and is still further increased if they come down unarmed. Prophets should only go unarmed into the market place if they think that their work is done, and are prepared to depart hence. Some prophets take to arms. Even where the original prophet does not, his disciples may do so. The organisation, which they build, will almost certainly do so. The Devil must be fought with the Devil's weapons. This is argumentatively sound but practically disastrous. For it means that the servants of God, the disciples of the idea, tend to descendto the Devil's level. As the oganisation grows it deteriorates. Its leaders are not the men they were.

Among the rank and file many things combine to keep them in the organisation, even when they become uneasily conscious that there is a dawning, and even a yawning, gap between organisation and idea. First there is the force of inertia. It is easier not to resign than to resign. Drift is easier than decision. Next there is the factor of personal humility, the tendency to assume that, difficult as the thing seems, the leaders, after all, probably know best. Next there is the factor of sentiment. All of us tend to project onto the organisation of which we are members the virtues we would like it to have, and to be blind to its defects. And, finally, men are gregarious creatures and dislike falling out of the ranks away from the comrades of years. Gradually the organisation changes. As it changes it attracts new elements, which approve the change. Not because of conscious calculation, which comes much later, when the idea has been deserted, but because organisation develops its own logic, its own raison d'être; and because men tend to become the prisoners of the organisation, the organisation can finish up by standing for the precise opposite of the idea which called it into being.

What is the moral to be drawn from all this? One moral, it would not be wholly facetious to suggest, might be that the first rule for any organisation should be a rule providing for its dissolution within a limited period of time. 'This organisation shall be dissolved not later than ...' But the deeper moral is concerned with our attitude to organisation as such. The moral is that even when we are members of an organisation, our attitude to it should be one of partial detachment. We must be above it even while we are in it. We should join it in the knowledge that there we may have no abiding place. We should be weekly tenants; not long lease holders. We should accept no such commitments as would prevent our leaving it when circumstances make this necessary. We should reckon on being in almost perpetual rebellion within it. Above all we should regard all loyalties to organisation as tentative and provisional. The whole concept of 'my party, right or wrong', 'my union, right or wrong', 'my Church, right or wrong', should be utterly alien to our thinking.

We must be Servants of the Spirit, not Prisoners of the Organisation. We must keep in touch with the sources of life, not lose ourselves in its temporary vehicles. And whenever the demand of the spirit, the categorical imperatives of the soul, conflict with the demands of the organisation, it is the first to which we must listen. But all this was said long ago. It is all contained in one of the legendary sayings of Jesus, which bears all the marks of authenticity:

"This world is a bridge. Ye shall pass over it. But ye shall build no houses upon it."

Bivouacs. Yes! Tents. Maybe! Houses. No!

*

Part III

KALEIDOSCOPE

*

2) SOCIO-POLITICO-ECONOMIC

*

● The 'ratcatcher' . . .

The truth about . . . Pied Piper's

EVERY Sunday morning during the summer tourist season, the Pied Piper legend is re-enacted in the town square of Hameln, or Hamelin, a small town near Hannover in Lower Saxony, West Germany. Pastries in the shape of rats are sold as part of the celebration.

But this is no mere show for visitors. Behind the festivities lies a historic tale that so shook the village that it has been retold for 700 years.

Even the exact date is recalled: June 26, 1284, when 130 children are said to have vanished from Hamelin.

Why did they leave? Was there really a Pied Piper?

Like many legends, there is a true story, whose origins become obscure and lost behind later embellishments. The evidence of the tale is revealed in more than the annual drama.

● There is a "Ratcatcher's House" in Hamelin, on which is written a graphic account of the children's disappearance, and other houses with such inscriptions.

● Even more intriguing is the "Street of No Noise" in the medieval quarter, an ancient alley where, for several hundred years, no parade, wedding procession, street dancing, or parties have been allowed – and where children are not allowed to play.

It was down just this alley that the sons and daughters of Hamelin left home, never to return.

ONE FAMOUS account of the fable is Robert Browning's poem, "The Pied Piper of Hamelin: A Child's Story," The dramatic poem recalls the terror of the . . .

"Rats!
They fought the dogs and killed the cats,
And bit the babies in the cradles,
And ate the cheeses out of the vats,
And licked the soup from the cooks' own ladles,
Split open the kegs of salted sprats,
Made nests inside men's Sunday hats,
And even spoiled the women's chats
By drowning their speaking
With shrieking and squeaking
In fifty different sharps and flats."

By FRED FOLDVARY

The villagers complained bitterly about inaction by the city governors:

"To think we buy gowns lined with ermine
For dolts that can't or won't determine
What's best to rid us of our vermin!"

To the rescue came a stranger, tall and thin, wearing a long pied (mottled) coat, and a playing pipe. For 1,000 guilders, he promised to rid Hamelin of all its rats. The astonished mayor and city council were more than glad to agree.

The Piper fluted his way down the streets as "out of the houses the rats came tumbling," until he led them to the Weser River, where all perished but one who swam across and warned all other rats to stay away from Hamelin.

Returning to city hall, the Piper asked for his 1,000 guilders. But the mayor, thinking "what's dead can't come back to life," refused to "pay the Piper," thus not only coining a now familiar phrase but setting the stage for the coming tragedy.

The flutist threatened to "pipe to another fashion," and the mayor mocked him. "Blow your pipe till you burst!"

The Piper played again, this time the "sweet soft notes" that roused the children, who left home to follow him to the nearby Koppelberg Hill, where the mountain opened and the Piper disappeared with the children. Only one child remained, lame and unable to dance the whole way. "Alas, alas for Hamelin!"

THE STORY of the search for the true history behind the tale is as fascinating as the fable itself.

It began in 1934, when Hamelin celebrated a Jubilee Year, the 650th anniversary of the event. The sponsors engaged Heinrich Spanuth, a school principal, to assemble historical material related to the legend. Spanuth discovered so much that it became a permanent museum and Spanuth its curator.

Spanuth, in fact, was a victim of contemporary vermin – the Nazis – and the Piper discovery is closely tied up with the march of events of the 1930s and 40s. He had been fired for being a liberal of the old school, unfit to teach the children of Nazi Germany. The city quietly then gave him this harmless post.

During the Hamelin Jubilee of 1934, there came one Wolfgang Wann, archivist of the city of Troppau (now Opava) in Moravia, central Czechoslovakia. Wann was among the descendents of German colonists who had settled in Czechoslovakia during the Middle Ages, and his mission was to trace the founding of Troppau by settlers from the Weser area. The two scholars agreed to collaborate in the project.

Two years later, they came upon a note written by the philosopher Leibnitz about a 14th century manuscript in Lueneburg, a city 90 miles north of Hamelin. There, in a chronicle called "The Golden Chain," written in Latin in 1370 by the monk Heinrich of Hereford, was a passage on the back of the last page written in English, with the title, Hamelin.

It described a "young man of about 30 years," who led 130 children "out of the East Gate." Also, "the mother of the deacon John of Luede saw the children leave town." John of Luede indeed lived during the mid 1300s and

'Out of the houses the rats came tumbling'

. . . June 26, 1284

. . . of Hamelin

promised land

his mother may have have been a child in Hamelin in the fateful year of 1284 – perhaps too young or lame to join the others?

There is no mention of rats in the Lueneburg account. They were injected much later by religious writers who felt that some divine purpose must have caused the loss of innocent children, and conjured the rats to explain it as punishment for the broken pledge to the "ratcatcher".

But if rats did not cause the exodus, what did?

WOLFGANG Wann's town of Troppau lies in a strategic valley known as the Moravian Gate, near the current Polish border. The town was established in the 13th century by Bishop Bruno, Count of Schaumburg. The main city in Moravia today is his namesake, Brno (sic). The Count wanted to secure this strategic gap by importing immigrants – from Germany. For Bruno himself was a German.

Schaumburg, Bishop Bruno's birthplace, lies on the Weser River just 10 miles from Hamelin. It was quite natural for him to send his recruiters to the Wesser region, promising the colonists new opportunities and land.

The Pied Piper was none other than one of these agents, who came to charm away colonists with his promises as well as by his colourful pied costume and his silver flute!

As Wann dug deeper into the records, he found evidence of former village names, such as Hamelinkow, near Troppau. He discovered still-living families with names such as Hamlinus, Hamler, and Hamel. What clinched the evidence was the uncovering of duplicate 13th century names in the archives of both Hamelin and Troppau, rare names not found elsewhere. Of course it was long known that the original settlers of Troppau were from the Weser land, but now it seemed clear that the exact origin was Hamelin.

Interestingly enough, Browning pointed to that very origin in his poem:

"And I must not omit to say
That in Transylvania there's a tribe
Of alien people who ascribe
The outlandish ways and dress
On which their neighbours lay such
stress
To their fathers and mothers
having risen
Out of some subterraneous prison
Into which they were trepanned
Long ago in a mighty band
Out of Hamelin town in Brunswick
land,
But how or why they don't
understand."

Transylvania is in Romania, not Czechoslovakia; otherwise, this section of Browning's account is remarkable.

Wann himself was a descendant of this German migration and, ironically, having spent a lifetime studying the trek of his ancestors to Czechoslovakia, he became part of the reverse migration from the Sudetenland back to Germany after World War II, when the Germans were expelled.

Among the 60 pounds of hand baggage permitted him were the historic documents of the Hamelin exodus.

But the great question remains: How or why did the Piper have such great success in Hamelin? If not the rats, what force led to the loss of such a great portion of the town's youth? Here is Dr. Wann's explanation:

"Hamelin in 1284 was a social pressure cooker, a walled town of 2,000 residents and growing fast. But to be a citizen, one had to be a burger, a property owner, and a few grasping patrician families held everything. They owned the crowded housing, and refused to expand the town walls. They owned all the woods around Hamelin, and reserved for themselves cutting privileges, fuel for the cold winters. Moreover, in land speculation, they had bought up all the open fields around Hamelin, thus driving into town many dispossessed peasants, an angry proletariat. These uprooted farmers, or, more likely, their land-hungry sons and daughters, were natural volunteers in the Piper's offer of a new deal.*

The "children", then, were young adults, who left the wretched conditions of Hamelin to settle on land of their own – this promise of land was the "music" that lured them away.

AN IRONY of the story is that in the legend, the city fathers caused the exodus by their greed.

In historical fact, after the departure of the "children", they smothered all record of it, fearing that it could happen again. Though the city archives were well kept, there is no mention of the exodus of June 26, 1284.

But the common folk of Hamelin, in anguish over their loss, kept the memory alive and passed it down to the present day.

One question remains – why June 26?

It was the date of the summer solstice celebration, still observed in Saxony. This long day was perfect for the departure, and the long summer daylight hours would allow more time for the journey. Wann's theory is that there was a mass nuptual then, with some 60 marriages and much feasting and dancing, just before the trek to the east, when the youths were led through the East gate by the triumphant Piper, to their promised land.

Today, when a bride is married in Hamelin, the wedding procession is silent when it passes through "The Street of No Drums and Trumpets."

What a testimony to the age-old curse of concentration of land and power in a few hands.

*The remarkable research by Dr's. Spanuth and Wann was reported in "What Happened to These Children?" by James P. O'Donnell, *Saturday Evening Post,* Dec. 24, 1955. It also appeared in "The Pied Piper of Hamelin: The True Story" by John Henry Richter, in *Topical Time,* March/April 1982, published by the American Topical Association (based on the earlier article). The stamp illustrated in the article was issued by West Germany in 1978. Robert Browning's poem appears in *The Poems and Plays of Robert Browning,* The Modern Library, New York, 1934.

There were no rats – just greedy landowners

Land and Liberty
(With acknowledgements.)

THE LAW OF RENT - becomes

-(see diagonal arrows on chart)-

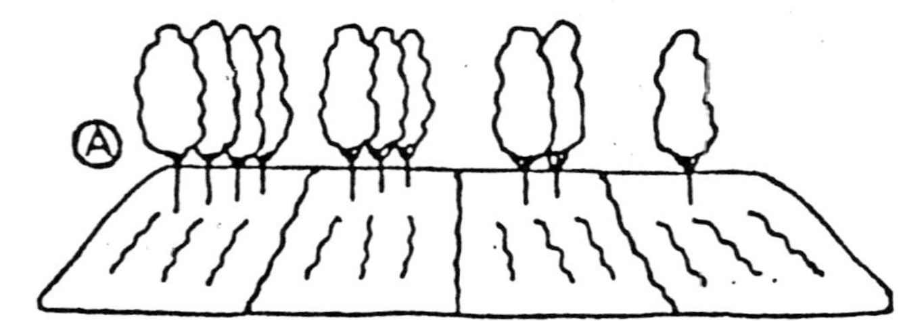

A — Different Grades of Land

Here are four sections of a piece of land, with fruit trees. For simplicity, let us assume you can get one bushel of fruit from each tree. On the best section, where four trees are growing (at left) you can get four bushels in one day. On the next section, with the same day's labor, you can get only three bushels. On the next land two, and on the worst (at right), only one.

B — First Comer — All Wages

So far, all this land is free. When the first man comes to pick fruit, which land will he appropriate? Naturally, the best. The best land is then the margin of production (indicated by the dotted line). With one day's labor he gathers four bushels. They are all his wages - the reward for his exertion.

C — Second Comer — Rent Begins

The next comer has to be content with the three-tree section. (This now becomes the margin of production). With one day's labor he can get only three bushels - they are his wages.

These two men work the same- still one gets four bushels, and the other only three. Why? Because of the difference of the land. The four-bushel land has a rent. Since it is one bushel superior, its rent is one (above the black line). Wages are three on both lands.

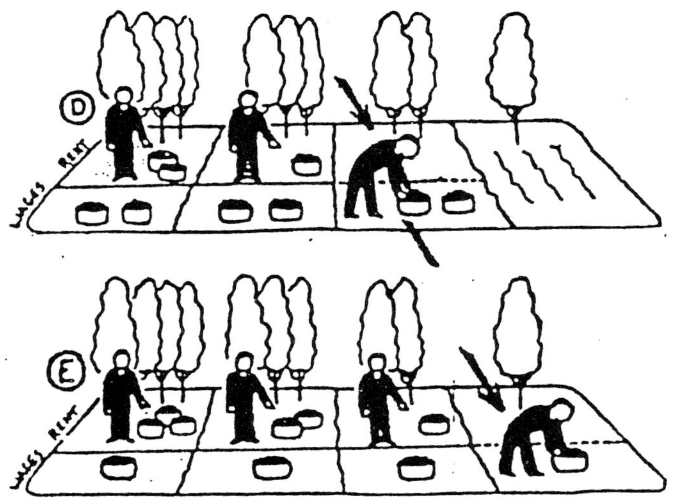

D — Third Comer — Further Rise of Rent

The third comer has to use the two-bushel land. (This land now becomes the margin.) The two bushels he gathers are his wages. The three-bushel land now has a rent of one, and the four-bushel land a rent of two. Wages on all lands are two. If this third comer wanted to work on the three-bushel land, its owner would give him only two wages and take one as rent. And if he were to work on the best land, that owner could demand a rent of two, leaving two as wages. That's all the third owner could get working for himself on his two-bushel land. The rent represents what the land-owners can get without working, but solely by virtue of their ownership.

E — Fourth Comer — All Land Used

The fourth comer arrives and the only land left is the worst land, on which he can get only one bushel. Now all the other lands have a rent in proportion to their superiority over this land (which is now the margin of production).

F — Other Natural Differences

The operation of rent applies with any factor that makes one piece of land superior to other lands. There are other besides agricultural differences. A good harbor makes land around it valuable. The land further away is less valuable.

— With acks. to the Henry George Foundation. (See Address List.) —

G — Growth of Population

Here is a good piece of agricultural land that yields four. People settle in one section of it, and a town grows up there. Though land within the town is no more fertile than the land outside, a productiveness of a new kind has arisen. Through cooperation and specialization of labor, that section of the land is of much greater productivity. It now yields forty instead of four. If the four land were free, rent within the town would be thirty-six.

H — Effect of Industrial Growth

Industries grow up, new machines are invented and much more can be produced. The productivity of industrial lands has become seventy, which is greater than the town's productivity of forty. Since more is produced, new materials are needed, and this extends the margin of production to land that yields only one. Wages then become one, and rent is the excess of all superior lands.

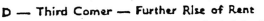

– THE LAW OF THE DEPRESSION OF WAGES.......

*

(As presented in my earlier "The Land Question", 1981.)

Kaleidoscope

476

To Members of the Scot. Land Consn.

LAND HOLDINGS TO BE ASSESSED ACCORDING TO SIZE? - OR VALUE?

T H E   T W O   D O   N O T   M I X

Do some of us hold the belief that we can go forward reforming land tenure on the basis of both size and value?

This is not a well thought-out belief.

To attempt to institute a land reform which mixes together assessments of land according to size as well as value will only prove the root of confusion.

The holding of one man may turn out to be of more value - (location, for access or other advantage? - quality of soil? - mineral deposits?) - than that of another which is twice its size. The holder of the larger area will then point out that the other man's holding should be reduced in size before his - and he will equally feel unjustly penalised at being "regulated", (by whatever regulatory "land use" bodies may have the misfortune to be set up),* when the far superior, smaller holding is exempted from such interference.

As in other spheres of life, radicalness goes hand in hand with SIMPLICITY.

A truly virtuous RADICAL reform does not ask for superficial regulatory devices to be imposed upon it - and will do ill with them.

The trouble is that our society has travelled so long the path of superficiality, (with which our education system is riddled),** that we do not recognise any more the nature of the radical, or what it can do for us, or teach us. (Excepting, that is to say, for those who have ventured on similarly radical pathways, such as natural healing, organic cultivation, etc.)

** See 'green' leaflet

Radical land reform will therefore require a considerable re-educational drive - while we allow it to disburden us, along its way, of all those false grants and other artificial props of our artificially constituted land-use practices today.

But if assessments according to size and value cannot be mixed, and it is value that is paramount even in the countryside - how much more is this so in our towns and in our cities, where the pre-eminent factor is so glaringly value, and where it affects by far the larger part of our population?

This, then, is part of the beauty of radical land reform: that it deals equally simply - and equally justly - with all land, wherever situated. And this is necessary of the land reform we choose, for "the land question is...a question that affects every man, every woman, and every child", and those who would set on foot land reform in Scotland must not be found to favour one section of the population above another.

May I leave you with "The Land for the People", from whose opening paragraph I have just quoted - one of the basic addresses by Henry George on this great question.

---

* We can do nothing better, or wiser, than to leave people alone - leave them to find out what kind of use of land they find their own way to making. What the land needs more than anything is the richest yield of imaginative ideas in the sphere of land use - to make up for the centuries of stultified thought reflected in our stultified landscape; and these ideas can only come from individuals, not from committees.

For any corporate body - a far better and more vital task lies right to hand: that is, to gather together and disseminate all information available on the pioneering projects that are already a-foot, and that we hear too little of; as in tree-planting, rock dust application, super-quality food production, environmental and low-cost housing, herbs for healing - (essential as drug-based therapies prove ever more problemmatical), etc. In short, there is plenty to be done by all, once the land is freed - and indeed, most of those who can only hope for "a job" on some land-use regulatory body today may well, under just land reform, find themselves more fulfilled being involved directly in land-use projects themselves.

This refers to what I had understood re the S.N.P.'s land policy proposals at that time. S.A.H. March 97.

THE ROCKS
PITLOCHRY
PERTHSHIRE PH16 5QZ

15 May 96

Birthright...and...Scotland Today

Shirley-Anne Hardy

Extracts from:
"Why the German Republic Fell" *

– by Austrian journalist, Bruno Heilig, a leading journalist of his time, who recorded Hitler's rise to power as foreign editor/correspondent of newspapers in Austria, Germany, Hungary and the Balkans, and later survived Dachau and Buchenwald to write his book, "Men Crucified".

* *(Published by **Land and Liberty**, an organ of the Henry George Foundation, U.K.)*

Germany, it seems to me, has provided a striking example supporting the theory that the private appropriation of the rent of land is the fundamental cause of industrial depression and of distress among those who labour in the production of wealth – the theory expounded by Henry George in his *Progress and Poverty*, a theory that some professed teachers of social science have been strangely slow in accepting, whether from ignorance or prejudice is for them to say. For my part, a conclusion has been arrived at not by prior theoretical study but rather by attendance upon the circumstances I have recounted. It was not until I had arrived in England as a refugee journalist that by good fortune the book fell into my hands, to be read with increasing interest and excitement for the light it shed upon what I had seen taking place. The economic demonstration was complete, at least I could discover in it no defect. Yet why had Germany taken the road from individual political liberty through mass hysteria to the surrender of all liberty and the despotic "leadership" of one man? Was there a link between the economic and the political collapse? Emphatically, yes. For as unemployment grew, and with it poverty and the fear of poverty, so grew the influence of the Nazi Party, which was making its lavish promises to the frustrated and its violent appeal to the revenges of a populace aware of its wrongs but condemned to hear only a malignant and distorted explanation of them.

......The wall painter and corporal was of course not to the taste of the German landlords but in the most important problem he has not betrayed his sponsors. He did not touch the land problem. He only added to the class of Junkers that of the "Erbhofbauern" (peasants owning land under entail and prohibited from mortgaging), thus creating a new hereditary class of middle-sized land monopolists. So we see how the land question repeatedly got into the hub of political life at every turn as the German Republic drove to its fate.

Similar conditions will be of the same effect everywhere. What happened in Germany will inevitably happen anywhere that similar conditions prevail. In some Continental countries it has happened already. The Nazi regime is not Hitler's, the man's, achievement. Nazidom has grown organically out of a rotten democracy, and the rottenness of that democracy is the natural consequence of unequal economic conditions: and unequal economic conditions obtain all over the world owing to the instituted private appropriation of the rent of land. Therefore every country is potentially a Fascist country. Germany is but the type of a development which no country can escape except by the establishment of the equal right to the occupation and use of land. therefore also there can be no lasting peace even after the defeat of Nazism if the present economic structure of the civilized countries remains. The private appropriation of the rent of land is the deadly enemy of mankind.

"SIZE OR VALUE?"

The Scottish Land Commission, set up by the Scottish National Party in the earlier 1990s, held meetings in a number of locations around Scotland, where they invited the local people to come and give their views on the land question.

I attended the session held in Pitlochry in April 1996, at the Atholl Palace Hotel, and spoke on land rent reform. Afterwards I sent to the Commissioners two or three lots of follow-up material - (seeing that this fundamental economic reform is not one that is widely known) - and was told by one of the Commissioners that it had been well received. I place here, to the left, that dated 15 May 96 on a fundamental aspect of the reform.

Birthright...and
...Scotland Today

"NAZI ROOTS OF THE EUROPLOT"

Such is the heading to a review, in The Ecologist of Nov-Dec 98, of a recently published book by John Laughland

"The Tainted Source, (Warner Books, ISBN 0-7515-2324-0, £8.99), shows that the concept of a United Europe "comes from the world of giant business, banking and power-broking; in short, not from the ordinary citizen body but from people whose gimlet eyes are on money or power or both. John Laughland proceeds in this remarkable book to spell it out in both historical and philosophical depth to a quite riveting degree, one which cannot fail to put the reader deeply in his debt."

As the reviewer, John Papworth, continues: "He makes it clear, and his reference sources alone run to over sixty pages, that in the modern era the concept has its roots unambiguously in Nazi Germany. The same slogans, the same arguments, the same anti-democratic attitudes of mind, the same contempt for people and the same gruesome assumption that economic consideration must take precedence over any other citizen concern all lead to the same conclusion: that its banner, a circle of gold stars on a blue background, is incomplete without a black Nazi swastika in its centre."

(With acknowledgements to John Papworth, and to The Ecologist.)

*

VIEW FROM CROATIA

A friend of mine found himself travelling on a bus last summer (98) in the company of a young Croatian man, who was over here with his wife visiting her family in Scotland.

The Croatian was a horticulturist and grew, especially, a lot of fruit. Asked how he found the fruit and vegetables bought in our shops over here, he replied that, to be honest, he found them watery and tasteless. "When I take a peach from my garden and dig my teeth into it, I know it's a peach I'm eating. It tastes like one."

Asked about the Common Market, and whether Croatia would be likely to join it, his reply was definite: "No. We live on the borders of Italy, and we see what it means to the Italian farmers. It may appear advantageous at first, but it ends in tying them up in knots."

(Just like chemical agriculture!)

THE EUROPEAN UNION

Letter published in
The Courier,
7th January, 1999.

With acknowledgements to
Mr William W. Scott
and The Courier

*

Betrayed by politicians

Sir,—Before 1972, the power in this country was held in the hands of the people. At election time that power was given to Parliament for a period of not more than five years when it was returned to the people who then had the opportunity to decide once again who best to trust.

The people trusted the politicians to hand that power back to them in its entirety when a general election was called and this they did until Ted Heath betrayed that trust. Margaret Thatcher, John Major and Tony Blair have followed in his treasonable footsteps.

In no manifesto were we told we would become citizens of a foreign state, that our territorial waters would be surrendered, that our laws would be subservient to a court furth our shores or that our taxes would be controlled by bankers in a foreign land. Indeed, since 1972, we have been assured there would be no loss of our sovereignty.

If our present Prime Minister takes us into the European Single Currency, then Ted Heath's ambition will have been fulfilled and it will be a waste of time voting in a general election.

The British people will, I am sure, be consumed by a terrible rage once they realise how they have been betrayed.

William W. Scott.
23 St Baldred's Road,
North Berwick.

*

Published in 1971, this article (speaking so particularly to Scotland) refers to the Common Market - the name by which the European Union was first marketed to us. (The Scots Secretariat is now no longer in existence. See Part II, ch. 1.)

THE COMMON MARKET AND SCOTLAND

By WILLIAM H. MARWICK

Published in the *Scottish Journal of Science* Volume 1, Part 3, pages 151-155 September, 1971

The Scots Secretariat
Jess Cottage, Carlops, Penicuik, Midlothian, Scotland.

THE COMMON MARKET is politically a combination of a few states, and economically an example of capitalist concentration, against the rest of the world. It seeks to maximise material production irrespective of social values. A true internationalism would comprise small self-governing nations, such as Scotland, abjuring power politics and developing their peculiar gifts, economically and culturally, for mutual benefit.

"NARROW NATIONALISM" is the parrot cry with which opponents of the Common Market are condemned by its partisans, who profess the higher virtue of "internationalism." No word is more misused in current controversies. Defined in the Oxford Dictionary as "existing, carried on between different nations," it implies as a pre-condition the existence and activities of NATIONS. Properly interpreted, nationalism and internationalism are complementary rather than contradictory. Most mischievous is the disingenuous practice of describing organisations comprising a few nation states such as NATO and the Common Market as "international." The limitation of outlook to Europe indeed indicates a narrow Continentalism.

Since the medieval dawn of the modern nation, the Scots have singularly exhibited a right relation between nationalism and internationalism. Their special contacts, political and cultural, with France, the Netherlands and Scandinavia are a particular example. In our own time such a man as Boyd Orr has personally illustrated their compatibility. There are absurd suggestions that entry will bring to the British people greater opportunities of cultural contacts. This is merely an appeal to those who are presumed to look to something higher than trade. It is dishonestly implied that to reject entry involves a self-centred and self-sufficing isolationism, a withdrawal from the official and voluntary organisations- e.g., ILO, FAO, the World Council of Churches, bodies of trade unionists, scientists, etc. Rather will British exclusion from the Common Market, which ties them to a sectional group, tend to strengthen its connections with Europe as a whole and the world at large.

The English, since their first aggression in Ireland have, despite the opposition of their finest spirits, tended to convert nationalism into imperialism, domination of other nations. Only now, when, as even such a jingo as Kipling, in a moment of truth forecast, "all our vaunted pomp and show is one with Nineveh and Tyre" and the British Lion, once monarch of the jungle, has become a tame performing animal in the Pentagon menagerie, have the former imperialists been reduced to seeking participation in the power and profits of other European nations.

U.S.A. has succeeded to Great Britain's former position, illustrated chiefly by its dealings with Latin America and Eastern Asia; an American flag has even been planted on the Moon.

American capital contributed largely to the economic recovery of Germany after both World Wars. It persistently penetrates the British economy, whether by new enterprises or the take over of native firms – particularly in Scotland. This is sometimes short-sightedly regarded as beneficial; the truth is that profits are meantime drained across the Atlantic, and the frequent abandonment of unprofitable sections chronically increases unemployment. Some of the Market's protagonists defend British participation as a means of escaping American domination. The continuing share of American capital, not only in Germany but in the other Western European states demonstrates the fallacy of this hope. Another example is the havoc caused within the Market by Nixon's manipulation of the Almighty Dollar. The domination of cosmopolitan (largely American) finance is in no way undermined by the Common Market, whose members retain their own currency systems; the financial link is the weakest in their chain. The financial monopoly ("never did so many OWE so much to so few") is unassailed. Not England but U.S.A. is the chief menace to genuine Scottish self-government.

In the earlier part of this century, British and German industrialists became rivals. The Germans, after twice vainly endeavouring to gain supremacy by military means, now seek to gain it by economic means. British industrialists waged an economic war with protective tariffs and after fomenting anti-German hysteria in both Wars, now seek partnership with the former enemy.

The notion of helping to create a "European Community" deceives some of the very elect, who with naive sentimentalism picture it as ending old animosities and promoting world peace. Religious apologists such as the British Council of Churches in their Report (1967, revised 1971) seek to sanctify it by sprinkling a little holy water over it; as they have sought to conscript the Lord to win their battles, now they would conscript him to ensure their entry to the Market. Some Scottish churchmen have shown a wiser appreciation of realities. George MacLeod founder of the Iona Community and the best known figure in the Church of Scotland, has devoted his rhetorical talent to damning the Market; another leader of the Kirk, Rev. John Gray, describes it as "a sordid conspiracy of the rich to exploit the poor" (*Scotsman*, 23/10/70).

Naive Cupidity

Many besides J.B. Priestley (*New Statesman*, 13/8/71) must have been disgusted by the vulgar advertising to "sell" the Market to the ordinary citizen by proclaiming the material advantages of joining. Their expensiveness betrays the sordid aims of the real promoters. He terms the Market "a tycooning job, a high pressure sales job, a big power block job." The Government's *Fact Sheets* seek popular support primarily by promises of "pie in the Market", as visionary as "pie in the sky." Its crude appeal to cupidity makes the naive idealists of European unity look foolish. Increasingly, pro-Market propaganda relies on forecasts of the future rather than present realities. Sometimes forecasts are given a pseudo-scientific form by a parade of statistics and their unscientific extrapolation. This reaches its nadir (e.g. *Edinburgh Post*, 26/8/71) by prophesying disaster unless we enter the Market; "it is a matter of sink or swim, prosper or perish"; seeking to intimidate the electorate by an appeal to their superstitious fears, much as the old time preacher threatened future torment to all who rejected his gospel.

Still more pernicious is the "American Way of Life," denounced as it is by the best social thinkers and creative writers of U.S.A. (e.g., Mumford, Galbraith). In the economic sphere, it advocates the "economics of growth," propounded by W.W. Rostow, an "adviser" of the Government, insisting on the perpetual increase of material production, irrespective of the social value of what is produced, and under what conditions. This has become orthodox doctrine for most British economists, with such notable exceptions as E.J. Mishan and E.F. Schumacher. It is the "philosophy" of the Common Marketeers. Its complement is the artificial encouragement of wasteful and harmful consumption, the exploitation of the "Affluent Sheep," and the destruction of irreplaceable natural resources and of environmental amenities, e.g., by pollution of the atmosphere. It is the superstition of "the bigger the better," the fallacy of "gigantism." Whether under private or state ownership, economic enterprises tend to monopolistic combination, destroying for the consumer whatever protection the former competition may have given him. The shameful destruction of "surplus" food, especially in France, in accordance with the regulations of the Market, is recurrently reported – (e.g., *Scotsman*, 24/8/71), "While millions starve, vast quantities of unwanted foodstuffs are piling up in the Common Market. . .Taxpayers are shelling out around £25 millions a year for produce that ends up on the rubbish tips" (*Observer*, 8/9/68). Supporters have had to admit that membership of the Market would involve increased cost of living; now it is cynically affirmed that that would happen anyway. The real economic problems, particularly that of inflation, are ignored, or referred to the magicians in Brussels or Strasbourg.

A more probable danger to the survival of civilisation than even the atomic bomb is that of population outrunning the means of subsistence, accelerated by the growing demands of the undeveloped countries for higher standards, at the expense of the Western World. The myth of ever-increasing standards of material livelihood, fostered by politicians of all parties, must be countered by asserting the superior value of a way of life which is "simple but beautiful."

Social Ethics

Scotland may well set an example of this; its own resources are adequate to provide a decent livelihood for present numbers, and it can export sufficient surplus to acquire some of the amenities of life. The "Market philosophy" of Affluence indeed runs counter to the traditional ethos of Scotland, which has "cultivated the muses on a little oatmeal." Catholicism and Calvinism at their best alike insisted on a SOCIAL ethic, not mere individual piety, but a righteous nation. Likewise both the medieval scholastics and the rationalists of the Enlightenment, such as Adam Smith and David Hume, regarded Political Economy as a branch of Moral Philosophy.

Whether the Union of 1707 was mainly responsible for Scottish later 18th century economic growth is doubted by some competent historians. It is at least plausible to argue that, like the Scandinavian countries, Scotland might have avoided part of the worst evils of rapid industrialisation if it had made its own slower but more balanced development.

It seems strange that Liberals, professing belief in freedom of trade, should advocate membership of an "economic community" which imposes tariff barriers against the rest of the world, and involves intricate government intervention, bureaucratic interference, and a further development of the pernicious policy of using indirect taxation as an arbitrary attempt to direct economic activity, rather than for its legitimate purpose of raising funds necessary to meet public expenditure. We have already suffered from this in the form of "protective" tariffs, purchase tax and S.E.T. Under the common Market we should be subjected to the still more vicious "Value-Added Tax," whose complicated mechanism would also involve an increase in unproductive personnel to administer it.

The Labour Party relies on the inherent anti-Conservatism of the Scottish people to prefer a party of the Left, however equivocal its policy. The late Government's "pragmatic" bolstering up of capitalism was a departure from the ethical basis of Scottish socialism, adumbrated in the chartist Churches, and inspiring the teaching of Keir Hardie and James Maxton. That nationalism and socialism are interdependent was their belief; and that, in their varied interpretations, was the faith of Cunninghame Graham, Roland Muirhead, John Maclean, James Barr and Hugh Macdiarmid. No misconception of Socialism is falser than Robens' definition (*Observer*, 22/8/71) as "the belief that the state should own the whole of the means of production, distribution and exchange," which has produced those travesties of Socialism, the "public corporations." The founding fathers of Socialism looked forward to the "withering away of the State," not to the proliferation of its tentacles which the Common Market further fosters with its bureaucratic centralisation.

Remote Control

By the terms of the Treaty of Rome, adhesion to the Common Market is declared irrevocable. No constitutional method of withdrawal exists. Any country strongly opposed to its policy can secede only forcibly, unless its inhabitants are all converted to Gandhism. This provision is more likely to promote strife than to abate it. There is no provision for the abolition of national armies. Demands on Britain might lead to the reintroduction of conscription, an accepted institution in the western European countries.

It is claimed with considerable force (whatever legal quibbles may be raised), that British acceptance of the Treaty of Rome involves yet another breach of the Treaty of Union between Scotland and England, of 1707.

The British Government's involvement in NATO has inflicted on Scotland the profanation of the Holy Loch and the destruction of the amenities of South Uist. Its economic complement, the common Market, will inflict similar disadvantages, determined by the bureaucratic oligarchy which administers it. Scotland has suffered the sabotage of its railways by Beeching, whose genius it required £24,000 a year to evoke, and which in practice resolved itself into the trite commonplace of reducing services and increasing charges. The still more remote control which Common Market direction implies, increases liability to neglect of Scotland's distinctive requirements.

George Younger incautiously admitted that while only 25 per cent of the public were in favour of E.E.C. entry, the majority of business men were (*Scotsman*, 26/6/71). A more recent estimate by its promoters confirms this for Scotland at any rate (*Scotsman*, 27/8/71). Denmark and Norway are so economically dependent on Britain that their Governments feel bound to follow suit in applying for entry. Their Social-Democratic parties, as compromising as our own, may genuinely approve, but there is growing opposition from those who adhere to Socialist principles; and indeed many conservatives also object.

The shallow cosmopolitanism which, by promoting similarity or identity, whether in food, clothing and housing, or in the arts and literature, is destroying all variety and diversity – a chief glory of creation, of nature and of man – must be challenged by an assertion of the peculiar gifts of each nation; the modern renascence of a native Scottish literature is one example. The assertion that the "day of small nations is over" was as premature as it is mischievous. Atomic weapons have produced a stalemate between the great power groups of NATO and the Warsaw Pact. The chief factor making for war is the repression of small nationalities within states, notably Biafra in Nigeria and Bangladesh in Pakistan. Examples nearer hand, as yet less violent, are the Bretons in France, the Flemings in Belgium, the Basques in Spain.

No historical generalisation is truer than Acton's:- "All power corrupts, absolute power corrupts utterly!" The power politics of the great states and alliances of states is a chief menace to humanity. A world state might eliminate liberty. The small nations, abjuring power politics, developing each its peculiar social and cultural gifts in the service of all, offer the happiest prospects.

REFERENCES

ANTI-COMMON MARKET LEAGUE, 1967, revised 1970. Joining the Common Market.
BRITISH COUNCIL OF CHURCHES, 1967, revised 1971. Christians and the Common Market S.C.M. Press.
DELL, S. 1963. Trade Blocs and Common Markets. Constable.
DENIAU, J.F. 1959, translated 1960, Third Edn., 1963. The Common Market. Barrie & Rockcliff.
EINZIG, P. 1971. The Case Against Joining the Common Market. Macmillan.
EVANS, DOUGLAS, Editor. 1971. Challenge or Crisis: A Symposium.

HENDERSON, W.O. 1962. The Genesis of the Common Market. F. Cass & co.
JAY, DOUGLAS. 1968. After the Common Market. Penguin Special.
JENSEN, W.G. 1967. The Common Market. Foulis.
KITZINGER, W. 1962. Challenge of the Common Market. Blackwood.
LIPPMAN, W. 1967. Western unity and the Common Market. Hamish Hamilton.
LOMAS, A. 1971. The Common Market; Why We Should Keep Out. London Co-op Society.
MISHAN, E.J. 1969. The Costs of Economic Growth. Pelican Books (first published 1967.)
NORTHERN FRIENDS' PEACE BOARD. 1971. Friends and the Common Market.
PINDER, J. 1961. Britain and the Common Market. Cresset Press.
RESTOW, W.W. 1960. The Stages of Economic Growth. Cambridge University Press.
SCHUMACHER, E.F. 1920. Economic Development and Poverty.
SCHUMACHER, E.F. 1970-71. Articles in Resurgence, vols. i and ii. 24 Abercorn Place, St. John's Wood, London, N.W.8.
STATIONERY OFFICE, H.M. 1970. Fact Sheets on Britain and Europe. Nos. 1 and 2.
STRAUSS, E. 1958. Common Sense and the Common Market. Allen & Unwin.

*

"SECRET GROUP THAT RULES THE WORLD?"

The *Scotsman* of 11th May (1998) described a "hugely influential and highly secretive 'shadow world government' which was meeting in Scotland. The Bilderberg group consists of between 115 and 120 of the world's most powerful businessmen, financiers and politicians (including some of our own), which in its 44-year history has been accused of creating business conglomerates more powerful than national governments and influencing the creation of the European superstate for its own ends.

Sounds like sensational fiction? It seems not. With its roots in Nazi Germany the group was created by Prince Bernhard of the Netherlands "with a vision of 'globalization' - a one-world government...The secretive group has been accused of creating the European Union, prompting wars and engineering the fall of unfriendly governments."

Why do we not hear more of this in the Press? It appears that one of the group's members, Hollinger plc, controls over 130 newspapers.

For the meeting in Scotland "they arrived in black limousines with smoked windows, protected by armed men and the kind of security reserved for people who rule the world." (*Scotsman* 15th May) If Bilderberg is a force for good, why is this necessary? Jim Tucker, veteran reporter of *The Spotlight*, Washington-based weekly, says "They are controlling the world and making decisions that influence the world with absolutely no democratic control."

Attenders at their meetings are often financed by the group and some are asked to attend officially by their governments (including our own), but no statements are ever made. It is all very intriguing, to say the least, and Rodney Ackland has published a great deal of information on Bilderberg in his book *"Europe: Full Circle"*.

Published by the Farm & Food Society: Newsletter, Sept. 1998.
4, Willifield Way, London NW11 7XT.

Extract from Ch.4 of

OUR ENEMY THE STATE

by A.J. Nock

First published in 1946.
Republished in 1973, by Free Life Editions In., N.Y.,
and in 1983 by
Hallberg Publishing Corp.,
Delavan, Wisconsin, USA.

*

After conquest and confiscation have been effected, and the State set up, its first concern is with the land. The State assumes the right of eminent domain over its territorial basis, whereby every landholder becomes in theory a tenant of the State. In its capacity as ultimate landlord, the State distributes the land among its beneficiaries on its own terms. A point to be observed in passing is that by the State system of land tenure each original transaction confers two distinct monopolies, entirely different in their nature in as much as one concerns the right to labour-made property, and the other concerns the right to purely law-made property. The one is a monopoly on the use value of land; and the other, a monopoly of the economic rent of land. The first gives the right to keep other persons from using the land in question, or trespassing on it, and the right to exclusive possession of values accruing from the application of labour to it; values, that is, which are produced by exercise of the economic means upon the particular property in question. Monopoly of economic rent, on the other hand, gives the exclusive right to values accruing from the desire of other persons to possess that property; values which take their rise irrespective of any exercise of the economic means on the part of the holder.[1]

Economic rent arises when, for whatsoever reason two or more persons compete for the possession of a piece of land, and it increases directly according to the number of persons competing. The whole of Manhattan Island was bought originally by a handful of Hollanders from a handful of Indians for twenty-four dollars' worth of trinkets. The subsequent 'rise in land values', as we call it was brought about by the steady influx of population and the consequent high competition for portions of the island's surface; and these ensuing values were monopolised by the holders. They grew to an enormous size, and the holders profited accordingly; the Astor, Wendel, and Trinity Church Estates have always served as classical examples for study of the State system of land tenure.

Bearing in mind that the State is the organisation of the political means – that its primary intention is to enable the economic exploitation of one class by another – we see that it has always acted on the principle already cited, that expropriation must

[1] *The economic rent of the Trinity Church Estate in New York City, for instance, would be as high as it is now, even if the holders had never done a stroke of work on the property. Landowners who are holding a property 'for a rise' usually leave it idle, or improve it only to the extent necessary to clear its taxes; the type of building commonly called a 'tax payer' is a familiar sight everywhere. Twenty five years ago a member of the New York City Tax Commission told me that by careful estimate there was almost enough vacant land within the city limits to feed the population, assuming that all of it were arable and put under intensive cultivation!*

precede exploitation. There is no other way to make the political means effective. The first postulate of fundamental economics is that man is a land animal, deriving his subsistence wholly from the land.[2] His entire wealth is produced by the application of labour and capital to land; no form of wealth known to man can be produced in any other way. Hence, if his free access to land be shut off by legal preëmption, he can apply his labour and capital only with the land holder's consent, and on the landholder's terms; in other words, it is at this point, and this point only, that exploitation becomes practicable.[3] Therefore the first concern of the State must be invariably, as we find it invariably is, with its policy of land tenure.

---

[2] *As a technical term in economics, land includes all natural resources, earth, air, water, sunshine, timber and minerals in situ, etc. Failure to understand this use of the term has seriously misled some writers, notably Count Tolstoy.**

* (In his use of terms, I would concede - as I have myself noted in his writings here and there; but not, I think, in his understanding of the principle. See "Tolstoy: Principles for a New World Order", by David Redfearn. Henry George Foundation catalogue - in Address List. S-A.H.)

[3] *Hence there is actually no such thing as a 'labour problem', for no encroachment on the rights of either labour or capital can possibly take place until all natural resources within reach have been preëmpted. What we call the 'problem of the unemployed' is in no sense a problem, but a direct consequence of State created monopoly.*

*

PRIZE QUOTATION OF 1986

"We want to see landlords being rewarded for letting land under security of tenure – tax grants for letting land.".

(*From a Scottish farming television programme.*)

Shirley-Anne Hardy, 15 Jan. 87.

*

Jim Crumley – A PERSONAL VIEW

A SIMPLE EQUATION

THE COURIER

6 Oct 98.

We have stepped this way before. The subject of national parks for Scotland has been visited so often in the last 50 years that it begins to resemble the morass of the erosion scars up Ben Lawers.

There remains this discernible difference: Ben Lawers still has a far-sighted and thought-provoking view from the top, whereas the summit of national park thinking has all the clarity and vision of a whiteout, but with none of that mountain phenomenon's elemental potency.

The new proposals from Scottish Natural Heritage are not new at all, but trample the same familiar ground, compounding the already barren wastes, aping the small-scale small-budget, small-minded approach to national parks in England and Wales where all that has prospered is the most demeaning species of car-dominated tourism, where staff spend their working hours and their working budgets on damage limitation instead of landscape conservation and where the "protected" landscapes wilt and wither under the relentless burdens of tourist promotion.

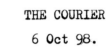

The word "wilderness" has been extinct for decades.

Is that what we want? It is what we are about to get if we buy what is on offer, if we swallow whole the latest proposals. Nothing is surer than they will be under-funded, and that the philosophies (and salaries) of bureaucrats and uniformed park wardens will supersede the needs of the landscape.

There is not a word about how the landscape will benefit. Not a word about how bureaucrats in Edinburgh (why do the Government's countryside advisers live in a city?) will improve the landscape of, to begin with, Loch Lomond and the Cairngorms, so that nature is in better heart than it is now.

Surprise, surprise. This is, after all, the organisation which declined to object to a funicular railway on Cairn Gorm with a projected visitor total of 250,000 a year. If Scottish Natural Heritage cannot man the barricades in the most resolute defence of the Cairngorms of all places, then it is not entitled to lay claim to any of the three words in its title.

The word "protection" is used as if there was some idea how protection would be achieved, as if there was a difficult problem to resolve.

In a place like the Cairngorms, the landscape needs protection from only one source: people. Only people have degraded the land, permitted its decline and sustained the decline. The national park model which is being pursued will have one consequence in particular. It will hugely increase the pressure of people.

Remove the pressure, and you remove the problem, or a least you begin to remove the problem. then, with the problem eased, you begin to assist the cause of nature by native tree planting, deer and sheep management (which bluntly means massive culls), and the restoration of every native habitat.

It is a simple equation. It does not need a national park. It needs a different approach to land and to nature, one which should be explored not by this tired and discredited regime but by the galvanising impetus for change which will be an inevitable consequence of the Scottish Parliament.

So the current SNH proposals are as ill-timed as they as ill-judged. It will not benefit our landscape that we enter a new era of our history having newly burdened ourselves with a philosophy of land management borrowed from the dregs of a failed system in England and Wales.

Let's wait until the shackles are cut, let's look around at our land and let's make a fresh start at looking after it.

So while we gather round the bonfire fuelled by every copy of the SNH report, it's worth considering what a Scottish Parliament might contemplate instead of what we have just consigned to the flames.

Change matters. Change is already happening. The pattern of land ownership is changing, and more community and conservation owned land is inevitable. Good. People working the land in a small, thoughtful way, will always be a better proposition than people not working it in a big, thoughtless way. In a small country like Scotland of all places, that is a truism. We should match the diversity of nature with diversity in land ownership and land use.

Given that the process is already begun, and has emerged from the people on the land itself rather than from bureaucrats and politicians, why don't we simply encourage the process?

Land ownership which BEGINS as a partnership between community and conservation will not need to have solutions thrust upon it from outside.

Such a fundamental change on the face of the landscape should also herald a change in the way the land itself is used. Both elements – conservation and community – are looking for new and better ways, better than deer forest and sheep, better than prairies and sitka spruce, better for people and better for nature.

The deer and the sheep have been disastrous for people and landscape in Scotland, and 200 years should be long enough to have assimilated the lessons.

One of the better ways of using the land is to pay people to practise conservation. Pay farmers to farm more thoughtfully, landowners to practise silviculture and land restoration, communities to think of conservation as socially desirable because it reinforces the old bond between people and landscape, humanity and nature.

So who pays?

We do. All of us. In the same way that at the moment we pay for sheep subsidies, in the same way that we threw tax incentives at spruce forests, in the same way we pay landowners not to plant spruce forests, in the same way that we are apparently ready to contemplate throwing millions of pounds a year to staff and administer a national park system, in the same way we pay for the salaries which have just fuelled the bonfire-full of national park reports.

Nature and landscape, in a country like Scotland of all places, are our responsibility, and therefore our Government's.

Now that we are about to have our own Government and now that the air crackles with the prospect of land reform, surely it is a wiser use of our resources – people, land, nature and money – to put the conservation and wise use of the Scottish landscape into the hands of those who live and work and want to be there because they love the place and the way of life, rather than put it in the hands of bureaucrats in Edinburgh, politicians, national park committees, uniformed careerists and all the coat-tail hangers-on whose ambitions reach no higher than to make a fast buck out of a national park badge, whether it's on a shirt or a landscape.

Who knows, if we get good enough at it, perhaps even the National Trust for Scotland will notice, rethink the way they exploit Ben Lawers and channel some of their considerable energies into how they might let it heal.

THIS LAND IS OUR LAND

The Struggle for Britain's Countryside by Marion Shoard

Gaia Books, 1997, 521pp, 212 x 138mm £12.50 inc. p&p.

Landowners, whether farmers or landlords, hold the countryside in a vice-like grip. Not only do they have an almost absolute right to do whatever they will with the land they own, they exercise a degree of legal and institutional control over the wider countryside which has hardly diminished since medieval times.

They are represented out of all proportion in both the House of Commons and local government. **They dominate the quangos which oversee such things as** nature conservation, forestry, national parks and the landscape. The influence of their lobbying organisations over legislation has led over the years to the quashing of watering down of any moves to restrict their absolute right to do what they will with the land, to exclude others from it, and to destroy it if they so please. Witness the present 'Labour' government's speedy reneging on their pledge to establish the right to roam over uncultivated land.

. Is it a wonder that it's almost impossible to buy a small piece of land on which to live and practice permaculture, or any kind of smallholding life?

This classic book, recently updated, not only lays out the picture of rural power in detail, but makes proposals for change. It is required reading for anyone who wants to understand the British countryside.

(Review by Patrick Whitefield, published in a 1998 issue of the Permaculture Magazine. No 18. Reprinted by kind permission. **Emphasis added.** S-A.H.)

*

REFLECTIONS.....

Upon watching the Farmers BBC TV programme on Sunday, 21 Dec. 86, introducing the public to the concept of the new E.S.A.s, (Environmentally Sensitive Areas); starting with Breadalbane.

. . . First – get economic monopoly established at the base of society.

. . . Next: watch this (land) monopoly steadily permeate the successive layers of capital from ground up – to the topmost banking and financial ones.

. . . Then, with land and capital in increasingly fewer hands – (for monopoly works increasingly to its own advantage) – watch the gradual take-over of farming, industry, housing, employment, health, education, etc., etc. – always strictly, of course, "in the name" or "for the benefit" of the people.

. . . Till finally, their economic viability – and hence freedom – destroyed to the point that most are only "viable" via State support: NOW – show your goodness, morality, public concern, environmental caringness, etc., by setting up all the phoney "development" bodies that you can – including, of course, all the S.S.S.I.s, E.S.A.s, etc., you can conjure up – whilst a bemused public beautifully carries the whole works forward for you. . .including, naturally, paying for it all!

Finally: sit back for a good laugh – they'll *never* work it out now! S-A.H. - *27 Dec. 86.*

* * * * * * * * * * * *

Simple and fresh and fair from winter's close emerging,
As if no artifice of fashion, business, politics, had ever been,
Forth from its sunny nook of shelter'd grass - innocent, golden, calm
as the dawn,
The spring's first dandelion shows its trustful face.

(Walt Whitman.)

Extracts from *The Restoration of the Peasantries*
by Dr. G.T. Wrench, M.D.
(Published by the C.W. Daniel Company Limited, London – 1939)

* * * * * * * * * *

An examination of the destructive effect of British rule upon the peasantries of her dominions – now 'the Third World' – following directly from that conversion of land from a community into a capital asset by which she had already destroyed her own peasantry and was fast destroying her own agriculture.

The progress of a peasantry depends upon which of ... two sets of values is adopted. History affords many examples of the two different paths they build, along which the destinies of the peasants pass. Two such historical paths stand out from the others, because of our greater knowledge of them. Upon the first of these, China pursued her course from the dawn of her history to the last century; upon the second passed the plentiful dominion of Rome to its final extinction.

An enormous weight of fate for the peasantry of India and for many other peasantries, therefore, hung upon the question as to which set of values the British brought to India and to other parts of their dominions ...

It is, therefore, essential to the understanding of the path upon which the Indian peasants entered, to review the path of the English peasants, because the effect of English leadership in India would be to make the Indian peasant pursue a course similar to that which the English peasants had already taken. When it is stated that England once had its ryots *(Indian term)*, or peasants with free access to the land, and that, in the course of time, these 'free' peasants had been practically eliminated, it will be seen how vital this question of the English agricultural path was and is to the Indian peasants ...

Originally the lord of the manor ... mingled with the peasants both as farmer and as a member of the village assembly. But, by the time of the Tudors, he had largely lost this intimate relation ... he had privileges that gave him ... a right to free labour ... a right to fold the peasants' sheep, as well as his own, upon his land and so secure the value of their manure ... lastly, he had a direct relation with the law-making power of government, where, in his own interests and experience, he stood for the superiority of private enclosed land as against the open field land of the peasant community.

... Whether the manor derived from the Roman villa or not, one thing is sure, namely that the agricultural path which England eventually took was that of Rome, that is to say it took the path of capitalistic farming for individual profit.

... As *trade in wool* grew, it gave the lords of the manors a growing temptation to separate out their share of the land and to maintain or increase its fertility by securing for it the major part of the manure. The good pasturage resulting ensured superior wool.

The wealth, which their wool brought them, eventually induced the large land owners to take advantage of their strong position in the State to pass laws giving them a right, under certain conditions, to take for their own private possession land actually belonging to the peasants. It will be remembered that the Roman aristocrats had done the same. The principal laws conferring this power upon the lords of the manors were the Statute of Merton, A.D. 1236 and the Statute of Westminster, A.D. 1285.

This was the first encroachment due to the new dominant idea of the use of land for private profit, though to the detriment of others. The old dominant idea in Western Europe and England had taught that private property should be used for mutual good; that the primary function of the land was to produce food and not profit ...

In the early Tudor period the new dominant idea of the use of property for its owner's individual gain challenged the old; King Henry the Eighth and his minister, Thomas Cromwell, supported by the big landowners and the rich traders, over‿threw the Church, abolished the Church's agricultural institutions, the monasteries, and took their land for themselves. They went further. They enclosed a large amount of village land for their own use and ejected the peasants, who had previously held and cultivated it.

This was the first of the heavy blows dealt to the English communities by their rival, the large estates or English latifundia. It was such a blow as fell upon the Roman peasants after the second Punic War.

The peasants never recovered ...

Land increased in value, rents rose, but prices rose even more. So great was the activity in agriculture between 1780 and 1813 that investment of money in land was as profitable as that in factories. Men, who had got wealth through industry, bought up land. Capitalistic farming became a sure road to fortune. Even the great landlords, who held their land, not to cultivate themselves but to get rents, sent their sons as pupils to farmers, that they might take an understanding part in cultivation, instead of leaving it to stewards, and so secure its profits more safely to themselves.

In this big movement, the peasants of the open field system were once more attacked ... enclosures of their land and its seizure by this means proceeded at a prodigious pace by means of the old processes and new laws. Like the Roman landlords, so now the English landlords gave themselves 'legal permission to buy out small-holders ... and with growing frequency to drive them out.' Small-holders and peasants of the open field system 'disappeared like raindrops in the sea,'...

At that time many of the labourers sank so low that they had to be supported by the parish funds. The parish or village officials even sold their labour. "Sometimes the paupers were paraded by the overseers on a Monday morning, and the week's labour of each individual was offered at auction to the highest bidder." *(Ernle)* The degradation of the peasants was complete. The English agricultural path had led to what the same path led to in Roman Italy, the elimination of the family cultivators and their agricultural system ...

"Had the gentlemen of England so chosen", ... writes *Mr. Gilbert Slater* in ... 'The Growth of Modern England', 1932, "the agricultural evolution of the eighteenth century could have been so controlled as to bring unexampled prosperity to the workers of the land. Actually it gave to those who had, and took away from those that had not even the little they thought they had ..."

Unfortunately then, the English, when they became paramount in India, were upon the second agricultural path, which had brought about the abolition of the small-holding peasants or English ryots. They brought with them the system of large private estates ... landlords, tenants, and labourers ...

The imposition of the English land system upon India was fortunately limited ... owing to stout opposition from Sir Thomas Munro (1761-1827), the Governor of madras ... throughout the forty seven years of his service ...

That which has gravely affected all the mis-valued Indian ryots has been the imposition upon them of the English view of debt.

Up to the time of the Tudors, usury in England had been restrained by a number of prohibitions. The chief of these was the Canon Law against usury ... This Law was rejected by the Puritans ... so when the English became permanent in India, debt and the right to recover it and its interest by law was a firmly established principle in England, both as regards things of the land and things of the city ...

It is now necessary to review the effect of this change ... upon the sowcar *Indian moneylender* and his fellow villagers. No one has described it with greater clarity than Sir Malcolm L. Darling, I.C.S. ...

Darling is quite clear about the change of the dominant idea. "Before British rule, the communal ownership of land made mortgage difficult." Money could not be raised on the security of land, because land was not private; only in a few parts of India, such as the valley of the Indus, was land held privately. Mortgage, the raising of money on land, awaited a new conception, that of private property in land. This conception of land the ruling English brought. All land in England at that time was private property; upon which all English land money could be raised with the land as security. So debt, which was common enough in India, came to be transvalued; it came to have a different effect and influence upon men to that which it had in the pre-British period. "If debt was as common then as it is today, the moneylender was not so powerful as he subsequently became under British rule." He lived under restraints, which the British rule removed or weakened ... "Kindly feeling ... prevailed between debtor and creditor till well into the sixties. In 1866, the Chief Court was established and pleaders were allowed to practice ... The rigid application of the law which ensued put the ignorant peasant entirely at the mercy of his creditor." ...

The result in India has been that the peasants have been placed upon the same path as the English peasants were placed on. In England the village communities were eventually completely broken up, and the rural workers sank to the degraded state which has been described. In India the panchyats have been much weakened and have been unable to preserve the land for the peasants ... who are almost as much serfs and slaves as were the English labourers, who were paraded on Mondays by the parish overseers and their labour sold for the week to the highest bidder...

In England, laws checked but failed to avert the eventual elimination of the peasants' system by that of large landed estates. The agricultural path remained that of Rome.

In British India, many laws have been passed and are still being passed for law-making is the means by which practical and sympathetic men strive to correct the 'evils' of a change of principle. The more evils it causes, the more laws they have to pass. Their very numbers show that in the new principle something social is lacking. When social principles are not lacking in a State's organisation, little law is needed; But in the industrial era no factories have been so busy as those which make laws. Nevertheless, though the laws mitigate a particular evil or set of evils, in general they failed, for they are checks within the ambit of the deeper causes of the evils.

Mr. Gandhi, with other men of vision, stands aghast at the foreboding picture which the world today presents ... He attacks modern civilisations at the very roots. He preaches a change of heart ... He has played a leading part in politics of the most modern kind. Supported by funds from large industrial interests, he organised a revolutionary movement upon the usual lines described in Chapter VI. He clothed the movement, it is true, with Indian emotionalism and ... the people's traditional religion ... But he entirely omitted any historical basis and seemingly any historical understanding, thereby confirming what Spengler pronounces as eminently characteristic of Indian culture, namely 'the perfectly ahistoric soul'. There is, he points out, no real historical literature in India. So Mr. Gandhi, though realising, almost as a peasant himself, the needs of the peasant, nevertheless has involved himself in movements and theories that have arisen from industrial conditions, and are not based upon an historical demonstration of the basis of peasant existence.

Nor, as far as I know, has any other Indian leader shown any comprehension of the peasants' position and value in terms of history, which relates them to a definite period and to the stories of peasantries in other lands. Being ahistorical, men belong to their times so confinedly that they can neither create nor understand the creation of such a foreshadowing as that of the restoration of the peasantries. They can only appreciate it when it becomes visible substance in the events of the day in which they themselves live.

*

Money and mechanism are the characters of our civilisation. But a yet greater reality than they is the soil. Historical periods of culture and civilisation come and go, but the soil, the producer of life, is lasting. It continues, while they wax and wane. And, if a civilisation is such that it degrades the soil, then it is the civilisation and not the soil that comes to an end.

Healthy life and vigour ... depend upon healthy agriculture. *But healthy agriculture has been neglected, peasants have been neglected, peasants have been uprooted, and the soil treated as a source of money rather than as a source of healthy crops ...*

*

In 1872 the *English agricultural labourers* ... started a trade union ... We find them going to the root of the matter in their attempts to free land from the dominance of money. They supported the Land Restoration League, which wished to put a tax upon rent and increase it progressively until it absorbed and eventually abolished rent, and thus achieve the aim of Henry George ...

Let Scotland take up the story again from here! And not just her Agricultural labourers – (what few of these remain) – but *her people as a whole.*

*

"When in the course of history we see the conquerors making chattel slaves of the conquered, it is always when population is sparse and land of little value, or where they want to carry off their human spoil. In other cases, the conquerors merely appropriate the lands of the conquered, by which means they just as effectually, and much more conveniently, compel the conquered to work for them."

Chapter "Slavery and Slavery", from "Social Problems" by Henry George.

*

OUR DESPAIRING FARMERS – AND LAND REFORM

Farmers – small farmers – today are in desperation. Some cannot think how land reform could help them. This is because they have not stopped to look at – (doubtless have not had *time to* stop to look at) – the picture *whole*.

If an entire building is of a rotten structure and is in process of collapsing, then it is understandable that those living in a particular wing, where the walls are more obviously caving in, are entirely focussed upon their own particular plight. Others, in an upper storey, are aware that *their* apartment is in great danger too – and send out desperate signals for *its* shoring up, by 'State aid' of whatever kind.

What needs to be faced is the fact that, with a fundamentally rotten structure, it is impossible for *any* part to be in a healthy state; and while by all means let emergency aid be directed where emergency aid is currently required, *no amount of such emergency aid is, in the long run, going to be of the slightest use*, because the *entire structure* is in process of collapse, and will bring to ruin every part of itself when it falls.

The most valiant of the farmers insist they do not in fact want State aid – only a 'fair price' for their produce. What we need to see is that there cannot, in fact, be *any* fair price for *any* product in a structure where a 'fair price' is skewed at the bottom line: that is – where the great mass of the people are having to pay a *monopoly* price for mere living space on this earth.

Once the 'fair price' question is settled *at the foundations* of the economic structure, it will have repercussions the whole way up. What is all-important is for those at present crying out from their *specific* anguishes, at the same time to give attention to the picture – the structure – *in its wholeness*, and so understand that their cry must reach out on behalf of the *whole* disorder, as well as just their own. Far from the structure not being the concern of those who function in different parts of it, *it is in fact their primary concern!*

"To obtain real solutions, one should no longer strive to deal with the symptom but its cause (which can usually be attributed to imbalance); for solutions often have nothing to do with the presented problems."

(Christopher Seebach, in "Living Water" by Olaf Alexandersson Gateway Books, 1990, on the work of Victor Schauberger.)

*

Perhaps today's farmers could stand back from the scene and take a longer look in other ways too. The article from *Aquarian Alternatives* opens up vistas... and not for farmers alone. So also does *Secrets of the Soil* by Peter Tompkins and Christopher Bird, (*Arkana, 1992*).

S-A.H., May 1998.

IRELAND

Land and Peace

By C.M. Hussey

(Published in *Progress*, Australia, Sept. - Oct. 1997.).

In unravelling the perennial northern crisis, the logical starting point is the plantation of Ulster. This plantation and the general conquest of Ireland involved two concomitant but distinct developments – dispossession and privatization. On the one hand, the clan inhabitants were dispossessed of their beneficial Gaelic type rights to the common free lands. On the other, the new Protestant planter usurpers became beneficiaries of privatised unencumbered land.

End of Common Ground

Thus land, common to all and used for the sustenance of all, was appropriated for the enrichment of some. When land becomes an assignable marketable asset without social duties, because it is in fixed supply and is vital for all production, it becomes a de facto monopoly. As such, all economic progress serves to boost land values, without any necessary input by its owners. Thus the conquest of Ulster entailed not just a one-off theft, like a house burglary, but a permanent and continuing theft and exclusion.

When the Gaelic system of common tenure prevailed in both countries, Scots and Irish were interchangeable and moved back and forth across the channel in joint endeavours and perfect amity for centuries on end. This perfect amity was based on actual and metaphorical "common ground".

Things changed radically when the English system of enclosure/dispossession spread like falling dominoes from England into Scotland onto Ireland and elsewhere. Then enmity replaced the previous amity and the previous common ground became a battleground.

Class and Clan

In southern England, the drier weather and more level terrain has made cultivation the usual land use. This type of livelihood leads to households being independent economic entities and the development of an individualist society. When such lands are privatised, there develops a hierarchical pyramid-shaped class society smoothly stratified on a largely individual basis.

In Scotland and Ireland, the natural conditions of high rainfall and uneven terrain have made cattle herding, and other pastoralist pursuits, the usual land use. This extensive land use leads to the development of interlocking obligations and ties among the beneficiaries of the land. Egalitarian and mutualist clans or tribes are the societal outcome of such conditions.

When such pastoralist clan lands are privatised, there can develop not just a hierarchy on an individual basis but also a hierarchy on a clan basis.

Ascendancy and War

In Ireland, therefore, with the conditions of dispossession, privatization and tribalism, there developed a dichotomised system of a landed Protestant clan ascendancy and a landless Catholic clan descendancy. More accurately, we should speak of a Protestant semi-clan with the proletariat compensated for their landlessness by a rigid preferential access to employment.

In English conditions, land monopoly entails an implicit exaction on the labour and capital of others. In Ulster conditions, land monopoly entails an implicit structural Protestant exaction on Catholic labour and capital.

Exclusion and exaction mean the easy escalation of division to tension, to conflict, to war. With its land unfree, Ulster will never be at peace.

Neo-colonialism and War

Not one single nationalist party opposes the land system imposed by the Tudor, Stuart, Cromwellian and Williamite English rulers. Despite heavy unemployment, emigration and public debt, labour is heavily taxed to subsidise land. The ratio of unearned land values to national income is reliably reported as the worst in the world and is getting worse with time. In independent Ireland the colonialist system has been retained and enhanced but with native ownership in classical neocolonialist fashion.

In an attempted united Ireland, therefore, the pressure, legal and illegal, for the land monopoly of Ulster to be retained but shifted to Catholic control would be irresistible. If such a change succeeded perchance, the present ascendancy/descendancy roles would invert, and with similar bitter and bloody results. So, equally, with its land unfree a united Ireland would never be at peace.

With land monopoly, Catholic wrongs cannot be righted without wronging Protestant rights. With land monopoly, both Catholic grievances and Protestant paranoia are entirely justified; so that intransigence becomes transmuted into wisdom and wisdom into intransigence. With land monopoly the problem resembles a drama with but two roses – prince or pauper.

Unity

This is not to oppose or delay a united country. Rather it is to illuminate the only possible path to unity and put rocket fuel into the engine of the project. The land monopoly is best broken by taxing land values – urban and rural – and other natural resources until they are virtually free, and by rolling back the taxes on labour and capital. Sharing the common land can then take the form of equal exchequer payments to all citizens. Parallel policies of a minimal state and of free markets complement the free land policy.

Privatised land has divided the people and the island of Ireland. Restoring the Gaelic common ground, either north or south, would soon unite both people and country. Then we would be not merely free and Gaelic but peaceful and prosperous as well.

Postscript: Land and Empire

Would a free land system lead to greater equality but unhappily to an equality of poverty? Even though highly stratified by class, was not Britain's industrial revolution, superior prosperity, world empire and top nation status, developed on the basis of privately appropriated land? Should not we copy their example and success?

The rolling appropriation of British land led to the growth of a landless proletariat there. These people in their millions found an outlet in colonizing the lately "discovered" and easily conquered new world territories. With the large economies of scale that a world wide enclosed market offered, British handicraft production developed into high capital industrial mass production.

Thus it was not landed proprietorship that made Britain "top nation". Rather was it the spreading frontier of free land, made available by military conquest, that the British Empire encompassed. . . . .

A free land system has a constantly renewed internal frontier of opportunity leading to a prosperous vibrant egalitarian harmonious society.

An appropriated land system leads to social and economic malfunction. and constant popular pressure for external frontiers of opportunity, leading to colonial and resource and trade wars, inter imperial conflicts and, presumably in the future, star land wars. All the while, weapons of mass destruction develop and proliferate.

Feel free to contact C.M. Hussey at 64 Manor Street, Dublin 7. Tel: 01-6771955.

Other Harp pamphlets available: *Land War in Northern Ireland, Land, Communism and Socialism, Land, wages and the state, Land! Peace! Freedom!, The Land for the People!*

Myths, Murder & the pursuit of virtual happiness

Paolo Bellarossi

THE LIE OF THE LAND
IRISH IDENTITIES
by Fintan O'Toole
Verso, £15

IRELAND is a metaphor for modern society. It is not a place, but rather an idea that is born of the displacement of people from their home territory.

Ireland's identity has as much to do with places like Boston (USA) and Birmingham (UK) as with the island off the coast of Europe, a culture with no spatial borders.

A sovereign nation, yes, but not sovereign at all, dependent on others for its existence, most readily seen in its economy. In 1996 the Republic produced more wealth per head of population than the UK. Cause for celebration? The achievement is a lie recognised for the charade that it is by one of Ireland's most talented journalists, Fintan O'Toole, who is currently in New York as drama critic of the *Daily News*. In the introduction to a collection of his essays he notes:

"Ministers may have gotten to spend the billions of pounds flowing in from the EU's regional and social funds, but the public knew that it had people outside the State - mostly German taxpayers - to thank for them. Ministers may have gotten to announce huge industrial investments like IBM's 3,000-job project for Dublin or Intel's $1.5 billion investment in Leixlip, but the public knew that the real decisions had been taken on the far side of the Atlantic". As with Scotland in the past

Ireland is a state of dependency. Three-quarters of its exports are owned by foreign corporations. What price sovereignty? How were the people of this island moulded into the first virtual reality nation, for which 28 people are bombed to death in the high street of a small market town on a summer's day, followed by an apology from the bombers that they didn't mean it.

In the North people govern their lives on the strength of the past. In the South they live in a future utopia. Economic subsidies from the East, cultural myths from the West.

Ireland, transit station in the global wealth production machine rather than integrated society, profits repatriated to tax havens, impoverishing the fabric of society of the resources that would otherwise enrich everyone's life. Ireland's most valuable export remains its children.

NO MYSTERY about the history. The colonial power dispossessed the people of their land, and political independence was a sham: the people were not re-integrated into the landscape. They were not allowed to reclaim their birthright.

Instead, they sought meanings for their lives through the myths of the Wild West, where Irish gunslingers dreamt of the green valleys back home even as they displaced the Indians from their territories...And the landless peasants of the West of Ireland dreamt of the riches that awaited them across the ocean.

Today, notes O'Toole, the American Indian and the Negro features in the mythology of Dublin youth who struggle with the pathology of their historical displacement, which has bequeathed to them a schizophrenic culture.

They retreat into the big screen myths created by Sam Shepherd who uses the American badlands as a metaphor for the social amnesia which was necessary for a people who could not confront the reality: liberation from Westminster did not liberate them from the institutionalised process of exploitation.

O'Toole's essays are an eloquent testimony to that pathological condition. In the America of the early 19th century the Irish were regarded as little better than the barbarous Indians who had to be displaced so that property rights could be consolidated. In fact, once the Indians had been driven back, they were replaced by the Irish from Belfast who, as backwoodsmen "blacked and disguised like Indians" fought for a place in the sun against the prejudices of the English settlers. To sur-

■ **Fintan O'Toole**

vive in the urban ghettos of Chicago and York the Irish had to create their equivale the Mafia - Tammany Hall, the poli machine that brushed aside democracy an imperative of the market to trade favour votes.

The celluloid image became the subst for the psychoanalysis. John Ford and Wayne provided the therapy, helping the on the emerald isle to construct a mytho which substituted for a real identity. O'T analyses the interaction beautifully, nc that "in this paradoxical manipulatio images the American West becomes the of Ireland, Ireland becomes the rich prom land of the American West. The dynamic memory and exile are not denied, they reversed".

WHEN will reality intrude? bereaving parents of the five dren who died in Omagh would to know.

But while the subsidies keep slushin from Brussels, Ireland will exploit the im which icons like J.F. Kennedy were happ illuminate in their quest for power. The ju position of America and Ireland is no O'Toole points out, simply a clash betwe traditional and a modern culture, but a complex interaction "in which America's tural sense of itself is partly an Irish crea and Ireland's sense of itself is partly American creation". The connections are tured by nostalgia and myth. Why sh Dubliners who have been enriched by boom in house prices heed O'Toole: "We to get out from under that myth. We nee turn the mirrors into windows"?

The moguls of cyberspace have fort invested in the technology that helps to serve the myths which dull the se O'Toole thinks that "the Indian metapho been taken on by contemporary Irish cu as a device which frees it from the burd identity and lets it loose to play games the world". But aren't we all just a attracted by the Indian metaphor? Don't w conspire to play games with the world ruse to avoid the realities of our identi There is precious little for any nation t proud about in the 20th century. The flick images on video provide quick-fix escap even for the President in the White House thinks he can virtually distance himself reality by "telling the truth" to a ca instead of eye contact with a grand jury.

But while we may manipulate the cu maps so that they tell convenient lies, mately the truth will emerge. It is delineat the landscape. Honest identities are hew of the land, and in the 21st century, if man is to retrieve its full sense of reality, it have to swear a new oath with nature. It i the lie of the land, but the lie of the peop the land that needs to be eliminated.

*

I found this letter from Denise Black - in speaking of Paolo Bellarossi's fine article on Fintan O'Toole's book - so interesting, and so illuminative of our whole scene, that I felt it must have a place in this book alongside it.

(With apologies to "Land and Liberty": I have had to reduce the spaces between the columns of the article to fit it on one page; nor was there time to check the exact date of issue. S-A.H.)

*

Dear Shirley-Anne,

I have enclosed a copy of the BBC Wildlife magazine article.

I was also reading the "Land and Liberty" magazine which was sent to us this morning. Although, there are many very interesting articles as usual, this one stood out to me. I felt that this article, not only explains Ireland's obsession with America, but in many ways it particularly relates to Scottish people.

I think that phrases like "social amnesia" explain a lot, why it is so hard to make people realise the truth even with it staring them in the face.

The point that the author has missed is what we spoke of last night, that this social amnesia will never be rectified until correction of the diet of people can resurrect their social and genetic memory.

Love Denise

x

Originally published in — "Progress" — Australia: Feb 1968.

SIR STAMFORD RAFFLES IN INDONESIA

LAND REVENUE SYSTEM APPLIED IN JAVA BEFORE HENRY GEORGE

by

A.R. Hutchinson, B.Sc., A.M.I.E.Aust.

*

(Alack that those so eager to "aid" the Third World today cannot, with their "compart-mentality" outlook, discern what the **holistic** view of Sir Stamford Raffles could not miss! One wonders if those who now visit the famous Raffles Hotel in Singapore have any idea of the real stature of the man it was named after... S-A.H.)

*

Indonesia is much in the news these days in an unfavourable light. It is timely to review events of an earlier period during which the system advocated by Henry George was put into practical operation in Java more than 60 years before his classic work, 'Progress and Poverty', was written. The circumstances are almost unknown to succeeding generations of his followers, though they provide the clearest vindication of the soundness of the land revenue system he advocated. Later history has underlined the lessons to be learnt from that experience.

The wealth of the 'Spice Islands' early attracted the Portuguese and the Dutch to the great chain of islands stretching from Malaya towards New Guinea in the East and Japan in the North. English traders also tried to establish trading stations there but were opposed ruthlessly by the Dutch.

After Holland was over-run by France in 1793, she was considered an enemy state by Britain, and the British fleet began to take over all her scattered and valuable overseas settlements – Cape Colony, Ceylon, the East Indies and various West Indian Islands. In 1795 a force from India captured Malacca, and later planned to completely destroy the port and transfer its inhabitants to Penang. This plan was abandoned on the advice of Stamford Raffles, who was to become a towering figure in many fields in his relatively short lifetime.

He had entered the service of the East India Company in London as a clerk at the age of 14. His active mind soon attracted the attention of the governors, and he was sent to a post in Penang. On the way out he learnt the Malay language, his mastery of which brought him both advancement in the Indian Service and a profound knowledge of and admiration for the Malay people. Within two years at Penang he became first Acting Secretary and then Secretary to the Administration. He became Chief Malayan translator with a staff of Malay assistants.

The British had long been interested in Java, the most prized tropical island in the world, but they believed it was too strongly held. Raffles knew differently. He knew that neither the Dutch nor the French had really conquered Java. The Javanese were unfriendly to both. The remaining Dutch residents and the Chinese traders, too, had good cause to aid another power. Raffles was able to give sound advice as a result of which the Governor-General of British India, Lord Minto, decided to seize Java and this was done without effective resistance on August 4th, 1811. On his departure in October of the same year, Lord Minto appointed Raffles Lieutenant-Governor of Java and its dependencies, the uncrowned king and overlord of some five millions of people, a position which he held until March 1816. He was to work with an Advisory Council consisting of the Commander-in-Chief Gillespie and the Dutchmen Cranssen and Muntinghe. In departing, Lord Minto said to him: "While we are in Java let us do all the good we can."

From that stems the story of a small nation elevated in a few short years to a degree of liberty and prosperity amazing and without parallel.

When Raffles took over his island empire the fifty thousand square miles of Java had a population of 100 to the square mile, whereas, in our days, it has over 800 to the square mile, with more than 41 million people.

This rise was achieved without obvious over population and cries for more living space. Raffles laid the foundations which made this possible by restoring the Way of Life which the Javanese had enjoyed before the coming of the French and the Dutch. He found the finances in a shocking state. Taxation and restrictions on trade were as rampant as in our world of today. The list of devices adopted by the Dutch and the French in order to sustain their monopoly over Javanese trade and industry would seem incredibly silly but for the fact that these same devices are adopted by Europeans wherever they obtain control. Tolls, taxes and restrictions lay across every activity of Javanese life.

TAXES BEFORE THE REFORM

There was a 15 per cent tax upon the production of rice, a poll tax upon families and market duties or tolls literally levied on every article produced by agriculture, manufacture or the petty arts. These somewhat resembled our Sales Tax and levies made by the Egg Boards, Dried Fruits Boards and similar bodies. There was a tax upon the slaughter of buffaloes, which affected the price of food and restricted the breeding of animals. There was a charge upon the cost of transport of baggage and stores of every description and upon the feeding of travellers. There were obligations to render free labour service for public works and forced contribution to the Government monopolies. Duties and charges on sea-born commerce amounted to 46 per cent *(which seems moderate compared to some of the imposts under which Australian trade is conducted)*. Under the onslaught of these ferocious taxes whole districts became de-populated. There was a drift from the land to the towns and villages and production of real wealth was rapidly declining. Amongst the first acts of Raffles, in agreement with Lord Minto, was the immediate abolition of nine tenths of these meddlesome and damaging laws.

RAFFLES' LAND RENT SYSTEM

Raffles himself plunged into Javan History. He soon discovered the reasons why a prosperous and glorious past on this great island had been effectively destroyed, not by invasion itself, but by the folly of the invading rulers, who were ignorant or regardless of the just land laws of the Malays and Javanese. Under these laws, landlordism did not exist, and there was no room for land speculation and land monopoly. Land might be held for use, provided the ground rent in full was paid over to the Government Authority. The Malays and Javanese had put into practice for many centuries the principles which were clearly seen by the physiocrats of France in the Eighteenth Century, and which Henry George was to expound to the Western World more than half a century later, in his classic works, 'Progress and Poverty', 'Free Trade or Protection', and 'The Condition of Labour'.

He divided Java up into 16 *landrostampts*, entitled residencies. The Resident carried out administrative and judicial functions and acted as collector of government revenue. Raffles' aim was to substitute the general tax on land value for all compulsory services, contingencies and forced deliveries. He declared the government the sole owner of the soil. The Javanese inhabitants thus became government tenants paying rent for the land they cultivated. The rent was levied not on individuals but on desas *(villages)*, and was to be assessed according to the productivity of the soil.

Average rent was estimated at two fifths of the yield. The cultivator had free disposal of the rest of his produce, which was rice in most cases. He could pay his dues in rice or money. If in money, payment was to the desa headman, and thence to the divisional office. If in rice, he had to convey it at his own expense to the Residency Headquarters.

This reduced the local Chief's opportunities for graft, since he no longer had a personal interest in the yield of the crops, and lost much of his power of demanding forced services. As a public servant he was to receive a fixed salary.

Raffles proceeded by diplomacy to overcome the opposition and to secure the co-operation and friendship of the established chiefs and rulers. When these people learned through his great Land Settlement Memorandum that he proposed to restore completely the ancient system of Java, they one by one accepted his authority without further question. He was approachable by high and low. Accompanied by his wife, he travelled over the island for the purpose of establishing his government and appointing suitable Javans to carry out the details of administration.

These changes involved a revolution in the lives of most people and could not be carried out overnight. It was not until 1813 that arrangements had gone far enough for a start to be made in practice. Raffles soon realised that the full improvement in revenue and in the position of the cultivator was not being realised because of the limitations of desa assessment. In this the headman still had too much power in the apportionment of lands among the inhabitants. He therefore changed over to the method of individual assessment. But this required a cadastral survey to work out individual assessments fairly. He initiated such a survey but it was not completed by the end of the occupation through lack of skilled staff and time for the work. Hence the revenue demand had to be fixed according to the arbitrary estimates of the Residents.

ADEQUACY OF THE REVENUE

Raffles believed that the introduction of the land rent system would provide a surplus, which would cover expenditure. The revenue did increase and more than covered the normal operations of Government, but it was not adequate to cover, in addition, two crippling burdens with which the administration was unfairly loaded. First was the payment of the cost of the wars of occupation. Second was the 'appalling handicap' of carrying out Lord Minto's promise to redeem, at the rate of 20 per cent discount, the paper money still circulating from the Dutch period. Raffles hoped that the island would continue to be held after the war was over, but recognised that neither the East India Company nor the British Government would want this unless it was self-financing, including these extra commitments superimposed upon a normal government. Hence there was an element of pressure continually exerted upon his administration. His evaluation was confirmed later, when it inevitably happened that these extra demands could not be fully covered from revenue. The Directors of the East India Company then accused him of rendering the occupation of Java a 'source of financial embarrassment to the British Government.' These extra burdens on the Treasury prevented him from carrying out fully his proposals to abolish the tollgates and free internal trade.

To meet these extra demands upon the Treasury, a small revenue tariff was maintained with a six per cent duty upon three articles only of import and three per cent upon four items only of export. This was a very close approach to absolute free trade, and even these exceptions were planned to be temporary only. He also had to agree, with great reluctance, to sell some of the Government lands, mainly to resident foreigners. As D.G.E. Hall says in *'A History of South East Asia'*, "The land sales, however, were merely a temporary expedient for dealing with an immediate need. His land revenue system must be judged by its long-term results. It was retained by the Dutch when Java was restored to them, and ultimately justified Raffles' own expectations. As Furnival, himself an expert in land revenue matters, puts it: "Raffle's calculations were not wrong, but merely too optimistic."

OTHER ACHIEVEMENTS

Raffles was not only outstanding in his introduction of the land rent system for public revenue in Java, but in many other fields. As a scientist, explorer, diplomat, administrator and author of a comprehensive book: 'The History of Java' – the volume and range of his work is amazing, particularly when it is remembered that he died at the age of only 43 years.

Raffles was a follower and associate of Wilberforce and committed to the abolition of slavery. He was unable to implement this part of his programme completely in Java in the brief time there, but proceeded in stages. He started in 1812 by imposing a tax on the keeping of slaves, and issued an order forbidding any further importation of slaves from the beginning of January 1813. Shortly afterwards he passed a regulation prohibiting the slave trade throughout the Archipelago. One long standing native evil, by which a debtor with his wife and family could be seized by a creditor and forced to work without pay, was abolished out of hand. The net result was that by the time of his recall, although slavery still existed, the numbers of slaves had been very greatly reduced.

Despite these shortcomings, the measure of application of Raffles' land rent system retained by the Dutch enabled extension of prosperity to increasing millions of Indonesians to be maintained until the Second World War. Land speculation was small or non-existent. There was no chronic poverty here of the type which characterises India and other Asian countries.

DETERIORATION SINCE INDEPENDENCE

The position has now changed with the attainment of independence by the Indonesians. The land tax was abolished in 1951 and replaced by an income tax payable only by those who previously paid land tax above a stated figure. This resulted in splitting holdings to escape the income tax. Then, in 1956, the previous 'right to use' land was converted to a 'right to own' it.

Selosoemardjan says in 'Social Patterns in Jogjakarta', that "up to the land reform of 1918 the farmer had only duties and no rights – from 1918 to 1951 he had both duties and rights – after the abolition of land tax in 1951 he had rights only and virtually no duties."

Results of these foolish and unjust measures have been disastrous. There has now emerged a landless class and much unrest in consequence. Without the stimulus to proper land use, previously given by a sufficiently high 'cost of holding land whether used or not' in the form of a land value tax, a premium is given to under-use, and productivity has fallen. Indonesia was previously a rice-exporting nation, but has now become a rice-importing nation.

On the financial front there has been unbridled inflation. The whole country has suffered in terms of real income but with the removal of all obligations from the peasants they are relatively far better off than others. Wage labourers and public servants are the sections most hit. Compared with the position in 1938, in terms of real wages, at 1958 the peasants' rice income remained approximately the same – the wage labourer dropped to about one half – the civil servant on an average to about one thirtieth. This last is disastrous, because it fosters corruption in the administration where the public servant cannot live on his official salary without supplementing it by graft. This is a short cut on the road to perdition.

In the last few years these various self-inflicted blows have turned the Javan paradise into a hell. There has been one of the worst blood baths in history with the slaughter of nearly half a million Indonesians in the name of 'anti-Communism'. How many were really Communists will never be known. Even if they were, the primary evil was the degeneration in the economic conditions without which Communism would have no attraction.

Only if and when Indonesia returns to the basic principle of land rent for public revenue can its citizens expect to raise their living standards above those under the Dutch or even return to them. It needs to be applied more fully and embrace the cities where site rents are highest as well as rural land. Simultaneously, taxes on buildings and other improvements, and on incomes, should be abolished. These act as deterrents to limit the national product and hence the well being of all who share it. This course is

Raffles had dreamed of making a new British Empire of the islands centred on Java. But soon after the introduction of his land rent system Napoleon fell and the Netherlands regained independence. At the convention of London in August 1814, Britain agreed to restore Java to the Netherlands. There was a temporary hitch in this with the escape of Napoleon from Elba, but it was carried out in August 1816. Before that, Raffles had been recalled to answer charges made by his associate, General Gillespie, who had never forgiven the upstart Secretary for Penang for his appointment as Governor over the military. The charges were all disproved shortly before the return of the island to the Dutch. Raffles proceeded on a tour of Europe and then returned to Indonesia as Governor of Bencoolen, on the island of Sumatra.

PUBLIC RECOGNITION

In England, his outstanding achievements and abilities were recognised, and a knighthood conferred upon him by the King. While in Europe he took the opportunity of calling on the King of the Netherlands to make intercessions in favour of his former Dutch colleagues at Batavia, as well as the Princes of Java. He was successful because the Dutch authorities had already reported favourably on the merits of the Raffles administration. Raffles observed afterwards, however: "The King and his leading Minister seem to mean well, but they have too great a hankering after profit, and *immediate* profit, for any liberal system to thrive under them." This may be significant in the light of later events. Whilst the Dutch in Java did leave his land policy untouched, or practically so, they initiated or restored many interferences with trade and industry of doubtful benefit and often of definite harm. They applied the land rent system fully to native and rural land, but not fully to the city lands as the system requires. It is in this area that the really spectacular potential of the land rent revenue system exists. There they applied a land tax (*verponding*) which is based not only on the rental value of the land alone, but upon the value of the buildings as well.

When Indonesia finally passed from Dutch control the rate of land tax was 7.5 per cent of the annual rental value. This is a long way short of the full revenue potential.

LAND RENT SYSTEM IN SUMATRA

When he went to Sumatra as Governor of Bencoolen, in 1818, the respectable East India Company derived its main income from slavery, gaming, and cockfighting farms, plus the enforced growing of a few tons of pepper. This was entirely inadequate to cover the £100,000 annually spent on the station. He wiped out these sources of income almost immediately on principle. Later he was reprimanded for disposing of the slaves, referred to officially as 'the property of the Company', with such precipitation. Not content with dealing with the Company's slaves in this way, Raffles also acquired the Island of Nias, off the coast, for the express purpose of completely eradicating the slave trade in all its forms.

Following his successful policy in Java, Raffles repealed all restrictions and taxation upon trade and secured the revenue of the Government upon ground rents. Owing to the under-development of the Island of Sumatra, which for richness and production could not be compared with Java, he did not follow in detail the direct collection of the ground rents, but obtained them through the princes and chieftains as feudal dues. The immediate result was a natural flow of trade which brought unexpected revenues to the Company, and the production of pepper – now produced for payment at market rates – increased many-fold. By the time this Island, too, was handed over to the Dutch, it had become almost a paying proposition, as well as a prosperous country for the native inhabitants. The withdrawal of the blight of governmental interference and repeal of the robbery through taxation upon trade, wages and industry – accompanied by the collection of ground rent for public revenue – must always have a similar result. Those who formerly thought themselves to be fortunate to possess the privilege of monopoly found that greater profit *for all* flows from unrestriction. Both production and consumption increased, creating two-way traffic instead of stagnation.

From here, Raffles went on to establish Singapore on the same principles, as a free trade open port, and it is for this that he is best known in the English speaking world.

How Raffles himself regarded his land rent system is summed up in his own words cited by Furnival: "I have the happiness to release several millions of my fellow creatures from a state of bondage and arbitrary oppression. The revenues of Government, instead of being wrung by the grasping hand of an unfeeling tax farmer from the savings of industry, will now come into the treasuries of Government direct and in proportion to the actual capacity of the country ...".

*

PARADISE BECOMES HELL

JAVA SINCE THE RAFFLES ERA

With the return of Java to the Dutch in 1816, in accordance with the decisions of the Convention of London, it was first governed by three Commissioners under Baron van der Capellen. Its Charter from the King was based on the principle of freedom of cultivation and trade. Within a month he issued a decree throwing open the trade of the Netherlands Indies.

THE LAND – RENT SYSTEM ENDORSED

The finances were a vital consideration so that there was an early review of the situation. This resulted in the decision to retain Raffles' land rent system, using the desa method of assessment. The system was to be improved by measuring up and valuing the land. To help the taxpayer to keep out of the hands of the moneylender he was allowed to pay his land rent in money or kind. These principles were embodied in Land Rent Ordinances published in 1818 and 1819.

Other measures from the Raffles period designed for protection of the native to prevent his exploitation were confirmed, including his regulations against slavery. But the safeguards were not effectively enforced.

The post war boom was followed by a slump and revenue dropped with the reduced trade. But the land revenue continued to increase, and it was a fall in revenue from other sources, which produced the deficit.

The Java War of 1825-30 was a revolt arising from dis-satisfaction over cancellation of land lease contracts and tolls levied at the boundaries between native and government territory. The cost of the Java War and outbreak of a revolt of Belgium against Holland at home caused a change in policy for the worse in the Indies.

THE FORCED 'CULTURE' SYSTEM

A new Governor General, van den Bosch, in 1830, put into effect the 'Culture System', which was really a return to the old system of forced deliveries and forced labour under a new name. Under it, the principle of free peasant cultivation was abandoned. The peasant was forced to devote a portion of his holding to cultivation of export crops as directed by government, which would take the product in lieu of land rent in cash. With it free trade was abandoned, the products being handled by Dutch merchants, using only Dutch ships, and sold in the Netherlands. It soon became a device for enriching Holland at Java's expense. The element of compulsion increased and the safeguards in the original scheme were abandoned. Those controlling the scheme received a percentage of the products and thus had an incentive to use means forbidden by government decrees. The original requirement that the cultivator devote only one fifth of his holding to export crops was extended and the cultivator compelled to cultivate the government land before his own. Forced labour was used for the upkeep of roads and bridges. In some districts the cultivator had to work more than 200 days a year for the government. During the years 1848-50, there was widespread famine in central Java for this reason.

Liberal ideas at work in Holland brought reaction against the culture system and agitation to get rid of it. Conditions were improved and the safeguards policed. The result of this agitation against the system resulted in legislation in 1870 providing for the government to withdraw from sugar cultivation in twelve annual stages from 1878. But the most profitable culture (*coffee*) remained forced till 1917. Even then the most profitable monopolies of opium, salt and pawnshops continued to 1927. The desire to free the native was there but the withdrawal of government from the controlled culture field in favour of private enterprise was largely pressed to give individual Dutchmen a greater share.

Much was done for the Indonesians by the Dutch from 1900 on, but there was too little development of education and little training or participation in the administration. Hence, few Indonesians were equipped for responsibilities when independence was gained.

in accordance with its own historical method restored by Raffles. We hope wiser councils prevail and they return to it.

READING REFERENCES

'The History of Java' by Sir Stamford Raffles
'Netherlands India' by J.S. Furnival
'A History of South East Asia' by D.G.E. Hall
'Social Patterns in Jogjakarta' by Selosoemardjan

*

We believe that this account of Sir Stamford Raffles' land rent system in Java, and of the later developments in that country, contains lessons from which the public administrators in all countries can learn. We invite your help in bringing it to the attention of those in a position to gain from it. For this further copies are available from the ***Henry George League,*** 31, Hardware St., ***Melbourne, Victoria,*** Australia.

*

CAN LAND VALUES BE MEASURED ACCURATELY?

Many people (and even some surveyors) believe that land values cannot be measured accurately. If land prices are changing as fast as they did in Japan in 1987 how can a value be fixed? If most urban land is sold with buildings on it how can land values be extracted? This view is false; it can be done because it is done. The Inland Revenue Directorate in Denmark has been predicting site values for land throughout Denmark to within 1% of market values for years. The British and American Inland Revenues however haven't got a clue how much their land is worth in aggregate. The British know less about it than William the Conqueror did in 1086 with his Domesday Book! Land values in Britain today are greater than the Gross National Product, but they are ignored by economic statisticians. The government must be persuaded to fund the provision of this vital data.

LAND & LIBERTY SUMMER 1997

DANISH HISTORY – 1957 - 1960

*(Extract from Knud Tholstrup's **Inflation** (1988), published in **Progress**, Australia, Oct. 1988. A shortened extract from that is presented here.)*

The Positive Experiences

After the election in 1957, when my party was in a key position, and recognising the economic basic laws, I took the initiative to create a three-party government, based on collecting land rent, which was well prepared by the leader of the Justice Party, Mr. Viggo Starcke's election speeches containing possible government constellations.

Knowing what land rent could lead to I said – speaking for my party (in the Parliament): "With the politics which now has to be effected, the inflation will stop and the interest will be reduced." This statement was met by laughter.

The following year the interest was reduced from $6^1/_4$ per cent to 5 per cent and in 1959 the inflation was 0 per cent and below 1 per cent a year in the period 1957 to 1960, compared to approx. 5 per cent per annum before and after.

During the period, 100,000 new jobs were created, and owing to low interest and without new taxes, the workers received the highest real payroll increases ever.

In addition, the balance of trade deficit became a surplus, and three-quarters of Denmark's foreign debt was repaid. Another year, and Denmark would have been free of debt.

The result was so sensational that the *New York Times* on October 2, 1960, wrote: "Big lesson from a small nation" in which article Professor Comager recommended other nations to learn from this.

At the election in 1960, the parties against land rent put all their efforts in getting the Justice Party destroyed by use of the hitherto biggest campaign in any election, strongly supported by the associations of land owners.

Because of more deaths and sickness in the parliament group, the Justice Party had weakened their agitational power and the party could not pass the limit for election. For personal reasons I left the Danish Parliament in 1958.

The Uncomprehensible Act

With Mr. J.O. Krag as Social Democratical Prime Minister from 1962 and his promise to repeal the law about land rent, the speculation went back with an accelerating speed. The law was repealed on April 30, 1964, and the inflation increased to 8 per cent.

While the gross national product (GNP) and the total real estate values (the land prices being an essential part) have increased 20 times since 1960, or 3 times as much as the consumer price index, the real estate values in Denmark in actual sales prices in the same period have increased from 17 billion DKK to more than 500 billion DKK, i.e. more than 30 times and more than 4 times as much as the consumer prices/inflation.

As the nation neglected to collect the rent from the socially created value increases, the Danish government suffered an annual loss of about 50 billion DKK, which, therefore, has had to be collected in additional taxes, which otherwise would not be necessary.

The additional taxes end up in higher commodity prices and cost each of the country's 5 million inhabitants 10,000 DKK a year as a part of the consumer prices and, beyond that, it leads to reduction in the competitive power.

Today, Denmark is confronted with the worst economic crisis ever.

We shall never get out of this crisis, if we do not get to the root of the problem – the reason for the lost competitive ability – and stop the land speculation against a future promise to demand land rent paid to the society so that the suffocating income taxes can be eliminated over a period of e.g. 10 years.

We do not, however, have to wait years for the effect of this. It will come immediately after a firm promise of making the necessary laws, exactly as it did in 1957 to 1960.

The neglect of the society to collect the society created land rent has necessitated a broad variety of taxes. The worst of these is the income tax which swallows up a large part of the fruit of effort.

It is worse, however, that the effect is a punishment on working, which especially hits the young people without any money who want to start up their own business. Barriers for a sound economic development are thereby created. The initiatives are killed from the beginning, which causes young entrepreneurs to suffer from interest and tax death, before their expansion actually gets started.

*

THE SINGLE TAX IS ENOUGH

Published in *Progress*, Australia – Aug. 1985

Eric, little by little, is beginning to see the light (B.D., August 10). Eric (Major Douglas) de Maré asks "where will the money originate to pay those single taxes?". From the same sources that now pay private ground rent, namely labour and capital. John Marshall, Chief Justice of the United States Supreme Court, put it more bluntly than Plato: "The power to tax is the power to destroy."

Present taxes destroy both capital and labour and only favour the landed interests. The application of the single tax will destroy the landed interest as a landed interest and free the people of the entire world to use their labour and capital on the free land. The single tax on the value of land will, by becoming the state's only income, limit the damage that state borrowing and profligate waste and debts entail on future generations.

Unfortunately the state now does control the creation of money. It has demonstrated that it uses such control to engender more and more debt and waste more and more resources. How can you by now printing even more money called "social credits" ever hope to free mankind from its slavery? Mankind is suffering a cancer, and social credit would pump more blood into the sick body politic. What is needed is surgery to vehemently cut out the cancer. The single tax is that surgeon's knife. Without that radical surgery civilisation will die. With it, it may just survive.

Meyer and de Maré are not so far apart. Eric proclaims the full impact of the disease, "the credit monopoly and the banking oligarchy", which now bleed the body politic, but the disease is the cancer of the vested interest in land. This the single tax will cure. The single tax is enough to cure the crisis. Only the single tax will do it. If this long exchange of letters has made even some of your readers aware of Henry George it has done its work. The rest will not be silenced.

Herbert Meyer, London, "*Building Design*", 31/8/84.

*

*(**Note:** "It is of more importance to the community,*
that regulations should be imposed on the proprietors of land,
than on the proprietors of money." William Ogilvie.)

Part III

KALEIDOSCOPE

*

3) BROADER PERSPECTIVES

*

LAD IN A TREE HOUSE

A VERY DES RES!

Adam McIntosh

"I think if every child had such a magical place of its own, there wouldn't be so many problems of young people hanging about on the streets. That would mean less crime and drugs."

Green house: Adam relaxes in the furnished, eco-friendly retreat he built on Craigencalt Farm, Fife. Picture: Nick McGowan-Lowe

How I branched out into a leafy des res

A treehouse takes you closer to nature and gives young people a bird's eye perspective on life, says *Adam McIntosh*, 14, who built his own

RECENTLY this newspaper had a big article about the fuss over a treehouse in Morningside. Neighbours were complaining about it. Some were saying, "I am worried about the effect it may have on the price of my property."

Well, I would like to ask such adults, what matters to you? Real estate? Or a real place where your children can learn from nature?

I am 14 and go to Firhill High School in Edinburgh. I have been interested in treehouses since I was very young. I first started studying building techniques at road protest sites like the M77 Pollok Free State in Glasgow. I then put these approaches to use in constructing my own treehouse.

The first was one that I built with some friends in woods between Firhill School and the City Hospital, but that was destroyed by local boys. My new treehouse is on an organic farm called Craigencalt, where my Dad lives in Fife.

By using rope techniques to tie beams of old timber to branches of a big sycamore, it meant that I didn't have to hurt the tree by hammering in nails.

After one week of hard work I had made the floor, four walls and the roof, but since then I have been adding to it.

The main features are a woodburning stove made from a five-gallon oil drum, a 3ft x 4ft glass window and a permaculture garden growing potatoes, parsley and peas inside natural hollows in the tree.

I also have a grass lawn and a four-person bed with pillows, sleeping bags and blankets. The treehouse has electric lighting, running water, a hammock and artwork. It is fully carpeted, with English oak-lined walls. I even have a stereo system rigged up to a Walkman.

Some visitors leave contributions, such as pictures and poems. One that relates to all this fuss about treehouses was done by a Fife bard called Barney McCormack. He wrote:

Child go break off from the herd
go beyond the lowlands
leave the valley of shed antlers
the elders are sick
it is your time now

Safety factors are very important, especially as we've had as many as ten people up there in one go. To hold the weight, I have the primary beams supported by primary and secondary ropes.

Then there are the secondary beams, which also have primary and secondary ropes in case the first lot break.

Every two weeks I abseil down the wall and check knots, ropes and beams.

An open stove in a treehouse could also be quite dangerous, so I have a fire guard, and heat-proof mats in treble thickness at both sides, to stop the walls from burning.

For climbing down from the treehouse, I have banisters and a rope net surrounding every gap, so I can't fall through.

It also makes it safe for some of my Dad's friends, who might be coming down a little tipsy after making music up there.

After parties, some friends and I will often sleep up there, even in January. What we do is stoke up the fire for the night, put the fire guard on, fold down the mattresses, tell stories and go to sleep to the sound of a waterfall outside and the smell of incense sticks inside.

I think if every child had such a magical place of its own, there wouldn't be so many problems of young people hanging about on the streets. That would mean less crime and drugs.

Just now in the West, the basic stages in life for your average person are to "make bucks, get rich, be better than everybody else, get fat and have a heart attack." But this could all be changed with the way future children are brought up.

We must ask ourselves, what is reality? Is it when the book I'm studying comes before enjoyment in nature? Or is it what a treehouse can teach you?

I have this question to put to people like the neighbours of Morningside. What do you want your children growing up with? Ecology? Ecstasy? Evolution?

Nicholson 24/6/92
I UNDERTAKE TO CREATE MORE JOBS..
I UNDERTAKE TO RESTART THE ECONOMY..
I UNDERTAKE TO MAKE THE COUNTRY EFFICIENT...
IS THAT WHY THEY CALL HIM THE UNDERTAKER?

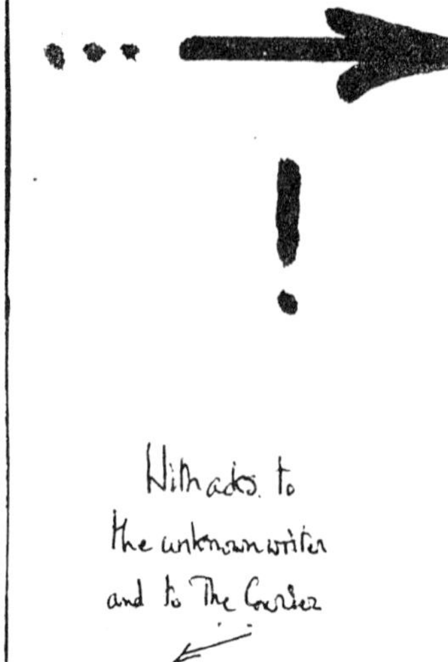

With acks. to the unknown writer and to The Courier

Time to return to basics

28 Aug 1998

Sir,—Last year I returned to primary teaching after the summer holidays, with some hope that the murmurings about "a return to basics" might bear some fruition.

Alas—my hopes were dashed! Already this year I see things are getting worse.

Teachers now have lists of "retraining" programmes which they must attend—no worries about money, plenty to pay the dozens of supply teachers. Having taught, with some credit, for over 20 years at the "chalk face", I now go to spend a day listening to an "expert" who has done no significant teaching for perhaps 10 years.

These people are "expert" only in modern jargon and airy-fairy methods, sadly proved as totally useless in day-to-day teaching.

The "retraining" should be the other way round.

Advisors, staff tutors, non-teaching promoted staff should be obliged to teach for significant blocks of time.

Get these people back to working with children in the real world of the classroom. Only then might these people see the result of their ineffectual, frankly laughable, new ideas.

Please don't print my name or I'll be forced to attend the latest course—"Don't tell the truth it might frighten them!"

Name and address supplied.

There is much I should like to have added to this inspiring cartoon - but there is hardly a moment left. The Courier has sparkled on education. In addition to the one on the right, there was Bob Smart on "targets only met by changing the goalposts", and "We have schools offering French and German to children who could barely pick a noun or adverb out of their own language", from "Please do not print my name as I am still a footsoldier!" (BRING BACK PARSING, is my cry! How can children have the full fun of language - let alone know how to use it properly - if they do not know what the building-blocks are. Make parsing FUN - it can be done!)

...Then on health: "We are now having people coming straight in from the universities, who have never done a day's nursing, and telling us what to do" - (an experienced nurse). And: "The Government and the majority of national health managers would not know what a patient is, even if they tripped over a bedpan", from R.C. McLagan...and Dr Ken Keddie, on retiring as a consultant psychiatrist, about over-emphasis being placed on whiz-kid technology - "It seems that in a world of electronics and computers, no one has time to listen to the heart-beat".

...And a cry from the heart by Graham Shand in the summer of 1997, about having lost "the purest and cleanest water in the whole of Britain" (Glendevon) as it is now "contaminated with chemicals...and literally stinks as it comes out of the tap".

...

Our UNDERTAKERS are well sandwiched between Adam McIntosh and Pure Genius!

*

The "PURE GENIUS" initiative of the campaigning body The Land Is Ours. Referred to in Pt.II, ch.1 of this book. The address of TLIO is Box E, 111 Magdalen Road, Oxford OX4 1RQ.

(With acknowledgements for the article both to TLIO, and to The Big Issue in whose magazine it was published on 12/8/96, and whose address in Scotland is 14 Albany St., Edinburgh EH1 3QB.)

INITIATIVE
Social Action in Action

Land and freedom

The controversial Pure Genius site has become home to *Big Issue* vendors, as Sarah Woodley reports

'YOURSELF THIS Way' points a sign welcoming newcomers to the 13-acre Pure Genius eco-village in Wandsworth, south London. The arid landscape of scorched grass, rubble and towering buddleias, set against the backdrop of an encroaching urban sprawl, may seem an unlikely place to find enlightenment, but the Guinness-owned site has been squatted by members of The Land Is Ours campaign since May.

And the 20-70 strong community seems to be flourishing in the wilderness. Since the media circus came and went a few months ago, they have been busy erecting teepees and yurts (Mongolian tribal shelters); cultivating their organic vegetable gardens; continuing their protest (a planning application has been lodged with Wandsworth Council to use the land for low-cost homes, an arts centre, nursery and nature reserve); and getting on with the business of living, under the shadow of an eviction order served by Guinness two-and-a-half months ago.

The land – a former gin distillery which has stood vacant for seven years – has become home to an assortment of engineers, builders, architects, travellers, ex-Newbury Bypass tree protestors – and recently *Big Issue* vendors. These latest additions include Scott and Dave who, like others on the site, return here rather than the streets after their day's selling. It's a reflection of The Land Is Ours' concern with one of the most pressing social issues of the day – homelessness.

A motif for the madness of modern housing policy – London alone has derelict land the size of the Borough of Westminster – is Michael's home in Pure Genius. A qualified builder and plasterer, he has constructed a raspberry-and-blue riverside hut, complete with boat launch and a pedallo made from wood and orange plastic chairs. Across the Thames lies Chelsea Harbour, to the right luxury apartments waiting to be sold – at £190,000 a throw. On the door of Michael's home is scrawled the word 'happy'.

Alex Macnaughton

Digging for the future: Land Is Ours campaigners in May

"We've got a good community. It's very relaxed, everybody's alive and there's no aggression. It's just a bunch of people living together"

"Being here is so much more positive than walking the streets," says Wilf, an ex-stage-lighting engineer for bands including ZZ Top and David Bowie. "We've got a good community. It's very relaxed, everybody's alive and there's no aggression. It's just a bunch of people living together." Reclining on a tattered sofa – locals have been very supportive, donating anything from food and clothes to timber and blankets – Wilf surveys his co-residents from inside an imposing wooden marquee which serves as a meeting area. A young girl plays with a battered, matted-haired doll, worn with too much affection; a slender, bare-chested man with long blonde hair arches his back into a yoga pose; a man and woman set industriously about the makeshift carpet with a dustpan and brush, and a sleepy, silky-haired spaniel curls up at its owner's feet.

Mariamne, 30, a *Big Issue* vendor considering living on the site (hostels she's tried so far have turned her away because of her dog, Zara – "a Doberlady"), is impressed with what she's seen so far. "Everyone's really friendly," she says, two long dreadlocks threaded with seashells swinging enthusiastically.

"For people who are homeless it's a very positive environment," she continues. "When you're poor you can't afford to think about things like recycling rubbish. Here you can learn to survive in an environmental way."

Behind the self-sustaining communal idyll – the healing area and the vegetarian kitchen; the 'compostloo' and eco-shower; the astrology workshops and the colourful noticeboards extolling the virtues of permaculture and woad – lies a sharply-honed direct action campaign which has won over the press and local community alike since its inception in October last year. "Homes For All", "Land For the People" and "People Not Profit" declare the banners at the main entrance, in front of a wooden reception hut complete with gatekeeper.

Putting homelessness and derelict land at the top of the agenda; calling for affordable housing and as much green public space as possible, The Land Is Ours – fronted by 33-year-old Oxford don, author and campaigner George Monbiot – adopts a pragmatic approach it is difficult to find fault with. "We only want to stay living on the land till another use for it comes up," says Will, simply. "Then we'll move on. But while it's laying empty we can do something with it."

Another resident, Horus, smiling sagely from behind his mane of waist-length black hair as he tells me about a cosmic wobble which could send the planet spinning off its axis in the year 2016, puts it another way. "If more people start living like this, in the correct way, we could save the planet," he says. When I ask how we can change he gestures towards the distant horizon. "When all the negative things like greed and environmental destruction disappear – all the madness going on out there."

I follow his gaze past the tops of teepees and the whirring energy windmills to the skyscrapers beyond – and I have to agree with him. Madness.

The Initiative pages give a voice to homeless people and report on innovative self-help projects which attempt to bring about social change

Birthright... and... Scotland Today

GANDHI ON WORK

. . . fit for human beings

"The truth is that man needs work even more than he needs a wage. Those who seek the welfare of the workers should be less anxious to obtain good pay, good holidays and good pensions for them than good work, which is the first of their goods.

For the object of work is not so much to make objects as to make men. A man makes himself by making something. Work creates a direct contact with matter and ensures him precise knowledge of it as well as direct contact and daily collaboration with other men; it imprints the form of man on matter and offers itself to him as a means of expression; it concentrates his attention and his abilities on one point or at least on a continuous line; it bridles the passions by strengthening the will. Work, bodily work, is for nine-tenths of humanity their only chance to show their worth in this world.

But in order that work itself, and not just payment for it, shall profit a man, it must be human work, work in which the whole man is engaged: his body, his heart, his brain, his taste. The craftsman who fashions an object, polishes it, decorates it, sells it, and fits it for the requirements of the person he intends it for, is carrying out human work. The countryman who gives life to his fields and makes his flocks prosper by work attuned to the seasons is successfully accomplishing the task of a free man.

But the worker enslaved in a serial production, who from one second to another repeats the same movement at the speed dictated by the machine, fritters himself away in work which has no purpose for him, no end, no taste, no sense. The time he spends there is time lost, time sold: he is not selling his creation, but his very lifetime. He is selling what a free man does not sell: his life. He is a slave.

The problem is not how to sweeten the lot of the proletarian so as to make it acceptable to him, but how to get rid of the proletariate, just as we got rid of slavery, since the proletariate is indeed slavery.

As for the whole peoples who are doomed to idleness, what is to be done with them, what will they do with themselves?

In reply to which people will tell you that the State (and if you don't know what the State is, I shall tell you: it is mechanised Providence), which will have solved the problem of work by complete industrialisation, will then only have to solve the problems of leisure and education. It will plan games and entertainment and will distribute learning to all.

But the pleasures of men without work have always been drunkenness and mischief. The State can offer them educational pleasures for all it is worth, they will still prefer drunkenness and mischief. The games will then have to become compulsory and for many will cease to be games and turn into discipline and duties, falsifications of work from which no good can come. It would have been better to plan work.

But there is a pleasure dearer to man than work, dearer than drunkenness and mischief, that of shouting 'Down with ...!' and setting fire to everything. That is a game which will quickly replace all others in the mechanised Paradise."

The teachings of Gandhi, from Ch. 'Wardha' in 'Return to the Source', by Lanza del Vasto (Rider & Company, London, 1971). Quoted with kind permission of the Publishers.

*

GANDHI ON EDUCATION

(From the same book)

"... The question was how to rid official teaching of its fundamental vice, which is that of all our culture, namely the divorce between practice, theory and morality.

Practice, says Gandhi, is the root and stem of the plant, science its foliage, virtue its flower and fruit. Separating disciplines is cutting up the plant.

The child should first be taught a craft, and from that stem the branches of his culture will grow.

The child's body should be busied, exercised and fortified at the same time as his intellect and heart.

No knowledge, no principle should be revealed to him without their point of application, their use, their connection with reality being made tangible to him.

Now, everything is connected with everything else. It is up to the educator to discover the joints. If he starts from spinning and weaving, for example, it is not difficult to spin and weave a whole history of the civilisations from that subject. The study of cotton leads on to botany, agriculture, political economy and so on.

The child should be taught the dignity of working with his hands, and from that, the dignity of working on himself and mastering his senses, which leads on to all duties and all the virtues.

From the outset the child should be made to understand the price of knowledge and he should earn it himself in the sweat of his brow. A school must be productive and self-supporting through the work of its pupils.

Boredom must be banished from school. Boredom is useless mortification by bodily idleness; it is dead science, dead principles forcibly inflicted on children. Children are the most lively creatures there are, the most open, the most inquiring on all subjects. Imposing silence, immobility, dead science and dead principles on them is not bringing them up. 'Dead' means 'cut off at the root'.

Quoted with kind permission of the Publishers, also.

HENRY GEORGE - *Progress & Poverty*

The Story of a Best-seller

In the Spring of 1879, when America was recovering from violent economic panic and corrupt political administration, Henry George was learning to use the typewriter and telephone. He organised under the banner of the Knights of Labour and watched the rise of Andrew Carnegie and John D. Rockefeller. A neat, holograph manuscript began to make the rounds of New York publishing houses. Written by this unknown West Coast newsman and printer, it was a revolutionary effort to solve the problems of depression, unemployment and poverty, through a step-by-step analysis that was both careful and inspirational. After refusals everywhere, it was accepted by D. Appleton & Co., provided the author bore the cost of making printing plates. This he did, and the next spring appeared ***Progress and Poverty.***

San Francisco papers derided it as a "hobby" of "little Harry George," other journals dismissed it as visionary, but in significant quarters, it gained immediate acclaim. "Little Harry George" sprang from obscurity to world renown. After reading *Progress and Poverty*, philosopher John Dewey said that you could count on your fingers "those who from Plato down, rank with Henry George among the world's great social philosophers."

The next quarter of a century saw *Progress and Poverty* become one of the top best sellers in all American publishing history. It went quickly into paper-bound editions and was translated into all the chief languages of Europe; by 1905, about 2 million copies had been sold. As America passed through World War I and into unmatched prosperity, its popularity waned, until the Robert Schalkenbach Foundation was organised in 1925 to promote George's philosophy. Its edition of the book expanded its market, spurred on perhaps by the Great Depression, and now accounts for a sale of 10,000 copies a year. That its acceptance goes beyond avowed Georgists is attested by its having sold 3 million by 1950. How many since then?

*

Introduction to

"ECOLOGISTS AND THE LAND"

An article by Dr E.F. Schumacher on "How to Abolish Land Speculation" appeared in the magazine Resurgence of September 1974 - just a quarter of a century ago; and I understand has recently been reprinted in a collection of his works entitled "This I Believe, and Other Essays". (Green Books publishers.)

It may therefore be timely to re-publish here the following article, which was written at the time in answer to Dr Schumacher's. As it was refused publication in Resurgence, I therefore published it myself in the spring of 1975. It was favourably reviewed in Land and Liberty (May-June 75), and stocked in their library at the time; while a quantity ordered by the well-known 'peace' bookshop, Housmans, in London N.1, also found a ready sale.

*

ECOLOGISTS AND THE LAND

by

Shirley-Anne Hardy

DR. SCHUMACHER'S LAND REFORM

"All right, if you don't like this scheme, will you kindly propose something better?" So ends an article on 'How to Abolish Land Speculation', by Dr. Schumacher, in a recent issue of *Resurgence* devoted entirely to the land question.

Taking up the challenge, it is not so much that one 'does not like' Dr. Schumacher's scheme as that it turns out to be quite inadequate. The reason is that he attempts to deal with only a part of land speculation, and that the less important part, because his view of land remains the conventional one – namely that of land as a saleable asset.

The first hint of this occurs in the opening paragraph where we find the names of Karl Marx and Henry George bracketed together with no suggestion at all that there is any important difference between their teachings on the land question, whereas the difference is vital and fundamental. Where Marx held that the basic economic categories are two – namely, capital and labour, Henry George postulated a third – and placed it first. In George's teaching land and labour are the two fundamentals, capital resulting only from a marriage between them. He therefore held that land, which antedates all human effort, is of a given quantity, and cannot be added to by human labour, should not be bought and sold like the things made with men's hands.

Because he does not see this Dr. Schumacher, while rejecting land nationalisation in favour of de-centralised ownership – and on good grounds – fails to challenge the commonly accepted idea that the land may rightfully be taken possession of by some to the exclusion of all other members of the community.

It is interesting that many early types of community seem to have had a natural understanding of the unique asset they possessed in the land and its resources. 'The Earth is our Mother, and we cannot sell our Mother' is an Iroquois saying. And Nyerere of Tanzania speaking today not only for Africans but for *all* the inhabitants of this planet, points out – (quoted on page seven of *Resurgence's* Land issue) – that every individual in society must have a right to the use of land, since without it man cannot make his living on earth, and it is self-evident that the right to life must carry with it the right to the means of maintaining life.

How then can we take as our starting point for any new land legislation (as Dr. Schumacher would have us take), a concept of land which inherently denies the right of vast numbers in our society to share in what nature has given freely to all? Any new land legislation that attempts to preserve the foundations of our unjust system of land tenure will succeed ultimately in but one thing, and that is in cementing present injustice yet more firmly into the structure of society.

In fact we have already seen what happens to legislation which fastens upon the speculation in land that takes place at the point of sale (however thoroughly it tries to tackle it here, as Dr. Schumacher's scheme does try). Both the Town and Country Planning Act and the more recent Land Commission attempted to deal with land speculation in just this way, and came to grief for the same reason – that their primary effect was to discourage the sale of land. What both overlooked – as Dr. Schumacher does likewise – is the *continuing* speculation that takes place in land *rental values*, where an individual is in the position of being able to grant others access, on monopoly terms, to land which he does not need, but they do. It was this that enabled Harry Hyams to increase his fortune from £27 million to £300 million in the space of six years – without making a single sale to do it. (And here one must note a rather strange statement by Dr. Schumacher – that most landowners are farmers and that nothing could be further from their real interests than land speculation).

DR. G.T. WRENCH ON RECONSTRUCTION BY WAY OF THE SOIL

Dr. Schumacher speaks as an ecologist and conservationist and it would be a pity if such people were to think of land speculation – and thus the land problem – only in this narrow and somewhat superficial sense. Fortunately one can point them to a man of their own choosing to take them to the heart of the matter – G.T. Wrench, author of 'Reconstruction by Way of the Soil'. For Wrench was one of the great pioneers of organic husbandry, and a firm advocate of the farming of the land by an independent peasant population. Writing about the period at the turn of the century, he reports: "We find them (the agricultural labourers unions) going to the root of the matter in their attempts to free land from the dominance of money. They supported the Land Restoration League, which wished to put a tax upon rent and increase it progressively until it absorbed and eventually abolished rent, and thus achieve the aim of Henry George."

Wrench went straight to the root of the land question. Ecologists, who sometimes confuse the two ideas, should note that he does not write of the proposal here as one to tax *land*, but as one to tax the *rental value* arising from land – that is, the exploitative element in land holding: the very thing ecologists should welcome. Turning to the problems of the Third World, with which ecologists are so greatly concerned, it is of course the screwing down of landless peasants by the extraction of rental payments (either in money or in kind) so as to leave them verging continually on a level below subsistence, which lies at the root of their situation – so uniquely illumined by George's teachings. Once the workings of the law of land rent have been grasped (known as Ricardo's Law of Rent, recognised – but not trumpeted – by orthodox economists), the cruelty of the system under which they likewise labour is readily seen.

THE MOVEMENT BACK TO THE LAND

Under a system of the annual collection of land rent, however, all land which is being held by its owner as a capital asset, and not used directly by him, would be forced onto the market, since no one is going to continue paying a rental demand on land which he cannot recoup by passing on – (though he will be actually selling on the market only the value of the man-made improvements). The monopoly power in land holding being thus removed, the 'price' of land would come tumbling – (that is to say, the price of its annual rental value to a member of the community) – since it is of the essence of a monopoly that it at once bestows an artificial price on things. This point should commend itself particularly to those seeking to return to the land, many of whose troubles currently spring from the fact that the price of land as capital is compelling them to embark on such ventures in conditions of unnaturally close proximity.

PUBLIC AND PRIVATE RIGHTS

Thus the tax upon land values, in going to the root of the land question, automatically eliminates land speculation in its wider as well as narrower sense – and without the need to resort to 'powers of compulsory purchase', as Dr. Schumacher admits his scheme would require. Indeed, the great virtue of Henry George's proposal is that it draws this fine and exact line between the spheres of public and private rights. Of no other system purporting to deal with the land question can this be said. The exactness of the line drawn is well illustrated in the following passage from George's writings: 'In truth, the right to the use of land is not a joint or common right, but an *equal* right. The joint or common right is to *rent* in the economic sense of the term. Therefore it is not necessary for the State to take land, it is only necessary for it to take rent.'

At a time when some form of public ownership of land is pressing itself so insistently upon people's attention, the clear line drawn here between necessary and unnecessary State intervention deserves our most careful study. Ecologists should surely be in the lead here.

SOURCES OF LAND ABUSE

We refer to the idea of land, of course, in its broadest sense, without any specifically agricultural meaning. 'Man is a land animal', as Henry George points out, and there is no single way he can engage his energies which does not require the use of land. It is the basic raw material of all human activities.

As to whether the individual is to be trusted on the question of land use, ecologists might note that abuses are perpetrated here not generally by those who employ only themselves or work in small co-operative ventures, but by men become irresponsible through long working for another, or by those giants who possess the magic wand of being able to 'provide' the masses with 'employment'.

ORIGINS OF UNEMPLOYMENT

Revealing as to the origins of our strange theories of unemployment today was an ITV series at the end of 1974 named 'The Disappearing World', in which we were shown the last few really isolated communities remaining in certain parts of the world. Now, where these communities are making contact with Western land capitalist society, they are falling rapidly under the power of their new 'providers' of work. However, these providers, one notes, first carefully provide themselves with the land of the indigenous peoples, upon which to play their conjuring trick! Here we see where the bogus philosophy of unemployment has its rise.

FALSE OR TRUE SOLUTIONS

Surely it is clear that power wielded, as under our land system, right at the basis of existence, over the economic and social activities of other men, must be corruptive whether wielded by separate individuals, by small hierarchies of individuals, or by that ultimate hierarchy the State? It was sad then to observe, in a journal which stands for the de-centralisation of power, that there were one or two articles in this Land issue which actually proposed further centralisation as the solution to our ills. Both the 'common ownership of land' and an increase in 'social ownership and control' were advocated. The over-simplification seems to be that there can be but two owners of the soil, either the State or private landlords, and it is because of this unreal choice that error leads to further error in propounding solutions.

Where the problems of mankind signal some basic idea as yet unperceived, how few are those who in the process of searching, and while remaining possibly long empty of answer, have the strength still to reject what they know will not do, and remain untempted by false solutions.

A false solution is invariably recognisable as one, which attempts in some way to substitute human manipulation for the workings of a natural law. To the individual engaged in rejecting false solutions, such a law, emerging in his researches, will immediately appeal, for his vision will not meanwhile have been engaged by false remedies.

Such a man was Henry George; and it was a law of this kind which, after years of searching, observation and questioning, he came to perceive at work shaping the economic and social circumstances of men.

But it is not only in its avoidance of false solutions that George's proposal attracts us. The workings of a natural law have, in addition, a peculiar power, commending to us a pattern of *liberty* – that in conformity with our true being; a concept well expressed in the seeming paradox, 'whom to serve is perfect freedom'.

Perhaps it is not surprising that ecologists in general should be so unacquainted with the teachings of Henry George. The crux of the matter is that Henry George is the enemy of centralisation – (as *Resurgence* itself claims to be) – and as such is inevitably rejected by the centralisers, who are in power today. One is surprised, however, to find in the editorial columns of this Land issue a warning against the 'ideologues' who 'believe that to settle the question of land is to settle everything else that relates to economic justice." It is not so much that to settle the land question is to settle everything else, but rather this – that until the land question is settled we do not know what else left to settle there may be.

For the law of liberty – (the *law* of liberty, be it emphasised) – possesses a unique power in working out the knots of human entanglement, since under its operation the unnatural distortions to human character – which are the source of so much restrictive legislation – are gradually effaced, and man in his truer image makes appearance.

Turning to the question of community land trusts, and the tremendous efforts currently being invested in these – (article by Stephen Bridge) – one is momentarily disheartened. In the first place – whilst fully respecting the sincerity of such efforts – however well intentioned and however successful in the short term such land trusts may be, by reason of their incidental commitment to the idea of land as capital they will, in the long run, but cement us more firmly into the present false structure of society. But in addition, their inherently hierarchical structure, controlling land use, raises certain questions: 'The leaseholder only loses his lease if he does not use his land productively.'[1] Who is to decide on the true definition of that last word? Clearly this responsibility rests with the trustees – with whom must lie ultimately also the interpretation of the 'specified social purposes' bearing on land use. It is open knowledge, however, that freedom and responsibility grow hand in hand – and grow

[1] *See 'The Community Land Trust: A new approach to land tenure'. Published by Warren, 3 Salubrious, Broadway, Worcs.*

strongest that way. Henry George's system would leave them space to do just this. Our aim should always be as far as possible to free ourselves from organisational structures, rather than bind fresh ones on our backs.

'No jail ... no crime ... no juvenile delinquency', we read in a book about the Hunza people.[2] Reading further under the chapter headings, we find the inevitable link: 'land is neither bought nor sold'. The Hunzakuts, living under a land system well suited to a more primitive society, likewise avoid the pitfall of exploitation, which is inseparable from the power conferred by the private appropriation of land rent.

Little is left over, as the passage above quoted indicates, for bureaucrats to busy themselves about amongst the people of Hunza, who are not a hunter-gatherer society, be it noted (such as is generally singled out by ecologists as the unexploitative type), but a settled community cultivating their land. This seems well to support Henry George's contention that where a just land system governs in a society there are few things left indeed for governments to perform which individuals will not far better accomplish, freely co-operating amongst themselves.

---

[2] *Hunza Health Secrets for Long Life and Happiness', by Renee Taylor. Tandem Books, London. Paperback.*

Birthright ... and ... Scotland Today

*

ANTONIA SWINSON - SCOTLAND ON SUNDAY

With kind permission from Antonia Swinson, weekly columnist in the Business section of "Scotland on Sunday" - the following extract from her article which appeared on 16th August, 1998.

*

"Don't talk about IT, we chorus. Another guest in marketing services suggests IT has reduced his productivity by 90% and makes him long for the old days when he had a secretary who would type. Another admits that she is often embarrassed by the huge fees she charges her clients for very low productive work. ...I suddenly have a vision of just how vulnerable the service economy now is. Is the current worship of IT a case of the emperor's clothes?"

*

EXTRACTS FROM

AN HISTORIAN'S CONCLUSIONS

by

John Peter, J.P., M.A., F.E.I.S.

During the first decade of this Century, the great politico-economic debate in Great Britain was Free Trade or Protection ... I was in my teens; and my interest in public affairs was from the first economic rather than political ... My family background was liberal ... Of course I was a Free Trader. I had read every available pamphlet on the Free Trade side of the question, and also most of what the other side had to say ... It appeared that foreigners had no right to be in our market, but that we had a peculiar and exclusive right to be in theirs ...

Meantime, the Socialists were ... assuring the working man that the question was of little consequence to him, and that he was exploited by the capitalists. I used to listen to the Clydeside 'rebels' on this theme when they visited my hometown.

It was at this time that a relative handed me a well worn paper covered copy of 'Protection or Free Trade' by Henry George ... I soon recognised that here was a thinker who had gone right down to fundamentals and shown that Free Trade was essential to economic well being – and that Free Trace was not enough! I was no longer worried as I had been about the 'displaced' worker. His opportunities were really unlimited – though he didn't (and doesn't) know it – if only access to them under just conditions were permitted.

In due course I became an undergraduate of the University of Edinburgh. From a school fellow, Matthew Wilson Paul, who had become attached to the then very active Scottish League for the Taxation of Land Values, I received a copy of Henry George's 'Progress and Poverty', which I still possess. Having already become familiar with economic terms and reasoning, I found it comparatively easy to grasp its main thesis. I soon realised that this analysis of the economic problem was unique and satisfying and that the solution presented was simple and just. I need hardly add I did not all at once grasp the full significance of the teachings of this book. Who ever did? But it was quite obvious that the author deserved the attention of all serious-minded people. Certainly, I was gripped.

The subjects which we 'took' (as we say in Scotland) in my degree course were all chosen so that, besides qualifying me to earn my living, they would help me to become a citizen competent to understand what was going on around him. Thus I became a member of Professor Shield Nicholson's class in Political Economy. In his lectures (and in his books) he explained the Law of Rent, as promulgated by Ricardo, perfectly. It was all exactly as I had understood it from reading Henry George (and others) and was illustrated by a diagram which I often used later on when I was speaking to audiences. What I could never understand, however, was his failure to draw the obvious conclusion from it. That, of course, was just exactly what Henry George did. The man who grasps the significance of the margin of land utilisation and its effect upon wealth distribution has in his hand the key to an understanding of the great economic problem of our time, indeed, of all time. The question of to whom 'rent' rightfully belongs was shirked or slurred over. Economists in established places are always anxious to declare their objectivity. They deal, they say, with things as they are. The realm of ethics and morals is one into which they claim it is not their business to enter. Usually they dismiss Henry George in a footnote without even trying to show wherein he was wrong. But Henry George will not be disposed of so easily. Practice proves.

At the conclusion of my war service, I was concerned, like thousands more, to know what beyond earning a living was a worthwhile aim in life. From the beginning I had felt that the way of life propounded by Henry George was for free men the best I knew. Advocacy of his teachings might put a worthy purpose into my life. Yet his way of things was frowned upon, or ignored, by the established economics teachers. I resolved to re-read his books systematically and critically. If there was a fallacy somewhere in his reasoning I would find it and that would be the end of the matter. As it was, far from finding error in George's teaching, I could not help seeing the errors in others'. Chief of these was imprecision in the use of terms, the crime – to the logician – of giving things that are essentially different, a generic name, e.g., property, and drawing conclusions that were not applicable to all things in the category. In short, they were illogical.

By this time I had extended the breadth of my reading considerably. I read the classical economists and the socialist propagandists – how hard it must be for a classical economist not to be a socialist! – and history of all types, particularly political and economic. It was borne in on me how almost all writers failed to see the connection between the system of land tenure and taxation in a country and the general well being of its people; and how obvious (throughout all history) the connection was to me. Cause and effect were there for all but the wilfully blind to see. I read scores of theses on economic subjects and discovered that these could be written without once using the word 'land', the very prerequisite of life itself. The word rarely appeared even in the most learned tones written by the most be-degreed men in the business, 'Capital' and 'poverty' were there alright, scattered all over the text, but never precisely defined. Yet accuracy of definition is the first essential to clear thinking.

By this time I had become a subscriber to 'Land and Liberty' and joined the Scottish League for the Taxation of Land Values. This brought me into contact with some of the stalwarts of the movement ... I had begun to write letters to the editor ... whenever I saw anything reported that invited comment. I did some speaking to groups of people under various auspices ... I was invited on one occasion to write the leading article in 'Land and Liberty' – and did ... and finally to speak for Scotland at two International Conferences, at Edinburgh and St. Andrews ...

The great merit of henry George's analysis of the economic problem (the equitable distribution of wealth) is that it is made in terms of real things, land, labour and capital, as opposed to 'finance'. George also assumes as fundamental, and demonstrates as true, that the distribution of wealth among the productive agents is, in free and just conditions, in accordance with natural law. This latter conception is beyond the unenlightened thinker who sees the problem – and how obvious! – as one of a shortage of purchasing power, particularly in certain individual hands, and thus a monetary one. This view has won most of our leading men in all parties; and though they see the danger of increasing purchasing power (paper currency and credit built thereon) they know no way out. All advanced nations are today inflating their currencies, with good intent, and hoping to dodge the consequences! We Georgists must understand this 'money business' for we are now being confronted by another attractive, specious and dangerous 'remedy' for the poverty malaise ...

NOTE: The above article was published in August 1959 in the 'Personally Speaking' series of the Journal 'Land and Liberty'. See Ref. List. John Peter, born in Stirlingshire, and a member of the teaching profession, was Vice-president of the Scottish league for Land Value Taxation, on the Executive of the Scottish Liberal Party, and a member of Falkirk Town Council.

*

Introduction to

"FOR GOD'S SAKE SET THE PEOPLE FREE AND END LEGALISED THEFT"

by

David A. MacMurchie

*

I am re-publishing here the above article by David MacMurchie, first published by him some twenty years ago, not only for its excellence but also in memory of the MacMurchie brothers, James and David, who helped keep alive in Scotland the movement for radical land reform through many less hopeful decades, while the Socialist experiment was running its course.

Both brothers lived long lives: David, in Dundee, well into his eighties; and James, in Easter Kilbride, well into his nineties. David, whom I came to know personally, was a skilled welder of angle-iron who had worked on the Tay Bridge. Later, as the work scene changed, through involuntary unemployment he experienced vividly at first-hand the deprivations of that state, and its effects on the full round of life. His gentle and generous spirit was matched by the depth of his feelings on social injustice. In his later years, David also wrote a small book containing vivid memoirs of Dundee, under the title "I Remember Princes Street".

Scotland should not forget the MacMurchie brothers, of whom a third - always averred by James and David as far outshining them in gifts - tragically for us was killed in the First World War. David's article is a fitting memorial to all three.

(Note: I have slightly edited the article, chiefly to replace the word State with Community - (used in places by David himself) - as more in keeping with our time. S-A.H.)

*

A Blue Print for Full Employment & National Prosperity

FOR GOD'S SAKE SET THE PEOPLE FREE AND END LEGALISED THEFT!

by

David A. MacMurchie

*

"WHAT MORE PREPOSTEROUS than that one tenant for a day of this rolling sphere should collect rent for it from his co-tenants or sell to them for a price what was here ages before him, and will be here ages after him"

Henry George

We're landless! Such was the anguished cry of the wild MacGregors. Today, that cry is echoed by the MacDonalds, Campbells, MacLeods, Robertsons, Smiths, Browns, Jones's and millions more throughout the world similarly afflicted. With only their labour to sell, the landless are haunted much of their lives by the fear of unemployment or sickened, frustrated and angered by the experience of it.

Men and women do not live to work but work to live and enjoy the full fruits of their labour. White collar and blue-collar workers should make common cause in the struggle for a better society as all landless are caught up in the rat race.

In industrialised countries the people have been driven or drained from rural to urban areas. Britain has witness these forces at work bringing disastrous consequences to the nation and down the years, leaving great tracts of land derelict. Unless this process is, in part at least, reversed – unless there is a fundamental change in our economic structure, hundreds of thousands will never find employment and so will be condemned to spend their lives in aimless idleness. All those who desire employment should, we believe, have useful and profitable employment open to them: production would then be immeasurably increased.

ACCESS TO LAND NECESSARY

Access to land is vitally necessary for houses, hospitals, schools, shops, factories, mines, farms, transport and every sort of urban and rural activity, including new enterprises. These amenities and activities would provide work not only for those engaged in construction but also for those in the service industries as well as for those involved in producing the consumer goods that go with a decent and satisfactory living for everyone; but this desirable situation is impossible on account of land monopoly. It has, therefore, become abundantly clear that, until land monopoly is abolished and access to land secured, unemployment cannot be remedied and must remain NUMBER ONE social problem.

In tackling unemployment, which for far too long has plagued the nation, the old pragmatic dosage, i.e., tariffs and quotas, job creation schemes, employment subsidies, etc., has failed and must always fail because it does not reach the root of the problem. To avoid the disappointment of enforced idleness experienced by school leavers and college graduates; a more practical approach is necessary. Bleak job prospects for the rising generation give cause for deep concern.

Equity demands that every human being has access to land. “By nature, every living creature, including man, has the right to this source of food. No man has a prior right. If by force, whether physical or legal, man is deprived of his natural rights, he loses his manhood, freedom and individuality, man’s most precious possessions. He necessarily becomes a tool in the hands of others ...”*

Evidently, eliminating the monopoly land-owning set-up is long overdue. This can best be done by requiring all landholders to remit the annual GROUND RENT to the community. This would end the holding of land for rental profit and none would occupy more land than he could directly put to use himself. Community living is natural to man, and GROUND RENT/SITE RENT is the naturally arising fund from community living. GROUND RENT can be seen as that spontaneous fund, or Social Dividend (not due to any action of the private landowners as such), owing to and created by the activities of the whole community and, by right, to be used by the Community as revenue. “All that is necessary to do,” said Henry George, "is to collect the annual (economic) GROUND RENT for the common benefit."” This GROUND RENT revenue ought to be used and completely exhausted before one-penny piece of direct or indirect taxation is imposed. This policy is advocated in the works of Adam Smith, Dr. F. Quesnay, Henry George, Patrick Dove and other eminent political economists.

Appropriating GROUND RENT for public expenses would be but a return to the ancient method of raising revenue. Theoretically, down the ages, the community has met the annual GROUND RENT charge, but instead of going into the community’s treasury that revenue has swelled the bank balances of private landowners. To make good the deficiency in revenue the government has had recourse directly and indirectly to taxing capital and labour. Again, apart from tax evasion, which is widespread, direct and indirect tax concerns only commercialised production: any production and exchange done clear of commerce escapes taxation. Therefore, in no way can United Kingdom revenue raising practices be said to operate with fairness. Besides seriously disrupting trade and industry, the present tax devices involve a huge army of tax gatherers and an improvised administration the whole imposing a vast financial burden, itself, upon the community.

Taxes, also, are improvised and altogether harmful from the sense of expedience, economics, ethically and from any sense from which one cares to judge the issue. Taxation is not a factor and has absolutely no function in the Science of Wealth (production and distribution). Taxation is a wholly unnecessary evil. Taxation is corrupt and corrupting. Taxation destroys. Taxation causes unemployment, poverty, crime, distress and all manner of social problems and brings War in its train. Taxation is unworkable – unless Havoc is deemed acceptable. On June 1st, 1976, Sir William Pile, Chairman of the Board of Inland Revenue, said, “I told the Government the system (of revenue raising) is breaking down.” What’s the sense in continuing the awful struggle with the unworkable? – Particularly, when the perfectly efficient economy is crying out to be operated?

Birthright ... and ... Scotland Today

INVOLUNTARY EMPLOYMENT *IS* HOME MADE

Should the government give the merest hint that it intended next year to revert to the ancient method of collecting the annual GROUND RENT as Community Revenue, that hint would at once neatly kill land speculation. In turn, it would open up all land for development with suitable jobs for the jobless. This would debunk statements that involuntary unemployment is the result of world trade slumps and prove that involuntary unemployment is largely home made. Bringing the maximum manpower into play would signal the millennium – the opposite to conditions, which prevail today. Keeping things as they are, with one and a half millions workless and its deplorably evil effects on the poor landless, is quite apparently an instrument of modern government policy. All the politicians' wartime promises of "making the United Kingdom a land fit for heroes" have been discarded. Why, then, should we not revert to the ancient method of collecting GROUND RENT for Revenue – so allowing the economy to function naturally? As Edmund Burke would have said, "Is this too sane and too simple"?

Either in town or country, those failing to put the land to the most profitable use would be obliged by economic pressure to release it for some more rewarding purposes.

Security of tenure ensuring the benefit of improvements is all that is necessary to make the best use of land. Private monopoly is a bad set up. Landowners keep land out of production for speculative gain; this entails rack-renting and is contrary to the community's interest. Like air and sunshine, land – as of its original state – is not wealth and so should not be subject to private ownership. The highest interest an individual may have in land is a tenancy in fee simple; the tenant holds the land 'in usufruct'.** In 1789, the French Assembly declare, 'Ignorance, neglect or contempt of Human Rights are the sole causes of public misfortune and corruption of government.'

Some States control land and industry, but this gives the State an overweening power over the individual. The aim must, therefore, be to end land monopoly; to free commercial and industrial enterprise from State interference, ownership or control; and to end shortages, privileges, quotas and subsidies. In brief, the target is the basis for real Democracy – Free Land; Free Trade and Free Men!

END LEGALISED THEFT

Once the landless know that GOUND RENT is the Community's share of production, the day of emancipation with all its benefits and blessings shall draw near. Having rid of penal taxation would, of itself, give abundant cause for national rejoicing.

The land, which is 'our Mother' from which we get all things necessary for life and living, must be restored to the nation. This shall be accomplished not by 'nationalisation', nor by sharing out land in small lots, but by collecting the rent of land (GROUND RENT) for Community Revenue; for this would prevent the holding of land by any beyond that amount which a man could directly utilise by his own labour (or men, in free co-operation together, by theirs).

The people must demand this reform. And the day of its accomplishment be declared a public holiday; this holiday, call it Jubilee Day, Emancipation Day or, Land Restoration Day, to be kept clear of other high days, holidays or Saint's Days, and celebrated annually as a reminder to future generations of the importance which 'Mother Earth' is to all men, and which holding the land in common is for each nation's well being and happiness.

The Mosaic Jubilee meant a 'clean slate' and a fresh start.*** With opportunity for work laid open, and higher wages for each according to ability, this nation would witness the speedy end of poverty and its attendant evils. Then, and only then, would the Millennium be ushered in, and that bright picture Sir Winston Churchill was wont to paint of this nation entering those broad meadows of peace and plenty become accomplished fact.

Demanding GROUND RENT for Community Revenue and No Taxation!

LIBERALS AND LABOUR PROMISED THIS REFORM 60 YEARS AGO!

---

* *The Land Question and Christian Justice by Rev. W.H. Howard.*

** *See Blackstone Commentaries on English and Scottish Law.*

*** *See Leviticus, Chap, 25, v.10.*

BY THE WAY...

By Lindy Davies

Published in the *Georgist Journal*, U.S.A. in 1997.

It is sometimes said that the endeavour of teaching political economy using so quaint a tool as simple deductive logic is practically useless, in this "information age". Without numbers, they say, what can we say for sure?

For instance: some of our academic colleagues are impatient with public-education efforts. Instead, they call for urgent, heavily-funded research on the amount of land rent in our national economy. Now, this is not such a terrible idea in itself. Questions are often raised about the revenue-raising sufficiency of land rent. And, it is evident that generous building depreciation allowances (far in excess of the buildings' market values) are reported in national income statistics – and can provide data for a broad, but credible, estimate of aggregate rent. (This is because the tax savings on buildings depreciated in excess of their true market values is indeed land rent; most of that rental income is generally not collected until it takes the form of a "capital gain" when the property is sold.)

To be sure, a well-planned, sensible commitment to research can only help to illustrate the fundamental truths that we are trying to make clear. But let's not fall into the trap that academic economists have always sought to lead us into, against which Henry George urgently warned in *Social Problems*: "We cannot safely leave politics to politicians, or political economy to college professors. The people themselves must think, because the people alone can act."

So let's think. No statistics now exist on the aggregate rental value of land. The economy is not accustomed to treating land as a distinct factor in the economy. Even if we could estimate the rental value of the land component of real estate, we would still leave out the value of minerals and other natural resources, of clean air and water, and preservation of natural diversity, and of broadcast frequencies and other natural opportunities. It's complex out there. Decoding all this mess, and coming up with an accurate quantification of the share of land rent in national income, would be an expensive task. But very worthwhile, no?

Perhaps – if we have plenty of money. But I believe that we can use logic – not expensive at all, in fact it's free for the using – to devise a model of aggregate land rent that is quite useful, and might even make our point quite strongly enough. To see how this could work, let's consider three points:

1) The magnitude of land costs to individuals and businesses is readily apparent. Hard as it is to come up with a solid number for this, we have a very good idea of the enormity of its effect. Consider a two-bedroom apartment (or a 1500 square foot store-front). Take the identical improvement, same building, same general level of infrastructure, etc., and place it in different locations. Place it in the centre of New York City, then in the depressed South Bronx, then in rural Virginia, then in the Nevada desert. It's the same, identical improvement, remember. The difference in its rental value in those various places can only be due to land rent.

2) The public collection of land rent would be self-quantifying. Private collection of land rent creates irresistible incentives to produce inaccurate, biased land assessments. If land rent were relied on for public revenue, however, and assessments were published in land-value maps, accurate market-value assessments would quickly become the norm. Rents set too high would make individual parcels unprofitable (just as speculative rents do today); rents set too low would encourage land speculation. And if assessment rolls were easy to find and understand, abuses on individual parcels would not long be tolerated by neighbours.

3) Aggregate land rent would be drastically affected by public rent collection and elimination of taxes on labour and capital. Even if we were able to come up with an accurate estimate of aggregate rent today, it would tell us very little about what would happen after our reform were enacted! Public collection of rent would remove the "speculative bubble" of land values which so interests real estate analysts; it would also remove the greatest source of volatility (not to mention unearned income) in the financial sector. Certainly such a sweeping reform would have profound and unpredictable effects on stock and bond markets. Couple that with the nearly-simultaneous removal of taxes, direct and indirect, from labour and productive capital. Is anyone proposing to accurately model that many variables?

No: we cannot quantify the probable effects of the single tax. But we can, using our wits and logic, make some confident statements about the positive directions in which it would lead society. Scholarly research is important; indeed it should be supported. But let us not be persuaded that we **must** quantify political economy in order to understand it. Clear logic tells us what has to be done to solve our seemingly intractable social problems.

*

Published in *Progress*, Australia – Aug. 1984

LETTER TO THE EDITOR

RESOURCES RENTAL TAX

(Extract)

In the controversy re the resources rental tax both sides have failed to consider one of the major set of benefactors of oil production and other forms of mining, namely, the owners of the sites and properties in the townships that develop to service the mining activities. As mining output increases in a particular area, there is an increased demand for housing, shops, banks, hotels, warehouses, industrial space, postal facilities etc. In the case of off-shore oil and gas exploitation, this development takes place in ports near the drilling areas. This increasing demand is reflected in huge increases in land prices rents and situational profits. It is these rental values that should be taken for the community. Our failure to do so means that the mass of people, as well as the mining companies, have to pay an ever-increasing tribute to land parasites for the right to produce and develop as well as bearing a crushing burden of taxation because governments fail to collect for the nation the economic rent of land.

It is doubtful whether the resources rental tax is the proper process for collecting economic rent. Most importantly the tax is only collected when the oil or other mineral is produced. This is a punishment for producing. The proper concept of economic rent, revenue is that you collect revenue whether production takes place or not. This revenue should be based on the potential for production in a particular area as determined by difficulty of access to the mineral, amount exploitable, transport distances etc. On the other hand there would be no tax on the actual production. Those who produced more for a given site potential would pay no more revenue than those who produced less or not at all. Such a system would give the maximum incentive to production and prevent the monopolisation of oil resources. *

Yours sincerely, C.H. Stowasser,
Secretary, Queensland Land Rent League.

---

* Note: While we heed Viktor Schauberger's warning that oil and gas resources should be left where they are (see Pt.II, ch.2), it is important that we reason aright regarding proposed resource rental taxes, in the present scenario. C.H. Stowasser's letter helpfully clarifies that scene.

Again, the "maximum production" referred to would not, as now, be propped up by false licence to rape the Earth of its resources through unsanctified title-deeds thereto. It would be limited to the input that was willing to be made of human effort. S-A.H.

THE FRUIT AND THE TREE

Two friends from their own differing internal standpoints are surveying today's social scene.

One, observing that the work ethos is not what it should be – that large numbers of people have become so corrupted by a work-shy mentality that they are happier to live on the dole, or by any other means, rather than engage in 'honest work' – viewing the scene from his particular angle, and feeling that such a social feature is alien to him and is a disgrace, becomes highly critical and judgmental of these 'lazy' ones, declaiming against them with indignation.

The other, viewing the scene from a different standpoint, sees that the thing, *within its own framework*, is in every feature exactly as it should be.

Wasting no energies upon indignation at these trivia, he recognises the scene as only a beautiful confirmation of one of the great teachings of all the masters, as expressed in the Bible in Matthew Ch.7:

"... every good tree bringeth forth good fruit, but a corrupt tree bringeth forth evil fruit. A good tree cannot bring forth evil fruit, neither can a corrupt tree bring forth good fruit ... Wherefore by their fruits ye shall know them."

Relating these words to the scene, he is now for the first time struck, too, by the last eight words quoted. He realises that they are no mere observation, but contain a *hidden injunction.* They warn us not to linger among the trivia of the scene that is presented to our gaze, but to allow these to lead us deeper, to the *structure upon which they rest.*

Now, too, he is for the first time struck by a further 'warning', woven into the above words practically wherever they appear. To quote from Luke this time (Ch.3):

"And now also the axe is laid to the root of the tree; every tree therefore which bringeth not forth good fruit is hewn down, and cast into the fire."

Unless we manage to wrest our gaze from absorption in the trivia of a situation, we will not see if the moment comes when the whole is cracking up around us from its innate rottenness. Like the proverbial attendant on the deck of the Titanic, we will remain busily rearranging the deckchairs while the waters are closing over our heads.

In the socio-economic scene, we have witnessed the colossal fall of one rotten tree over the major part of what is called Eastern Europe, and the attendant pains and anguish that must follow from the collapse of a whole social order. Are we sure that the 'tree' of socio-economic order in the West is really so much more secure than that of the East has proved?

Let us look at the West's situation in the light of that succinct saying, 'Where some people get something for nothing, others get nothing for something."'

A major part, or rather, to be accurate, *the* major part of any enterprise in the West, whether it be house building, the setting up of a business, creation of sports facilities – or whatever human activity may be involved – is the obtaining of the necessary land upon which to establish it.

In a society where land is treated as a person's capital, money must be paid to acquire it.

Now, what did the land cost to produce? Nothing.

Without going into the more precise mechanics of who precisely is robbing whom, it is clear that the socio-economic structure of the West contains, then, in huge measure, this inbuilt flaw of some 'getting something for nothing' – and hence also its inseparable obverse of 'others getting nothing for something', or; working without getting a full return for their labours – (since all production involves human labour of some kind).

Whilst the features of this robbery may not be clearly seen, nor its mechanism readily identified, a subterranean sense of its presence inevitably pervades the whole of society, corrupting those on the advantaged, as equally those on the disadvantaged, side of things.

As for the disadvantaged – the great mass of people, who must pay for access to land and have nothing to pay with but the wages of their labours – they know very well that something is amiss; or, in more down-to-earth terms, that somewhere they are being robbed.

Could anything be more calculated to create what may euphemistically be described (on *both* sides) as, a 'work-shy' mentality?

'Some people get something for nothing, and others get nothing for something.' Could anything more simply summarise the essence of an unjust society which contains the fatal seeds of its destruction within itself?

Can the West, then, still hope to escape the kind of upheaval that the East has seen?

We may re-phrase this: Can enough people awaken in enough time from their fixation with the details of the scene to join in the push for real, fundamental change?

Why do so many remain obsessed with particulars, and resist examination of *the whole*?

It seems that the painfulness of the outcome of such resistance is, at any rate, one of the pathways of learning for humankind ... as the invincible Law of Love finally, in its own time, moves to remove root and branch what has become fruitless for society.

To return then to the question, can there be sufficient awakening, in sufficient time, from the obsession with particulars, to cease resisting examination of THE WHOLE? Ancient Greek has a verb, which enables you to say very neatly, in about half the number of words; *I had not noticed that I have overlooked* – something very important.

Shirley-Anne Hardy

5th May 1991

*

"When the missionaries first came to Africa they had the Bible and we had the land. They said 'Let us pray.' We closed our eyes. When we opened them, we had the Bible and they had the land."

Desmond Tutu

(With acknowledgements to Harry Alderslade for suggesting the apt quotation at the end!)

*

SUPERSTITION IS THE ENEMY - EDUCATION IS THE KEY

Extracts from an article by George Charles Hawthorn

"Progress", Australia March-April, 1999

. . . The power of the superstitious organizations came and still comes about because the leaders themselves were and are ignorant and reason was and is beyond them. There is exception to this in that for personal power those leaders who profess to be ignorant, do so for their own gain.

This powerful force, for force it is, ruled supreme until about the 16th and 17th centuries when the human race took on a new system that of using reason to ask what is the nature of things. Galileo was the end product of thought from Copernicus and Kepler. These people used reason to explain the nature of the universe instead of blindly accepting superstition to govern people's lives.

The superstitious power of his day so embarrassed Galileo that he nearly lost his life, which was the fate of so many before him.

Many thinkers which included Isaac Newton and others ushered in what is now known as the age of enlightenment. Which movement has continued right up to the present time and is now known as the technology age?

The search began by using reason to find natural laws to increase food supplies and later spread to embrace all the technical discoveries which give us what we have at this time the end of the 20th century.

These discoveries also were the source of an increase in the gap between the rich people and the poor because it was only the rich who had the financial resources to exploit the new discoveries. This exploitation not only affected the means of producing material things – it also exploited people.

All the useful advances in the past 200 to 300 years have been in the physical sciences. The social sciences or the science which affected the gap between the ruling elite were held in abeyance until the arrival of Henry George in the latter part of the 19th century. This time lag was owing to the fact that the development of this study was thought to have been against the financial interests of those who had the power to discriminate or prevent dissemination of knowledge.

It is very important to recognize that Henry George was not a traditional academic and he was freely and ruthlessly vilified by the traditional superstitious academics; the result is that society today is ruled by what has become known as economic rationalism which is falsely built upon falsity because the system has no relation whatever to natural law or rational thought. This theory can give no solutions to economic troubles. But the term economic rationalism, does serve to give a false authority to it because academia ratifies and teaches the subject in schools and universities to try and bring it into line with the physical sciences.

As America was developing and Ireland was in such dire poverty, Henry George observed and developed the logical and rational nature of the science of economics from observations of naturally occurring phenomena.

The factors give perfectly obvious examples to establish a science based upon reason without the tradition and superstition which until then ordered the economic systems of the nations.

. . . . .

To pursue the work of scientific economists can be very frustrating because the dissemination of true economics meets with so much ignorant opposition; it is only by being aware of the enormous nature of the situation that the best that can be made of what resources are available to continue the work so ably begun over 100 years ago. (By Henry George.) S-A H.

Indeed, to understand the reality of the situation is to have confidence when taking any step to further the interests of what is today the foremost problem of the planet earth.

It is not a luxury; it is an absolute necessity . . . . .

VIVISECTION

There is a verse of a hymn - (which will be familiar to many) - that I once used to regard as somewhat far-fetched in its use of the word "once":-

Once to every man and nation
Comes the moment to decide,
In the strife of truth with falsehood,
For the good or evil side.

(James Russell Lowell.)

I came upon it again, however, in the summer of 1997, when looking through some papers on vivisection, and was struck by its peculiar application in this context - its devastating truth.

For once "a nation" has made the choice of this pathway, it proves very difficult to move off it. That is because the very pathway we have taken is progressively destructive to that vital "biological thinking" which Viktor Schauberger speaks of: our sense of contact with the animals, and hence with the Earth Mother, who nurtures and cherishes the animal kingdom as her very own children, just as she cherishes the human one.

But just as it was - is - a pathway to hell for the animals, so it has proved a veritable pathway to hell for the humans as well...who had thought to build themselves a nice, safe passageway to heaven by it. Our entire poisoned and chemicalized agriculture, all of the false drugs with which we "medicate" ourselves, (which only suppress symptoms...to our worser fate, and destroy the body's natural energies and immune systems), the whole of the nuclear business - of the fluoridation business - right on to the latest GMO "hallelujah" business: all, ALL, are reared upon the fundamental business of animal exploitation. (But the WHOLE, of course - including the destruction of their biological thinking - roots back to the original dispossession of the people from their land.)

Here, then, are some of the quotations I came upon in that summer of 1997 - (when I was just making my deeper acquaintance with the Seven Wise Masters, and soon to start on Ogilvie's Essay!) - and which I would like to share with you now:-

"When animal experimentation became luridly notorious about the middle of the nineteenth century, practically every great moral thinker of that age denounced it on ethical grounds. Carlyle, Browning, Tennyson, Victor Hugo, Tolstoy, Ruskin, (Cardinal) Manning, Russell Wallace, to mention only a few...One and all of them condemned vivisection as a moral iniquity which could not possibly be mitigated by any hopes or promises of its yielding knowledge helpful to medical science or calculated to alleviate the physical suffering of mankind... These were not hysterical cranks, but the wisest and most far-seeing thinkers of their era.

(Dr George Wilson, LL.D., Medical Officer of Health.)

"Man is responsible for his own diseases, and to employ animals in the endeavour to prevent or cure them is an attempt to evade Nature's just penalty... True health cannot be attained in this manner." (Bertrand P. Allinson, M.R.C.S., L.R.C.P.)

"I despise and abhor the pleas on behalf of that infamous practice, vivisection." (Robert Browning.)

"I consider that vivisection is unscientific and at variance with the highest moral standards, which are the manifestation of love, compassion and pity. The man or woman who carries out such cruel experimentation...exhibits the mind that is out of touch with the great realities." (Gordon Latto, M.B., Ch.B. A Scot - and brilliant doctor of wide reputation, who practised in the south. Just passed away. He used a wide variety of natural healing methods - and once put me on my feet again, with the herb Parsley Piert and a week's fasting!)

"These scientific pursuits are now defiantly, provokingly, insultingly separated from the science of religion; they are all carried on in defiance of what has hitherto been held to be compassion and pity, and of the great link which binds together the whole creation, from its Maker to the lowest creature."

(John Ruskin, from a Speech at Oxford, 1884. Ruskin resigned his chair in 1885 as Slade Professor of Fine Arts, in the University of Oxford, as a protest against the inclusion of vivisection among the methods of teaching at the University.)

"I believe I am not interested to know whether vivisection produces results that are profitable to the human race or doesn't.

"To know that the results are profitable to the race would not remove my hostility to it. The pains which it inflicts unon unconsenting animals is the basis of my enmity toward it, and it is to me sufficient justification of the enmity without looking further."

(Mark Twain.)

"My own life has been one of great bodily suffering, and I am, therefore, well acquainted with pain of this nature. But all the many and various physical torments I have undergone are as nothing when compared with the mental suffering which has been caused me by the knowledge of the practices and principles of vivisection..."

(Dr Anna Kingsford. From a letter to the Press.)

"Nothing can justify, no claim of science, no conjectural result, no hope of discovery, such horrors as these... I do not believe this to be the way that the All-wise and All-good Maker of us all has ordained for the discovery of the Healing Art, which is one of His greatest gifts to man." (Cardinal Manning. Speech, 21 June 1882.)

"Mr Carlyle has received your letter and read it carefully. He bids me say that ever since he was a boy, when he read the account of Majendie's atrocities, he has never thought of the practice of vivisecting animals but with horror."

(Thomas Carlyle, dictated to a niece, in answer to a correspondent, 28 Aug 1875.)

"It was the spiritual determination and courage of the gallant few who finally obtained the abolition of child-slavery, bear-baiting, cock-fighting and other abominations. Very few, if anybody, today would attempt to question the right of such legislation; yet at the time almost all, including the Church, were part of the opposition."

(H.P. Kilsby, L.L.M., L.R.C.P.I., L.R.C.S.I.)

"There will come a time when the world will look back to modern vivisection, in the name of science, as they do now to burning at the stake in the name of religion."

(Dr Henry J. Bigelow, late Professor of Surgery, Harvard Medical School.)

*

Note: The above quotations are taken, with acknowledgement, from two pamphlets, "In the Company of Anti-Vivisectionists", and "Medical Opinions Against Vivisection", both published by the Scottish Society for the Prevention of Vivisection, now re-named Animal Advocates, of 10 Queensferry Street, Edinburgh EH2 4PG.

Scenes from laboratory life

by George Target

When she was seven she had a pet cat called Gandalf, a short-haired grey with orange eyes and mysterious ways.

On her fourteenth birthday her parents gave her a golden retriever puppy with floppy ears, galumphing paws, and a tail with a life of its own. She called him Bilbo Baggins, and loved him like the younger brother she never had.

At home she read by the hour, at school she was top of the form in English and Literature, got seven O-levels, and wanted to take an Arts Course in the Upper Fifth and Lower Sixth.

'You want something a bit more practical,' said her father, who was something in the City.

So, after a lot of argument and tears and hard work, she got three A-levels in Science subjects, and it was decided that she would go in for Medicine.

She was twenty-two when she left university with just about a second-class degree and little chance of Medical school. She tried – but competition was fierce, and she simply wasn't well-enough qualified. True, there was always Nursing. . . .

'What prospects are there in that?' said her father.

The thought of Teaching appalled her – and as for getting married to any one of four possibles . . . well, she wasn't all that desperate!

And so, eventually, after dozens of applications and interviews and disappointments, she managed to get a post as a Laboratory Assistant (Third Grade) in a Medical Research Establishment: reasonable salary and conditions of service, pension scheme, good prospects.

'And you'll be doing something pretty damned useful,' said her father. 'Unlike these Weary Willies with long hair!'

The first time she had to kill a white rat at the end of a six-day testing process she was upset. Yes, almost dead, anyway, only a mercy to put it out of its obvious misery . . . yet it looked up at her so piteously, its flanks heaving, the blood and mucus dribbling from its mouth and anus.

Merely took a second, of course, and she dropped the body into the sterile disposal-bin . . . but needed that cup of coffee at break.

'Don't tell us you're green about the gills already?' said her colleagues. 'Wait till you start on the new series next month!'

And she was offered a friendly cigarette, and accepted it gratefully.

Within six months such things no longer bothered her.

Well, not very much, anyway.

True, she was now working with cats, and sometimes the experimental subject was more of a kitten, really, and it would purr when she picked it up, and look at her with orange eyes . . . but they bothered her less and less. After all, it was in the Cause of Medical Science, wasn't it? And the sufferings of humanity were going to be alleviated . . . or wasn't that the general idea?

At the end of her first year she was smoking twenty a day.

At the end of her third year she was the Personal Assistant to the Head of the Department, and in direct charge of the latest series of improved tests on dogs which had survived the previous series.

But, quite frankly, these tests were running into deep trouble: six fatalities out of ten per batch. Which was costing money, as the supply of such pre-conditioned experimental subjects wasn't exactly easy to maintain at such a rate of demand.

'Beats me,' said the Head of the Department. 'Perhaps we should increase the dosage?'

'Already tried that,' she said. 'Merely shortens the convulsions.'

'And this vocalisation is a bloody nuisance,' said the Head of the Department. 'Gets on my nerves. Never could stand senseless barking.'

'Suppose we try terminating immediately after the main period of convulsions?' she said, 'but prior to the final spasms? That way we could ascertain the condition of the surrounding tissues before the bruising damages too many cells, yes?'

'Good thinking,' said the Head of the Department . . . and, after seventy minutes careful observation, they selected a subject from several possibles, had it removed from the cage, and placed in the standard set of restraints on the operating surface.

'Shall I terminate?' she said, reaching for the hypodermic-pack.

'No need,' said the Head of the Department. 'Already in coma. . . . This'll be enough.'

And he made the primary incision.

Which, of course, was enough, as termination ensued before any possible recovery of consciousness.

True, it bothered her just that little bit . . . but not for long, as the resulting absence of chemical agents in the blood made the usual preparation of sections for microscopic examination much easier.

At twenty-seven she married the Chairman of the local Young Farmers, son of the second-largest egg-producer in the area: twelve battery-houses, five thousand hens in each, two houses for broilers.

Took six months leave of absence to have their first and only child, a girl. . . .

'One's enough, thank you. Not going through that again!'

At thirty she was Head of the Department, personally responsible for instigating original lines of research, smoking a steady forty a day, enjoying more than the occasional social drink, her marriage no longer quite what it used to be.

'Mummy?' said her six-year-old daughter one evening. . . .

'What do you want?'

'Could I have a little baby kitten for my birthday?'

'Wouldn't you rather have that sort of video-game thing we saw?'

'The big one?' said the child. 'Oh! Mummy! Could I really?'

True, it cost rather more than a kitten – but, as she explained to her husband, it would be a lot less bloody trouble.

Lines from "Turning"
by Rainer Maria Rilke,

as translated by J.B. Leishman,
in his edition of Rilke's Poems: 1906-26,
published by the Hogarth Press, November, 1957.
(With acknowledgement.)

*

...Animals trustfully entered
his open glance as they pastured,
and the imprisoned lions
stared as into incomprehensible freedom.
Birds flew straight through him,
kindly soul. Flowers
gazed back into him
large as to children.....

*

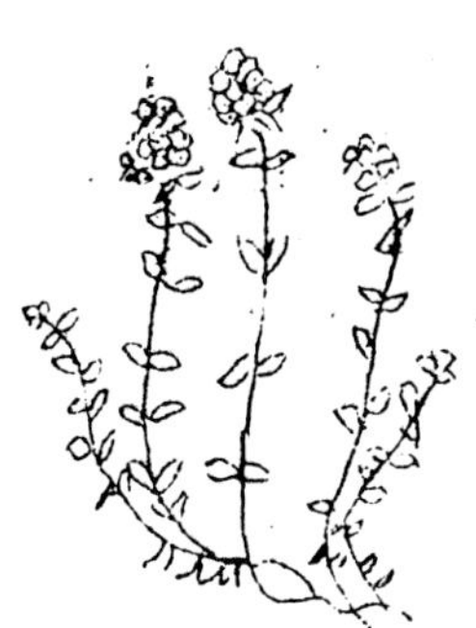

(Completed Easter Sunday, 1999.)

"THE PROPHET OF SAN FRANCISCO"

So Henry George was once sneeringly dubbed by the Duke of Argyll, but it has since become for him an endearing title of praise – and of quite prophetic accuracy! S-A.H.

*

Reflections from Russia

The cold war has ended. Our so called 'free market' system triumphed over what might loosely be called the 'command economies'. It is timely to remind ourselves however that currently, 29 separate wars rage throughout the globe. Most are being fought over land (or resources) issues, and the wealth that ownership will bring.

Within many of the richest nations on earth riots continue to stretch the resources of the government. For those who have read a great classic *'Progress and Poverty', by Henry George*, this process has been well described. From the *chapter: "How Modern Civilisation may Decline*":

"The very foundations of society are being sapped before our eyes while we ask how it is possible that such a civilisation as this, with its railways, and daily newspapers, and electric telegraphs, should ever be destroyed? While literature breathes but the belief that we have been, and for the future must be, leaving the savage state farther and farther behind us, there are indications that we are actually turning back again toward barbarism.

Though we may not speak it openly, the greatest faith in democratic institutions, where they have reached their fullest development, is narrowing and weakening; it is no longer the confident belief in democracy as the source of national blessings that it once was. Thoughtful men are beginning to see its dangers, without seeing how to escape them. . . The people at large are becoming used to the growing corruption; the most ominous political sign is the growth of a sentiment which either doubts the existence of an honest man in public office or looks on him as a fool for not seizing his opportunities. That is to say, the people themselves are becoming corrupted.

Where this course leads is clear to whoever will think. As corruption becomes chronic; as public spirit is lost; as traditions of honour, virtue and patriotism are weakened; as law is brought into contempt and reforms become hopeless; then in the festering mass will be generated volcanic forces which will shatter and rend when seeming accident gives them vent. Strong, unscrupulous men, rising up upon occasion, will become the exponents of blind popular desires or fierce popular passions, and dash aside forms that have lost their vitality. The sword will again be mightier than the pen, and in carnivals of destruction brute force and wild frenzy will alternate with the lethargy of a declining civilisation.

Whence shall come the new barbarians? Go through the squalid quarters of great cities, and you may see, even now, their gathering hordes. . .

The tendency to inequality, which is the necessary result of material progress where land is monopolised, cannot go on much farther without carrying our civilisation into that downward path which is so easy to enter and so hard to abandon. Everywhere the increasing intensity of the struggle to live, the increasing necessity for straining every nerve to prevent being thrown down and trodden underfoot in the scramble for wealth, is draining the forces that gain and maintain improvements. . . But as sure as the turning tide must soon run full ebb, as sure as the declining sun must bring darkness, so sure it is that though knowledge yet increases and invention marches on, and new states are being settled, and cities still expand, civilisation has begun to wane when, in proportion to population, we must build more and more prisons, more and more almshouses, more and more insane asylums. It is not from top to bottom that societies die; it is from bottom to top.

Fred Harrison in Russia.
Published in ***Progress****, Australia – Feb. 1994.*

SOME FAMOUS WORDS ON HENRY GEORGE

"It would require less than the fingers of two hands to enumerate those who, from Plato down, rank with Henry George among the world's finest social philosophers."

John Dewey, Prof. of Philosophy, Columbia Univ., 1904-30.

"Men like Henry George are rare, unfortunately. One cannot imagine a more beautiful combination of intellectual keenness, artistic form, and fervent love of justice."

Albert Einstein (1879-1955), winner of Nobel Prize in Physics.

"I believe that Henry George was one of the really great thinkers produced by our country."

Franklin D. Roosevelt, President o the United States, 1933-45.

"People do not argue with the teaching of George, they simply do not know it. The teaching of George is irresistibly convincing in its simplicity and clearness. He who becomes acquainted with it cannot but agree."

Leo Tolstoy, (1828-1910).

"Henry George was a master of English, one of the greatest that ever used a pen. . . He was one of the real prophets of the world. . . His was a wonderful mind; he saw a question from every side; his philosophy appealed to every school. . ."

Clarence Darrow, American trial lawyer and famous defence attorney, (1857-1938).

"Probably no other writer has ever made the study of economics so interesting to so many readers as Henry George."

Harry Gunnison Brown, (1880-1975), Professor of Economics, University of Missouri.

"Henry George was a great man – great in his economic, prophetic insight; great in his faith, his hope, his love. He gave his message to the world and passed on, scourged, depressed, undone, because the world did not accept the truths he voiced. . . All for which he strived and struggled will yet come true – his prayer will be answered. Of all modern prophets and reformers, Henry George is the one whose arguments are absolutely unanswerable and whose forecast is sure."

Elbert Hubbard.

Part III

KALEIDOSCOPE

*

4) THE NATURAL WORLD

Ragwort

Bracken

If an Ox Eats Meat - Rudolf Steiner

Plants for a Future

The Purpose of Disease

The Criminal-Mineral Link

Problems of Modern Food Production and the Importance of Trees - Eric K. Yapp

Aquarian Alternatives - the Work of Carl Weschke

Soil Remineralization and Climate Shift - Cameron Thomson

Blueprint for a New Health Service! - The Templegarth Trust

*

Ragwort

I would like to pass on something that happened to my grandmother many years ago. She had a poisoned hand. It did not respond to the doctor's treatment, but got steadily worse. It got so bad that she was to go into hospital to have the hand removed.

My grandfather, going home one day, met an old countryman who begged him to collect Ragwort and make a poultice of it. This he did. They applied it and kept it on for a few days. When the time came for the operation the hand was healed.

My grandmother used to show me her hand and tell me this story when I was a small child. She always remembered how nearly she lost her hand, and felt grateful all her life for the "miracle" that saved it.

Mrs E. Lewis, Woking, Surrey.

By courtesy of "Grace" magazine, Smr. 97

How far we have strayed! Of Ragwort, a herb, of miraculous external use, (but not to be taken internally), we hear nothing but ill today. If it is poisonous to animals who graze it - this simply shows how far we have managed to re-create such animals in our own debased image, eradicating in them the original natural instinct to avoid it in feeding.

Ragwort

"The flowers of Ragwort have important forces which magnetize and remove deep-seated impurities and which also dissolve swellings." (Juliette de Bairacli Levy in "The Illustrated Herbal Handbook". Faber, 1974. She advises external use only.)

I can add my own testimony to this. It completely dissolved over one weekend - and without leaving a trace - a nasty abcess in my mouth, which started one Friday evening. I consulted Juliette's book - and was fortunate, for the Ragwort was in bloom. I masticated some flowers and held them, as a poultice, with my tongue. The result was miraculous indeed!

Since writing the above a few days ago, I have just caught a newsflash following the Farmers' Weekly Weather on BBC 1 TV (March 6th) - that Ragwort is being found in hay this winter, making it a danger to horses and other animals fed it. It was referred to in the usual ignorant manner as "that ghastly pernicious weed" - (the customary pest vocabulary brought into play). It was also reported that there had been whole fields full of it last summer (98).

If there are fields full of Ragwort, then the Ragwort is telling us something. Just like the Bracken - (see on). It is telling us that we have fields going to waste...in our countryside of dedicated agro-business farming, 'sport' and 'conservation'; and that the land is crying out for its true guardians to inhabit it once more - the people of Scotland overlong squeezed out.

In fact, the Ragwort is telling us a second thing. It is telling us the state of the soil where it has run so rampant. Nature is always trying to achieve a balancing-up; and so the Ragwort will be there trying to heal the soil of some deficiency state.

So, once more, we need to look, to listen...and to re-inhabit the land.

One thing for definite - NO MORE POISONS!...with cancer now running at one in three in Scotland (or whatever those latest statistics are). Or are we demented? Have we totally lost the capacity of putting an elementary two and two together? Let permaculture and herbalism - via radical land reform - restore Ragwort to its rightful place in our lives - and hearts.

Bracken

Not "Away with bracken!" - but A WAY with bracken!
And indeed, more than one way...

"The old inhabitants of these inland townships (of the Scottish highlands) had also a way of growing potatoes as well as oats on the cultivated patches away up in the glens, where no sea-ware could be procured, and where it was impossible to carry the manure from their byres and stables in the township, because it was all required for the cropping of what was then known as the "infield" land round their houses.

One way of growing potatoes up in the wilds was by substituting bracken for sea-ware, and making "lazy beds" of it where the soil was fairly deep and moist. The bracken was cut with the sickle in July when at its richest, and the ground given a thick coating of it; ditches were then opened about six feet apart and the soil from the ditches put on the bracken, so that it had a covering of six or eight inches of earth on it. Thus it was left for some nine months to decay, till the spring came round again, when holes were bored in the beds with a "dibble" and the seed potatoes dropped into them..."

(Taken from an old sheet I have come across out of a book - title not marked, but clearly written many decades ago, by one who could still remember these ways. From ch. XIII - "Agriculture".)

*

The young fronds of bracken can also be eaten like asparagus; and bracken makes a very useful garden mulch - (the second "quilt" layer on the raised beds I have described).

*

In the summer of 1997, following a course in permaculture, Alan Torrance was speaking to me about the bracken that has gradually been creeping over the land of Scotland for a long time now; and of how the kind of plants that are flourishing - and the condition of those plants - are both showing us the nature of the land. Bracken indicates **exhausted soil**.

As Alan put it - our soil is suffering from a monoculture of 250 years, and that monoculture is SHEEP. The bracken is telling us - **stop putting sheep on the soil.** But the landed interest, instead of listening to the plantlife on the land and what it is telling us, simply want to kill it. As Alan said, it illustrates so well the saying that "a man who has too much land is poor - a man who has enough land is rich".

Anthony Wigens - who was "rich" (in a **clandestine** way!) - tells us in his book "The Clandestine Farm" (Granada, 1981), how he successfully eradicated bracken from a certain area where he wanted to grow vegetables, simply by cutting it at a time crucial for its growth.

We need to humble ourselves sufficiently to learn once more to **look** - and so, to read the landscape aright. We shall then see that what the bracken is crying out to us for is, in every way, a **return of the people to the land.**

Let us see the bracken as a forerunner! As Alan remarked: "The bracken is creeping back over the land almost like the way that the people will be creeping back"...

*

IF AN OX EATS MEAT

by

Rudolph Steiner

You know that there are some animals that are simply gentle vegetarian beings. There are animals that do not eat meat; they also eat only plants. Now, you must be clear that an animal not only absorbs food but is also constantly shedding what is inside its body. Among birds you know there is something called molting. The birds lose their feathers and must replace them with new ones. You know that deer drop their antlers. You cut your nails, and they grow back. What appears outwardly so visible here is part of a continuous process. We constantly shed our skins ... During a period of approximately seven to eight years, our entire bodies are shed and replaced with new ones. This is also the case with animals.

Consider a cow or an ox. After some years the flesh within it has been entirely replaced. With oxen the exchange takes place even faster than with human beings. A new flesh is therefore made. From what did this flesh originate, however?... The ox itself has produced the flesh in its body from plant substances. The animal's body is therefore capable of producing meat from plants. Now, you can cook cabbage as long as you like, bur you won't turn it into meat... [*Producing meat*] cannot be done with outer skills, but, taken fundamentally, the animal's body can accomplish inwardly what one can't do outwardly. Flesh is produced in the animal's body, and to do this forces have to be present in the body. With all our technological forces, we have none by which we can simply produce meat from plants. We don't have that, but in our bodies and in animal bodies there are forces that can make meat substance from plant substance.

Now, this is a plant (*sketching*) that is still in a meadow or field. The forces that have been active up to this point have brought forth green leaves, berries, and so forth. Think of a cow devouring this plant. When the cow devours this plant it becomes flesh in her. This means that the cow possesses the forces that can make this plant into meat.

Now imagine that an ox suddenly decided that it was too tiresome to graze and nibble plants, that it would let another animal eat them and do the work for it, and then it would eat the animal. In other words the ox would begin to eat meat though it is able to produce the meat by itself. It has the inner forces to do so. What would happen if the ox were to eat meat directly instead of plants. It would leave all the forces unused that can produce the flesh in him. Think of the enormous amount of energy that is lost when the machines in a factory in which something or other is manufactured are all turned on without producing anything. There is a tremendous loss of energy. But the unused energy in the body of the ox cannot simply be lost, so the ox is finally filled with it, and this pent-up force does something in him other than produce flesh from plant substances... The energy remains; it is present in the animal, and so it produces waste products. Instead of flesh, harmful substances are produced. Therefore, if an ox were suddenly to turn into a meat eater, it would fill itself with all kinds of harmful substances such a uric acid and urates.

Now urates have their specific effects. These are expressed in a particular affinity for the nervous system and the brain. *The result is that if an ox were to consume meat directly, large amounts of urates would be secreted; they would enter the brain and the ox would go crazy.* If an experiment could be made in which a herd of oxen were suddenly fed with pigeons, it would produce a completely mad her of oxen.

Health and Illness, Vol. 2, Lecture of 13 January 1923

EDITOR'S NOTE: *We are grateful to the reader and contributor, Roy Wilkinson who sent in the above article by Rudolph Steiner, first published in the 1920's.*

*

With acknowledgements to
The Science of Thought Review, Boston House, Chichester, Sussex. (A 1996 issue)

*

PLANTS FOR A FUTURE

Edible and Useful Plants
for a Healthier World

by Ken Fern
Foreword by Joy Larkcom

"It is hard to over-estimate the importance and likely impact of this book. Plants For A Future hugely widens the range of edible species which we can, with confidence, grow in temperate climates. It shows us how to use land more efficiently and sustainably than ever before, and it brings to our sadly limited cuisine a vast new range of remarkable foods, all around the year. It is, in short, the first shot in an impending horticultural revolution. The result of an insatiable curiosity and years of painstaking research, this book is comparable in stature only to the works of Evelyn and Culpeper."
Professor George Monbiot, environmental campaigner, founder of The Land Is Ours.

The way we currently produce our food is damaging both to ourselves and our planet. We need to create gardens, woodlands and farms which are in harmony with nature. Natural ecosystems are good models, but many of the plants they contain are not edible. So we need to discover a wide variety of easily grown perennials and self-seeding annuals which provide delicious and healthy food.

Describing edible and other useful plants, both native to Britain and Europe and from temperate areas around the world, this book includes those suitable for: the ornamental garden, the lawn, shady areas, ponds, walls, hedges, agroforestry and conservation.

In this thoroughly useful book, Ken Fern shares his experiments and successes in growing herbs, vegetables, flowers, shrubs and trees. Packed with information, personal anecdote and detailed appendices and indexes, this pioneering book takes gardening, conservation and ecology into a new dimension.

Available from: Permanent Publications,
Hyden House Ltd., The Sustainability Centre,
East Meon, Hampshire GU32 1HR.

£19 incl. p & p.
ISBN: 1 85623 011 2

(Above notice quoted from
Permanent Publications sheet,
with acknowledgements.)

THE PURPOSE OF DISEASE

In the end Nature always takes us in hand and teaches us that it does not pay to disregard her rules. Disease is her reply to those whose actions are in flagrant contradiction to her laws, one of which is the law of return. This law holds good in crops, in live stock, and in mankind. The relation of disease to the law of return must therefore be understood.

Disease is not created by mankind. It occurs in Nature and always has and always will. It is a part of the Creation. It is met with everywhere – in the primeval forest; on the prairies; in streams, rivers, lakes, and the ocean; it is by no means unknown among wild animals. Disease has a very definite place in the natural order. This is significant. For this reason man cannot hope to eliminate it.

Disease is the means adopted by Nature for the removal of the unfit. It is also the normal accompaniment of old age when the organism is worn out. It is perhaps most easily seen at work on old trees where the diseased condition steadily advances until finally the tree ceases to live. Because the tree is so well furnished with reserve food and very effective arrangements for resisting parasites, its death is a slow process and one which can easily be watched. But smaller plants and, in particular, the microscopic forms of the vegetable kingdom are not so well provided with defences and perish much more dramatically.

The commonest agents involved in plant diseases are insects and fungi: in animals and man, various types of bacteria are the usual invaders.

The course run by disease is generally the same. A struggle for the mastery takes place between the host and the parasite. It is not a case of two organisms living together, but a battle.

Disease is the beginning of Nature's composting. The inefficient or worn-out organism is converted into material from which humus can be synthesized to feed a new generation of plants. The insects, fungi, or bacteria involved in this work may be regarded as Nature's censors whose duty it is to mark down the imperfect organism, condemn it, and then start the execution of the sentence by preparing it for transformation into lower forms of life from whose wastes and remains humus can be synthesized for re-starting the wheel of life.

Now we see why Nature has no arrangements like the burning of infected material, poison sprays, insecticides, sera, or vaccines for checking disease. Why should she fight what is her own arrangement? Why should she burn diseased material or institute quarantine arrangements? The diseased plant or animal continues in free and close contact with its fellows who are always exposed to full infection. The infection spreads only to what is already unfit. If it could spread to the fit, all life would soon cease. the parasites would overrun their victims like a forest fire. But life does nothing of the sort, it continues rightly and abundantly. This is the one proof we need to tell us that disease cannot attack the healthy organism. Why, therefore, should be fear it?

Disease is no enemy: it is part of the natural cycle: it has a definite and useful function in Nature: it enters into the wheel of life. All that mankind can do by means of agencies like the medical and veterinary professions is to help the valuable but stricken organism to become whole and to have a fresh start.

But the alleviation and cure of disease do not end the matter. We are only dealing with a portion of the subject – the casualties, most of which need never have occurred. One important question has still to be answered: How does disease arise?

We have dealt with the apparent causes – insects, fungi, and bacteria; but what is that invites them to attack certain hosts only and leave the rest alone? If we could answer this question, we could take up preventive measures with every hope of success.

A satisfactory answer has, I consider, been found. It has been furnished by the work of Mr. J.E.R. McDonagh, one of the pioneers in medical research. This investigator considers that the nature of disease is to be found in a study of the protein complex, that constituent of the vegetable and animal kingdoms in which life resides. In a note dated September 8th, 1944, printed in full in Chapter XI of *Farming and Gardening for Health or Disease*, Mr. McDonagh summed up his life work. This brief summary has since been expanded by the author in the paper which begins on p. 71 of this issue. It will be evident that in plant diseases everything depends on the way the proteins are formed in the green leaf by methods which conform closely to those in operation in Nature. Nothing more is needed to keep diseases in check. But the moment we try to improve on Nature's methods or attempt short cuts, trouble begins. The introduction of a substitute phase (in the form of artificial fertilizers) in the nitrogen cycle is one certain method of bringing about improperly synthesized protein followed by loss of quality and finally disease.

Mr. McDonagh's detailed presentation of the normal working of the green carpet and his explanation of the irreparable damage now being done by artificial manures constitute a challenge.

This challenge has already been taken up by a few of the pioneers in the farming community. The practical results obtained on the land amply confirm the theory.

Albert Howard.

THE CRIMINAL-MINERAL LINK

Contributed by the National Health Federation

In the 1970s, William J. Walsh, Ph.D., was conducting chemistry and physics research at Argonne National Laboratory, near Chicago. He was also doing volunteer work with inmates at the Stateville Penitentiary in Joliet, Illinois. Most of the violent criminals had very troubled childhoods, but Walsh questioned whether their behaviour was entirely the result of upbringing.

Walsh compared the mineral levels of forty-eight pairs of brothers, mostly teenagers. In all cases, one brother was considered an "all-American boy" and the other very violent. The experiment was a "fishing expedition," because Walsh wasn't sure what he would find, he told doctors attending the 25th annual Nutritional Medicine Today Conference. But the finding were significant. The violent brothers had one of two distinct patterns of mineral imbalances. These patterns remained consistent, regardless of race, when Walsh went on to compare mineral levels between violent imprisoned criminals and normal, law-abiding people.

One of the criminal patterns was a high copper-to-zinc ratio; low levels of sodium, potassium and manganese; and high levels of lead and cadmium, which are toxic. People with this mineral pattern generally displayed extreme mood swings, poor responses to stress and occasional violent behaviour. They did, however, feel remorse about their actions.

The other mineral pattern consisted of very low copper, very high sodium and potassium; high lead, cadmium, iron and calcium; and low zinc. These people often very violent, pathological liars, cruel and fascinated by fire. They also exhibited no conscience or remorse for their actions.

Published in Remineralize the Earth,
Spring – Northern Hemisphere: 1998.

HEALTHY AGRICULTURE

Published 21 years ago in the journal of the Men of the Trees (now The Tree Soc. Internat.), this article by Eric Yapp is right up-to-date with our need to know, and to understand, the damage being wrought to health all round - to soil, plant, animal and man - by our State-sponsored chemical agriculture. (I have not attempted to obliterate the markings made long years ago.) Note the reference to R.H. Elliot, whose farm in the Borders became a showpiece, and whose book "The Clifton Park System of Farming" was published by Fabers...

Spring 1978

Problems of Modern Food Production and The Importance of Trees

by ERIC K. YAPP

The food for all the organisms of the world comes from the soil. This soil varies incredibly in its many forms; it is always richer in the valleys and lower ground than on surrounding hills from which it may have moved very slowly through the ages. Unless real care is taken to maintain the soils of the world, the food supplies for plants, animals, man and all the invertebrate flora and fauna will diminish, and in my view this may occur far more quickly and suddenly than most people can possibly expect.

After the ice age a large part of the northern hemisphere was slowly covered by forests of trees which brought up a continuous supply of food from deep in the soil, and every year the surface of the land was covered by a rich humus with the fall of the leaves from these trees. A wide and varied flora and fauna developed in this humus, gradually changing and eventually bringing man.

At first man had no tools to use and he lived a very primitive life, but in due course he invented tools to aid him in his use of the world. This development made it easier for man to use and interfere with nature more and more, and since history began this use has been steadily speeded up, until now world supplies are disappearing at an alarming rate, particularly as the sciences have been developed during the recent century without real thought of the consequences.

Man has used the soils for food production and destroyed a dangerous amount of natural flora, particularly trees, and interfered with far too much of the soil surface. The need for trees as the basic makers of humus for providing a balanced supply of the many chemicals from the earth for the plants, animals and man is absolutely vital. Yet, to-day, the cover, shelter and fertility of the land for growing food is vastly reduced and there are too few trees still growing or being planted. The extra supply of oxygen needed by the increase in human population comes essentially from trees, which also use excess available carbon dioxide.

To-day a very new danger has arisen with the disappearance of mixed and balanced farming methods and too much specialisation. Science has produced fertilisers, sprays and unnecessarily heavy machinery, which are undermining healthy food production. This has been extraordinarily and unfortunately increased since the start of the heavy use of artificial fertilisers during the last war when food became desperately short, and spraying has since become too common.

'In upsetting the equilibrium of the mineral elements in the soil, we upset the equilibrium of the mineral elements in the blood.'—says André Voisin, in his book *Soil, Grass and Cancer*. For example, lack of magnesium aids the development of cancer and thrombosis.

Voisin was a French scientist and farmer who tackled the problems of modern food production, health and illness, and backed his arguments with an unusual amount of reference to work done by other workers and scientists. He states that the three main elements of fertilisers are doing a lot of damage as they prevent the plants absorbing the equally vital minor elements; e.g., copper cannot be absorbed by the plants when too much nitrogen is used, iron is kept out by too much phosphorus, and magnesium by too much potassium. Unbalanced soils result. (And blood.)

Insufficient supplies of copper in plant foods lowers the milk yield and the weight of beef and dairy stock, and also reduces the fertility of the animals. Copper is needed to keep ryegrass and timothy erect and prevent rotting of their bases, and for the full development of clover. Copper and iron form a remarkable association for fighting disease in animals and man. Iron is vital in haemoglobin in the blood for absorbing oxygen and removing carbon dioxide, which are respectively supplied and used by trees and to a much lesser degree by smaller plants, to keep the air balanced. Iron, copper and cobalt are unavailable in soils treated with too heavy an application of slurry. This causes more trouble than lack of magnesium as it can prevent the soil, crops and microfauna, including worms, from breathing. Lack of magnesium, as well as cancer and thrombosis, causes hypomagnesaemia in stock, particularly when potassium is put on with nitrogen; it also causes mental disorders and tetany, which is most noticable when stock are put on young leys. These troubles have greatly increased with the ploughing up of permanent pasture.

The effect of the use of nitrogen is only surreptitious. But after 15 years the plants become quite changed. The unused nitrates getting into the soil water must be accepted as a very real danger, as the plants can only absorb a proportion of them, and the excess is wastefully dissolved. Some will certainly be moved and may reach wells and reservoirs as well as streams and the sea.

For many years I farmed on the Hastings Sands with the lovely oakwoods of Battle Abbey along one boundary. This farm only had pastures with small grasses whose yields I tried to improve by ploughing up and planting mixed leys based on ryegrass and clover, and I used artificial fertiliser. It was not a success.

I later discovered the Clifton Park system based on deep-rooting grasses, herbs and clover, which made a tremendous difference. The Clifton Park system was originated by R. H. Elliot, who chose to work on the highest and poorest farm on his estate in Roxburghshire towards the end of the last century to tackle the problems. He states: 'The cheapest, deepest and best tillers, drainers and warmers of soil are roots.' To-day deep-rooted leys are far too little used. . . . .

The importance of herbs has been overlooked. They contain many minerals which are not absorbed by grass or clover, and should always be included in ley mixtures and sown over the whole area in order to provide more balanced food. Trees contain a much heavier supply of the minerals available in the soil than any field plant, so the value in their autumn leaves cannot be ignored and they should be encouraged all round the field in the hedges, which also help. The fall of the leaves adds humus to the land around for the good of all and reduced disease. The smaller fields are much better than the large ones, as their hedges provide more fertility, more shelter for the stock and prevent a lot of erosion by the wind of the fertile top soils.

THE PRESS

It has been 17 years since Carl Weschke died. Carl was a unique Jonny Appleseed for our era. Last month, we turned to a sprightly newsletter, Aquarian Alternatives, *for an update of sorts on what was once fabulous experiment. Art Rosenblum operates Aquarian Alternatives, $25.00 a year, 12 issues sent first class or by donation, address 5620 Morton Street, Philadelphia, Pennsylvania 19144. Any way, here is what Rosenblum has to say.*

AQUARIAN ALTERNATIVES

THE NEWSLETTER OF THE AQUARIAN RESEARCH FOUNDATION

A prophet-making organization

REPLACING THE RAINFORESTS

While in Indiana, I took time to fly to Wisconsin (450 miles, four hours) to visit with Dan Carlson at his research farm 40 miles southeast of Twin Cities.

What I saw there was unforgettable. Few nut trees do well in the cold Wisconsin climate, But early in this century Carl Weschke thought he could introduce nut growing to the area. He brought nut trees from all over the world, grafted and cross-pollinated, producing combinations you never heard of but never sold a nut.

He died leaving an intricate hand-hewn cave, a massive log dwelling, deep wells, hundreds of nut trees (many with labels), special buildings and a monument to commemorate the new varieties of nuts he produced.

Weschke's abandoned farm was bought by Dan Carlson. Dan says he was especially interested because he had previously found that, using his Sonic Bloom technology, a nut tree could be grown from seedling to a mature nut bearing tree in only two to three years.

Dan met me at a little college airport nearby and we were soon at the farm. First he took me to a monument: a huge piece of petrified wood. Below were inscriptions about Weschke's work and the crossbred nuts (like "Buttercans") he had created.

Then he pointed at the trunk of an old evergreen, which was similar to old pines I had seen elsewhere. Live green needles were only near the top and below then were very dead branches, mostly only stumps. But here, at every dead branch, where it came from the tree, there was a bright green shoot emerging! I looked at another old pine and another; on every one the exact same phenomena! It was clear to see from the ground; no climbing or special efforts were required.

Then Dan took me on a tour of the place and showed me nut trees, which were all over. There must have been thousands – all kinds. Every tree appeared to be in outstanding good health with clear bright green leaves. But then he pointed out the older leaves that had been there a while, and compared them to the newer ones.

New leaves were at least three times the length of the old ones; perhaps six times the area. Dan said the size of a tree's fruit is proportional to the size of the leaves, so he was expecting larger nuts than usual. He then pointed to the nuts, which were already developing. Many were coming on in clusters of three or four or more. Dan said nuts usually come on singly. The size of his harvest seems likely to be exceptional.

Dan won't sell his harvest, except for seed. He'll have thousands of seedlings which will also be raised with the Sonic Bloom process and if Dan is right he will soon have new nut trees bearing nuts of exceptional size and quality.

I wondered how to make a video proving how fast a tree grows. Then a beautiful idea came to me. Wouldn't it be great if you could show a new born baby grasping a nut followed by a scene of the baby watching the nut being planted, seeing a shoot come up, and the tree developing as the baby also grows into a child that begins to walk and talk and gather nuts under his tree! It would certainly present a moving story for the miracle of Sonic Bloom.

Dan said he believed devastated rainforests could be replaced with millions of nut trees to produce vast amounts of food for the planet in a very few years. At the same time they would take a tremendous amount of carbon dioxide from the atmosphere and help to counter the dangerous greenhouse effect.

Sonic Bloom is a combination of special sounds similar to the mating calls of birds and a spray applied to the leaves of the plant. The spray contains minerals and a growth hormone, all of which is non-toxic and entirely safe. The sound has the effect of opening the stomata of the plant so it can absorb the nutrients and use them at once. It also lets the plants take in far more carbon dioxide from the air than with closed pores.

Since our atmosphere today has about twice as much carbon dioxide as it did a century or two ago, a tremendous acceleration of growth is produced, along with improvement in nutrition and many other qualities and better seeds. The improvement in seed quality means that after plants are treated with Sonic Bloom for several generations, the seed they produce creates far better plants even if the new system is not longer used.

Dan's discoveries suggest a direct relationship between the presence of millions of birds (before Europeans invaded) and the verdant growth they encountered:

"To those who followed Columbus and Cortez, the New World truly seemed incredible because of the natural endowments. The land often announced itself with a heavy scent miles out into the ocean. Giovanni di Verrazano in 1524 smelled the cedars of the East Coast a hundred leagues out. The men of Henry Hudson's Half Moon were temporarily disarmed by the fragrance of the New Jersey shore, while ships running farther up the coast occasionally swam through large beds of floating flowers. Wherever they came inland they found a rich riot of color and sound, of game and luxuriant vegetation. Had they been other than they were, they might have written a new mythology here. As it was, they took inventory," quote Frederick Turner.

NEW VIDEO: 'GROW WITH SOUND AND SPRAY'

Aquarian Alternatives now has a 29 minute video showing trees in Wisconsin and garden crops in Colorado. Dan's 75 minute slide lecture is added. It sells or rents with a $25 deposit.

Birthright ... and ... Scotland Today

SOIL REMINERALIZATION AND ITS REASIBLE ROLE IN STABILISING THE CLIMATE SHIFT

Extracts from Cameron Thomson's fine article, referred to in Part II ch. 2.

During the last 2 million years the Earth has experienced 20 glaciations, each lasting around 90,000 years, and 20 inter-glacials, each lasting around 10,000 years.

THIS IS MORE THAN COINCIDENCE

These cycles are Gaia's fertility cycles. Glaciation is similar to menstruation in that it is a necessary part of a cycle which prepares the organism - woman or Gaia - to support life.

Just as a woman is fertile for only 36 hours every 28 days (approximately), Gaia is fertile for approximately 10,000 thousand years every 100,000 years (or more specifically, for only 2 or 3 thousand years, during the Mesocratic - Post-Glacial Climatic Optimum - phase of the inter-glacial). It is true to say that the present Climate Shift is no more than Gaia's pre-menstrual (glaciation) tension.

The excess carbon and other gases in the atmosphere cannot remain there. Gaia will recycle them - with earthquakes and cooling higher latitude oceans acting as 'sinks' for atmospheric carbon.

Floods, droughts, hailstones, early and late frosts and snowfalls, hurricanes and tornadoes, earthquakes and volcanoes, forest fires ... are all becoming the norm.

Extremes become the norm at the end of the Telocratic phase..

As the SEER Centre see it...

Our choice is to utilise our technology and resources, as **TOOLS** rather than weapons, to **SIMULATE** Earth's natural remineralisation process, to grow soil to grow biomass to bring global CO2 levels down from 365 ppm (parts per million) to 270 - 280 ppm ...

Or to continue into the harsh end of inter-glacial conditions which are becoming more extreme, more obvious with each day and **WILL** lead to a **NATURAL REMINERALISATION PROCESS**, i.e.,

GLACIATION . . .

Every quarry or sand/gravel pit has rock dust and silt available. Silt (glacial deposit) is 'surplus to requirements' and **IS TRANSPORTED** and dumped into local landfill sites. I suggest that it be dumped into local set-aside fields, generally the poorest, most minerally depleted, chemically polluted land which, too, is 'surplus to requirements'.

Imagine what could be achieved if District/County Councils throughout Britain were to recycle this rock dust and silt, incorporating it into their compost heaps. A 'soil conditioner' would become a 'soil fertiliser' and could compete with NPK!

Imagine what could be achieved if this remineralised compost were to be incorporated into set-aside fields to heal and regenerate the soil, and establish 3 million acres of tree nurseries on every farm in Britain, and throughout other First World Countries. **REAL** jobs could be created for the young unemployed who, too, seem to be 'surplus to requirements' under present political policies. We could, in fact, go a long way in recycling carbon from the atmosphere (Agenda 21).

Consider the time, energy (fossil fuel), and labour expended gathering stones from our fields, either by hand or by machine (stone separating) and dumping them.

If this assortment of stones was crushed by mobile rock pulverisers (which have been designed by a N.A.S.A. engineer and are manufactured in U.S.) and returned to the soil; each field would receive something approaching the perfect mixture of stone types, providing most of the whole spectrum of minerals and trace minerals...

Our Remineralised Permaculture Demonstration Garden, its vigorous growth, bumper crops and (climate shift) hardiness have convinced many, from various professional walks of life of the potential, locally and globally, **SOIL REMINERALISATION** has to offer.

Cabbages, once grapefruit sized, now grow to football sized; peas, which once grew 4 feet high, now grow to 8 feet high!

Our Garden is 'Open' throughout the Summer season. Visits by appointment/SAE. **ALL WELCOME.**

CAMERON THOMSON

Sustainable Ecological Earth Regeneration Centre Trust
(SEER Centre)

Ceanghline, Straloch,
Enochdhu,
Perthshire PH10 7PH,
Scotland.

"When you look at the chances of getting the vitamins and minerals we need from our food nowadays, I think we are lucky if we get anything! There have been lots of studies done where researchers have tested oranges, for example, and found no vitamin C at all"

Breakthroughs in Nutrition 3

With acknowledgements to Beyond Nutrition Press,
27 Old Gloucester Street, London WC1N 3XX.

BLUEPRINT FOR A NEW HEALTH SERVICE!

*

"No major investment,
new technology or bureaucracy
is required... It will be fun
to be a part of." See on!
S-A.H.

*

WHAT DO WE STAND FOR?

Templegarth *Trust*

Reg. Charity No. 511704

Our national medical service - the NHS - has been in decline since long before the current proposals to restructure it. It never did live up to its name. It has never had anything much to do with health.

All sorts of people can see this - parents, teachers, priests; even some individual doctors and nurses. But the medical and nursing professional bodies and the business managers who direct the NHS show no prospect of grasping the truth. They cling to ideas about the nature of disease that are way out of date. They do not take seriously the increasing environmental hazards and diminishing personal vitality which now challenge health on an epidemic scale.

So the kind of medicine provided for us - even most so-called preventive medicine - is increasingly out of step with the real needs of most ordinary people. If we are ever going to have a real Health Service, we shall have to construct it ourselves.

This Lincolnshire Charity was founded in 1981 by a family doctor, a dentist, a priest and several teachers as a modest but genuinely independent attempt to explore this possibility. We have listened to thousands of people in trouble, talked to many hundreds of groups, researched scores of issues, conducted dozens of practical experiments, set up and advised a string of clubs and self-help services. We have set out our ideas in three books, scores of articles, numerous broadcasts and over 200 self-help leaflets and pamphlets.

We now know what is needed to make a start. No major investment, new technology or bureaucracy is required. It will cut back drastically our reliance on expensive medical and surgical services. It will be fun to be a part of!

WHAT DO I NEED FOR HEALTH?

- A clear idea of what health consists of and how good yours is
- Lots of detailed information about how to live well and get rid of obstacles to good living
- Easy access to all the supplies and practical facilities you may need

HOW CAN I GET ALL THESE?

- Through one of our Good HealthKeeping schemes

We now offer a choice of schemes under the Good HealthKeeping banner. Information on WholeCare, ReAlive and ***HealthScore*** may be found in separate leaflets, available on request.

HOW CAN I HELP?

- Let us know you are interested. We like to keep in touch with anyone whose interests run parallel to our own, and are glad to exchange newsletters with other organisations on a complimentary basis.

- Subscribe to the Trust annually, preferably by Deed of Covenant. A minimum of £10 is suggested. We circulate occasional newsletters to keep you in touch with progress. Covenant and Banker's Order forms are available on request.

- Enrol in one of our Good HealthKeeping schemes

FURTHER DETAILS

Templegarth *Trust* is a registered charity number 511704. Its trustees are Peter Mansfield (family doctor), Robert Borrill (dental surgeon), Pamela Mansfield (teacher) and Celia Monument (Trust secretary). Patrons include:

Geoffrey Cannon Author and Journalist
Lord Donaldson one-time Minister for the Arts
Yehudi Gordon Consultant Obstetrician
Susan Hampshire Actress
Leslie Kenton Author and Broadcaster
Sue MacGregor Broadcaster
Lady Micklethwait past President, National Childbirth Trust
Lord Young of Dartington Founder, The Consumers Association

Templegarth *Trust* is scrupulously independent of pressure groups, political parties, official agencies and commercial interests of any kind and most of its income will in future be covenanted to it by Good HealthKeeping.

Good HealthKeeping exists in support of Templegarth *Trust* and its profits are covenanted to the Trust in full. Directed by Peter Mansfield, Good HealthKeeping publishes, produces and distributes Trust literature, promotes products and services recommended by the Trust, and manages the Good HealthKeeping schemes.

Templegarth *Trust*, Thames Street, LOUTH, Lincs LN11 7AD  100% recycled paper

Part III

KALEIDOSCOPE

*

5) A FEW FANDANGOS ... AND FLUORIDATION!

On the Scottish Office's Land Reform Policy - S-A.H.

On the Scottish Office's "Towards a Healthier Scotland" Policy - S-A.H.

Fluoridation... S-A.H.

Fluoride, Teeth and the Atomic Bomb, by Joel Griffiths and Chris Bryson.

(Published here by kind permission of the Authors, and with grateful acknowledgements also to the National Pure Water Association.)

*

The Rocks Pitlochry Perthshire PH16 5QZ

The Secretary of State for Scotland,
St Andrews House, (The Scottish Office),
Edinburgh EH1.

29 Apr 98

(For delivery by hand to The Scottish Office on April 30th, closing date of consultation period.)

Dear Donald Dewar,

Land Reform for Scotland

In response to your consultation on the question of land reform for Scotland, may I write you as follows:-

(1) The only land reform that is consistent with justice is that which enables the redistribution of land to follow from the collection annually of the rental value of the land from every occupant.

(2) The rental value of land is a community-created value. By returning to the community what rightly belongs to the community - that wealth which is created by the community - we discover to hand a fund specifically designed to meet society's needs, whilst allowing the ineptitude of taxation - (that hits production on the head) - to be done away with.

(3) The monopoly of land underlies the monopoly of capital. (We live not in a capitalist society, but in a monopoly capitalist society.) This reform, by reaching to the root of capital monopoly, would reach to the root of the present appalling, and ever-widening, gap between rich and poor, effecting a radical redistribution of wealth.

(4) Hence this reform would institute social justice at the very root of the social structure, as well as bringing to an end the monopoly of land.

(5) Millions of pounds of taxpayers' money, required to deal with the complexities and absurdities of our present taxation system would be saved. Land cannot be moved, hide itself, or run away. Once the initial valuation rolls are set up - (with regular updating as required by society) - the collection of the land's rental values would be simplicity itself.

(6) This land reform is indigenous to Scotland, having been promulgated by many of Scotland's finest thinkers, including William Ogilvie, Thomas Spence and Patrick Edward Dove. On this account also it is particularly to be looked to by the Scots as their very own concept both of economic justice and of justice in land reform.

(7) For the above reasons, this land reform is the land reform pre-eminently consistent with common sense as well as with justice - and is hence uniquely fit to be adopted by the Scots, besides being their very own.

I enclose "The Land Question", (now translated into Danish), as a testimony to my own studies in this field; with a few accompanying papers.

Finally, I enclose a s.a.e., and would ask you kindly to acknowledge to me receipt of this communication.

Yours sincerely,

Shirley-Anne Hardy

(Mrs S-A. Hardy)

P.S. I am glad to see that this proposal figures in the response to your Consultation of my own Perth & Kinross Council.

The Rocks Pitlochry Perthshire PH16 5QZ

9 Sept 98

Dear [The Sec. of State for Scotland + the 11 Members of the Group, individually]

Land Reform Policy Group:
Identifying the Solutions (Sept 1998).

As one who addressed you on Land Reform, you have kindly sent me the results of your Group's deliberations - published under the above heading.

I am sorry to have to say it, but I find your publication to be of content trivial, an almost complete defence of the status quo - and all in all presenting a travesty of the word "vision" which is sprinkled so freely through its pages.

I enclose a further copy of my letter to you on this matter, dated 29 Apr 98, from which I am sure you will understand what I mean.

Yours sincerely,

Shirley-Anne Hardy

(Mrs S-A. Hardy)

The Rocks Pitlochry Perthshire PH16 5QZ

Assistant Secretary to the Land Reform Policy Group,
The Scottish Office,
Pentland House,
47, Robb's Loan,
Edinburgh EH14 1TY.

27 Sept 98

Dear Alison Morris,

Land Reform for Scotland

Thank you for your letter of 22nd September, saying that "I understand your main interest lies in the subject of land value taxation...discussed on p.21 of the consultation paper, that the "second paper contains the Group's emerging thinking and provisional view of all options discussed, including that of taxation", that the Group "will consider the responses" to this second paper in preparing its final document, and that you will send me a copy of that final document when it is published.

I must clarify a misunderstanding. I do not have any interest in the promotion of a reform by the name of "land value taxation". The reform referred to in my letter of April 29th is that of land rent for revenue - (sometimes also referred to as community ground rent). My letter makes no mention of "land value taxation".

The term "rent" - more precisely "rental value" - is the essential term descriptive of this reform. The reason is that rental values are community-created. The collection of community-created values to finance the community's needs is thus in accordance with natural law of an elementary kind. In the sphere of revenue-raising, natural law stands for those higher laws which are infallible and non-manipulative, as compared with human ones which are both manipulative and fallible. There can therefore be no questioning of the fact that these rental values, originating from the community, must be returned to the community from which they originate. To sum up:-

(1) The dedicating to the community's needs of the rental values it has itself created meets a moral imperative as well as a practical one.

(2) The applying to the commonuty's needs of its own rental values strengthens and empowers the community and every member of it.

(3) The financing of the community's needs from its own rental values (as opposed to taxation), promotes a background of stability against which society can successfully operate - arbitrary human tax-devisings forming no part of that scene.

(4) The setting out of the question of revenue thus, in its correct terms, also enlightens and educates the public on a matter of primary importance for their well-being - a matter upon which there has been a long and artful cover-up.

In contrast - I have come to recognize over the years that the term "land value taxation" - whether used mistakenly by its promoters (and I gather most have written to you under this term), or deliberately by its opposers - is essentially a term of concealment, since it places this reform within the brackets of a tax.

The nature of a tax is essentially as follows:-

(a) It is an arbitrary demand: that is, a demand which accords with the dictates merely of a collection of - entirely fallible - human beings. It is thus the opposite of moral.

Please Turn Over

(b) It is imposed from above, and is therefore essentially contrary to the idea of community empowerment.

(c) It has no certainty of continued operation - taxes change notoriously from one year, and from one budget, to another. This makes a ruinous background for human activity, including business activity, being essentially de-stabilising.

(d) It is dis-educative of the people as to a fundamental right - that of enjoying the values which they themselves create; and amounts (as stated above) to a term of concealment.

In short, by the term "land value taxation", the land rent reform is indeed trivialised.

Given (a), (b), (c) and (d) - with the stack of confusions that must follow therefrom - it is no wonder that your conclusion regarding "land value taxation", in your second paper ("Identifying the Solutions"), does not rise above: "Maybe, but not yet; a lot more study needed" - ! You will now be into that third study...

Yours sincerely,

Shirley-Anne Hardy

(Mrs S-A. Hardy)

The Rocks Pitlochry Perthshire PH16 5QZ

The Secretary of State for Scotland,
The Scottish Office,
St Andrews House,
Edinburgh EH1.

13 Jan 99

Dear Donald Dewar,

Land Reform Policy Group
Your 3rd Paper: Recommendations for Action

You have now completed your deliberations on the subject of Land Reform, and have kindly sent me a copy of your Final Paper, "Recommendations for Action", dated January 1999.

In response to this, I find that I have nothing to add to my earlier communications to you, dated 29th April, and 9th and 27th September, 1998, of which I enclose reminder copies for you here.

Yours sincerely,

Shirley-Anne Hardy

(Shirley-Anne Hardy)

Copies to:

Lord Sewel, Chairman of the Group,
and Alison Morris, its Assistant Secretary.

The Rocks Pitlochry Perthshire PH16 5QZ

The Scottish Office (Department of Health),
Public Health Policy Unit,
St Andrews House,
Edinburgh EH1 3DG.

21 Feb 99

Dear Sirs,

"Towards a Healthier Scotland"

I am in receipt of your letter of 17th February with White Paper of the above title, of which you have sent me a copy as one of those who addressed you on this matter.

In response, I have to say this:

A government which actively promotes the use of artificial fertilizers and poison sprays in agriculture; the fluoridation of public water supplies; and the use of genetically modified organisms in food and on the land, amongst many other evils; and which also cements poverty, hence malnutrition, into the lives of the great mass of the people at base, by upholding the false economic and social structure of land monopoly *: such a government does not have the first beginnings of a genuine interest in the health of the population.

I can only regard your Report, therefore, as a cover-up, and a **WASTE** of the paper on which it is written.

There is this to add: that a government which resorts to (or maintains) the subterfuge of setting up its own appointed "Health" Boards, (as similarly, Water Boards, etc.), as a means of underhandedly removing power over their health from the people themselves in order to serve various commercial and political interests behind the scenes instead - such a government clearly has no intention whatsoever of fulfilling the wishes of the people, and all its protestations in this regard likewise amount to no more than a further gross DECEPTION AND COVER-UP.

Yours truly,

Shirley-Anne Hardy

(Mrs S-A. Hardy)

* For my responses to the government's policy papers on Land Reform, you may consult with the relevant department at the Scottish Office.

The Rocks Pitlochry Perthshire PH16 5QZ

[Name erased]
To: . . . .
The Scottish Office,
(Public Health Policy Unit),
St Andrews House,
Edinburgh EH1 3DG.

(No further reply received) STAH

Your Ref: NJC/7/2

7 June 98

Dear . . . .,

Fluoridation - "THE GREATEST CASE OF SCIENTIFIC FRAUD OF THIS CENTURY - IF NOT OF ALL TIME"

(Dr Robert Carlton, U.S. E.P.A. scientist.)

Thank you for your letter of 1st June - but at the very start of it you have dropped a major "clanger".

The substance with which it is proposed to fluoridate water supplies is not that which occurs naturally, and the two substances vary in their behaviour, (as you can discover from scientific literature).

This error in turn invalidates your argument that - fluoridation is not mass-medication. The addition of a highly toxic and corrosive industrial waste to water supplies for purposes of fluoridating them is not merely mass-medication - it is more truly enforced poisoning of the entire population.

The deliberate falsification of the whole fluoridation issue at its very foundations, in this way, by those who dishonestly take the path of misrepresentation and cover-up, must invalidate every further argument in favour of fluoridation which is officially presented to us. The world is of course now awash - following decades of this heinous experiment - with scientific evidence warning against fluoridation; not "outwith scientific journals, but within them. Please catch up on today's scene!

The World Health Organization which you refer to ALSO - (but somehow you forgot it!) - warns us that ere schemes of artificial fluoridation are contemplated, the level of intake of fluoride already endured by the population from our vastly-polluted-today environment should be carefully measured. So why not tell us of the grim findings of Dr Peter Mansfield, who has already set such an assessment on foot? (What Doctors Don't Tell You, June 1998.)

As for the typically dishonest government wording of that 1992 poll you are so unwise as to quote: may I remind you that Dr Robert Weaver - (upon whose famous North Shields and South Shields studies of teeth, government fluoridation proposals in this country majorly took off) - additionally found that in the more highly fluoridated South Shields community (1.40 ppm) as compared with the North Shields one (.25 ppm), life expectancy was lower AND INFANT MORTALITY HIGHER.

Who's for a set of teeth like the grin on the face of the Cheshire Cat - and no baby ?

Yours truly,

Shirley-Anne Hardy

(Mrs S-A Hardy, B.A. Hons.)

The Rocks Pitlochry Perthshire PH16 5QZ

The Editor,
The Dundee Courier,
80, Kingsway East,
DUNDEE DD.

Letter published 13 Mar 98
- but minus verse.
So for the sake of the verse
I am adding it here!
- and as an introduction to what follows.

4 Mar 98

Dear Sir,

Fluoridation

Dr [Name here erased] 's pro-fluoridation message (19th February) doesn't quite add up. If the "majority of people" wish fluoridation, it would have been slapped down our throats long ere this. It is precisely because the (vast) majority does not wish it, that Labour is now toying with draconian steps to impose it - with Dr....... an acknowledged ally! (Enforced medication requires legislating against in Scotland's Bill of Rights.)

The fraud and fibbery that the ordinary public have always known lay behind fluoridation has now received - if I may so describe it - full frontal exposure. Recently de-classified 1940s U.S. secret military documents reveal that the fluoridated communities of Britain have been serving nicely as - yes! - guinea-pigs for America's atomic bomb research programme!

All honour to the Scots for having formed small part of that! - on account of their sharp-witted refusal to accept - and tireless beatings back of - this medical FRAUD. There's plenty more I could add, but perhaps the following verse will suffice:-

Oh fluoride, oh fluoride -
We'll take them on a fluo-ride!
They'll never guess - we'll say it means
Good teeth - the truth we'll sneak and hide.
Now someone's gone and spilt the beans!
Our pleasant game of "Open wide!"
Has boomeranged,
And now it seems -
Full frontal secrets open pried -
We're hoist on our own fluo-ride!

Yours truly,

Shirley-Anne Hardy

(Shirley-Anne Hardy)

Special Edition of WATERSHED
Vol. 3, No. 3, October, 1997
Published by the National Pure Water Association,
12, Dennington Lane, Crigglestone, Wakefield WF4 3ET, U.K.

"If you shut up the truth and bury it under the ground,
it will but grow and gather to itself such explosive power
that the day it bursts through it will blow up everything in its way." – Zola.

*

Massive United States cover-up of fluoride toxicity revealed by declassified 1940's secret military documents. U.S. editors consider the following article "too sensitive" for publication. There are 6,000,000 reasons for publishing it in Britain.

Why was a dentist involved in the "MANHATTAN PROJECT"? Why were the military affiliations of key fluoridation-promoters concealed for FIFTY YEARS? Why do "government advisers" *deliberately deny* the mass of peer-reviewed, published scientific evidence on the adverse health effects of fluoridation?

FLUORIDE, TEETH AND THE ATOMIC BOMB

© By JOEL GRIFFITHS and CHRIS BRYSON

New York, July 1997

Joel Griffiths *is a medical writer who lives in New York. Author of a book on human radiation experiments cited in Congressional Hearings and used as a basic reference in environmental publications, Mr. Griffiths has also contributed hundreds of articles for Medical Tribune, as well as numerous articles for Parents' Magazine, the Village Voice, Manhattan Tribune, Covert Action, etc.*

Chris Bryson, *who holds a Masters degree in Journalism, is an independent reporter with ten years professional experience. He has worked with BBC Radio and Public Television in New York, plus numerous publications, including the Christian Science Monitor and the Mansfield Guardian.*

Some fifty years after the United States began adding fluoride to public water supplies to reduce cavities in children's teeth, declassified government documents are shedding new light on the roots of that still controversial public health measure, revealing a surprising connection between fluoride and the dawning of the nuclear age.

Today, two thirds of U.S. public drinking water is fluoridated. Many municipalities still resist the practice, disbelieving the government's assurances of safety.

Since the days of World War II, when this nation prevailed by building the world's first atomic bomb, U.S. public health leaders have maintained that low doses of fluoride are safe for people, and good for children's teeth.

That safety verdict should now be re-examined in the light of hundreds of once-secret WWII documents obtained by Griffiths and Bryson – including declassified papers of the Manhattan Project, the U.S. military group that built the atomic bomb.

Fluoride was the key chemical in atomic bomb production, according to the documents. Massive quantities of fluoride – millions of tons – were essential for the manufacture of bomb-grade uranium and plutonium for nuclear weapons throughout the Cold War. One of the most toxic chemicals known, fluoride rapidly emerged as the leading chemical health hazard of the U.S. atomic bomb program – both for workers and for nearby communities, the documents reveal.

Other revelations include:

- Much original proof that fluoride is safe for humans in low doses was generated by A-bomb programme scientists, who had been secretly ordered to provide "evidence useful in litigation" against defence contractors for fluoride injury to citizens. The first lawsuits against the U.S. A-bomb programme were not over radiation, but over fluoride damage, the documents show.
- Human studies were required. Bomb program researchers played a leading role in the design and implementation of the most extensive U.S. study of the health effects of fluoridating public drinking water – conducted in Newburgh, New York from 1945 to 1956. Then, in a classified operation code-named "Programme F," they secretly gathered and analyzed blood and tissue samples from Newburgh citizens, with the co-operation of State Health Department personnel.
- The original secret version – obtained by these reporters – of a 1948 study published by Programme F scientists in the Journal of the American Dental Association shows that evidence of adverse health effects from fluoride was censored by the U.S. Atomic Energy Commission (AEC) – considered the most powerful of Cold War agencies – for reasons of national security.
- The bomb program's fluoride safety studies were conducted at the University of Rochester, site of one of the most notorious human radiation experiments of the Cold War, in which unsuspecting hospital patients were injected with toxic doses of radioactive plutonium. The fluoride studies were conducted with the same ethical mind-set, in which "national security" was paramount.
- The U.S. government's conflict of interest – and its motive to prove fluoride "safe" – has not until now been made clear to the general public in the furious debate over water fluoridation since the 1950's, nor to civilian researchers and health professionals, or journalists.

The declassified documents resonate with a growing body of scientific evidence, and a chorus of questions, about the health effects of fluoride in the environment.

Human exposure to fluoride has mushroomed since World War II, due not only to fluoridated water and toothpaste, but to environmental pollution by major industries from aluminium to pesticides: fluoride is a critical industrial chemical.

The impact can be seen, literally, in the smiles of our children. Large numbers of U.S. young people – up to 80 per cent in some cities – now have dental fluorosis, the first visible sign of excessive fluoride exposure, according to the U.S. National Research Council. (The signs are whitish flecks or spots, particularly on the front teeth, or dark spots or stripes in more severe cases.)

Less-known to the public is that fluoride also accumulates in bones – "The teeth are windows to what's happening in the bones," explains Paul Connett, Professor of Chemistry at St. Lawrence University (N.Y.). In recent years, paediatric bone specialists have expressed alarm about an increase in stress fractures among U.S. young people. Connett and other scientists are concerned that fluoride – linked to bone damage by studies since the 1930's – may be a contributing factor. The declassified documents add urgency: much of the original proof that low-dose fluoride is safe for children's bones came from U.S. bomb program scientists, according to this investigation.

Now, researchers who have reviewed these declassified documents fear that Cold War national security considerations may have prevented objective scientific evaluation of vital public health questions concerning fluoride.

"Information was buried," concludes Dr. Phyllis Mullenix, former head of toxicology at Forsyth Dental Center in Boston, and now a critic of fluoridation. Animal studies Mullenix and co-workers conducted at Forsyth in the early 1990's indicated that fluoride was a powerful central nervous system (CNS) toxin, and might adversely affect human brain functioning, even at low doses. (New epidemiological evidence from China adds support, showing a correlation between low-dose fluoride exposure and diminished I.Q. in children.) Mullenix's results were published in 1995, in a reputable peer-reviewed scientific journal.

During her investigation, Mullenix was astonished to discover there had been virtually no previous U.S. studies of fluoride's effects on the human brain. Then, her application for a grant to continue her CNS research was turned down by the U.S. National Institutes of Health (NIH), where an NIH panel, she says, flatly told her that "fluoride does not have central nervous system effects."

> *"Clinical evidence suggests that uranium hexafluoride may have a rather marked central nervous system effect"*

Declassified documents of the U.S. atomic-bomb program indicate otherwise. An April 29, 1944 Manhattan Project memo reports: "Clinical evidence suggests that uranium hexafluoride may have a rather marked central nervous system effect. . . . It seems most likely that the F [code for fluoride] component rather than the T [code for uranium] is the causative factor."

The memo – stamped "secret" – is addressed to the head of the Manhattan Project's Medical Section, Colonel Stafford Warren. Colonel Warren is asked to approve a program of animal research on CNS effects: "Since work with these compounds is essential, it will be necessary to know in advance what mental effects may occur after exposure . . .

This is important not only to protect a given individual, but also to prevent a confused workman from injuring others by improperly performing his duties."

On the same day, Colonel Warren approved the CNS research program. This was in 1944, at the height of the Second World War and the nation's race to build the world's first atomic bomb. For research on fluoride's CNS effects to be approved at such a momentous time, the supporting evidence set forth in the proposal forwarded along with the memo must have been persuasive.

This proposal, however, is missing from the files of the U.S. National Archives. "If you find the memos, but the document they refer to is missing, it's probably still classified," said Charles Reeves, chief librarian at the Atlanta branch of the U.S. National Archives and Records Administration, where the memos were found. Similarly, no results of the Manhattan Project's fluoride CNS research could be found in the files.

After reviewing the memos, Mullenix declared herself "flabbergasted." She went on, "How could I be told by NIH that fluoride has no central nervous system effects when these documents were sitting there all the time?" She reasons that the Manhattan Project did do fluoride CNS studies – "that kind of warning, that fluoride workers might be a danger to the bomb program by improperly performing their duties – I can't imagine that would be ignored" – but that the results were buried because they might create a difficult legal and public relations problem for the government.

The author of the 1944 CNS research proposal was Dr. Harold C. Hodge, at the time chief of fluoride toxicology studies for the University of Rochester division of the Manhattan Project. Nearly fifty years later at the Forsyth Dental Center in Boston, Dr. Mullenix was introduced to a gently ambling elderly man brought in to serve as a consultant on her CNS research – Harold C. Hodge. By then Hodge had achieved status emeritus as a world authority on fluoride safety. "But even though he was supposed to be helping me," says Mullenix, "he never once mentioned the CNS work he had done for the Manhattan Project."

The "black hole" in fluoride CNS research since the days of the Manhattan Project is unacceptable to Mullenix, who refuses to abandon the issue. "There is so much fluoride exposure now, and we simply do not know what it is doing," she says. "You can't just walk away from this."

Dr. Antonio Noronha, an NIH scientific review advisor familiar with Dr. Mullenix's grant request, says her proposal was rejected by a scientific peer-review group. He terms her claim of institutional bias against fluoride CNS research "farfetched". He adds, "We strive very hard at NIH to make sure politics does not enter the picture."

Split Atoms and Split Peaches' – A massive Manhattan Project pollution incident in New Jersey sparks secret wartime U.S. research on fluoride safety.

Fluoride and National Security

The documentary trail begins at the height of World War 2, in 1943, when a severe pollution incident occurred downwind of the E.I. du Pont Nemours Company chemical factory in Deepwater, New Jersey. The factory was then producing millions of pounds of fluoride for the Manhattan project, the ultra-secret U.S. military program racing to produce the world's first atomic bomb.

The farms downwind in Gloucester and Salem counties were famous for their high-quality produce – their peaches went directly to the Waldorf Astoria Hotel in New York. Their tomatoes were bought up by Campbell's Soup.

But in the summer of 1943, the farmers began to report that their crops were blighted, and that "something is burning up the peach crops around here."

Poultry died after an all-night thunderstorm, they reported. Farm workers who ate the produce they had picked sometimes vomited all night and into the next day. "I remember our horses looked sick and were too stiff to work," these reporters were told by Mildred Giordano, who was a teenager at the time. Some cows were so crippled they could not stand up, and grazed by crawling on their bellies.

Their account was confirmed in taped interviews, shortly before he died, by Philip Sadtler in 1996 of Sadtler Laboratories of Philadelphia, one of the nation's oldest chemical consulting firms. Sadtler had personally conducted the initial investigation of the damages in 1943-44.

Although the farmers did not know it, the attention of the Manhattan Project and the federal government was riveted on the New Jersey incident, according to once-secret documents obtained by these reporters. After the war's end, in a secret Manhattan Project memo dated March 1, 1946, the Project's chief of fluoride toxicology studies, Harold C. Hodge, worriedly wrote to his boss Colonel Stafford L. Warren, Chief of the Medical Division, about "problems associated with the question of fluoride contamination of the atmosphere in a certain section of New Jersey. There seem to be four distinct (though related) problems," continued Hodge;

"1. A question of injury of the peach crop in 1944.

2. A report of extraordinary fluoride content of vegetables grown in this area.

3. A report of abnormally high fluoride content in the blood of human individuals residing in this area.

4. A report raising the question of serious poisoning of horses and cattle in this area."

The New Jersey farmers waited until the war was over, then sued du Pont and the Manhattan Project for fluoride damage -- reportedly the first lawsuits against the U.S. A-bomb program.

> *"If the farmers won, it would open the door to further suits, which might impede the bomb program's ability to use fluoride."*

Although seemingly trivial, the lawsuits shook the government, the secret documents reveal. Under the personal direction of Manhattan Project chief Major General Leslie R. Groves, secret meetings were convened in Washington, with compulsory attendance by scores of scientists and officials from the U.S. War Department, the Manhattan Project, the Food and Drug Administration, the Agriculture and Justice Departments, the U.S. Army's Chemical Warfare Service and Edgewood Arsenal, the Bureau of Standards, and du Pont lawyers. Declassified memos of the meetings reveal a secret mobilization of the full forces of the government to defeat the New Jersey farmers:

These agencies "are making scientific investigations to obtain evidence which may be used to protect the interest of the Government at the trial of the suits brought by owners of peach orchards in ... New Jersey," stated Manhattan Project Lieutenant Colonel Cooper B. Rhodes, in a memo c.c.'d to General Groves.

"27 August 1945

"Subject: Investigation of Crop Damage at Lower Penns Neck, New Jersey
To: The Commanding General, Army Service Forces, Pentagon Building, Washington D.C.

"At the request of the Secretary of War the Department of Agriculture has agreed to cooperate in investigating complaints of crop damage attributed... to fumes from a plant operated in connection with the Manhattan Project."

Signed, L.R. Groves, Major General U.S.A.

"The Department of Justice is co-operating in the defence of these suits," wrote General Groves in a Feb. 28, 1946 memo to the Chairman of the U.S. Senate Special Committee on Atomic Energy.

Why the national-security emergency over a few lawsuits by New Jersey farmers? In 1946 the United States had begun full-scale production of atomic bombs. No other nation had yet tested a nuclear weapon, and the A-bomb was seen as crucial for U.S. leadership of the postwar world. The New Jersey fluoride lawsuits were a serious roadblock to that strategy.

"The specter of endless lawsuits haunted the military," writes Lansing Lamont in his acclaimed book about the first atomic bomb test, "Day of Trinity."

In the case of fluoride, "If the farmers won, it would open the door to further suits, which might impede the bomb program's ability to use fluoride," said Jacqueline Kittrell, a Tennessee public interest lawyer specializing in nuclear cases, who examined the declassified fluoride documents. (Kittrell has represented plaintiffs in several human radiation experiment cases.) She added, "The reports of human injury were especially threatening, because of the potential for enormous settlements -- not to mention the PR problem."

Indeed, du Pont was particularly concerned about the "possible psychologic reaction" to the New Jersey pollution incident, according to a secret 1946 Manhattan Project memo. Facing a threat from the Food and Drug Administration (FDA) to embargo the region's produce because of "high fluoride content," du Pont dispatched its lawyers to the FDA offices in Washington, where an agitated meeting ensued. According to a memo sent next day to General Groves, Du Pont's lawyer argued "that in view of the pending suits...any action by the Food and Drug Administration... would have a serious effect on the du Pont Company and would create a bad public relations situation." After the meeting adjourned, Manhattan Project Captain John Davies approached the FDA's Food Division chief and "impressed upon Dr. White the substantial interest which the Government had in claims which might arise as a result of action which might be taken by the Food and Drug Administration."

There was no embargo. Instead, new tests for fluoride in the New jersey area would be conducted -- not by the Department of Agriculture, but by the U.S. Army's Chemical Warfare Service because "work done by the Chemical Warfare Service would carry the greatest weight as evidence if...lawsuits are started by the complainants." The memo was signed by General Groves.

Meanwhile, the public relations problem remained unresolved -- local citizens were in a panic about fluoride.

The farmer's spokesman, Willard B. Kille, was personally invited to dine with General Groves -- then known as "the man who built the atomic bomb" -- at his office at the War Department on March 26, 1946. Although he had been diagnosed with fluoride poisoning by his doctor, Kille departed the luncheon convinced of the government's good faith. The next day he wrote to the general, wishing the other farmers could have been present, he said, so "they too could come away with the feeling that their interests in this particular matter were being safeguarded by men of the very highest type whose integrity they could not question."

In a subsequent secret Manhattan project memo, a broader solution to the public relations problem was suggested by chief fluoride toxicologist Harold C. Hodge. He wrote to the Medical Section chief, Col. Warren: "Would there be any use in making attempts to counteract the local fear of fluoride on the part of residents of Salem and

Gloucester counties through the lectures on F toxicology and perhaps the usefulness of F in tooth health?" Such lectures were indeed given, not only to New Jersey citizens but to the rest of the nation throughout the Cold War.

The New Jersey farmers' lawsuits were ultimately stymied by the government's refusal to reveal the key piece of information that would have settled the case --how much fluoride du Pont had vented into the atmosphere during the war. "Disclosure... would be injurious to the military security of the United States," wrote Manhattan Project Major C.A Taney, Jr. The farmers were pacified with token financial settlements, according to interviews with descendants still living in the area.

"All we knew is that du Pont released some chemical that burned up all the peach trees around here," recalls Angelo Giordano, whose father James was one of the original plaintiffs. "The trees were no good after that, so we had to give up on the peaches." Their horses and cows, too, acted stiff and walked stiff, recalls his sister Mildred. "Could any of that have been the fluoride?" she asked. (The symptoms she detailed to the authors are cardinal signs of fluoride toxicity, according to veterinary toxicologists.)

The Giordano family, too, has been plagued by bone and joint problems, Mildred adds. Recalling the settlement received by the Giordanos, Angelo told these reporters that "my father said he got about $200."

> *". . . work done by the Chemical Warfare Service would carry the greatest weight as evidence if . . . lawsuits are started by the complainants."*

The farmers were stonewalled in their search for information, and their complaints have long since been forgotten. But they unknowingly left their imprint on history -- their claims of injury to their health reverberated through the corridors of power in Washington, and triggered intensive secret bomb-program research on the health effects of fluoride. A secret 1945 memo from Manhattan Project Lt. Col. Rhodes to General Groves stated: "Because of complaints that animals and humans have been injured by hydrogen fluoride fumes in [the New Jersey] area, although there are no pending suits involving such claims, the University of Rochester is conducting experiments to determine the toxic effect of fluoride."

Much of the proof of fluoride's safety in low doses rests on the postwar work performed by the University of Rochester, in anticipation of lawsuits against the bomb program for human injury.

Fluoride and the Cold War

Delegating fluoride safety studies to the University of Rochester was not surprising. During World War Two the federal government had become involved, for the first time, in large-scale funding of scientific research at government-owned labs and private colleges. Those early spending priorities were shaped by the nation's often-secret military needs.

The prestigious upstate New York college, in particular, had housed a key wartime division of the Manhattan Project, studying the health effects of the new "special materials", such as uranium, plutonium, beryllium and fluoride, being used to make the atomic bomb. That work continued after the war, with millions of dollars flowing from the Manhattan Project and its successor organization, the Atomic Energy

Commission (AEC). (Indeed, the bomb left an indelible imprint on all U.S. science in the late 1940's and 50's. Up to 90% of federal funds for university research came from either the Defense Department or the AEC in this period, according to Noam Chomsky's 1996 book "The Cold War and the University.")

The University of Rochester medical school became a revolving door for senior bomb program scientists. Postwar faculty included Stafford Warren, the top medical officer of the Manhattan Project, and Harold Hodge, chief of fluoride research for the bomb program.

This marriage of military secrecy and medical science bore deformed offspring. The University of Rochester's classified fluoride studies -- code-named Program F -- were conducted at its Atomic Energy Project (AEP), a top-secret facility funded by the AEC and housed in Strong Memorial Hospital. It was there that one of the most notorious human radiation experiments of the Cold War took place, in which unsuspecting hospital patients were injected with toxic doses of radioactive plutonium. Revelation of this experiment in a Pulitzer prize winning account by Eileen Welsome led to a 1995 U.S. Presidential investigation, and a multimillion-dollar cash settlement for victims.

Program F was not about children's teeth. It grew directly out of litigation against the bomb program and its main purpose was to furnish scientific ammunition which the government and its nuclear contractors could use to defeat lawsuits for human injury. Program F's director was Harold C. Hodge, who had led the Manhattan Project investigation of alleged human injury in the New Jersey fluoride-pollution incident.

Program F's purpose is spelled out in a classified 1948 report. It reads: "To supply evidence *useful in the litigation* arising from an alleged loss of a fruit crop several years ago, a number of problems have been opened. Since excessive blood fluoride levels were reported in human residents of the same area, our principal effort has been devoted to describing the relationship of blood fluorides to toxic effects." (Emphasis added.)

The litigation referred to, of course, and the claims of human injury were against the bomb program and its contractors. Thus, the purpose of Program F was to obtain evidence useful in litigation against the bomb program. The research was being conducted by the defendants.

The potential conflict of interest is clear. If lower dose ranges were found hazardous by Program F, it might have opened the bomb program and its contractors to lawsuits for injury to human health, as well as public outcry.

Comments lawyer Kittrell: "This and other documents indicate that the University of Rochester's fluoride research grew out of the New Jersey lawsuits and was performed in anticipation of lawsuits against the bomb program for human injury. Studies undertaken for litigation purposes by the defendants would not be considered scientifically acceptable today", adds Kittrell, "because of their inherent bias to prove the chemical safe."

Unfortunately, much of the proof of fluoride's safety rests on the work performed by Program F scientists at the University of Rochester. During the postwar period that university emerged as the leading academic center for establishing the safety of fluoride, as well as its effectiveness in reducing tooth decay, according to Dental School spokesperson William H. Bowen, MD. The key figure in this research, Bowen said, was Harold C. Hodge-- who also became a leading national proponent of fluoridating public drinking water.

Program F's interest in water fluoridation was not just "to counteract the local fear of fluoride on the part of the residents" as Hodge had earlier written. The bomb program needed human studies, as they had needed human studies for plutonium, and adding fluoride to public water supplies provided one opportunity.

The A-Bomb Program and Water Fluoridation

Bomb-program scientists played a prominent -- if unpublicized -- role in the nation's first-planned water fluoridation experiment, in Newburgh, New York. The Newburgh Demonstration Project is considered the most extensive study of the health effects of fluoridation, supplying much of the evidence that low doses are safe for children's bones, and good for their teeth.

> *Their military affiliations were kept secret. Hodge was described as a pharmacologist, Barnett as a pediatrician. . . Ast had participated in a key secret wartime conference on fluoride held by the Manhattan Project . . .*

Planning began in 1943 with the appointment of a special New York State Health Department committee to study the advisability of adding fluoride to Newburgh's drinking water. The chairman of the committee was Dr. Hodge, then chief of fluoride toxicity studies for the Manhattan Project.

Subsequent members included Henry L. Barnett, a captain in the Projects Medical Section, and John W. Fertig, in 1944 with the U.S. Office of Scientific Research and Development, the Pentagon group which sired the Manhattan Project. Their military affiliations were kept secret: Hodge was described as a pharmacologist, Barnett as a paediatrician. Placed in charge of the Newburgh project was David B. Ast, chief dental officer of the State Health Department. Ast had participated in a key secret wartime conference on fluoride held by the Manhattan Project, and later worked with Dr. Hodge on the Project's investigation of human injury in the New Jersey incident, according to once-secret memos.

The committee recommended that Newburgh be fluoridated. It also selected the types of medical studies to be done, and "provided expert guidance" for the duration of the experiment. The key question to be answered was: "Are there any cumulative effects -- beneficial or otherwise, on tissues and organs other than the teeth -- of long-continued ingestion of such small concentrations...?" According to the declassified documents, this was also key information sought by the bomb program, which would require long-continued exposure of workers and communities to fluoride throughout the Cold War.

In May 1945, Newburgh's water was fluoridated, and over the next ten years its residents were studied by the State Health Department. In tandem, Program F conducted its own secret studies, focusing on the amounts of fluoride Newburgh citizens retained in their blood and tissues - key information sought by the bomb program, "Possible toxic effects of fluoride were in the forefront of consideration," the advisory committee stated. Health Department personnel co-operated, shipping blood and placenta samples to the Program F team at the University of Rochester. The samples were collected by Dr. David B. Overton, the Department's chief of paediatric studies at Newburgh.

The final report of the Newburgh Demonstration Project, published in 1956 in the *Journal of the American Dental Association*, concluded that "small concentrations" of fluoride were safe for U.S. citizens. The biological proof -- "based on work performed ... at the University of Rochester Atomic Energy Project" -- was delivered by Dr. Hodge.

Today, news that scientists from the atomic bomb program secretly shaped and guided the Newburgh fluoridation experiment, and studied the citizens' blood and tissue samples is greeted with incredulity.

Today, news that scientists from the atomic bomb program secretly shaped and guided the Newburgh fluoridation experiment, and studied the citizen's blood and tissue samples, is greeted with incredulity.

"I'm shocked -- beyond words," said present-day Newburgh Mayor Audrey Carey, commenting on these reporters' findings. "It reminds me of the Tuskegee experiment that was done on syphilis patients down in Alabama."

As a child in the early 1950's, Mayor Carey was taken to the old firehouse on Broadway in Newburgh, which housed the Public Health Clinic. There, doctors from the Newburgh fluoridation project studied her teeth, and a peculiar fusion of two finger bones on her left hand she had been born with. Today, adds Carey, her granddaughter has white dental-fluorosis marks on her front teeth.

Mayor Carey wants answers from the government about the secret history of fluoride, and the Newburgh fluoridation experiment. "I absolutely want to pursue it," she said. "It is appalling to do any kind of experimentation and study without people's knowledge and permission."

Contacted by these reporters, the director of the Newburgh experiment, David B. Ast, says he was unaware Manhattan Project scientists were involved. "If I had known, I would have been certainly investigating why, and what the connection was," he said. Did he know that blood and placenta samples from Newburgh were being sent to bomb program researchers at the University of Rochester? "I was not aware of it," Ast replied. Did he recall participating in the Manhattan Project's secret wartime conference on fluoride in January 1944, or going to New Jersey with Dr. Hodge to investigate human injury in the du Pont case--as secret memos state? He told the reporters he had no recollection of these events.

A spokesperson for the University of Rochester Medical Center, Bob Loeb, confirmed that blood and tissue samples from Newburgh had been tested by the University's Dr. Hodge. On the ethics of secretly studying U.S. citizens to obtain information useful in litigation against the A-bomb program, he said, "that's a question we cannot answer." He referred inquiries to the U.S. Department of Energy (DOE), successor to the Atomic Energy Commission.

A spokesperson for the DOE in Washington, Jayne Brady, confirmed that a review of DOE files indicated that a "significant reason" for fluoride experiments conducted at the University of Rochester after the war was "impending litigation between the du Pont company and residents of New Jersey areas." However, she added, "DOE has found no documents to indicate that fluoride research was done to protect the Manhattan Project or its contractors from lawsuits."

On Manhattan Project involvement in Newburgh, the spokesperson stated, "Nothing that we have suggests that the DOE or predecessor agencies -- especially the Manhattan Project - -authorized fluoride experiments to be performed on children in the 1940's."

When told that the reporters had several documents that directly tied the Manhattan Project's successor agency at the University of Rochester, the AEP, Newburgh experiment, the DOE spokesperson later conceded her study was confined to "the available universe" of documents. Two days later spokesperson Jayne Brady faxed a statement for clarification: "My search only involved the documents that we collected as part of our human radiation experiments project -- fluoride was not part of our research effort.

"Most significantly," the statement continued, relevant documents may be in a classified collection at the DOE Oak Ridge National Laboratory known as the Records Holding Task Group. "This collection consists entirely of classified documents removed from other files for the purpose of classified document accountability many years ago," and was "a rich source of documents for the human radiation experiments project," she said.

The crucial question arising from this investigation is: Were adverse health findings from Newburgh and other bomb-program fluoride studies suppressed? All AEC-funded studies had to be declassified before publication in civilian medical and dental journals. Where are the original classified versions?

> *"Either those documents are still classified, or they've been 'disappeared' by the government."*

The transcript of one of the major secret scientific conferences of World War Two – on "fluoride metabolism" – is missing from the files of the U.S. National Archives. Participants in the conference included key figures who promoted the safety of fluoride and water fluoridation to the public after the war – Harold Hodge of the Manhattan Project, David B. Ast of the Newburgh Project, and U.S. Public Health Service dentist H.Trendley Dean, popularly known as the "father of fluoridation." "If it is missing from the files, it is probably still classified," National Archives librarians told these reporters.

A 1944 World War Two Manhattan Project classified report on water fluoridation is missing from the files of the University of Rochester Atomic Energy Project, the U.S. National Archives, and the Nuclear Repository at the University of Tennessee, Knoxville. The next four numerically consecutive documents are also missing, while the remainder of the "M-1500 series" is present. "Either those documents are still classified, or they've been 'disappeared' by the government," says Clifford Honicker, Executive Director of the American Environmental Health Studies Project in Knoxville, Tennessee, which provided key evidence in the public exposure and prosecution of U.S. human radiation experiments.

Seven pages have been cut out of a 1947 Rochester bomb-project notebook entitled "Du Pont litigation." "Most unusual," commented chief medical school archivist Chris Hoolihan.

Similarly, Freedom of Information Act (FOIA) requests by these authors over a year ago with the DOE for hundreds of classified fluoride papers have failed to dislodge any. "We're behind," explained Amy Rothrock, FOIA officer for the Department of Energy at their Oak Ridge operations.

Was information suppressed? These reporters made what appears to be the first discovery of the original classified version of a fluoride safety study by bomb program scientists. A censored version of this study was later published in the August 1948 *Journal of the American Dental Association.* Comparison of the secret with the published version indicates that the U.S. AEC did censor damaging information on fluoride – to the point of tragicomedy.

This was a study of the dental and physical health of workers in a factory producing fluoride for the A-bomb program, conducted by a team of dentists from the Manhattan Project.

The secret version reports that most of the men had no teeth left.
The published version reports only that the men had fewer cavities.

The secret version reports that most of the men had no teeth left. The published version reports only that the men had fewer cavities.

The secret version says the men had to wear rubber boots because the fluoride fumes disintegrated the nails in their shoes. The published version does not mention this.

The secret version says the fluoride may have acted similarly on the men's teeth, contributing to their toothlessness. The published version omits this statement.

The published version concludes that "the men were unusually healthy, judged from both a medical and dental point of view."

Asked for comment on the early links of the Manhattan Project to water fluoridation, Dr Harold Slavkin, Director of the National Institute for Dental Research, the U.S. agency which today funds fluoride research, said "I wasn't aware of any input from the Atomic Energy Commission." Nevertheless, he insisted, fluoride's efficacy and safety in the prevention of dental cavities over the last fifty years is well-proved. "The motivation of a scientist is often different from the outcome," he reflected. "I do not hold a prejudice about where the knowledge comes from."

After comparing the secret and published versions of the censored study, toxicologist Phyllis Mullenix commented, "This makes me ashamed to be a scientist." Of other Cold War-era fluoride safety studies, she asks, "Were they all done like this?"

The dangers of fluoride ingestion were well known even before the Manhattan Project. "Fluorine is a general protoplasmic poison, but the most important symptoms of chronic fluorine poisoning known at present are mottling of the teeth and interference with bone formation . . . when the threshold value is exceeded, as it is in drinking water containing one or more parts of fluorine per 1,000,000, detectable signs of toxicity appear." - *Journal of the American Dental Association*, Vol.XXIII, p574; 1936. *Fluoride is more poisonous than lead and only marginally less toxic than arsenic.* AWARE of published adverse evidence, WHY did the US PUBLIC HEALTH SERVICE give MILLIONS of American tax-payers' dollars to many countries - including Canada, Denmark, Netherlands, Norway, Sweden, Switzerland, Eire and the UK - to promote fluoridation? The UK and Eire received AT LEAST the following $ sums:

	1958	1960	1963
EIRE	19,078	62,250	78,730
UK	232,035	900,048	2,751,215

Attempts are being made by the US National Academy of Sciences to classify fluoride as an "essential nutrient." The following is the text of a Press Release dated 23 September, 1997 by the Union of government employees (NFFE - Local Branch 2050) at the US Environmental Protection Agency HQ, Washington, DC. The NFFE contact is J. William Hirzy, PhD, Senior Vice-President.

NATIONAL FEDERATION OF FEDERAL EMPLOYEES

The document, "Dietary Reference Intakes, Prepublication Copy" (DRI) is seriously flawed and deficient as an instrument to justify a public policy to establish fluoride as an "essential nutrient". The DRI document is rife with inadequacy, error and deceptive information, only some of which can be touched upon here.

For example, the only adverse effects of fluoride exposure discussed in DRI are enamel and skeletal fluorosis. These effects are only cursorily and deceptively touched upon, and no connection is made between them, as though they were independent effects and fluoride affinity for and damage to enamel is not a biochemical window on what is happening in bone.

While DRI lays out the parameters for conducting risk assessments in Chapter 3, it ignores application of those parameters particularly egregiously with respect to fluoride in purporting to establish a "tolerable upper intake level". One component of risk assessment is hazard identification, whose components include addressing evidence of adverse effects in humans. DRI attempts to deceive the public into believing the only identified adverse effects of fluoride exposure of significance are those mentioned above. The DRI document omits any mention of studies in humans showing increased risk of hip fractures and bone cancer and decreased IQ in children in areas with artificially fluoridated water or other sources of dietary fluoride that result in fluoride intakes that are below the "tolerable upper intake level". Neither does the DRI document properly address use of animal data in the hazard and risk assessments on fluoride. There are recent (1990-1995) animal data supporting concern for both cancer and central nervous system effects.

Even if one grants as accurate the statement at page 8-15 in the prepublication copy of DRI, "Most research has indicated that an intake of at least 10mg/day for 10 or more years is needed to produce clinical signs of the milder forms of the condition" (skeletal fluorosis), consider the simple mathematics of this "tolerable upper intake" level. That level is set at *10/mg/day* for individuals aged 9 years and up. At age 39, the individual who has received the "tolerable upper intake" since age 9 will have accumulated *3 times* the amount of fluoride needed, according to the DRI, to put him or her at high risk of skeletal fluorosis - not to mention bone fracture, cancer and decreased mental capacity.

When a chemical manufacturer wants to make a new chemical to use, for example, as an additive in motor oil, all existing toxicological data must be presented to the Environmental Protection Agency for review of potential risks before manufacture and use can begin. In the DRI we see risk assessment principles as applied to a major public policy issue flouted - even the existence of a massive body of information on adverse effects of fluoride is ignored, let alone discussed. And this for a chemical the National Academy recommends we purposely *add to our diets,* not our motor oil.

Furthermore, the claimed benefits from the "adequate intake" level have been shown to be based on biased or otherwise flawed studies. Not a single one of those studies was a randomized control trial.

In summary, our union members' review of the literature over the last 11 years has led us to conclude that a causal link exists between fluoride exposure and cancer, increased risk of hip fracture, and damage to the central nervous system. For the National Academy of Sciences to attempt to anoint this substance an "essential nutrient" is a travesty and a matter of shame for the US science community.

National Federation of Federal Employees Local 2050 represents and is comprised of scientists, lawyers, engineers and other professionals at Headquarters, US Environmental Protection Agency, Washington, DC.

Central Nervous System References:

1 Li, X.S., Zhi, J.L., Gao, R.O. Effect of fluoride exposure on intelligence in children. *Fluoride* 28:4, 189-192 (1995).
2 Zhao, L.B., Liang, G., Zhang, D., Lu-Liang, X. Wu. Effect of a high fluoride water supply on children's intelligence. *Fluoride* 29:4, 190-192 (1996).
3 Mullenix, P.J., Denbesten, P.K., Schunior, A., Kernan W.J. Neurotoxicity of sodium fluoride in rats. *Neurotoxicology and Teratology* 17:2, 169-177 (1995).

*

TEXT of a two-page NPWA PRESS RELEASE and NOTES FOR EDITORS syndicated on 7 July, 1997 *FOR IMMEDIATE RELEASE*

United States Government Scientists take stand against fluoridation of drinking water

The National Federation of Federal Employees, (NFFE), Union of Government scientists of the United States Environmental Protection Agency, Washington DC, voted unanimously to co-sponsor a California Initiative to ban fluoridation. Their statement on 2 July, 1997 reads:

"Our members' review of the body of evidence over the last eleven years, including animal and human epidemiology studies, indicate a causal [NB CAUSAL] link between fluoride/fluoridation and cancer, genetic damage, neurological impairment and bone pathology."

The Union membership consists of the toxicologists, chemists, physical scientists, statisticians, biologists, engineers, attorneys and other professionals at *Environmental Protection Agency headquarters in Washington DC*. The members are responsible for evaluating technical and scientific knowledge in areas that lie at the core of all EPA's scientific and technical determinations, with specific responsibilities under the US Safe Drinking Water Act.

According to NFFE: "*. . . the health and welfare of the public is not served by the addition of this substance (fluoride) to the public water supply . . . for which there is virtually no evidence of significant benefits . . . and substantial evidence of adverse effects."*

For more than a decade, the professionals directly responsible for assessing the scientific information relating to fluoride have protested EPA management conclusions and "independent" contractor reviews, which the Union members allege were performed by "hired guns". After numerous attempts to correct EPA management conclusions that were not supported by available facts, the Union attempted to join a lawsuit against their own employer in 1986, citing "fraudulent alterations of data and negligent omission of fact to arrive at predetermined Agency political positions regarding fluoride."

Dr. Wm. L. Marcus, Senior Science Adviser, Standards and Compliance Division in EPA's Office of Drinking Water was fired for a 1990 whistle-blowing memo calling for a review of the cover-up of the National Toxicological Program study that shows fluoride is a "probable human carcinogen". That finding alone would prohibit the addition of fluoride to the public water supply. Although Dr Marcus won his whistle-blower lawsuit, with punitive damages, and returned to work at the EPA, the classifications were never reviewed.

NOTES FOR EDITORS:

ABOUT SIX MILLION PEOPLE IN UK DRINK ARTIFICIALLY FLUORIDATED WATER, MAINLY IN THE WEST MIDLANDS AND THE NORTH EAST.

Fluoride is a ***cumulative****, protoplasmic poison.* We excrete about 50% of the fluoride we ingest. The rest is stored, mainly in the bones and other tissues of the body. Fluoride is ubiquitous in the environment - we ingest it from food, beverages, toothpaste, mouth rinses, drops, tablets, medicines, pesticides, herbicides and from the air we breathe. Recent evidence from the *Templegarth Trust* (Contact Dr Peter Mansfield, 01507 327842) shows that *15% of the British population is ingesting much more fluoride than the "safe levels" recommended by the Department of Health.*

The US Food and Drugs Administration issued a directive in April 1997 that fluoride toothpaste and other fluoride products must carry warnings; for example, on toothpaste tubes and packaging: "If you accidentally swallow more than used for brushing, seek professional help or contact a poison control center immediately."

This warning is currently being down-played by members of the American Dental Association, who receive massive sums in "endorsements" of fluoride products, and by some local poison control centres in the United States. The British Dental Association also makes considerable sums of money from "endorsements" of fluoride products.

In 1994, the World Health Organisation warned: "Dental and public health administrators should be aware of the total fluoride exposure in the population before introducing any addittional fluoride programme for caries prevention."

This warning is being completely ignored. Moreover, attempts are currently being made by the British Dental Association, the British Medical Association and NAHAT to persuade MPs to change the law to COMPEL water companies to fluoridate at the request of health authorities.

Northern health authorities have just been given leave for a judicial review of the decision of Northumbrian Water plc not to extend fluoridation in its area. The law is permissive - it says that water companies MAY fluoridate at the request of health authorities. The proponents read "may" as "must"!.

VISIT WEBSITE AT http://www.sonic.net/~monty/fluoride.htm

Contact: Jane Jones, NPWA, 01924 254433 or J. William Hirzy, PhD, 001 202 260 2383

*

Part III

KALEIDOSCOPE

*

ASPECTS OF THE TASK!

There is no pain like the pain of a new idea.
(William James.)

Truth is always present; it only needs to lift the iron lids of the mind's eye to read its oracles.
(Emerson.)

No feats of heroism are needed to bring about the greatest and most important changes in the life of humanity, neither the arming of millions of men, neither the construction of new railways, nor Trade Unions, nor revolutions, nor barricades...and so forth. All that is necessary is a change in public opinion. (Leo Tolstoy.)

There is a dire need today, in almost any area of human affairs, for men to speak the truth.

Having regard to our subject, this is required in the form of a re-statement of the significance to mankind of land and its rent... This significance...has been forgotten, and people need reminding. This work of reminding...is a work indeed. (John Tippet, in Progress, Nov 89.)

"'Rent as Revenue' is as natural as breathing. 'That source of income is the earth itself, with its innumerable sites and abundant natural resources... Here in a nutshell is why the rich get richer and the poor poorer... This is common sense, so common in fact, that one is appalled when so few people grasp its significance.'" (From a review of Rent as Revenue: the Enemy of Interest, by Les Hemingway; in Land and Liberty, Jan-Feb 91.)

*

This simple truth [concerning the power bestowed by land monopoly], in its application to social and political problems, is hid from the great masses of men partly by its very simplicity. (Henry George in Progress and Poverty, ch. 14.)

As one not knowing that a golden treasure lies buried beneath his feet, may walk over it again and again, yet never find it... (From the Hindu Upanishads, Indian scriptures of 800-600 B.C.)

The great and fundamental questions of existence are all very simple and everyone is able to understand them. Small details are often complicated and difficult of understanding. Some people cannot see that. They are so absorbed in details of small things that they do not see the great things at all. The shrewd Italian statesman Machiavelli...said: "People are always provoked by small injustices but never by great injustices." (Dr Viggo Starcke, in Our Daily Bread.)

The majority believes that everything hard to comprehend must be very profound. This is incorrect. What is hard to understand is what is immature, unclear and often false. The highest wisdom is simple and passes through the brain directly into the heart. (Viktor Schauberger.)

It appears to be a universal law that the truth is simple, and the further we stray from the truth the more complex things become. (Mark Hasses, in "Progress", Sept-Oct 97.)

All ideas of immense consequence are always simple. (Leo Tolstoy.)

There are a thousand hacking at the branches of evil to one who is striking at the root. (Thoreau.)

*

Prophets and sages of old pointed out the evil and injustice of private property in land thousands of years ago...(This) truth is continually appearing more and more clearly, but [interested parties] try to distort it, suppress it, or extinguish it, and if they cannot succeed in this, then they try to hush it up...

Henry George...the remarkable man who appeared towards the end of the last century...devoted his immense mental powers to elucidating the injustice and cruelty of the institution of landed property and to indicating means of rectifying that injustice... The chief method of opposing Henry George was...the method always employed against irrefutable and self-evident truths...that of ignoring it.

(Leo Tolstoy, ch. "A Great Iniquity" in his Recollections and Essays, O.U.P., World's Classics Series.)

The Stratagem to Defeat Henry George. A professor of economics has nailed the plot to thwart the popular democratic demand for a change to a rational system of public finance.

Mason Gaffney of the University of California turned sleuth to uncover the truth behind the remarkable campaign to silence public debate about the Single Tax...

The full story of this disgraceful episode in the history of economic thought is told by Professor Gaffney in The Corruption of Economics...published by Shepheard-Walwyn (Publrs.) Ltd...

Professor Gaffney indicts neo-classical economists for the damage they continue to inflict on students: "Systematic, universal brainwashing is the crime, tendentious mental conditioning calculated to mislead students, to impoverish their mental ability, to bend their minds to the service of a system that funnels power and wealth to a parasitic minority." (Report in Land and Liberty, Jul-Aug 94.)

*

In all the attention given to Mrs Thatcher's Conservative Party conference speech, one point has been missed. This was when she said: "There is no public money - only taxpayers' money. She is mistaken.

There is a vast source of public money, created by the public, attached to land. It stems directly from population and from industrial growth and activity. The unearned income which attaches to land is the rightful property of the community. To allow this value to be appropriated by individuals means that the community is robbed of its wealth.

Mrs Thatcher puts herself forward, among other things, as a champion of law and order. How can she and her party claim this when they fail to recognise this robbery built into our legal system? (George Curtis, Dist. Orgnsr., TGWU Agric. Trade Group, Brigg: Obs. 23 Oct 83.)

We cannot safely leave politics to politicians, or political economy to college professors. The people themselves must think...(Henry George.)

*

You have slept for unnumbered ages,
This morning will you not wake? (Kabir.)

We live in a world where cruelty is honoured, where dishonesty is rewarded, where power is taken by the vicious and the brutal, and where the inept, the incompetent and the uncaring prosper. We live in a world where integrity is sneered at, where honesty is described as controversy, where passion is regarded as an embarrassment and where truth is a dangerous commodity...

We have dirtied our land and polluted our air and water. We live in a filth of our own making; a filth that gets worse each day and which contaminates our very lives...If you feel that something is wrong, and you feel passionately that something ought to be done about it, then stand up for your principles, shout and make your voice heard. (Dr Vernon Coleman. *)

It is infinitely difficult to begin where mere words must move a great block of inert matter. But there is no other way when you have none of the material strength on your side. And a shout in the mountains has been known to start an avalanche.
(Solzhenitsyn.)

One of the problems of our society at present is that people are not writing songs of protest, and so there isn't effective protest against things that should be protested against. (Radio Scotland, 5 Aug 96.)

Count this book as a song! (S-A.H.)

*

---

* From his book "How to Stop Your Doctor Killing You". Quoted from a review in The Ecologist of Nov-Dec 98, by Tuula E. Tuormaa, of his further book, "Betrayal of Trust", which "exposes the utter uselessness of animal experiments in medical research". "Vernon Coleman, doctor of medicine, journalist and author of over 70 books, which have been translated into 21 languages and sold in more than 50 countries, has been described in the press as having "the sharpest mind in medical journalism and the calmest voice of reason."

THE GIFT OF THE GAFFE

Praise be to Radio Scotland for providing us with such a wonderful header into the New Year of 1999!

NEW YEAR'S DAY NEWS BULLETIN:

A Euro spokesman on the birth of the Euro currency in January 99. Clearly meant to be speaking constrUctively on this grand matter, but alas for his foreign accent - what we got was:-

"I think it is an important new step in the
European ConstrIctions" - !

Immortal prophecy!

The late (10 p.m.) news - while, one noted, not cheating us of a replay of this most awful gaffe - carefully preceded it with a Scottish voice - getting the pronunciation "right"!

But was it **really** right?

Too late, too late,
At any rate,
For resurgent bellyfuls of New Year laughter! -
An unconstrIcted laugh
At this unconstrUcted gaffe -
And be it so remembered ever after!

*

Labour will "never waver in its commitment to social justice". (Radio Scotland, 3 Oct 97. Closing speech of their annual conference.)

"Tackling the problem of social exclusion is our number one social policy priority in Scotland... We are determined to crack the problem of social exclusion." (Donald Dewar, reported in The Courier, 3 Feb 98.)

*

GOTCHA! At the end of writing the Gosabe section (in Part II, ch. 2) last year, I mentioned having heard the famous words -

"government of the people, for the people,
by the people" -

spoken by Labour with the **last vital three missing.** I have just now come upon them recorded in The Courier of 13 May 98.

And who could ever have guessed the context? What was it that Mr Dewar was talking about as representing -

"government of the people, for the people" -
and full stop?

QUANGOS!

"Quangos, said Mr Dewar, represented 'government of the people for the people'."

PRECISELY!

Best of all, Mr Dewar also happened to remark - (on this occasion of publishing a "glossy brochure" describing quangos "in glowing terms") - that Labour, after six months of studying the quango question (six months!) had come up with the findings that "the overwhelming argument" about quangos "didn't come down to whether they could be abolished", but "how they could be made..." - guess what? **"More accountable"** - !

That is quite simply, of course - made to **look** as though those last three words hadn't been bitten off after all!

..."You are so twisted up in knots" !

On with the Quango-tango! ...Or Quangle-tangle, maybe!

A Matter of "CONFUSION"

Re the Glasgow area water cock-up of winter 1997-98 - a major "water-fouling" incident, with 3-4 days' delay in informing certain areas of the population: this was put down to "confusion in the complex water distribution system" - (radio news bulletin at the time).

"Confusion"? We seem to have heard that word before! But it's doubtful if the confusion was **in the pipes**!

The verdict of an experienced retired country plumber: "The people in charge now are people up in book-learning - but **not hands-on.**"

Well - we did away with those down-to-earth apprenticeships of course, didn't we? In favour of the tech trek...

But then, how **could** those apprenticeships have been allowed to continue? "In the old days your master-tradesman might well give a clip on the ear to any young apprentice that was behaving cheekily."

Allowing blue-collar workers to wear the mantle of virtual "elders of the community"!

Away with it! And if we find ourselves in a state of confusion ever, we can always say it was **confusion in the pipes**!

Another Leak!

"We didn't have many of the answers", says a scientist. "Rather than explain that to the general public, it was thought better to give the impression that we had everything under control."

Radio Times of 15 Feb 98, reporting on the scandal of the government's handling of the BSE business.....and no doubt thoroughly savoured by those Glasgow folk who suffered a similar 'hiatus' of information regarding their water supplies!

"Tax Harmonization in Europe!"

Newly announced proposal by the Euro-rulers, in a radio bulletin of 1 Dec 98.

(Not exactly the PR exercise for a people attuned to **land-rent-for-revenue!**)

*

Community Right to Buy Land

The continual harping of the government on this - (now enshrined in their Land Reform Policy paper: "Recommendations for Action - Jan 99") - has always struck me as rather strange. I have never noticed that **land-owners** live in communities...

"GAMBLING WITH SCOTLAND - Dewar's lottery law on land."

Heading on the front cover of "Land and Liberty", Spring 1999.

The soil of Scotland is sold for silver -
Thirty pieces and more..... (S-A.H.)

*

Birthright...and...Scotland Today

SCOTLAND'S YEAR OF LEARNING LAUNCHED

Reported a year ago in The Courier (6 Jan 98).

"Scottish Enterprise has declared 1998 Scotland's Year of Learning..."

Still waiting for it!

...Come to think of it - what **was** that Year of Learning **for?**

"To build a world-class skills base in Scotland."

Still time! - for 1999...

It starts with **mapping**, of course!

*

SOME FAVOURITE PIECES AND SPECIAL LOVES

O TEMPORA! O MORES!

"Each new set of exchancellor's memoirs unfailingly reveals a world where ministers and their officials live in a statistical fog, in which all forecasts are wrong and nobody really understands how the economy works anyway." John Plender, "Financial Times", 19 June 93. (Acks. to the Land Value Taxation Campaign, Brentwood, Essex.)

Neo-classical economics, forged as a stratagem to discomfort Henry George and Georgists, is intellectually, morally and practically bankrupt. (Professor Mason Gaffney.)

*

Citizenship in our country is not an inalienable natural right for every human being born on its soil. It is a kind of coupon controlled by an exclusive clique of people who have in no way proved, by anything they have done, that they have a greater right to the Russian soil. This clique can declare a citizen deprived of his homeland if it does not approve of his convictions. (Or simply of his presence? Plenty of land clearances throughout history. S-A.H.) I leave it to you to find a word for such a social structure.

(Solzhenitsyn.)

"THE LAND FOR THE PEOPLE" - (graveyard scene)

"Your portion make the best of it
The Landlords have the rest of it."

(Acks. to Cynicus Art Publishing Co. See illustration set into DCM's Biog. Notes.)

Man did not make the earth...neither did the Creator of the earth open a land office, from which the first title-deeds should issue. (Thomas Paine.)

*

Health. (Health?)

There is already some direct evidence that we can be literally doctored to death, For example, when doctors in Israel went on strike for a month the death rate dropped by 50 per cent - the largest drop since the previous doctors' strike 20 years earlier. Much the same happens whenever doctors have gone on strike. In Bogota, Colombia, doctors went on strike for 52 days and there was a 35 per cent fall fall in mortality rates, while in Los Angeles a doctors' strike resulted in an 18 per cent reduction in mortality statistics, which returned to normal as soon as the strike was over. (Tuula E. Tuormaa in "The Ecologist" - already referred to.)

Now what was that saying about -
"if all the medicines were at the bottom of the seas..." ? (See Part II, ch. 2!)

- And Education

Labour want more "educational psychologists" - to help, in schools, with children with special needs.

"We have to ask them what **they** want,
and listen to what **they** have to say."

Yes - safe enough now! Now that State 'agriculture', State 'health' and State 'education' have done their ruinous work!

*

Fighting Fo - (Dario Fo, referred to in Pt.II:1.)

...Fo has another career, what's more, as a solo performer. Here he purveys a similar line in revolutionary burlesque, and enjoys the mass appeal of a pop idol...

(Audiences are) treated to an athletic combustible variant of the stand-up comedian's art. Fo takes apart Bible stories and traditional fables, cementing them together again with ribaldry and topical reference. He storms around the stage, mimicking, miming in the fashion characteristic of Italy's streets... But beneath the studiously rough, even vulgar, exterior is an arsenal of skills that have been painstakingly fine-tuned over the years...

Fo himself was once challenged to a duel by an artillery officer who claimed he had slandered the honour of the Italian army. Fo accepted on condition they fight under the rules of Thai wrestling. The officer was never seen again. Against this background, alternately risible and terrifying, he sees it as his job to put theatre's weight behind popular causes. Wherever there's a strike, factory occupation or controversial trial in Italy, you will probably find Dario Fo, tailoring his improvised performances to the matter in hand... (From article in the "Radio Times", dated 25 Feb 84.)

The Theatre of Dario Fo

Dario Fo is unique in world theatre. Playwright, actor, clown, teacher and philosopher, he is an international celebrity.... and a great hero of the Italian Left....

Arena filmed DARIO FO against the background of medieval Italy, working with students in Umbria, at home in Milan and against the colourful backdrop of the Venice Carnival, where he performed his triumphant one-man comic show, *Mistero Buffo*.

Life does not belong to the barbarians, even when absolute authority does belong th them. Life belongs to human beings, life goes forward because of them. This is the source of my hope.
(George Mangakis.)

Intelligent men don't govern - they create and transform. Governmental power is a dead horse. (Solzhenitsyn.)

Beware of paddling in the ocean of God's truth, when you should be out in it, swimming. (Oswald Chambers.)

*

The Great Spirit, in placing people on the earth, desired them to take care of the ground and to do each other no harm.
(Young Chief of the Cayuses.)

They are taking all our young warriors and making them into soldiers. (A N. American Indian, at the time of the Viet Nam war. Acks. to Alan Torrance.)

You become a warrior. then a poet, and then a holy person. (An ancient teaching of the Picts. Acks. to Alan Torrance.)

...A poor society may be a very happy and contented society. A rich society may be a very unhappy and discontented society. (R.H. Tawney's "Commonplace Book".)

The angels keep their ancient places -
Turn but a stone and start a wing!
'Tis ye, 'tis your estranged faces
That miss the many-splendour'd thing.
(Francis Thompson.)

*

MORE!
LOVE
1ST

MORE!
LOVE
1ST

"The Tangle o' the Isles"

"The Scotsman" 6 Feb 63

A sad story

Minewood House, Abercrombie Drive, Bridge of Allan, January 31, 1963

Sir,—The following sad little story, which may amuse those of your readers with a fondness for Hebridean place-names, was found among my late father's effects. It would appear to be original in theme, to say the least.

Once upon a time there was a man called Ben Becula who was much Harris-sed lest he might Lewis his life. Soay took a cocktail of Eigg and Rum, though it seemed Eriskay drink, especially as he wasn't Uist to it, and anything might Appin.

Shortly he said. "Iona feel a little Tiree"—and he knew he Shuna swallowed the Muck—"so Islay me down and en-Jura little pain." Later he was heard to Colonsay, "I hear my final Coll."

So his soul went to Skye and they took his body away in a Barra and made it into a Little Minch.

As for his poor wife, she Canna believe it and it's a wonder the shock has St. Kilda.—I am &c.

A. R. Edge.

Sad tale of a man of the Hebrides

The Scots

18 Abercromby Place, Edinburgh, February 6, 1963

Sir,—As joint author of the above "Sad Tale," concocted many years ago—and suggested by the chance remark of a steward on a MacBrayne steamer—I was interested to see it reappear in your Points of View today.

Several years ago, I sent it in to A Scotsman's Log, where it duly appeared with the admirable alternative title of "The tangle o' the Isles," which I attributed to Mr Wilfred Taylor.

Mr Edge may like to know that, in a revised edition of the "Tale" the last paragraph reads: "As for his poor wife Lis—more she canna bear, being so a Knoydart. Indeed, it's a wonder the shock of his being thus Stornoway has St Kilda."—I am &c.

W. Watson Davidson.

"The Scotsman" 8 Feb 63

Words written by Donald G. Clayton (Scots Magazine of August 1979) as a guide to pronunciation of the Island of Gigha

Jock Mackay, of the Island of Gigha,
At boating was quite without figha;
He knew how to sail,
To luff & to bail,
But he had no idigha how to stigha.

Now Mrs Mackay, the old digha,
Had a hate for the sea quite sincigha;
She once was afloat
In a very small boat
But complained that it made her feel quigha!

As sent to me by my sister, Marigold Readman, in 1979.

Part III

KALEIDOSCOPE

*

9) WHO ARE THEY?

Harry Beston

Evelyn Underhill

CHOO - Ann Smith

The Carp and the Butterfly
 - Briony Vanessa Lill

Who Are They? -
 Stephanie Sorrell

Juniper

Who Are They?

*

"For the animal shall not be measured by man.
In a world older and more complete than ours, they
move finished and complete, gifted with extensions
of the senses we have lost or never attained, living by
voices we shall never hear. They are not brethren;
they are not underlings; they are other nations, caught
with ourselves in the net of life and time, fellow prisoner
of the splendour and travail of the earth."

Henry Beston

*

Ackd. to: The Protesters Animal Inf. Network Ltd.,
The Lodge, Broadhurst Manor, Horsted Keynes,
West Sussex RH17 7BG.

I come in the little things...
Yea, on the glancing wings
Of eager birds, the softly
pattering feet
Of furred and gentle beasts,
I come to meet
Your hard and wayward heart.

(Evelyn Underhill)

*

THE STORY OF CHOO
Introduction

I lost CHOO for more than twenty years.

When I moved back up to Scotland in 1975, I thought that I had carefully packed to bring with me all the written material I valued - but somehow the story of CHOO turned out not to be there. For a time I hunted, disbelieving - but to no avail. As it was already some years since this moving story had appeared in the magazine of the Campaign Against All Cruelty To Animals (CAACTA), I felt unable to ask my friends there to search for me through so many past issues. But the memory of CHOO would still surface in my mind from time to time...

Then suddenly, in October 1997 a circular letter from EarthKind (CAACTA's successor) announced that their forthcoming annual general meeting would include a display covering all of EarthKind's work, accomplishments **and history!** My resolve was **instantly made**...and when presently a large envelope arrived bearing EarthKind's stamp on the outside, I knew before opening it that I was to be reunited with my **Choo!** He was, of course, Ann Smith's Choo, but to all who meet him through the words of her story, he inevitably belongs also, in the inner way of things.

By the autumn of 1997 this book was already well on the way, and I at once decided to include the story of CHOO in it - both to celebrate my finding of him again, (since it is a special story to share), and also for its remarkable testimony to Harry Beston's words placed at the start of this section. I think no one can emerge from a reading of this story without a feeling of reverence for the world of the animal...from which it is so very hard to turn back to today's scene, with all our betrayals of the animals that it involves.

There is a third reason for re-publishing it. For who knows if it might come into the hands of Ann Smith or her family again, so that one might hear some more stories about Choo, and also the other friends she writes about, such as those "very naughty Gibbon apes"!...

*

THE STORY OF CHOO

Re-published from 'With Sword and Shield', Nov-Dec 1966
Magazine of Crusader Against All Cruelty to Animals,
by kind permission of
Earthkind (formerly C.A.A.C.T.A.)
Avenue Lodge, Bounds Green Road, London, N22 4EU

CRUSADER OWES HER LIFE TO THE MOST FEROCIOUS ANIMAL OF THE JUNGLE ...

According to the reference books, black leopards, often referred to as panthers, are not a distinct species but are the offspring of the ordinary variety of leopard. The black panther is generally reputed to be even more ferocious than his spotted relation.

*

Most people are familiar with the world-renowned true story of Joy Adamson and Elsa the lioness, which she reared from a cub into a full-grown animal, which lived as one of the family. Few people who have seen the film of this story called **BORN FREE** starring Crusade Patron, Virginia McKenna and her husband, Bill Travers, will have fully realised that perhaps something even greater was accomplished in the making of this picture. As it had to be completed in less than twelve months, there was no time for our two stars to rear a female cub and so befriend the animal from babyhood for several years.

Several lions of varying ages had therefore to be used to play the part of Elsa growing up, the adult one being Mara, a fully grown wild and untrained animal who responded in a very short time to the love and trust extended to her by the two stars – so much so that she slept on their bed! They tell the wonderful story of this friendship in their book **ON PLAYING WITH LIONS**.

We publish another remarkable true story by a Crusader of the love and devotion shown to her by an allegedly untameable creature – reputed to be the most ferocious animal of the jungle – a black panther .....*Editor*.

*

CHOO AND HIS FAMILY

by Ann Smith

I had been walking through dense jungle darkness for a whole week. Tired, footsore, utterly weary, I had waded through rivers, climbed hills, fought red ants and dodged ugly black scorpions; slimy leeches had clung to my feet. Eventually from the darkness of the forest we emerged into a large clearing which was the mining camp. I could see many native huts and there high on the hill overlooking the whole camp a large white bungalow like a jewel in the sun.

The jungle had been ruthlessly hacked back and there stood my home perched high on top of concrete pillars. A wide veranda circled the whole bungalow and concrete steps led up to the entrance where there was great excitement. Down the steps ran four white-clad Chinese servant boys, at the foot stood a line of Sikh police who were our special bodyguards. I was to find out later they were a necessity in the jungle. Everybody was smiling a welcome – just like delighted children.

A new life for me had just begun in this strange land. I had recently arrived from England and my husband had met me at Singapore. He was a mining engineer and manager of a group of tin and wolfram mines here in Northern Malaya so I was quite prepared to find I must live far away from civilisation.

I had arrived at Singapore ten days previously and for the first three days we had travelled by car up through this beautiful country – land of tropical palms, white sands and sapphire blue seas, tin mines, rubber plantations, sultans and their palaces, mosques, Chinese temples, Buddhist priests, rice fields, kampongs and exotic people. Tom had lived in this country for many years so he talked, pointing out places of interest. I enjoyed this part of the journey; it held all the romance of the East. · But soon we reached Alor Star, capital city of northern Kedah – from here we must walk. Leaving the car at a Chinese garage we made our way to the Rest House where after a meal and change of clothes we set off towards the jungle.

Looking at my new home I felt it was worth all the discomfort. I climbed the wide steps, then stepped across the highly polished veranda and entered my first home in Malaya. It was pleasantly furnished and a meal was cooked ready to be served. We bathed, changed our clothes, ate a meal and afterwards sat admiring the view. A vast panorama of green jungle stretched out before us; below was the long winding road up which we came, a road which ended at the bungalow; from here it was virgin jungle. Quite close to one end of the veranda a large tree grew and monkeys leapt from bough to bough.

The nights were hot, a humid heat, and I lay awake listening to the call of wild animals, the sound of the crickets, hooting of the owls, whooping of monkeys and the distant roar of the tiger. I tossed and turned inside my mosquito net, and longed for a cool breeze, which I knew would not come. During the day the heat was suffocatingly intense.

Here in this impenetrable jungle I found happiness, days flew by as if on wings. There were times after a recent rainfall when during my walks the leeches clung to my feet and legs but even this failed to damp my happiness. I soon learned that no visitors ever came up that winding narrow road. It would take me a week to walk to my nearest neighbour.

The labour force on the mine was mainly Chinese with a couple of hundred headhunters from Borneo and some Indians so it was essential to learn Chinese, Malay and Hindustani. Two Sikh police were my special bodyguards; they must accompany me everywhere I go. They taught me how to use a gun and insisted I carry a small revolver in my belt for my own protection in case of attack from any rogue animal or perhaps a lone bandit.

A walk in the jungle is fraught with many dangers, the most common being a bite from a mischievous monkey, but carrying a light cane was most effective. A swish of my cane and they either gave me a broad grin and climbed up the nearest tree or sat in the long grass grinning at me. I have spent many hours watching them at play. The infinite variety of plant life is very beautiful, wild orchids grow in profusion.

On one of my walks I saw what I thought at first was a monkey in the tall grass but venturing a little closer I saw what seemed to be a ball of fur with two frightened yellow eyes and an extraordinary long tail. I tried to pick him up but, how he hissed and spat...

The Sikh said, "Don't touch him, Mem! *(Madam)* It's the fiercest animal in the jungle – It's a black panther!"

And so it was, but only a baby one – not more than a few weeks old.

I decided to take him home so the guards helped me to release him from the iron cage trap in which he had been caught. The front paws were badly injured, they had been jammed in the hinge of the trap door, and were still bleeding. The tiny animal had obviously struggled to free himself and was panting with exhaustion. It was clear that he was in great pain so we gave him a piece of bamboo to chew and wrapped him in my short linen coat. Returning to the bungalow with the still struggling panther, we halted several times and laid him down on the grass, but it was pitiful to watch him trying to get away.

On the way back to the camp I had plenty to think about. The cage, which had been roughly made – perhaps by a native who wanted to trap some animal to sell to the City Zoo – was a wild concoction of twisted, galvanised wire. Who, I wondered, was responsible for this? With a labour force of several hundreds of Chinese and headhunters from Borneo, it was impossible to find out.

I was determined to save this little creature and decided to keep him safe away from other animals so on arrival home the Sikhs made him a strong pen underneath the building. He licked his wounds and we fed him on milk and soups from a baby's bottle.

Some days later when we opened his pen, he was able to run about, we expected to see him run for the shelter of the jungle, but, oh dear no, he stayed, and became a great pet. In a matter of days he was chasing me around the bungalow. When I sat on the veranda he sat down at my feet and chewed holes in my slippers. Siesta time was also siesta time for Choo, as we called him, and he slept beside my bed.

He would lie on the rug watching my every movement, his head resting on his paws – those paws with their soft velvet pads hiding dangerously long, sharp claws, his big mysterious yellow eyes so thoughtful and perplexed. He wandered through and around the bungalow, sleek and graceful. When I was swimming in the pool at the bottom of the garden, he liked to come too and swim beside me, the whole length of the pool, afterwards lazily stretching himself full length on a flat ledge of rock. Here he would lie apparently asleep, but not a sound escaped him. Even here Choo and I were guarded by Sikh police, always with a gun. As he grew (and how he grew!) he was given the freedom of the jungle as well as my home.

He followed me everywhere. When I paused to look about me, Choo paused too. I would laugh at him and he grew to dislike anyone doing that so he grunted and growled and tried to frighten me. But there was one thing he liked and that was my voice. I simply had to keep talking or even singing and whistling as I walked and that would please him. I found out very soon that everything I did when Choo was around must be done slowly. When I walked I must walk always at a slow pace and never run; even when picking up something from the ground, I was to do it slowly.

We had a pet frog who lived under the icebox in the drip tray; only in the evenings did he come out hunting for mosquitoes. Choo, lying on the veranda at my feet, waited for him. He would watch every leap the frog made as it came across the dining room towards him, every few seconds its long tongue darting out to catch a mosquito.

I believe Choo thought it would be great fun if he was allowed to play with Freddie the frog but one look – "a don't you dare" look from me – and Choo would watch the frog leap over his paws, still catching mosquitoes, until, feeling that Freddie was having all the attention, he would get up and go back into the dining room and from the top of the long sideboard take down in his jaws a box of chocolates, bring it to me, and after shaking it to and fro, drop it in my lap. This was a regular thing. Choo liked chocolates and he knew he would get one if he did this party trick.

Sometimes at mating time he disappeared for days but always returned the same playful Choo as before, sleek, graceful and soft-footed. Then ... it must have been two years later, I awoke one early morning to hear something like a thousand squealing cats chasing each other ...

Lula Singh outside my window said, "Mem, it's Choo with his friends ..."

I didn't understand.

"Mem, it's Choo brought back his mate and two leopard cubs!"

I rushed out to the veranda in my dressing gown and slippers. The Sikhs were ready with loaded rifles ...

"Oh no, please don't shoot! They will do no harm. Just leave them to me!"

I sat perfectly motionless on the top step, watching for a movement from the leopards, but apparently they were bored with the situation. Perhaps this mate of Choo's was one of those I could often see from my window gazing at me through the branches of the nearby tree. At last Choo came in sight. I kept silent.

After gazing up with those yellow eyes of his, he decided to come closer, then I noticed the adorable fat little cubs chasing him. One flicked his tail, the other nibbled it between his tiny teeth – it was so like kittens at play. I tried to think of them as ferocious little animals, but I could not.

Leopards are not usually a danger to human beings. They keep as far away from us as possible. I decided to move slowly towards Choo – he waited until I was close enough to rest my hand on his head. There was no hesitation with him ... he rubbed his head against my leg affectionately.

I now decided to sit down on the step talking softly the whole time. It was not long before the mother leopard ventured closer, and then the cubs gambolled around my feet. They climbed on to Choo's back and he didn't seem to mind when one nibbled his ear. Mother leopard watched and waited, her eyes never left me. Choo seemed quite indifferent. The mother suddenly gave a hiss and a grunt, half snarled, struck out with one paw, then rolled over on the lawn and apparently settled down to rest, her eyes half closed, but not for long; the cubs were up again and wanted to play. There was no tension ...

I came indoors, dressed, and went for my usual walk. I sat on a huge boulder, the cats rested too ... but always watching. Later that day I again walked up into the hills, this time taking with me two tiger cubs, which I had reared, when they were found abandoned in the jungle. The only weapon I ever carried when the animals were with me was a thin cane.

I had been walking perhaps fifteen minutes – one did not watch the time for any particular reason in the jungle. Suddenly, the ground was slipping away beneath me and, looking up, I knew what had happened. The natives had dug a tiger trap and I had fallen into it.

Mandy and Tessa had fallen with me. They struggled to climb up the sides but we were all trapped. I was wondering how on earth we could get out when looking up I was face to face with the biggest tiger I had ever seen. He was on the very edge of the pit, his two front paws dangling over the edge, his enormous head held on one side, his long tongue lopping over cruel yellow teeth.

My cubs were evidently frightened. They jumped about making it almost impossible for me to stand and in their restlessness Mandy tore my arm which bled profusely.

I knew by the look of the tiger he could smell the blood, so tearing off my short linen coat, I hastily wrapped it around the wound, but the blood oozed through. Mandy and Tessa were watching the tiger who had now begun to pace around trying to find an easy way to reach us. The earth was giving way under his weight. I tried to keep as motionless as possible but I was facing a man-eater and I was more than frightened – I was terrified. Any moment now he would spring ... already he was poised ready to leap ...

I heard the rustle of long grass and a blood curdling full-throated roar ... then I was fascinated by what followed. The panther and his mate sprang from a nearby tree on to the enemy. I saw Choo's teeth sink well into the tiger's neck and watched the blood gush like a rivulet down his massive chest. It was a fierce battle but it was a losing battle for the King of the Jungle against the leopards.

His career as a man-eater was soon over – with a shudder he lay with his throat ripped wide open.

Monkeys were screaming with terror but when they sensed that all danger was over they ventured closer. The animals, then well satisfied with their conquest, disappeared from view and whilst I was wondering "What next?" I heard many voices, loud shouts of "Mem, Mem." I knew then I was safe ... it was the camp Police.

They had received a warning that I had gone walking in the danger area. A native woman had been badly mauled the previous night and had since died. Armed with rifles and ropes they all set off to find the Mem before the tiger did.

I was in a bad state of shock – trembling in every limb. By the time I was hauled to the top with my frightened cubs, Choo and his family had disappeared. Two men cut long bamboo poles and the dead animal was soon on his way back to the camp.

We quickly reached home but Choo was there before me. He was alone up in the tree licking his wounds. It was days later before the leopard family returned and when they did, they also took up residence in the tree.

But Choo was even more watchful than before; wherever I went he held on to the hem of my dress or my cane. The incident had no other influence on the cubs except that now they disappeared for hours in the hinterland hunting, sometimes dragging part of their kill back with them. Quite often it was a large bamboo rat, sometimes a snake, but apparently they wanted me to know that they could also kill.

I had to watch for their return for fear of them bring their kill on to the highly polished veranda which the Chinese boy took such a pride in polishing every morning. If that happened we should all be in trouble; so I sat with the Sikh guards and watched...

One of these men remarked. "Mem, you will never be without animals around you now. You seem to have an uncanny influence over them."

"Oh no, Beda Singh," I said, "Nothing uncanny. They just know I love them."

I was shortly to sail to England for my holiday. On my return to the jungle I was told that Choo had pined for me, refused to move away from the veranda and there he had died.

*

TRAGEDY STRIKES AGAIN

Readers may be wondering how it is that although we have published pictures with this truly amazing article we have no picture of Choo himself. Surely something as unique as this story deserves a photograph of the leading character? Were no photographs taken of Choo with his mistress? The answer is a decided yes – many. But perhaps it would be better if Ann Smith tells you the rest of the story herself ... *Editor*

My love for animals is part of me. There seems nothing unusual in it. After all, ten years is a long time to live amongst them. I watched them, they watched me and we trusted each other. The animals were all around us, one could not live apart from them; some of them followed me wherever I walked, others peeped from behind tall trees and lay watching in the long grass. I think most of the time I was a bore to them; quite often they fell asleep watching. We did have many photographs of our own special tiger cubs and of Choo, also four cheetahs, which we called Matthew, Mark, Luke and John, but Choo was a special pet.

As a mining engineer my husband and I were quite used to living away from other human beings. We had lived in many parts of the Far East jungles. This particular tin and wolfram mine was on the borders of Thailand. The first manager of the mine was Chinese and then the Kuala Lumpur company decided to send a European manager to take over – he was brutally murdered there. The second European manager met a violent death too – rumour had it that he was poisoned. My husband, Tom, was the next to die there. He had been shot but was recovering from his wounds when tropical typhus and typhoid struck him. He died the second day. I entered hospital in the nearest city for observation and six weeks later was on a liner bound for England.

In that six weeks during my stay in hospital everything I possessed was burnt, even our home reduced to ashes to check any outbreak of typhus in the mining camp. Broken-hearted, I returned to England to my two children who were at school in Cornwall wearing the only dress I possessed – a black one, which had been hurriedly made for me by a local tailor in Malaya.

Life was so entirely different here back in England. I missed my animals, I longed for the jungle – oh, how I longed! I received word from Malaya that all my pets were being looked after by the Sikhs. I could imagine it because I knew how they too adored them but it did not ease my aching heart for the sight of them. I longed to see those very naughty Gibbon apes who sat on my veranda at precisely four o-clock every afternoon for their mug of sweet tea. I never once thought I would need photographs of them all. I had often sketched them but the photos and the sketches were all thrown into the flames which devoured my home …

I will never forget Choo. I think everyone agrees that a black panther is the fiercest animal one can face in the jungle and most people would say as a household pet they are impossible. I agree up to a point but there was something about Choo … Yes, Choo was the only wild animal who really accepted me. Living amongst every kind of wildlife in the dense jungles of Malaya and Borneo, I had many wild pets, but none like Choo. I will always remember him.

*

Ann Smith is now happily re-married and living in England, her family grown up around her. This remarkable true story leaves no one in doubt as to her sincerity and courage – courage which must have stood her in good stead during another episode in her life in the jungle. At one period she was kidnapped and tortured by terrorists, held to ransom and found blind by her husband and a search party. Her sight returned after six months and she tells me that she can never forget the joy of seeing Choo lying on the veranda … *Editor.*

THE CARP & THE BUTTERFLY

For over twenty years we owned a beautiful carp named Henry. He was very special to us and was extremely tame and friendly, often taking his food from our fingers, and at times even allowing us to stroke him. He lived in our pond along with various other species of fish. We were often quite concerned for their safety as foxes had been seen in and around our garden, and on two occasions had taken some of the smaller fish. And so it was with great sadness when one day we discovered that Henry had mysteriously disappeared.

Being large it would have been impossible for him to have remained undetected for too long, were he still there, for his sleek shining back would now and then break through the surface of the water, often followed by loud splashing sounds from his joyous leaps between the lilies.

We thought there might be a possibility that he was somewhere in the deeper area of the pond, but in spite of much searching which lasted for days, we finally decided that a fox must have taken him, and so, feeling very disheartened, we gave up. We felt that the garden would never quite be the same again without our loveable companion, and everything seemed so quiet and still apart from the gentle singing of the birds.

About a week later, as Mother and I stood beside the pond recalling fond memories of him, a Red Admiral butterfly appeared and flew towards a large water lily leaf. After encircling the latter, the butterfly gently alighted upon it. A moment later it flew up into the air and down again, once more settling upon this leaf. For several moments more it continued to behave in a similar manner. We were fascinated as we watched the butterfly's movements and its strange pre-occupation with the leaf. It brought to our minds the many occasions when God had comforted and helped me, through unusual appearances of these beautiful creatures.

Suddenly a thought came to me – could it be that the strange actions of the butterfly were somehow His way of showing us that Henry was in fact still in the pond, and that he was perhaps in some kind of difficulty? Becoming increasingly convinced of this possibility, Mother and I decided to step out in faith.

I remember my Father's puzzled expression, as we tried to persuade him to empty the pond on the strength of the butterfly's behaviour! But I am so glad he finally agreed, for there, right at the bottom of the deep end, stuck pitifully in the mud, was our dear friend, only just alive and barely breathing.

The pond was thoroughly cleaned, and with care Henry gradually recovered, living happily for a further two years. There is no doubt that, had he remained in the mud just a short while longer, he would not have survived. God knew this, and that is why on that summer's morning, a beautiful butterfly alighted upon a certain water lily leaf – **DIRECTLY ABOVE** where Henry lay!

Briony V. Lill
[By kind permission of the Author]

*

Who Are They?

These creatures who share our lives,
Who follow us with their wise gaze
Who pad silently through the hours
and gently tame us with their trust,
Where do they come from?

These creatures who slip out
from the folds of time,
Who teach us the dignity
of their silent language,
Who pierce us with a glance
Where do they go?

STEPHANIE SORRÉLL

*

Tribute to JUNIPER - (also known as ISLA),
who taught me so much.

*

I lost my beloved Juniper last week. She just gradually ceased to eat, and so quietly took her way.

Eighteen years is a long time companioning, and so I cancelled everything for the next few days - to have time to be alone with her, to try to understand something more of her wondrous ways...

At the end of the third day, she spoke to me, so clearly and distinctly that my tears were dried on the instant. I could feel her joyous presence all around.

That morning, so amazingly, I had received a book catalogue, and my eye being drawn by the title of one, I found myself reading the words in the extract attached.

What an amazing little dog! Juniper was - **and is** - a miracle in my life!

*

Extract from "The Faithful Gardener"
by Clarissa Pinkola Estes

"'What is this faithful process of spirit and seed that touches empty ground and makes it rich again? Its greater workings I cannot claim to understand. But I know this: Whatever we set our days to might be the least of what we do, if we do not also understand that something is waiting for us to make ground for it, something that lingers near us, something that loves, something that waits for the right ground to be made so it can make its full presence known.

I am certain that as we stand in the care of this faithful force, that what has seemed dead is dead no longer, what has seemed lost, is no longer lost, that which some have claimed impossible, is made clearly possible...'

*

These tales of loss, survival, and fierce rebirth centre around Dr Estes's uncle, a war-ravaged Hungarian peasant and refugee, a faithful gardener who was one of the 'dancing fools, wise old crows, grumpy sages, and almost saints', who made up the old people in Estes's childhood. "The Faithful Gardener" is, at its core, the story of an open-hearted child who listened well to her elders and grew up to remember, to bear witness, and, as one of the foremost storytellers of our time, to remind people of all ages of 'that faithful force which can never die'."

(With acknowledgements to Clarissa Pinkola Estes,
and to Cygnus booklist, April 96.)

*

Easter, 1996.

S-A.H., The Rocks,
Pitlochry.

*

EXTRACT FROM AN ARTICLE IN THE SUNDAY POST
- 19th August, 1979 -

"One of Scotland's most enthusiastic hill climbers is - a dog! She's Isla, the one year old black terrier" (actually collie-poodle) "belonging to Tom and Shirley-Anne Hardy, Rocks cottage, Pitlochry. The cottage is on the track that leads up to the 1300 ft. hill, Craigower...

Isla sits at a vantage point in the garden, waiting for climbers. When a group appears, she trots along in front of them right to the top of Craigower. She's so keen on the hill climb, that one day she was six times up to the top!

She's a favourite with tourists, and has had her photograph taken at the top of the mountain many times..."

*

Here is one such picture of her, standing by the cairn at the top, kindly sent to us with - written on the back of it: "Juniper, our Guide up the hill. (S)he was marvellous".

We took to calling her the Craigower Courier!

Part III

KALEIDOSCOPE

*

PHOTOGRAPHS

People tell me that pictures add interest to a book. I know they do for me ~ and so I have found a few to add here. I was determined to find one of our Sutherland holiday any way! ~ and luckily an old album was to hand . . .

Juniper with Tom. On a visit to friends at Killiecrankie, which she always enjoyed.

Juniper with two special Pitlochry friends – Neil McIntyre and Leisa Scott.

The three of us ~ snapped unawares!
A favourite picture, owed to Janie Morrison of Pitlochry. 1988.

At Farr Bay ~ our unforgettable holiday in Sutherland, at Bettyhill. 1935.

Underneath this photo was written ~ "Papa with our beloved Garry" . . . perched on a barrow of garden clippings! At our house in Colinton, near Edinburgh. Early 1940s.

Somewhere in the highlands ~ summer of 1937.
My sisters, Marigold and Diana, on the left and right of our mother.
I remember our father had just bought one of those cameras on a tripod which you could ***set*** *– and then you rushed back to join the family before it snapped!*

Early days at The Rocks, with some good friends.
Left to right: *Colin Graham, Jimmy Ross, George Ross, Bryan Smith and Alastair Wilson. My hand was resting on the head of the lovely collie-spaniel we had at that time – Shuna, but she has just missed the picture. Mid-1970's.*

*

From
'Twenty Minutes of Reality'
by
Margaret Prescott Montague

Macalester Park Publishing Co., 1947
[First appeared in 1916 in 'The Atlantic Monthly']

It happened to me about two years ago, on the day when my bed was first pushed out of doors to the open gallery of the hospital. I was recovering from a surgical operation. I had undergone a certain amount of physical pain, and had suffered for a short time the most acute mental depression, which it has ever been my misfortune to encounter. I suppose that this depression was due to physical causes, but at the time it seemed to me that somewhere down there under the anaesthetic, in the black abyss of unconsciousness, I had discovered a terrible secret, and the secret was that there was no God; or if there was one, He was indifferent to all human suffering.

Though I had hardly re-established my normal state of faith, still the first acuteness of that depression had faded, and only a scar of fear was left when, several days later, my bed was first wheeled out to the porch. There other patients took their airing and received their visitors; busy internees and nurses came and went, and one could get a glimpse of the sky, with bare grey branches against it, and of the ground, with here and there a patch of melting snow.

It was an ordinary cloudy March day. I am glad to think that it was. I am glad to remember that there was nothing extraordinary about the weather, nor any unusualness of setting – no flush of spring or beauty of scenery – to induce what I saw. It was, on the contrary, almost a dingy day. The branches were bare and colourless, and the occasional half melted piles of snow were a forlorn grey rather than white. Colourless little city sparrows flew and chirped in the trees, while human beings, in no way remarkable, passed along the porch.

There was, however, a wind blowing, and if any outside thing intensified the experience, it was the blowing of that wind. In every other respect it was an ordinary commonplace day. Yet here, in this everyday setting, and entirely unexpectedly (for I had never dreamed of such a thing), my eyes were opened, and for the first time in all my life I caught a glimpse of the ecstatic beauty of reality.

I cannot now recall whether the revelation came suddenly or gradually; I only remember finding myself in the very midst of those wonderful moments, beholding life for the first time in all its young intoxication of loveliness, in its unspeakable joy, beauty, and importance. I cannot say exactly what the mysterious change was. I saw no new thing, but I saw all the usual things in a miraculous new light – in what I believe is their true light. I saw for the first time how wildly beautiful and joyous, beyond any words of mine to describe, is the whole of life. Every human being moving across that porch, every sparrow that flew, every branch tossing in the wind, was caught in and was a part of the whole mad ecstasy of loveliness, of joy, of importance, of intoxication of life.

It was not that for a few keyed-up moments I *imagined* all existence as beautiful, but that my inner vision was cleared to the truth so that I *saw* the actual loveliness which is always there, but which we so rarely perceive; and I knew that every man, woman, bird, and tree, every living thing before me, was extravagantly beautiful, and extravagantly important. And, as I beheld, my heart melted out of me in a rapture of love and delight. A nurse was walking past; the wind caught a strand of her hair and blew it out in a momentary gleam of sunshine and never in my life before had I seen how beautiful beyond all belief is a woman's hair. Nor had I ever guessed how marvellous it is for a human being to walk. As for the internees in their white suits, I had never realised before the whiteness of white linen; but much more than that, I had never so much as dreamed of the mad beauty of young manhood. A little sparrow chirped and flew to a nearby branch, and I honestly believe that only 'the morning stars singing together, and the sons of God shouting for joy' can in the least express the ecstasy of a bird's flight. I cannot express it, but I have seen it.

Once out of all the grey days of my life I have looked into the heart of reality; I have witnessed the truth; I have seen life as it really is – ravishingly, ecstatically, madly beautiful, and filled to overflowing with a wild joy, and a value unspeakable. For those glorified moments I was in love with every living thing before me – the trees in the wind, the little birds flying, the nurses, the internees, the people who came and went. There was nothing that was alive that was not a miracle. Just to be alive was in itself a miracle. My very soul flowed out of me in a great joy.

No one can be as happy as I was and not have it show in some way. A stranger passing paused by my bed and said, "What are you lying here all alone looking so happy about?" I made some inadequate response as to the pleasure of being out of doors and of getting well. How could I explain all the beauty that I was seeing? How could I say that the grey curtain of unreality had swirled away and that I was seeing into the heart of life? It was not an experience for words. It was an emotion, a rapture of the heart.

Besides all the joy and beauty and that curious sense of importance, there was a wonderful feeling of rhythm as well, only it was somehow just beyond the grasp of my mind. I heard no music, yet there was an exquisite sense of time, as though all life went by to a vast, unseen melody. Everything that moved wove out a little thread of rhythm in this tremendous whole. When a bird flew, it did so because somewhere a note had been struck for it to fly on; or else its flying struck the note; or else again the great Will that is Melody willed that it should fly. When people walked somewhere they beat out a bit of rhythm that was in harmony with the whole great theme.

Then, the extraordinary importance of everything! Every living creature was intensely alive and intensely beautiful, but it was as well of a marvellous value. Whether this value was in itself or a part of the whole, I could not see; but it seemed as though before my very eyes I actually beheld the truth of Christ's saying that not even a sparrow falls to the ground without the knowledge of the Father in heaven. Yet *what* the importance was, I did not grasp. If my heart could have seen just a little further I should have understood. Even now the tips of my thoughts are forever on the verge of grasping it, forever just missing it ...

Certainly that unspeakable importance had to do with our relationship to the great Whole; but what the relationship was, I could not tell. Was it a relationship of love toward us, or only the delight in creation? But it is hardly likely that a glimpse of a cold Creator could have filled me with such an extravagant joy, or so melted the heart within me. For those fleeting, lovely moments I did indeed, and in truth, love my neighbour as myself. Nay, more: of myself I was hardly conscious, while with my neighbour in every form, from wind tossed branches and little sparrows flying, up to human beings, I was madly in love! ...

"Five years ago I had a beautiful experience which set me on a road that has led to the writing of this book. I was sitting by the ocean one late summer afternoon, watching the waves rolling in and feeling the rhythm of my breathing, when I suddenly became aware of my whole environment as being engaged in a gigantic cosmic dance.

Being a physicist, I knew that the sand, rocks, water and air around me were made of vibrating molecules and atoms, and that these consisted of particles which interacted with one another by creating and destroying other particles. I knew also that the Earth's atmosphere was continually bombarded by showers of 'cosmic rays', particles of high energy undergoing multiple collisions as they penetrated the air. All this was familiar to me from my research in high-energy physics, but until that moment I had only experienced it through graphs, diagrams and mathematical theories.

As I sat on that beach my former experiences came to life; I 'saw' cascades of energy coming down from outer space, in which particles were created and destroyed in rhythmic pulses; I 'saw' the atoms of the elements and those of my body participating in this cosmic dance of energy; I felt its rhythm and I 'heard' its sound ..."

Opening paragraph to preface from
"The Tao of Physics", by Fritjof Capra

Morning in Spring
by
Louis Ginsberg

One morning when I went downtown,
I felt such sunlight capsize down
That streets were glutted with more gold
Than all my heart could ever hold.
I thought a glory much like this
Must have been poured from Genesis.
I had not noticed until now
Such glittering of leaf and bough.
Not for a moment could I doubt
Telephone poles might start to sprout.
Brilliant gas stations, like bazaars,
Were jubilating with the cars.
The traffic in some triumph went
In pageant of astonishment.
And all the things in all the stores
Were like abundant metaphors.

More than the sun illumined sight;
More than the sun and more than light
Seeped on the avenue a wonder
That everything grew porous under.
Houses and people, trees and I
Replied to each, as earth to sky.
I felt all objects linked and set
As in a vast, transparent net;
I felt that everything was part
Of rapture, answering my heart;
Until I knew, until I knew
I was the world I wandered through.

(Published in the Atlantic Monthly, April 1955)

FROM
"LONG DAY'S JOURNEY INTO NIGHT"

by

Eugene O'Neill

You've just told me some high spots in your memories. Want to hear mine? They're all connected with the sea.

Here's one. When I was on the Squarehead square-rigger, bound for Buenos Aires. Full moon in the Trades. The old hooker driving fourteen knots. I lay on the bowsprit, facing astern, with the water foaming into spume under me, the masts with every sail white in the moonlight, towering high above me. I became drunk with the beauty and singing rhythm of it, and for a moment I lost myself – actually lost my life. I was set free! I dissolved in the sea, became white sails and flying spray, became beauty and rhythm, became moonlight and the ship and the high dim-starred sky! I belonged, without past or future, within peace and unity and a wild joy, within something greater than my own life, or the life of Man, to Life itself! To God, if you want to put it that way …

And several other times in my life, when I was swimming far out, or lying alone on a beach, I have had the same experience. Become the sun, the hot sand, green seaweed anchored to a rock, swaying in the tide. Like a saint's vision of beatitude. Like the veil of things as they seem drawn back by an unseen hand. For a second you see – and seeing the secret, are the secret.

If the doors of perception were cleansed,
everything would appear to man as it is, infinite.

*

THE LIGHT LAWS AND THE LAND QUESTION

Just before lying down to sleep last night, I was reading in W.E. Butler's book about the aura – more particularly about the 'light' body of the astro-mental aura, and how this is built by the individual.

It thrilled me deeply, revealing to me something further of the underlying laws which had been at work during that string of apparent 'miracles' of healing of 1978 – connecting with those words about the advanced yogi *re-arranging at will the light atoms of the universe*, in 'Autobiography of a Yogi' (which I had been reading at the time).

In the early hours of the morning I awoke from a vision of the working of these *light laws* which was deeply thrilling to me.

As I lay there, I began to recollect about the book I had been reading before lying down to sleep. It was then that the real thrill of the vision came over me, for it had related – not to the structure of the forms of the universe, but in some heightened level of perception of the workings of the *underlying social law relating to land tenure* – (as expounded especially by Henry George in our time, but glimpsed and put into practice with blessing for man through the ages).

I lay there trying to take in the profundity of the revelation of the *burning land question* to me in this way. All I could remember was the indelible writing of it amongst these laws of light. The specific features of the vision were beyond my recollection by then – for upon first awakening the unusualness of it had not struck me at all. Just the concepts of *the law of light* and *holy* remained with me.

Shirley-Anne Hardy
12 February 1980
(As recorded at the time)

And - a Few Words in Farewell!

I am only one; but I am one.
I can't do everything, but I can do something,
And what I can do, and what I should do,
By the grace of God I will do.

(*Source unknown*)

*

The Spirit blows where it will,
but it only fills sails already spread.

(*Source unknown*)

*

... "If the longing for the achievement of the goal is powerfully alive within us, then we shall not lack the strength to find the means for reaching the goal, and for translating it into deeds."

(*Einstein*)

*

(*John G. Stein*, on being asked the secret of his success): "Bite off a bit more than you can chew ... and start chewing."

*

The world stands out on either side,
Wider than the heart is wide.

On he whose soul is flat, the sky
will cave in on him by and by

(*Edna St. Vincent Millais*)

Life is mostly froth and bubble,
Two things stand like stone:
Kindness in another's trouble,
Courage in your own.

(*Adam Lindsay Gordon*)

*

Daily you pour your blessings on us, Lord,
Yet we turn to the ash-heap of yesterday,
Pawing through the ruins, searching for you.
Help us to remember that You don't live in yesterday
Any more than we do.
Teach us to receive all your NEW blessings
Even when they're cleverly disguised
As unsolvable problems.

(*Susan Lenzkes*)

*

For every hill I've had to climb,
For every stone that bruised my feet,
For all the blood and sweat and grime,
For blinding storms and burning heat,
My heart sings but a grateful song –
These were the things that made me strong!

(*Anon*)

Modern civilisation is enveloped in a rising crescendo of noise, which can only be pierced by the soul-illuminated mind in unison with the open heart devoted to the good of mankind. Modern man has to discover the note of the soul, the voice of the silence, and the silence that sounds in the noise of the world.

But when he does so, his words will gather power and his thought will resonate throughout the planet. The world is transformed by the power of thought conforming to the livingness of great spiritual ideas and humanitarian principles brought down to earth by men and women of goodwill and applied to human living.

(*Triangles Bulletin, 1965*)

*

The truly religious person is not concerned with reform. He is seeking what is true, and that very search has a transforming effect on society.

(*Krishnamurti*)

*

The master ideas – the great moral, religious, and metaphysical teachings, which are the foundation of culture – are based on no information whatever.

(*Theodore Roszak*)

*

All true knowledge comes only from within ourselves, in silent communication with our own Soul.

Doctrines and civilisation have robbed us of the Silence, have robbed us of the knowledge that we know all within ourselves.

We have been led to believe that we must be taught by others, and our own Spiritual Selves have become submerged.

The acorn, carried hundreds of miles from its mother-tree, knows without instruction how to become a perfect Oak. The fish of the sea and rivers lay their spawn and swim away. The same with the frog. The serpent lays its eggs in the sand, and goes on its journey;

and yet within the acorn, and the spawn, and the eggs, is all the knowledge necessary for the young to become as perfect as their parents.

Young swallows can find their way to their Winter quarters hundreds of miles away, whilst parent birds are still busy with the second brood.

We need so much to come back to the knowledge that within ourselves lies all truth. To remember that we need seek no advice, no teaching but from within.

The Christ taught us that the lilies of the field, though they neither toiled nor spun, were more perfectly arrayed than Solomon in all his glory.

And the Lord Buddha taught us that we were all on the path to our self-realisation once we became rid of the priests and the books.

(*Edward Bach, 21st May, 1936*)

*

That only which we have within, can we see without.
If we meet no gods, it is because we harbour none.

(*Ralph Waldo Emerson*).

The light of the world comes and goes, it is unstable. The Light that is eternal can never be extinguished. By this Light you behold the outer light and everything in the universe; it is only because It shines ever within you, that you can perceive the outer light. Whatever appears to you in the universe is due solely to that great Light within you, and only because the Supreme Knowledge of the essence of things lies hidden in the depths of your being is it possible for you to acquire knowledge of any kind.

(*Anandamayi Ma*)

*

Let Thy wish become my desire
Let Thy will become my deed;
Let Thy word become my speech, Beloved,
And let Thy love become my creed.
Let my plant bring forth Thy flowers,
Let my fruits produce Thy seed.
Let my heart become Thy lute, Beloved,
And my body Thy flute of reed.

(*Hazrat Inayat Khan*)

*

This must be a combined operation, since time has run out - the book is about to go to the printers!

My consolation is - that there is a considerable amount of information, both addresses and reading-matter, scattered throughout the book. I shall therefore confine myself to essantial information here.

*

1) The Henry George Foundation,
427, London Fruit Exchange,
Brushfield St., London E1 6EL.

Publishers also of the bi-monthly "Land and Liberty".

Send £1, to receive their catalogue, packed with information on reading matter. (I should add: if anyone wishes a copy of my earlier booklet, "The Land Question", it is listed in the catalogue.)

2. The Robert Schalkenbach Foundation,
149, Madison Avenue, Suite 601,
New York,
N.Y. 10016-6424, U.S.A.

3) Tax Reform Australia,
31, Hardware St.,
Melbourne,
Victoria 3000,
Australia.

Publishers of monthly "Progress". Also, I am sure, stockists of Graham Hart's book on Banking, Currency and Inflation, (which I was glad to cite in my Part I).

4) To obtain A.J. Nock's "Our Enemy the State", write to Robert Thornton, The Nockian Society, 42 Leathers Road, Fort Mitchell, Kentucky 41017, U.S.A. There are reductions on bulk supplies.

*

I am aware there are a few items I said in the course of the book would be in Part III - but it has been impossible to manage everything. However, I would like to make the page from Sinton (see Part I) available, as also "Land Health" by Lady Eve Balfour, and "My Debt to Nature Cure" by a G.P. Also the information about Henry George's considerable, (though hidden-up) influence on world history. This latter I came to include something about in my response to the "Dingwall Agenda" (an initiative from the Crofters Union). My simplest plan is, I think, to place copies of these four items, at any rate, along with my book, with the National Library of Scotland, the Reference Dept. of Perth Central Library, (The A.K. Bell Library, York Place, Perth), and similarly with the Pitlochry branch of it. ...I see that space has run out, as well as time! - but I hope these few notes are of help. S-A.H. -(Printers Day, 6 Apr 99).

*

Immortal Love, forever full,
   Forever flowing free,
Forever shared, forever whole,
   A never ebbing sea -

Our outward lips confess the name
   All other names above;
But love alone knows whence it came,
   And comprehendeth Love.

The letter fails, the systems fall,
   And every symbol wanes:
The Spirit overbrooding all,
   Eternal Love, remains.

(John Greenleaf Whittier)

*